Paradise Road

First published in 2003
by Blue Fish
7 New Street, Henley-on-Thames, Oxon RG9 2BP, England
bluefishpress@aol.com

© Bob Mee, 2003

ISBN 0-9546197-0-6

The moral rights of the author are asserted in accordance with the
Copyright, Designs and Patent Act, 1988.

All rights reserved. No part of this publication may be reproduced, stored in
a retrieval system, or transmitted, in any form or by any means, electronic,
mechanical, photocopying, recording or otherwise without the prior
permission in writing of the copyright holder.

Cover painting by Bob Mee

Printed by Lithocraft, 35a Dane Road, Coventry, West Midlands CV2 4JR

Paradise Road

Bob Mee

Blue Fish

For Janet

ACKNOWLEDGEMENTS

Thanks to those editors who have published some of these poems for their tolerance, energy and enthusiasm – and to those who have not, and who also battle away in the thankless job of making contemporary poetry available to those who want to find it.

The poem Texas was awarded first prize in the 2003 Bank Street Writers competition.

Contents

Ada Ellis, 1917	9
Charles Binning, 1868	10
Emily Binning, 1944	11
If You Were Here What Difference Would it Make?	13
The Dinner Party	14
Lightning Louie	15
We Didn't Cross the Road to See Dannie Abse	16
The Birdman of Hullcatraz	18
The Point	20
According to Certain Theories	21
Mother's Burial	22
Ways of Dying	23
School Play	26
Ten Years Old	27
Copse	28
The Way It Is	29
Sons	30
Buddleia	32
Elegy for Alison	33
Snow	34
Kipper	35
Swans, and Jeffrey in the Pub	36
Doris Lessing at the Harper Collins Party	38
Train	40
If I Stay on This Train I Can Go to Nuneaton	42
Five Minutes Near Milton Keynes	43
Pete	44

Brian, Who Are We to Remember?	46
Above Olden Lake	47
Brekke, Norway	48
Views	49
Beatrice	50
A Potted History	51
For the Time We Have	52
This Blessed Bordeaux	54
Customs	56
If	58
Don't Tell Me Anybody Could Write My Poems, Don't Tell Me They Go Nowhere, Do Nothing. What the Hell Do You Expect?	60
Subsidence	61
Passing Through Peterborough	62
Christmas Wine	64
Night Out	65
Lorna	66
The Nurse	67
History Dream No. 1	68
History	69
Science	70
Persecution	71
Going There	72
Smile the Weird Joy	74
The Figures Are Probably False	76
Driving into Fog	78
Prisoners	80

Somewhere East of Sunset

Atlantic City	82
Jazz Bar	83
1996, Leo's Bar	84
Manhattan	86
New Orleans, 1892	87
Texas	88
Advice for Young Women by the Ladies of the Daughters of the Republic of Texas	90
Dog	91
Elvis, Vegas, 2001	92
At the Time of Nuclear Testing in Nevada	93
Somewhere East of Sunset	94
George from the Andes	96
Rest Home and a Man Swimming	97
On the Beach at Malibu	98
Kingfish Levinsky	99
Driving, USA	100
Notes	103

ADA ELLIS, 1917

I was peeling potatoes for a stew that would last me all week.
My dad came in and took off his cap, so I knew something was up.
Sit down, Ada, he said. *I've something to tell thee.*
And at the little kitchen table, in Benjamin's chair
He took my hand and said: *He's not coming back, love.*
He passed me the letter. They were supposed to be private
But he was tired of it all, my dad, and he'd opened it when
Miss Edgar had said: *This is for your Ada, I hope it's not bad news.*
I sat staring at the words: *I regret to inform you that Pte Benjamin John Ellis…*
I kept looking at his precious name, kept looking at the words -
Benjamin John Ellis – kept willing them to change
So I could look up at my dad and say: *No, look, it's not Benjamin.*
Dad put his hand on mine, gripped it, said: *I'll fetch Laura.*
But when he'd gone I went out walking, kept walking, out of the town
And up to the hills and sat on a boulder that was white in the moon
And the sky was purple and yellow and deep dark blue
And the heavens raced as if the earth were spinning too fast.
I rocked back and forward and asked God why. We'd been married
At St Michael and All the Angels 15th October 1916 and I thought
St Michael and all his angels would bless us and bring him back.
And we'd been together two weeks before they took him off on the train
And we'd been married eight weeks in all. And I'd lain awake at night
And prayed with all my might: *God keep him safe, God please keep him safe.*
But he hadn't.

Laura came to live with me, to watch out for me. I kept his clothes ironed
And folded in our chest of drawers. I hadn't finished
The little silk token I was making for him and I wouldn't do it then.
Laura and I would sit reading at night and then I'd hear the guns
And I'd begin to panic and she'd say to me: *No, Ada, it's just the trains.*
And once she said: *Anyway the guns can't hurt him any more.*
And I cried like a baby for Benjamin and for all the babies we'd never have.

CHARLES BINNING, 1868

Oh, she's a love. Clever? Too sharp for me.
And, you know what? Never down in the dumps.
It's a marvel really. Don't know how she does it.
How did we start? You mean, how come a pretty
schoolteacher ended up with a lump like me?
It's all right, no offence taken. We were
at the vicarage for a feed-up to do with
the summer fair – who would do what and that -
and Emily was sitting by me. We'd been friendly,
I'd walked her home once or twice from church
and I got a bit bold, nudged her leg with mine
a time or two, and it was all going along nicely
when she put down her knife and fork and said:
*Charles Binning, if you love me, say so. Don't
keep rubbing your boot up and down my leg.*
Red! I've never blushed so much. Even the vicar
set off laughing. I felt a right fool but outside
I stood with my cap in my hands and asked
if she would walk out with me. I thought
What the heck, I can't be any more embarrassed
than I've already been. She said yes. And we did.
And it went along smashing and we married last May.
We've never looked back. Now I've gone
and caught this damned chest cold. Stupid thing.
Just a spot of tug-o-war on a Saturday with my pals
and we lost and I fell in the brook. Didn't
think nothing of it. Didn't go home to change.
Well, it was a nice day and it only turned chilly later.
Now I can't seem to shake it off. To be honest,
I feel right rough. I'll get better in a week or so,
I should think. Nothing to worry about.

EMILY BINNING, 1944

They say I was a disgrace but I can't remember.
Who on earth can or should? It was Christmas
and it was my job to bring the goose. I forgot
but got lucky. There was one left over at market.
I should have plucked it, but you know how it is.
Or I hope you do. You've had no salt in your life
if you don't. I met someone, a good honest drinker.
And I had a few sherries with him, then some
nettle wine, and we went dancing in the garden.
That got the nets-a-twitching, but what do I care?
And by the time I caught the bus to Kate's
it was Christmas Eve afternoon and the sun
was low and white, and the cold was settling in.
I'm afraid the rest has gone, but I believe
I flung open the front door, the goose flapping
around my neck – it was in a bag when I left,
I'm sure – tripped over the mat and fell splat
on my face under the parlour table.
They say they fetched the goose from under me
and put a pillow under my head and left me there.
Kate was po-faced all through Christmas Day,
the misery. Just because she'd got herself
a husband who was tight-arsed and frightened
of his own shadow. And I told him so, once.
He looked as if he could strangle me, but smiled
and I thought, yes, I know you, don't you
think I don't. When did the drinking start?
When I was teaching at Newton. Nice enough job
but not many of them wanted to learn and
at harvest none of them came. One day I was
at the vicarage and the vicar asked if I'd like a sherry.
I'd never tasted anything like it. Glorious.
I liked it so much – and what it did to me – he sent
a little barrel round, so I could take a glass
at my leisure. He might have wanted a little
something in return. I've been daft in my life
but not that daft. Anyway he had a cast in his eye

and you never knew who he was looking at.
Which was all right if he was giving a sermon
but no good if he was trying to make eyes at a girl.
And I liked the bottle so much I didn't need a man.
I hadn't felt the same way about men anyway
since my Charles died. Silly bugger, I'll never
forgive him. A game of bloody tug-o-war, I ask you.
He died smiling and saying he'd be better soon.
Anyway, once school had finished for summer
I took to my bed with my barrel, and when that ran out
I made wine from dandelions, nettles, elderflower,
whatever took my fancy. Sometimes it was so strong
it made my lips go numb, but it did me no harm
and I've lived to be 96. I've agreed to cut back now –
one glass in the morning and one at night. That's
because I fell in the grate while the ashes were hot
and singed my hair. To be honest, the taste's not the same
anyway. I know I've been lucky. I've outlived
all those miseries who tut-tutted away their lives
and never knew how to dance even a little bit.
And I've still got my wits and I can read my Bible
and sing a hymn or two.

IF YOU WERE HERE WHAT DIFFERENCE WOULD IT MAKE?

if you were here
we could eat oysters
we could grow extra fingers at night
we could smell the wheat after rain
we could astound each other and the world
we could discover comets
       take fifteen more years to watch herons on the severn
                          red admirals in our hair
                              red caves in the trunks of huge trees

if you were here
we could make love giggling and shushing
as if the children or our parents were behind chipboard walls

if you were here
the mountain roads would be just as dangerous
the mysteries of the river would stay mysteries even as we slept
dim skies would roll over and see us for what we are

THE DINNER PARTY

We are not supposed to know Wilf has an alternative wife in a corner shop in Warwick

We are not supposed to know Catherine says things at work like *second guessing the future in a planning window of five years is certainly complex*

We are not supposed to know she also hears voices behind walls calling her to drift in the shallows beneath the willows and wait and listen and say nothing

We are not supposed to know she dropped the prawn tostadas, about which we make such approving grunts, on the kitchen floor exactly where the dog pissed this afternoon

And how could we know Wilf once tied forget-me-nots in Catherine's hair in the warm rain of summer

We are not supposed to know he scratches the eczema on his wrists in his sleep and drives her mad

We are not supposed to know the company for which we all work is embarking on a programme of rationalisation and she knows exactly whose jobs will go

We are not supposed to know the stuffed parrot they inherited from a potty aunt and kept on the backroom mantelpiece as a joke burst from its case, exploded in a dust of feathers and glass as Wilf's parents, over for last weekend, watched TV

We are not supposed to know his parents are still there, the glass embedding itself a little further each day as their flesh decays, the feathers fragrant as peace

How could we know any of this as Wilf cheerfully uncorks another red and Catherine serves seconds of mousse

LIGHTNING LOUIE

Lightning Louie's working the corner in
his England shirt and pork-pie hat, handing
up the spit bucket, rinsing the gumshield.
Louie flits either side of the ringpost
fists flickering in a staccato of
memory – he was no Panama Al,
nor even a Brian London but he
was twice as good as these kids, scuffling round
for six rounds in this hall full of chancers
and gamblers and boys who dodge cameras

And even here nobody messes with
Lightning Louie. Everybody respects
a man who's mad enough to get thrown out
of the French Foreign Legion. Twice.

WE DIDN'T CROSS THE ROAD TO SEE DANNIE ABSE

John and I were going to hear Dannie Abse read his poetry
but got there early
and popped in for a swift one
at The Prince of Wales across the road

The Prince of Wales where you can find Fred
who's just done a good deal on a hundred quid Volvo
who's growing his own water cress now the wild stuff's gone

The Prince of Wales where Bill
lowering his voice
will tell you
Henry Weston Black Top's not a drink
but an anaesthetic

The Prince of Wales where nobody can quite remember
the name of the first man around here
to get done for drink-driving
but everybody agrees he lived up in the forest
and drove a Robin Reliant

The Prince of Wales where Wilf with half his teeth left
and a hat he got from a Bavarian tourist
says he's got to go but he'll just
have one for the ditch

The Prince of Wales where Cedric
is proud of his new purple shirt
and of his wife
who is a barrister a teacher
an income tax collector
and related to Dylan Thomas
and who, when he rings up to ask, does
actually tell him the Hobo Poet
was W H Davies

And talking of poets John's just remembering
it was Adrian Mitchell
who first said
Philip Larkin was really Eric Morecambe

and
given this
we estimate that
if Dannie Abse is really Ernie Wise
by now
he must be about halfway through
Bring Me Sunshine

THE BIRDMAN OF HULLCATRAZ

From the sill of his cell at the Royal Hotel
the Birdman of Hullcatraz feeds pigeons
with room service leftovers.
The pigeons pick at the gifts and consider
whether or not it would be absurdly passé
to take the children to Greece this year.
Ah, says the wise one, dismissing the idea,
I've been through this leaving thing before.
The generations sing at the Polar Bear
and the poets gather to talk of technique, syntax
and who's having who, while in an unlamented boozer
off the Hessle Road a Manilow lookalike serenades
the blessed in no particular key.
And on the Marina wall the Home Guard ghosts watch
for the way death rolls in from a grey sea,
at every sunset repeat in the log:
Nothing to Report. Visibility Good.
Across the road the bleak trees reach into themselves
and a bag lady applauds
as a busker finishes A Whiter Shade Of Pale.
Behind him in a fashionable bar a bore
bestows his jokes upon an old man who has a pint of mild
and wax in his ears who catches words like leaves
as circles of silvery bark spin into the wet sky
which is hot with the momentum of so many years.
The Birdman of Hullcatraz remembers the nape of the neck
of the girl who talked to friends in a better bar where
flame-grilled burgers were at a knockdown price
and the middle aged drunk dried Sarah's tears and held her hand.
Sarah's children have new shoes now
and Bill from the bookshop has eight widows on the go,
three of them named Joy.
The Birdman's phone rings at three in the morning
but nobody's there. Grey as a gravestone -
put it down to morphine - he makes a pot of tea,
packs, checks out, drives to the bridge,
stacks his clothes and flies.

On the long swoop
as dawn breaks into rain
he becomes anxious that all he was,
all that all of us were, should not be lost.
And he smiles at the absurdity of that
as the river rises.
A fisherman on the bank
wondering whether or not
to sell his collection
of Tigers' programmes
and how much he might get
is really pissed off
by the splash.

THE POINT

Mr Eli Charles
was old, fit, not an ounce of excess flesh.
All his own teeth.
Pulled the old girls and,
it was said, the odd (very odd)
young one too.

Mr Eli Charles
said the secret
of his great strength and keen mind
was a raw egg in a glass of sherry
last thing at night.

Yes,
said my father,
sucking on a Park Drive.
He lived to be 92.
But he died in the end.

ACCORDING TO CERTAIN THEORIES

According to certain theories
my father feels less emotion than he did.
At 76 his brain is shrinking, his body drying out
his neuro-chemicals playing him up,
which could explain the grin he carries with him
when he plods between the headstones counting his mates.
According to Biblical rule of thumb, my father's life has over-run,
is measured in smiles that say he knows fear of dying
is the prerogative of the comparatively young.
My father smokes but doesn't inhale, believes Baptist
drinks halves of bitter when male relatives (not many left) come south.
He waits for a grandson to save the line
(but if you ask he'll say what he's got already's fine)
and upstairs with his holy books he draws and redraws the frontiers
of his Strict and Particular war with God.
At 76, he's outgrown the fantasy of declining years in the ancestral village
(my mother protested: *But no-one will know us there*)
and now the garden's too big he wants a smaller place not far away.
At 76, the task of earning a shilling has been replaced
with a family tree dating back to 1611.
Gone the rows (and us kids)
gone too the faith-accompli of Right, Wrong and God Willing.
According to certain theories
my father feels less restriction than he did,
which could explain why, for his daily bread, he ignores the road
and treads the tarmacked path between the dead,
clambers through a gap in the cemetery fence
and cuts through the council yard.
Arriving home, he shoulders his way through the creosoted gate
that's never fitted at the top,
and in his hard chair at the kitchen table
remembers the rush
and thinks when all's said and done
there's not much left to see that's worth a fuss
even if his brain is shrinking
according to certain theories.

MOTHER'S BURIAL

my father left the grave
which one day
would be his own

and walked
in the drizzle
across the mud

to where the sexton stood
(in brown waterproofs
by John Oswin's stone)

and thanked him

WAYS OF DYING

Some people die almost without knowing it. Lot's wife, for example. There she was trudging up the hill. Paused for breath and either forgot what Lot had said – *Don't look back, love* – or ignored it. As he was walking ahead, droning on about a madcap vision of retribution, he didn't notice she'd stopped. She enjoyed the moment of peace, turned to watch the red sun going down on the rooftops of Gomorrah. Everywhere was shining and glowing and the whole place seemed to be in flames. Then it happened.
    "*Lot!*" she cried out, incredulous. "*I taste salt…*"
And that was that.

And I'm thinking about this as I swing the car off the motorway, on to the ring road north for a mile or two and into the hospital car park. I park every time in roughly the same place by the hospital social club, a small, rectangular hut painted white and green. I go into the ward and two nurses are helping him into the toilet, so I go back out and stand and watch two magpies darting between a lawn and an old fir tree. When I go back, he's in his chair. He ignores me, his eyes paler than yesterday, his skin somewhere between yellow and grey. He looks down, folds and unfolds his hands. The right one works much better than the left because of the stroke that the doctors say should have killed him. He looks at himself in a mirror on the other side of the room. The nurses tell us he was lucky to get a room on his own. It happened when they re-shuffled the men and women last week. They are right, of course, if luck comes into any of this.

This is my father in two-thousand-and-two, knackered out, as he said with difficulty, before the descent began.

When I talk he looks at me coldly and shakes his head as if I don't understand that I've interrupted him. I bend to catch the words that are distorted by his inability to control his tongue and by the tube that's passing through his nose and throat to his stomach. At the third try I understand he's saying:
    "*I don't know you.*"
Then he reaches out with his good hand, and I grasp the yellow clawed fist that is dotted with purple bruises and I block out the memories of how I used to reach up to hold that hand, but I don't do it well enough and there's the smell of Saturdays at nearly five o'clock as we're walking

the quarter-mile home from Oadby football club to hear the results of the big games on the radio. I can hear one now: *Leicester City 8, Manchester City 4*. And the smell is of autumn fog settling in and bonfire smoke and Bovril and tea the colour of bricks and fatty bacon sizzling in a pan. And today his grip is still tight, and his chest heaves and I hug his shoulders lightly and I smooth the white hair on his grey head.

He whispers at me again and I make out the word Bible. I reach into his cabinet and take out the battered, dog-eared book that has shaped his ninety years. The next words are low and painful for him to say as the fluid on his chest brims into his throat. I distinguish '*Read*' from the rest of the noise and, I kid you not, the book opens at Genesis Chapter Nineteen and I start reading at Verse Twenty-Three:
    "The sun was risen upon the earth when Lot entered into Zoar. Then the Lord rained upon Sodom and upon Gomorrah brimstone and fire from the Lord out of heaven...but his wife looked back from behind him and she became a pillar of salt."

And I look up and he's asleep and I kiss his head and go.

When I reach my car there is a single dim light in the hospital social club and through the net curtains I can make out figures sitting at what might be the bar. I drive away, not looking back, and head home with the radio off and no need to stop.

And I'm in a pub having a quiet drink with Tony when the call comes and he's gone and nobody had told me he'd been put on morphine that day and I'm angry and sad and don't know what's right. An hour later the nurse in the check top and black trousers lets me in through the door that's locked at night and we walk down the corridor saying nothing and I go into his room.

And there's a white lily on his chest, dear God.

And I stroke his cold white hair and run my fingertip along the stitches still smudged with blood where he fell from his chair last week.

The nurse brings me sweet strong tea in a plastic cup and says: *Take as long as you like.*

I hear her through the door trying to persuade a woman to use the commode.
Do it for me, she says.

And I lay the back of my hand against his cold waxen head.

And I know my sister will have him buried in his brown suit with his check cap in his hand and peppermints in his pocket because that's how he dressed for church on Sundays.

And I go without goodbyes.

It begins to snow huge, slow flakes that settle and quieten the tyres on the road and make me sleepy. And in a layby I get out and climb a fence and stand in a field and let the snow touch my face and I breathe it all and turn my face to the sky and the universe and all I've ever known.

SCHOOL PLAY

In the 50s our teachers
had a minimalist approach
to nativity plays.
Our parents
had to imagine
the rope
I dragged along the floor
was a camel
and the strange hat
my sister sat up
half the night making
from cardboard
and a pile of dusters
made me a king.

TEN YEARS OLD

The boy
sees a muntjac
in the far field

runs in
with two heads
of green corn
and a stick

grabs
his binoculars
and dashes out

COPSE

When the year turns and shadows burn without release
a woman rushes to your heart and holds you.
                              In the deep of some half-recalled,
coiling copse we see the light go out, far ahead,
in the wet ruins that downwind you smell crumbling.
These places nourish madness. Sense it and it spreads.
The soft dead know, among the roots, becoming roots.

THE WAY IT IS

We dig a row of potatoes, my patient, persistent son and I.
The weeds pull easily with a touch from our spades when the soil is dry.

The harvest begins and in an hour the vast fields are reclaimed from the brown, impenetrable waves of rape that have hemmed us in for weeks.

The neighbours' black Scottie, who'd look good stuffed and mounted on wheels, thunders by on his little kneeless legs.

And you lie in the hammock with your skirt wrapped around you, reading The Man Who Mistook His Wife For A Hat. (And I hope I never do.)

Tonight we will light the tall bonfires that must not be lit until the harvest is in because of how hot and dry everything is.

The rise of the hill almost hides the red tractor, but little Jack sees its roof glistening in the sun.

Its driver rests, swigging a flagon of cider. The ghosts have their ways of taking us back and it is not our place to understand or appreciate why the fist-sized chunk of cheese and Annie's barley loaf, moistened by yesterday's dripping, alter the way we perceive history in all its harvested glory.

A lark oversees it all, then and now, too high to hear.

You get up and go to the kitchen to change the mint that draws off the flies.

SONS

In the dry, cracked bed of the bottom field I disturbed
a lapwing, which swirled around and swooped away,
and in the pale, dry stalks of last year's cabbages
at the edge of the bindweed in the ditch by the oaks
a hare ducked out of sight. The dog rooted about.

I know the confident pull the years make,
here and beyond Hanging Hill;
sometimes at dusk a stag will frame itself
against the sky and the black curve
of the land. And then it will turn
and run, as if disturbed by the ghosts
who walk up here from the village
to bear dreadful witness to God's grace.

On autumn evenings I can smell
the stench of dead flowers beneath the hanging
bodies of men and women everyone knew,
as colours move and blend. Crows
pick them clean and maggots burst
from the bellies like the flesh of figs
until they are ploughed into the earth.

I dig near the house with my father's spade
as he did, deliberately, without hurry.
One summer we dug a vegetable patch –
cut down tall weeds,
dug out couch, dock and daisy,
and explored for yards the roots of nettles;
digging, forking, hoeing and,
it seemed to me, planting in no particular
or pre-conceived pattern; moving
as the mood took.

Those were the free years
when I followed dreams
as kingfishers do streams.

We hacked at grasses to let raspberries breathe
and mowed beneath the apples and plums.
My father showed me how to understand clouds;
his veined, lined hands,
his big shape against the sun
and his unconditional pride in me.

In the young wood the fallen leaves cleared the ground
as each autumn and winter passed.
I planted a pine for joy, a birch for sorrow.
They are full-grown now; my father dead.
The ghosts who walk Hanging Hill
accept us both as their own.

BUDDLEIA

To amuse the buddleia
where the butterflies are social enough
I take the secateurs
and clip the wings of Mrs Wise Owl,
leader of the Brownie pack,
slice up and string together
the sheet-music of Bach and Purcell
to keep pigeons off my peas.
This ruins today's weddings
so depriving the blustering
rector of his extras.
I prune the nose of the neighbour
who peeps a fraction too far
from behind her 'nets',
and trim a finger or two
from the ladies of the WI.
Marvellous how they stiffen a soup
or, mashed, add a little edge
to a soufflé. I dead-head
the dog-walkers and fork over
with dung all those who assert
the governmental right to roam
the boundaries of my wilderness.
And the buddleia is satisfied
and hums the ecstatic anthems
of delirious honey-bees
while the butterflies
ignore everyone as if
they're the only
ones in heaven
with wings.

ELEGY FOR ALISON

Iron deficiency leaves pits in the skull.
Protein excess fuses vertebrae.
Passion is not an option.
Is it freedom to miss you so much?

A lapwing rose from the blue flowers of flax
And you saw a fox on the track.
It was first light on the first day of summer.
There was no way back.

You danced in the candlelight
As the poets, making nothing of something,
Quoted Ginsberg; and the eagles of time
Circled the ruins of the century

Like helicopters at Jericho. Each day
The corpses are carried to the tombs
To await those who will use them
To analyse diet and levels of pollution

In 1998.

SNOW

The couple kissing in the snowfield
as a Swiss train trundled
through Austria in '78

are still there; wrapped around each other
in overcoats, scarves, thick trousers,
boots. The cold still thrills them, makes the heat

of their breathing, softness of their mouths
so impossibly exciting.
They have not married, raised children, fought,

made up, grown bored, strayed, divorced, died. Not
once has one of them stepped back, let
hands and fingers go so gently, said:

This is all there is.
I don't know what I hoped to find.
I think it was more than this.

KIPPER

Kipper's 50p's on trap six in the 11.07 at Catford
and that six-dog hits the first bend clear
and there's trouble behind:
the one slides on the bend and takes out two
which clips the heels of four,
three's no good and five's got a belly full of oats
and Kipper's six bounds in by eight lengths.

By which time Kipper is singing
the theme from 'The Dambusters'
his old arms out like wings
tilting in honour of fallen comrades
from the Black Dog and the Greyhound Inn
and the Red Lion and the Two Feathers
and the Prince of Wales
and the Legion
where the beer's cheaper than anywhere
if you can stand the soapy tang
from the pipes
improperly cleaned by
the lazy steward called Reg.

Kipper's won
and winning is beating them
and his mad beam is for all of us to share
in the fight against disillusion and defeat
and we're with him all the way
to the 11.16 at Romford.

SWANS, AND JEFFREY IN THE PUB

The talk turned to the swans
whose two cygnets nobody
had seen for days.

Last year their eggs
were swept away
in a flood, yet

they nested again
on the island
in the middle of the pond

which Jeffrey, who would
love to be squire, carved
from a buttercup meadow

to mark his 50th birthday.
He's OK, Jeffrey, even
if he's somehow perpetually

strapped for cash.
I like a man daft enough
to wear a clip-on bowtie

and fake tweed, who
likes to ride
the biggest horse.

I don't know, he said
with deliberate whimsy
sipping another free beer,

*What's on
the third floor
of my house.*

I like Jeffrey
because he knows
he has nothing to say

but says it anyway.
Bert came in
for last orders

and said a fox got
the cygnets
on Wednesday.

DORIS LESSING AT THE HARPER COLLINS PARTY

I've written a book about bare-knuckle boxing and Harper Collins have bought it and paid me for it.

And the invitation to their Authors Of 2000 Party has dropped through the letterbox and Nelly the dog has grabbed it and waved it around a bit.

You say you know it's not my scene but the party might be the sort of thing I should go to, and I do, after moaning about having to do a 200-mile round trip and not being able to drink. And I get there after the queues on the M4 and on the slip road at Hammersmith and pull up at the electric iron gates and persuade the man in the crisp white shirt and Donald Duck tie I'm worth a parking space.

Inside I hand over my invitation and two men in black give me a name tag and I pin it on and in I go and there they are, holding their nibbles in fingers like tweezers and the sound of Miles Davis is coming out of somewhere and they've all got full glasses which means none of them is drinking and I walk around the room twice and I don't know anybody and nobody knows me.

So I sit on a bar stool with an orange juice and Doris Lessing's there in an overcoat with a big brooch and she's smiling and nodding and her eyes are twinkling with all the attention as people jostle to be with her and one boldly touches her sleeve as if she were a precious relic which I suppose she is. And I can't stand the babbling any more and ten minutes after getting there I'm swinging the car back on to Fulham Palace Road and up to the M4 and away to the west and north.

I ring you and tell you about it and you say the kids have eaten and shall we eat together later. And I enjoy saying *I'll get the take-away, you warm the plates* because there's a sing-song rhythm to it.

At a service station near Oxford I stop for a coffee and resist an urge to eat an all-day breakfast. I sit in the corner away from where two boys with billiard-ball heads are impressing girls with purple lips and white faces and one of the boys turns and belches into the face of an old man who is waiting for a pot of tea.

The two of them swap slaps and the old guy drags up the memory of a stiff jab that's not a prod or a poke but a real step-in-behind-it and drill-it-through-your-face job, then he rolls in with a left hook and the boy's nose is broken and he howls and backs off and the bleak girls laugh. The old man tosses coins on the counter and struts off, the fire of the boy's youth in his watery eyes. And the boy dabs at his nose and says it wouldn't have been right to hit an old man.

And I go out and the stars are spreading wonder across the lives of any of us who choose to lean back and look. And I stand for a moment and breathe in the dry cold ache of joy and I wonder what Doris is doing now.

TRAIN

The delayed 8.16 from Manchester Piccadilly to Portsmouth Harbour
gets bored
turns left at Heaton Chapel
to avoid Stockport
thinks to itself
Ah, the M56 could be fun on a Sunday morning
glides off its rails, bumps and rocks down the embankment
and clatters off into the middle lane.

Then it spots a sign for the airport
and heads up the slip road towards Wythenshawe
smashes through the perimeter fence
squeezes between a Ryan Air to Jersey
and a British Midland to Tenerife
accelerates up runway three with a terrifying, glorious roar
and we lurch into the air.

The Virgin West Coast steward arrives, wide-eyed, and sobs:
I have claim forms for anyone who wants to complain.
And she tells us
there are no hot drinks in the buffet
and the first class coach
fell off
somewhere over Congleton, Cheshire.

An albatross
flies alongside for a while.
It taps on the window.
Good luck, I have to go back now
and it falls away,
disintegrating into bones
which unloose
into a small cascade of dust.

By now we've levelled out
and I see coming up to meet us
the countryside of North Staffordshire:

shallow, fast streams with white water over smooth boulders
and dew on grass as the mist rises where perfect white sheep and
perfect white horses graze together in the sun.
And a girl throws a stick for a dog, a great joyous miscreant mongrel of a dog.
The stick hangs teetering on the edge of the field
and the great dog dashes at full pelt to fetch it,
digs in its claws and tips up North Staffordshire

And all of North Staffordshire's bits fall off,
slithering away in a glittering shower of limbs
and open mouths and stunned wide eyes.
I watch the perfect sheep the perfect horses, the girl, the dog
getting smaller

And as we change to a lower gear
to climb another hill of air
we come to a cloud
where an old man riddled with melanomas
sits with bandages on the holes where his waxen wings used to be.
I'm Icarus, he says. *I can't get down*.
And there's nothing any of us can do.

And I guess I'm here for the journey
whether it turns left at Heaton Chapel or not
ends at Portsmouth, North Staffordshire
or a cloud too close to the sun.
And I just sit and wait
to go higher and further.

IF I STAY ON THIS TRAIN I CAN GO TO NUNEATON

If I stay on this train I can go to Nuneaton, says the guard,
then get the cross-country connection to Coventry.

If I stay on this train I can read a guide to what's on next week.

If I stay on this train I can see the slinky seductive shapes of this season's swimsuits
           can indulge in idle chit-chat with Bukowski and
           Larkin over a tandoori chicken sandwich from
           the food counter. Larkin will get the beers in
           and we'll analyse the day's racing. Bukowski
           will say *Where the bloody hell is Wincanton?*

If I stay on this train I can paint stillness
           dress in scarlet and black
           beguile and shock

If I stay on this train I can be wrong about the blood on the ceiling
           sip Darjeeling with lemon
           become a citizen of eternity
           pluck the feathers of a pig

If I stay on this train I can display granite-like stoicism when given out caught behind off my thigh
           can smell honeysuckle in your hair
           agree to meet again in thirty years
           beneath the lions in Trafalgar Square

If I stay on this train I can photograph echoes
           grow my own kangaroos
           breed swallows
           start fires with my footprints
           swim the Sahara
           ride a camel across the Channel
           meet myself coming back

           go to Nuneaton
           catch the connection to Coventry

FIVE MINUTES NEAR MILTON KEYNES

The train has stopped again. I count
the young birch trees on the embankment.
I reach a hundred and twenty six.
We edge forward a few yards.
I lose my place.

The woman opposite has a bundle
of papers laid out on the table.
I read them upside down -
a pipeline proposal
for Mozambique.

She taps her lips with her pen, turns
a page, looks at a series of maroon
graphs, puts down the pen.
Slides her wedding ring up
and down her finger.

PETE

Pete has a wife a daughter a bad back and a shed for pigeons
        has gold-capped teeth a bootlace tie a tartan hat
          and a moustache he pencils on each morning

Pete went every Sunday to the Polish church the Polish club and the park
        spent the afternoon with his pigeons
        sang to them
        knew them all by name

Then one day his wife
        who collects coffee jar labels for charity
        who can't sleep for fear of sleeping forever
        told him the pigeons had to go
        because her friend Frances
        whose husband had pigeons
        had just got cancer

Pete carried his pigeons away in a huge basket

Pete spent hours digging and weeding the garden
        mending the guttering
        repointing the chimney
        doing the jobs
        that had needed doing for years

And his wife
        more frightened than ever
        cooked unfathomable Polish dishes Pete couldn't eat
        now he'd got used to chips with everything

And she took to sleeping downstairs on the sofa
And she hid behind the curtains watching people come back from the pub
And she lay and listened for burglars until the birds began to sing
And in the mornings she shouted in Polish
        that Pete's bootlace tie was ridiculous and soon
        she wouldn't be able to buy Brylcreem any more
        who did he think he was
        Elvis or Gable

And today Pete
        came back from church the club and the park
        ignored his daughter his wife and his dinner
        sat in his empty scrubbed out disinfected shed
        and slowly painted green bars on the windows

Now he's inside
        has been there hours
        with a bottle of vodka
        we can hear him laughing
        and can see the smoke from his Woodbines
        and he's laughing and sitting and smoking and shouting
        SCREW YOU
        over and again
        again and again

His wife is outside
        wringing her hands
        and pleading
        and rubbing her rosary
        but it won't do any good

Pete is ruling his roost.

BRIAN, WHO ARE WE TO REMEMBER?

Oh, those nights we put the world to rights over a pint or five
Split a couple of quid in the fruit machine at the death
Then stumbled still ranting down the hill
You in shirt sleeves whatever the weather
And me in love with what was left of my youth.
Sometimes we'd stay on and talk long into the night
Until we began to repeat ourselves
And then, sadly, would call our own time.
Once, on the way home, as the sky lightened
I stopped to piss, by accident, on Mrs Edkin's roses.
The next day a judge from the Best Kept Village Competition
Sniffed them and savoured the aroma like fine brandy.
Our village did not win, and I wondered if,
In a roundabout way, I had anything to do with it.
Oh, those nights that have set me writing tonight
Now the cancer's finished you.

ABOVE OLDEN LAKE

Sunlight explodes on the snow above the clouds
bounces the peaks and breaks into white waterfalls
that spill all the way to the lake

A car on the track intrudes and appals
and further below gulls screech and swerve and stall
while above, where a glacier keeps its nerve
as it wrestles time for a better footing,
a heron arrows and glides on its latest journey to provide.

Already we are used to the way the raspberries climb the silver birch
to the way the leaves of the ash rustle in the breeze as the boughs bend
to the way rain filters through the turf and drops off the end of our log roof
and to the way we immerse ourselves in the faith
that this devotion has no end
until sometimes there is nothing to say nor write
that will not diminish what it is to be here.

BREKKE, NORWAY

Rain from this afternoon's heavy showers filters through the turf and off the edge of the log roof in steady drops to the gravel path.

Small grey birds pick at the wet earth.

The light on the fjord is dancing, now a waltz, now a jive!

On the bed you sit in your pink towelling dressing gown and write your diary.

The warm rain drips: A perfect sound as a waterfall is perfect and a tap is not.

Almost as far as it's possible to distinguish water from mountain, a boat is moving from left to right.

You wrap a blanket around your legs and brush your fringe from your eyes. You pause with one end of the pen resting on your bottom lip.

On the wall by the door is a painting of a dead mermaid floating. Behind her an oil rig sets fire to the night.

Tomorrow we drive on.

It's possible, and we must always believe it, that our luck will hold.

VIEWS

Stiff-backed in tweed and gaiters, Mallory
gazed over Tibet, accommodated
the inconvenience of failure, wept
for his children, ached for what he would miss;

not sentimentality, but pure joy
you understand, a magical triumph
for the years go on and we shall not.
We shall beat them, every one of us.

I fly above white, uninhabited
lands, find love in wind and hail on high ground,
where faces like Mallory's free themselves
and learn to concentrate on flow and ebb

until there is no more to say, no one
to say it to, and eagles pluck our eyes.

BEATRICE

I should have worked it out and phoned
but I was just another messed up kid
with weird ideas and not much sense.

And I didn't have the brains
to follow up the kiss
outside the Black Dog
that night in the autumn
of '71 when we saw Beatrice
for the last time.

Maybe it was because
I didn't know
what a kiss like that meant
and maybe you didn't either
though I think you did

And I hope Beatrice found out
before she drowned
off the Scottish coast
trusting, as she always would,
that those who sail boats
know how and when to sail.

I remember her blue eyes
deep as seas.

A POTTED HISTORY

It's thirty years on, for pity's sake,
and we would have had something
if you hadn't got pregnant by the pet shop manager
with the fast car and the smile that said:
*I'm a man of the world. Let me
give you the whole wide world.*

We were young and it wasn't your fault.
How could you wait even for a boy as mad on you
as I was, who carried your bags and tied
the flowers in your hair, and who said *I love you*
as if we were stealing plums.

Today we buried my mother.
Afterwards I walked around the village,
saw the house where I was born,
heard the voices of the dead calling

and didn't think of you
until I saw the pet shop,
more or less as it was.
It needed new paint on the door
and the sun had faded
the adverts for birdseed
and the RSPCA.

I peered in like a fat ghost.
And you were leaning on the counter, chatting,
a steaming mug in both hands.
Your hair was still parted
in the same place, and still the colour of chestnuts.

That smile, those brown eyes dancing.

A child at your feet.

I walked on.

FOR THE TIME WE HAVE

War put too many acres under plough,
separated us. We made do, somehow.
When I came back, limping,
the kids shrank behind your skirts.

(The slow water ignores us, as it must;
concentrates on its skill, craftsmanship,
pride, rhythm.
We are here; were; will be.
A swan cuts patterns in the weed.)

There were rosehips in the hedgerows.
You picked them to make syrup.
We planted tulips and wild seed,
trusted something would thrive.
We mowed ourselves back
to what we hoped we were.

(Feather-brush the stones. Breathe lightly on them.
Crack them open and you'll find honeycombs,
centuries.)

Now you are a girl, gathering clover.
I split logs. You bake bread. The children
chatter around the long kitchen table.
We look through the window and see them
running with their kites on the hill
where the sweet weeds used to be:
Corncrake, poppy, charlock.
Heavy yield has choked them all.

And we learn, forget, relearn peace.

There are things I should have said to you.

Now my legs hurt. The pain crawls
into my gut, explores my bladder
and I piss blood. I flush it, tell no-one.

You talk to our grandson on the phone.

Our voices are small.

THIS BLESSED BORDEAUX

And so to bed, said Alice
with a bottle of red, two glasses,
and a jazz band
below.

Later she lay her face
on my shoulder and slept
and the lights of a passing car
crossed the ceiling
as others had done
in my room
in my parents' house
in those days
when cars had gaps between them
and when the Howes
next door
complained
that my music
was shaking the ornaments
on their mantelpiece
and when mother told them
I was going through
a difficult phase.

Not as difficult, I guess,
as Mr Howe
who hanged himself
in the cellar
listening to a tape
of a Strict Baptist choir
nor Mrs Howe
who dropped dead
in the butchers
ordering faggots.

The warmth of Alice's hand and arm
across my belly, the curve
of her hip and leg as she
spread herself around me
brings alive
this blessed Bordeaux
at this old table
in this messy kitchen
as the mid-winter mad-hattters swirl
and chatter and thud.

And Alice is there
and the world
for all its crimes is
warm and good.

CUSTOMS

All day the customs man,
head and shoulders behind a glass cage,
stamps blue books with a block of red ink.

When his shift is over
and the airport is empty
but for two old ladies
with malicious, patient eyes
knitting woollen angels
and two lads playing football with a rag,
the customs man leaves his desk.

He wears carpet slippers
and has a plastic leg.

He waits quietly for buses
does not curse when he misses a connection
does not talk to other travellers
does not react even when the joyful girl who dances
in a felt Santa hat along Main Street
pauses halfway through Hark! The Herald Angels Sing
to kiss his cheek
does not, in short,
let thought invade
his sense of proportion.

Home, he pats the dog
kisses his son
carries him to bed after tea
hobbles downstairs
and slumps into a chair
where his devoted wife
opens his mouth
touches the flowers that grow there
and waters them.

In the corner her father,
for he is blind,
reads the braille edition
of Playboy.

IF

If I told you
Hitler was a shepherd in Cornwall
two kids, wife, cottage
spent his days on a hillside
a pint or two on Fridays
never went far
except for chapel outings

If I told you
Goebbels
emigrated in '33
took a chance on a new life
alongside Cagney, Gable
and Edward G.
smoked like Bogart
married his very own Garbo
ended up the best
snake-oil salesman in Alabama

If I told you
Goering was a plumber in Bolton
Franco a postman with a passion
for bottle-neck and slide
Mussolini had a cafe near the Angel
and followed the Arsenal

If I told you
Stalin shot himself because a woman left him
Molotov ran a hostel for the homeless
Lenin kept bees

If I told you
Nixon was a Buddhist
by the time he was 20
spent years barefoot in Nepal

If I told you Pol Pot was into stamp collecting and
stayed at home with his mum

If I told you
Milosevic was a cricket freak
meticulously filled out scorecards every day
dreamed in a Zagreb bar
of googlies and late cuts

If I told you Amin
was an elegant dwarf
who ran the Ugandan branch of the Tom Waits fan club.

And if I were right
If all of these things were true
It wouldn't have changed a thing

Someone else
would still have come along
and fucked it all up

DON'T TELL ME ANYBODY COULD WRITE MY POEMS, DON'T TELL ME THEY GO NOWHERE, DO NOTHING. WHAT THE HELL DO YOU EXPECT?

You want iambic pentameters, haiku, villanelles

and in the small hours beyond the edge of
the white of the dark and the mist
I want poetry reckless and real as jazz
and poems that breathe and die
and are wild horses careering through graveyards
and are all of us
and you sitting here tonight
hoping to get through without being touched.

Write me a sonnet, you said.
And I did and neither of us liked it.
Countless times we rewind the clock
beyond despair, past anger and frustration
past all there was
to the beginning of all that was said for effect
past the lies and the need to trust
to forever, whatever and wherever we were
in the outpouring wild everything that a poem should be.
No, you said. *I don't want that.*

And I look at you, sipping tea and picking up
Rilke (collected poems of),
and I don't know
what to say or do.

SUBSIDENCE

We get smaller, the past gets bigger.
Pile the wet rocks, the sandbags three deep.
Chunks of cliff slither into the sea.
There is the smallest splash.
Houses, farms, forests will fall too.
It's in the way the earth rotates,
and the old prophets told us
there would be holes in the sky.
Let's drink our tea, that's it -
cup your hands around the mug.
Here, let me help.

PASSING THROUGH PETERBOROUGH

The barmaid tells me
the bar is empty
because
the hotel is full
of ex-prisoners of war
who are here
for a convention.

*They only drink
during Happy Hour*,
she says.

The next morning
I see them
in the lobby
with photo albums
and name tags
like Helmut,
Heinrich,
Fritz and
for some reason
Jeff.

They catch
their bus and go.

I work all morning
in my room
and come out
for lunch
just in time
to see
another bus
draw up.

Everybody
who gets off
has
a handlebar
moustache.

CHRISTMAS WINE

You order the Christmas wine on
Barclaycard and it comes in a
cardboard box and I drink it
by the end of November
- sometimes
I
just
can't
help
but
piss
y o u
o f f

NIGHT OUT

The young man in me clambers out of me
and we go out for the night.
We have a few pints in the pub.
I keep up with him but then
hang around at the bar while he chats up
two women in tight skirts and half-open shirts
drinking something pink and fizzy.
He goes off with them.
I take my pint to a chair in the corner
decide I've had enough
and catch the bus home.
When I get there I lock up
switch off the lights and go to bed.
In the early hours I'm awoken
by the young man in me coming home.
He swears because the door's locked
bangs on it with his fists, raps
the door knocker. I think:
Sod you mate, you can stay outside,
and a few minutes later I hear him
close the gate and trudge off,
the sound of his footsteps receding.

LORNA

Whenever we went to see Lorna
it was autumn
and everywhere was wet.
The hens would be pissed
on fallen apples.
She would walk around naked
hen-shit on her feet
singing hymns.

Once we found her on the roof
of the hen-house
blue with cold, beaming
and smoking something green.
If the weather got so bad
the mud was too deep for the van
she'd take the canoe on the river
to the village shop
for food and wine.

Last night I saw her on TV
on a programme about decorating
called Changing Rooms
presented by a pregnant woman in pink
who waved her arms and smiled a lot.

Lorna who, according
to the programme, lived
in a semi in Worthing,
didn't like her. I hoped
she'd do something
inappropriate -
trash the room
or pull off her lurid orange shirt -
but of course
the programme
like the rest of us
had been edited.

THE NURSE

The nurse unbolts my head and lifts the lid.
Out comes the usual nonsense: sunsets, women,
a bottle or three of Barolo, a gallon of Bombardier
then with a slithering thump at her feet a lizard in aspic.
The nurse grimaces, rolls up her sleeve
and plunges in her hand up past the wrist,
foraging about. *Ah*, she says, and
extricates a piece of driftwood labelled
Found on Mount Ararat, piece of Noah's Ark.
Behind that come sounds in a whoosh –
my mother's voice as she speaks to me for the last time
Go home and look after those children;
the chunk of my dad's spade on a piece of flint
as he digs the potato patch in 1959;
blue tits on the lonicera, bees on the foxgloves,
and finally, for this session at least, the sound
of bombs and flames in Baghdad.

The nurse closes the lid of my head, presses it down tight,
slides the bolts into place and steps back.

I'll just rinse my hands, she says, *then let's see
what's been going on in your trousers.*

HISTORY DREAM NO. 1

on the Town Hall steps Hart's in his topper announcing his gift to the city of a fountain and marble lions

but he can't compete with the rattle and clop of double-decker horse trams that ferry lunchtime concert-goers from the Assembly Rooms to Burgess's

where coffee is a penny a pint and
where out of the top windows you can see the back steps of Cheap John's

where John is taking a gin break and negotiating a flutter on the pigeons with Buckler the one-eyed tobacconist

and Buckler thinks it's a bad do that as it's Thursday the Association for Clothing Destitute Children will be lining up 86 scallywags for kitting out outside the Wesleyan chapel

where Eli Wright last week hanged himself from the balcony because of the rising price of tea

and even worse says Cheap John is the plan to let the inmates of Trinity play one-stump cricket in the park on Tuesday mornings

a sign he says of things to come

HISTORY

Am I to worship time or these drunken gods whose roguish laughs give me love to grasp and wrestle as if I were no man, but a tame mammoth for all of my long, short days?

Am I not to tell you history is a corpse in a ditch, a soaking field full of the fresh dead?

History! It's down to the rules, to the way we step out to the scratch each morning until at last no amount of brandy or champagne will bring us back.

Once they put a sock in my mouth to quiet the moans and pushed me back up, and I stumbled but did not fall. On I went in my colours of blue and bird's eye. On and bloody well on.

There were days when nothing went right, mind you. When history and my place in it didn't matter as much as the quickest way to get rid of migraine, when I thought *Look it doesn't matter what anyone thinks, if I get the milk-train home, it will come right. And the sadness and horror, pain and sleaze of the whole damn business will be erased.*

And it's true. I found a haphazard, wondrous way to win, at least for now, as the competent and devious do.

Don't expect, that's the thing. Make it pay and to hell with the spread of the belly and the monstrous flecks of grey that come in September or when you're asleep.

Don't expect. And to hell with it.

SCIENCE

Examine the slide.
Here's the microscope:
Things get fierce in there, and it's up to you to make sense
of the shapes the bald, wriggling cells make.
Hear them splashing about,
shifting, eating, thinking, shitting.
Over in that corner a virus is sulking.
That old coughing disease is turning on its side to take in air.
It won't last long.
Watch the others converge upon it and eat their fill.
It will squeal,
poor, wretched thing
but put that from your mind now.
Take off your spectacles, my son.
It's easier to see with your eye pressed tight

PERSECUTION

The villagers walk south along the snow line.
They stop for the night when the weak tire
and burn rags to keep warm, but the wood is wet,
the small trees too alive, and the child
freezes to death in her father's arms.

GOING THERE

Nitrates and phosphates illuminate the wilderness.
Dogs yap by the river
where the wrecked boat is beached on the mud
and the wind drives in from the west.

Above, a helicopter transports heat, colour, sex, noise, power.

Inside the house
your body follows the route of its spine.
as daylight fades and you step, steaming, from your bath.
You speak in the curious dialect of the young.
I paint the way your face moves.

Outside it's getting worse.
There was a riot downtown.
The muzzle is back on free speech.
The phones are tapped.
The linguistic detector vans rumble across the red earth towards us,
in formation, black against the dropping of the sun.
The interrogators know there is always a confession that cannot be made.
I boast that I shall defend us, even though it should be understood
that because I have taught the art of irrelevance
to cheerful students with nothing to lose
and the list of my failures remains pinned to the staffroom wall
I tend to lose track of the point of the struggle.
And my left jab is not what it was.

Yet with wine I forget and flaunt education again.
The textures of language send me swaggering through the house
and I catch a whiff of bacon cooking.
You rub my neck and shoulders
until the phone rings
and a friendly voice asks if we belong.
To what? I say. *Life is not a library, old chum.*
The joke is wasted.

Night comes. The noises change into those some perceive as silence.
You look out, see the glow of the burning city and say we must go.
We pack clothes, soap, pens, paper, a box of books, the smallest paintings
and we drive and drive, and drive.
Drive is a word you can sleep with.

We stop and stretch our legs as the sun rolls above the hills.
And we hear the exodus
hear the advance of the creatures
fossilised in the cracking boulders
wriggling beneath the tall grasses
hear the terrific armies of aphids gathering in the drying mud
hear our finger ends crackling
hear our eyes changing colour to fit the habitat
hear us holding each other
hear the collective energy of resistance
hear us whispering our languages

We are going! We are going there!

SMILE THE WEIRD JOY

This land has no name.

No one has crossed the water.

The storms have abated.

The sun freshens the ice.

Experiences begin to quicken. There is a bridge to another world.
Today we will move, either toward it, or further away.
Ideas like this neither matter, nor change the way we behave.

The keeper of the flame sings.
His voice bears us to the next hour, the next age.
We believe with him, not in or because of him.
In the evening we sit by our fire, as the sun burns.

This morning the dogs sit up, ears pricked,
as if there are hooves, or war has broken out.
We gather handfuls of snow, melt it, and drink.

The salt water brings gifts of wood
and food enough until the slow beasts come.

Inside the ice we have buried our dead.
We have dug them in well.
Inside the ice our sons, or the winter,
will bury us.

Our bodies will travel south,
a yard or two a year, then as the earth warms
a mile in a month

until we shall roll on the tide of the water,
smiling the weird joy of those who go clear.

The dogs, convinced something is happening,
throw back their heads and howl.
The keeper of the flame begins his song.

Maybe today we shall see the bridge,
a day's walk away, becoming larger.

We are strong, not tired.

THE FIGURES ARE PROBABLY FALSE

Shadows dance.

I do not know where you are.

Facts are agents of comfort: the sun is a flame, mercury burns on one side, jupiter and saturn contain ammonia and methane, mars is a freezing landscape of craters and crags.

The window is open but the bars do not shift in the breeze.

Men wait to be hanged and men wait to hang them. Our jailers idle their lives with poker and whist. Fate is a simple decision to twist.

Radioactive dust interrupts mealtimes and people, hearing the reports of the fire, run this way and that, gathering children and spare clothing and covering their heads.

Governments admit to round numbers of dead.

The wind deceives us into believing lovers will come to whisper at the wire, that no-one else will be listening, that the noise just then was not a key turning in the door. That beyond stretches not the motionless eternity of nothingness.

And I want to live. I want to tell you this.

We strain to listen, and hear, out among the laughter and memories, another pulse.

There are the bruised and the tortured, the bullied and the matter-of-factly abused; there are those who embrace themselves; there are those who say despite everything tanks will be replaced by tractors and people will walk through walls.

There are mistakes.

Shadows dance.

There are people clearing up.

The figures are probably false.

I do not know where you are.

DRIVING INTO FOG

There is a dark side to fog
drivers plunge into it
brake too late

Inside it's quiet and heavy
nothing moves
nobody speaks

Get the flask
pour the whisky
celebrate
wait for flares glowing
somewhere

Let time justify itself
let summer pass
winter come
let your girlfriends precede
each other

Put on the radio
shut your eyes
listen to the old songs
getting younger

Let the girls you loved
with their beads and rings
and cool breath
lie on your shoulder
for as long as it lasts
as if this wasn't fog at all

as if there were still picnics
in the warm mist by the river
where the boats of youth
float

If you can't
I don't know
what will happen
to you
and to those who
follow you

PRISONERS

We take the bay out of the landscape, set it in the woods.
This takes time, and is tricky. The slightest spillage could be
                              ruinous.
And the axes have seen sharper days.
Our stomachs need tightening, too, but that's a paler story.
Birds wonder what the fuss is about, scatter then return to circle us,
peering and chattering.
We are puzzled, too, for we did not plan this.
There was no way of anticipating it.
(I shall always be cautious with these memories
for the future has its own horizons.)
We toil. The sun goes up and down.
The curved line of sky gets closer.
The shape of it fills out.
A parabola, says Thomas, who thinks that's important.
Nobody answers.
We are getting closer. As a group, even as inmates or if you like workers, we
have more unity than we did.
But closer to an end? I don't know.
Why did we take the bay and put it here?
How did we find the strength to lift it?
It came out easily enough, with just a wrench or two at the edges.
And what for? Are we ruining or creating,
and is the cost too great? Ask the birds.
But hurry. They are leaving.
If you find out tell us.

Somewhere East of Sunset

Poems written while working
(and playing) in the U.S.A.

ATLANTIC CITY

Because of the jazz
Because of the bar where the piano plays itself
Because of New Jersey and nowhere and nobody
and all of us and you and I
Because Ferlinghetti wrote *The Old Italians Dying*
and I bought a book with that poem in yesterday
and because it's alive
Because the trombone player blasts out
Oh Come All Ye Faithful
on the Boardwalk a block south of
where the limbless woman lies on a cushion
and plays *Amazing Grace* on a keyboard with her tongue

Because of how it gets dark in ten minutes flat
and of how the sun rises like a gift each day
Because of Corona beer with a slice of lime in the rim
Because of the little man who plays the flute and his friend who won't stop
talking about himself to Lucy with her fathomless eyes
as I eat salsa and drown
And because outside it seems people
maybe Italians maybe just everybody
really are dying just a little bit in the backs of cabs all over town
or drifting between casinos or lying in the shadows

And because so soon it's five in the morning
and a singing man wearing a Father Christmas hat pleads for love
And because of the songs we always said we'd write
And because none of this has anything to do with numbers or facts
or Christmases or days or distances between you and I
Because of the nights that fly
and of all the angels who bounce off the walls of the night
who go home but never arrive
Because of what should happen but does not
Because of all of this and more
we must go on celebrating and worshipping
always
promise me that
wherever you are

JAZZ BAR

In a jazz bar
in a bad part of town
the girl holds back her hair
and accepts a light
from the small man
who talks incessantly
about himself.

She smiles, inhales.
He throws the match
into the ash-tray
and gestures with his hands
to illustrate the point
he is making.

Meaningless details?
We have wings.
Or at least the crumbling,
chaotic morality
dipping and rising
in the darkness.

Another man asks if she wants to leave.
She takes his hand.
Why?
We don't know.

1996, LEO'S BAR

In a bar in Crystal City one
stormy night in December,
you talked about God and death.

I stuck it for an hour.
You had eyes big as dreams,
a body warm as a beach.

Then I pulled my coat
over my head and ran six blocks
in the rain to Leo's

where Charlie sat, drunk
and smiling in the gloom.
Leo poured my beer,

whistled, said *Even Gene Kelly
wouldn't go out
on a night like this.*

Charlie said: *She's left me
And didn't say why.*
I bought him another beer.

We sat like that for an hour
until Razors came in
from a prayer meeting.

Razors was smiling because
he was Born Again - *Without
even a fair trial!* as he liked to say.

Razors is a nice guy
even if he did
crucify a man once.

Then at last you came back
the way I knew you would.
This one wore a blue blazer

and said his name was Jesus.
I shook hands, but Charlie said
Tell me something. Tell me why

you didn't want me for a sunbeam.
Jesus looked lost. You took him upstairs.
We inherit the world. It is good.

MANHATTAN

Ahead of us, Manhattan
The rest a memory tomorrow
May bring:
The old man selling water-colours in the rain
And you, and our hurried, clumsy hug
Like drowning folk clutching at the sea

The sun on your hair, making it yellow,
The crickets on Rhode Island
In the field that ran down to the sea.
And the day the whole world went to Boston just to see it,
But we sat under a tree in Albany and read Joyce.
Too pretentious, you said, and sprawled out on your back.
I watched you fall asleep.

Now, travelling in from JFK with newer friends
A shadow, a past that has hidden itself
For 25 years rises again
From where the street-saints sleep
Like the ghost-owl at home floating between the yews
And swooping by the graves of the gamblers with their soaring souls

And we ride the 59th Street Bridge and sing the song
Not knowing we will end the day drunk in a bar
With a woman who has perfect eyebrows
Who will tell us
Each of us
Is meant to rescue the world.

NEW ORLEANS, 1892
JAMES J. CORBETT KNOCKED OUT JOHN L. SULLIVAN IN 21 ROUNDS

It was over. You could smell September: the mugginess between storms, no break in the clouds.

When he fell, flags were tossed in the air. One arced into the ring and fell across his body like a shroud. Some madcap was blowing a horn.

Corbett gazed arrogantly into the tumult and shrivelled in the applause, taking note of the fickleness of crowds.

And slowly fat old John L. sat up, his consciousness given back to him.

He had finally done it then: betrayed himself. All that nonsense about the best shape of his life. Why, the only roadwork he'd done was with Clara Tuthill, described in the papers as "a local beauty". The boys here all know her well: she has a past and a pock-marked face. Et-Three, Brutus! as the poet said.

A fruitcake called Rufus took it upon himself to predict the end of the world before the year was out. Our Willie said: *Good, I'll drink myself daft with no fear of liver-rot or gout.*

Someone else sang an old song in a sad, passionate tenor.

John L. looked down at his fists trapped in those new-fangled gloves and knew it was done. *If I lost*, he said, *I'm glad it was to an American.*

We all roared. And yes he was adored, that red-eyed, crazy god. In the ten long years of his prime, ever since he broke big Paddy Ryan in Mississippi like a man chops down dead wood, he beat his chest and boasted: *I can lick any son of a bitch in the house!*

But now he was more ridiculous than sublime.

You could smell September. You really could.

TEXAS

In Sabinal Canyon, America, a man will kill a hog only if the moon is half-full.

And Gary took us to dinner and next day dropped dead of stress in his uplink truck.

Maria, let's ride the dirt roads out to the canyon, lie on our backs and see the buzzards and remember all those days

Or maybe not stop until we reach the Last Chance and watch the poor wetbacks from the bridge.

Don't look at me like that from wherever you are.

I know man cannot join what God and mothers have put asunder.

And Gary took us to dinner and next day dropped dead of stress in his uplink truck. And Billy got knocked out in round eight in the open air on the hot lawn outside the town hall.

Historians are living prophets looking back.

Three miles north west of Utopia, from Powderhouse Hill, they can see the trapped, moving figures on the Alamo walls.

And what does Abel's father do, dying at his cabin at Blanket Creek, wishing he was with his friends in the Mission, going out with honour instead of lying afraid and alone, a wasted way of going if ever there was one? What can he do?

I can taste the dry dirt in my father's throat.

Hitch the horse to Abel's plough and work the fields, steady now, straight, don't think, don't worry. There will be black-eyed peas and string beans. It will rain.

And don't remember when you were young when the river had 'em all: sunfish, catfish, bass. And when you went to school with Abel and May, and learned your gazintas and tutums.

Five gazinta ten twice. Tutums two is four.

And Gary took us to dinner and next day dropped dead of stress in his uplink truck. And Billy got knocked out in round eight in the open air on the hot lawn outside the town hall. And back home Portsmouth were relegated and Ian hung off the balcony pointing his aerial to the sky and catching the result on the World Service.

And all those years ago, chin deep in the cold creek, you did your best to hold your breath.

And as you came out they sang those old hymns, all those ghosts, all those grandfolks.

Shall we gather at the river? The beautiful, the beautiful river?

No longer, dear friends. The grass is horse high.

When we came here my father said softly: You survive the bears, the wolves, the floods, the droughts and this land is yours, my son.

And I have but it isn't and never will be.

And my Baptist father told me: Give it everything ya got. It's All or Nothing.

And don't underestimate Nothing, said my mother, pinafored and pragmatic.

And another thing, said my mother. Don't marry that Maria.

And Gary didn't. In one day, one strange and meaningless, long-way-from-home day in Sabinal Canyon, America, where a man will kill a hog only if the moon is half-full, Portsmouth were relegated, Billy got knocked out, and Gary dropped dead.

And whatever we did, why and when, it came to this.

ADVICE FOR YOUNG WOMEN BY THE LADIES OF THE DAUGHTERS OF THE REPUBLIC OF TEXAS

Stout ladies should avoid dainty and spindly chairs and furniture that accentuates their bigness. They should wear hats with wide brims.

Remove tan and freckles with a mixture of new milk, brandy and lemon juice. But rub it on your face. Don't drink it!

To remedy baldness, rub the patch morning and evening with onions until it is red, and afterward with honey.

If you add a cup of sweet milk to boiling water, it will flavour roasted pigs-ears if you drop them into it for half a minute.

Very fat bacon or salt pork strapped to a boil will draw the infection.

Scrapple and Hopping John are fine breakfasts by themselves.

You can't be too liberal with tomatoes. They're good for the liver, and a sovereign remedy for dyspepsia and indigestion.

But go easy on clabber, popcorn balls, horehound candy - and kisses.

For croup, hold the baby over the smoke of a fire doused in turpentine and white whiskey.

Don't let your husband go to bed with cold feet and, as for yourself, whatever he says to the contrary, for men sometimes have the instincts of blue bugs in a henhouse, don't try to get along without flannel underclothing in winter.

DOG

The dog of your sanity takes off at an even pace
block by block
out of town
on and on over the hills
over the snow peaks
and down
into the heat and the red rocks
where the kids dream their dreams
and America's
through the valley where the red dust burns its feet
and unborn cities glow in the night sky.
Nothing, not even death, stops the dog.
Even when the flesh has fallen from it
and the skeleton is bleached by the sun
it trots on at the same pace
the imaginary flesh of its tongue lolling
the eyes in their holes staring

on and on to where the day stretches into memory
on and on beneath a thrilling sky

on and on
the dog of your 30,000 days

ELVIS, VEGAS, 2001

he's at the bus stop on Paradise Road

his sequined suit's in his bag
he's not fat

he's not on dope
not into women younger than his daughter

he knows what day it is
he's had his hips replaced

and a room is a room is a room
and his voice is an echo

that just about handles the on-beat
and tonight

he's struggled through Heartbreak Hotel
in the Talking Horse bar at the MGM

and he wonders what the hell it was
that made him enter

the Elvis-Look-Alike contest
and he feels like shit

because he came fourth.

AT THE TIME OF NUCLEAR TESTING IN NEVADA

You can get a view of the explosion
from pretty much anywhere in town.
They come in from some place to watch.
Sheila says: *Hey, what else can they do?*

On Paradise the bride chews gum.
Hey baby, yells Sweet Pete,
*your jeans are so tight
I can read the date on the nickel
in your back pocket.*
She gives him the finger.

It's cold in the desert.
Friends die or get hooked.
And women walk the bleak night,
and some survive, but the way Sheila does.
Last night she wept beneath the Bourbon St. sign.
We have all come, as the girl said when I was young,
to fear the beating of the drum.

The explosion draws people from
wherever they leave, and when it's done
they talk about it, loudly with flushed
faces, as they walk to their cars
and we crawl back to our bars,
thinking at least the stars, the great
magnificent echoes of the glorious,
deafening unknown, go on. We'll see
them later.

SOMEWHERE EAST OF SUNSET

… and Ben's sober because he's driving but he's dafter than I am and I'm tucking into Caffreys while he's talking to a Tanzanian woman who is gracious and dignified and there's baseball on the TV above the bar and I still can't fathom out how the damn game works…

… and a girl is shouting at her man with the pony-tail and the hairy bit under his bottom lip who is sorry for himself and swilling tequilas and ready to fight anybody who doesn't like him or who likes his girl…

… and there are men who don't know why they've left home tonight and there are women who hold themselves with pride and solitude who have nothing to be ashamed of and nothing to be proud of and women who are going nowhere too, yes, and isn't it good?…

… and I still can't see why the Red Sox are beating the Blue Jays and the Tanzanian woman is nibbling Ben's ear and he's beaming and singing along as the juke box plays Losing My Religion and the wrinkled thin man next to him is playing air guitar and at the end of the song they all hug…

…and I pass the magic gallon of Caffreys and the girl from the argument talks to me about the way the world is and should be and shouldn't be and for an hour there's the two of us with nothing more than now and everything and the jubilant mess of wonder and tenderness…

… and she flings her arms around me and a punch lands in my back and the boyfriend is curling his silly lip and Ben's stopped promising to buy dinner just as the Tanzanian woman says she wants to cook for him…

… and Ben's hurling out words and waving his arms and I'm cursing and the boyfriend is backing off and there are faces and open mouths and hot beer breath and drinks spilling and the girl wants to hold my hand and take us out of this place…

…and Ben's calling to the barman *Ace, another Tequila for my new friend* and the boyfriend can't understand what he's objecting to and really wants the tequila and doesn't want the girl and everything would be good if he didn't maul her tits…

…oh, and she spits in his face and it all kicks off and somewhere in the whirl the boyfriend is sitting on the floor with his tequila crying out *But it's my birthday* and his girl asks where I'm staying and gives me her number and I give her mine and nothing's the same and Ben says can we get a cab because he's been drinking vodka…

…and we go and I know this is real and right and the only way to go out of the chaos and I get into my room and crack open a last beer and write it all down with the girl's number on the bedside table by the lamp and it's getting light and I stand at the window looking at the view…

… and the girl phones and says I know it's early but what do you say we go down to the beach to watch the waves and the whole damn thing and I say great let's do it and the glory begins again…

GEORGE FROM THE ANDES

George came from the Andes to Santa Monica
and is on the pier playing his pipes
working the tunes with the tide and the setting sun

and I lean on the pier rail and inhale
George's generosity
and you're with me again and it's just us

and you hold my arm and look up at me
and George is playing
for the Pacific and the sky
for the Navajo rug sellers
for the tattooists
for the toddlers proudly steering their first dodgem cars in circles
for you and for me

and then it's a bar and George has gone and so have you and
whatever you were is an ocean away
and there's soccer on the TV
and Christa the waitress brings me
green drinks that keep me sane
and I speak to no one except Christa
who is proud of her newly pierced navel
who has a boyfriend somewhere
and who sticks her cleavage in my face
in honest pursuit of her tip

and the jukebox has on it crazy things
like Forever by Roy Harper and I play it
and it's a quarter of a century ago
and it doesn't have to be any other way
when alcohol and exhilaration make love
on a day that begins and ends well

when George is on his way
from the Andes to somewhere
via Santa Monica pier.

REST HOME AND A MAN SWIMMING

The old folk who pay over the odds for a sea view
grip plastic beakers as they walk on the ship of the carpet
and the waves dance them to the land of youth
and all of geography and science and love and heat
goos up their bibs.

And I can't watch, sitting on the wall of their garden
to wait while you use the unisex loo by the beach huts
beyond which children hoot and scream and
a beachball bobs up into the sky.

And a man in fatigues runs into the waves
waving and yelling
and plunges around in the surf
then comes out and I guess when the burning begins
it doesn't stop and that's pretty much the end of you.
And people avoid him and he grins at the sky
or whatever he sees up there and runs off.

And in the rest home
a piano sets up.

And the old folk
begin to sing.

ON THE BEACH AT MALIBU

The surf's good but keep off the rocks and don't swim too far left
because the drain spills out there.

A Mexican couple with a toddler ask me to take their picture.
Where they're sitting the light will be all wrong. I don't know
how to tell them in Spanish but I move around
until the sun's behind us and they move with me,
beaming all the time.

The wind tugs the yachts away
to Santa Monica, Venice and the south.

And the sea smells of oil and the gulls won't dive into it.

And a man with an extremely long thin head comes by selling melons
and a woman in a shawl buys one
sits on a boulder, takes a knife from her cloak and eats.

And a lean kid skims smooth stones on the foul sea
and a bi-plane advertises a mobile phone company
and on the radio someone talks about world famine
between the jingles.

And I go to the bar with its blue and white chairs
and drink a beer and pick at a plate of white fish.

In the hills
a boy flies a red kite.

KINGFISH LEVINSKY

Kingfish Levinsky knows we've all laid back on a bed and wondered what in hell happens next.

Kingfish Levinsky looks at the words LENA DEAD PLEASE PHONE and now he has he wishes he hadn't.

Kingfish Levinsky remembers carrying boxes of fish at the docks on those cold winter mornings with pa's grin as fierce as the wind, remembers ma telling him *Harry, Look After Your Sister.*

Kingfish Levinsky smells the grey hairs sprout at his temples.

Kingfish Levinsky sees Lena as a girl playing marbles and hop-scotch.

Kingfish Levinsky says *Lena did me proud.*

Kingfish Levinsky hears Lena say: *Some you lose, one or two you draw and that's about it with love.*

Kingfish Levinsky says she was right all along.

Kingfish Levinsky remembers her telling him she's got him 30 grand to fight Joe Louis, remembers telling her *Gee Lena, we've got it made.*

Kingfish Levinsky feels the fear stiffening his legs and hears them say get undressed and he's shaking too much to do it and then they do it for him and the next thing he knows he's on the ropes and it's over and he's pleading *Don't Let Him Hit Me Again*

Kingfish Levinsky hears Lena's body floating in the river around the bend beneath the bridge that carries trains north.

Kingfish Levinsky weeps, says *The Queen is gone and I ain't the King no more.*

Kingfish Levinsky knows the road stretches out long and lonely and going home is just one more stop.

DRIVING, USA

I drive past Jumpin' Jimmy's and Automatic Slim's
    past the motels and diners, junkyards and second hand car lots
    past the Welcome To Mississippi sign that looks like a Klan hood

I drive through the cotton fields and swamps
    where dead tree trunks are framed against the sunrise

I stop at a gas station and a clown in full make-up pours the gas
    and talks of the terrible stress of making people laugh

I drive past the twins who have to be finger-printed to tell them apart
    who sit on the bridge where the road forks
    to Nineveh and Nameless

I drive through Utah where the trains are on time but the people have
    broken down
    on and on
    into Omaha where Ellie waits at tables seven-to-six in the Pea
    Soup Diner
    and means it when she says *Try our new chicken melt...*

I drive into cities where beggars dance to the tunes of their bones
    where girls in gingham play with hoola-hoops
    where poems walk solemnly behind the coffins of poets

I give lifts to men called Yogi and Shooter and Buck
    who rename French fries Freedom fries
    in protest at the French stance on the war in Iraq
    who take weekends in the wilderness to hunt wild boar
    with grenades

I drive past a man with a sign that says Terror Alert High
    and another that says The Wages of Sin Mean It's a Job Like Any
    Other

I drive past a naked man-and-woman
    who are mad with each other

        mad because the car's got a flat tyre
        mad because the police are arresting them
        mad because of the price of oranges
        mad because people don't get naked enough
        and persecute those who do
        mad about Cuba Afghanistan and God
        about Kingfish Levinsky
        Katherine Hepburn
        Neil Armstrong
        Babe Ruth
        loneliness

I drive past men who owe everything they have
        men who orbit their own earth
        women who grow beards and clip them to look serious

I drive past City Lights
        up Nob Hill to the Fairmont
        where Tony Bennett sang *I Left My Heart In San Francisco*
        where you get a beautiful view of Alcatraz -
        where the ghosts gaze at the glow of the city
        where the Birdman waits for his birds
        where Machine Gun Kelly mends the movie projector
        where Capone mutters *No Respect No Respect*

I circle the graveyards at Colma
        where Boshter Bill fought Tommy Burns
        and lasted 129 seconds

I drive on into the valley where the oranges grow
        where the flat fields end at the edge of the road
        and I slow down and buy orchids from a child
        at the only lights between here and Arkansas
        and a woman in a Dodge Durango blows me a kiss

And where is she going? And where am I?
        I haven't a clue

Except
    right out of this day
    right out of this century

    and on and on
    I drive
    right out
    as fast as I can
    right out of reasons and love and joy
    right out of death
    right out of America

NOTES

Lightning Louie: Panama Al Brown (1902-51), world bantamweight champion 1929-35. The phrase 'he was no Panama Al' derives from the writings of the great sportswriter A J Liebling. Brian London of Blackpool fought Floyd Patterson and Muhammad Ali for the world heavyweight title and also held the British and Empire championships. He once said: "I'm only a prawn in the game."

Texas owes a great deal to ***Bear Meat 'N Honey***, ed. Greg Walton, Acorn 1991, and Orlando Canizales v Billy Hardy, Laredo, Texas, 1991.

Advice for Young Women is indebted to *A Pinch of This and a Handful of That, Historic Recipes of Texas*, 1988.

Kingfish Levinsky was a heavyweight boxer and later a travelling salesman in America in the 1930s. His real name was Harry Krakow. He was managed by his sister Lena.

Driving, USA. There is a *Welcome To Mississippi* sign on Highway 61 just outside Memphis that from a distance looks like a Ku Klux Klan hood. Nameless is in Tennessee. Most of the other references can easily be looked up, should anyone be interested, but Boshter Bill is Bill Squires of Australia who travelled to Colma, just outside San Francisco, to box Tommy Burns for the world heavyweight title on 4 July 1907 and was knocked out in 129 seconds. Afterwards when asked by journalists what he thought, he said: "I got a bloody good lickin' and I'm goin' home."

DIAGNOSTIC ISSUES IN DEPRESSION AND GENERALIZED ANXIETY DISORDER

Refining the Research Agenda for DSM-V

DIAGNOSTIC ISSUES IN DEPRESSION AND GENERALIZED ANXIETY DISORDER

Edited by

David Goldberg, D.M., FRCPsych
Kenneth S. Kendler, M.D.
Paul J. Sirovatka, M.S.
Darrel A. Regier, M.D., M.P.H.

Published by the
American Psychiatric Association
Arlington, Virginia

Note: The authors have worked to ensure that all information in this book is accurate at the time of publication and consistent with general psychiatric and medical standards, and that information concerning drug dosages, schedules, and routes of administration is accurate at the time of publication and consistent with standards set by the U.S. Food and Drug Administration and the general medical community. As medical research and practice continue to advance, however, therapeutic standards may change. Moreover, specific situations may require a specific therapeutic response not included in this book. For these reasons and because human and mechanical errors sometimes occur, we recommend that readers follow the advice of physicians directly involved in their care or the care of a member of their family.

The findings, opinions, and conclusions of this report do not necessarily represent the views of the officers, trustees, or all members of the American Psychiatric Association. The views expressed are those of the authors of the individual chapters.

Copyright © 2010 American Psychiatric Association
ALL RIGHTS RESERVED

Printed in the Canada on acid-free paper
14 13 12 11 10   5 4 3 2 1
First Edition

Typeset in Adobe's Frutiger and AGaramond.

American Psychiatric Publishing, Inc.
1000 Wilson Boulevard
Arlington, VA 22209-3901
www.appi.org

Mixed Sources
Product group from well-managed forests, and other controlled sources
www.fsc.org Cert no. SW-COC-002358
© 1996 Forest Stewardship Council

Library of Congress Cataloging-in-Publication Data
Diagnostic issues in depression and generalized anxiety disorder : refining the research agenda for DSM-V / edited by David Goldberg ... [et al.]. -- 1st ed.
    p. ; cm.
  Includes bibliographical references and index.
  ISBN 978-0-89042-456-8 (pbk. : alk. paper)
  1. Anxiety disorders–Diagnosis–Congresses. 2. Depression, Mental—Diagnosis—Congresses. I. Goldberg, David P. II. Diagnostic and statistical manual of mental disorders.
  [DNLM: 1. Depressive Disorder—diagnosis—Congresses. 2. Anxiety Disorders—classification—Congresses. 3. Anxiety Disorders—diagnosis—Congresses. 4. Depressive Disorder—classification—Congresses.
WM 171 D53558 2010]
  RC531.D543 2010
  362.196'852206—dc22
                                                                    2009046835

British Library Cataloguing in Publication Data
A CIP record is available from the British Library.

CONTENTS

CONTRIBUTORS ix

PREFACE xvii
    Darrel A. Regier, M.D., M.P.H.

1 THE PROBLEM: CHARGE TO THE CONFERENCE 1
    Kenneth S. Kendler, M.D.

2 THE NOSOLOGIC RELATIONSHIP BETWEEN GENERALIZED ANXIETY DISORDER AND MAJOR DEPRESSION 15
    John M. Hettema, M.D., Ph.D.

COMMENTARY ON "THE NOSOLOGIC RELATIONSHIP BETWEEN GENERALIZED ANXIETY DISORDER AND MAJOR DEPRESSION" 41
    Jules Angst, M.D.
    Alex Gamma, Ph.D.
    Vladeta Ajdacic, Ph.D.
    Wulf Rössler, M.D., M.A.

3 THE BIOLOGY OF GENERALIZED ANXIETY DISORDER AND MAJOR DEPRESSIVE DISORDER: COMMONALITIES AND DISTINGUISHING FEATURES 45
    Elizabeth I. Martin, Ph.D.
    Charles B. Nemeroff, M.D., Ph.D.

4 WHAT (NO) DIFFERENCES IN RESPONSES TO THREE CLASSES OF PSYCHOTROPICS CAN TEACH US ABOUT DISTINCTIONS BETWEEN GENERALIZED ANXIETY DISORDER AND MAJOR DEPRESSIVE DISORDER 71
    Toshi A. Furukawa, M.D., Ph.D.
    Norio Watanabe, M.D., Ph.D.
    Ichiro M. Omori, M.D., Ph.D.

COMMENTARY ON "THE BIOLOGY OF GAD AND MDD" AND "WHAT (NO) DIFFERENCES IN RESPONSES TO THREE CLASSES OF PSYCHOTROPICS CAN TEACH US ABOUT DISTINCTIONS BETWEEN GAD AND MDD" 105
    David J. Kupfer, M.D.
    Ellen Frank, Ph.D.

5 PSYCHOMETRIC ASPECTS OF ANXIETY AND DEPRESSION 109
    David Goldberg, D.M., FRCPsych

COMMENTARY ON "PSYCHOMETRIC ASPECTS OF ANXIETY AND DEPRESSION" 125
    Patrick E. Shrout, Ph.D.

6 THE BOUNDARY BETWEEN GENERALIZED ANXIETY DISORDER AND THE UNIPOLAR MOOD DISORDERS: DIAGNOSTIC AND PSYCHOMETRIC FINDINGS IN CLINICAL SAMPLES 131
    Timothy A. Brown, Psy.D.

7 MAJOR DEPRESSION AND GENERALIZED ANXIETY DISORDER IN THE NATIONAL COMORBIDITY SURVEY FOLLOW-UP SURVEY... 139
    Ronald C. Kessler, Ph.D.
    Michael Gruber, M.S.
    John M. Hettema, M.D., Ph.D.
    Irving Hwang, M.A.
    Nancy Sampson, B.A.
    Kimberly A. Yonkers, M.D.

8 THE RELATIONSHIP OF GENERALIZED ANXIETY DISORDER AND MAJOR DEPRESSION OVER TIME 171
    Valery N. Krasnov, M.D.

9 GENERALIZED ANXIETY DISORDER AND MAJOR DEPRESSION: COMMON AND RECIPROCAL CAUSES 179
    D. M. Fergusson, Ph.D.
    L. J. Horwood, M.Sc.

10 CONFIRMATORY FACTOR ANALYSIS OF COMMON MENTAL
DISORDERS ACROSS CULTURES............................191
    K. S. Jacob, M.D., Ph.D., MRCPsych
    Martin Prince, M.D., MRCPsych
    David Goldberg, D.M., FRCPsych

    COMMENTARY ON "CONFIRMATORY FACTOR ANALYSIS
    OF COMMON MENTAL DISORDERS ACROSS CULTURES".........211
        Dan J. Stein, M.D., Ph.D.
        Vikram Patel, M.Sc., MRCPsych, Ph.D.
        Gerhard Heinze, M.D.

11 GENERALIZED ANXIETY DISORDER AND DEPRESSION:
CHILDHOOD RISK FACTORS IN A BIRTH COHORT FOLLOWED TO
AGE 32 YEARS..217
    Terrie E. Moffitt, Ph.D.
    Avshalom Caspi, Ph.D.
    HonaLee Harrington, B.A.
    Barry Milne, Ph.D.
    Maria Melchior, Sc.D.
    David Goldberg, D.M., FRCPsych
    Richie Poulton, Ph.D.

12 ARE THERE EARLY ADVERSE EXPOSURES THAT DIFFERENTIATE
DEPRESSION AND ANXIETY RISK?............................241
    Marcus Richards, Ph.D.
    David Goldberg, D.M., FRCPsych

13 EPISODES AND DISORDERS OF GENERAL ANXIETY
AND DEPRESSION..257
    Ian M. Goodyer, M.D.

14 ARE MAJOR DEPRESSION AND GENERALIZED ANXIETY DISORDER
THE SAME OR DIFFERENT DISORDERS? DISCUSSION OF THE
DUNEDIN AND MEDICAL RESEARCH COUNCIL BIRTH COHORT
STUDIES AND THE THREE-GENERATION HIGH RISK STUDY........271
    Myrna M. Weissman, Ph.D.
    Virginia Warner, M.P.H.
    Priya Wickramaratne, Ph.D.

15 TOWARD A PRIMARY-CARE FRIENDLY DSM-V CLASSIFICATION OF
EMOTIONAL DISORDERS: AN INTEGRATIVE APPROACH 285
J. Ormel, Ph.D.
M. J. Manley, Ph.D.

16 PSYCHOSOCIAL ORIGINS OF DEPRESSIVE AND ANXIETY
DISORDERS 303
George W. Brown, Ph.D.

COMMENTARY ON "PSYCHOSOCIAL ORIGINS OF DEPRESSIVE
AND ANXIETY DISORDERS," PART 1 333
Sidney Zisook, M.D.

COMMENTARY ON "PSYCHOSOCIAL ORIGINS OF DEPRESSIVE
AND ANXIETY DISORDERS," PART 2 347
Donna E. Stewart, M.D., FRCPC

17 THE RELATIONSHIP BETWEEN GENERALIZED ANXIETY DISORDER
AND MAJOR DEPRESSIVE EPISODE 355
David Goldberg, D.M., FRCPsych

INDEX 363

CONTRIBUTORS

Vladeta Ajdacic, Ph.D.
Research Associate, Department of General and Social Psychiatry, Zurich University Psychiatric Hospital, Zurich, Switzerland

Jules Angst, M.D.
Professor and Head, Research Department, Zurich University Psychiatric Hospital, Zurich, Switzerland

George W. Brown, Ph.D.
Health Service and Population Research, Institute of Psychiatry, Kings College London, London, United Kingdom

Timothy A. Brown, Psy.D.
Professor, Department of Psychology, Boston University, Boston, Massachusetts

Avshalom Caspi, Ph.D.
Edward M. Arnett Professor, Departments of Psychology and Neuroscience and of Psychiatry and Behavioral Sciences, and Institute for Genome Sciences and Policy, Duke University, Durham, North Carolina

D. M. Fergusson, Ph.D.
Research Professor and Director, Christchurch Health and Development Study, Department of Psychological Medicine, University of Otago, Christchurch, New Zealand

Ellen Frank, Ph.D.
Professor of Psychiatry and Psychology, Department of Psychiatry, University of Pittsburgh School of Medicine, Pittsburgh, Pennsylvania

Toshi A. Furukawa, M.D., Ph.D.
Professor and Chair, Department of Psychiatry and Cognitive-Behavioral Medicine, Nagoya City University Graduate School of Medical Sciences, Nagoya, Japan

Alex Gamma, Ph.D.
Research Assistant, Research Department, Zurich University Psychiatric Hospital, Zurich, Switzerland

David Goldberg, D.M., FRCPsych
Professor Emeritus, Health Service and Population Research, Institute of Psychiatry, King's College London, London, United Kingdom

Ian M. Goodyer, M.D.
Foundation Professor of Child and Adolescent Psychiatry, University of Cambridge, Cambridge, England

Michael Gruber, M.S.
Programmer/Analyst, Department of Health Care Policy, Harvard Medical School, Boston, Massachusetts

HonaLee Harrington, B.A.
Associate in Research, Departments of Psychology and Neuroscience and of Psychiatry and Behavioral Sciences, and Institute for Genome Sciences and Policy, Duke University, Durham, North Carolina

Gerhard Heinze, M.D.
Professor, Jefe del Departamento de Psiquiatriá y Salud Mental, Facultad de Medicina, Ciudad Universitaria, Universidad Nacional Autónomade México, Delegación Coyoacán, D.F., Mexico

John M. Hettema, M.D., Ph.D.
Associate Professor, Virginia Institute for Psychiatric and Behavioral Genetics, Department of Psychiatry, Virginia Commonwealth University, Richmond, Virginia

L. J. Horwood, M.Sc.
Associate Professor, Department of Psychological Medicine, University of Otago, Christchurch, New Zealand

Irving Hwang, M.A.
Programmer/Analyst, Department of Health Care Policy, Harvard Medical School, Boston, Massachusetts

K.S. Jacob, M.D., Ph.D., MRCPsych
Professor and Head, Department of Psychiatry, Christian Medical College, Vellore, India

Kenneth S. Kendler, M.D.
Professor of Human Genetics; Director, Virginia Institute for Psychiatric and Behavioral Genetics; and Rachel Brown Banks Distinguished Professor of Psychiatry, Virginia Commonwealth University, Richmond, Virginia

Ronald C. Kessler, Ph.D.
Professor, Department of Health Care Policy, Harvard Medical School, Boston, Massachusetts

Valery N. Krasnov, M.D.
Director, Moscow Research Institute of Psychiatry, Moscow, Russian Federation

David J. Kupfer, M.D.
Thomas Detre Professor, Department of Psychiatry, University of Pittsburgh School of Medicine, Pittsburgh, Pennsylvania

M. J. Manley, Ph.D.
Researcher, Interdisciplinary Center for Psychiatric Epidemiology, Department of Psychiatry, University Medical Center Groningen, University of Groningen, Groningen, the Netherlands; Department of Epidemiology and Public Health, Yale University School of Medicine, New Haven, Connecticut

Elizabeth I. Martin, Ph.D.
Research Associate, Peptide Biology Laboratory, Salk Institute for Biological Studies, La Jolla, California

Maria Melchior, Sc.D.
INSERM, Université Paris XI, Hôpital Paul-Brousse, Villejuif, France

Barry Milne, Ph.D.
Research Data Manager, Growing Up in New Zealand, University of Auckland, Tamaki Campus, Auckland, New Zealand

Terrie E. Moffitt, Ph.D.
Kurt Schmidt Nielsen Professor, Departments of Psychology and Neuroscience and of Psychiatry and Behavioral Sciences, and Institute for Genome Sciences and Policy, Duke University, Durham, North Carolina

Charles B. Nemeroff, M.D., Ph.D.
Reunette W. Harris Professor, Department of Psychiatry and Behavioral Sciences, Emory University School of Medicine, Atlanta, Georgia

Ichiro M. Omori, M.D., Ph.D.
Department of Psychiatry and Cognitive-Behavioral Medicine, Nagoya City University Graduate School of Medical Sciences, Nagoya, Japan

J. Ormel, Ph.D.
Professor, Interdisciplinary Center for Psychiatric Epidemiology, Department of Psychiatry, University Medical Center Groningen, University of Groningen, the Netherlands

Vikram Patel, M.Sc., MRCPsych, Ph.D.
Professor of International Mental Health and Wellcome Trust Senior Clinical Research Fellow in Tropical Medicine, Centre for Global Mental Health, London School of Hygiene and Tropical Medicine and Sangath, Goa, India

Richie Poulton, Ph.D.
Professor and Director, Dunedin Multidiscplinary Health and Development Research Unit, Department of Preventive and Social Medicine, Dunedin School of Medicine; Co-Director, National Centre for Lifecourse Research, University of Otago, Dunedin, New Zealand

Martin Prince, M.D., MRCPsych
Professor of Epidemiological Psychiatry, Centre for Public Mental Health, Health Service and Population Research Department, David Goldberg Centre, Institute of Psychiatry, London, United Kingdom

Darrel A. Regier, M.D., M.P.H.
Executive Director, American Psychiatric Institute for Research and Education; Director, Division of Research, American Psychiatric Association, Arlington, Virginia

Wulf Rössler, M.D., M.A.
Professor of Clinical and Social Psychiatry, Research Department, Zurich University Psychiatric Hospital, Zurich, Switzerland

Nancy Sampson, B.A.
Project Director, Department of Health Care Policy, Harvard Medical School, Boston, Massachusetts

Patrick E. Shrout, Ph.D.
Professor, Department of Psychology, New York University, New York, New York

Dan J. Stein, M.D., Ph.D.
Professor, Department of Psychiatry and Mental Health, University of Cape Town, Cape Town, South Africa

Donna E. Stewart, M.D., FRCPC
University Professor and Chair of Women's Mental Health, University Health Network, University of Toronto, Toronto, Ontario, Canada

Virginia Warner, M.P.H.
Research Scientist III, Department of Psychiatry, College of Physicians and Surgeons, Columbia University, New York, New York

Norio Watanabe, M.D., Ph.D.
Assistant Professor, Department of Psychiatry and Cognitive-Behavioral Medicine, Nagoya City University Graduate School of Medical Sciences, Nagoya, Japan

Myrna M. Weissman, Ph.D.
Professor of Epidemiology in Psychiatry, Department of Psychiatry, College of Physicians and Surgeons, Columbia University, New York, New York

Priya Wickramaratne, Ph.D.
Assistant Professor, Department of Psychiatry, College of Physicians and Surgeons, Columbia University, New York, New York

Kimberly A. Yonkers, M.D.
Associate Professor, Department of Psychiatry, Yale University School of Medicine, New Haven, Connecticut

Sidney Zisook, M.D.
Professor and Director, Residency Training Program, Department of Psychiatry, University of California, San Diego, La Jolla, California

The following contributors to this book have indicated a financial interest in or other affiliation with a commercial supporter, a manufacturer of a commercial product, a provider of a commercial service, a nongovernmental organization, and/or a government agency, as listed below:

Darrel A. Regier, M.D., M.P.H.—The author, as Executive Director of American Psychiatric Institute for Research and Education (APIRE), oversees all federal and industry-sponsored research and research training grants in APIRE but receives no external salary funding or honoraria from any government or industry.

Jules Angst, M.D.—The author has served on the advisory board for Eli Lilly and Janssen, and has served on the speakers' bureau for Eli Lilly, GlaxoSmithKline, AstraZeneca, Lundbeck, and Pfizer.

George W. Brown, Ph.D.—The author has received research support from the Medical Research Council of the United Kingdom.

Ellen Frank, Ph.D.—The author has served on the advisory board of Servier. The author has received grant support from the Forest Research Institute, and she receives royalties from Guilford Press.

Toshi A. Furukawa, M.D., Ph.D.—The author has received research support and speaking fees from Asahi Kasei, Astellas, Dai-Nippon Sumitomo, Eisai, Eli Lilly, GlaxoSmithKline, Janssen, Kyowa Hakko, Meiji, Nikken Kagaku, Organon, Otsuka, Pfizer, and Yoshitomi. The author has received research support from the Japanese Ministry of Education, Science, and Technology and the Japanese Ministry of Health Labor and Welfare.

David Goldberg, D.M., FRCP—The author has received consulting fees from Lundbeck and Bristol Meyers. The author has received travel reimbursement from Eil Lilly.

Ronald C. Kessler, Ph.D.—The author has received consulting fees from AstraZeneca, Bristol-Myers Squibb, Eli Lilly, GlaxoSmithKline, Pfizer, Sanofi-Aventis, and Wyeth Pharmaceuticals. The author has received research support from Bristol-Myers Squibb, Eli Lilly, Ortho-McNeil, Pfizer, and the Pfizer Foundation.

Valery Krasnov, M.D.—The author has received consultative and technical research assistance from the National Institute of Mental Health (NIMH), consultative assistance from APIRE/American Psychiatric Association (APA), and grant support from U.S. Civilian Research and Development Foundation/Agency for Healthcare Research and Quality. The author has participated in clinical trials on schizophrenia, depressive disorders, anxiety disorders, and dementia sponsored by Eli Lilly, Pfizer, GlaxoSmithKline, and AstraZeneca, as well as an epidemiology study of Mental Health in Chechen Republic (Russia) sponsored by the World Health Organization (WHO) and UNICEF. The author has participated on the AstraZeneca Young Minds Awards Committee, sponsored by APIRE/APA.

Contributors

Terrie E. Moffitt, Ph.D.—The author has no financial conflicts of interest to disclose. However, the author's work in this volume was supported by the New Zealand Health Research Council, NIMH grants MH45070 and MH49414, the William T. Grant Foundation, and U.K. Medical Research Council grant G0100527.

Charles B. Nemeroff, M.D., Ph.D.—The author has served as a consultant to, served on the speakers' bureau and/or Board of Directors, has received grant support, and/or owned equity in one or more of the following: Abbot Laboratories, Acadia Pharmaceuticals, American Foundation for Suicide Prevention (AFSP), APIRE, AstraZeneca, BMC-JF LLC, Bristol-Myers-Squibb, CeNeRx, Corcept, Cypress Biosciences, Cyberonics, Eli Lilly, Entrepreneur's Fund, Forest Laboratories, George West Mental Health Foundation, GlaxoSmithKline, i3 DLN, Janssen Pharmaceutica, Lundbeck, National Alliance for Resesarch on Schizophrenia and Depression (NARSAD), Neuronetics, NIMH, National Foundation for Mental Health (NFMH), NovaDel Pharma, Otsuka, Pfizer, Quintiles, Reevax, UCB Pharma, and Wyeth-Ayerst. The author serves on the Scientific Advisory Board for AstraZeneca, Johnson & Johnson, Pharma Neuroboost, Forest Laboratories, Quintiles, and NARSAD. The author has received grant support from National Institutes of Health (NIH), NARSAD, and AFSP. The author serves on the Board of Directors of AFSP, APIRE, NovaDel Pharmaceuticals, and the George West Mental Health Foundation. The author owns equity in CeNeRx and Reevax. The author owns stock or stock options in Corcept, Cypress Biosciences, and NovaDel.

Wulf Rössler, M.D., M.A.—The author has served on several advisory boards for Eli Lilly, Janssen-Cilag, and Bristol-Myers Squibb. The author has also served on the speakers' bureau for Eli Lilly, GlaxoSmithKline, Astra Zeneca, Lundbeck, Pfizer, and Bristol-Myers Squibb.

Patrick E. Shrout, Ph.D.—The author has consulted with Hector R. Bird, M.D., of Columbia University Medical Center and he intends to pay a small fee from a grant from McNeil Pediatrics Division of McNeil PPC, Inc. No oversight of work was provided or required.

Dan J. Stein, M.D., Ph.D.—The author has received research grants and/or consultancy honoraria from Astra Zeneca, Eli Lilly, GlaxoSmithKline, Lundbeck, Orion, Pfizer, Roche, Servier, Solvay, Sumitomo, and Wyeth Pharmaceuticals.

Donna E. Stewart, M.D., FRCPC— The author has served on the Global Advisory Board for Antidepressants for Eli Lilly and on the National Advisory Board for Venalafaxine/ Desmethylvenlafaxine for Wyeth.

Norio Watanabe, M.D., Ph.D.—The author has received a speaking fee from GlaxoSmithKline.

Kimberly A. Yonkers, M.D.—The author has received grant/research support from

Eli Lilly, Wyeth Pharmaceuticals, NIMH, National Institute on Drug Abuse, NARSAD, and National Institute of Child Health and Human Development.

Sidney Zisook, M.D.—The author has served on the advisory board for GlaxoSmithKline. The author has served as a member of the speaker's bureau and received honoraria from GlaxoSmithKline and Forest Laboratories. The author has received grant support from Aspect Medical Systems, PemLab, the Jed Foundation, NIMH, and the Veterans Administration Health Care System.

The following contributors to this book do not have any conflicts of interest to disclose:

Vladeta Ajdacic, Ph.D.
Timothy A. Brown, Psy.D.
Avshalom Caspi, Ph.D.
D.M. Fergusson, Ph.D.
Alex Gamma, Ph.D.
Ian Goodyear, M.D.
Michael Gruber, M.S.
HonaLee Harrington, B.A.
Gerhard Heinze, M.D.
John M. Hettema, M.D., Ph.D.
L. J. Horwood, M.Sc.
Irving Hwang, M.A.
K.S. Jacob, M.D., Ph.D., MRCPsych
Kenneth S. Kendler, M.D.
David J. Kupfer, M.D.
M. J. Manley, Ph.D.
Elizabeth I. Martin, Ph.D.
Maria Melchior, Sc.D.
Barry Milne, Ph.D.
Ichiro M. Omori, M.D., Ph.D.
J. Ormel, Ph.D.
Vikram Patel, M.Sc., MRCPsych, Ph.D.
Richie Poulton, Ph.D.
Marcus Richards, Ph.D.
Nancy Sampson, B.A.
Virginia Warner, M.P.H.
Myrna M. Weissman, Ph.D.
Priya Wickramaratne, Ph.D.

PREFACE

Diagnostic Issues in Depression and Generalized Anxiety Disorder: Refining the Research Agenda for DSM-V was born from the 10th conference in a series of 13 funded by the National Institutes of Health (NIH), collectively titled, "The Future of Psychiatric Diagnosis: Refining the Research Agenda." Under the leadership of conference co-chairs Kenneth S. Kendler, M.D., and David Goldberg, D.M., FRCPsych, 23 scientists from around the world convened to discuss the biologic and psychosocial evidence both separating and conjoining generalized anxiety disorder (GAD) and major depressive disorder (MDD). The conference series was convened by the American Psychiatric Association (APA) in collaboration with the World Health Organization (WHO) and the NIH.

The APA/WHO/NIH conference series represents a key element in a multiphase research review process designed to set the stage for the fifth revision of the *Diagnostic and Statistical Manual of Mental Disorders* (DSM-V). In its entirety, the project entails 13 work groups, each focused on a specific diagnostic topic or category, and two additional work groups dedicated to methodological considerations in nosology and classification.

Within the APA, the American Psychiatric Institute for Research and Education (APIRE), under the direction of the author (D.A.R.), held lead responsibility for organizing and administering the diagnosis research planning conferences. Members of the Executive Steering Committee for the series included representatives of the WHO's Division of Mental Health and Prevention of Substance Abuse and of three NIH institutes that jointly funded the project: National Institute of Mental Health (NIMH), National Institute on Drug Abuse (NIDA), and National Institute on Alcohol Abuse and Alcoholism (NIAAA).

APA published the fourth edition of the DSM in 1994 (American Psychiatric Association 1994) and a text revision in 2000 (American Psychiatric Association 2000). Although DSM-V is not scheduled to appear until 2012, planning for the fifth revision began in 1999 with collaboration between APA and NIMH, designed to stimulate research that would address identified opportunities in psychiatric nosology. A first product of this joint venture was preparation of six white papers that proposed broad-brush recommendations for research in key areas; topics included developmental issues, gaps in the current classification, disability and impairment, neuroscience, nomenclature, and cross-cultural issues. Each team that developed a paper included at least one liaison member from NIMH, with the intent—largely realized—that these members would integrate many of the work groups' recommendations into NIMH research support programs. These white papers were published in *A Research Agenda for DSM-V* (Kupfer et al. 2002). This volume has been followed by a second compilation of white papers (Narrow et al. 2007) that outline diagnosis-related research needs in the areas of gender, infants and children, and geriatric populations.

As a second phase of planning, the APA leadership envisioned a series of international research planning conferences that would address specific diagnostic topics in greater depth, with conference proceedings serving as resource documents for groups involved in the official DSM-V revision process. We, in collaboration with colleagues at WHO, developed a proposal for the cooperative research planning conference grant that NIMH awarded to APIRE in 2003, with substantial additional funding support from NIDA and NIAAA. The conferences funded under the grant are the basis for this monograph series and represent a second major phase in the scientific review and planning for DSM-V.

The conferences that constituted the core activity of this phase of preparation had multiple objectives. One was to promote international collaboration among members of the scientific community with the aim of eliminating the remaining disparities between DSM-V and the International Classification of Diseases (World Health Organization 1992b) Mental and Behavioural Disorders section (World Health Organization 1992a). The WHO has launched the revision of ICD-10 that will lead to publication of the 11th edition in approximately 2014. A second goal was to stimulate the empirical research necessary to allow informed decision-making regarding deficiencies identified in DSM-IV. A third was to facilitate the development of broadly agreed upon criteria that researchers worldwide may use in planning and conducting future research exploring the etiology and pathophysiology of mental disorders. Challenging as it is, this last objective reflected widespread agreement in the field that the well-established reliability and clinical utility of prior DSM classifications must be matched in the future by a renewed focus on the validity of diagnoses.

The APA attaches high priority to ensuring that information and research recommendations generated by each of the work groups are readily available to investigators who are concurrently updating other national and international classifications of mental and behavioral disorders. Moreover, given the vision of an ultimately unified international system for classifying mental disorders, members of the Executive Steering Committee have made strenuous efforts to realize the participation of investigators from all parts of the world in the project. Toward this end, each conference in the series had two co-chairs, drawn respectively from the United States and a country other than the United States; approximately half of the experts invited to each working conference were from outside the United States, and half of the conferences were convened outside the United States.

The group of international experts that convened in London in June 2007 was charged with clarifying the relationship between GAD and MDD among clinical, epidemiological, and multicultural samples. It will serve as a major reference document for the relevant DSM-V Work Groups in mood and anxiety disorders as they progress through field trials and finalizing criteria changes.

Toward DSM-V and ICD-11

Even as the conference series was in progress, attention shifted to assembly of the DSM-V Task Force, whose members would be charged both with serving as chairs of the individual work groups and with nominating the work group members that drive the revision process. In 2006, formation of the task force was initiated with the announcement of David J. Kupfer, M.D., as chair and Darrel A. Regier, M.D., M.P.H., as vice-chair. They were joined by other leaders at APA, as well as NIH, in overseeing the development of DSM-V. With approval from the Board of Trustees, the task force completed establishment of the 13 work groups in 2008. These experts in science and clinical practice were intentionally selected to bring their unique perspectives from disciplines in psychiatry, psychology, neurology, sociology, social work, nursing, and epidemiology/statistics.

Construction of DSM-V is being completed with an eye on creation of the next edition of the *International Classification of Diseases* (ICD-11) as a congruent and complementary classification of all medical conditions. There is a demonstrable gap between multicultural perspectives on psychiatric phenomena and the way diagnosis of these phenomena are currently represented in DSM-IV. International inclusion is undoubtedly a priority for the task force and work groups, and any potential changes must be considered in light of making DSM-V parallel to the forthcoming ICD-11. The APA has maintained international representation among its groups for the dual purpose of encouraging worldwide discourse as well as ensuring integration of these global viewpoints into the revision process.

The first meetings of the work groups took place in 2007, signaling the official start of the revision process. Work group members are mindful that although there are no preset limitations to what type of and how many changes they may enact, DSM-V must be supported by a foundation of empirical data and peer-review literature, and it must also preserve clinical continuity and utility on its surface.

As development of DSM-V progresses towards the May 2012 deadline, ensuring the validity of diagnostic categories by providing criteria that accurately reflect the complex presentation of mental disorders has become of central focus. The two disorders described in this volume provide an excellent case in point for why such an approach is necessary. Although biologic and psychosocial evidence for MDD and GAD currently support their continued separation, it is clear that they exist as mixed states in many individuals, and failure to recognize them as closely related entities may delay clinician response in diagnosing and providing treatment. Their separation also hinders scientific progress, as researchers and epidemiologists are often constrained to examining disorders within the confines provided by DSM. In order to generate greater empirical evidence as to the true relationship between these disorders, DSM must demonstrate more flexibility in its classification approach by creating better awareness of overlapping diagnoses and symptoms and facilitating the detection and treatment of such.

The subject of disorder boundaries is particularly pertinent to the current work underway by the DSM-V Task Force and Work Groups in developing field trials for criteria revisions. Among the most prominent changes under scrutiny is the utility of dimensional assessments to better capture variations within and across psychiatric disorders. Diagnostic dimensions will improve validity, stimulate research to clarify the nature of disorders with shared validators, and enhance clinician recognition of comorbid, subsyndromal, mixed, and atypical presentations. At the disorder level, this includes assessing for severity and chronicity of individual symptoms, as well as calling attention to specific disorders of relevance to a given diagnosis—the utilization of mood dimensions among patients diagnosed with anxiety, for example, would be especially beneficial. As reflected in this volume, the degree of relatedness between MDD and GAD offers compelling evidence for why dimensional approaches should be an integral part of psychiatric diagnosis and how they may provide some much-needed answers to the questions and problems raised in these chapters.

The American Psychiatric Association greatly appreciates the contributions of all participants in this research planning work group and the interest of our broader audience in this topic.

Darrel A. Regier, M.D., M.P.H.
Executive Director
American Psychiatric Institute for Research and Education

References

Alexander FG, Selesnick ST: The History of Psychiatry: An Evaluation of Psychiatric Thought and Practice from Prehistoric Times to the Present. New York, Harper & Row, 1966, pp 388–401

American Psychiatric Association: Diagnostic and Statistical Manual of Mental Disorders, 4th Edition. Washington, DC, American Psychiatric Association, 1994

American Psychiatric Association: Diagnostic and Statistical Manual of Mental Disorders, 4th Edition, Text Revision. Washington, DC, American Psychiatric Association, 2000

Kupfer DJ, First MB, Regier DA (eds): A Research Agenda for DSM-V. Washington, DC, American Psychiatric Association, 2002

Narrow WN, First MB, Sirovatka P, et al (eds): Age and Gender Considerations in Psychiatric Diagnosis: A Research Agenda for DSM-V. Arlington, VA, American Psychiatric Association, 2007

World Health Organization: The ICD-10 Classification of Mental and Behavioural Disorders: Clinical Descriptions and Diagnostic Guidelines. Geneva, World Health Organization, 1992a

World Health Organization: International Statistical Classification of Diseases and Related Health Problems, 10th Revision. Geneva, World Health Organization, 1992b

THE PROBLEM: CHARGE TO THE CONFERENCE

Kenneth S. Kendler, M.D.

In this chapter I aim to set the stage for the conference "The Future of Psychiatric Diagnosis: Refining the Research Agenda for Depression and Generalized Anxiety Disorders" and provide a historical and theoretical overview of the empirical and conceptual issues that face psychiatry today as we move toward DSM-V.

A Background Historical Sketch

Generalized anxiety disorder (GAD) began its peripatetic nosologic history in 1975 with the publication of the Research Diagnostic Criteria (RDC; Spitzer et al. 1975), wherein GAD was described as an "illness in which the most prominent disturbance is generalized anxiety without panic attacks." In addition to a persistent generalized anxious mood, only one of five specific symptoms was required to meet diagnostic criteria, and the minimal required duration was 2 weeks.

In DSM-III (American Psychiatric Association 1980), GAD underwent a substantial metamorphosis. Minimal duration was increased to 1 month and symptoms were now required from at least three of four categories: "motor tension," "autonomic hyperactivity," "apprehensive expectation," and "vigilance and scanning." These categories were illustrated by a listing of approximately 43 individual symptoms or signs. GAD was placed within the category of "Anxiety Disorders." The introduction to this section made it clear that the underlying logic of this categorization was symptomatic resemblance; these disorders were placed together because anxiety was a core feature of the GAD condition.

In DSM-III-R (American Psychiatric Association 1987), the description of GAD again underwent rather major alterations. Its required minimal duration continued its upward climb, reaching 6 months. Unrealistic worry about two or more life circumstances was now required. The list of 43 individual symptoms in DSM-III was reduced to 18 specific criteria, of which a minimum of 6 were required.

GAD did not escape yet another large overhaul in DSM-IV (American Psychiatric Association 1994). The 18 specific symptomatic criteria were reduced to 6, with 3 or more required to make the diagnosis. As with many other diagnoses, the symptoms had to cause significant distress or impairment. DSM-IV also added the criterion that "the person finds it difficult to control the worry."

By comparison with GAD, the diagnosis of major depressive disorder (MDD) has, in modern times, had an untroubled and stable history. It began as "depression," one of the two "primary affective disorders" in the Washington University, or "Feighner," criteria (Feighner et al. 1972). It was given the modifier "major" in the RDC (because that system contained a minor depressive disorder). The term "major depression" has persisted despite the fact that "minor depression" disappeared from our manuals some time ago.

There have been some modest changes in criteria over the years; for example, the duration went from 1 month in the Washington University criteria to 2 weeks in all subsequent systems and the RDC; subsequent DSM editions added weight gain; and, in DSM-III-R, "diminished interest or pleasure" was added as a possible required symptom (to what had previously been solely "depressed mood"). However, the nine symptomatic criteria for MDD have had a remarkably stable history through multiple permutations of our diagnostic manual. It is worthwhile noting that the introduction to the DSM section on affective disorders states "The essential feature of this group of disorders is a disturbance of mood" (American Psychiatric Association 1980, p. 205).

Focus of This Book

The path to this book began with a series of findings from twin studies—in Australia (Kendler et al. 1987), Virginia (Kendler 1996; Kendler et al. 1992), and most recently, Sweden (Kendler et al. 2006)—all of which suggest, with rather compelling consistency, that MDD and GAD share all, or at least most, of their genetic risk factors. Coupled with other emerging evidence—well reviewed in Chapter 2 of this volume, "The Nosologic Relationship Between Generalized Anxiety Disorder and Major Depression," by Jack Hettema—for similarities between the two disorders, the organizers of the series of pre-DSM-V conferences felt that some potentially important things could be learned by a thorough examination of the nosologic relationship between MDD and GAD.

This concept resulted in a quite focused work assignment. Compared with many of the other workgroups, our goals have been narrower and, perhaps, deeper. One way to think of this assignment is as a single "case study" of a diagnostic problem, with the goals of "throwing everything we can at it" to see what we can learn and then using the knowledge gained to help explore some important conceptual issues within our nosology.

In thinking about the goals of this meeting, it is useful to divide them into two categories: empirical and conceptual. I treat these two broad sets of issues in turn.

Empirical Issues

To put it simply, we want to review everything we can about the interrelationship of MDD and GAD, try to summarize all this work into a few broad conclusions, and then reflect on the implications of these findings for future nosologic efforts.

In the tradition of modern psychiatric nosology, the empirical inquiries in this conference are organized around the concept of *validators,* as originally articulated by Robins and Guze (1970). In this approach, the aim was to review similarities and differences between MDD and GAD from the perspective of meaningful empirical studies that shared the feature of independence of the diagnostic process itself. There are a number of typologies of validators for psychiatric illnesses, from the original set proposed by Robins and Guze in 1970 (e.g., course of the illness, response to treatment, family history) to an expansion that I suggested some years ago (Kendler 1984) with the three major classes of antecedent, concurrent, and predictor validators.

The particular typology is probably of little import. Our goal in this conference is to try to study all the validators that can be applied to the question of an interrelationship between MDD and GAD. Our work group sought to include all the major classes of validators, for which the field had produced enough data to help illuminate the question at hand. We review data from the perspectives of genetics, biology, treatment, development, course, predictors, disability, and psychosocial stressors.

What should the empirical output of this conference look like? One intuitive way to organize conclusions would be in the form of a box score, which would look like Table 2–4 in this volume. Rows would be different validators, and columns would be a summary score that reflects the degree to which MDD and GAD resemble one another for that validator. There will surely be subtleties and disagreements in the interpretation of these results, because studies will use different methods, samples, assessment tools, generations of DSM, and so on. No one who has worked long in the DSM process will expect unanimity across studies. Our science is simply not yet at that level. Instead, we should be looking, as nosologists, at broad empirical trends rather than getting caught up in specifics.

It is useful to ponder a moment about what results we might expect. In particular, is it likely we will see a high level of consistency for the degree of resemblance of GAD and MDD across various classes of validators? Although such a result is intuitively appealing, I suggest it is unlikely. I know little of systematic research in this area, but let me give a few examples of the kinds of issues we are likely to confront in our discussions.

Along with Ming Tsuang and Alan Gruenberg, I took part in a systematic study of different subtyping systems for schizophrenia (Kendler et al. 1984, 1985, 1988). We found that the Tsuang-Winokur subtypes best predicted outcome, whereas the ICD-9 criteria did a better job of predicting long-term stability and familial aggregation. So which is the better subtyping system? Although treatment outcome is an appealing validator, we all know that treatment response can be quite nonspecific. Antipsychotic drugs can reduce delusional thinking in schizophrenia, affective psychosis, and psychotic symptoms associated with dementias. Would we wish to claim, on that basis, that these different disorders should be classified together in a nosologic system? Several early environmental traumatic experiences, such as childhood sexual abuse, have been shown to increase risk for mood, anxiety, eating, and drug use disorders. Would these findings constitute evidence of a close etiological relationship between these disorders?

In the final stage of our empirical efforts, we attempt to integrate results from research on all these diverse validators to come up with a single "bottom-line" recommendation as to whether MDD and GAD are best considered as 1) different forms of the same disorder, 2) closely related disorders, or 3) distally related disorders. Then, we review what implications our findings have for DSM-V.

David Goldberg and I sketched out several possible outcomes of our workgroup deliberations. MDD and GAD could be 1) considered as they are in DSM-IV and DSM-IV-TR (American Psychiatric Association 2000), in separate categories; or 2) classified in the same category as subforms or subtypes of the same disorder. If the choice were #2, then should GAD be moved into the "mood disorders" category and MDD moved into "anxiety disorders" or a new category be created for both?

Finally, we address the question of what new kinds of data could be gathered that would help to address the relationship between MDD and GAD more definitively.

Conceptual Issues

An examination of the similarities and differences between MDD and GAD raises a number of conceptual issues, nine of which are reviewed here.

CRITERIA FOR RESULTS FROM VALIDATORS

How should we define results from validators that support each of the three possible conclusions mentioned above? Are they 1) different forms of the same disorder, 2) closely related disorders, or 3) distally related disorders? That is, how different can different forms of the same disorder be? How much difference in results from validators would be required for us to conclude that the findings support the concept that MDD and GAD are at best distally related?

A logical response to these questions would be "What, precisely, do you mean by 'different forms of the same disorder' or 'closely related disorders'?" One approach to answering this question is to look through DSM-IV-TR for guidance. Would we want to define criteria for "different forms of the same disorder" like those for other syndromes considered to be subtypes or subforms of the same disorder?

Two examples come to mind. First, take the category of simple phobias, which includes animal, situational, and blood injury phobias. Although these phobias share certain features (irrational fears, avoidance behaviors, and so on), some aspects of these phobias are strikingly different. In particular, exposure to the phobic stimulus in individuals with animal and situational phobias results in increased sympathetic activity (i.e., heightened pulse and blood pressure). Exposure to the phobic stimulus in individuals with blood-injury phobia results in the exact opposite response, with reduced pulse and blood pressure and often fainting. Yet DSM-IV-TR considers them to be different forms of the same disorder.

Second, consider the subtypes of schizophrenia. We know that although they share a number of common symptoms, such as delusions and hallucinations, these subtypes differ in average age at onset, symptom patterns, and outcomes. So if we used phobias and schizophrenia as paradigmatic examples, we would have to conclude that closely related disorders *do not* need to be highly similar on all potential validators.

What guidelines might we have for defining closely related disorders? One approach could be to consider disorders classified in the same overall grouping in DSM-IV-TR. The problem with this approach is that a brief examination of DSM-IV-TR suggests that the underlying logic of these groupings is quite heterogeneous. For many disorders, as noted earlier, categories seem to group disorders by prominent symptoms, with some implications of an etiological relationship (i.e., "mood," "anxiety" "schizophrenia and other psychotic disorders"). Other categories, however, seem to define very broad classes of conditions, such as "sleep disorders" or "sexual and gender identity disorder," for which the organizing principle appears more to reflect the domain of functioning affected. I do not think we would want to argue that narcolepsy and circadian rhythm sleep disorder should be considered paradigmatic "closely related disorders" even though they are both in the "dyssomnias" section of primary sleep disorders. So, we might be on our own when it comes to developing criteria for "closely related disorders."

Left to their own devices, different investigators are likely to have different intuitions about the degree of difference required for two disorders to be classified as closely related or distinct disorders. Those who are by nature "lumpers" will have higher thresholds than those who are "splitters." How would we begin to establish a consistent set of results that could not only help us with the MDD/GAD question but also apply more broadly across other DSM categories?

RELEVANCE OF RESULTS ON SYMPTOMS OF ANXIETY AND DEPRESSION

A huge literature in psychology and psychiatry examines the interrelationships of symptoms of anxiety and depression, as measured on a wide range of self-report instruments. How relevant should these findings be for our deliberations about GAD and MDD? We could decompose this global question into at least two more-specific questions. First, how good a proxy for the clinical diagnosis of major depression is self-reported depressive symptoms? A range of studies have examined this question. On average, the relationship is certainly highly significant. However, depending on the specific self-report scale used, it is clear that there are some very unhappy people out there who do not meet DSM criteria for MDD. Using typical cutoffs, one can screen for major depression by self-report scales, but it is typically not possible to obtain both high sensitivity and high specificity from this screening. The item content for many self-report scales differs from the "A" criteria for DSM-IV-TR major depression, emphasizing the cognitive and mood aspects of depression more than the vegetative and psychomotor changes. However, there is a second part to this question. In many studies, MDD and GAD are examined on a lifetime basis. So it is a further stretch from current self-report symptoms to lifetime diagnoses.

To the best of my knowledge, the association between the wide range of self-report symptom scales and the diagnosis of GAD has been subjected to less research than is the case with MDD. All of the problems noted earlier for screening scales for depression apply to GAD as well. Many self-report scales for anxiety include items that might reflect panic, phobic, or even obsessive-compulsive symptoms better than they reflect GAD.

So, a question we need to address is whether self-report symptom scales are a close enough proxy for MDD and GAD that the information derived is informative for our overall purposes. I expect the conference participants will have a diversity of responses to this query.

WEIGHTS OF DIFFERENT CLASSES OF VALIDATORS

An especially weighty conceptual issue that I broached earlier and that we cannot avoid confronting is: In our final deliberations, how do we weigh different classes of validators if, as we expect, they do not all agree?

Although it might be politically correct to argue that all validators are created equal, this is unlikely to be a sustainable position. Most researchers confronting this kind of problem have an implicit hierarchy of the various classes of validators. That is, most of us have an idea about which validators are most important—and should be given the greatest sway in influencing our ultimate nosologic decisions—and which are "more minor" and can be safely "down-weighted" in the deliberations. I suspect that there will be a tendency among us to regard the area in which *we* work—be it genetics, follow-up studies, biological findings, or treatment response—to be the most important validators. However, looking beyond that parochialism is it possible to establish a deeper set of principles that might be applied in other areas of DSM-V about how different validating perspectives should be valued?

I have previously argued that the development of a hierarchy of validators for nosologic decisions is not fundamentally an empirical exercise (Kendler 1990). That is, there is no study we could design that, in itself, could tell us what validators were most important in trying to decide the nosologic relationship between MDD and GAD. To pick validators, we have to decide, *a priori,* what we want our diagnoses to do.

Of the many possible schemas available to us, I outline two. One could argue that the validators that most closely reflect etiology are to be most valued. Putting aside the deep problems of defining what we mean by "most closely reflect etiology," is that a principle worth adopting? It is, if we want DSM editions to move toward an etiologic-based model—which was specifically rejected as an approach in prior DSM editions. (For those further interested in this issue, the philosopher Dominic Murphy argues, powerfully, that psychiatry has to move toward etiologically based diagnoses [Murphy 2006].) Alternatively, one might plausibly argue that nosologic manuals are ultimately supposed to help clinicians practice, and therefore, we should value those validators that best reflect the practical aspects of clinical work, especially treatment response and prognosis.

RULES FOR ASSIGNING DISORDERS INTO CATEGORIES

What should be the basis by which individual disorders are assigned to categories in DSM? A number of rules might be proposed, but I think it likely that two will dominate our discussion: clinical similarity and etiology. (There may be some who would advocate that treatment response should be the organizing principle, but, for reasons noted earlier, I doubt this position will have many strong advocates.) As mentioned earlier, a brief read through DSM-III makes clear that the architects of that document were using the criteria of clinical similarity in designing their categories. More specifically, they were deciding, *a priori,* that certain key clinical domains—in our case, mood and anxiety—were the proper organizing principles.

A quite different approach on which to base a nosologic classification is etiology. The reactions to this simple proposal can be strikingly diverse. Some will see this as the obvious way for psychiatric nosology to develop, and the wave of the future. I have heard talk with much anticipation about the day when we will be able to diagnose different forms of schizophrenic illness on the basis of specific genetic etiologies.

Others see the idea of developing an etiologically based system in quite a different light. To paraphrase a colleague, does that mean you would take three patients with depression and highly similar symptoms and put them into different categories because you could attribute their illnesses, in one case, to high genetic loading; in another case, to having been mugged in the street; and in a third case, to having given birth to a child? It would be crazy, wouldn't it?

This debate has an interesting parallel in the history of classification in biology in the twentieth century (Hull 1990). The original pre-Darwinian approach to the classification of species was on the basis of morphological similarity—that is, similarity in body size, shape, color, and so on. However, the twentieth century saw the rise of cladistics, a philosophy of classification that suggests the sole criteria for arranging organisms in a hierarchy should be the rules of common descent, as captured by the branching of the evolutionary tree. Ultimately, of course, this approach will be based on DNA-sequence comparisons. So, in summary, the question is "Should we classify animals on the basis of how they look or their degree of evolutionary relationship, as indexed by DNA sequence comparisons?"

Let's do a thought experiment and imagine that we are primitive biologists with no knowledge of evolution or DNA and are developing our first "nosologic" manual for species around us. We decide that two of our major classifications will be "animals with fur that live on land and give birth to live young" and "animals that live in the sea and have streamlined bodies with flippers." In the first classification would be land mammals. In the second would be fish and aquatic mammals such as dolphins and whales. So, one way to pose the problem we are facing at this meeting is that, if mood disorders are like the furry land animals, and anxiety disorders are like streamlined sea creatures with flippers, is GAD similar to a dolphin that "looks like a fish" but "isn't a fish"?

RELATIVE MERITS OF CLINICAL VERSUS EPIDEMIOLOGIC SAMPLES

The issue of clinical versus epidemiological sampling is "smaller" than some we face but nonetheless is of practical import in our discussions. We will be seeing samples obtained in clinical and in community settings. Sometimes the results will not agree. Can we say anything consistent about the relative merits of these two sampling approaches? The problems with clinical samples are well known. Clinical samples are biased, for example, demonstrating higher rates of comorbidity than would be expected in the community (Berkson 1946). With mental health delivery systems differing so widely across countries, there is little likelihood that clinical samples from different sites would closely resemble one another because of local differences in referral patterns. However, clinical samples have one tremendous advantage: they simulate the world in which clinicians—who after all are the main users of DSM—live and work.

Epidemiologic samples, if properly constructed, can eliminate the problem of representativeness. However, although this is debated and probably differs across disorders, on average, individuals meeting diagnostic criteria in epidemiological samples are more mildly ill than those that are seen in clinics. In fact, one can long debate whether the individuals identified in epidemiological samples are "real" cases.

APPROACHES OF OTHER BRANCHES OF MEDICINE TO SIMILAR PROBLEMS

It is tempting to hope that other areas in medicine have confronted and solved the problems with which we in psychiatry are struggling. I claim no deep expertise in medical nosology. However, I have wandered through the ICD-10 Web site (World Health Organization 2008) enough to realize that the ICD uses a wide array of classificatory rules. Disorders are classified on the basis of the organ they affect (arthritis of the hip, knee, and first carpometacarpal joint are in separate categories within the Arthrosis); the microbe involved (e.g., different forms of bacterial pneumonia); etiologic principles ("primary generalized osteoarthrosis" versus "secondary multiple arthrosis post-traumatic polyarthrosis"); and pathologic appearance (acute renal failure with acute cortical necrosis vs. acute renal failure with tubular necrosis). Disorders reflecting shared etiologic processes are not always classified together. Myocardial infarction and thrombotic stroke are both the result of atherosclerosis but are classified in different sections ("ischaemic heart diseases" and "cerebrovascular diseases"). A number of genetic risk factors predispose to a range of different types of cancer, but cancers are listed by anatomic site under the category "Malignant Neoplasms." Although I am happy to defer to those with greater expertise in this area, I doubt that we can simply turn to the rest of medicine for widely accepted solutions to the issues with which we are struggling.

SHARED RISK FACTORS VERSUS CAUSAL INTERRELATIONSHIPS

The typical approach to evaluating nosologic interrelationships (including the genetic models that I described at the start of this chapter) assumes a shared risk factor model. That is, a given risk factor (be it environmental events, genes, or personality) predisposes to both MDD and GAD. What if this model is wrong? What if, for example, having GAD directly increases the subsequent risk for developing MDD? The prior literature has generally suggested that, in comorbid cases,

GAD precedes MDD much more often than the other way around (Breslau et al. 1995), but several papers at this conference question that assumption. If a causal relationship were to exist between these two disorders, how would it change our thinking?

CAN WE KEEP OUR NOSOLOGIC CHANGES LOCAL?

Could you make isolated changes for MDD and GAD in as complex and interrelated a system as DSM-V without the effects of these changes rippling out into other important areas of the manual? In our deliberations about where MDD and GAD should be placed (e.g., together in a new "distress disorders" category), how concerned should we be about the strong research literature linking MDD to bipolar disorder? Although our group might feel quite comfortable at relocating MDD out of the mood disorders, bipolar researchers might have quite a different opinion. Hettema's review in Chapter 2, "The Nosologic Relationship Between Generalized Anxiety Disorder and Major Depression," makes a rather strong case that the close relationship between MDD and GAD is not so different from that seen between MDD and the other anxiety disorders. Should we be pushing for panic disorder or phobias to be moved also?

It is worth pondering whether a highly defined "surgical intervention" is possible for DSM-V, or will any change set off a chain reaction throughout the system, raising all sorts of problems that we might not anticipate?

ASYMMETRY OF ATTEMPTING CHANGE IN DIAGNOSTIC SYSTEMS

The last conceptual issue I want to highlight is the inherent asymmetry in the nosologic process, which can be neatly summarized as "It is much easier to propose than dispose." As anyone who has worked on a grant budget can testify, it is a lot easier to add than cut. The example also applies to diagnostic manuals. When diagnoses are created, they create their own constituencies. Drug companies try to develop treatments. Clinics open up specializing in their care. We should not underestimate the impact of DSM out there in the real world.

All of these factors create inertia in the system. This does not mean that diagnoses cannot be dropped. This was done, famously, in the United States for homosexuality. Yet that was a special case. I know of no lay groups protesting the inclusion of MDD or GAD in our diagnostic manuals. For more typical diagnoses, the inertia is hard to resist. I have no solution, but as in psychotherapy, insight can be the first step on the road to behavior change.

Backburner Issues

In this final section of this chapter, I would like to get even more general. Of the multitude of "deep" conceptual and even philosophical issues that underpin our thoughts about nosology, I want to highlight two questions that will be lurking in the background in our discussions. In so doing, I rely heavily on a recently published essay I wrote with Peter Zachar (Zachar and Kendler 2007).

Are categories of psychiatric disorder defined by their underlying nature (essentialism), or are they practical categories identified by humans for particular uses (nominalism)? Essentialists believe that psychiatric disorders, like elements in the periodic table, exist independent of our classifications. Our job as nosologists is to discover them. Advocates of essentialism argue that psychiatric disorders, like gold and oxygen, are part of the inherent structure of our universe and that taxonomies should represent that structure. Radical nominalists argue that we should pick our categories for their utility, with no expectation that they will reflect any deeper truths about our world. Moderate nominalists agree with essentialists that there is some structure of psychiatric illness "out there in the world"; they disagree with them in the conclusion that there is one unique categorization that stands above the others on *a priori* grounds but feel that some categories might be preferable to others, on practical grounds.

I would suggest the following thought experiment. All the contributors to this conference should try to assign themselves to one of these three categories: essentialists, radical nominalists, or moderate nominalists. I would predict that the participants' approaches to a number of the conceptual issues outlined here would line up as well—that is, that the deep ideas we have about the underlying nature of our diagnostic categories drives the way we see many nosologic issues.

Are psychiatric disorders best understood as illnesses with discrete boundaries (categorical) or the pathological ends of functional dimensions (continuous)? Those who advocate the categorical viewpoint in psychiatry argue that psychiatric disorders are, like species, discrete categories that are defined by nonarbitrary boundaries between what is inside and what is outside. These people would argue that our concepts of psychiatric illnesses should be modeled on that of the categorical or "taxonic" medical conditions, such as infectious diseases, cancer, and degenerative neurologic disorders. Advocates of the continuum viewpoint, by contrast, would start by noting that a category such as "tall" is not an objective class. There is certainly an objective continuum called *height,* but on this continuum, the difference between short and tall is quantitative, a difference of degree rather than kind. Advocates of the continuum perspective tend to point to a different class of medical disorders, such as hypertension and osteoporosis, as more realistic models for psychiatric disorders. How does it matter, if at all, for our deliberations about the relationship between MDD and GAD if these disorders are truly categorical versus continual?

A Final Observation

The status of our nosology, circa 2007, resembles the situation we were in with respect to psychiatric diagnosis pre-DSM-III. We can probably agree pretty well on the individual scientific findings that we will be reviewing. This is roughly analogous to the pre-DSM-III observations that psychiatrists were rather reliable on assigning the presence or absence of basic psychiatric symptoms and signs. However, we probably will not agree as well on the rules whereby we go from those scientific findings to nosologic recommendations. This is analogous to the evidence that the internal algorithms that pre-DSM-III psychiatry used for making diagnoses out of signs and symptoms differed widely. Following this logic, we should now be developing operationalized criteria for nosologic decisions—clear, reliable guideposts of how to go from data to diagnostic recommendations.

Conclusion

This conference represents an interesting experiment. Nosology is a funny kind of thing. In many ways, making nosologic decisions is like setting social policy. It should be informed by science, but many parts of it are not fundamentally scientific. In designing this conference, we hoped for a lively interchange between individuals who are approaching one problem (the relationship of MDD and GAD) from a wide range of perspectives. We hope to see an active discussion around scientific issues, the interpretation of results, and efforts to understand differences in findings across studies. However, we also hope to see an active interchange between the empirical and conceptual parts of our efforts. We cannot hope to "solve" the conceptual efforts. Indeed, their nature does not permit a solution in any direct sense.

More realistically, we can at least hope that we can move the field forward in thinking clearly about these issues in ways that can inform the rest of the DSM process. To do good nosology requires good data that are well collected and interpreted and clear and realistic thinking about the conceptual issues that are involved in going from data to nosologic recommendations. We hope that we can achieve both—lots of good data and clear thinking—in one meeting!

References

American Psychiatric Association: Diagnostic and Statistical Manual of Mental Disorders, 3rd Edition. Washington, DC, American Psychiatric Association, 1980

American Psychiatric Association: Diagnostic and Statistical Manual of Mental Disorders, 3rd Edition, Revised. Washington, DC, American Psychiatric Association, 1987

American Psychiatric Association: Diagnostic and Statistical Manual of Mental Disorders, 4th Edition. Washington, DC, American Psychiatric Association, 1994

American Psychiatric Association: Diagnostic and Statistical Manual of Mental Disorders, 4th Edition, Text Revision. Washington, DC, American Psychiatric Association, 2000

Berkson J: Limitations of the application of fourfold table analysis to hospital data. Biometrics 2:47–53, 1946

Breslau N, Schultz L, Peterson E: Sex differences in depression: a role for preexisting anxiety. Psychiatry Res 58:1–12, 1995

Feighner JP, Robins E, Guze SB, et al: Diagnostic criteria for use in psychiatric research. Arch Gen Psychiatry 26:57–63, 1972

Hull DL: Science as a Process: An Evolutionary Account of the Social and Conceptual Development of Science. Chicago, IL, University of Chicago Press, 1990

Kendler KS: Paranoia (delusional disorder): a valid psychiatric entity? Trends Neurosci 7:14–17, 1984

Kendler KS: Toward a scientific psychiatric nosology: strengths and limitations. Arch Gen Psychiatry 47:969–973, 1990

Kendler KS: Major depression and generalised anxiety disorder: same genes, (partly) different environments—revisited. Br J Psychiatry Suppl June (30):68–75, 1996

Kendler KS, Gruenberg AM, Tsuang MT: Outcome of schizophrenic subtypes defined by four diagnostic systems. Arch Gen Psychiatry 41:149–154, 1984

Kendler KS, Gruenberg AM, Tsuang MT: Subtype stability in schizophrenia. Am J Psychiatry 142:827–832, 1985

Kendler KS, Heath AC, Martin NG, et al: Symptoms of anxiety and symptoms of depression: same genes, different environments? Arch Gen Psychiatry 44:451–457, 1987

Kendler KS, Gruenberg AM, Tsuang MT: A family study of the subtypes of schizophrenia. Am J Psychiatry 145:57–62, 1988

Kendler KS, Neale MC, Kessler RC, et al: Major depression and generalized anxiety disorder: same genes, (partly) different environments? Arch Gen Psychiatry 49:716–722, 1992

Kendler KS, Gardner CO, Gatz M, et al: The sources of co-morbidity between major depression and generalized anxiety disorder in a Swedish national twin sample. Psychol Med 37:453–462, 2006

Murphy D: Psychiatry in the Scientific Image (Philosophical Psychopathology). Cambridge, MA, MIT Press, 2006

Robins E, Guze SB: Establishment of diagnostic validity in psychiatric illness: its application to schizophrenia. Am J Psychiatry 126:983–987, 1970

Spitzer RL, Endicott J, Robins E: Research Diagnostic Criteria for a Selected Group of Functional Disorders, 2nd Edition. New York, New York Psychiatric Institute, 1975

World Health Organization: International Classification of Diseases, 10th Edition. Available at http://www.who.int/classifications/icd/en/. Accessed July 28, 2008.

Zachar P, Kendler KS: Psychiatric disorders: a conceptual taxonomy. Am J Psychiatry 164:557–565, 2007

2

THE NOSOLOGIC RELATIONSHIP BETWEEN GENERALIZED ANXIETY DISORDER AND MAJOR DEPRESSION

John M. Hettema, M.D., Ph.D.

Major depressive disorder (MDD) and generalized anxiety disorder (GAD) have many areas of association and overlap, bringing into question the validity of their separation as distinct diagnostic entities. Given the general acceptance of MDD, compared with GAD, this could also be restated as an inquiry into whether GAD can stand as a valid, separate disorder from MDD. Despite the fact that GAD has undergone major revisions over the past two decades (Barlow and Wincze 1998), its empirical basis, although improved, remains somewhat unsatisfactory (Brown et al. 1994).

Particularly relevant to this inquiry is the evolution of the associated-symptom criteria for GAD; this disorder has gone from possessing a cluster of nonspecific panic-like autonomic symptoms (e.g., sweating, heart pounding, gastrointestinal

---

Copublished, with permission of the American Psychiatric Association, as Hettema JM: "Nosologic Relationship Between Generalized Anxiety Disorder and Major Depression." *Depression and Anxiety* 25:300–316, 2008.

distress)—as a carryover from its origins within "anxiety neurosis"—to having a more restricted symptom group that appears more MDD-like (insomnia, fatigue, difficulty concentrating). When an association is found between two disorders with overlapping diagnostic criteria, it is impossible to disentangle the nature of their relationship without external validators. Therefore, this review follows an approach similar to that used by Kendler (1980) for examining the validity of simple delusional disorder: it compares categories of antecedent, concurrent, and predictor validators between GAD and MDD. However, because other authors in this volume have provided in-depth coverage of several validator categories, this chapter focuses primarily on antecedent validators.

This chapter is not meant to be an exhaustive treatment of antecedent validators. There has been an enormous amount of research accumulated, and many thoughtful opinions expressed, on the relationship between depression and anxiety that cannot all be reasonably represented herein. I limit my focus here to the relationship between MDD and GAD, based upon the validator concept, including data from other anxiety disorders as a suggestive guide for when data for GAD are sparse, or as a comparison between MDD in relation to GAD versus other anxiety disorders, to determine specificity. I cite conclusions from meta-analyses or reviews of particular validators for the relevant conditions, when available. Given the changes in diagnostic criteria for GAD, I have only included studies using DSM-III (American Psychiatric Association 1980) criteria or later. I also limit this review to adult studies, because child psychopathology tends to be less stable and therefore prognostically less reliable. In addition, one needs to exert caution in drawing general conclusions from studies that have included treated patients, because many individuals with GAD do not seek treatment until after they have developed comorbid MDD or panic disorder, suggesting a potential for bias in these studies. Therefore, I preferentially review outcomes from large community studies, to the extent that such studies are available.

Antecedent Validators

FAMILIAL AGGREGATION AND GENETICS

Several early studies of GAD-like syndromes found little evidence for familial aggregation or genetics, likely due to poor diagnostic definition or lack of power due to small sample sizes. Meta-analyses from more recent studies show that MDD and GAD exhibit modest familial aggregation (MDD summary OR=2.8; GAD summary OR=6.1) and heritability (MDD, 37%; GAD, 32%) (Hettema et al. 2001; Sullivan et al. 2000), with less precision on the estimates for GAD due to fewer studies. I first consider analyses of samples from which one can draw inferences on the familial and genetic relationships between MDD and GAD.

Family Studies

Four family studies, summarized in Table 2–1, compared risk of GAD and MDD in relatives of probands; two of these were family history studies with their inherent potential biases (Kendler et al. 1991). Skre et al. (1994) performed a small family study that compared relatives of probands with anxiety disorders with those of probands with mood disorders and probands with substance use disorders, with no control probands. Their hierarchy for assigning proband groups allowed anxiety-disorder probands to have any disorder, mood probands could have substance use disorders but not anxiety disorders, and substance use–disorder probands could have neither mood disorders nor anxiety disorder. As indicated in Table 2–1, GAD was significantly more prevalent in relatives of anxiety-disorder probands (22%) than relatives of mood-disorder probands (9%) but not those of substance use–disorder (15%) probands. MDD had a nonsignificant preponderance in relatives of anxiety-disorder probands compared with other proband groups, but the majority of anxiety-disorder probands were cases of comorbid anxiety and depression. Thus, there may be some specificity for aggregation of GAD in families with anxiety disorders compared to mood disorders, but no conclusions about aggregation of mood disorders can be made in this study, given proband comorbidity.

The family study by Mendlewicz et al. (1993), although focused on panic disorder, compared morbidity risks in the first-degree relatives of four age- and sex-matched patient proband groups (N_p=25 each): panic disorder without agoraphobia, GAD, MDD, and healthy control subjects. Although no significant differences were observed, there was an increasing trend for GAD to be found in the relatives of control probands (1.9%), and upward for panic disorder (4.0%), MDD (4.9%), and GAD probands (8.9%). A similar trend was seen in rates of MDD in the respective proband groups, with less clear differences between the GAD and panic disorder relatives and relatives of healthy control probands. We note that significantly higher morbidity risk for panic disorder was found in relatives of panic-disorder probands than the other proband groups (not shown). Comorbidity in the GAD and MDD proband groups was not described. Within the context of this limitation, this study suggests that GAD may share some of its familial risk with MDD but not panic disorder.

Using the family history method, Reich (1995) examined the distribution of MDD and GAD in relatives of four non-overlapping (male-only) proband groups: lifetime MDD without GAD (N_p=54), GAD without MDD (N_p=16), comorbid MDD/GAD (N_p=20), and healthy control subjects (N_p=29). As Table 2–1 shows, rates of GAD were twice as high in GAD relatives (12.7%) as in MDD relatives (6.8%), both of which were higher than rates in control relatives (1.9%). There were similarly elevated rates of MDD in relatives of MDD (7.5%) and GAD (7.7%) proband groups compared with relatives of control subjects (1.9%). Interestingly, rates of MDD in relatives of the mixed MDD+GAD proband group were not elevated (1.4%), and GAD was only modestly elevated (4.2%). Interpreted

TABLE 2–1. Findings of family studies comparing rates of generalized anxiety disorder (GAD) and major depressive disorder (MDD)

Study	Probands (N)	GAD in FDR (% or OR), by proband diagnosis	MDD in FDR (% or OR), by proband diagnosis
Skre et al. 1994	Anxiety disorder[a] (33)	Anxiety disorder: 22%	Anxiety disorder: 29%
	Mood (20)	Mood: 9%	Mood: 18%
	Substance use disorder (6)	Substance use disorder: 15%	Substance use disorder: 15%
		($P=0.05$, anxiety disorder>mood)	Nonsignificant differences
Mendlewicz et al. 1993	GAD (25)	GAD: 8.9%	GAD: 4.4%
	MDD (25)	MDD: 4.9%	MDD: 8.8%
	Panic disorder (25)	Panic disorder: 4.0%	Panic disorder: 5.1%
	Healthy control subjects (25)	Healthy control subjects: 1.9%	Healthy control subjects: 3.8%
		Nonsignificant differences	Nonsignificant differences
Reich 1995[b,c]	MDD (54)	GAD: 12.7%	GAD: 7.7%
	GAD (16)	MDD: 6.8%	MDD: 7.5%
	MDD/GAD (20)	MDD/GAD: 4.2%	MDD/GAD: 1.4%
	Healthy control subjects (29)	Healthy control subjects: 1.9%	Healthy control subjects: 1.9%
		($P<0.001$)	($P<0.005$)

TABLE 2–1. Findings of family studies comparing rates of generalized anxiety disorder (GAD) and major depressive disorder (MDD) *(continued)*

Study	Probands (*N*)	GAD in FDR (% or OR), by proband diagnosis	MDD in FDR (% or OR), by proband diagnosis
Kendler et al. 1997[c]	Probands: 5,877 NCS respondents; FDR: 10,331 parents	GAD[d]: OR[e]=1.75 ($P<0.001$) MDD: OR[e]=1.55 ($P<0.001$)	GAD[d]: OR[e]=1.06 (NS) MDD: OR[e]=1.88 ($P<0.001$)

Note. FDR=first-degree relative; NCS=National Comorbidity Survey; NS=not significant; OR=odds ratio.
[a]Probands were organized according to a comorbidity hierarchy: Anxiety disorder probands could also have mood or substance use disorders; mood probands could also have substance use disorders; substance use disorder probands had neither anxiety nor mood disorders.
[b]Male probands only.
[c]Family History Study.
[d]GAD criteria: at least 1 month of anxiety or worry plus either 1) treatment for such, or 2) three or more of: i) keyed up/on edge, ii) irritability, iii) restlessness, iv) initial insomnia, v) tiring easily.
[e]OR quoted is the authors' OR, which has been adjusted for sociodemographic correlates and other diagnoses in probands and parents.

with caution, due to potential biases in the family history method, this study also indicates at least a partial overlap of familial risk between MDD and GAD.

Kendler et al. (1997) obtained diagnoses by family history of MDD, GAD, antisocial personality, alcohol use disorders, and drug use disorders for 10,331 parents of 5,877 respondents of the National Comorbidity Survey (NCS). These investigators found significant familial aggregation for MDD and GAD even after adjusting for demographic covariates and comorbidity in both probands and parents. Similarly, familial co-aggregation *between* MDD and GAD remained significant after these adjustments, albeit at a somewhat lower level. In particular, proband GAD-only significantly predicted parental GAD (OR=1.75), but proband MDD predicted parental MDD (OR=1.88) and GAD (OR=1.55). A factor analysis of these syndromes best fits the data using an internalizing-externalizing dichotomy suggesting partially overlapping familial risk between MDD and GAD.

Twin Studies

Kendler and colleagues have used twin studies to produce the largest body of data examining the relationship between MDD and GAD. Bivariate analyses between both 12-month (Kendler 1996) and lifetime (Kendler et al. 1992b) MDD and GAD in female twins from the Virginia Twin Registry (VTR), as well as lifetime MDD and GAD in same-sex male and female and opposite-sex twins from the Swedish Twin Registry (STR) (Roy et al. 1995) produced identical findings: MDD and GAD shared the majority of their genetic risk but had only a modest proportion of environmental risk factors in common. This was recently replicated in a larger sample of more than 37,000 twins from STR, estimating the gender-specific genetic correlation between MDD and GAD to be about 1.0 for females and 0.74 for males (Kendler et al. 2007). These findings have prompted some authors to consider MDD and GAD comorbidity as an example of "genetic pleiotropy" (Gorwood 2004).

Genetic Relationships Between Major Depressive Disorder, Generalized Anxiety Disorder, and Other Anxiety Disorders

To put the relationship between MDD and GAD into the larger context of overall psychiatric comorbidity, several large, population-based, phenotypic factor-analytic studies have found evidence for a single, higher-order "internalizing" factor that accounts for correlations among anxiety and depressive disorders and differentiates itself from an "externalizing" factor that relates to substance use and antisocial personality disorders (Krueger 1999; Slade and Watson 2006; Vollebergh et al. 2001). The internalizing factor is made up of two lower, highly correlated factors: the first roughly corresponds to an "anxious misery" factor that loads most strongly on MDD, dysthymia, and GAD, and the second corresponds to a "fear" factor that loads primarily on panic and phobic disorders. In a twin analysis examining that structure, Kendler et al. (2003) found that *genetic risk* could be broadly defined as internalizing (primarily affecting MDD, GAD, and phobias) and externalizing (primarily affecting alcohol dependence, illicit drug dependence, adult antisocial behavior, and conduct disorder). The internalizing genetic factor was further broken down into "anxiety-misery," loading primarily on MDD and GAD—with MDD-GAD genetic correlation approximately 1.0, consistent with earlier analyses in the VTR—and "fear," loading primarily on animal and situational phobias. Panic disorder was intermediate but closer to MDD and GAD, with the MDD-panic disorder genetic correlation approximately 0.8. This is similar to observations from the study in the NCS by Krueger (1999) cited earlier with somewhat higher phenotypic correlations between MDD and GAD (0.59) than MDD and panic disorder (0.50) or MDD and simple or social phobias (0.46 and 0.40, respectively). Analyses from another large twin dataset, the Vietnam Era Twin Registry, found significant genetic correlation between GAD and panic disorder (Scherrer et al. 2000) and between these syndromes and posttraumatic stress disorder (PTSD) (Chantarujikapong et al. 2001). We note that analyses in both the VTR and Vietnam Era Twin Registry suffer from the potential limitation of using broadened definitions of GAD and panic disorder that could weaken specificity.

Summary of Familial Aggregation and Genetics Studies

Family and twin studies all indicate that GAD and MDD share some, if not most, of their genetic risk factors. However, similar sources of data suggest that this may not be a unique relationship—that is, other anxiety disorders, particularly panic disorder, may share genetic risk with both GAD and MDD, although perhaps not to the same degree.

CHILDHOOD ENVIRONMENT

A range of variables, representing key aspects of the family environment experienced by a child during development, has been tested for association with adult MDD and, to a lesser extent, anxiety disorders.

Early Parental Loss or Separation

Early parental loss or separation has been implicated in adult risk of MDD in a fair number of studies, with most studies finding that disruption of parental care (separation, neglect) is more specifically predictive of adult depression than loss (death), per se (Agid et al. 1999; Bifulco et al. 1987; Furukawa et al. 1999; Harris et al. 1986; Oakley Browne et al. 1995b; Roy 1985; Veijola et al. 2004). Few large samples examined the effects of parental loss or separation in both GAD and MDD. In their analysis of data from the Early Developmental Stages of Psychopathology Study, Wittchen et al. (2000) found that early parental separation increased risk for most anxiety disorders, including GAD. They did not find association of parental separation with MDD, likely because many of the respondents (aged 14–24 years at baseline) had not gone through the risk period for MDD. Kendler et al. (1992a) examined the effects of parental loss before age 17, due to death or separation, on adult MDD, GAD, panic disorder, and phobias in 1,033 female-female twin pairs from the VTR. Parental death significantly predicted only panic disorder (relative risk=1.8), whereas separation predicted MDD, GAD, and panic disorder, with overall comparable risks (1.4–1.8).

Kessler et al. (1997) analyzed the effects of 26 specific childhood adversities categorized as interpersonal loss (e.g., death), interpersonal trauma (e.g., abuse), parental psychopathology, and miscellaneous traumas (e.g., natural disasters) on adult psychopathology in the NCS sample. Most bivariate adversity-diagnosis associations had an odds ratio greater than 1, with 67% significant at the 0.05 level, so most adversities were diagnostically nonspecific. The most consistent predictors across diagnoses were parental psychopathologies (93% significant), followed by interpersonal traumas (79% significant). The most consistently significant loss event across diagnoses was parental separation or divorce, with death of either parent showing few associations with adult outcomes, including MDD and GAD. Controlling for multiple adversities and prior disorders attenuated most associations; for example, no loss events remained (significantly) positively associated with MDD or any anxiety disorder. The authors cautioned against overinterpretation of studies that analyze effects of single adversities on single disorders.

Parenting Style

Parenting style, including parental bonding, has been investigated as a risk factor for psychopathology, with several studies reporting reduced parental care and, possibly, elevated overprotection during childhood in relation to MDD (Enns et al. 2000; Mackinnon et al. 1993; Oakley-Browne et al. 1995a; Parker et al. 1995; Sato et al. 1997). Only two studies compared parenting styles in MDD and GAD. In the first, Leon and Leon (1990) compared Parental Bonding Instrument ratings (using a quadrant assignment system based upon parental care and protection scores) across four clinical groups: MDD ($n=30$), GAD ($n=30$), panic disorder ($n=60$), and healthy control subjects ($n=30$). These authors found statistically significant distribution differences between control subjects and each patient group, with patients tending to rate their parents more in the low-care, high-protection quadrant (40%–60% of subjects) than control subjects (20%). In the second study, factors of parental coldness, protectiveness, and authoritarianism derived from multi-informant reports of items from the Parental Bonding Instrument were analyzed in relation to multiple adult psychiatric outcomes in female twins from the VTR (Kendler et al. 2000b). Multivariate analyses controlling for other covariates, including the other parenting dimensions and comorbid diagnoses, found modest

(~1.2–1.4) but significant and similar odds ratios between parental coldness and MDD, GAD and phobia, and parental protectiveness and GAD and phobia but not MDD.

Childhood Abuse

A number of studies have examined the effects of childhood abuse on risk for adult MDD and anxiety disorders as a group (Brown and Harris 1993; Brown et al. 1993; Burnam et al. 1988; Fergusson et al. 1996; Gibb et al. 2003; Levitan et al. 2003; Mullen et al. 1993) and have found comparable strengths of association between childhood abuse and either MDD or anxiety disorder. Only a handful of studies specifically included adult GAD as one of the outcomes. In a sample of 650 patients with mood and anxiety disorders, Young et al. (1997) reported high rates of childhood adversity (abuse, divorce, separation, parental psychopathology or substance use disorder), with a trend for lower overall abuse in GAD (17%) compared with MDD, panic disorder, phobia, or obsessive-compulsive disorder (~35%). Libby et al. (2005) analyzed the effects of childhood sexual abuse and physical abuse on outcomes of depression (MDD/dysthymia), anxiety (GAD/panic), and PTSD in two American Indian community samples ($N=3,084$). Controlling for other individual and parental predictors, these investigators found comparable, significant odds ratios (~2–3) between each type of abuse and each outcome in one sample, with less consistent results in the other. Kendler et al. (2000a) estimated similar odds ratios (~2–3) for any type of childhood sexual abuse in female twins from the VTR in relation to MDD, GAD, panic disorder, and alcohol and drug dependence, with stronger effects found for more severe forms. These effects were only mildly attenuated when adjusted for family functioning and parental psychopathology, suggesting that childhood sexual abuse is an independent risk factor for a wide range of psychiatric conditions. In 2,921 female respondents from the NCS, Molnar et al. (2001) found modest (OR~1.5) association between childhood sexual abuse and MDD and each anxiety disorder except PTSD (higher OR=10.2) using multivariate analyses controlled for parental psychopathology and other forms of abuse, although the relationship with GAD and specific phobia did not reach statistical significance. Among males ($N=2,945$), only PTSD and substance use disorders were significantly related to childhood sexual abuse.

Summary of Childhood Environment Studies

Studies that have examined childhood environmental measures of parental loss, parenting style, and abuse converge in their findings of modest associations of each of these predictors with both adult MDD and GAD. These findings are highly nonspecific, however, because they occur in the larger context of similar associations between these risk factors and other anxiety disorders both individually and as a group.

STRESSFUL LIFE EVENTS AND SOCIAL SUPPORT

Several excellent reviews exist that delineate the role for recent stressful life events in risk of MDD (e.g., Kessler 1997 and Paykel 1994). Comparing types of stressful life events for differential risk of psychiatric outcomes, early studies from Brown and colleagues reported that recent stressful life events involving "loss" were more often related to cases of depression, whereas ones involving "danger" (threat of loss) were more often related to anxiety, with comorbid conditions tending to involve both (Brown 1993; Brown et al. 1993; Finlay-Jones and Brown 1981).

A handful of studies compared the effects of stressful life events on GAD and MDD. Newman and Bland (1994) compared Life Events Scale scores in 222 subjects with MDD and 234 with GAD from 3,070 community survey respondents in Edmonton, Canada (cross-sectional). These authors observed a significantly increasing trend for total Life Events Scale scores and certain subscales of events ("entrance," "undesirable," and "marital")—no MDD or GAD < GAD-only < MDD-only < both MDD and GAD—however, they found no diagnostic specificity for types of events (which were not grouped by "loss" or "danger"). Pine et al. (2002) assessed 23 stressful life events and various internalizing and externalizing disorders in an epidemiological sample of 760 subjects ages 11–20 years, at baseline and again 6 years later. Significant cross-sectional associations were seen between total number of stressful life events at baseline and most baseline psychopathology (MDD, GAD, phobia, obsessive-compulsive disorder, panic disorder, attention-deficit/hyperactivity disorder, conduct disorder). Stressful life events at baseline were the main predictor variable for psychopathology at follow-up, controlling for age, gender, socioeconomic status, and diagnosis at baseline. Adolescent stressful life events significantly predicted only adult MDD with a trend for GAD (categorical diagnoses), with significant correlations found for MDD and GAD symptom scales (the latter for females only).

Schoevers et al. (2005) prospectively assessed risk factors for onsets of MDD and GAD at the 3-year follow-up point in 1,915 subjects without baseline psychopathology in an elderly (ages 65–84 years) Dutch community sample. Only prior history of depression/anxiety predicted onsets of pure GAD in multivariate analyses (no effects of stressful life events). Onsets of pure MDD or MDD with comorbid GAD had largely overlapping risk profiles, including stressful life events such as loss of spouse and recent decrease in activities of daily living.

Kendler et al. (1998) examined the effects and specificity of 15 classes of stressful life events for predicting onsets of MDD or a 2-week-duration generalized anxiety syndrome in the year prior to interview of female subjects from the VTR. Out of the 15 classes, 13 were significantly associated with MDD risk in the month of occurrence, with odds ratios ranging from 2.5 (network illness) to 18 (assault). Similarly, most events were also associated with risk for generalized anxiety syndrome (OR=2.2 for network illness to 10 for assault). Specificity, as indexed by a ratio of odds ratios predicting MDD versus generalized anxiety syndrome, was noted for some events. One event (network death) was the most specific for MDD (ratio 7.6); five events (assault, divorce/separation, and serious financial, housing, or network relationship problems) were modestly specific for MDD (ratios 1.3–2); three (loss of confidant and work or legal problems) were modestly specific for generalized anxiety syndrome (ratios 0.4–0.7); and six lacked specificity (ratios 0.8 to 1.2).

Social support has been found to reduce overall the risk of MDD in most studies (Paykel 1994), with little support for the "buffering theory of social support" that postulates that effective social support specifically lessens the depressogenic effects of stressful life events (Aneshensel and Stone 1982; Wade and Kendler 2000). Comparatively little study has been devoted to the effects of social support on risk for anxiety disorders in general and for GAD in particular.

Summary of Stressful Life Event and Social Support Studies

Stressful life events have been consistently implicated in risk for MDD and, to a lesser extent, GAD or GAD-like syndromes. There appears to be only partial overlap between the types of stressful life events that predispose to the two conditions, consistent with findings from twin studies of modest environmental correlation between these conditions. Little data are available for the other anxiety disorders, so it is unclear whether any overlap with stressful life event risk for MDD is specific to GAD. In addition, although social support has been consistently shown to be protective against MDD, insufficient data for GAD exist to make an adequate comparison.

PERSONALITY

Although most of the studies from which the available data are derived assessed current personality traits and disorders, I include here such qualities as (theoretically) longstanding and premorbid—and thus antecedent—validators.

Personality Traits

Neuroticism, a personality trait reflecting a tendency toward states of negative affect (Costa and McCrae 1980), together with extroversion and psychoticism constituted the three key dimensions of personality according to Eysenck (Eysenck and Eysenck 1985). Neuroticism has been included in most theories of personality since its introduction. Studies have consistently demonstrated associations between neuroticism level and likelihood of having symptoms or syndromes of depression, anxiety, or both, including MDD and GAD (for reviews, see Brandes and Bienvenu 2006; Widiger and Trull 1992). Data from a number of studies, including two large, population-based, longitudinal samples (Kendler et al. 1993; Ormel et al. 2004), have indicated that neuroticism acts as a premorbid vulnerability trait for MDD.

Some studies have attempted to identify the sources of correlation between neuroticism and anxiety and depressive symptoms and disorders. A study in the

Australian Twin Register that examined neuroticism and self-report symptoms of anxiety and depression concluded that genetic variation in these symptoms is largely dependent on the same factors as those affecting neuroticism (Jardine et al. 1984). Two analyses in the VTR have extended these findings to the disorder level: the first examined the genetic and environmental sources of covariation between neuroticism and MDD (Fanous et al. 2002) and the second examined those between neuroticism and GAD (Hettema et al. 2004). Each of those analyses found substantial genetic correlation between neuroticism and the respective psychiatric disorder (MDD, 0.55; GAD, 0.80). A study of more than 37,000 twins from the STR that examined the role neuroticism may play in MDD-GAD comorbidity found somewhat lower genetic correlation between neuroticism and MDD (~0.4) and GAD (~0.5), likely due to the use of neuroticism measured about 25 years earlier than MDD and GAD (Kendler et al. 2007).

Some researchers suggest that neuroticism (or something related to it) may function as a general vulnerability factor of negative affect that nonspecifically increases risk across mood and anxiety disorders (e.g., see the Tripartite Model of Clarke and Watson [1991]). Along those lines, a small number of studies have examined the role that neuroticism may play in explaining the findings of high levels of comorbidity between mood and anxiety disorders. Andrews et al. (1990) analyzed patterns of comorbid neurotic disorders and neuroticism scores in the Australian Twin Registry, finding that higher neuroticism scores predicted the number of internalizing disorders diagnosed in a subject. Bienvenu et al. (2004) used multivariate analyses to examine the relationship between factors and facets of the NEO Personality Inventory–Revised in 731 individuals from the Baltimore Epidemiologic Catchment Area sample and found higher neuroticism significantly associated with MDD and most anxiety disorders, including GAD. In a related analysis from that group, neuroticism was found to be the strongest predictor of comorbidity (Bienvenu et al. 2001). Phenotypic analyses in the VTR generally supported this, where neuroticism accounted for significant proportions of disorder comorbidity (Khan et al. 2005).

In a study that examined the genetic and environmental relationships between neuroticism and seven internalizing disorders (including MDD, GAD, panic disorder, and phobias) in the VTR, Hettema et al. (2006b) found high sex-averaged genetic correlation between MDD and GAD ($r=0.96$), about equally accounted for by neuroticism-related and non-neuroticism-related genetic factors, respectively. However, substantial total genetic correlations were also estimated between MDD and panic disorder ($r=0.99$), agoraphobia ($r=0.66$), and social phobia ($r=0.72$), making this a somewhat nonspecific finding. We note that the proportion of genetic correlation between MDD and GAD accounted for by neuroticism was a bit higher in this study than was recently found by Kendler et al. (2007) in the larger STR study cited earlier.

Personality Disorders

A review summarizing the relationship between MDD and personality disorders using clinical data reported an overrepresentation of Cluster B (particularly borderline and histrionic), generally low prevalence of Cluster A, and a great variability across studies for prevalence of Cluster C personality disorders in MDD (Corruble et al. 1996). Two large clinical samples examined personality disorders in GAD patients. In 1,448 total Greek outpatients, Garyfallos et al. (1999) reported that about half of subjects with GAD met criteria for at least one personality disorder, mostly within Cluster C. In 622 patients from the longitudinal Harvard/Brown Anxiety Research Project, personality disorders were compared in MDD, GAD, social phobia, and panic disorder (Dyck et al. 2001). In a multivariate model including each Axis I disorder, MDD, GAD, and social phobia had similar associations with having at least one personality disorder (OR= ~2); Cluster C and borderline personality disorder were the most commonly associated. MDD was primarily associated with Cluster B pathology.

Several large community samples report personality pathology in relation to MDD and anxiety disorders. Grant et al. (2005a) examined the relationships between DSM-IV-TR (American Psychiatric Association 2000) personality disorders and current (12-month) mood and anxiety disorders in the 43,000 individuals interviewed in the National Epidemiologic Survey on Alcohol and Related Conditions (NESARC). They found significant odds ratios between virtually all personality disorders and each mood disorder or anxiety disorder, with particularly strong but nonspecific associations between Cluster C avoidant and dependent personality disorders, respectively, and MDD (OR=10.6, 12.2), dysthymia (OR=12.6, 18.4), mania (OR=14.5, 22.0), GAD (OR=14.2, 18.6), social phobia (OR=27.3, 17.2), and panic disorder with agoraphobia (OR=21.0, 37.2). Lenzenweger et al. (2007) performed similar analyses in the 5,692 respondents from the NCS Replication (NCS-R) and found significant associations between each personality disorder cluster and each mood disorder or anxiety disorder (overall, Cluster B > Cluster C > Cluster A), but specific results are reported for only antisocial and borderline personality disorder, two of the strongest predictors of both types of Axis I comorbidity.

SUMMARY OF RESEARCH ON PERSONALITY TRAITS AND DISORDERS

In agreement with some psychological theories, a personality trait of negative affect, such as neuroticism, seems to function as a general risk factor for MDD, GAD, and possibly other anxiety disorders, accounting for a substantial portion of their comorbidity in several phenotypic studies. Data from two large twin studies suggest that GAD and MDD each exhibit moderate genetic correlation with neuroticism and that genetic factors shared between MDD and GAD are partially, but not completely, accounted for by genes for neuroticism. The finding in one of these studies (subject to replication) of a similar basis for overlap of genetic risk with other anxiety disorders, together with the majority of phenotypic studies, suggests that the mediating effects of neuroticism are not specific to the relationship between MDD and GAD.

Findings are less consistent regarding the comorbidity of personality disorders with MDD and GAD, however. Data from clinical studies suggest a higher prevalence of Cluster B disorders in MDD but of Cluster C disorders in GAD and other anxiety disorders. However, two large community surveys report somewhat discrepant results. The NESARC found higher Cluster C pathology in both mood disorders and anxiety disorders, in general, whereas the NCS-R found stronger association of these syndromes with Cluster B than Cluster C disorders. Both of these surveys find significant associations of both mood and anxiety disorders with a broad range of personality pathology, confirming that there are extensive, although somewhat nonspecific, relationships between Axis I and Axis II disorders.

Concurrent Validators

DEMOGRAPHICS

Gender has been found to be a reliable risk factor for both MDD and GAD (and for most anxiety disorders), with female risk about 1.5–2 times male risk. Several other demographic variables showed remarkable consistency between the large, population-based surveys, NESARC and NCS/NCS-R, as summarized in Table 2–2. Identical correlates of being female, middle-adult aged, widowed/separated/divorced, and low income or unemployed were positively associated with illness in both surveys, regardless of whether the diagnosis was MDD, GAD, or panic disorder, suggesting that some of these correlates may be nonspecific indices of internalizing disorders.

DISABILITY

Analyses that have compared disability and impairment in MDD and GAD generally have found significant, independent associations for both disorders (for a review, see Stein 2004), with levels of impairment of roughly equal magnitude (Kessler et al. 1999). However, this appears to be the case for other anxiety disorders as well (Ormel et al. 1994), suggesting that disability may be a nonspecific marker of illness.

The Nosologic Relationship Between GAD and Major Depression

TABLE 2–2. Demographic correlates of 12-month or lifetime MDD and GAD (compared with panic disorder) from large U.S. community surveys

					Demographic correlates			
Study	Outcome	Female	Mid-adult age (30–44)	WSD	Lower income	Unemployed	Lower educational levels	Hispanic or black
NCS-R (Kessler et al. 2003)	MDD	+	+	+	+	+	+	
NCS (Wittchen et al. 1994)	GAD	+	+	+		+	NA	
NCS-R (Kessler et al. 2006)	PD	+		+		+		−
NESARC (Hasin et al. 2005)	MDD	+	+	+	+	NA		−
NESARC (Grant et al. 2005b)	GAD	+	+	+	+	NA		−
NESARC (Grant et al. 2006)	PD	+	+	+	+	NA		−

Note. GAD=generalized anxiety disorder; MDD=major depressive disorder; NA=correlate was not assessed or not analyzed; NCS/NCS-R=National Comorbidity Survey/Replication; NESARC=National Epidemiologic Survey on Alcohol and Related Conditions; PD=panic disorder; WSD=widowed/separated/divorced; +=significantly increases risk; −=significantly decreases risk.

Predictive Validators

LIFETIME COMORBIDITY

Anxiety disorders overall are highly comorbid with each other and with MDD. Several consistent features have been identified from a long history of studies of the relationships between MDD and anxiety disorders, as a whole, that also apply specifically to GAD (reviewed by Maser and Cloninger 1990). First, the risk of depression in patients with anxiety disorder is greater than the risk of anxiety disorder in patients with depression. Second, depressive disorders are more likely to remain free of comorbid anxiety over time than anxiety disorders are to remain free of depression. Most studies find MDD to be temporally secondary to anxiety disorders, including GAD (de Graaf et al. 2003; Kessler et al. 2003; Merikangas et al. 1998; Regier et al. 1998), and the presence of both active and remitted anxiety disorders are potent risk factors for MDD. Several large epidemiological surveys found prior GAD to be the strongest other disorder predictor of MDD onset (Andrade et al. 2003; Bittner et al. 2004; Hettema et al. 2003; Kessler et al. 1996), whereas one survey found GAD to be an independent risk factor for MDD onset, after controlling for stressful life events (Hettema et al. 2006a).

Table 2–3 lists the rates of some disorders comorbid with MDD and GAD from the NCS; panic disorder without agoraphobia (NCS-R) is included for comparison. About 90% of subjects with lifetime GAD had lifetime comorbidity with other mental or substance use disorders; the highest rates were with MDD (62%) (Wittchen et al. 1994). A somewhat lower level of 74% lifetime comorbidity of MDD was found in the NCS (72% in the NCS-R), with anxiety disorders overall representing the highest rates of comorbidity (58%); GAD had a rate of only about 17%, lower than those for phobias and substance use disorders (Kessler et al. 1996). High comorbidity rates were also reported for panic disorder without agoraphobia in the NCS-R (83%), but the comorbidity of panic disorder with lifetime MDD was only about half that found for MDD comorbidity in GAD (Kessler et al. 2006). Similar overall comorbidity rates were reported in the NESARC for 12-month GAD (Grant et al. 2005b) and MDD (Hasin et al. 2005) (90% and 71%, respectively). That survey also found high overall comorbidity rates (>80%) for other anxiety disorders such as panic disorder and social phobia.

There are some interesting patterns of comorbidity for MDD, GAD, and panic disorder observable in Table 2–3. Surprisingly, GAD possesses higher comorbidity with dysthymia than does MDD, the latter of which is similar to that of panic disorder. Otherwise, patterns of comorbidity across anxiety disorders and substance use disorders are quite similar between the three index disorders when adjusted for total rates of comorbidity.

TABLE 2–3. Comorbidity rates of lifetime MDD and GAD from NCS (compared with lifetime PD from NCS-R)

Disorder	Study	Overall	MDD	GAD	PD	Dysthymia	Social phobia	Specific phobia	AUD	DUD
MDD	Kessler et al. 1996	74		17	10	7	27	24	28	20
GAD	Wittchen et al. 1994	90	62		24	40	34	35	38	28
Panic disorder	Kessler et al. 2006	83	35	21		10	31	34	25	18

Note. AUD=alcohol use disorder; DUD=drug use disorder; GAD=generalized anxiety disorder; MDD=major depressive disorder; NCS/NCS-R=National Comorbidity Survey/Replication.
[a]Rounded to nearest %.

Discussion

A substantial amount of data have accumulated on the relationship between GAD and MDD. Depending on the category of validator, a greater or lesser proportion of the data derive from large, population-based samples, either cross-sectional or, in a few cases, longitudinal. Some studies have included other anxiety disorders that may be used for comparison to determine whether particular validators have a unique or specific association with MDD and GAD, with the most data available for panic disorder. Although there are generally fewer data for GAD than for MDD, the data reviewed herein can be used to begin to address the nosologic validity of GAD in relation to MDD.

Table 2–4 summarizes the findings for each validator class, rated according to the strength of overlap in association between that validator and GAD/MDD and the specificity of that association, as well as the availability of data to support each. (Details of several validator classes listed in the table were not covered in the final text due to space constraints.) For many of the other validators, at least two well-done studies exist to examine these questions of overlap and specificity. Two overarching observations can be made.

1. For all of the validators, except social support and course of illness, there is a moderate-to-strong degree of overlap between GAD and MDD. The strongest overlap appears in those validators that may be conceived of as truly "predisposing," for example, familial/genetic factors, childhood environment, and personality traits, the latter of which may just be an early manifestation of the influence of the first two on risk for developing MDD or GAD.
2. Most validators display generally nonspecific associations across MDD, GAD, and other anxiety disorders, particularly panic disorder. Where specificity is found (familial/genetic factors, stressful life events, personality), it is only partial, suggesting that these factors may broadly elevate risk across several related disorders. So although the use of external validators has confirmed significant overlap between GAD and MDD, over and above their shared diagnostic features, it also has highlighted similar overlap with some other anxiety disorders that have diagnostic features quite distinct from those of MDD.

Conclusion

In summary, the literature relevant to the question of GAD as a valid psychiatric condition distinct from MDD was reviewed using a set of external validators. The literature supports a strong overlap between GAD and MDD based upon familial/genetic, childhood environment, personality trait, and demographic data. However, for many of these correlates, the relationship to MDD overlaps substantially

The Nosologic Relationship Between GAD and Major Depression   33

TABLE 2–4. Summary of validator findings for generalized anxiety disorder (GAD) and major depressive disorder (MDD)

Validator category	Validator	MDD-GAD overlap		Specificity for MDD-GAD	
		Available data[a]	Overlap strength[b]	Available data[a]	Specificity degree[c]
Antecedent	Familial aggregation	++	+	+	++
	Genetic factors	++	++	++	+
	Parental loss/separation	++	++	++	–
	Parenting style	++	++	++	–
	Childhood abuse	++	++	++	–
	Stressful life events	++	+	+	+
	Social support	+	–	+	N/A
	Personality traits	++	++	++	+
	Personality disorders	++	+	++	+
Concurrent	Biological studies	+	+	+	–
	Demographic factors	++	++	++	–
	Disability	++	++	++	–
Predictive	Comorbidity	++	+	++	–
	Course of illness	++	–	+	N/A
	Pharmacological response	++	+	++	–

Note. N/A=not assessed or not analyzed.
[a]++=two or more well-done studies comparing relevant conditions; +=one well-done study comparing relevant conditions; –=no well-done studies comparing relevant conditions. [b]++=near-complete overlap in associated validator; +=partial overlap in associated validator; –=no overlap in associated validator. [c]++=association not seen with other disorders; +=association more specific to MDD-GAD than to other disorders; –=associations of similar strength to other disorders.

with other anxiety disorders, suggesting that the association is somewhat nonspecific, with the strongest evidence for panic disorder in this regard. Data from life events, personality disorders, biology, comorbidity, and pharmacology are mixed, showing some areas of similarity between GAD and MDD but also some clear differences, again with some degree of nonspecificity for GAD versus other anxiety disorders. Thus there appears to be little more reason to question the nosologic validity of GAD than that of some other anxiety disorders.

References

Agid O, Shapira B, Zislin J, et al: Environment and vulnerability to major psychiatric illness: a case control study of early parental loss in major depression, bipolar disorder and schizophrenia. Mol Psychiatry 4:163–172, 1999

American Psychiatric Association: Diagnostic and Statistical Manual of Mental Disorders, 3rd Edition. Washington, DC, American Psychiatric Association, 1980

American Psychiatric Association: Diagnostic and Statistical Manual of Mental Disorders, 4th Edition, Text Revision. Washington, DC, American Psychiatric Association, 2000

Andrade L, Caraveo-Anduaga JJ, Berglund P, et al: The epidemiology of major depressive episodes: results from the International Consortium of Psychiatric Epidemiology (ICPE) surveys. Int J Methods Psychiatr Res 12:3–21, 2003

Andrews G, Stewart G, Morris-Yates A, et al: Evidence for a general neurotic syndrome. Br J Psychiatry 157:6–12, 1990

Aneshensel CS, Stone JD: Stress and depression: a test of the buffering model of social support. Arch Gen Psychiatry 39:1392–1396, 1982

Barlow DH, Wincze J: DSM-IV and beyond: what is generalized anxiety disorder? Acta Psychiatr Scand 98:23–29, 1998

Bienvenu OJ, Brown C, Samuels JF, et al: Normal personality traits and comorbidity among phobic, panic and major depressive disorders. Psychiatry Res 102:73–85, 2001

Bienvenu OJ, Samuels JF, Costa PT, et al: Anxiety and depressive disorders and the five-factor model of personality: a higher- and lower-order personality trait investigation in a community sample. Depress Anxiety 20:92–97, 2004

Bifulco AT, Brown GW, Harris TO: Childhood loss of parent, lack of adequate parental care and adult depression: a replication. J Affect Disord 12:115–128, 1987

Bittner A, Goodwin RD, Wittchen HU, et al: What characteristics of primary anxiety disorders predict subsequent major depressive disorder? J Clin Psychiatry 65:618–626, quiz 730, 2004

Brandes M, Bienvenu OJ: Personality and anxiety disorders. Curr Psychiatry Rep 8:263–269, 2006

Brown GW: Life events and affective disorder: replications and limitations. Psychosom Med 55:248–259, 1993

Brown GW, Harris TO: Aetiology of anxiety and depressive disorders in an inner-city population, 1: early adversity. Psychol Med 23:143–154, 1993

Brown GW, Harris TO, Eales MJ: Aetiology of anxiety and depressive disorders in an inner-city population, 2: comorbidity and adversity. Psychol Med 23:155–165, 1993

Brown TA, Barlow DH, Liebowitz MR: The empirical basis of generalized anxiety disorder. Am J Psychiatry 151:1272–1280, 1994

Burnam MA, Stein JA, Golding JM, et al: Sexual assault and mental disorders in a community population. J Consult Clin Psychol 56:843–850, 1988

Chantarujikapong SI, Scherrer JF, Xian H, et al: A twin study of generalized anxiety disorder symptoms, panic disorder symptoms and post-traumatic stress disorder in men. Psychiatry Res 103:133–145, 2001

Clark LA, Watson D: Tripartite model of anxiety and depression: psychometric evidence and taxonomic implications. J Abnorm Psychol 100:316–336, 1991

Corruble E, Ginestet D, Guelfi JD: Comorbidity of personality disorders and unipolar major depression: a review. J Affect Disord 37:157–170, 1996

Costa PT Jr, McCrae RR: Influence of extraversion and neuroticism on subjective well-being: happy and unhappy people. J Pers Soc Psychol 38:668–678, 1980

de Graaf R, Bijl RV, Spijker J, et al: Temporal sequencing of lifetime mood disorders in relation to comorbid anxiety and substance use disorders: findings from the Netherlands Mental Health Survey and Incidence Study. Soc Psychiatry Psychiatr Epidemiol 38:1–11, 2003

Dyck IR, Phillips KA, Warshaw MG, et al: Patterns of personality pathology in patients with generalized anxiety disorder, panic disorder with and without agoraphobia, and social phobia. J Personal Disord 15:60–71, 2001

Enns MW, Cox BJ, Larsen DK: Perceptions of parental bonding and symptom severity in adults with depression: mediation by personality dimensions. Can J Psychiatry 45:263–268, 2000

Eysenck HJ, Eysenck MJ: Personality and Individual Differences: A Natural Science Approach. New York, Plenum Press, 1985

Fanous A, Gardner CO, Prescott CA, et al: Neuroticism, major depression and gender: a population-based twin study. Psychol Med 32:719–728, 2002

Fergusson DM, Horwood LJ, Lynskey MT: Childhood sexual abuse and psychiatric disorder in young adulthood, II: psychiatric outcomes of childhood sexual abuse. J Am Acad Child Adolesc Psychiatry 35:1365–1374, 1996

Finlay-Jones R, Brown GW: Types of stressful life events and the onset of anxiety and depressive disorders. Psychol Med 11:803–815, 1981

Furukawa TA, Ogura A, Hirai T, et al: Early parental separation experiences among patients with bipolar disorder and major depression: a case-control study. J Affect Disord 52:85–91, 1999

Garyfallos G, Adamopoulou A, Karastergiou A, et al: Psychiatric comorbidity in Greek patients with generalized anxiety disorder. Psychopathology 32:308–318, 1999

Gibb BE, Butler AC, Beck JS: Childhood abuse, depression, and anxiety in adult psychiatric outpatients. Depress Anxiety 17:226–228, 2003

Gorwood P: Generalized anxiety disorder and major depressive disorder comorbidity: an example of genetic pleiotropy? Eur Psychiatry 19:27–33, 2004

Grant BF, Hasin DS, Stinson FS, et al: Co-occurrence of 12-month mood and anxiety disorders and personality disorders in the US: results from the National Epidemiologic Survey on Alcohol and Related Conditions. J Psychiatr Res 39:1–9, 2005a

Grant BF, Hasin DS, Stinson FS, et al: Prevalence, correlates, co-morbidity, and comparative disability of DSM-IV generalized anxiety disorder in the USA: results from the National Epidemiologic Survey on Alcohol and Related Conditions. Psychol Med 35:1747–1759, 2005b

Grant BF, Hasin DS, Stinson FS, et al: The epidemiology of DSM-IV panic disorder and agoraphobia in the United States: results from the National Epidemiologic Survey on Alcohol and Related Conditions. J Clin Psychiatry 67:363–374, 2006

Harris T, Brown GW, Bifulco A: Loss of parent in childhood and adult psychiatric disorder: the role of lack of adequate parental care. Psychol Med 16:641–659, 1986

Hasin DS, Goodwin RD, Stinson FS, et al: Epidemiology of major depressive disorder: results from the National Epidemiologic Survey on Alcoholism and Related Conditions. Arch Gen Psychiatry 62:1097–1106, 2005

Hettema JM, Neale MC, Kendler KS: A review and meta-analysis of the genetic epidemiology of anxiety disorders. Am J Psychiatry 158:1568–1578, 2001

Hettema JM, Prescott CA, Kendler KS: The effects of anxiety, substance use and conduct disorders on risk of major depressive disorder. Psychol Med 33:1423–1432, 2003

Hettema JM, Prescott CA, Kendler KS: Genetic and environmental sources of covariation between generalized anxiety disorder and neuroticism. Am J Psychiatry 161:1581–1587, 2004

Hettema JM, Kuhn JW, Prescott CA, et al: The impact of generalized anxiety disorder and stressful life events on risk for major depressive episodes. Psychol Med 36:789–795, 2006a

Hettema JM, Neale MC, Myers JM, et al: A population-based twin study of the relationship between neuroticism and internalizing disorders. Am J Psychiatry 163:857–864, 2006b

Jardine R, Martin NG, Henderson AS: Genetic covariation between neuroticism and the symptoms of anxiety and depression. Genet Epidemiol 1:89–107, 1984

Kendler KS: The nosologic validity of paranoia (simple delusional disorder): a review. Arch Gen Psychiatry 37:699–706, 1980

Kendler KS: Major depression and generalised anxiety disorder, (partly) different environments: revisited. Br J Psychiatry Suppl 168:68–75, 1996

Kendler KS, Silberg JL, Neale MC, et al: The family history method: whose psychiatric history is measured? Am J Psychiatry 148:1501–1504, 1991

Kendler KS, Neale MC, Kessler RC, et al: Childhood parental loss and adult psychopathology in women: a twin study perspective. Arch Gen Psychiatry 49:109–116, 1992a

Kendler KS, Neale MC, Kessler RC, et al: Major depression and generalized anxiety disorder: same genes, (partly) different environments? Arch Gen Psychiatry 49:716–722, 1992b

Kendler KS, Neale MC, Kessler RC, et al: A longitudinal twin study of personality and major depression in women. Arch Gen Psychiatry 50:853–862, 1993

Kendler KS, Davis CG, Kessler RC: The familial aggregation of common psychiatric and substance use disorders in the National Comorbidity Survey: a family history study. Br J Psychiatry 170:541–548, 1997

Kendler KS, Karkowski L, Prescott CA: Stressful life events and major depression: risk period, long-term contextual threat and diagnostic specificity. J Nerv Ment Dis 186:661–669, 1998

Kendler KS, Bulik CM, Silberg J, et al: Childhood sexual abuse and adult psychiatric and substance use disorders in women: an epidemiological and cotwin control analysis. Arch Gen Psychiatry 57:953–959, 2000a

Kendler KS, Myers J, Prescott CA: Parenting and adult mood, anxiety and substance use disorders in female twins: an epidemiological, multi-informant, retrospective study. Psychol Med 30:281–294, 2000b

Kendler KS, Prescott CA, Myers J, et al: The structure of genetic and environmental risk factors for common psychiatric and substance use disorders in men and women. Arch Gen Psychiatry 60:929–937, 2003

Kendler KS, Gardner CO, Gatz M, et al: The sources of co-morbidity between major depression and generalized anxiety disorder in a Swedish national twin sample. Psychol Med 37:453–462, 2007

Kessler RC: The effects of stressful life events on depression. Annu Rev Psychol 48:191–214, 1997

Kessler RC, Nelson CB, McGonagle KA, et al: Comorbidity of DSM-III-R major depressive disorder in the general population: results from the US National Comorbidity Survey. Br J Psychiatry Suppl (30):17–30, 1996

Kessler RC, Davis CG, Kendler KS: Childhood adversity and adult psychiatric disorder in the US National Comorbidity Survey. Psychol Med 27:1101–1119, 1997

Kessler RC, DuPont RL, Berglund P, et al: Impairment in pure and comorbid generalized anxiety disorder and major depression at 12 months in two national surveys. Am J Psychiatry 156:1915–1923, 1999

Kessler RC, Berglund P, Demler O, et al: The epidemiology of major depressive disorder: results from the National Comorbidity Survey Replication (NCS-R). JAMA 289:3095–3105, 2003

Kessler RC, Chiu WT, Jin R, et al: The epidemiology of panic attacks, panic disorder, and agoraphobia in the National Comorbidity Survey Replication. Arch Gen Psychiatry 63:415–424, 2006

Khan AA, Jacobson KC, Gardner CO, et al: Personality and comorbidity of common psychiatric disorders. Br J Psychiatry 186:190–196, 2005

Krueger RF: The structure of common mental disorders. Arch Gen Psychiatry 56:921–926, 1999

Lenzenweger MF, Lane MC, Loranger AW, et al: DSM-IV Personality Disorders in the National Comorbidity Survey Replication. Biol Psychiatry 62:553–564, 2007

Leon CA, Leon A: Panic disorder and parental bonding. Psychiatr Ann 20:503–508, 1990

Levitan RD, Rector NA, Sheldon T, et al: Childhood adversities associated with major depression and/or anxiety disorders in a community sample of Ontario: issues of co-morbidity and specificity. Depress Anxiety 17:34–42, 2003

Libby AM, Orton HD, Novins DK, et al: Childhood physical and sexual abuse and subsequent depressive and anxiety disorders for two American Indian tribes. Psychol Med 35:329–340, 2005

Mackinnon A, Henderson AS, Andrews G: Parental 'affectionless control' as an antecedent to adult depression: a risk factor refined. Psychol Med 23:135–141, 1993

Maser JD, Cloninger CR: Comorbidity of Mood and Anxiety Disorders. Washington, DC, American Psychiatric Press, 1990

Mendlewicz J, Papadimitriou GN, Wilmotte J: Family study of panic disorder: comparison with generalized anxiety disorder, major depression and normal subjects. Psychiatr Genet 3:73–78, 1993

Merikangas KR, Mehta RL, Molnar BE, et al: Comorbidity of substance use disorders with mood and anxiety disorders: results of the International Consortium in Psychiatric Epidemiology. Addict Behav 23:893–907, 1998

Molnar BE, Buka SL, Kessler RC: Child sexual abuse and subsequent psychopathology: results from the National Comorbidity Survey. Am J Public Health 91:753–760, 2001

Mullen PE, Martin JL, Anderson JC, et al: Childhood sexual abuse and mental health in adult life. Br J Psychiatry 163:721–732, 1993

Newman SC, Bland RC: Life events and the 1-year prevalence of major depressive episode, generalized anxiety disorder, and panic disorder in a community sample. Compr Psychiatry 35:76–82, 1994

Oakley-Browne MA, Joyce PR, Wells JE, et al: Adverse parenting and other childhood experience as risk factors for depression in women aged 18–44 years. J Affect Disord 34:13–23, 1995a

Oakley Browne MA, Joyce PR, Wells JE, et al: Disruptions in childhood parental care as risk factors for major depression in adult women. Aust N Z J Psychiatry 29:437–448, 1995b

Ormel J, Vonkorff M, Ustun TB, et al: Common mental disorders and disability across cultures: results from the WHO Collaborative Study on Psychological Problems in General Health Care. JAMA 272:1741–1748, 1994

Ormel J, Oldehinkel AJ, Vollebergh W: Vulnerability before, during, and after a major depressive episode: a 3-wave population-based study. Arch Gen Psychiatry 61:990–996, 2004

Parker G, Hadzi-Pavlovic D, Greenwald S, et al: Low parental care as a risk factor to lifetime depression in a community sample. J Affect Disord 33:173–180, 1995

Paykel ES: Life events, social support and depression. Acta Psychiatr Scand Suppl 377:50–58, 1994

Pine DS, Cohen P, Johnson JG, et al: Adolescent life events as predictors of adult depression. J Affect Disord 68:49–57, 2002

Regier DA, Rae DS, Narrow WE, et al: Prevalence of anxiety disorders and their comorbidity with mood and addictive disorders. Br J Psychiatry Suppl (34):24–28, 1998

Reich J: Family psychiatric histories in male patients with generalized anxiety disorder and major depressive disorder. Ann Clin Psychiatry 7:71–78, 1995

Roy A: Early parental separation and adult depression. Arch Gen Psychiatry 42:987–991, 1985

Roy M-A, Neale MC, Pedersen NL, et al: A twin study of generalized anxiety disorder and major depression. Psychol Med 25:1037–1049, 1995

Sato T, Sakado K, Uehara T, et al: Perceived parental styles in a Japanese sample of depressive disorders: a replication outside Western culture. Br J Psychiatry 170:173–175, 1997

Scherrer JF, True WR, Xian H, et al: Evidence for genetic influences common and specific to symptoms of generalized anxiety and panic. J Affect Disord 57:25–35, 2000

Schoevers RA, Deeg DJ, van Tilburg W, et al: Depression and generalized anxiety disorder: co-occurrence and longitudinal patterns in elderly patients. Am J Geriatr Psychiatry 13:31–39, 2005

Skre I, Onstad S, Edvardsen J, et al: A family study of anxiety disorders: familial transmission and relationship to mood disorder and psychoactive substance use disorder. Acta Psychiatr Scand 90:366–374, 1994

Slade T, Watson D: The structure of common DSM-IV and ICD-10 mental disorders in the Australian general population. Psychol Med 36:1593–1600, 2006

Stein MB: Public health perspectives on generalized anxiety disorder. J Clin Psychiatry 65(suppl):3–7, 2004

Sullivan PF, Neale MC, Kendler KS: Genetic epidemiology of major depression: review and meta-analysis. Am J Psychiatry 157:1552–1562, 2000

Veijola J, Maki P, Joukamaa M, et al: Parental separation at birth and depression in adulthood: a long-term follow-up of the Finnish Christmas Seal Home Children. Psychol Med 34:357–362, 2004

Vollebergh WA, Iedema J, Bijl RV, et al: The structure and stability of common mental disorders: the NEMESIS study. Arch Gen Psychiatry 58:597–603, 2001

Wade TD, Kendler KS: Absence of interactions between social support and stressful life events in the prediction of major depression and depressive symptomatology in women. Psychol Med 30:965–974, 2000

Widiger TA, Trull TJ: Personality and psychopathology: an application of the five-factor model. J Pers 60:363–393, 1992

Wittchen HU, Zhao S, Kessler RC, et al: DSM-III-R generalized anxiety disorder in the National Comorbidity Survey. Arch Gen Psychiatry 51:355–364, 1994

Wittchen HU, Kessler RC, Pfister H, et al: Why do people with anxiety disorders become depressed? A prospective- longitudinal community study. Acta Psychiatr Scand Suppl (406):14–23, 2000

Young EA, Abelson JL, Curtis GC, et al: Childhood adversity and vulnerability to mood and anxiety disorders. Depress Anxiety 5:66–72, 1997

Commentary

COMMENTARY ON "THE NOSOLOGIC RELATIONSHIP BETWEEN GENERALIZED ANXIETY DISORDER AND MAJOR DEPRESSION"

Jules Angst, M.D.
Alex Gamma, Ph.D.
Vladeta Ajdacic, Ph.D.
Wulf Rössler, M.D., M.A.

In Chapter 2, "The Nosologic Relationship Between Generalized Anxiety Disorder and Major Depression," John Hettema reviewed the relevant literature comprehensively and concluded that there is insufficient empirical evidence for unifying generalized anxiety disorder (GAD) with major depressive disorder (MDD), although the two diagnostic groups share many characteristics, most of which are diagnostically unspecific.

Comorbidity

Although Hettema's review focused on GAD and MDD, we would like, in addition, to broaden the scope of inquiry to include major mood disorders—embracing bipolar I/II disorders and MDD—and the associations of these disorders with GAD, panic disorder, and repeated panic attacks. Considering the association of bipolar disorder could shed extremely informative light on the question of whether GAD and MDD should be kept as separate diagnostic entities; however, there is a surprising dearth of literature on this association. In 1993, we described an association between GAD and hypomania (Angst 1993). Our newer cumulative data from an age cohort that was followed prospectively from ages 20–40 years (1979–1999) in the Zurich Study suggest that GAD is more strongly associated with bipolar II disorder than with MDD. Of 105 cases of DSM-III GAD (American Psychiatric Association 1980), 27 (25.7%) overlapped with MDD (OR=2.8; 95% CI 1.6–4.8) and 34 of 105 (32.4%) overlapped with bipolar II disorder, as defined by broad Zurich criteria (OR=4.3; 95% CI 2.6–7.4). These odds ratios were computed by comparing the diagnostic groups with the rest of the total sample.

We present below the odds ratios of several diagnostic subgroups versus both one another and the same control group, which consisted of subjects without major or minor mood disorders. This approach allows us to compare three mutually exclusive subgroups of mood disorders: DSM-IV bipolar disorder (American Psychiatric Association 1994), broad bipolar disorder II (Zurich definition; Angst et al. 2003), and MDD. Applying this method, 1-month DSM-III GAD was more strongly associated with DSM-IV bipolar disorder than with the broader bipolar disorder concept, with its weakest association being with MDD. The same was also true for DSM-III panic disorder and panic attacks—that is, the stricter the definition of bipolar disorder, the stronger the association with GAD and panic. Table 1 illustrates the odds ratios, computed in two ways (i.e., vs. the rest of the sample and vs. subjects without mood disorders).

It is remarkable that even our limited data on 6-month DSM-III-R GAD (N=35; American Psychiatric Association 1987), with a follow-up of 10 years (from ages 30–40 years), show a similar trend. These findings further demonstrate a variety of other psychiatric disorders to be more closely associated with bipolar disorder than with MDD—for instance, phobias, obsessive-compulsive disorder, alcohol use disorders (Angst et al. 2006), and other substance use disorders (data not shown).

A similar trend within bipolar disorders is also apparent in the latest analyses of the National Comorbidity Survey Replication. Merikangas et al. (2007) described a stronger lifetime association of DSM-IV GAD with bipolar I than with bipolar II or subthreshold bipolar disorder (ORs [95% CI]: 9.4 [6.2–14.2], 7.7 [5.1–11.7], and 4.3 [2.8–6.7], respectively).

Characteristics of GAD and MDD

In further analyses, we sought, unsuccessfully, to establish differences between GAD and MDD in many other clinical characteristics, including a family history for mania and depression, early childhood adversity, stressful life events, mastery,

TABLE 1. Odds ratio of mutually exclusive bipolar (BP) and major depressive disorders (MDD), adjusted for sex

Disorder	Diagnoses vs. single control group (N=230)			Diagnoses vs. rest of sample (N=490–575)		
	DSM-IV BP	ZH BP-2	MDD	DSM-IV BP	ZH BP-2	MDD
N	16	77	101	16	77	101
DSM-III GAD	15.2*	11.9*	7.9*	3.6*	2.9*	1.8*
DSM-III-R GAD	10.9*	9.2*	5.6*	2.2	2.7*	1.1
Panic disorder	9.3*	6.0*	4.0*	3.1	2.4*	1.6
Panic attacks	10.7*	6.3*	4.2*	3.8*	2.6*	1.6
Phobias	7.9*	4.2*	4.0*	3.2*	1.9*	1.9*
OCD	15.5*	5.0*	3.4	6.5*	2.0	1.1
Alcohol use disorder	57.4*	8.5*	2.5*	5.8*	4.8*	1.0

Note. OCD=obsessive-compulsive disorder; ZH=Zurich broad criteria (Angst et al. 2003).
*$P<0.05$, unweighted for stratified sampling.

temperament, personality traits, and the Symptom Checklist-90-R. We were unable to find any significant differences between the two diagnostic groups (data not shown), with one exception: at 40 years of age, subjects with GAD-only scored higher ($P<0.05$) on the Symptom Checklist-90-R depression subscale than did subjects with MDD-only, whereas both groups had the same scores at earlier interviews. Overall, our results confirm Hettema's conclusions.

Conclusion

Compatible with the review of Hettema, our data fail to provide any evidence for merging GAD with MDD. A primary argument against unification is the stronger association of GAD with bipolar disorders than with MDD.

References

American Psychiatric Association: Diagnostic and Statistical Manual of Mental Disorders, 3rd Edition. Washington, DC, American Psychiatric Association, 1980

American Psychiatric Association: Diagnostic and Statistical Manual of Mental Disorders, 3rd Edition, Revised. Washington, DC, American Psychiatric Association, 1987

American Psychiatric Association: Diagnostic and Statistical Manual of Mental Disorders, 4th Edition. Washington, DC, American Psychiatric Association, 1994

Angst J: Comorbidity of anxiety, phobia, compulsion and depression. Int Clin Psychopharmacol 8:S21–S25, 1993

Angst J, Gamma A, Benazzi F, et al: Toward a re-definition of subthreshold bipolarity: epidemiology and proposed criteria for bipolar-II, minor bipolar disorders and hypomania. J Affect Disord 73:133–146, 2003

Angst J, Gamma A, Endrass J, et al: Is the association of alcohol use disorders with major depressive disorder a consequence of undiagnosed bipolar-II disorder? Eur Arch Psychiatry Clin Neurosci 256:452–457, 2006

Kessler RC, Brandenburg N, Lane M, et al: Rethinking the duration requirement for generalized anxiety disorder: evidence from the National Comorbidity Survey Replication. Psychol Med 35:1073–1082, 2005

Merikangas KR, Akiskal HS, Angst J, et al: Lifetime and 12-month prevalence of bipolar spectrum disorder in the National Comorbidity Survey Replication. Arch Gen Psychiatry 64:543–552, 2007

3

THE BIOLOGY OF GENERALIZED ANXIETY DISORDER AND MAJOR DEPRESSIVE DISORDER

Commonalities and Distinguishing Features

Elizabeth I. Martin, Ph.D.
Charles B. Nemeroff, M.D., Ph.D.

Generalized anxiety disorder (GAD) commonly occurs comorbid with other anxiety disorders and with major depressive disorder (MDD). As syndromes, GAD and MDD share many symptoms, and there are several treatments that are effective for both. However, despite this remarkable overlap, there are many distinguishing features of the individual disorders that are discordant with the hypothesis that GAD and MDD represent a single neurobehavioral disorder and thus should be described as such in DSM-V. In this chapter, we describe the key biological similarities and differences between MDD and GAD, information essential for determining whether MDD and GAD will remain distinct diagnoses in DSM-V.

Supported by National Institutes of Health grants MH-77083, MH-69056, MH-58922, MH-39415, MH-42088, and RR-00039.

Functional Neuroanatomy

Symptoms of mood and anxiety disorders are thought to result, in part, from disruption in the balance of activity in emotional, limbic centers of the brain relative to higher cognitive centers (Table 3–1). To paraphrase the late neuroanatomist Walle J. H. Nauta, in certain psychiatric disorders, the cerebral cortex is "too loose a saddle" on the limbic system. Recent advances in neuroimaging now permit elucidation of functional and anatomical alterations in patients with neuropsychiatric disorders. Unfortunately, remarkably few imaging studies have examined functional and structural central nervous system (CNS) disruptions in GAD. Comparisons between different studies are made difficult due to variations in patient samples and diagnostic criteria, specific techniques employed, and methods of data analysis. Some discrepancies among earlier studies may have resulted from lack of resolution, making it difficult to identify differential activation of brain subregions.

FRONTAL CORTEX

Cortical activity is differentially disrupted in GAD and MDD in a subregion-specific manner. The frontal cortex can be divided into numerous subregions, some of which exert unique effects upon normal (and pathological) mood and anxiety. The orbital frontal cortex (OFC) codes information, controls impulses, and regulates mood. In healthy control subjects, anxiety-inducing autobiographical memory scripts, but not sadness-inducing scripts, increase regional cerebral blood flow (rCBF) in the left OFC. This result supports previous data demonstrating OFC activation in posttraumatic stress disorder (PTSD) and panic disorder patients during symptom provocation (Liotti et al. 2000). In patients with MDD, OFC volume has been reported to be decreased (Lacerda et al. 2004). A role for the frontal cortex in MDD relapse vulnerability is suggested by data showing that acute mood challenge reduced rCBF in the OFC and medial prefrontal cortex (mPFC) in nonmedicated, acutely depressed and remitted patients with MDD compared with never-depressed control subjects (Gemar et al. 2007; Liotti et al. 2002).

Successful treatment with antidepressant drugs influences frontal cortical activity in patients with MDD and those with GAD. In patients with GAD, successful treatment with paroxetine resulted in a diffuse set of metabolic changes; in patients with MDD, paroxetine treatment demonstrated a more focused effect, decreasing OFC metabolism (Kilts 2003). Brain activity changes after cognitive-behavioral therapy have also been studied in patients with MDD. Prior to treatment, the mPFC was hyperactive in patients who were depressed, but successful cognitive-behavioral treatment decreased dorsal, ventral, and medial PFC activity. In contrast, paroxetine increased prefrontal cortex metabolism (Goldapple et al.

2004). Antidepressant treatment has also been shown to increase right dorsal prefrontal cortical activity (Mayberg et al. 1999), and acute sadness induction in healthy subjects was shown to deactivate this region, suggesting dorsal prefrontal cortex (dPFC) hypoactivity may be involved in symptoms of depression (Liotti et al. 2000). This hypothesis is supported by numerous studies showing hypometabolism and hypoperfusion in the dPFC (for review, see Mayberg 1997), although other studies have reported no change in right prefrontal cortex activity in euthymic or acutely depressed patients with MDD during sadness induction (Liotti et al. 2002).

The ventromedial subregion of the PFC (vmPFC) is believed to be associated with MDD and the ventrolateral subregion (vlPFC) with both GAD and MDD. The vmPFC was involved in reward processing (Keedwell et al. 2005) and in the visceral response to emotions, which were enhanced by the right vmPFC and inhibited by the left vmPFC (Drevets 2001). Disruption of the vmPFC in patients with MDD was a potential neural correlate of anhedonia; in patients with MDD, vmPFC activity was elevated in response to "happy" stimuli, whereas these stimuli had the opposite effect in healthy subjects (Keedwell et al. 2005). In response to sadness induction, vlPFC activity was increased in euthymic and acutely depressed patients with MDD compared with healthy control subjects (Liotti et al. 2002), and vlPFC volume was decreased in patients with MDD (Lacerda et al. 2004). In adolescent patients with GAD, under resting conditions, vlPFC activity was also elevated relative to healthy control subjects. This elevation may represent a compensatory response rather than an underlying cause of GAD, because within patients with GAD, PFC activation correlated negatively with symptom severity (Monk et al. 2006).

LIMBIC AND PARALIMBIC REGIONS

The insular cortex integrates the sensory, affective, and cognitive components of pain and processes information regarding the internal bodily state. Like the frontal cortex, the insular cortex and cingulate cortex are divided into subregions distinguished by cytoarchitectonic, connectivity, and functional differences (Liotti et al. 2000). The dorsal insula is granular, has major connections to the somatosensory cortex, and is activated by acute sadness. The ventral insula is agranular, involved in visceral sensation and autonomic responses via connections with the OFC and amygdala, and activated by anxiety (Liotti et al. 2000).

The cingulate cortex also plays a role in the emotional components of pain perception. This structure can be divided into anterior (ACC) and posterior (PCC) segments. The ACC can be divided further into pregenual and subgenual sections. The pregenual ACC is deactivated in euthymic, remitted patients with MDD but activated in patients with acute depression during provoked sadness (Liotti et al. 2002). Activity in the subgenual ACC was unchanged during a depressive episode

TABLE 3–1. Summary of select neuroanatomical and neuroimaging studies in major depressive disorder (MDD), generalized anxiety disorder (GAD), and normal sadness and anxiety

Brain region	MDD and normal sadness	GAD, other anxiety disorders, and normal anxiety
Orbital frontal cortex	Decreased volume in MDD	Increased rCBF in left orbital frontal cortex in acute anxiety
	Decreased rCBF in euthymic and acute MDD	Overactivity during symptom provocation in PTSD, panic disorder
	Decreased metabolism after SSRI treatment	
	No effect in acute sadness	
Medial prefrontal cortex	Decreased rCBF in euthymia and acute MDD	
	Hyperactive in MDD	
	Decreased metabolism after cognitive-behavioral therapy	
	Increased metabolism after SSRI	
Dorsal prefrontal cortex	Increased after antidepressant treatment	
	Hypometabolic in MDD	
Ventromedial prefrontal cortex	Increased activity in MDD for happy stimuli but decreased in control subjects	
Ventrolateral prefrontal cortex	Increased activity for acute sadness in euthymic and acute MDD	Overactivity in adolescent GAD patients as compensatory mechanism
	Decreased volume in MDD	Activation correlates negatively with severity
Insular cortex	Activation of dorsal insula by acute sadness	Activation of ventral insula by acute anxiety

TABLE 3–1. Summary of select neuroanatomical and neuroimaging studies in major depressive disorder (MDD), generalized anxiety disorder (GAD), and normal sadness and anxiety *(continued)*

Brain region	MDD and normal sadness	GAD, other anxiety disorders, and normal anxiety
Cingulate cortex	Deactivation of pregenual ACC in euthymic MDD	No effect on ACC but deactivation of PCC in acute anxiety
	Activation of pregenual ACC in acute MDD	
	Normal subgenual ACC in acute MDD but hypoactive in remitted MDD patients	
	Activation of ACC and PCC by acute sadness	
Amygdala	Overactivity at rest in primary mood disorders	No overactivity at rest
	Activity magnitude correlates to severity	Overactivity during symptom provocation
	Overactivity without conscious perception	Activity of right amygdala most relevant to anxiety
	Normal activity after treatment	
	Decreased volume of left amygdala vs. controls	

Note. "Treatment" refers to successful treatment.
ACC = anterior cingulate cortex; GAD = generalized anxiety disorder; MDD = major depressive disorder; PCC = posterior cingulate cortex; PTSD = posttraumatic stress disorder; rCBF = regional cerebral blood flow; SSRI = selective serotonin reuptake inhibitor.

but exhibited reduced activity during remission. Subgenual cingulate hypoactivity may result from treatment-induced compensatory changes—a reestablishment of homeostasis at a new set-point—designed to better control intrusive thoughts and acute depression (Liotti et al. 2002; Mayberg et al. 1999). These and other data support the idea that ACC activity provides a marker for refractory MDD and is involved in emotion-attention interactions (Liotti et al. 2002). Subgenual ACC activity also increased following sadness induction but not anxiety induction in healthy subjects. In contrast, the PCC was deactivated by both sadness and anxiety compared with neutral memories (Liotti et al. 2000); in remitted patients with MDD, PCC activity was increased (Mayberg et al. 1999).

The amygdala organizes the emotional response to stress; it is overactive in patients with GAD and patients with MDD, potentially underlying rumination on aversive or guilt-provoking memories that is common to both mood and anxiety disorders (Drevets 2001). Interestingly, some studies have suggested that the left amygdala is most relevant to mood disorders, whereas the right amygdala, which is more closely associated with fear and distress, plays a more prominent role in anxiety (for reviews, see Anand and Shekhar 2003; Rauch et al. 2003). The amygdala is highly interconnected with brain regions responsible for interpreting social behavior. As such, amygdalar hyperactivity may be associated with inaccurate interpretations of social behavior, a frequent symptom of GAD, via interactions with the superior temporal gyrus, thalamus, and prefrontal cortex (Rauch et al. 2003).

Remarkably, an increase in resting amygdalar cerebral blood flow may be specific to primary mood disorders; patients with obsessive-compulsive disorder (OCD), phobias, or other neuropsychiatric conditions did not demonstrate increased resting amygdalar activity (Drevets 2003). The magnitude of increased rCBF and metabolism in the amygdala correlated with the severity of neurovegetative and emotional symptoms of a depressive episode (Anand and Shekhar 2003; Drevets 2001, 2003). Amygdalar overactivity in patients with MDD persisted, even in the absence of conscious processing, as evidenced by sleep studies (Drevets 2003), or in response to split-second presentation of fearful facial stimuli (Anand and Shekhar 2003). This overactivity normalized after successful antidepressant treatment (Drevets 2003). Some studies have suggested that the left amygdala is functionally overactive, although anatomically smaller, in patients with MDD (Anand and Shekhar 2003); other studies have shown that the amygdala is enlarged (e.g., Weniger et al. 2006). Unfortunately, volumetric studies have tended to be relatively inconsistent due to diverse patient samples and different methodologies used, and this inconsistency has rendered data interpretation difficult.

Although resting amygdala activation appears to be specific for mood disorders, symptom-provocation paradigms have revealed anxiety-induced amygdalar activation, particularly in the right hemisphere (Liotti et al. 2000). Unfortunately, of the few imaging studies in patients with GAD, most were performed in the basal state and failed to identify GAD-related changes in brain activity. Additional mood-challenge studies that specifically compare patients with GAD to patients with MDD will likely be necessary to provide direct and much-needed comparative data.

CORTICAL-LIMBIC NEURAL NETWORKS

Distinct cortical-limbic neural networks mediate GAD and MDD. Improved neuroimaging techniques, as well as our increasing understanding of the complicated interactions between brain regions, highlight the importance of moving beyond simple examination of regional changes. To identify relevant distinctions between MDD and GAD, more research is needed to focus on identifying neural networks responsible for these disorders. Normal sadness and anxiety are thought to recruit completely separate cortical-limbic pathways; sadness is associated with a *dorsal* cortical deactivation whereas anxiety is associated with *ventral* cortical deactivation (Liotti et al. 2000). Future studies identifying neural network activity in GAD and MDD are expected to reveal similar distinctions between pathological sadness and anxiety.

Moreover, shifts in limbic-cortical networks may influence the transition between euthymic and episodic states in patients with MDD. Both transient and chronic changes in negative mood may influence the direction of these limbic-cortical shifts. For example, connectivity between subregions of the cingulate cortex—along with links to the brainstem, hypothalamus, and spinal cord—and ascending projections to the OFC, mPFC, and dPFC provide a neural network through which primary autonomic information can influence learning, memory, reward, and reinforcement (Keightley et al. 2003). Sadness-induction studies support a role for this cingulate-prefrontal cortex connection in depression; patients with MDD, but not healthy control subjects, experienced decreased activity in the dorsolateral PFC associated with sadness-induced elevations in the subgenual ACC (Mayberg et al. 1999). Because these limbic-cortical connections are necessary for normal range and expression of emotion, disruption at any point in this network may result in symptoms of mood and anxiety disorders. Cognitive, pharmacological, and neurosurgical interventions may return homeostasis to this network via top-down or bottom-up effects (Mayberg et al. 1999).

Neuroendocrinology

Neuroendocrine systems have been intensively studied in mood and anxiety disorders, including the hypothalamic-pituitary-adrenal (HPA), hypothalamic-pituitary-gonadal (HPG), and hypothalamic-pituitary-thyroid (HPT) axes (Table 3–2).

TABLE 3–2. Summary of select endocrine and neuropeptide disruptions in major depressive disorder (MDD), generalized anxiety disorder (GAD), and normal sadness and anxiety

System	MDD and sadness	GAD, other anxiety disorders, and normal anxiety
HPA axis	Hyperactivity Dexamethasone nonsuppression Blunted response to CRF stimulation	Normal or slight elevation in GAD Associated with anxiety-like behavior in animals
CRF	Overexpressed in hypothalamic and extrahypothalamic regions Increased CSF concentrations	Normal CSF concentrations in GAD Overexpression in PTSD and OCD
HPG axis	Hypoactivity Increased susceptibility, not direct causality	Hypoactivity Increased susceptibility, not direct causality
HPT axis	Hypoactivity in some patients Blunted TSH response to TRH Increased CSF TRH concentrations	Unchanged Normal CSF TRH concentrations Blunted TSH response to TRH in OCD Elevated TSH response to TRH in PTSD Hyperthyroidism in panic disorder
Neuropeptide Y	Decreased plasma concentrations Lower CSF neuropeptide Y in first-episode MDD patients vs. recurrent MDD patients Decreased in prefrontal cortex of bipolar patients Concentration of CSF neuropeptide Y inversely proportional to anxiety scores in MDD	Unchanged Elevated neuropeptide Y may confer resiliency to PTSD after combat exposure in men

TABLE 3–2. Summary of select endocrine and neuropeptide disruptions in major depressive disorder (MDD), generalized anxiety disorder (GAD), and normal sadness and anxiety *(continued)*

System	MDD and sadness	GAD, other anxiety disorders, and normal anxiety
Cholecystokinin	Unchanged	Cholecystokinin hypersensitivity Overexpression in panic disorder; causes panic in healthy control subjects
Galanin	Elevated in MDD	Unclear, highly context-dependent Modulatory, not causal

Note. CRF=corticotropin-releasing factor; CSF=cerebrospinal fluid; GAD=generalized anxiety disorder; HPA=hypothalamic-pituitary-adrenal; HPG=hypothalamic-pituitary-gonadal; HPT=hypothalamic-pituitary-thyroid; MDD=major depressive disorder; OCD=obsessive-compulsive disorder; PTSD=posttraumatic stress disorder; TRH=thyrotropin-releasing hormone; TSH=thyroid-stimulating hormone.

THE HYPOTHALAMIC-PITUITARY-ADRENAL AXIS

HPA axis hyperactivity characterizes MDD but not GAD. The HPA axis is composed primarily of corticotropin-releasing factor (CRF), with cell bodies in the paraventricular nucleus of the hypothalamus, adrenocorticotropic hormone (ACTH) from the anterior pituitary, and glucocorticoids from the adrenal cortex. This system is known to mediate the mammalian response to stress (e.g., Schulkin et al. 1998; Swanson and Simmons 1989). In many patients with MDD, particularly those with severe or psychotic depression, the HPA axis exhibits marked hyperactivity, as evidenced by the observations that follow.

1. Plasma ACTH and cortisol concentrations are elevated at rest in patients with MDD compared with healthy volunteers.
2. Plasma ACTH and cortisol (and other glucocorticoids) are not suppressed by dexamethasone, a synthetic glucocorticoid, suggesting that HPA-axis negative feedback is disrupted in patients with MDD.
3. Plasma ACTH concentrations are blunted in patients with MDD, compared with healthy control subjects, when CRF is administered in a standard CRF stimulation test.
4. Plasma ACTH and glucocorticoid concentrations were elevated in patients with MDD, compared with control subjects, upon administration of dexamethasone followed by CRF (the Dex/CRF test), generally considered the most sensitive measure of HPA axis activity (reviewed by Holsboer 2000).
5. Cerebrospinal fluid (CSF) CRF and cortisol concentrations were elevated in patients with depression.
6. Concentrations of CRF peptide and CRF mRNA expression were elevated in the paraventricular nucleus of the hypothalamus of suicide victims who were depressed.
7. CNS CRF_1 receptor mRNA expression was decreased in suicide victims who were depressed.

HPA axis hyperactivity in MDD has been hypothesized to result from decreased sensitivity to glucocorticoid negative feedback and increased activity of hypothalamic CRF neurons. Evidence suggests that, during a depressive episode, CRF is overexpressed in both hypothalamic and extrahypothalamic regions, including the amygdala and bed nucleus of the stria terminalis. This overexpression is believed to result in elevated CSF CRF concentrations (e.g., see Arato et al. 1989; Bremner et al. 1997; Heim et al. 1997a, 1997b; Holsboer 2003). Elevated CSF CRF concentrations and HPA axis hyperactivity normalized upon recovery from depression, suggesting that these are state markers for a depressive episode rather than trait markers for MDD (Plotsky et al. 1998). It has been hypothesized that a return to normal HPA axis function is a shared property of all antidepressant treatments (e.g., Holsboer and Barden 1996; Owens and Nemeroff 1999; Stout et al. 2002).

Copious preclinical and clinical data support the hypothesis that CRF and stress play a causal role in symptoms of anxiety and depression (e.g., Claes 2004; Dunn and Berridge 1990; Koob and Bloom 1985; Nestler et al. 2002; Owens and Nemeroff 1991). In experimental animals, either chronic stress or direct CNS CRF administration led to symptoms remarkably similar to those observed in patients with MDD (for review, see Nemeroff 1988). Chronic antidepressant treatment prevented CRF activation and stress-induced behavioral responses but produced no such effect in unstressed control subjects, supporting the hypothesis that antidepressant efficacy depends on altered CRF signaling (Stout et al. 2002).

Importantly, in the few studies available, patients with GAD exhibited normal HPA axis activity and CRF secretion (Nutt 2001). Thus, patients with GAD exhibited neither hypercortisolism nor nonsuppression in the dexamethasone suppression test. HPA-axis disruption and elevated CSF CRF concentrations have, however, been observed in other anxiety disorders, most notably PTSD (for reviews, see de Kloet et al. 2006; Fossey et al. 1996; Nutt 2001; Risbrough and Stein 2006). That CRF and the HPA axis appear to play a less prominent role in GAD than in other anxiety disorders and in MDD is somewhat surprising, given the plethora of studies describing a role for CRF in anxiety-like behavior in experimental animals. There could be several explanations for this discrepancy: 1) more extensive GAD studies are required before concluding that CRF hyperactivity does not occur in GAD, or 2) animal models based on stress-reactivity cannot adequately model GAD. Despite the lack of evidence of a role for CRF circuits in the pathophysiology of GAD, CRF antagonists have been demonstrated to possess anxiolytic as well as antidepressant activity.

THE HYPOTHALAMIC-PITUITARY-GONADAL AXIS

The HPA and HPG axes are interlinked; the HPG axis is inhibited by CRF and glucocorticoids during the response to stress, and promoter elements in the CRF gene are regulated by sex steroids (for review, see Tsigos and Chrousos 2002). Evidence suggests that the HPG axis is underactive in MDD, as evidenced by decreased plasma concentrations of sex steroids (for reviews, see Hendrick et al. 2000; Swaab et al. 2005). Furthermore, gonadal hormone replacement can reduce depression symptom severity in men who are hypogonadal and who are unresponsive to selective serotonin reuptake inhibitors (SSRIs) (Seidman and Rabkin 1998).

Some evidence suggests that HPG axis activity is also decreased in patients with GAD (Cameron and Nesse 1988; Semeniuk et al. 2001). In men, anxiety associated with hypogonadism reportedly may be treated with testosterone supplementation (Cooper and Ritchie 2000). However, HPG axis alterations neither predicted treatment outcome nor correlated with anxiety symptoms in patients with GAD, suggesting a lack of a causal relationship between GAD and HPG axis alterations (Kaneda and Fujii 2001).

Preclinical data suggest that female sex hormones influence anxiety, but very few clinical studies have specifically examined this relationship (for review, see Le Melledo and Baker 2004). Estrogen directly interacts with neuropeptide and neurotransmitter systems involved in the regulation of mood and anxiety in humans and experimental animals, and estrogen receptors are found in brain regions relevant to mood and anxiety (for reviews, see Rubinow and Schmidt 2006; Walf and Frye 2006). In women, there is considerable evidence that estrogen exerts antidepressant effects, particularly in postpartum depression (Gregoire et al. 1996; Sichel et al. 1995) and in the perimenopausal period (Schmidt et al. 2000). This evidence does not necessarily support a direct causal role for estrogen in mood or anxiety disorders. The cyclicity of female sex hormone secretion may contribute to the susceptibility for mood and anxiety disorders by compounding genetic and environmentally induced risk factors in other neural systems, such as CRF neurons and the HPA axis. The individual response to this enhanced sensitivity is highly context dependent and likely depends on individual-specific alterations in other systems associated with anxiety and depression (discussed by Rubinow 2005).

THE HYPOTHALAMIC-PITUITARY-THYROID AXIS

HPT axis alterations are common in MDD but not in GAD. Hypothyroidism is relatively common in patients with MDD and may represent a trait marker in such patients. Unlike HPA axis disturbances, which identify the state of a depressive episode, HPT axis alterations have been demonstrated to be present even in euthymic patients with MDD (Musselman and Nemeroff 1996). There is considerable evidence that HPT axis disturbances play a causal role in MDD. Higher baseline plasma thyroxine (T_4) concentrations predicted better outcomes in patients with depression, and T_4 concentrations normalized with effective treatment. Recent evidence from the large STAR*D study (Rush et al. 2006) that augmenting antidepressants with triiodothyronine (T_3) in nonresponders improved treatment response confirms several previous findings (Abraham et al. 2006; Lifschytz et al. 2006), although T_3 increased neither the rapidity nor the magnitude of the response in unselected patients treated with SSRIs (Garlow et al., in press).

HPT axis function is best assessed by using the thyrotropin-releasing hormone (TRH) stimulation test. One of the most reliable findings in patients with MDD has been the blunted thyroid-stimulating hormone (TSH) response to TRH (Cameron and Nesse 1988). CSF concentrations of TRH have been reported to be elevated in depressed patients, and such an elevation might, in part, explain the blunted TSH response (for review, see Musselman and Nemeroff 1996). There is also a very high prevalence rate of symptomless autoimmune thyroiditis (grade IV hypothyroidism) in patients with MDD, as well as other types of hypothyroidism. Indeed, primary hypothyroidism remains the leading medical cause of refractory depression (Custro et al. 1994; Nemeroff et al. 1985).

There is virtually no evidence of HPT axis alterations in GAD (Cameron and Nesse 1988; Munjack and Palmer 1988). CSF TRH concentrations were unaltered in patients with GAD, panic disorder, and OCD (Fossey et al. 1993). However, the TSH response to TRH was blunted in OCD and panic disorder but enhanced in patients with PTSD (reviewed by Schatzberg and Nemeroff 2000).

Neuropeptides

In addition to CRF, other neuropeptides, such as neuropeptide Y, cholecystokinin, and galanin, influence mood and anxiety (Table 3–2).

NEUROPEPTIDE Y

Neuropeptide Y is decreased in MDD and may be a neural correlate of resiliency to mood and anxiety disorders. It is involved in the physiology of feeding behavior and is abundantly expressed in the CNS, where it is co-localized with norepinephrine in several brain regions known to modulate emotion, including the hypothalamus, hippocampus, and amygdala (Schatzberg and Nemeroff 2000). Neuropeptide Y exerts an antidepressant-like effect in animal models of depression and may be involved in the pathophysiology of depression (see Karl and Herzog 2007 for a review). Evidence supporting such a role includes reports that patients with depression had low plasma concentrations of neuropeptide Y that were normalized by treatment with antidepressants (Hashimoto et al. 1996). Interestingly, neuropeptide Y concentrations in CSF were significantly lower in first-episode patients with MDD than in patients with MDD in a recurrent episode, suggesting that it may be a valuable marker, and perhaps a predictor, of a first depressive episode (Hou et al. 2006).

No clear role for neuropeptide Y in the etiology of anxiety disorders has been established (Griebel 1999), and there are no published reports that have examined it in GAD. In experimental animals, neuropeptide Y exerted anxiolytic effects (Heilig 2004), potentially due to interactions with the CRF system (Sajdyk et al. 2004). Neuropeptide Y and CRF are co-localized in, and have opposing effects on, the amygdala, locus coeruleus, and periaqueductal gray. CRF receptor antagonists can prevent the anxiogenic effects of neuropeptide Y receptor antagonists, and neuropeptide Y can block CRF-induced anxiety (Sajdyk et al. 2004). In humans, men *without* PTSD who were combat-exposed tended to have higher concentrations of plasma neuropeptide Y than combat-exposed men *with* PTSD, suggesting that neuropeptide Y could be a neural correlate of resiliency (Yehuda et al. 2006).

CHOLECYSTOKININ

Cholecystokinin provokes panic and anxiety but not depression. It is found in the gastrointestinal system and vagus nerve and is located centrally in the amygdala, hippocampus, periaqueductal gray, substantia nigra, and dorsal raphe nucleus (for a review, see Schatzberg and Nemeroff 2000). Remarkably, cholecystokinin agonists, when administered to healthy human subjects, evoked severe anxiety symptoms—similar to a short-lived panic attack—that could be reduced with benzodiazepine treatment. Chronic administration of the antidepressant imipramine, also an effective treatment for panic disorder, decreased the acute anxiogenic effects of cholecystokinin (Schatzberg and Nemeroff 2000).

Cholecystokinin has been hypothesized to play a role in GAD but not in MDD; patients with GAD were hypersensitive to cholecystokinin agonists, whereas patients with MDD were not (Brawman-Mintzer et al. 1997; Koszycki et al. 2004). These data suggest that cholecystokinin receptor–selective antagonists could represent a novel class of anxiolytics. However, such drugs have been developed and have not been demonstrated to possess anxiolytic efficacy (Pande et al. 1999). Such drugs would be unlikely to possess antidepressant properties.

GALANIN

Galanin has depressogenic effects and may modulate anxiety. Galanin also influenced learning and memory, nociception, feeding, and neuroendocrine and cardiovascular regulation (Schatzberg and Nemeroff 2000). Galanin is co-localized with monoamines in brainstem nuclei and inhibits firing in norepinephrine, 5-HT, and dopamine neurons. Galanin overexpression or administration in experimental animals has been reported to increase depression-like behavior. Importantly, intracerebroventricular administration of the nonselective galanin antagonist M35 produces antidepressant effects. Orally active non-peptidergic galanin antagonists are being developed and also appear to possess antidepressant properties (Ogren et al. 2006). The role of galanin in anxiety, if any, appears to be context dependent and will require additional study (Barrera et al. 2005; Karlsson and Holmes 2006).

Neurotransmitters

Myriad studies have scrutinized classical neurotransmitter systems in experimental animal models and patients with psychiatric disorders, revealing a complex interaction between neurochemistry and emotional and behavioral output (Table 3–3).

The aforementioned increases in CNS activity observed in patients with GAD could result from decreased inhibitory or increased excitatory neurotransmission.

TABLE 3–3. Summary of select neurotransmitter abnormalities in major depressive disorder (MDD), generalized anxiety disorder (GAD), and normal sadness and anxiety

Neurotransmitter	MDD and sadness	GAD, other anxiety disorders, and normal anxiety
GABA	Inconsistent $GABA_A$ agonists not approved by U.S. Food and Drug Administration for MDD	Decreased $GABA_A$ receptor density in GAD $GABA_A$ agonists are anxiolytic Affinity for $GABA_A$ predicts efficacy of benzodiazepines
Serotonin	Decreased CSF 5-HIAA concentrations in suicide victims Normal in nonsuicidal MDD patients Blunted prolactin response to 5-HT agonists	Decreased 5-HIAA CSF concentrations in some studies
Serotonin transporter	Decreased density in midbrain Density correlates negatively with anxiety symptoms in MDD	Density correlates negatively with anxiety symptoms in GAD
$5\text{-}HT_{1A}$		Anxiolytic as dorsal raphe nucleus autoreceptors Anxiogenic as hippocampus postsynaptic receptors
$5\text{-}HT_2$	Desensitized by antidepressants	Anxiogenic Antagonists are anxiolytic
Norepinephrine	Elevated in CSF and plasma of severe melancholic MDD patients Unchanged in nonmelancholic MDD patients Blunted growth hormone response to clonidine Blunted REM response to clonidine	Unchanged in GAD

Note. CSF=cerebrospinal fluid; GABA=γ-aminobutyric acid; 5-HIAA=5-hydroxyindoleacetic acid; REM=rapid eye movement.

Dysregulation of γ-aminobutyric-acid (GABA) inhibitory neurotransmission has been documented in several anxiety disorders (for review, see Nemeroff 2003). The observed $GABA_A$ receptor downregulation in patients with GAD is thought to play a role in the etiology of this illness (reviewed by Nutt 2001), and symptoms of GAD, including excessive worry, hypervigilance, and psychomotor agitation, are effectively treated with GABA receptor ($GABA_A$) agonists such as benzodiazepines and barbiturates (Nemeroff 2003).

Data that support a role for GABAergic disruption in MDD are minimal and less consistent (see Kalueff and Nutt 2007 for review). Neuroimaging studies have identified reduced GABAergic activity and a reduced number of GABA neurons in the OFC of patients with MDD (reviewed by Taylor et al. 2005), and some studies have suggested that GABAergic agonists may be effective in the treatment of depression. However, the U.S. Food and Drug Administration rejected the application for adinazolam, a triazolobenzodiazepine, as an antidepressant. Thus, unlike SSRIs, benzodiazepines appear to be effective treatments for anxiety disorders but not for major depression.

Evidence suggests that chronic antidepressant treatment may downregulate the excitatory amino acid *N*-methyl-D-aspartate (NMDA) receptor, which might be overexpressed in patients with MDD. NMDA receptor downregulation could reduce brain excitability in anxiety patients. In depressed patients, antidepressant-induced elevations in rates of neurogenesis could result from decreased glutamate-induced excitotoxicity secondary to NMDA receptor downregulation (reviewed by Simon and Gorman 2006). Recently, the NMDA antagonist ketamine has been reported to possess antidepressant properties (Zarate et al. 2006).

Since the serendipitous finding that monoamine depletion after reserpine treatment for hypertension caused depression in some patients, it has been suggested that monoamine circuit disruption may be involved in the pathophysiology of mood disorders. SSRIs and tricyclic antidepressants are effective antidepressants and anxiolytics, leading to the original hypothesis that 5-HT is deficient in patients with MDD and with GAD. Early studies found that brain concentrations of 5-HT, and its metabolite 5-hydroxyindoleacetic acid (5-HIAA), are decreased in suicide victims who were depressed (Shaw et al. 1967). More recent data have shown that CSF 5-HT and 5-HIAA concentrations were normal in nonsuicidal patients with MDD and decreased in patients with GAD (reviewed by Nutt 2001).

Further evidence in support of a segregated role for 5-HT circuitry in MDD and GAD etiology comes from challenge tests with 5-HT agonists. The $5\text{-}HT_{2A}/5\text{-}HT_3$ agonist *m*-chlorophenylpiperazine (mCPP) elicited anxiety and anger symptoms in patients with GAD but had no such behavioral effects in patients with MDD (Nutt 2001). In healthy subjects, administration of mCPP, the serotonin precursor L-tryptophan (Porter et al. 2003), or the $5\text{-}HT_{1A}$ agonist ipsapirone increased cortisol, ACTH, and prolactin concentrations. Compared with control subjects, patients with MDD exhibited a blunted prolactin response in the mCPP and L-tryptophan tests and a blunted cortisol response to ipsapirone challenge. Patients with primary anxiety disorders did not exhibit the blunted response to ipsapirone, even those patients with anxiety disorder who had subsyndromal depressive symptoms (Riedel et al. 2002).

Midbrain serotonin transporter (SERT) density has been measured in MDD and GAD and was found to be decreased in MDD and to be negatively correlated with anxiety symptoms in both disorders (Malison et al. 1998; Maron et al. 2004). More recent studies replicated the negative correlation between symptom severity and SERT density between patients with GAD and control subjects (Maron et al. 2004). Additional studies that measure SERT density in patients with GAD, before and after treatment, would be of interest.

Some of the confusion regarding the role of 5-HT in anxiety may be explained by variability in target regions and receptor subtypes among 5-HT pathways (reviewed by Kent et al. 2002). For example, presynaptic 5-HT$_{1A}$ autoreceptor activation in the dorsal raphe nucleus is believed to be anxiolytic, but postsynaptic 5-HT$_{1A}$ receptor activation in the hippocampus is believed to be anxiogenic. Activation of 5-HT$_{2A}$ receptors increased stress hormone release, and 5-HT$_{2A}$ antagonists were anxiolytic. Similarly, 5-HT$_{2C}$ antagonists were anxiolytic, 5-HT$_{2C}$ receptor agonists were anxiogenic, and some of the anxiolytic properties of antidepressants may have resulted from 5-HT$_2$ receptor desensitization (Kent et al. 2002).

Although serotonergic transmission, in general, is thought to be decreased in MDD and GAD, norepinephrine neurotransmission commonly is thought to be elevated in these disorders. Increases and decreases in norepinephrine metabolites have been identified in MDD; however, anxiety symptoms have been associated with increases in norepinephrine metabolites (for review, see Ressler and Nemeroff 2000). It has been hypothesized that norepinephrine signaling is elevated due to increased noradrenergic locus coeruleus neuron firing and/or receptor "supersensitivity." Elevations in norepinephrine neurotransmission may indirectly contribute to MDD and GAD symptoms via amygdala overactivity and CRF overexpression (reviewed by Ressler and Nemeroff 2000).

In response to chronic antidepressant treatment, norepinephrine and norepinephrine metabolite concentrations are decreased in CSF and β-adrenergic receptors are downregulated. The effect on the norepinephrine system is the same whether the antidepressant has acute effects on 5-HT (SSRIs) or norepinephrine (serotonin norepinephrine reuptake inhibitors [SNRIs]) receptors (reviewed by Ressler and Nemeroff 2000). The ability of SSRIs and SNRIs to elevate 5-HT and decrease norepinephrine neurotransmission supports the hypothesis that both of these classes of drugs act to "reset" neurotransmitter systems that are dysregulated in MDD and GAD (Ressler and Nemeroff 2000).

As with 5-HT agonists, patients with MDD and GAD responded differently to challenge tests with adrenergic and dopaminergic agonists. Clonidine, the presynaptic α_2 partial agonist, and apomorphine, a dopaminergic agonist, elicited growth hormone release in healthy subjects. The response to both of these drugs was blunted in patients with MDD (Ansseau et al. 1988), potentially due to a defect in catecholamines. Some studies have also identified a blunted growth hormone response to clonidine in anxiety disorders (reviewed by Coupland et al. 1992) and a blunted growth hormone response to apomorphine in OCD, but overall, the data do not support the hypothesis of dopaminergic alterations in anxiety disorders (Pitchot et al. 1996). In patients with MDD, the growth hormone response to apomorphine correlated negatively with total duration of illness (Meltzer et al. 1984). Clonidine, administered during sleep, increased the interval between rapid eye movement (REM) stages of sleep. This response was blunted in patients with MDD compared with healthy control subjects, patients with GAD, and subjects with subsyndromal depressive symptoms (Schittecatte et al. 1995). These results are thought to reflect a deficit in central α_2-adrenergic receptor signaling in MDD (Krishnan et al. 1988).

Neuroanatomical connections between circuits for neurotransmitters and neuropeptides complicate any interpretation of the roles of individual neurotransmitters and neuropeptides in the etiology of MDD and GAD. For example, 5-HT modulated GABAergic signaling within the prefrontal cortex, but preclinical studies revealed that CRF enhanced the effect of 5-HT on prefrontal cortex GABA neurons (Tan et al. 2004), providing a pathway by which stress-induced CRF activation may influence both 5-HT and GABA. This hypothesis is supported by previous data that CRF modulated brainstem serotonergic projections to forebrain regions (Price and Lucki 2001), resulting in functional alterations in depressive-like behavior (Price et al. 2002).

Noradrenergic signaling is also influenced by 5-HT and CRF. Brainstem monoamine nuclei are reciprocally connected; serotonergic projections from the dorsal raphe nucleus decrease norepinephrine cell firing in the locus coeruleus, whereas noradrenergic projections from the locus coeruleus increase 5-HT cell firing in the dorsal raphe nucleus. Noradrenergic locus coeruleus neurons interact with CRF systems coordinating the mammalian autonomic, endocrine, and behavioral response to stress (Nutt 2001). It has been proposed that SSRIs, by increasing 5-HT availability, decrease activation of amygdala CRF neurons by locus coeruleus norepinephrine projections and that this decrease in amygdala activation may reduce anxiety and depressive symptoms (Kent et al. 2002).

These data suggest that 1) although 5-HT and norepinephrine abnormalities exist in both MDD and GAD, the specific disturbances are quite different; 2) 5-HT and norepinephrine systems can influence mood through numerous pathways; and 3) the therapeutic effects of antidepressants result from complex effects on these systems.

Somatic Symptoms

GAD and MDD are characterized by distinct somatic symptoms. Somatic symptoms of these disorders may result from neuroanatomical, neuroendocrine, and neurotransmitter disturbances, and these symptoms may also influence neural activity. One symptom common to all anxiety disorders is increased muscle tension. In contrast, psychomotor retardation and physical pain are common symptoms in depression, although psychomotor agitation is not infrequent. People with GAD have also reported excessive sweating, heart rate, and blood pressure when objective measures of these variables revealed no such alterations. After treatment, these patients reported decreases in heart rate and muscle tension, despite the fact that no changes in heart rate and muscle tension occurred, suggesting that successful treatments "repaired" the brain's ability to interpret internal bodily states (Hoehn-Saric and McLeod 2000).

Further support for the existence of somatic differences between GAD and MDD is derived from neuroimaging data. Invoking sadness increased motor and premotor cortex activity, whereas acute anxiety activated the supplementary motor cortex and bilateral primary somatosensory cortex, thought to result from intense feedback from somatic sensations, which likely contributed to incorrect interpretation of the body's internal state (Liotti et al. 2000).

Sleep polysomnography studies have shown that, compared with healthy control subjects and patients with GAD, patients with MDD exhibited severe sleep disturbances, including increased awakenings and increased shifts in sleep stage. Patients with MDD also exhibited longer durations of REM and shorter REM latency periods. In contrast, patients with GAD exhibited longer sleep-onset latency, shorter total sleep time, and shorter stage 2 sleep compared with healthy control subjects (Papadimitriou et al. 1988).

Additional biological distinctions between MDD and GAD include evidence that MDD is an inflammatory state, as is illustrated, for example, by increases in inflammatory cytokines (Dantzer 2006; Pace et al. 2007; Raison et al. 2006). However, no such data exist for GAD.

Summary and Implications for Research

Because MDD and GAD are characterized by a variety of neuroendocrine, neurotransmitter, and neuroanatomical disruptions, identifying the most functionally relevant differences is no easy task. Disruptions of neurotransmitter systems in MDD and GAD are complicated by the high degree of interconnectivity between neurotransmitter- and neuropeptide-containing circuits in limbic, brainstem, and higher cortical brain areas. The well-documented effectiveness of SSRIs in the treatment of depression and anxiety disorders likely results from the diverse role of

5-HT in the CNS and the manifold effects of SSRIs, rather than a common underlying pathophysiology of serotonergic circuits in MDD and GAD (Nutt 2001; Vaswani et al. 2003).

Similarly, common neuroendocrine and neuropeptide systems are disrupted in MDD and GAD, but the magnitude and nature of those disruptions in symptom etiology is quite distinct. Patients with MDD often exhibit a hyperactive HPA axis, as measured by elevations in ACTH, cortisol, and CRF. These patients also commonly exhibit a hypoactive HPG axis and numerous HPT axis alterations. In contrast, the HPA, HPG, and HPT axes are largely unchanged in patients with GAD. Patients with MDD appear to exhibit galanin hyperactivity; however, the role of galanin in anxiety, if any, remains obscure. Neuropeptide Y activity may influence resiliency to stress and decreased susceptibility for MDD and GAD, and although cholecystokinin hypersensitivity is strongly implicated in anxiety disorders, it appears to play no role in depression.

Neuroanatomical studies also identify some similarities as well as clear differences between patients with GAD and those with MDD. Nutt (2001) reviewed neuroanatomical findings in MDD and GAD and suggested that GAD, in general, is associated with overactive neural circuitry, whereas neural circuitry tends to be underactive in patients with MDD. Modern neuroimaging research in psychiatric patients must examine not only regions of interest but also interactions between brainstem, limbic, and higher cognitive centers and the neurotransmitters and neuropeptides involved in those interactions. The amygdala, in particular, is a key structure in which CRF, monoamines, and psychological stress interact to potentially initiate symptoms of depression or anxiety (Goldstein et al. 1996). Some researchers have suggested that amygdalar hyperactivity in patients with MDD is secondary to decreased prefrontal cortex activity (for review, see Anand and Shekhar 2003). Decreases in information processing in higher cognitive centers and increases in limbic centers may cause inaccurate perceptions of environmental and internal conditions, a symptom common to MDD and GAD (Anand and Shekhar 2003). Reciprocal limbic-cortical networks clearly play an important role in emotional processing, and additional research must dissect the network changes responsible for normal anxiety and sadness as well as for pathological mood and anxiety disorders.

Additional studies must also employ highly selective inclusion criteria in order to avoid confounds caused by comorbidity between both syndromal GAD and MDD as well as take into account patients with GAD who have prominent depressive symptoms, and the converse. It is not unlikely that conflicting data in much previous neuroimaging research result from overlapping subject populations in MDD and GAD studies rather than a real similarity in the etiology of anxiety and depression. Importantly, despite the varied methodological differences between neuroimaging studies, provoked anxiety across diagnoses involves neural circuitry quite segregated from depression and normal sadness (Mayberg et al.

1999), and continued research in this area is likely to identify additional distinguishing features of normal and pathological anxiety compared with normal and pathological sadness.

The decision to classify MDD and GAD as distinct disorders must be based not only on clinical phenomenology but also on pathophysiology, genetics, course of illness, and treatment response data. Neuroendocrine, neurotransmitter, and neuroanatomical differences between patients with MDD and with GAD, and between patients and healthy control subjects, must be interpreted with care. Brain regions and neurotransmitter systems implicated in mood and anxiety disorders have wide-ranging functions, many of which may be unrelated to the etiology of psychiatric disorders.

Finally, both of these disorders clearly represent complex gene-environment interactions. The clinical phenotype, GAD or MDD, may well be determined largely by individual differences in multiple genes that exhibit functional polymorphisms.

References

Abraham G, Milev R, Stuart Lawson J: T3 augmentation of SSRI resistant depression. J Affect Disord 91:211–215, 2006

Anand A, Shekhar A: Brain imaging studies in mood and anxiety disorders: special emphasis on the amygdala. Ann NY Acad Sci 985:370–388, 2003

Ansseau M, Von Frenckell R, Cerfontaine JL, et al: Blunted response of growth hormone to clonidine and apomorphine in endogenous depression. Br J Psychiatry 153:65–71, 1988

Arato M, Banki CM, Bissette G, et al: Elevated CSF CRF in suicide victims. Biol Psychiatry 25:355–359, 1989

Barrera G, Echevarria DJ, Poulin JF, et al: One for all or one for one: does co-transmission unify the concept of a brain galanin "system" or clarify any consistent role in anxiety? Neuropeptides 39:289–292, 2005

Brawman-Mintzer O, Lydiard RB, Bradwejn J, et al: Effects of the cholecystokinin agonist pentagastrin in patients with generalized anxiety disorder. Am J Psychiatry 154:700–702, 1997

Bremner JD, Licinio J, Darnell A, et al: Elevated CSF corticotropin-releasing factor concentrations in posttraumatic stress disorder. Am J Psychiatry 154:624–629, 1997

Cameron OG, Nesse RM: Systemic hormonal and physiological abnormalities in anxiety disorders. Psychoneuroendocrinology 13:287–307, 1988

Claes SJ: Corticotropin-releasing hormone (CRH) in psychiatry: from stress to psychopathology. Ann Med 36:50–61, 2004

Cooper MA, Ritchie EC: Testosterone replacement therapy for anxiety. Am J Psychiatry 157:1884, 2000

Coupland N, Glue P, Nutt DJ: Challenge tests: assessment of the noradrenergic and GABA systems in depression and anxiety disorders. Mol Aspects Med 13:221–247, 1992

Custro N, Scafidi V, Lo Baido R, et al: Subclinical hypothyroidism resulting from autoimmune thyroiditis in female patients with endogenous depression. J Endocrinol Invest 17:641–646, 1994

Dantzer R: Cytokine, sickness behavior, and depression. Neurol Clin 24:441–460, 2006

de Kloet CS, Vermetten E, Geuze E, et al: Assessment of HPA-axis function in posttraumatic stress disorder: pharmacological and non-pharmacological challenge tests, a review. J Psychiatr Res 40:550–567, 2006

Drevets WC: Neuroimaging and neuropathological studies of depression: implications for the cognitive-emotional features of mood disorders. Curr Opin Neurobiol 11:240–249, 2001

Drevets WC: Neuroimaging abnormalities in the amygdala in mood disorders. Ann NY Acad Sci 985:420–444, 2003

Dunn AJ, Berridge CW: Physiological and behavioral responses to corticotropin-releasing factor administration: is CRF a mediator of anxiety or stress responses? Brain Res Brain Res Rev 15:71–100, 1990

Fossey MD, Lydiard RB, Ballenger JC, et al: Cerebrospinal fluid thyrotropin-releasing hormone concentrations in patients with anxiety disorders. J Neuropsychiatry Clin Neurosci 5:335–337, 1993

Fossey MD, Lydiard RB, Ballenger JC, et al: Cerebrospinal fluid corticotropin-releasing factor concentrations in patients with anxiety disorders and normal comparison subjects. Biol Psychiatry 39:703–707, 1996

Gemar MC, Segal ZV, Mayberg HS, et al: Changes in regional cerebral blood flow following mood challenge in drug-free, remitted patients with unipolar depression. Depress Anxiety 24:597–601, 2007

Goldapple K, Segal Z, Garson C, et al: Modulation of cortical-limbic pathways in major depression: treatment-specific effects of cognitive behavior therapy. Arch Gen Psychiatry 61:34–41, 2004

Goldstein LE, Rasmusson AM, Bunney BS, et al: Role of the amygdala in the coordination of behavioral, neuroendocrine, and prefrontal cortical monoamine responses to psychological stress in the rat. J Neurosci 16:4787–4798, 1996

Gregoire AJ, Kumar R, Everitt B, et al: Transdermal oestrogen for treatment of severe postnatal depression. Lancet 347:930–933, 1996

Griebel G: Is there a future for neuropeptide receptor ligands in the treatment of anxiety disorders? Pharmacol Ther 82:1–61, 1999

Hashimoto H, Onishi H, Koide S, et al: Plasma neuropeptide Y in patients with major depressive disorder. Neurosci Lett 216:57–60, 1996

Heilig M: The NPY system in stress, anxiety and depression. Neuropeptides 38:213–224, 2004

Heim C, Owens MJ, Plotsky PM, et al: Persistent changes in corticotropin-releasing factor systems due to early life stress: relationship to the pathophysiology of major depression and post-traumatic stress disorder. Psychopharmacol Bull 33:185–192, 1997a

Heim C, Owens MJ, Plotsky PM, et al: The role of early adverse life events in the etiology of depression and posttraumatic stress disorder: focus on corticotropin-releasing factor. Ann NY Acad Sci 821:194–207, 1997b

Hendrick V, Gitlin M, Altshuler L, et al: Antidepressant medications, mood and male fertility. Psychoneuroendocrinology 25:37–51, 2000

Hoehn-Saric R, McLeod DR: Anxiety and arousal: physiological changes and their perception. J Affect Disord 61:217–224, 2000

Holsboer F: The corticosteroid receptor hypothesis of depression. Neuropsychopharmacology 23:477–501, 2000

Holsboer F: Corticotropin-releasing hormone modulators and depression. Curr Opin Investig Drugs 4:46–50, 2003

Holsboer F, Barden N: Antidepressants and hypothalamic-pituitary-adrenocortical regulation. Endocr Rev 17:187–205, 1996

Hou C, Jia F, Liu Y, et al: CSF serotonin, 5-hydroxyindolacetic acid and neuropeptide Y levels in severe major depressive disorder. Brain Res 1095:154–158, 2006

Kalueff AV, Nutt DJ: Role of GABA in anxiety and depression. Depress Anxiety 24:495–517, 2007

Kaneda Y, Fujii A: Effects of tandospirone, a serotonin-1A agonist, on the hypothalamo-pituitary-gonadal axis of male patients. Neuro Endocrinol Lett 22:243–247, 2001

Karl T, Herzog H: Behavioral profiling of NPY in aggression and neuropsychiatric diseases. Peptides 28:326–333, 2007

Karlsson RM, Holmes A: Galanin as a modulator of anxiety and depression and a therapeutic target for affective disease. Amino Acids 31:231–239, 2006

Keedwell PA, Andrew C, Williams SC, et al: The neural correlates of anhedonia in major depressive disorder. Biol Psychiatry 58:843–853, 2005

Keightley ML, Seminowicz DA, Bagby RM, et al: Personality influences limbic-cortical interactions during sad mood induction. Neuroimage 20:2031–2039, 2003

Kent JM, Mathew SJ, Gorman JM: Molecular targets in the treatment of anxiety. Biol Psychiatry 52:1008–1030, 2002

Kilts C: In vivo neuroimaging correlates of the efficacy of paroxetine in the treatment of mood and anxiety disorders. Psychopharmacol Bull 37(suppl):19–28, 2003

Koob GF, Bloom FE: Corticotropin-releasing factor and behavior. Fed Proc 44:259–263, 1985

Koszycki D, Copen J, Bradwejn J: Sensitivity to cholecystokinin-tetrapeptide in major depression. J Affect Disord 80:285–290, 2004

Krishnan KR, Manepalli AN, Ritchie JC, et al: Growth hormone-releasing factor stimulation test in depression. Am J Psychiatry 145:90–92, 1988

Lacerda AL, Keshavan MS, Hardan AY, et al: Anatomic evaluation of the orbitofrontal cortex in major depressive disorder. Biol Psychiatry 55:353–358, 2004

Le Melledo JM, Baker G: Role of progesterone and other neuroactive steroids in anxiety disorders. Expert Rev Neurother 4:851–860, 2004

Lifschytz T, Segman R, Shalom G, et al: Basic mechanisms of augmentation of antidepressant effects with thyroid hormone. Curr Drug Targets 7:203–210, 2006

Liotti M, Mayberg HS, Brannan SK, et al: Differential limbic-cortical correlates of sadness and anxiety in healthy subjects: implications for affective disorders. Biol Psychiatry 48:30–42, 2000

Liotti M, Mayberg HS, McGinnis S, et al: Unmasking disease-specific cerebral blood flow abnormalities: mood challenge in patients with remitted unipolar depression. Am J Psychiatry 159:1830–1840, 2002

Malison RT, Price LH, Berman R, et al: Reduced brain serotonin transporter availability in major depression as measured by [123I]-2 beta-carbomethoxy-3 beta-(4-iodophenyl)tropane and single photon emission computed tomography. Biol Psychiatry 44:1090–1098, 1998

Maron E, Kuikka JT, Ulst K, et al: SPECT imaging of serotonin transporter binding in patients with generalized anxiety disorder. Eur Arch Psychiatry Clin Neurosci 254:392–396, 2004

Mayberg HS: Limbic-cortical dysregulation: a proposed model of depression. J Neuropsychiatry Clin Neurosci 9:471–481, 1997

Mayberg HS, Liotti M, Brannan SK, et al: Reciprocal limbic-cortical function and negative mood: converging PET findings in depression and normal sadness. Am J Psychiatry 156:675–682, 1999

Meltzer HY, Kolakowska T, Fang VS, et al: Growth hormone and prolactin response to apomorphine in schizophrenia and the major affective disorders: relation to duration of illness and depressive symptoms. Arch Gen Psychiatry 41:512–519, 1984

Monk CS, Nelson EE, McClure EB, et al: Ventrolateral prefrontal cortex activation and attentional bias in response to angry faces in adolescents with generalized anxiety disorder. Am J Psychiatry 163:1091–1097, 2006

Munjack DJ, Palmer R: Thyroid hormones in panic disorder, panic disorder with agoraphobia, and generalized anxiety disorder. J Clin Psychiatry 49:229–231, 1988

Musselman DL, Nemeroff CB: Depression and endocrine disorders: focus on the thyroid and adrenal system. Br J Psychiatry Suppl (30):123–128, 1996

Nemeroff CB: The role of corticotropin-releasing factor in the pathogenesis of major depression. Pharmacopsychiatry 21:76–82, 1988

Nemeroff CB: The role of GABA in the pathophysiology and treatment of anxiety disorders. Psychopharmacol Bull 37:133–146, 2003

Nemeroff CB, Simon JS, Haggerty JJ Jr, et al: Antithyroid antibodies in depressed patients. Am J Psychiatry 142:840–843, 1985

Nestler EJ, Barrot M, DiLeone RJ, et al: Neurobiology of depression. Neuron 34:13–25, 2002

Nutt DJ: Neurobiological mechanisms in generalized anxiety disorder. J Clin Psychiatry 62(suppl):22–7, discussion 28, 2001

Ogren SO, Kuteeva E, Hokfelt T, et al: Galanin receptor antagonists: a potential novel pharmacological treatment for mood disorders. CNS Drugs 20:633–654, 2006

Owens MJ, Nemeroff CB: Physiology and pharmacology of corticotropin-releasing factor. Pharmacol Rev 43:425–473, 1991

Owens MJ, Nemeroff CB: Corticotropin-releasing factor antagonists in affective disorders. Expert Opin Investig Drugs 8:1849–1858, 1999

Pace TW, Hu F, Miller AH: Cytokine-effects on glucocorticoid receptor function: relevance to glucocorticoid resistance and the pathophysiology and treatment of major depression. Brain Behav Immun 21:9–19, 2007

Pande AC, Greiner M, Adams JB, et al: Placebo-controlled trial of the CCK-B antagonist, CI-988, in panic disorder. Biol Psychiatry 46:860–862, 1999

Papadimitriou GN, Kerkhofs M, Kempenaers C, et al: EEG sleep studies in patients with generalized anxiety disorder. Psychiatry Res 26:183–190, 1988

Pitchot W, Hansenne M, Moreno AG, et al: Growth hormone response to apomorphine in obsessive-compulsive disorder. J Psychiatry Neurosci 21:343–345, 1996

Plotsky PM, Owens MJ, Nemeroff CB: Psychoneuroendocrinology of depression: hypothalamic-pituitary-adrenal axis. Psychiatr Clin North Am 21:293–307, 1998

Porter RJ, Gallagher P, Watson S, et al: Elevated prolactin responses to L-tryptophan infusion in medication-free depressed patients. Psychopharmacology (Berl) 169:77–83, 2003

Price ML, Lucki I: Regulation of serotonin release in the lateral septum and striatum by corticotropin-releasing factor. J Neurosci 21:2833–2841, 2001

Price ML, Kirby LG, Valentino RJ, et al: Evidence for corticotropin-releasing factor regulation of serotonin in the lateral septum during acute swim stress: adaptation produced by repeated swimming. Psychopharmacology (Berl) 162:406–414, 2002

Raison CL, Capuron L, Miller AH: Cytokines sing the blues: inflammation and the pathogenesis of depression. Trends Immunol 27:24–31, 2006

Rauch SL, Shin LM, Wright CI: Neuroimaging studies of amygdala function in anxiety disorders. Ann NY Acad Sci 985:389–410, 2003

Ressler KJ, Nemeroff CB: Role of serotonergic and noradrenergic systems in the pathophysiology of depression and anxiety disorders. Depress Anxiety 12(suppl):2–19, 2000

Riedel WJ, Klaassen T, Griez E, et al: Dissociable hormonal, cognitive and mood responses to neuroendocrine challenge: evidence for receptor-specific serotonergic dysregulation in depressed mood. Neuropsychopharmacology 26:358–367, 2002

Risbrough VB, Stein MB: Role of corticotropin releasing factor in anxiety disorders: a translational research perspective. Horm Behav 50:550–561, 2006

Rubinow DR: Reproductive steroids in context. Arch Womens Ment Health 8:1–5, 2005

Rubinow DR, Schmidt PJ: Gonadal steroid regulation of mood: the lessons of premenstrual syndrome. Front Neuroendocrinol 27:210–216, 2006

Rush AJ, Trivedi MH, Wisniewski SR, et al: Acute and longer-term outcomes in depressed outpatients requiring one or several treatment steps: a STAR*D report. Am J Psychiatry 163:1905–1917, 2006

Sajdyk TJ, Shekhar A, Gehlert DR: Interactions between NPY and CRF in the amygdala to regulate emotionality. Neuropeptides 38:225–234, 2004

Schatzberg A, Nemeroff CB: The American Psychiatric Publishing Textbook of Psychopharmacology. Washington, DC, American Psychiatric Publishing, 2000

Schittecatte M, Garcia-Valentin J, Charles G, et al: Efficacy of the 'clonidine REM suppression test (CREST)' to separate patients with major depression from controls: a comparison with three currently proposed biological markers of depression. J Affect Disord 33:151–157, 1995

Schmidt PJ, Nieman L, Danaceau MA, et al: Estrogen replacement in perimenopause-related depression: a preliminary report. Am J Obstet Gynecol 183:414–420, 2000

Schulkin J, Gold PW, McEwen BS: Induction of corticotropin-releasing hormone gene expression by glucocorticoids: implication for understanding the states of fear and anxiety and allostatic load. Psychoneuroendocrinology 23:219–243, 1998

Seidman SN, Rabkin JG: Testosterone replacement therapy for hypogonadal men with SSRI-refractory depression. J Affect Disord 48:157–161, 1998

Semeniuk T, Jhangri GS, Le Melledo JM: Neuroactive steroid levels in patients with generalized anxiety disorder. J Neuropsychiatry Clin Neurosci 13:396–398, 2001

Shaw D, Camps FE, Eccleston EG: 5-Hydroxy tryptamine in the hind-brain of depressive suicides. Br J Psychiatry 113:1407–1411, 1967

Sichel DA, Cohen LS, Robertson LM, et al: Prophylactic estrogen in recurrent postpartum affective disorder. Biol Psychiatry 38:814–818, 1995

Simon AB, Gorman JM: Advances in the treatment of anxiety: targeting glutamate. NeuroRx 3:57–68, 2006

Stout SC, Owens MJ, Nemeroff CB: Regulation of corticotropin-releasing factor neuronal systems and hypothalamic-pituitary-adrenal axis activity by stress and chronic antidepressant treatment. J Pharmacol Exp Ther 300:1085–1092, 2002

Swaab DF, Bao AM, Lucassen PJ: The stress system in the human brain in depression and neurodegeneration. Ageing Res Rev 4:141–194, 2005

Swanson LW, Simmons DM: Differential steroid hormone and neural influences on peptide mRNA levels in CRH cells of the paraventricular nucleus: a hybridization histochemical study in the rat. J Comp Neurol 285:413–435, 1989

Tan H, Zhong P, Yan Z: Corticotropin-releasing factor and acute stress prolongs serotonergic regulation of GABA transmission in prefrontal cortical pyramidal neurons. J Neurosci 24:5000–5008, 2004

Taylor C, Fricker AD, Devi LA, et al: Mechanisms of action of antidepressants: from neurotransmitter systems to signaling pathways. Cell Signal 17:549–557, 2005

Tsigos C, Chrousos GP: Hypothalamic-pituitary-adrenal axis, neuroendocrine factors and stress. J Psychosom Res 53:865–871, 2002

Vaswani M, Linda FK, Ramesh S: Role of selective serotonin reuptake inhibitors in psychiatric disorders: a comprehensive review. Prog Neuropsychopharmacol Biol Psychiatry 27:85–102, 2003

Walf AA, Frye CA: A review and update of mechanisms of estrogen in the hippocampus and amygdala for anxiety and depression behavior. Neuropsychopharmacology 31:1097–1111, 2006

Weniger G, Lange C, Irle E: Abnormal size of the amygdala predicts impaired emotional memory in major depressive disorder. J Affect Disord 94:219–229, 2006

Yehuda R, Brand S, Yang RK: Plasma neuropeptide Y concentrations in combat exposed veterans: relationship to trauma exposure, recovery from PTSD, and coping. Biol Psychiatry 59:660–663, 2006

Zarate CA Jr, Singh JB, Carlson PJ, et al: A randomized trial of an N-methyl-D-aspartate antagonist in treatment-resistant major depression. Arch Gen Psychiatry 63:856–864, 2006

4

WHAT (NO) DIFFERENCES IN RESPONSES TO THREE CLASSES OF PSYCHOTROPICS CAN TEACH US ABOUT DISTINCTIONS BETWEEN GENERALIZED ANXIETY DISORDER AND MAJOR DEPRESSIVE DISORDER

Toshi A. Furukawa, M.D., Ph.D.
Norio Watanabe, M.D., Ph.D.
Ichiro M. Omori, M.D., Ph.D.

Diagnosis is a servant to treatment. When the effective treatments are identical for two disorders, unless they describe phenomenologically distinct entities with or without clearly differentiated pathoetiologies, clinicians would prefer to call

---

We would like to thank Hugh McGuire of the Cochrane Collaboration Depression, Anxiety, and Neurosis Group for searching their trials register. We also thank Corrado Barbui and Andrea Cipriani for their helpful comments on the manuscript.

them by one name. Because the other chapters have dealt with phenomenological overlaps and/or pathoetiological distinctions between generalized anxiety disorder (GAD) and major depressive disorder (MDD), our task for this chapter is to examine treatment specificity of GAD and MDD by comparing treatment responses of these two disorders with different classes of pharmacological agents.

Three classes of psychotropics—antidepressants, benzodiazepines, and azapirones—have been suggested to be effective for GAD (Allgulander et al. 2003; Ballenger et al. 2001). This chapter, therefore, examines how effective these same agents are for GAD and MDD and, through this examination, compares treatment specificity of GAD and MDD.

Methods

The true underlying effect of an intervention can only be estimated through comprehensive review of relevant randomized, controlled trials (RCTs). We therefore set out to identify relevant trials for these disorders through systematic literature search.

CRITERIA FOR STUDIES CONSIDERED FOR THIS REVIEW

Types of Studies

RCTs that compared an antidepressant, a benzodiazepine, or an azapirone against placebo in the acute-phase treatment of GAD or MDD were selected. Quasi-randomized trials, such as those that allocated by using alternate days of the week, were excluded.

Types of Participants

Participants were patients aged 18 years or older, of both sexes, with a primary diagnosis of GAD or MDD. Secondary diagnoses of other anxiety or mood disorders were allowed. Patients with cognitive disorders, psychotic disorders, bipolar disorder, recent or current substance dependence or substance abuse disorders, and serious physical illnesses were excluded. The diagnostic criteria for GAD were limited to those of DSM-IV (American Psychiatric Association 1994), because successive versions of DSM have introduced some substantive changes in the operationalization of this disease entity. Diagnostic criteria for MDD were also limited to DSM-IV. However, as it turned out, we were able to locate no trial that examined benzodiazepines in the treatment of DSM-IV major depression and measured the outcome through the Hamilton Rating Scale for Depression (HAM-D; Hamilton 1960) and/or Hamilton Rating Scale for Anxiety (HAM-A; Hamilton 1959), and only one such trial in the case of azapirones. We therefore included studies that used diagnostic criteria before DSM-IV in the case of benzodiazepine and azapirone treatment of depression because, with regard to MDD, various operational diagnostic criteria since the Feighner criteria or the Research Diagnostic Criteria have adopted essentially the same items.

Types of Interventions

Antidepressants evaluated included classical tricyclic/heterocyclic antidepressants; monoamine oxidase inhibitors; selective serotonin reuptake inhibitors such as citalopram, escitalopram, fluoxetine, fluvoxamine, paroxetine, and sertraline; serotonin-noradrenaline reuptake inhibitors such as venlafaxine, duloxetine, and milnacipran; and other newer agents such as mirtazapine, reboxetine, and bupropion.

Benzodiazepines included a group of two-ring heterocyclic compounds, consisting of a benzene ring fused to a diazepine ring. Any degree of hydrogenation, any substituents, and any H-isomer was permitted. Typical benzodiazepines studied were diazepam, chlordiazepoxide, and lorazepam. Alprazolam, a triazolobenzodiazepine, is also included here, but, in view of the attention once given to triazolobenzodiazepines as antidepressants, the validity of the decision to include alprazolam was examined in a sensitivity analysis.

Azapirones, or azaspirodecanediones, included buspirone, gepirone, and tandospirone. They are all 5-HT_{1A} receptor partial agonists.

Trials in which one of these drugs was compared with an active comparator, without a placebo arm, were excluded. Trials in which these agents were employed as an augmentation strategy were also excluded.

Types of Outcome Measures

We established two a priori primary outcomes for GAD and MDD trials. The first primary outcome for GAD trials was the HAM-A. The second primary outcome for GAD trials was the HAM-D or Montgomery-Åsberg Depression Rating Scale (MADRS; Montgomery and Åsberg 1979) or any other depression scale. The standard HAM-D is the 17-item version, but we accepted 21-item, 24-item, and other modifications of the original HAM-D.

The two primary outcomes for MDD trials were the HAM-A and the HAM-D, MADRS, or any other depression scale.

As a secondary outcome for all these comparisons, we pooled "treatment discontinuation for any reason" as a robust, pragmatic outcome, indicating overall treatment acceptability or desirability. When the trials were long and/or provided these outcomes at various time points (e.g., 2 weeks, 4 weeks, 8 weeks, and 24 weeks), we selected the time points closest to 8 weeks. This represents the typical length of a trial, and we would also expect the greatest differentiation in treatment effectiveness between active treatments at the end of the acute phase treatment.

SEARCH STRATEGY FOR IDENTIFICATION OF STUDIES

We searched the Cochrane Collaboration Depression, Anxiety, and Neurosis Group (CCDAN) Registers in December 2006. This comprehensive register is updated regularly, adding the results on searches of The Cochrane Library, MEDLINE (1966–), EMBASE (1980–), CINAHL (1982–), PsycINFO (1974–), PSYNDEX (1977–), and LILACS (1982–1999) and hand searches of major psychiatric and medical journals and conference proceedings. The register currently contains more than 24,000 records on trials that compare treatment options within the scope of depression, anxiety, and other related neurotic disorders. The register is being coded continuously with respect to characteristics of studies, such as diagnostic criteria used, intervention details, and outcome measures employed, by looking through the full articles of relevant studies manually. The studies already coded are being stored in CCDANCTR-Studies.

Search terms to locate all trials that examined DSM-IV GAD were:

Diagnosis = Generalized Anxiety Disorder and Main Diagnostic Criteria = DSM-IV

Search terms to locate all trials that examined DSM-IV MDD using HAM-A as an outcome measure were:

Diagnosis = Major Depression and Main Diagnostic Criteria = DSM-IV and Intervention = Antidepress* or "Monoamine Oxidase Inhibitors" or "Selective Serotonin Reuptake Inhibitors" or "Tricyclic Drugs" or Acetylcarnitine or Alaproclate or Amersergide or Amiflamine or Amineptine or Amitriptyline or Amoxapine or Befloxatone or Benactyzine or Brofaromine or Bupropion or Butriptyline or Caroxazone or Chlorpoxiten or Cilosamine or Cimoxatone or Citalopram or Clomipramine or Clorgyline or Chlorimipramine or Clovoxamine or Deanol or Demexiptiline or Deprenyl or Desipramine or Dibenzepin or Diclofensine or Dothiepin or Doxepin or Duloxetine or Escitalopram or Etoperidone or Femoxetine or Fluotracen or Fluoxetine or Fluparoxan or Fluvoxamine or Idazoxan or Imipramine or Iprindole or Iproniazid or isocarboxazid or Litoxetine or Lofepramine or Maprotiline or Medifoxamine or Melitracen or Metapramine or Mianserin or Milnacipran or Minaprine or Mirtazapine or Moclobemide or Nefazodone or Nialamide or Nomifensine or Nortriptyline or Noxiptiline or Opipramol or Oxaflozane or Oxaprotiline or Pargyline or Paroxetine or Phenelzine or Piribedil or Pirlindole or Pivagabine or Prosulpride or Protriptyline or Quinupramine or Reboxetine or Rolipram or Sertraline or Setiptiline or SSRI* or Teniloxine or Tetrindole or Thiazesim or Thozalinone or Tianeptine or Toloxatone or Tomoxetine or Tranylcypromine or Trazodone or Trimipramine or Venlafaxine or Viloxazine or Viqualine or Zimeldine or Buspirone or

Gepirone or Tandospirone and Outcome=Hamilton Anxiety Scale (HAS)

Because the above search for trials with DSM-IV MDD found no trial with benzodiazepines and only one with azapirones, we ran a supplemental search with the following terms to locate all trials that used benzodiazepines or azapirones in the treatment of depression:

Diagnosis=Depress* or Dysthymi* or "Adjustment Disorder*" or "Mood Disorder*" or "Affective Disorder" or "Affective Symptoms" Intervention=Benzodiazepine* or Alprazolam or Bentazepam or Bromazepam or Brotizolam or Camazepam or Chlordiazepoxide or Clobazam or Clonazepam or Clorazepate or Clotiazepam or Cloxazolam or Diazepam or Estazolam or Etizolam or Flumazenil or Flunitrazepam or Flurazepam or Flutoprazepam or Halazepam or Ketazolam or Loflazepate or Lorazepam or Lormetazepam or Medazepam or Metaclazepam or Mexazolam or Midazolam or Nitrazepam or Nordazepam or Oxazepam or Prazepam or Propazepam or Quazepam or Ripazepam or Serazapine or Temazepam or Tofisopam or Triazolam or Buspirone or Gepirone or Tandospirone

METHODS OF REVIEW

Selection of Trials and Data Extraction

Two independent reviewers (T.A.F. and N.W.) identified studies that administered antidepressants or benzodiazepines to patients with DSM-IV GAD and three independent reviewers (T.A.F. and N.W. or T.A.F. and I.M.O.) extracted the mean-change scores on the HAM-A and HAM-D (or MADRS or any other depression rating scale) and standard deviations using a standard data-extraction spreadsheet. Any disagreement was resolved by consensus of reviewers.

Again, two independent reviewers (T.A.F. and N.W.) identified studies that administered antidepressants or benzodiazepines to patients with DSM-IV major depression and, at the same time, measured the HAM-A; three independent reviewers (T.A.F. and N.W. or T.A.F. and I.M.O.) extracted the mean-change scores on the HAM-D (or MADRS or any other depression-rating scale) and HAM-A and standard deviations. Any disagreement was resolved by consensus. We further searched for trials that administered benzodiazepines to patients with depression diagnosed by any operational diagnostic criteria.

We performed an additional search for trials that administered azapirones to patients with DSM-IV GAD or with depression by any operational diagnostic criteria.

We extracted change scores of these outcome measures from baseline to post-treatment, because unpaired t-test of change scores is statistically more powerful than unpaired t-test of endpoint scores when the correlation between baseline scores and endpoint scores is greater than 0.5 (Norman 1989). When change scores were not available, we extracted endpoint scores.

Data Analysis

Extracted data were entered into RevMan 4.2.8 software for meta-analysis, prepared and provided by the Cochrane Collaboration (Review Manager 2003). When there were missing data and the method of *last observation carried forward* (LOCF) was used in the original report of the trial, these LOCF data were used.

The primary analysis was the standardized mean difference (SMD), using the random effects model (DerSimonian and Laird 1986), because this method allows the most conservative estimates of treatment effectiveness (Furukawa et al. 2002). Fixed-effect analyses were done routinely in order to investigate the effect of choice of meta-analytic methods.

When the trial was a three (or more)-armed trial in which both an antidepressant and a benzodiazepine (or two antidepressants or two benzodiazepines) were compared with placebo, all comparisons of active drug versus placebo were entered into meta-analysis. However, in order to avoid double counting of the placebo arm patients and, thus, artificially inflating the sample size, we divided the number of patients of the placebo arm accordingly.

Heterogeneity between studies was investigated by I-squared (I^2) statistics (Higgins et al. 2003), and values equal to, or more than, 50% were considered indicative of heterogeneity.

Missing Data

When only the standard error or t statistics or P values were reported, standard deviations were calculated according to Altman and Bland (1996). When none of these values were reported, standard deviations of the HAM-A and HAM-D change scores were imputed from other included studies that did report standard deviations on the same instrument according to a validated imputation method (Furukawa et al. 2006). For a few studies, it was not possible to calculate mean-change scores because only endpoint scores were reported; in such cases, we used endpoint scores, because it has been shown empirically that it is possible to safely mix change and endpoint scores in estimating treatment effects (Banerjee and Wells 2006). However, we examined the validity of these assumptions in a sensitivity analysis.

Funnel-Plot and Sensitivity Analyses

Funnel-plot analyses were performed to check for existence of small study effects, including study publication bias (selective publication of studies with "significant" outcomes) and outcome-reporting bias (selective reporting of "significant" outcomes, within a publication).

As already noted, the following sensitivity analyses were planned a priori:

- Excluding trials that used triazolobenzodiazepines
- Excluding trials for which change scores were not available or for which standard deviations were not reported and had to be imputed

Results

STUDY DESCRIPTIONS

The search for DSM-IV GAD trials in the CCDANCTR-Studies database yielded 360 records, 139 of which included a placebo arm. By going through these records, we identified 26 records that examined an antidepressant, a benzodiazepine, or an azapirone in comparison with placebo. We obtained full texts of these studies and finally arrived at 19 RCTs that compared an antidepressant, a benzodiazepine, or an azapirone against placebo in the treatment of DSM-IV GAD; these are shown in Table 4–1. Most of the trials, except for Silverstone and Salinas (2001), limited the patients to "clean" GAD patients, either by excluding patients scoring above a certain cutoff on HAM-D and/or Raskin Depression Scale (Raskin et al. 1969) and/or by excluding current or recent MDD. The baseline average HAM-A scores ranged from 23 to 28, whereas the baseline average HAM-D scores were in the range of 12–17, except for Silverstone and Salinas (2001). There were 16 trials, involving 4,417 patients with GAD, that included an antidepressant arm; three trials (440 patients) that included a benzodiazepine arm; and two trials (366 patients) that included an azapirone arm (one trial included both antidepressant and benzodiazepine arms, another included both antidepressant and azapirone arms). The median length of trial was 8 weeks (range, 4–24 weeks). All trials measured and reported HAM-A scores, but only seven reported depression measures (two used HAM-D, four used MADRS, and one reported the Hospital Anxiety and Depression Scale depression subscale).

The search for MDD trials that had used HAM-A in the CCDANCTR-Studies database yielded 243 records, of which 54 used DSM-IV; of these, 22 included a placebo arm. We obtained full texts of these studies and finally identified 10 studies that had compared an antidepressant with placebo among patients with DSM-IV MDD and measured the HAM-A score (shown in Table 4–2). None of the studies had excluded GAD, except for Silverstone and Salinas (2001), which focused on MDD without GAD. All in all, a total of 3,122 patients with MDD were involved in these nine RCTs. The baseline average HAM-A scores ranged from 15 to 26, and those for HAM-D were from 18 to 27. The median length of trial was 8 weeks (range, 6–24 weeks).

Because this search identified no trial with a benzodiazepine arm and only one with an azapirone arm, we decided, post hoc, to extend eligibility criteria for any

TABLE 4–1. Placebo-controlled randomized controlled trials (RCTs) of antidepressants, benzodiazepines, or azapirones for DSM-IV GAD

Study	Baseline characteristics		Length (weeks)	Interventions	Outcomes	
	Anxiety	Depression		Drugs	Anxiety	Depression
Allgulander et al. 2001; Montgomery et al. 2002	HAM-A=26.5	—	8	a) Venlafaxine 37.5 mg/d b) Venlafaxine 75 mg/d c) Venlafaxine 150 mg/d	HAM-A	HADS depression subscale
Brawman-Mintzer et al. 2002, 2006	HAM-A=24.3	MADRS=12.6	10	Sertraline 149.1 mg/d	HAM-A	MADRS
Dahl et al. 2005; Steiner et al. 2005	HAM-A=24.8	MADRS=10.8	12	Sertraline 50–150 mg/d	HAM-A	MADRS
Davidson et al. 1999; Rolland et al. 2000	HAM-A=23.6	—	8	a) Venlafaxine 75 mg/d b) Venlafaxine 150 mg/d c) Buspirone 30 mg/d	HAM-A	HADS depression subscale not reported[a]
Davidson et al. 2004	HAM-A=23.4	HAM-D=12.2	8	Escitalopram 10–20 mg/d	HAM-A	HAM-D
Gelenberg et al. 2000	HAM-A=25.0	—	8	Venlafaxine 75–225 mg/d	HAM-A	HADS depression subscale not reported[a]

TABLE 4–1. Placebo-controlled randomized controlled trials (RCTs) of antidepressants, benzodiazepines, or azapirones for DSM-IV GAD *(continued)*

	Baseline characteristics		Interventions		Outcomes	
Study	Anxiety	Depression	Length (weeks)	Drugs	Anxiety	Depression
Goodman et al. 2005[b]; Stein et al. 2005	HAM-A=22.9	HAM-D=12	8	Escitalopram 10–20 mg/d	HAM-A	HADS depression subscale not reported[a]
Goodman et al. 2005[b]; Stein et al. 2005	HAM-A=22.9	HAM-D=12	8	Escitalopram 10–20 mg/d	HAM-A	HADS depression subscale not reported[a]
Hackett et al. 2003	HAM-A=28.0	—	8	a) Diazepam 15 mg/d b) Venlafaxine 75 mg/d c) Venlafaxine 150 mg/d	HAM-A	HADS depression subscale not reported[a]
Lenox-Smith and Reynolds 2003	HAM-A=28	MADRS=16	24	Venlafaxine 75–150 mg/d	HAM-A	MADRS
Montgomery et al. 2006	HAM-A=26.7	HAM-D=12.4	6	Venlafaxine 75 mg/d	HAM-A	HAM-D
Nimatoudis et al. 2004[c]	HAM-A=27.8	—	8	Venlafaxine 75–150 mg/d	HAM-A	HAM-D measured but not reported

TABLE 4–1. Placebo-controlled randomized controlled trials (RCTs) of antidepressants, benzodiazepines, or azapirones for DSM-IV GAD *(continued)*

Study	Baseline characteristics		Interventions		Outcomes	
	Anxiety	Depression	Length (weeks)	Drugs	Anxiety	Depression
Pollack et al. 2001	HAM-A=24.2	HADS depression subscale=14.4	8	Paroxetine 20–50 mg/d	HAM-A	HADS depression subscale not reported[a]
Rickels et al. 2000	HAM-A=24.2	—	8	a) Venlafaxine 75 mg/d b) Venlafaxine 150 mg/d c) Venlafaxine 225 mg/d	HAM-A	HADS depression subscale not reported[a]
Rickels et al. 2003; see also McCafferty et al. 2000	HAM-A=24.1	—	8	a) Paroxetine 20 mg/d b) Paroxetine 40 mg/d	HAM-A	HADS depression subscale not reported[a]
Silverstone and Ravindran 1999; Silverstone and Salinas 2001[d]	HAM-A=25.7	HAM-D=27.9	12	a) Venlafaxine 75–225 mg/d b) Fluoxetine 20–60 mg/d	HAM-A	HAM-D
Feltner et al. 2003; Pande et al. 2000, 2003	HAM-A=24.8	HAM-D=13.5	4	Lorazepam 6 mg/d	HAM-A	HAM-D

TABLE 4–1. Placebo-controlled randomized controlled trials (RCTs) of antidepressants, benzodiazepines, or azapirones for DSM-IV GAD *(continued)*

Study	Baseline characteristics		Interventions		Outcomes	
	Anxiety	Depression	Length (weeks)	Drugs	Anxiety	Depression
Rickels et al. 2005	HAM-A=24.8	HAM-D=13.3	4	Alprazolam 1.5 mg/d	HAM-A	HAM-D
Lader 1999; Lader and Scotto 1998	HAM-A=26.5	MADRS=16.8	4	a) Buspirone 15 mg/d b) Hydroxyzine 37.5 mg/d	HAM-A	MADRS

Note. All trials had used DSM-IV diagnostic criteria for GAD. GAD=generalized anxiety disorder; HADS=Hospital Anxiety and Depression Scale; HAM-A= Hamilton Rating Scale for Anxiety; HAM-D=Hamilton Rating Scale for Depression; MADRS=Montgomery-Åsberg Depression Rating Scale.
[a]HADS depression subscale not reported but should be available.
[b]Goodman et al. (2005) reports two RCTs not reported elsewhere.
[c]HAM-D measured only at baseline; outcome measured but not reported.
[d]Subjects were patients with GAD and MDD simultaneously.

TABLE 4–2. Placebo-controlled randomized controlled trials (RCTs) of antidepressants, benzodiazepines, or azapirones for DSM-IV MDD

Study	Baseline characteristics		Length (weeks)	Interventions	Outcomes	
	Anxiety	Depression		Drugs	Anxiety	Depression
Silverstone and Salinas 2001[a]	—	—	12	a) Venlafaxine 75–225 mg/d b) Fluoxetine 20–60 mg/d	HAM-A	HAM-D
Burke et al. 2002; Lepola et al. 2004[b]	—	HAM-D=25.5	8	a) Citalopram 40 mg/d b) Escitalopram 10 mg/d c) Escitalopram 20 mg/d	HAM-A	HAM-D
Coleman et al. 1999[c]	—	31-item HAM-D=34.4	8	a) Sertraline 50–200 mg/d b) Bupropion 150–400 mg/d	—	HAM-D31
Detke et al. 2004	HAM-A=18.1	HAM-D=20.1	8	a) Paroxetine 20 mg/d b) Duloxetine 80 mg/d c) Duloxetine 120 mg/d		
Goldstein et al. 2004	HAM-A=14.8	HAM-D=17.9	8	a) Duloxetine 40 mg/d b) Duloxetine 80 mg/d c) Paroxetine 20 mg/d	HAM-A	HAM-D
Ranga and Krishnan 2002[c]	—	HAM-D=25	6	Paroxetine 20 mg/d	—	HAM-D
Loo et al. 2002	HAM-A=26.5	HAM-D=27.4	8	Paroxetine 20 mg/d	HAM-A	HAM-D

TABLE 4–2. Placebo-controlled randomized controlled trials (RCTs) of antidepressants, benzodiazepines, or azapirones for DSM-IV MDD *(continued)*

	Baseline characteristics			Interventions		Outcomes	
Study	Anxiety	Depression	Length (weeks)	Drugs		Anxiety	Depression
Rudolph and Feiger 1999c	—	HAM-D$_{21}$=25	8	a) Venlafaxine 75–225 mg/d b) Fluoxetine 20–60 mg/d		HAM-A	HAM-D
Stahl 2000	HAM-A=16.8	HAM-D=26.5	24	a) Citalopram 20–60 mg/d b) Sertraline 50–150 mg/d		HAM-A	HAM-D
Trivedi et al. 2001	HAM-A=19	HAM-D$_{21}$=25.1	8	a) Sertraline 50–200 mg/d b) Bupropion 150–400 mg/d		HAM-A	HAM-D21
Beutler et al. 1987d	—	HAM-D=22.7	4–6	Alprazolam 0.5–8 mg/d		—	HAM-D
Borison et al. 1989	—	HAM-D=23.3	6	a) Alprazolam 3 mg/d b) Alprazolam 6 mg/d		—	HAM-D
Feigner et al. 1983a, 1983b	HAM-A=26.4	Diagnosed by Feighner criteria HAM-D=25.9	6	Alprazolam 1.0–4.5 mg/d		HAM-A	HAM-D
Laakman et al. 1995, 1996	HAM-A=23.3	Diagnosed by ICD-9 HAM-D=19.7	6	a) Lorazepam 2.5–10 mg/d b) Alprazolam 1–4 mg/d		HAM-A	HAM-D

TABLE 4–2. Placebo-controlled randomized controlled trials (RCTs) of antidepressants, benzodiazepines, or azapirones for DSM-IV MDD *(continued)*

Study	Baseline characteristics		Length (weeks)	Interventions	Outcomes	
	Anxiety	Depression		Drugs	Anxiety	Depression
Mendels and Schless 1986	—	Diagnosed by Feighner criteria; HAM-D	6	Alprazolam 1–5 mg/d	—	HAM-D
Rickels et al. 1985	HAM-A=23.6	Diagnosed with DSM-III HAM-D=25.8	6	Alprazolam 1.5–4.5 mg/d	HAM-A	HAM-D
Rickels et al. 1987	—	Diagnosed with DSM-III HAM-D=25	6	a) Alprazolam 1.5–4.5 mg/d b) Diazepam 15–45 mg/d	—	HAM-D
Rickels et al. 1991	—		7	Diazepam 30–60? mg/d	—	HAM-D
Fabre 1990	HAM-A=23.9	Diagnosed by DSM-III, 25-item HAM-D=30.2	8	Buspirone 10–90 mg/d	HAM-A	HAM-D
Feiger 1996[e]	—	Diagnosed by DSM-III-R HAM-D=24	8	Gepirone 10–60 mg/d	—	HAM-D

TABLE 4–2. Placebo-controlled randomized controlled trials (RCTs) of antidepressants, benzodiazepines, or azapirones for DSM-IV MDD *(continued)*

Study	Baseline characteristics		Length (weeks)	Interventions	Outcomes	
	Anxiety	Depression		Drugs	Anxiety	Depression
Feiger et al. 2003	—	Diagnosed by DSM-IV HAM-D=22.7	8	Gepirone 20–80 mg/d	—	HAM-D
Jenkins et al. 1990[e]	HAM-A=22.6	Diagnosed by RDC HAM-D=25.7	8	a) Gepirone 5–45 mg/d b) Gepirone 10–90 mg/d	HAM-A	HAM-D
Schweizer et al. 1998	HAM-A=20.7	Diagnosed by DSM-III-R HAM-D=24.0	8	Buspirone 10–60 mg/d	HAM-A	HAM-D
Wilcox et al. 1996[e]	—	Diagnosed by DSM-III-R HAM-D=22.6	8	a) Gepirone 10–50 mg/d b) Gepirone 20–100 mg/d	HAM-A	HAM-D

Note. All trials for antidepressants used DSM-IV diagnostic criteria for MDD; for trials with benzodiazepines and azapirones, any operational diagnostic criteria were accepted.
[a]Both HAM-A and HAM-D measured at baseline but only change scores reported. [b]HAM-A measured at baseline but only change scores reported.
[c]HAM-A measured both at baseline and endpoint but not reported. [d]This study had cognitive therapy arms but these were not included in the current systematic review. [e]HAM-A measured but not reported.

Study or sub-category	N	Treatment Mean (SD)	N	Control Mean (SD)	SMD (random) 95% CI	Weight %	SMD (random) 95% CI
01 Antidepressants							
Allgulander2001a	138	−12.00(7.71)	44	−10.10(7.71)		3.17	−0.25 [−0.59, 0.09]
Allgulander2001b	130	−13.80(7.71)	43	−10.10(7.71)		3.02	−0.48 [−0.83, −0.13]
Allgulander2001c	131	−14.50(7.71)	43	−10.10(7.71)		3.00	−0.57 [−0.92, −0.22]
Brawman-Mintzer2006	164	−12.71(7.17)	162	−11.15(7.32)		7.73	−0.21 [−0.43, 0.00]
Dahl2005	182	−11.70(8.09)	188	−8.00(8.23)		8.61	−0.45 [−0.66, −0.25]
Davidson1999a	87	−10.70(7.71)	49	−8.10(7.71)		2.95	−0.34 [−0.69, 0.02]
Davidson1999b	87	−9.20(7.71)	49	−8.10(7.71)		2.99	−0.14 [−0.49, 0.21]
Davidson2004	154	−11.30(7.45)	153	−7.40(7.42)		7.08	−0.52 [−0.75, −0.30]
Gelenberg2000	115	−12.70(7.71)	123	−8.50(7.71)		5.47	−0.54 [−0.80, −0.28]
Goodman2005a	124	−9.60(6.68)	128	−7.70(3.39)		5.92	−0.36 [−0.61, −0.11]
Goodman2005b	143	−9.20(5.98)	138	−7.60(5.87)		6.64	−0.27 [−0.50, −0.03]
Hackett2003b	185	−14.00(7.71)	33	−11.70(7.71)		2.66	−0.30 [−0.67, 0.07]
Hackett2003c	169	−12.80(7.71)	32	−11.70(7.71)		2.56	−0.14 [−0.52, 0.24]
Lenox-Smith2003	107	−13.90(7.71)	97	−12.00(7.71)		4.82	−0.25 [−0.52, 0.03]
Montgomery2006	110	−14.10(8.39)	100	−11.60(8.00)		4.94	−0.30 [−0.58, −0.03]
Nimatoudis2004	24	−19.20(7.71)	22	−10.80(7.71)		0.95	−1.07 [−1.69, −0.45]
Pollack2001	161	−12.10(7.71)	163	−10.10(7.71)		7.67	−0.26 [−0.48, −0.04]
Rickels2000a	86	−11.22(8.50)	32	−9.51(8.50)		2.22	−0.20 [−0.61, 0.21]
Rickels2000b	81	−12.36(8.50)	32	−9.51(8.50)		2.16	−0.33 [−0.74, 0.08]
Rickels2000c	86	−11.52(8.50)	32	−9.51(8.50)		2.21	−0.23 [−0.64, 0.17]
Rickels2003a	188	−12.50(8.40)	90	−9.30(8.70)		5.72	−0.38 [−0.63, −0.12]
Rickels2003b	197	−12.20(8.80)	90	−9.30(8.70)		5.83	−0.33 [−0.58, −0.08]
Silverstone2001a	32	−13.20(7.71)	13	−8.80(7.71)		0.85	−0.56 [−1.22, 0.10]
Silverstone2001b	33	−11.30(7.71)	12	−8.80(7.71)		0.83	−0.32 [−0.98, 0.35]
Subtotal (95% CI)	2914		1868			100.00	−0.35 [−0.41, −0.29]

Test for heterogeneity: Chi² = 20.01, df = 23 (P = 0.64), I² = 0%
Test for overall effect: Z = 11.27 (P < 0.00001)

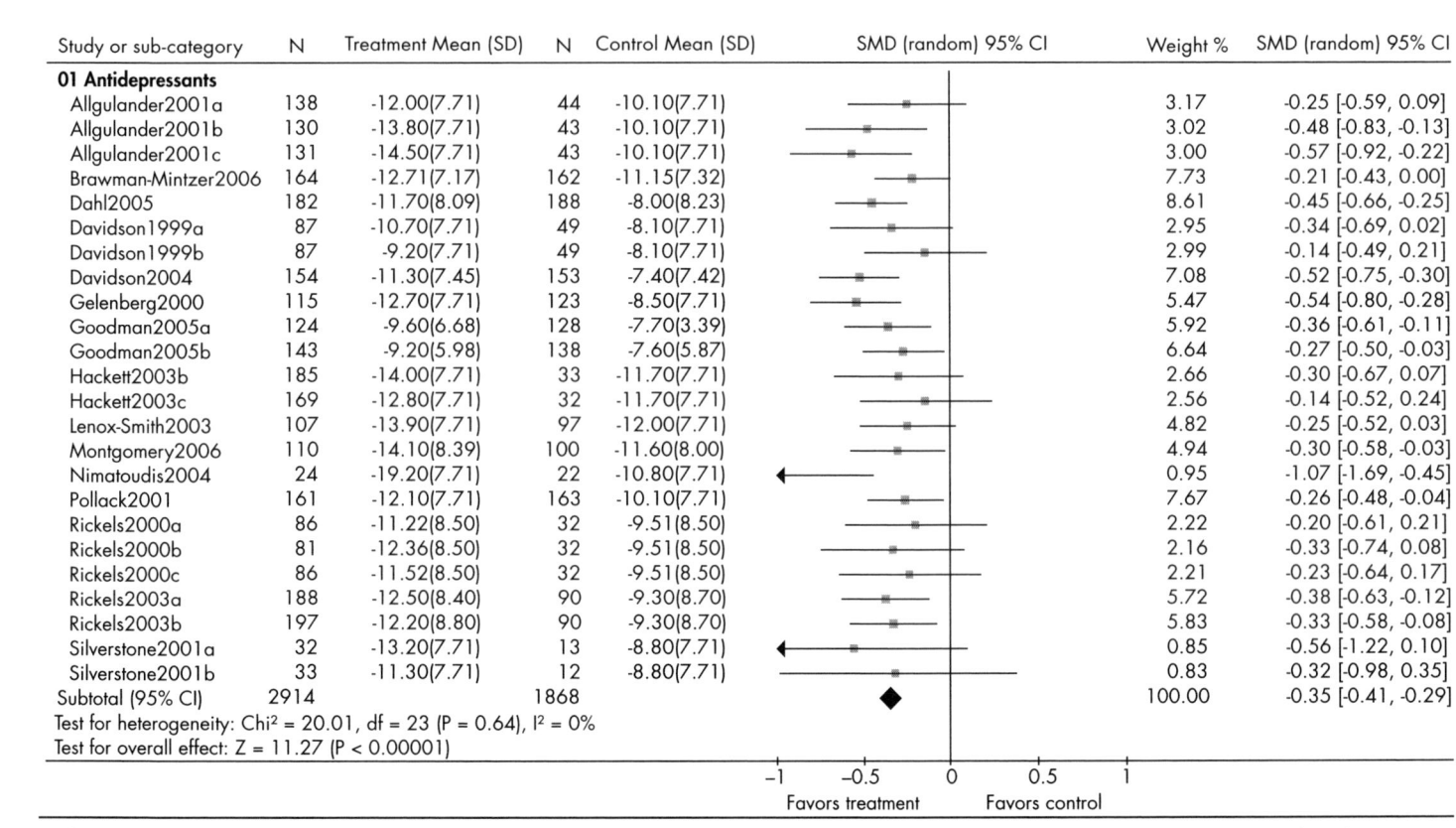

−1   −0.5   0   0.5   1
Favors treatment   Favors control

FIGURE 4–1. Changes in Hamilton Rating Scale for Anxiety (HAM-A) scores among patients with generalized anxiety disorder (GAD).

What (No) Differences in Responses to Classes of Psychotropics Can Teach Us   87

Study or sub-category	N	Treatment Mean (SD)	N	Control Mean (SD)	SMD (random) 95% CI	Weight %	SMD (random) 95% CI
02 Benzodiazepines							
Feltner2003	64	-11.60(6.85)	66	-9.30(6.85)		32.77	-0.33 [-0.68, 0.01]
Hackett2003a	89	-14.80(7.16)	32	-11.70(7.16)		23.64	-0.43 [-0.84, -0.02]
Rickels2005-alp	88	-10.90(7.50)	85	-8.35(7.38)		43.59	-0.34 [-0.64, -0.04]
Subtotal (95% CI)	241		183			100.00	-0.36 [-0.56, -0.16]
Test for heterogeneity: Chi² = 0.15, df = 2 (P = 0.93), I² = 0%							
Test for overall effect: Z = 3.56 (P = 0.0004)							
03 Azapirones							
Davidson1999a	93	-9.70(7.75)	98	-8.10(7.75)		53.94	-0.21 [-0.49, 0.08]
Lader1998	82	-8.80(7.80)	81	-7.20(7.70)		46.06	-0.21 [-0.51, 0.10]
Subtotal (95% CI)	175		179			100.00	-0.21 [-0.41, 0.00]
Test for heterogeneity: Chi² = 0.00, df = 1 (P = 1.00), I² = 0%							
Test for overall effect: Z = 1.93 (P = 0.05)							

-1 -0.5 0 0.5 1
Favors treatment   Favors control

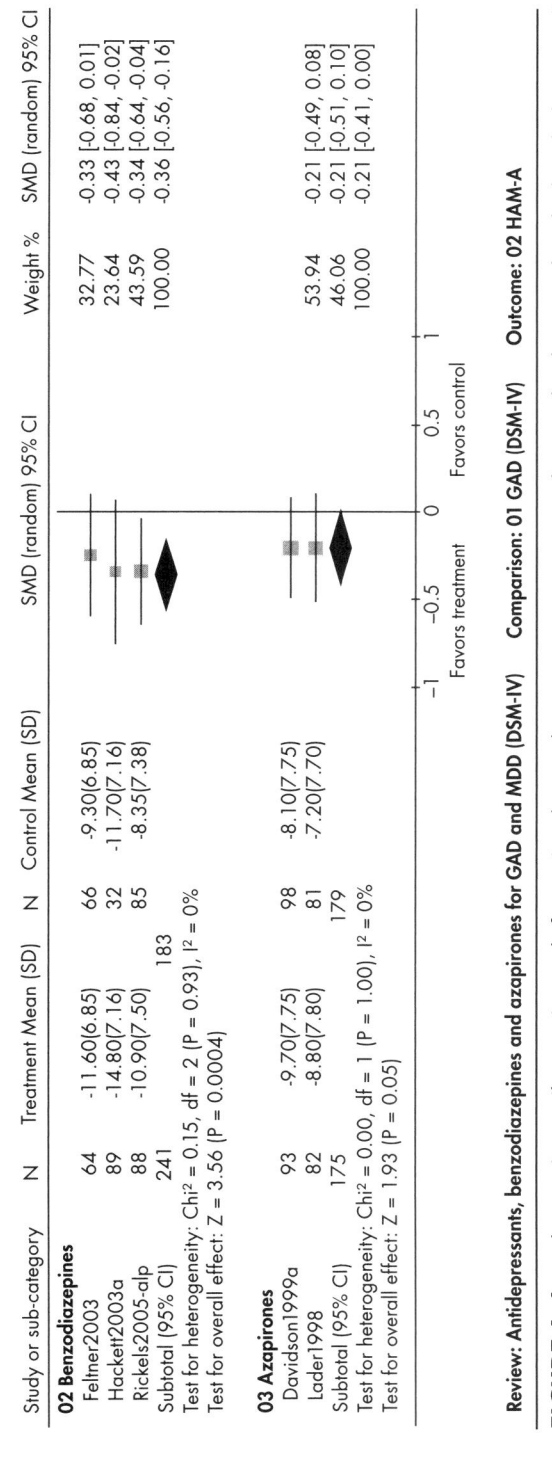

Review: Antidepressants, benzodiazepines and azapirones for GAD and MDD (DSM-IV)   Comparison: 01 GAD (DSM-IV)   Outcome: 02 HAM-A

FIGURE 4–1. Changes in Hamilton Rating Scale for Anxiety (HAM-A) scores among patients with generalized anxiety disorder (GAD). *(continued)*

diagnosis of depression when we evaluated the effectiveness of benzodiazepines or azapirones for depression. The CCDANCTR-Studies search yielded 206 records, 52 of which had used a placebo arm, 30 of which had administered either HAM-A or HAM-D. We obtained full texts of these studies and, excluding trials that had primary diagnoses other than major depression or those that administered the drug in question as an adjunct treatment, we obtained eight studies that had administered a benzodiazepine and six studies that had administered an azapirone to patients with depression and also measured HAM-A and/or HAM-D (Table 4–2). The benzodiazepine trials involved 1,567 patients with MDD and the azapirone trials involved 823 patients. The baseline average HAM-A scores were between 23 and 26, and those for HAM-D were between 20 and 26. All of the trials lasted 6–8 weeks.

CHANGES IN HAM-A AND HAM-D SCORES IN GENERALIZED ANXIETY DISORDER (DSM-IV)

Figure 4–1 shows changes in HAM-A scores under antidepressants, benzodiazepines, or azapirones among patients with DSM-IV GAD.

Acute-phase treatment of GAD with antidepressants was more effective than placebo in reducing HAM-A scores (SMD = –0.35; 95% CI, –0.41 to –0.29; $P<0.00001$). No heterogeneity was observed ($I^2 = 0\%$). Acute-phase treatment of GAD with benzodiazepines was also more effective than placebo in reducing HAM-A scores (SMD = –0.36; 95% CI, –0.56 to –0.16; $P=0.0004$). There was no heterogeneity ($I^2 = 0\%$), and a sensitivity analysis, which excluded a trial that administered a triazolobenzodiazepine, yielded a very similar SMD (–0.38; 95% CI, –0.64 to –0.11; $P=0.005$). Azapirones also proved to be more effective than placebo in reducing HAM-A scores (SMD = –0.21; 95% CI, –0.41 to 0.00; $P=0.05$); I^2 was 0% again.

Changes in HAM-D or other depression measures among patients with GAD are shown in Figure 4–2. Antidepressants reduced depression severity in comparison with placebo. The SMD was –0.48 (95% CI, –0.61 to –0.34; $P<0.00001$), and statistical heterogeneity was negligible ($I^2 = 38.2\%$). Benzodiazepines were also able to reduce HAM-D scores of GAD patients with an effect size (SMD) of –0.40 (95% CI, –0.63 to –0.18; $P=0.0005$). Although there was no statistical heterogeneity ($I^2 = 0\%$), removing a trial that used a triazolobenzodiazepine left only one study, which showed an SMD of –0.32 (95% CI, –0.66 to –0.03). One trial that examined an azapirone showed it was more effective than placebo (SMD = –0.50; 95% CI, –0.81 to –0.18; $P=0.002$).

Study or sub-category	N	Treatment Mean (SD)	N	Control Mean (SD)	SMD (random) 95% CI	Weight %	SMD (random) 95% CI
01 Antidepressants							
Allgulander2001a	138	6.10(3.64)	44	7.00(3.76)		9.60	-0.24 [-0.58, 0.10]
Allgulander2001b	130	5.10(3.76)	43	7.00(3.76)		9.20	-0.50 [-0.85, -0.15]
Allgulander2001c	131	4.80(3.78)	43	7.00(3.76)		9.16	-0.58 [-0.93, -0.23]
Dahl2005	182	-4.80(5.39)	188	-1.10(5.48)		19.76	-0.68 [-0.89, -0.47]
Davidson2004	154	-4.40(6.20)	153	-1.40(4.95)		17.70	-0.53 [-0.76, -0.31]
Lenox-Smith2003	122	-1.50(7.96)	122	0.00(7.58)		15.38	-0.19 [-0.44, 0.06]
Montgomery2006	110	-5.10(5.24)	100	-3.00(5.00)		13.57	-0.41 [-0.68, -0.13]
Silverstone2001a	32	-16.20(5.00)	13	-11.40(5.00)		2.79	-0.94 [-1.62, -0.27]
Silverstone2001b	33	-13.90(5.00)	12	-11.40(5.00)		2.84	-0.49 [-1.16, 0.18]
Subtotal (95% CI)	1032		718			100.00	-0.48 [-0.61, -0.34]
Test for heterogeneity: Chi² = 12.95, df = 8 (P = 0.11), I² = 38.2%							
Test for overall effect: Z = 6.95 (P < 0.00001)							
02 Benzodiazepines							
Feltner2003	64	-5.60(4.40)	66	4.20(4.40)		44.52	-0.32 [-0.66, 0.03]
Rickels2005-alp	88	-4.90(4.69)	85	-2.70(4.61)		55.48	-0.47 [-0.77, -0.17]
Subtotal (95% CI)	152		151			100.00	-0.40 [-0.63, -0.18]
Test for heterogeneity: Chi² = 0.44, df = 1 (P = 0.51), I² = 0%							
Test for overall effect: Z = 3.48 (P = 0.0005)							
03 Azapirones							
Lader1998	82	-6.35(7.50)	81	-2.97(6.00)		100.00	-0.50 [-0.81, -0.18]
Subtotal (95% CI)	82		81			100.00	-0.50 [-0.81, -0.18]
Test for heterogeneity: not applicable							
Test for overall effect: Z = 3.11 (P = 0.002)							

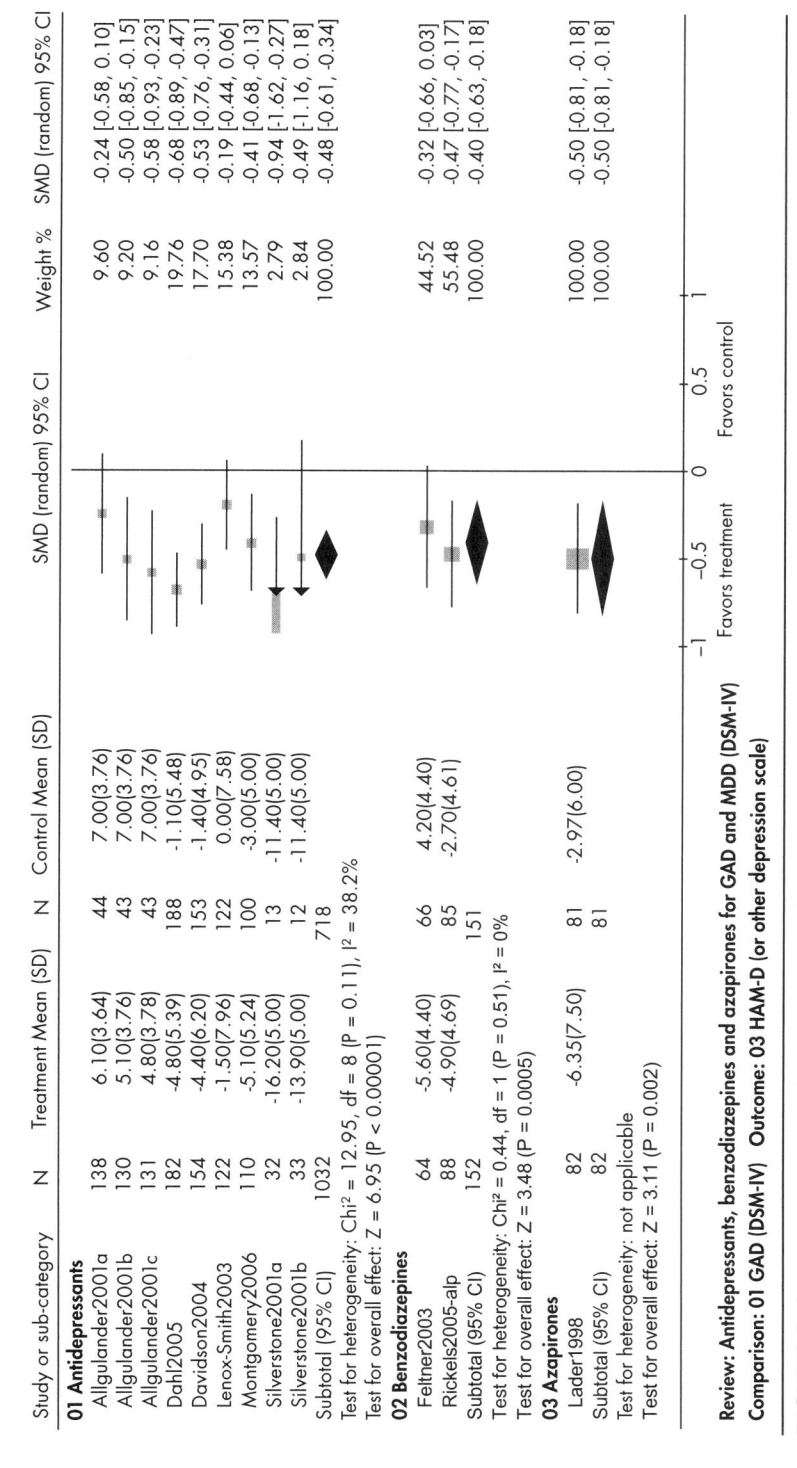

Review: Antidepressants, benzodiazepines and azapirones for GAD and MDD (DSM-IV)
Comparison: 01 GAD (DSM-IV) Outcome: 03 HAM-D (or other depression scale)

FIGURE 4–2. Changes in Hamilton Rating Scale for Depression (HAM-D) scores and other depression measures among patients with generalized anxiety disorder (GAD).

CHANGES IN HAM-A AND HAM-D SCORES IN MAJOR DEPRESSIVE DISORDER

Figure 4–3 shows the changes in HAM-A scores during the acute-phase treatment of depression with antidepressants, benzodiazepines, or azapirones. Surprisingly enough, all three classes of psychotropics reduced HAM-A scores to a statistically significant degree, in comparison with placebo. The SMD for antidepressants was −0.34 (95% CI, −0.42 to −0.26; $P<0.00001$). The SMD for benzodiazepines was −0.84 (95% CI, −1.11 to −0.58; $P<0.00001$). Although there was substantial heterogeneity among trials with benzodiazepines, the heterogeneity is more of a quantitative, rather than a qualitative, nature and leaves no doubt as to the superiority of benzodiazepines over placebo, although the point estimate of this effectiveness may be somewhat uncertain. Deleting all triazolobenzodiazepine trials left only one trial with a statistically significant result (SMD = −1.17; 95% CI, −1.60 to −0.73). The SMD for azapirones was −0.38 (95% CI, −0.64 to −0.12; $P=0.004$). Again, I^2 was 0%.

Figure 4–4 shows the changes in HAM-D and other depression measures among patients with DSM-IV MDD who were treated with antidepressants, benzodiazepines, or azapirones. Not surprisingly, antidepressants were more effective than placebos in reducing depression severity (SMD = −0.36; 95% CI, −0.43 to −0.29; $P<0.00001$), with no statistical heterogeneity among trials ($I^2=0$%). Surprisingly, benzodiazepines showed an even greater SMD (−0.78; 95% CI, −0.96 to −0.60; $P<0.00001$). Deleting all triazolobenzodiazepine trials left only three trials, but the SMD remained similarly large and statistically significant (−0.76; 95% CI, −1.14 to −0.38; $P=0.0001$). In both of these meta-analytic summaries for benzodiazepines, there was substantial heterogeneity ($I^2=45.5$% in the former and 80.3% in the latter), but these values represent, again, a quantitative, rather than qualitative, variability in effect sizes, and we can remain assured of the effectiveness of benzodiazepines for major depression in terms of HAM-D. The SMD for azapirones was again of similar and significant magnitude, at −0.35 (95% CI, −0.49 to −0.20; $P<0.00001$).

OVERALL ACCEPTABILITY OF TREATMENTS

Dropouts for any reason—a proxy measure of overall acceptability or desirability of treatment—did not differ significantly for any of the active treatments for either GAD or MDD in comparison with placebo treatments. For GAD, the relative risk was 1.02 (95% CI: 0.87–1.18), 1.21 (0.81–1.82), and 0.87 (0.60–1.24) for antidepressants, benzodiazepines, and azapirones, respectively. For major depression, the relative risk was 0.93 (0.81–1.09), 0.79 (0.61–1.01), and 1.05 (0.82–1.33).

Study or sub-category	N	Treatment Mean (SD)	N	Control Mean (SD)	SMD (random) 95% CI	Weight %	SMD (random) 95% CI
01 Antidepressants							
Burke2002b	118	−1.10(4.10)	40	0.00(4.10)		5.41	−0.27 [−0.63, 0.09]
Burke2002c	123	−2.60(4.10)	39	0.00(4.10)		5.32	−0.63 [−1.00, −0.26]
Detke2004a	85	−9.70(4.61)	31	−6.90(4.82)		4.70	−0.60 [−1.01, −0.18]
Detke2004b	93	−8.90(4.82)	31	−6.90(4.82)		4.80	−0.41 [−0.82, 0.00]
Detke2004c	93	−10.10(4.82)	31	−6.90(4.82)		4.74	−0.66 [−1.07, −0.24]
Goldstein2004a	84	−1.12(6.20)	30	0.00(6.20)		4.71	−0.18 [−0.60, 0.24]
Goldstein2004b	86	−2.24(6.30)	29	0.00(6.30)		4.64	−0.35 [−0.78, 0.07]
Goldstein2004c	84	−0.90(6.30)	29	0.00(6.30)		4.65	−0.14 [−0.56, 0.28]
Krishnan2002	68	−8.30(5.17)	64	−6.30(5.17)		5.61	−0.38 [−0.73, −0.04]
Loo2002	144	−13.39(5.17)	136	−10.98(5.17)		7.15	−0.46 [−0.70, −0.23]
Rudolph1999a	95	−10.60(5.17)	49	−7.70(5.17)		5.53	−0.56 [−0.91, −0.21]
Rudolph1999b	103	−8.40(5.17)	48	−7.70(5.17)		5.64	−0.13 [−0.48, 0.21]
Silverstone2001a	90	−14.50(7.68)	47	−11.20(7.68)		5.46	−0.43 [−0.78, −0.07]
Silverstone2001b	86	−12.80(7.68)	46	−11.20(7.68)		5.43	−0.21 [−0.57, 0.15]
Stahl2000a	103	−7.50(5.17)	51	−4.80(5.17)		5.67	−0.52 [−0.86, −0.18]
Stahl2000b	106	−6.10(5.17)	53	−4.80(5.17)		5.80	−0.25 [−0.58, 0.08]
Trivedi2001a	225	−9.40(7.90)	117	−8.40(7.90)		7.36	−0.13 [−0.35, 0.10]
Trivedi2001b	234	−9.90(7.90)	116	−8.40(7.90)		7.37	−0.19 [−0.41, 0.03]
Subtotal (95% CI)	2020		987			100.00	−0.34 [−0.42, −0.26]

Test for heterogeneity: Chi² = 19.17, df = 17 (P = 0.32), I² = 11.3%
Test for overall effect: Z = 7.96 (P < 0.00001)

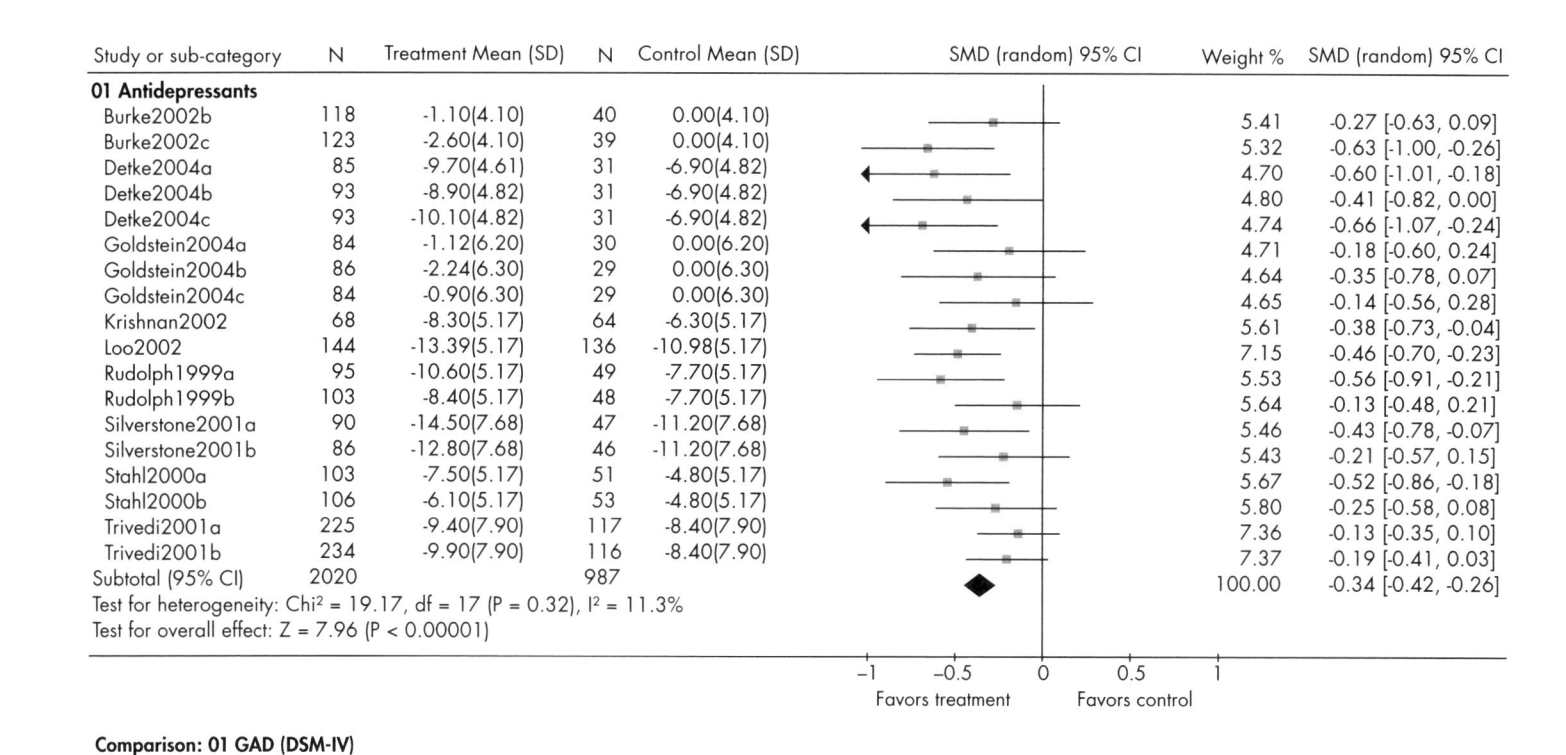

Comparison: 01 GAD (DSM-IV)

FIGURE 4–3. Changes in Hamilton Rating Scale for Anxiety (HAM-A) scores among patients with major depressive disorder (MDD).

Study or sub-category	N	Treatment Mean (SD)	N	Control Mean (SD)	SMD (random) 95% CI	Weight %	SMD (random) 95% CI
02 Benzodiazepines							
Feighner1983-alp	236	-10.30(6.95)	243	-4.70(6.95)		32.89	-0.80 [-0.99, -0.62]
Laakman1995a	66	-14.20(7.20)	37	-5.90(6.80)		18.83	-1.17 [-1.60, -0.73]
Laakman1995b-alp	70	-13.50(7.00)	37	-5.90(6.80)		19.24	-1.09 [-1.51, -0.66]
Rickels1985-alp	126	-9.68(6.95)	130	-6.13(6.95)		29.04	-0.51 [-0.76, -0.26]
Subtotal (95% CI)	498		447			100.00	-0.84 [-1.11, -0.58]
Test for heterogeneity: Chi² = 9.68, df = 3 (P = 0.02), I² = 69.0%							
Test for overall effect: Z = 6.14 (P < 0.00001)							
03 Azapirones							
Fabre1990	58	-9.00(9.50)	64	-5.60(9.50)		50.99	-0.36 [-0.71, 0.00]
Schweizer1998	54	-9.30(9.20)	58	-5.50(9.20)		49.01	-0.41 [-0.78, -0.04]
Subtotal (95% CI)	112		122			100.00	-0.38 [-0.64, -0.12]
Test for heterogeneity: Chi² = 0.04, df = 1 (P = 0.84), I² = 0%							
Test for overall effect: Z = 2.89 (P = 0.004)							

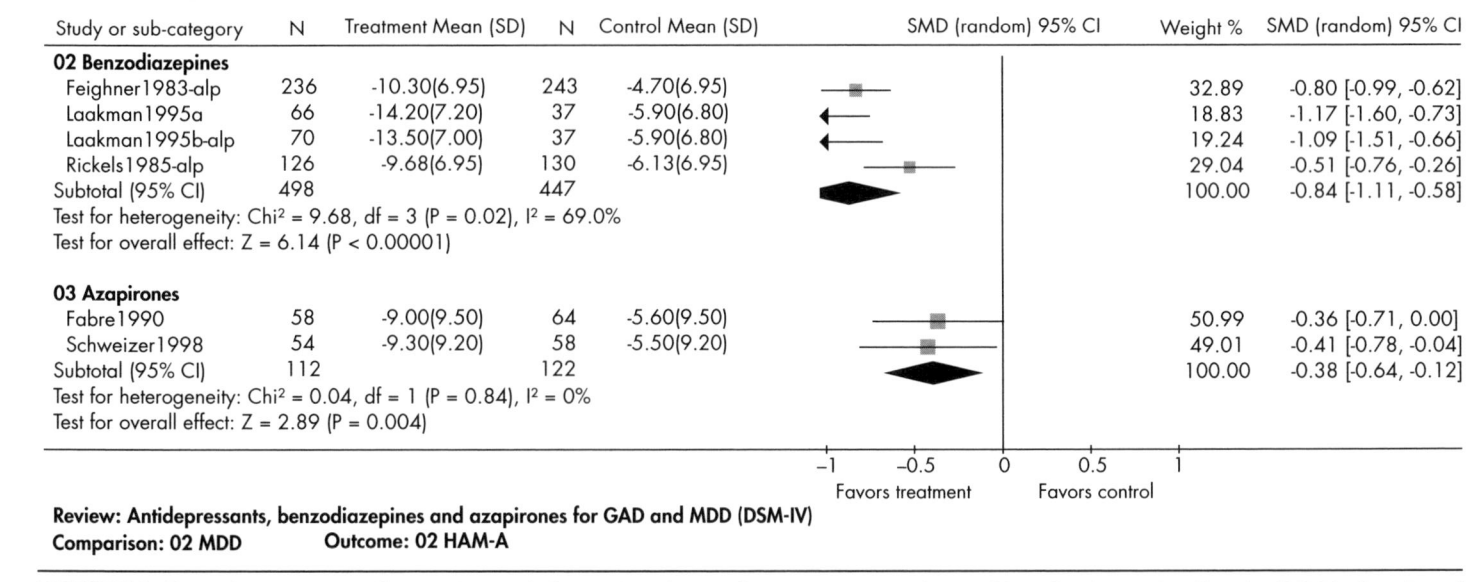

Review: Antidepressants, benzodiazepines and azapirones for GAD and MDD (DSM-IV)
Comparison: 02 MDD   Outcome: 02 HAM-A

FIGURE 4–3. Changes in Hamilton Rating Scale for Anxiety (HAM-A) scores among patients with major depressive disorder (MDD). *(continued)*

FUNNEL-PLOT ANALYSES

Visual inspection of the funnel plots for studies using antidepressants did not demonstrate gross asymmetry. There were not enough studies that used benzodiazepines or azapirones for GAD or MDD to make meaningful funnel-plot analyses.

SENSITIVITY ANALYSES

As explicated already, in each section, excluding trials that used triazolobenzodiazepines left only a handful of relevant RCTs, but their pooled-point estimates were very similar to those obtained by pooling all benzodiazepines.

Excluding trials with endpoint scores only, or with imputed standard deviations, also produced very similar pooled estimates, although naturally their 95% CIs were wider.

Discussion

A systematic and comprehensive review of currently available best evidence demonstrated that three classes of psychopharmacologically distinct agents—namely, antidepressants, benzodiazepines, and azapirones—had more or less the same magnitude of effectiveness across two supposedly distinct psychopathological dimensions of two arguably distinct disorders. Table 4–3 summarizes results of the meta-analyses.

There are seven theoretical possibilities to accommodate these findings:

1. It may be that GAD and MDD represent the same disease entity, at least as far as treatment recommendations are concerned.
2. Our findings may simply reflect the nature of the matter that GAD is always accompanied by subsyndromal depression, whereas MDD is accompanied by subsyndromal general anxiety. This interpretation, however, leads us to a natural doubt as to why we would not put them together under one broader category. In other words, this possibility represents only a subtle, and perhaps useless, modification of the first possibility, namely, that GAD and MDD are one and the same disease entity.
3. Another major possibility is that the HAM-A and HAM-D, our most often used measures of anxiety and depression, respectively, are confounded and contaminated with each other. We know that this is at least partly true, because HAM-A does contain items that would be elevated in depression and HAM-D does contain anxiety-related items. One old study found a correlation of 0.77 between HAM-A and HAM-D scores in a clinical trial with "neurotic" patients (Johnstone et al. 1980). Moreover, HAM-A does not tap the dimension of excessive or uncontrollable worry, which is the key GAD criterion

Study or sub-category	N	Treatment Mean (SD)	N	Control Mean (SD)	Weight %	SMD (random) 95% CI
01 Antidepressants						
Burke2002a	125	-9.90(10.06)	40	-7.60(8.73)	4.05	-0.23 [-0.59, 0.12]
Burke2002b	118	-10.20(7.60)	40	-7.60(8.73)	3.97	-0.33 [-0.69, 0.03]
Burke2002c	123	-11.70(8.87)	39	-7.60(8.73)	3.90	-0.46 [-0.83, -0.10]
Coleman1999a	109	-19.60(7.98)	59	-17.20(7.98)	5.09	-0.30 [-0.62, 0.02]
Coleman1999b	118	-20.90(7.98)	58	-17.20(7.98)	5.10	-0.46 [-0.78, -0.14]
Detke2004a	85	-11.70(4.61)	31	-8.80(4.82)	2.94	-0.62 [-1.04, -0.20]
Detke2004b	93	-11.00(4.82)	31	-8.80(4.82)	3.06	-0.45 [-0.86, -0.04]
Detke2004c	93	-12.10(4.82)	31	-8.80(4.82)	2.99	-0.68 [-1.10, -0.26]
Goldstein2004a	84	-7.40(7.56)	30	-4.96(7.74)	2.94	-0.32 [-0.74, 0.10]
Goldstein2004b	86	-8.70(7.65)	29	-4.96(7.74)	2.85	-0.48 [-0.91, -0.06]
Goldstein2004c	84	-6.30(7.56)	29	-4.96(7.74)	2.89	-0.17 [-0.60, 0.25]
Krishnan2002	68	-12.90(13.20)	64	-9.30(13.20)	4.39	-0.27 [-0.61, 0.07]
Loo2002	144	-14.21(8.24)	136	-12.06(8.24)	9.32	-0.26 [-0.50, -0.02]
Rudolph1999a	95	-12.50(8.21)	49	-10.20(8.04)	4.31	-0.28 [-0.63, 0.07]
Rudolph1999b	103	-11.80(8.28)	48	-10.20(8.04)	4.38	-0.19 [-0.54, 0.15]
Silverstone2001a	90	-15.40(7.98)	47	-11.10(7.98)	4.02	-0.54 [-0.89, -0.18]
Silverstone2001b	86	-15.40(7.98)	46	-11.10(7.98)	3.90	-0.54 [-0.90, -0.17]
Stahl2000a	103	-14.50(8.89)	54	-10.00(9.06)	4.63	-0.50 [-0.83, -0.17]
Stahl2000b	106	-13.00(9.02)	53	-10.00(9.06)	4.69	-0.33 [-0.66, 0.00]
Trivedi2001a	225	-14.20(7.98)	117	-11.80(7.98)	10.24	-0.30 [-0.52, -0.08]
Trivedi2001b	234	-14.10(7.98)	116	-11.80(7.98)	10.33	-0.29 [-0.51, -0.06]
Subtotal (95% CI)	2372		1147		100.00	-0.36 [-0.43, -0.29]

Test for heterogeneity: Chi² = 11.62, df = 20 (P = 0.93), I² = 0%
Test for overall effect: Z = 9.77 (P < 0.00001)

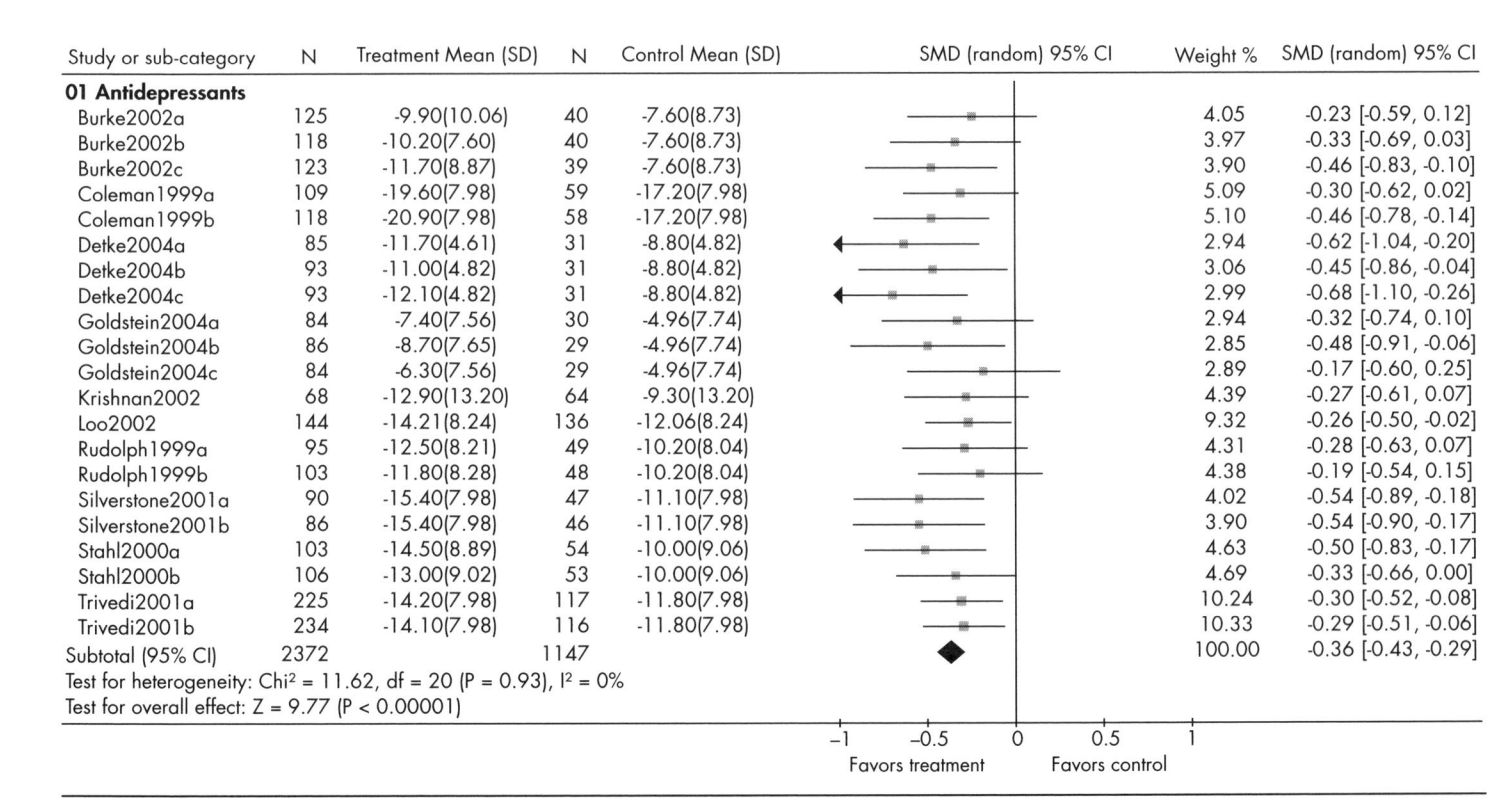

-1   -0.5   0   0.5   1
Favors treatment   Favors control

FIGURE 4–4. Changes in Hamilton Rating Scale for Depression (HAM-D) scores and other depression measures among patients with major depressive disorder (MDD).

Study or sub-category	N	Treatment Mean (SD)	N	Control Mean (SD)	SMD (random) 95% CI	Weight %	SMD (random) 95% CI
02 Benzodiazepines							
Laakman1995a	66	-11.10(5.70)	37	-4.80(5.10)		29.50	-1.14 [-1.57, -0.71]
Rickels1987b	59	-7.40(5.60)	30	-5.00(5.60)		27.99	-0.42 [-0.87, 0.02]
Rickels1991	62	-10.00(5.60)	64	-6.00(5.60)		42.50	-0.71 [-1.07, -0.35]
Subtotal (95% CI)	187		131			100.00	-0.76 [-1.14, -0.38]
Test for heterogeneity: Chi² = 5.20, df = 2 (P = 0.07), I² = 61.5%							
Test for overall effect: Z = 3.88 (P = 0.0001)							
03 Azapirones							
Fabre1990	58	-11.10(12.80)	64	-6.70(12.80)		16.49	-0.34 [-0.70, 0.02]
Feiger1996	41	-10.00(8.40)	40	-6.30(8.40)		10.87	-0.44 [-0.88, 0.00]
Feiger2003	101	-9.77(7.11)	103	-7.43(6.64)		27.65	-0.34 [-0.62, -0.06]
Jenkins1990a	42	-8.10(7.50)	19	-5.00(7.50)		7.06	-0.41 [-0.96, 0.14]
Jenkins1990b	41	-8.30(7.40)	19	-5.00(7.40)		6.99	-0.44 [-0.99, 0.11]
Schweizer1998	54	-11.40(9.30)	58	-8.10(9.30)		15.14	-0.35 [-0.73, 0.02]
Wilcox1996a	44	-8.51(7.94)	24	-6.70(7.85)		8.49	-0.23 [-0.73, 0.27]
Wilcox1996b	32	-8.78(7.94)	23	-6.70(7.85)		7.30	-0.26 [-0.80, 0.28]
Subtotal (95% CI)	413		350			100.00	-0.35 [-0.49, -0.20]
Test for heterogeneity: Chi² = 0.65, df = 7 (P = 1.00), I² = 0%							
Test for overall effect: Z = 4.70 (P < 0.00001)							

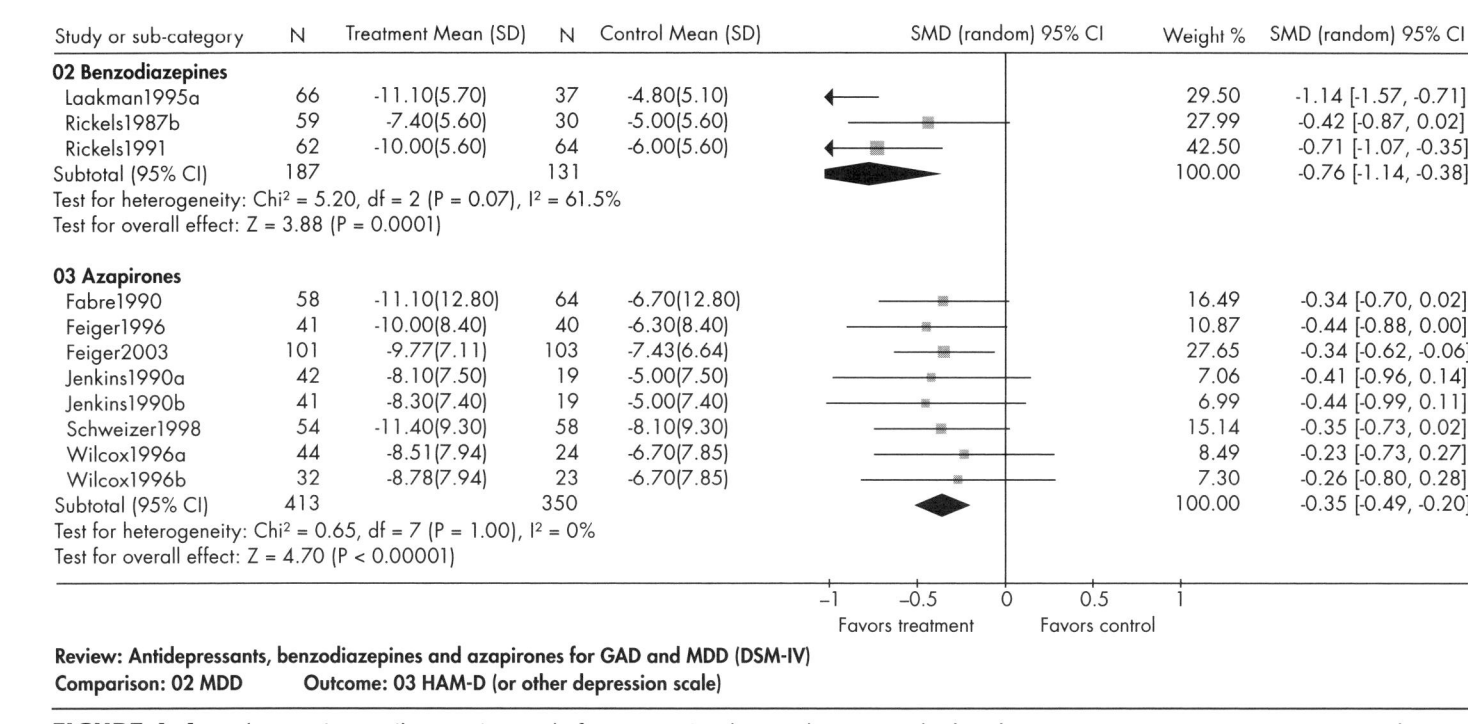

Review: Antidepressants, benzodiazepines and azapirones for GAD and MDD (DSM-IV)
Comparison: 02 MDD   Outcome: 03 HAM-D (or other depression scale)

FIGURE 4–4. Changes in Hamilton Rating Scale for Depression (HAM-D) scores and other depression measures among patients with major depressive disorder (MDD). *(continued)*

TABLE 4–3. Summaries of the standard mean differences (SMDs) of effects of three classes of psychopharmacologic drugs on two aspects of two disorders, generalized anxiety disorder (GAD), and major depressive disorder (MDD)

Drug class	GAD		MDD	
	HAM-A (95% CI)	HAM-D (95% CI)	HAM-A (95% CI)	HAM-D (95% CI)
Antidepressants	−0.35 (−0.41 to −0.29)	−0.48 (−0.61 to −0.34)	−0.34 (−0.42 to −0.26)	−0.36 (−0.43 to −0.29)
Benzodiazepines	−0.36 (−0.56 to −0.16)	−0.40 (−0.63 to −0.18)	−0.84[a] (−1.11 to −0.58)	−0.78[a] (−0.96 to −0.60)
Azapirones	−0.21 (−0.41 to 0.00)	−0.50 (−0.81 to −0.18)	−0.38[a] (−0.64 to −0.12)	−0.35[a] (−0.49 to −0.20)

Note. Rating scales for depression included HAM-D, MADRS, and the depression subscale of HADS; 95% confidence intervals calculated according to random-effects model.
[a]Diagnoses of MDD for these estimates included operational criteria before DSM-IV; for all other estimates, studies included dealt only with DSM-IV GAD or MDD.

(Shear et al. 2006), and HAM-D has been severely criticized for its several mismatches with DSM-IV diagnostic criteria items (Bagby et al. 2004). These considerations would cast grave doubt over the whole exercises of current GAD trials, all of which use the HAM-A as their primary outcome measure, and of current MDD trials, many of which use the HAM-D.

4. At a deeper level, our findings may come as no surprise if we consider the psychometric fact that depression and anxiety have almost never been shown to be clearly distinct from each other since the old days of the Great Debate in the United Kingdom (Roth and Barnes 1981). In other words, it is not the scales that are confounded, but the concepts that cannot be meaningfully differentiated. HAM-A seems to correlate not only with HAM-D but also with other depression measures. For example, one study found a correlation coefficient of 0.58 between changes in HAM-A and the Raskin Depression Scale among patients treated for their depression (Maier et al. 1988). Clark and Watson (1991) used symptom scales of depression and anxiety without overlaps and still found correlation coefficients around 0.40 among clinical, as well as general, populations. Dohrenwend (1990), who developed more than 25 questionnaires in his more than 20 years' career as psychiatric epidemiologist, once recalled that he found distinct factors of depression and anxiety in none of those questionnaires. Again, if this interpretation is correct, then it would also cast doubt on the results of the current clinical trials with current measurement scales.

5. GAD, in itself, may exist as a separate entity, but the current diagnostic criteria for GAD (and/or possibly MDD) are inappropriate, so they cannot properly distinguish what, in nature, is distinct.

6. Although we were unable to confirm or negate small study effects, including study publication bias and outcome reporting bias, among our identified trials, the continual evidence of their presence in the medical literature (see Furukawa et al. 2007; Hall et al. 2007) warns us that these effects may be at play in our meta-analyses and may have led to overestimation of treatment effectiveness.

7. Last, an unlikely explanation (we hope) for all these findings is that, with current psychopharmacological clinical trials methodology, any psychoactive substance with noticeable effects and/or side effects can beat placebo, with an effect size around 0.3 or 0.4, which after all represents a small treatment effect only (Cohen 1988), and when the problem of statistical power is overcome, as in meta-analysis, this small effect can become statistically significant. As a matter of fact, although our meta-analyses pointed to statistically significant superiority of active drugs over placebo in all the comparisons we made, it is important to note that for HAM-A for GAD, 11 out of 24 randomized comparisons of antidepressants failed to show statistically significant differences against placebo; and for HAM-D for MDD, 8 out of 21 randomized compar-

isons of an antidepressant against placebo were nonsignificant. In other words, slight trends in favor of an active drug, introduced by biased methodology, may well lead to "statistically significant" pooled estimates. The finding that relative risks in the rates of treatment discontinuation, for any reason, were comparable for all of the comparisons, and all included 1.0, appears to strengthen the fifth and/or sixth possibilities—namely, that any of these treatments are not particularly good or acceptable to the patients.

A few caveats are in order before we conclude. First, benzodiazepines showed the greatest effect sizes in reducing both HAM-A and HAM-D for MDD. This should be interpreted with caution because the constituent trials had employed depression-diagnostic criteria before DSM-IV. Older trials could have been of lesser methodological rigor and thus have overestimated the treatment effect. The visual inspection of the funnel plots and HAM-A and HAM-D under benzodiazepines or azapirones, ordered by year, did not reveal any decreasing tendency in effect size over the years since 1983 (Figures 4–3 and 4–4).

Second, this review demonstrated convergent validity of GAD and MDD as far as treatment responses are concerned. However, diagnostic validity hinges not only on convergent validity but also on divergent validity. We therefore need to examine whether GAD and MDD differentiate themselves similarly from phobic and panic disorders, on one hand, and from bipolar disorder, on the other. If GAD and MDD behave similarly, vis-à-vis these other disorders, they are more likely to be one entity; if, on the other hand, their relationships with phobic disorders and/or bipolar disorder can be differentiated, we will have more reason to keep the two separate.

Third, should there remain any phenomenological and/or pathophysiological specificities to GAD, another possibility is to conceptualize it as a specifier for MDD and other anxiety disorders, such as "with generalized anxiety." This was not discussed in the present paper but may well be a viable alternative.

With these caveats in mind, and in waiting for phenomenological and pathoetiological data that may show otherwise, our findings demonstrate a lack of pharmacodissection between GAD and MDD and suggest that the disorders represent the same, or at least closely overlapping and/or related, disorders.

IMPLICATIONS FOR THEORY

If there remain any phenomenological and/or pathophysiological specificities to GAD, despite the observed similarities in response to three classes of psychotropics, an alternative is to conceptualize GAD as a specifier for MDD and other anxiety disorders, such as "with generalized anxiety." This proposal is compatible with the interpretations outlined in possibilities numbers 1, 2, and 4 outlined earlier. Furthermore, if interpretation number 5 should hold, we would need to redefine GAD.

IMPLICATIONS FOR RESEARCH

Our findings, all in all, call for two types of research in the future. One type will be a reanalysis of existing databases. We can reanalyze all GAD and MDD trials that have measured HAM-A and HAM-D, at the same time. We can first run factor analyses of these two scales together and possibly delineate a pure "depressive" factor and a pure "general anxiety" factor and then examine if the treatment effectiveness of three classes of psychotropics may be more differentially summarized than in our Table 4–3. Another urgently needed research task, if we are to retain GAD as a disease entity, is development of a GAD-specific assessment tool. We already have several forerunners (Brown et al. 1992; Meyer et al. 1990; Shear et al. 2006), and we now need to accumulate evidence on their relative validities.

References

Allgulander C, Hackett D, Salinas E: Venlafaxine extended release (ER) in the treatment of generalised anxiety disorder: twenty-four-week placebo-controlled dose-ranging study. Br J Psychiatry 179:15–22, 2001

Allgulander C, Bandelow B, Hollander E, et al: WCA recommendations for the long-term treatment of generalized anxiety disorder. CNS Spectr 8:53–61, 2003

Altman DG, Bland JM: Detecting skewness from summary information. BMJ 313:1200, 1996

American Psychiatric Association: Diagnostic and Statistical Manual of Mental Disorders, 4th Edition. Washington, DC, American Psychiatric Association 1994

Bagby RM, Ryder AG, Schuller DR, et al: The Hamilton Depression Rating Scale: has the gold standard become a lead weight? Am J Psychiatry 161:2163–2177, 2004

Ballenger JC, Davidson JR, Lecrubier Y, et al: Consensus statement on generalized anxiety disorder from the International Consensus Group on Depression and Anxiety. J Clin Psychiatry 62(suppl):53–58, 2001

Banerjee S, Wells G: Caveats in the meta-analysis of continuous data: a simulation study, Poster 143 presented at the XIV Cochrane Colloquium, Dublin, Ireland, October 2006

Beutler LE, Scogin F, Kirkish P, et al: Group cognitive therapy and alprazolam in the treatment of depression in older adults. J Consult Clin Psychol 55:550–556, 1987

Borison RL, Sinha D, Albrecht JW, et al: Double-blind comparison of 3- and 6-mg fixed doses of alprazolam vs. placebo in outpatients with major depressive disorder. Psychopharmacol Bull 25:186–189, 1989

Brawman-Mintzer O, Rickels K, Rynn M, et al: A placebo-controlled, double-blind, flexible dosage study to evaluate the efficacy and tolerability of sertraline in the treatment of DSM-IV generalized anxiety disorder. Eur Neuropsychopharmacol 12:S365, 2002

Brawman-Mintzer O, Knapp RG, Rynn M, et al: Sertraline treatment for generalized anxiety disorder: a randomized, double-blind, placebo-controlled study. J Clin Psychiatry 67:874–881, 2006

Brown TA, Antony MM, Barlow DH: Psychometric properties of the Penn State Worry Questionnaire in a clinical anxiety disorders sample. Behav Res Ther 30:33–37, 1992

Burke WJ, Gergel I, Bose A: Fixed-dose trial of the single isomer SSRI escitalopram in depressed outpatients. J Clin Psychiatry 63:331–336, 2002

Clark LA, Watson D: Tripartite model of anxiety and depression: psychometric evidence and taxonomic implications. J Abnorm Psychol 100:316–336, 1991

Cohen J: Statistical Power Analysis in the Behavioral Sciences. Hillsdale, NJ, Erlbaum, 1988

Coleman CC, Cunningham LA, Foster VJ, et al: Sexual dysfunction associated with the treatment of depression: a placebo-controlled comparison of bupropion sustained release and sertraline treatment. Ann Clin Psychiatry 11:205–215, 1999

Dahl AA, Ravindran A, Allgulander C, et al: Sertraline in generalized anxiety disorder: efficacy in treating the psychic and somatic anxiety factors. Acta Psychiatr Scand 111:429–435, 2005

Davidson JR, DuPont RL, Hedges D, et al: Efficacy, safety, and tolerability of venlafaxine extended release and buspirone in outpatients with generalized anxiety disorder. J Clin Psychiatry 60:528–535, 1999

Davidson JR, Bose A, Korotzer A, et al: Escitalopram in the treatment of generalized anxiety disorder: double-blind, placebo controlled, flexible-dose study. Depress Anxiety 19:234–240, 2004

DerSimonian R, Laird N: Meta-analysis in clinical trials. Control Clin Trials 7:177–188, 1986

Detke MJ, Wiltse CG, Mallinckrodt CH, et al: Duloxetine in the acute and long-term treatment of major depressive disorder: a placebo- and paroxetine-controlled trial. Eur Neuropsychopharmacol 14:457–470, 2004

Dohrenwend BP: Notes on some epidemiologic studies of comorbidity, in Comorbidity of Mood and Anxiety Disorders. Edited by Maser JD, Cloninger CR. Washington, DC, American Psychiatric Press, 1990, pp 177–185

Fabre LF: Buspirone in the management of major depression: a placebo-controlled comparison. J Clin Psychiatry 51(suppl):55–61, 1990

Feiger AD: A double-blind comparison of gepirone extended release, imipramine, and placebo in the treatment of outpatient major depression. Psychopharmacol Bull 32:659–665, 1996

Feiger AD, Heiser JF, Shrivastava RK, et al: Gepirone extended-release: new evidence for efficacy in the treatment of major depressive disorder. J Clin Psychiatry 64:243–249, 2003

Feighner JP, Aden GC, Fabre LF, et al: Comparison of alprazolam, imipramine, and placebo in the treatment of depression. JAMA 249:3057–3064, 1983a

Feighner JP, Meredith CH, Frost NR, et al: A double-blind comparison of alprazolam vs. imipramine and placebo in the treatment of major depressive disorder. Acta Psychiatr Scand 68:223–233, 1983b

Feltner DE, Crockatt JG, Dubovsky SJ, et al: A randomized, double-blind, placebo-controlled, fixed-dose, multicenter study of pregabalin in patients with generalized anxiety disorder. J Clin Psychopharmacol 23:240–249, 2003

Furukawa TA, Guyatt GH, Griffith LE: Can we individualize the "number needed to treat"? An empirical study of summary effect measures in meta-analyses. Int J Epidemiol 31:72–76, 2002

Furukawa TA, Barbui C, Cipriani A, et al: Imputing missing standard deviations in meta-analyses can provide accurate results. J Clin Epidemiol 59:7–10, 2006

Furukawa TA, Watanabe N, Omori IM, et al: Association between unreported outcomes and effect size estimates in Cochrane meta-analyses. JAMA 297:468–470, 2007

Gelenberg AJ, Lydiard RB, Rudolph RL, et al: Efficacy of venlafaxine extended-release capsules in nondepressed outpatients with generalized anxiety disorder: a 6-month randomized controlled trial. JAMA 283:3082–3088, 2000

Goldstein DJ, Lu Y, Detke MJ, et al: Duloxetine in the treatment of depression: a double-blind placebo-controlled comparison with paroxetine. J Clin Psychopharmacol 24:389–399, 2004

Goodman WK, Bose A, Wang Q: Treatment of generalized anxiety disorder with escitalopram: pooled results from double-blind, placebo-controlled trials. J Affect Disord 87:161–167, 2005

Hackett D, Haudiquet V, Salinas E: A method for controlling for a high placebo response rate in a comparison of venlafaxine XR and diazepam in the short-term treatment of patients with generalised anxiety disorder. Eur Psychiatry 18:182–187, 2003

Hall R, de Antueno C, Webber A: Publication bias in the medical literature: a review by a Canadian Research Ethics Board [Biais de publication dans la litterature medicale : un compte rendu d'un Comite d'ethique de recherche canadien]. Can J Anaesth 54:380–388, 2007

Hamilton M: The assessment of anxiety states by rating. Br J Med Psychol 32:50–55, 1959

Hamilton M: A rating scale for depression. J Neurol Neurosurg Psychiatry 23:56–62, 1960

Higgins JP, Thompson SG, Deeks JJ, et al: Measuring inconsistency in meta-analyses. BMJ 327:557–560, 2003

Jenkins SW, Robinson DS, Fabre LF Jr, et al: Gepirone in the treatment of major depression. J Clin Psychopharmacol 10:77S-85S, 1990

Johnstone EC, Owens DG, Frith CD, et al: Neurotic illness and its response to anxiolytic and antidepressant treatment. Psychol Med 10:321–328, 1980

Laakman G, Faltermaier-Temizel M, Bossert-Zaudig S, et al: Treatment of depressive outpatients with lorazepam, alprazolam, amitriptyline and placebo. Psychopharmacology (Berl) 120:109–115, 1995

Laakman G, Faltermaier-Temizel M, Bossert-Zaudig S, et al: Behandlung des leicht bis mittelschwer depressiven symptoms: plazebokontrollierte Doppelblinduntersuchung zur therapie mit benzodiazepinen oder antidepressiva. Munch med Wschr 138:69–74, 1996

Lader M: Anxiolytic effect of hydroxyzine: a double-blind trial versus placebo and buspirone. Hum Psychopharmacol 14:S94–S102, 1999

Lader M, Scotto JC: A multicentre double-blind comparison of hydroxyzine, buspirone and placebo in patients with generalized anxiety disorder. Psychopharmacology (Berl) 139:402–406, 1998

Lenox-Smith AJ, Reynolds A: A double-blind, randomised, placebo controlled study of venlafaxine XL in patients with generalised anxiety disorder in primary care. Br J Gen Pract 53:772–777, 2003

Lepola U, Wade A, Andersen HF: Do equivalent doses of escitalopram and citalopram have similar efficacy? A pooled analysis of two positive placebo-controlled studies in major depressive disorder. Int Clin Psychopharmacol 19:149–155, 2004

Loo H, Hale A, D'Haenen H: Determination of the dose of agomelatine, a melatoninergic agonist and selective 5-HT(2C) antagonist, in the treatment of major depressive disorder: a placebo-controlled dose range study. Int Clin Psychopharmacol 17:239–247, 2002

Maier W, Buller R, Philipp M, et al: The Hamilton Anxiety Scale: reliability, validity and sensitivity to change in anxiety and depressive disorders. J Affect Disord 14:61–68, 1988

McCafferty J, Bellew K, Zaninelli R, et al: Paroxetine is effective in the treatment of generalized anxiety disorder: results from a randomized placebo-controlled flexible dose study. Eur Neuropsychopharmacol 10:S348, 2000

Mendels J, Schless AP: Comparative efficacy of alprazolam, imipramine, and placebo administered once a day in treating depressed patients. J Clin Psychiatry 47:357–361, 1986

Meyer TJ, Miller ML, Metzger RL, et al: Development and validation of the Penn State Worry Questionnaire. Behav Res Ther 28:487–495, 1990

Montgomery SA, Åsberg M: A new depression scale designed to be sensitive to change. Br J Psychiatry 134:382–389, 1979

Montgomery SA, Mahe V, Haudiquet V, et al: Effectiveness of venlafaxine, extended release formulation, in the short-term and long-term treatment of generalized anxiety disorder: results of a survival analysis. J Clin Psychopharmacol 22:561–567, 2002

Montgomery SA, Tobias K, Zornberg GL, et al: Efficacy and safety of pregabalin in the treatment of generalized anxiety disorder: a 6-week, multicenter, randomized, double-blind, placebo-controlled comparison of pregabalin and venlafaxine. J Clin Psychiatry 67:771–782, 2006

Nimatoudis I, Zissis NP, Kogeorgos J, et al: Remission rates with venlafaxine extended release in Greek outpatients with generalized anxiety disorder: a double-blind, randomized, placebo controlled study. Int Clin Psychopharmacol 19:331–336, 2004

Norman GR: Issues in the use of change scores in randomized trials. J Clin Epidemiol 42:1097–1105, 1989

Pande AC, Crockatt JG, Feltner DE, et al: Three randomised, placebo-controlled, double-blind trials of pregabalin treatment of generalized anxiety disorder (GAD). Eur Neuropsychopharmacol 10:S344, 2000

Pande AC, Crockatt JG, Feltner DE, et al: Pregabalin in generalized anxiety disorder: a placebo-controlled trial. Am J Psychiatry 160:533–540, 2003

Pollack MH, Zaninelli R, Goddard A, et al: Paroxetine in the treatment of generalized anxiety disorder: results of a placebo-controlled, flexible-dosage trial. J Clin Psychiatry 62:350–357, 2001

Ranga K, Krishnan R: Clinical experience with substance P receptor (NK1) antagonists in depression. J Clin Psychiatry 63(suppl):25–29, 2002

Raskin A, Schulterbrandt J, Reatig N, et al: Replication of factors of psychopathology in interview, ward behavior and self-report ratings of hospitalized depressives. J Nerv Ment Dis 148:87–98, 1969

Review Manager (RevMan) [Computer program], Version 4.2 for Windows. Copenhagen, The Nordic Cochrane Centre, The Cochrane Collaboration, 2003. Available at http://www.cc-ims.net/revman/revman/. Accessed August 28, 2008.

Rickels K, Feighner JP, Smith WT: Alprazolam, amitriptyline, doxepin, and placebo in the treatment of depression. Arch Gen Psychiatry 42:134–141, 1985

Rickels K, Chung HR, Csanalosi IB, et al: Alprazolam, diazepam, imipramine, and placebo in outpatients with major depression. Arch Gen Psychiatry 44:862–866, 1987

Rickels K, London J, Fox I, et al: Adinazolam, diazepam, imipramine, and placebo in major depressive disorder: a controlled study. Pharmacopsychiatry 24:127–131, 1991

Rickels K, Pollack MH, Sheehan DV, et al: Efficacy of extended-release venlafaxine in nondepressed outpatients with generalized anxiety disorder. Am J Psychiatry 157:968–974, 2000

Rickels K, Zaninelli R, McCafferty J, et al: Paroxetine treatment of generalized anxiety disorder: a double-blind, placebo-controlled study. Am J Psychiatry 160:749–756, 2003

Rickels K, Pollack MH, Feltner DE, et al: Pregabalin for treatment of generalized anxiety disorder: a 4-week, multicenter, double-blind, placebo-controlled trial of pregabalin and alprazolam. Arch Gen Psychiatry 62:1022–1030, 2005

Rolland PD, Kablinger AS, Brannon GE, et al: Treatment of generalized anxiety disorder with venlafaxine XR: a randomized, double-blind trial in comparison with buspirone and placebo. Clin Drug Invest 19:163–165, 2000

Roth RM, Barnes TR: The classification of affective disorders: a synthesis of old and new concepts. Compr Psychiatry 22:54–77, 1981

Rudolph RL, Feiger AD: A double-blind, randomized, placebo-controlled trial of once-daily venlafaxine extended release (XR) and fluoxetine for the treatment of depression. J Affect Disord 56:171–181, 1999

Schweizer E, Rickels K, Hassman H, et al: Buspirone and imipramine for the treatment of major depression in the elderly. J Clin Psychiatry 59:175–183, 1998

Shear K, Belnap BH, Mazumdar S, et al: Generalized anxiety disorder severity scale (GADSS): a preliminary validation study. Depress Anxiety 23:77–82, 2006

Silverstone PH, Ravindran A: Once-daily venlafaxine extended release (XR) compared with fluoxetine in outpatients with depression and anxiety. Venlafaxine XR 360 Study Group. J Clin Psychiatry 60:22–28, 1999

Silverstone PH, Salinas E: Efficacy of venlafaxine extended release in patients with major depressive disorder and comorbid generalized anxiety disorder. J Clin Psychiatry 62:523–529, 2001

Stahl SM: Placebo-controlled comparison of the selective serotonin reuptake inhibitors citalopram and sertraline. Biol Psychiatry 48:894–901, 2000

Stein DJ, Andersen HF, Goodman WK: Escitalopram for the treatment of GAD: efficacy across different subgroups and outcomes. Ann Clin Psychiatry 17:71–75, 2005

Steiner M, Allgulander C, Ravindran A, et al: Gender differences in clinical presentation and response to sertraline treatment of generalized anxiety disorder. Hum Psychopharmacol 20:3–13, 2005

Trivedi MH, Rush AJ, Carmody TJ, et al: Do bupropion SR and sertraline differ in their effects on anxiety in depressed patients? J Clin Psychiatry 62:776–781, 2001

Wilcox CS, Ferguson JM, Dale JL, et al: A double-blind trial of low- and high-dose ranges of gepirone-ER compared with placebo in the treatment of depressed outpatients. Psychopharmacol Bull 32:335–342, 1996

Commentary

COMMENTARY ON "THE BIOLOGY OF GAD AND MDD" AND "WHAT (NO) DIFFERENCES IN RESPONSES TO THREE CLASSES OF PSYCHOTROPICS CAN TEACH US ABOUT DISTINCTIONS BETWEEN GAD AND MDD"

David J. Kupfer, M.D.
Ellen Frank, Ph.D.

This commentary is an opportunity to review two very different empirical approaches to addressing the key issue for this conference: namely, whether MDD and GAD are 1) different forms of the same disorder; 2) closely related disorders; or 3) distally related disorders.

Over the past 8 years, the ongoing development of a research-driven agenda for DSM-V has better prepared us to address this issue. The two chapters considered here—Chapter 3 by Martin and Nemeroff and Chapter 4 by Furukawa,

Watanabe, and Omori—provide important data, the first from neurobiology and clinical neuroscience and the second from treatment-outcome studies.

If we could turn the clock back to 1970, we would encounter the cogent arguments made by Robins and Guze (1970) that pointed to five validators of diagnostic categories: clinical description, laboratory studies, delimitation from other disorders, follow-up studies, and family investigations. Based on the succeeding 40 years of research, we now might adopt a more contemporary interpretation of these validators in evaluating the arguments made in DSM-V (American Psychiatric Association 2002). To do this, we would want to highlight the following features: clinical characteristics and course (behavioral phenotype); neurobiological profile; genetics/familial pattern; context/environment; treatment response and follow-up studies. Although these five characteristics are related to the earlier framework of Robins and Guze, they embrace the advances in both behavioral and clinical neuroscience. Thus, a neurobiological profile might include data derived from the following types of studies: susceptibility genes, pharmacogenomics, pharmacological response, neuroimaging, and other neurobiological features.

One can delineate a number of common features and questions that must be addressed in evaluating both of these chapters. The quality of data and sensitivity of the methods utilized to collect the information are important key variables to consider. Second, what is the nature of the sample studied?—that is, from what patient or community population are the data derived? How much information do we have about a broader or deeper behavioral phenotype beyond a DSM-III (American Psychiatric Association 1980) or DSM-IV (American Psychiatric Association 1994) diagnosis? Have we utilized both biological and treatment outcome measures, with reasonably sophisticated methodological approaches such as meta-analysis? Finally, what are the implications for future studies?

When we review Chapter 3 by Martin and Nemeroff, which raises the question of the value of neurobiological validators applied to GAD and MDD, there are both commonalities and distinguishing features. The authors examined the follow sets of data: 1) anatomy of GAD and MDD, 2) endocrinology, 3) neuropeptides, 4) neurotransmitters, and 5) distinct somatic symptoms, including sleep. They provided a superb literature review and sought to provide conclusions that can be easily reviewed in Table 4–1.

After reviewing their report and tables, one is left with the impression that there is much to be gained from connecting the neurobiological validators to treatment outcome, both psychological and pharmacological. For example, there are early efforts in this direction, primarily from neuroanatomical and neuroimaging studies. Particularly promising is work highlighting the amygdala and the notion of reciprocal limbic-cortical networks. Other areas of emphasis include the utilization of challenge paradigms and an attempt to separate out sadness/depression from provoked anxiety. One obvious shortcoming raised by these authors is the difficulty in identifying short-term versus persistent changes. They also demonstrate that research groups working in different domains, with different techniques, are not necessarily conducting the same types of studies, thereby reducing the generalizability of these findings.

In turning to Chapter 4 by Furukawa, Watanabe, and Omori, we encounter an entirely different set of issues, and yet there are commonalities with the previous report. In this chapter, we have an important historical lesson in the examination of the effects of three classes of psychotropics (benzodiazepines, antidepressants, and azapirones) on both GAD and MDD, based on measurement with the two classic scales developed by Max Hamilton (Hamilton Rating Scale for Depression [HAM-D]/Hamilton Rating Scale for Anxiety [HAM-A]). The authors utilized meta-analysis as their analytic tool, which, appropriately, reduced the available number of studies. They sought to include only studies that provided active drug versus placebo differences. The studies selected were conducted over a 30-year period. This, of course, raises the issue of different diagnostic criteria, since these diagnoses were made throughout a period covered by both DSM-III and DSM-IV. Second, there have likely been improvements in the rigor of studies over that time period, although that same period has seen a steady decline in active drug/placebo differences (Kupfer and Frank 2002). Third, the meta-analytic methods chosen did not include some of the newer tools of evidence-based medicine, such as number needed to treat (Kraemer et al. 2005).

In their discussion, the authors raise a number of questions that could account for their findings. Reorganizing their list, one might first raise the basic question of whether GAD and MDD represent the same disease entity. Even though other sets of data suggest that benzodiazepines would not be useful in the treatment of MDD, the authors' meta-analysis indicates a similar level of efficacy for benzodiazepines as for more-traditional antidepressants. A second possibility raised by the authors is that GAD is always accompanied by subsyndromal depression and MDD by subsyndromal general anxiety. Although this may be true, it probably should be approached not in a cross-sectional way, but by examining the longitudinal course of the disorders in question. The third point they raise is that depression and anxiety have almost never been shown to be clearly distinct from each other. It is difficult to conclude whether this is strictly due to a measurement issue or to a real convergence of symptoms that cross diagnoses in a somewhat ongoing fashion.

On the other hand, it may be that methodological issues are driving either pseudo-differences or pseudo-convergences. For example, it is well known that the HAM-A and the HAM-D are confounded and contaminated with each other. Thus, these particular measures can never provide an answer to our overriding question. Second, the choice of studies used in this meta-analysis, and the relatively small sample sizes available in such studies, often lead to publication and reporting biases that tend to overestimate treatment effects. Of course, we have also learned that many unpublished sets of data on these topics have never been appropriately analyzed.

Finally, it can be argued that clinical trials are so flawed methodologically and in terms of execution that almost any psychoactive substances can beat a placebo, at least with a small effect size. Yet one of the most frustrating problems in clinical trials in the past 10 years has been the frequent inability to separate active compound from placebo in a robust fashion (Walsh et al. 2002). Furthermore, the need to assess clinical significance, not simply statistical significance, makes it even more important to strive for a medium effect size (Kraemer et al. 2005).

The overarching question raised by these two excellent reviews relates to strategies for future analyses and new studies. The question is whether the past can be helpful to us anymore—that is, can review of existing databases and reanalysis be useful to us? We do realize now that we probably have not utilized psychosocial interventions for "diagnostic dissection" as well as have studies of pharmacological interventions. Our lack of attention to developmental issues and acknowledgment of the importance of age at onset also has led to several misleading conclusions. Finally, if we think of psychiatric comorbidity as a cumulative process, then the long-term course of illness must be taken into account when we seek to validate distinctions between or among diagnoses.

References

American Psychiatric Association: Diagnostic and Statistical Manual of Mental Disorders, 3rd Edition. Washington, DC, American Psychiatric Association, 1980

American Psychiatric Association: Diagnostic and Statistical Manual of Mental Disorders, 4th Edition. Washington, DC, American Psychiatric Association, 1994

American Psychiatric Association: A Research Agenda for DSM-V. Edited by Kupfer DJ, First M, Regier DA. Washington, DC, American Psychiatric Association, 2002

Kraemer HC, Lowe KK, Kupfer DJ: To Your Health: How to Understand What Research Tells Us About Risk. New York, Oxford University Press, 2005

Kupfer DJ, Frank E: Placebo in clinical trials for depression: complexity and necessity (editorial). JAMA 287:1853–1854, 2002

Robins E, Guze SB: Establishment of diagnostic validity in psychiatric illness: its application to schizophrenia. Am J Psychiatry 126:983–987, 1970

Walsh BT, Seidman SN, Sysko R, et al: Placebo response in studies of major depression: variable, substantial, and growing. JAMA 287:1840–1847, 2002

5

PSYCHOMETRIC ASPECTS OF ANXIETY AND DEPRESSION

David Goldberg, D.M., FRCPsych

This chapter begins with relevant data from two sorts of pencil and paper tests: symptom scales and personality scales. Analyses of these data show that there is much common variance between symptoms of anxiety and depression, and although in theory personality scales measure stable aspects of functioning, in practice, there is a problem of disentangling measures of stable traits from those of unstable states when responses are influenced by the presence of a mental disorder.

The succeeding section takes a conventional clinical approach: it uses categorical diagnoses obtained by standardized research interviews and explores relationships between the diagnoses currently recognized by DSM-IV (American Psychiatric Association 1994). Studies that have linked psychological dimensions and clinical categories are then considered.

It is also possible to use individual symptoms, rather than diagnostic labels, as units of analysis. Item-response theory can create a multivariate space, produced by the symptoms themselves, and clinical diagnoses can be projected upon it. This allows calculation of the psychometric characteristics of the diagnostic categories currently in vogue.

Finally, this chapter considers pros and cons of adding dimensional models to diagnostic categories; the chapter ends by summarizing what has been learned and flagging areas that need further work.

Self-Report Scales for Symptoms of Anxiety and Depression

Self-report scales that purport to measure anxiety have substantial correlations with those that intend to measure depression; this observation applies to a wide range of scales and has been reviewed by Clark and Watson (1991). These effects are shown, both in patient and nonpatient samples, with discriminant validity only slightly lower than convergent validity (for nonpatients, 0.70 against 0.71–0.80; for patients, 0.66 against 0.73–0.84).

It is possible to reduce these correlations somewhat through judicious pruning of items loading on both scales, but even when this has been done, substantial correlations remain, so that correlations of 0.77 between the original Hamilton Rating Scale for Depression and Hamilton Rating Scale for Anxiety can be reduced to 0.39 with the revised scoring (Riskind et al. 1987).

A problem that test constructors face is that many items relevant to depression and anxiety load on both scales and must be eliminated or reduced in order to lower correlations.

Multivariate Analyses of Self-Report Personality Scales

A distinction can be made between two rather different uses of information about personality: 1) measuring personality traits that are relatively stable over time or 2) trying to account for common variance between symptoms during an episode of mental disorder. Clark et al. (2003) argued that scores on personality inventories can be decomposed into stable (trait) components and variable (state and error) components. The unstable variance may mask the stable variance when clients are depressed.

Investigators who have reported multivariate analyses of self-report instruments find a large general distress factor running across items, and this has been named, variously, "anxious-misery" (Kendler et al. 2003), "neuroticism" (Eysenck 1964 and many other authors), "negative emotionality" (Harkness et al. 1995), and negative affect (Watson et al. 1984).

Watson's negative affect has several features often thought of as being typical of depression, such as sad, guilt, and ideas of reference, as well as other features often thought of as typically anxious, such as worry and fear. In the Iowa Depression and Anxiety Scales, the general factor is called the "dysphoria scale" and contains typically depressive items—such as hopelessness, guilt, and worthlessness (Watson 2006)—that make a general psychiatrist uneasy.

Researchers who have reported negative affect also have shown that another dimension, designated positive affect, is more or less orthogonal to negative affect;

positive affect is a bipolar dimension that runs from loss of interest or pleasure to psychomotor retardation, apathy, extreme fatigue, and lethargy (Watson et al. 1984). Positive affect, but not negative affect, shows both diurnal and seasonal fluctuations. Despite the name assigned to it, it is clear that the positive affect dimension of symptoms may also reflect a biological change in bodily functions rather than mere absence of positive experience. Furthermore, the idea of negative affect as an almost-universal component in common mental disorders smudges over the distinction between relatively stable temperamental traits and highly labile state measures. Thus, although the "positive-negative" tags seem neat, they also serve to distract attention from the distinction between traits and states and the important neurovegetative changes that accompany severe depressive illness.

Clark and Watson (1991) factor-analyzed several scales that measure depression and anxiety and described three factors: a "general neurotic factor" (similar to negative affect); a "specific anxiety factor" that measures hyperarousal, nervous tension, and other autonomic symptoms; and a "specific depression factor" that reflects a severe depressive change (similar to low positive affect). Their "tripartite model" reflects these three factors. Brown et al. (1997) also found this with the Depression Anxiety Stress scales. Christensen et al. (1999) carried out structural equation modeling on two established scales of anxiety and depression and concluded that "anxiety and depression are two highly correlated *but distinct* entities" (p. 338).

Stable Traits or Labile States?

People consult mental health professionals at times of crises in their lives when they have high symptom levels that typically resolve—either with treatment or with time. There is, therefore, a large labile component in negative affect, and there is also a labile component in Eysenck's "neuroticism" (or "n" score).

Coppen and Metcalfe (1965) showed that depressed patients' whole pretreatment neuroticism scores had a mean of 30.5 but dropped to 18.7 posttreatment, whereas their extraversion scores rose from 17.3 to 20.6. Kendell and diScipio (1968) inserted an additional sentence: "try to disregard your illness when answering these questions and answer 'YES' or 'NO' according to how you feel or behave when you are your usual self" (p. 767). With this minor adjustment, the change in neuroticism scores before and after treatment became small and nonsignificant. Many problems could have been avoided had these prescient instructions become widespread when people consult mental health professionals at times of crisis in their lives.

However, provided that neuroticism is measured at times independent of medical consultation, the same scores reflect an individual's usual level of symptoms. Duncan-Jones et al. (1990) reported results of three longitudinal studies, in three different countries, in order to model patterns of stability and change in common symptoms. They showed that all three studies obeyed a model in which stable symptom levels were predicted by neuroticism with correlation of between +0.79 and +0.93, with the remainder of the variance being due to environmental events.

Ormel and Rijsdijk (2000) administered the same neuroticism questionnaire on five occasions over a period of 18 years in a population-based sample in order to shed further light on the stability of neuroticism over time. They found variation on neuroticism scores over time and concluded that the stability found by others in two-wave studies may have mistakenly been interpreted as reflecting traits. They argued that neuroticism is not immutable over time but acts as a state measure, with a much lower rate of change than a current symptom measure.

Jeffrey Gray (1973) postulated that there were two different brain systems related to approach and avoidance, which he called the behavioral activation system (BAS) and the behavioral inhibition system (BIS). The former is an approach-related, positive-incentive motivation system, and the latter regulates sensitivity to threat and non-reward. Although Gray was concerned with anxiety systems, his ideas have been applied more recently to depression as well, with depression being characterized by deficits in the BAS and high BIS functioning (similar ideas to positive affect and negative affect) (Depue and Iacono 1989). To measure BIS and BAS in human subjects, Carver and White (1994) produced their BAS/BIS scales, consisting of only 20 items assessed on four-point true/false scales that are aimed at assessing typical reactions in certain situations. Scores on the BAS can be subdivided into three subscales: reward responsiveness (BAS-RR), drive (BAS-D), and fun seeking (BAS-Fun).

These scales have provided a different solution to the trait/state problem. Kasch et al. (2002) carried out a fairly small study of 62 depressed people and 27 non-depressed control subjects using the BAS/BIS scales and a range of scales of depressive symptoms, both before and after cognitive therapy. They were able to support three hypotheses: 1) depressed people were found to have high BIS and low BAS scores compared with nondepressed subjects; 2) these scale scores were found to be stable over time; and 3) higher BIS and lower BAS scores pretreatment were found to be associated with a poorer outcome. This was especially true of BAS-RR but also the other two subscales to a lesser extent. BIS, on the other hand, did not predict any clinical variable. At first interview, however, BIS scores were positively—and BAS scores, negatively—correlated with severity of symptomatology, number of previous episodes, and Global Assessment of Functioning score. The stability over time suggests the possibility that these measures are unaffected by emotional state.

These arresting findings have been taken forward by Brown (2007), who derived latent variables of what he calls neuroticism/behavioral inhibition (N/BI) and behavioral activation/positive affect (BA/P). The first of these is derived from three scales: Eysenck's neuroticism; the BIS items; and the negative affect scale of the Positive and Negative Affect Schedule (PANAS); whereas the last, BA/P, is from the BAS and positive affect from the PANAS. The PANAS questions are answered with the all-important proviso "complete these as you would, in general."

These two personality variables, N/BI and BA/P, were assessed alongside three DSM-IV diagnoses—major depression, generalized anxiety disorder (GAD), and social phobia—over three time points, in a group of 606 patients attending an anxiety disorders clinic. In this study, levels of N/BI dropped with treatment, but BA/P remained temporally invariant after treatment. The high initial levels of N/BI predicted smaller improvement in both GAD and social phobia, but there was no such relationship with symptom loss in depression, nor did initial levels of BA/P predict symptom loss in depression. However, change in N/BI over treatment accounted for all the parallel changes seen in clinical diagnoses, observed over time.

Relationships Between Anxiety and Depression Derived From Clinical Research Interviews

When clinicians conduct research interviews, they may be more concerned than are patients to discriminate between anxiety and depression. For example, in the original version of Wing's Present State Examination, if both anxiety and depression were found to be present, the clinician was instructed to "find out which is primary" and given a special page to assist in this task. Nevertheless, correlations do not disappear; when a latent-trait analysis was used on an interview derived from the 40-item version of the Present State Examination, the correlation between the latent trait for anxiety and that for depression was found to be +0.70 (Goldberg et al. 1987). Similar findings resulted from other research interviews; rating scales derived for each from the Diagnostic Interview Schedule (Robins et al. 1981) correlated +0.43 with one another in a large community sample (Eaton and Ritter 1988).

Relationships Between Categorical Diagnoses Found by Factor Analysis

Although the DSM-IV classification assigned depression and anxiety to different classes of disorder, more recent studies involving confirmatory-factor analysis and latent-structure analysis have shown a very close relationship between these two disorders. Krueger (1999) used confirmatory-factor analysis on the U.S. National Comorbidity Survey and produced a solution in which one first makes a distinction between externalizing disorders—such as drug and alcohol disorders and antisocial personality—and internalizing disorders. The latter are further subdivided into two broad groups: "anxious misery disorders" comprising major depressive episode, dysthymia, and GAD; and "fear disorders" such as panic disorder and the various subtypes of phobia. These relationships have been confirmed in the Dunedin study and the Dutch Nemesis Study (Krueger et al. 1998; Vollebergh et al. 2001).

The replication of the National Comorbidity Survey in the United States produced comparable results; exploratory-factor analysis confirmed a two-factor solution, with externalizing disorders loading on one dimension and internalizing disorders on the other (Kessler et al. 2005). These relationships were broadly confirmed by exploratory-factor analysis of studies that used the Composite International Diagnostic Interview, Primary Care Version, followed by confirmatory-factor analysis, on a large data-set collected in general healthcare settings in 14 different countries. In these studies, a two-factor model with internalizing and externalizing disorders provided the best fit for the data. A three-factor model, with depression and anxiety on one "anxious misery" factor and neurasthenia, somatization, and hypochondriasis loading on a "somatization factor" also provided a reasonably good fit, although correlations between these two factors were substantial: around +0.70 (Krueger et al. 2003).

The highly common component of negative affect was seen as responsible for the high levels of comorbidity reported between depression and anxiety in the United States (Kessler et al. 1996), Australia (Hunt et al. 2002), and Holland (Vollebergh et al. 2001).

Kendler et al. (2003) confirmed these findings in studies of Virginia twins and described the ways in which genetic factors are involved. After describing differences between externalizing and internalizing disorders, these investigators then modeled five internalizing disorders and found that one genetic factor loaded most heavily on major depression and GAD and another loaded most strongly on animal and situational phobia. The former was called "anxious-misery" and the latter, fear. They concluded that the pattern of lifetime comorbidity of common psychiatric and substance use disorders results largely from the effects of genetic risk factors.

Whether or not these risk factors can be approximated by assessing negative affect remains an open question, as such a measure (assessed during a period of relative health!) constitutes the product of genetic factors and features of an individual's unique environment—such as quality of maternal attachment and sequelae of childhood abuse—features that may, on their own, provide more sensitive indicators than genetic factors.

Linking Psychological Dimensions and Clinical Categories

So far, we have considered psychological dimensions on one hand and clinical categories on the other. Brown et al. (1998) administered a large battery of psychological tests, as well as a structured clinical interview designed to establish DSM-IV clinical diagnoses, to 350 patients who sought treatment for anxiety. The clinical diagnoses revealed the usual substantial correlations between depression and generalized anxiety (+0.63) and somewhat lower correlations between depression and other diagnoses: panic/agoraphobia (+0.44), obsessive-compulsive disorder (+0.43), and social phobia (+0.39). These investigators considered various competing models for studying relationships between categorical diagnoses and psychological dimensions of positive affect, negative affect, and autonomic arousal. Negative affect was significantly related to all categories as well as to autonomic arousal. However, autonomic arousal was only significantly related to panic/agoraphobia, whereas low positive affect was significantly related to depressive episode and social phobia. In this model, therefore, depression and social phobia emerged as being the product of both negative affect and low positive affect, but depression had a far higher component of negative affect (+0.87). Panic/agoraphobia emerged as a product of negative affect and autonomic arousal, whereas GAD was a result of negative affect on its own (+0.74). Thus, GAD can be either a remnant of depression after the low positive affect has resolved or a step in the development of what may be a later depression, waiting only for a low positive affect.

In a later paper, Watson (2005) presented the earlier tripartite model, alongside the "integrative hierarchical model" (Mineka et al. 1998), in which each disorder also contains both a general and a specific component. Mineka et al. (1998) concluded their review by speculating that depressive states are associated with memory biases for negative information about the self, whereas anxiety is associated with automatic attentional biases for threatening material. However, similar to Brown et al. (1998), anxious arousal was the specific component of panic disorder and no longer appeared to be mentioned in GAD. Thus, once more, GAD was only distinguished from depression by the absence of low positive affect.

Low positive affect is also seen as not being confined to depression but shared with social phobia. Arguments are advanced for recruiting GAD to the "distress disorders," consisting of major depression, dysthymia, and posttraumatic stress disorder. These arguments rely on genetic studies, on high comorbidity between the disorders, and on the demonstration mentioned earlier that internalizing disorders can be divided into "anxious misery" disorders and fear disorders (Krueger 1999).

Exploring Clinical Diagnoses With Latent-Trait Analyses

Latent-trait analysis is derived from item-response theory and aims to provide information about dimensions underlying observable phenomena, which cannot be observed directly. Latent-trait analysis offers a number of advantages over factor analysis: it is especially suitable for data that are either present or absent (like symptoms), and it provides more information about each symptom than do mere factor loads in conventional factor analysis. Specifically, it provides information about the *severity* of that symptom (the "threshold"), the position on the underlying dimension where 50% of patients will endorse the symptom, as well as the ability of that symptom to *discriminate between individuals* at that point (the "slope"). If the probability of endorsement of a symptom rises sharply at the threshold, the slope will be higher than if the probability rises only slowly over the whole range of the latent trait.

An early application of this technique to relationships between anxiety and depression was described by Goldberg et al. (1987); this study applied a two-dimensional adaptation of latent-trait analysis to the 36 symptoms used by either the DSM-III (American Psychiatric Association 1980) system or the European ID-Catego system; this adaptation was used to produce diagnoses from the Present State Examination. In this study, phobic avoidance was not included because it is a behavior rather than a symptom; in addition, 12 additional symptoms had to be excluded because fewer than 10 subjects reported them.

Two latent traits were extracted, one corresponding to anxiety and the other to depression; however, they were correlated +0.70 with each other. The two-dimensional solution was superior to the one-dimensional solution, and the three-dimensional solution offered no significant advantages over the two-dimensional. This technique demonstrates the relative position of various symptoms in a two-dimensional space, defined by anxiety and depression; it also allows the identification of those symptoms that are good discriminators.

A later paper from this group also included categorical diagnoses and considered these on the latent space defined by the two dimensions (see Table 5–1). This allowed a consideration of the validity of two current taxonomies, DSM-III and ID-Catego, and compared these taxonomies with the general practitioners' own diagnoses (Grayson et al. 1987).

In Table 5–1, if we start with the general practitioners' assessments, we see that the "direction" of their three assessments was good: the "depressed" label is 57° away from the anxiety latent trait; "anxious depression" is almost exactly halfway between the two latent traits; and "anxiety" is a full 79° away from the depression latent trait. We see that the thresholds for these three assessments were generally higher than those for the psychiatric categories, reflecting the fact that general practitioners are more likely to diagnose severe cases. It can be seen that, inevitably, there is a rough correspondence between the number of conditions diagnosed and the "threshold." The general practitioners were undone by their low slopes, inevitable because so many cases were missed.

Where anxiety disorders were concerned, the ID-Catego system detected more severe disorders than did DSM, but the directions of each were good, and the slopes better than the general practitioners, with ID-Catego having a better slope. Where depressive disorders were concerned, major depressive disorder was very close to the depression latent trait, but "neurotic depression" was intermediate between the two latent traits. Major depressive disorder and "retarded depression" both have good slopes, but they are both fairly mild disorders.

TABLE 5–1. Categorical diagnoses of common mental disorders in primary care, compared in two dimensions

	N	Direction	Slope	Threshold
Anxiety diagnoses				
DSM-III generalized anxiety disorder	16	−34°	1.97	0.69
ID-Catego—"anxiety neurosis"	5	−38°	1.94	2.07
General practitioner—"anxious patient"	15	−33°	0.79	1.70
Depressive diagnoses				
DSM-III major depressive disorder	13	41°	5.00	1.16
DSM-III dysthymic disorder	3	16°	0.59	3.78
ID-Catego—neurotic depression	12	20°	1.20	1.56
ID-Catego—retarded depression	10	66°	4.41	1.34
General practitioner—depressed patient	3	57°	0.59	3.78
General practitioner—anxious depression	5	25°	0.62	3.05

Note. Latent trait for anxiety was set at 0° and for depression at 46°. DSM-III diagnoses are compared with ID-Catego diagnoses and with judgment of the general practitioner who saw the patient. The direction, slope, and threshold for each diagnosis are shown.

Ormel et al. (1995) used the same interviews—but included phobic avoidance and omitted the DSM-III extra symptoms—in Manchester with two Dutch data sets, one in the community and one in primary care. This time, the symptoms studied were just those included in the short Present State Examination, so that 32 symptoms were included. The inclusion of somewhat different symptoms now produced three latent traits: the original two, representing depression and anxiety, and a third, representing phobic anxiety and avoidance. In the two-dimensional solution, anxiety and depression were collapsed onto a single dimension, and phobic anxiety and avoidance were on the other. Dimensions of depression and anxiety were correlated between +0.52 and +0.58 in all centers, but the phobic dimension had relatively low correlations with the first two.

These papers may provide a tool with which to compare variations in possible syndrome definition in DSM-V.

Latent Class Analysis

Latent class analysis assumes sick and well categories and recruits patients to similar underlying classes, as in clinical diagnoses. Croudace et al. carried out a latent class analysis on their large data set collected for the National Hospital Discharge Survey (T. Croudace, I. Colman, P. Jones: "The Latent Structure of PSE Symptoms in a Birth Cohort," manuscript in preparation, 2007). This produced five classes of patients, including a large class of asymptomatic individuals (61.1% of those interviewed); a much smaller class of subclinically distressed, mildly anxious people (17.6%); and three groups of symptomatic people. The largest of these three groups (11.2%) had phobic symptoms, 6.1% had predominantly depressive symptoms, and 4% had the most-severe symptoms, including both anxious and depressive symptoms.

Should Diagnostic Categories Be Supplemented With Dimensions?

Clinical categories are here to stay; the problem is, should each category be supplemented by a dimensional scale, or should dimensions be supplemented by categories so that the decision to offer treatment can be adjusted according to severity of the disorder? The latter should be the ultimate goal, using dimensions based on temperament, personality, and genetics, but there are problems in proceeding directly toward this goal.

There are numerous strong arguments in favor of dimensions that have been set out by Brown and Barlow (2005), including the greater reliability of dimensions over categories, the loss of clinical information inevitable with binomial classifications, the elimination of hierarchical rules still built into taxonomic frameworks, and the conveyance of information about severity of a disorder. To these arguments, Widiger and Samuel (2005) make the additional important point that using the term *comorbidity* implies two distinct pathological processes, whereas "co-occurrence" suggests a common shared pathology. Various authors (Clark and Watson 1991; Katon and Roy-Byrne 1991) have argued for the existence of "mixed anxiety-depression"; however, this categorization ceases to be a problem with dimensional models, because it then becomes a milder form of general distress, or "co-occurrent anxiety and major depression."

There are formidable obstacles to overcome before these dimensional dreams become reality. First, if working clinicians are expected to use dimensions in their daily work, this necessitates use of scales—an impracticable task in, for example, primary medical care. Also, dimensions cannot be used in "lifetime" assessments or latent-structure analyses—they are intrinsically cross-sectional assessments. In addition, dimensions, ipso facto, are not more reliable than categories—one has only to remember the poor reliability of the Global Assessment of Functioning (di Nardo et al. 1993). However, the biggest problem concerns the number and selection of constituent items to be used, because both these factors will influence the structure of dimensions that emerge. As an illustration of this, consider the classification of personality disorders, for which dimensions are the principal methods in use. Widiger and Simondsen (2005) reviewed 18 such dimensional structures and had to discard 8 of these as not being readily assimilable to the remaining 10. Even with 10, there was no agreement about the number or names to be assigned to the dimensions. These authors proposed a complex four-level structure of dimensional schemes, with criteria for diagnostic categories at the lowest level, described thus: "At the highest level could be the two broad domains of internalization and externalization…immediately beneath…would be three to five broad domains of personality functioning…beneath these…would be personality trait scales, and at the lowest level would be the more behaviorally specific diagnostic criteria" (Widiger and Simondson 2005, p. 18).

There is a problem here, because diagnostic criteria cannot possibly be nested under such a hierarchy—this would imply that all cases with a particular diagnosis can be nested under a single one of the three (or five) domains. Where, for example, would depression appear? It may be more common in one of the "broad domains" than others but can occur in all of them. Indeed, even externalizers can become depressed!

There is a disturbing lack of agreement about the broad domains, because many of the 18 schemas considered by Widiger and Simondsen cannot be assimilated to the broad schema advocated. Indeed, before we can make categories subservient to dimensions, it is clear that personality theorists must agree about the exact model to be adopted.

This having been said, a start can be made by producing dimensional scales for anxious symptoms and depressive symptoms. Goldberg et al. (1988) used two short scales derived from latent-trait analysis of patients who were seeking care in primary care settings. More complex dimensional scales for depression have been proposed more recently (Andrews et al. 2007; Slade and Andrews 2005).

Conclusion

1. Positive affect is an important personality trait that can be reliably measured, even during episodes of illness. Whether it is appropriately named is more arguable, because many of the items that characterize it have a biological content and, alone among personality traits, it is affected by diurnal rhythms and seasonal variations.
2. Negative affect (or Eysenck's "neuroticism"), measured during a period of relative health, is probably the best overall measure of shared vulnerability to both

GAD and major depressive episode, but during episodes of disorder, the trait variance is masked by state variance. Either measure is a good measure of vulnerability to stress; however, such vulnerability is determined by unique environmental variables (such as quality of maternal attachment and experience of childhood abuse) as well as genetic variables. The latent variable N/BI is another contender that might be even more reliable as a vulnerability indicator, although at present it is extracted from three inventories and also suffers from state effects during illness episodes. Negative affect is an important source of common variance among all internalizing disorders and is associated with autonomic arousal. Low positive affect makes an important additional contribution to depression and a smaller contribution to social phobia. GAD is only affected by negative affect, whereas panic/agoraphobia is affected by negative affect and autonomic arousal.

3. When factor analyses use categorical diagnoses as units of analysis, common mental disorders divide themselves into two broad groups, externalizing and internalizing disorders. Internalizing disorders may be further subdivided into "anxious-misery" (or anxious depression?) and fear disorders.

4. Latent-trait analysis uses individual symptoms as units of analysis and is able to compare the effects of varying the rules for a diagnostic category to consider the effects on severity of disorder, assessed by the category (threshold) and the power of that category to distinguish between patients at that point in multivariate space. Unfortunately, the use of "skip-outs" in many standardized interviews invalidates the data for a latent-trait analysis. Several data sets, derived from latent-trait analyses of community samples, indicate that dimensions of anxiety and depression are so closely correlated that it is superfluous to distinguish between them. However, consulting samples usually show correlation between anxious symptoms and depressive symptoms of between +0.52 and +0.70, so the distinction may well be worthwhile.

5. GAD can be thought of in two ways in longitudinal data: 1) as a step in the pathway toward depression, which may occur in a person who also has low positive affect when depressive cognitive processes occur in response to a loss; or 2) as a remnant of a depressive episode after treatment. Note that low positive affect, although associated with depression, is said to be unaffected by treatments for depression because it is a trait measure that reflects vulnerability to depression. Treatments for depression reduce general distress or negative affect.

6. Although there are real problems in constructing dimensional scales, these problems can be overcome. Already there are useful dimensional scales for both anxiety and depression.

References

American Psychiatric Association: Diagnostic and Statistical Manual of Mental Disorders, 3rd Edition. Washington, DC, American Psychiatric Association, 1980

American Psychiatric Association: Diagnostic and Statistical Manual of Mental Disorders, 4th Edition. Washington, DC, American Psychiatric Association, 1994

Andrews G, Brugha T, Thase ME, et al: Dimensionality and the character of major depressive episode. Int J Methods Psychiatr Res 16(suppl):S41–S51, 2007

Brown T: Temporal course and structural relationships among dimensions of temperament and DSM-IV anxiety and mood constructs. J Abnorm Psychol 116:313–328, 2007

Brown T, Barlow DH: Dimensional versus categorical classification of mental disorders in the fifth edition of the Diagnostic and Statistical Manual of Mental Disorders and beyond: comment on the special section. J Abnorm Psychol 114:551–557, 2005

Brown T, Chorpita BF, Korotitsch W, et al: Psychometric properties of the Depression Anxiety Stress Scales (DASS) in clinical samples. Behav Res Ther 35:79–89, 1997

Brown T, Chorpita BF, Barlow DH: Structural relationships among dimensions of the DSM-IV anxiety and mood disorders and dimensions of negative affect, positive affect and autonomic arousal. J Abnorm Psychol 107:179–192, 1998

Carver CS, White TL: Behavioural inhibition, behavioural activation, and affective responses to impending reward and punishment: the BIS/BAS scales. J Pers Soc Psychol 67:319–333, 1994

Christensen H, Jorm AF, Mackinnon AJ, et al: Age differences in depression and anxiety symptoms: a structural equation modelling analysis of data in a general population sample. Psychol Med 29:325–339, 1999

Clark LA, Watson D: Tri-partite model of anxiety and depression: psychometric evidence and taxonomic implications. J Abnorm Psychol 100:316–336, 1991

Clark LA, Vittengl JR, Kraft D, et al: Shared, not unique, components of personality and psychosocial functioning predict depression severity after acute-phase cognitive therapy. J Pers Disord 17:406–430, 2003

Coppen A, Metcalfe M: Effect of a depressive illness on MPI scores. Br J Psychiatry 111:236–239, 1965

Depue RA, Iacono WG: Neurobehavioral aspects of affective disorders. Annu Rev Psychol 40:457–492, 1989

di Nardo PA, Moras K, Barlow DH, et al: Reliability of DSM-III-R anxiety disorder categories using the Anxiety Disorders Schedule Revised ADIS-R. Arch Gen Psychiatry 50:251–256, 1993

Duncan-Jones P, Fergusson D, Ormel HJ, et al: A model of stability and change in minor psychiatric symptoms: results from three longitudinal studies. Psychol Med Monogr Suppl 18:1–28, 1990

Eaton WW, Ritter C: Distinguishing anxiety from depression in field survey data. Psychol Med 18:155–166, 1988

Eysenck HJ: The measurement of personality: a new instrument. Journal of the Indian Academy of Applied Psychology 1:1–11, 1964

Goldberg DP, Bridges K, Duncan-Jones P, et al: Dimensions of neuroses seen in primary care settings. Psychol Med 17:461–470, 1987

Goldberg DP, Bridges K, Duncan-Jones P, et al: Detecting anxiety and depression in general medical settings. Br Med J 297:897–899, 1988

Gray JA: The behavioural inhibition system: a possible substrate for anxiety, in Theoretical and Experimental Bases of the Behavioural Therapies. Edited by Feldman MP, Broadhurst A. London, England, Wiley, 1973, pp 1–41

Grayson D, Bridges K, Duncan-Jones P, et al: The validity of diagnostic systems for common mental disorders: a comparison between the ID-Catego and the DSM-III systems. Psychol Med 17:933–942, 1987

Harkness AR, McNulty JL, Ben-Porath YS: The Personality Psychopathology Five (PSY-5): constructs and MMPI-2 scales. Psychol Assess 7:104–114, 1995

Hunt C, Issikadis C, Andrews G: DSM-IV generalised anxiety disorder in the Australian National Survey of Mental Health and Well-Being. Psychol Med 32:649–659, 2002

Kasch KL, Rottenberg J, Arnow BA, et al: Behavioural activation and inhibition systems and the severity and course of depression. J Abnorm Psychol 111:589–597, 2002

Katon W, Roy-Byrne PP: Mixed anxiety depression. J Abnorm Psychol 100:337–345, 1991

Kendell RE, diScipio W: Eysenck Personality Inventory scores of patients with depressive illness. Br J Psychiatry 114:767–770, 1968

Kendler KS, Prescott CA, Myers J, et al: The structure of genetic and environmental risk factors for common psychiatric and substance use disorders in men and women. Arch Gen Psychiatry 60:929–937, 2003

Kessler R, Nelson CB, McGonagle KA, et al: Co-morbidity of DSM-III-R major depressive disorder in the general population. Arch Gen Psychiatry 168(suppl):17–30, 1996

Kessler R, Chiu WT, Demler O, et al: Prevalence, severity, and comorbidity of 12-month DSM-IV disorders in the National Comorbidity Survey Replication. Arch Gen Psychiatry 62:617–627, 2005

Krueger RF: The structure of common mental disorders. Arch Gen Psychiatry 56:921–926, 1999

Krueger RF, Caspi A, Moffitt TE, et al: The structure and stability of common mental disorders (DSM-III-R): a longitudinal-epidemiological study. J Abnorm Psychol 107:216–227, 1998

Krueger RF, Chentsova-Dutton YE, Markon KE, et al: A cross-cultural study of the structure of comorbidity among common psychopathological syndromes in the general health care setting. J Abnorm Psychol 112:437–447, 2003

Mineka S, Watson D, Clark, LA: Comorbidity of anxiety and unipolar mood disorders. Annu Rev Psychol 49:377–412, 1998

Ormel J, Rijsdijk FV: Continuing change in neuroticism during adulthood: structural modelling of a 16-year, 5-wave community study. Pers Individ Dif 28:461–478, 2000

Ormel J, Oldehinkel AJ, Goldberg DP, et al: The structure of common psychiatric symptoms: how many dimension of neurosis? Psychol Med 25:521–532, 1995

Riskind JH, Beck AT, Brown G, et al: Taking the measure of anxiety and depression: validity of the reconstructed Hamilton Scales. J Nerv Ment Dis 175:474–479, 1987

Robins L, Helzer R, Croughan J, et al: National Institute of Mental Health Diagnostic Interview Schedule: its history, characteristics and validity. Arch Gen Psychiatry 38:381–389, 1981

Slade T, Andrews G: Latent structure of depression in a community sample: a taxometric analysis. Psychol Med 35:489–497, 2005
Vollebergh WA, Iedema J, Bijl RV, et al: The structure and stability of common mental disorders: the NEMESIS study. Arch Gen Psychiatry 58:597–603, 2001
Watson D: Re-thinking the mood and anxiety disorders: a quantitative hierarchical model for DSM-V. J Abnorm Psychol 114:522–536, 2005
Watson D, Clark LA, Tellegen A: Cross-cultural convergence in the structure of mood: a Japanese replication and comparison with U.S. findings. J Pers Soc Psychol 47:127–144, 1984
Watson D, O'Hara MW, Simms LJ, et al: Development and validation of the Inventory of Depression and Anxiety Symptoms (IDAS). Psychol Assess 19:253–268, 2007
Widiger TA, Samuel DB: Diagnostic categories or dimensions? A question for the Diagnostic and Statistical Manual of Mental Disorders–fifth edition. J Abnorm Psychol 114:494–504, 2005
Widiger TA, Simondsen E: Alternative dimensional models of personality disorder: finding a common ground. J Personal Disord 19:110–130, 2005

Commentary

COMMENTARY ON "PSYCHOMETRIC ASPECTS OF ANXIETY AND DEPRESSION"

Patrick E. Shrout, Ph.D.

Professor Goldberg provides a stimulating review of psychometric issues and evidence relevant to competing answers to the question of whether major depressive disorder (MDD) and generalized anxiety disorder (GAD) are different forms of the same disorder, closely related disorders, or distinct disorders. He notes that commentaries on this question draw on data from the personality and mood literatures, as well as the clinical literature. He also reviews a number of statistical and psychometric approaches that have been used to interpret patterns in these data.

An implicit theme in his review is that the data do not map neatly onto our questions about the disorder or disorders. Kraemer et al. (2007) noted that disorders must be distinguished from diagnoses. Disorders are health conditions of patients, which may or may not be evident, whereas diagnoses are attempts by professionals to determine whether one or more disorders are present in a patient. Assessment data reflect reported symptoms, reported personality patterns, and diagnoses based on compilations of those symptoms—not the disorders themselves—and this presents a psychometric challenge.

Latent-variable models have been used in attempts to identify the underlying process—or processes—that give rise to the data. These latent variables can be represented as categorical or continuous and are often represented as being free of measurement error. Examining the degree of association among GAD and MDD latent variables is one way to approach the question at hand. As Professor Goldberg notes, there are many reports that argue that these latent variables are strongly associated, but few empirical studies conclude that these variables are redundant.

Another theme in Professor Goldberg's review is the distinction between stable traits and varying states. GAD is conceived in trait-like terms, and diagnoses based on this conception tend to be related to neuroticism traits but not stressful events or states. In contrast, MDD is episodic, and episodes may be related to stressful events. However, there is a trait component to depression processes, such that persons who have had an episode of depression tend to have recurrences. Persons with recurrences tend to be higher on neuroticism. Perhaps for this reason, Goldberg emphasizes the trait components of measures. He is especially impressed with measures that attempt to override state episode variation with instructions that emphasize one's "usual self." This brings the focus of his review to the trait portion of depression/anxiety comorbidity, such that once a person experiences depression he/she is always counted as "depressed." A question left unanswered is whether persons with single episodes of major depression have the same disorder as those with multiple episodes.

In this commentary, I reflect on these two themes of Professor Goldberg's review, with a focus on the implications of these themes on the measurement of anxiety and depression. A number of other contributors to this volume have reviewed clinical, genetic, and epidemiological findings regarding overlap of anxiety and depression, but these reports typically adopt operational definitions of anxiety and depression that treat the measures/diagnoses of these disorders as proxies of the disorders themselves. The goal of this chapter is to consider what goes into these measures.

Dimensions and Categories

When considering any measurement strategy, a preliminary issue is whether we should focus on dimensions or categories. Professor Goldberg reviews the many good reasons for considering dimensions of anxiety and depression, but he expresses the conservative view that dimensional measures may be impractical in primary care. I prefer to consider practicality as a technical issue to solve and instead focus on the fundamental features of anxiety and depression measurement.

From a basic perspective, anxiety and depression symptoms are always conceived in dimensional terms, and categories follow from some immediate applications of cutpoints. Consider, for example, the DSM-IV (American Psychiatric Association 1994) criteria of GAD and MDD, which include multiple cutpoints on implied continua. Diagnoses of GAD are based on reports such as *excessive* anxiety/worry occurring *more days than not* for at least *6 months* about a *number* of activities. Similarly, for MDD we have *markedly diminished* interest in *almost all* activities in a *2-week period or longer, most of the day, nearly every day* in the period.

Both of these examples show how categories can be defined by setting cutpoints on severity, duration, and consistency. In practice, clinicians would probably consider the cutpoints to be flexible if, for example, a distressed patient had only experienced excessive worry for 20 weeks rather than the prescribed 24 weeks for GAD. From this perspective, it seems advisable to collect dimensional observations whenever possible. The technical question that remains is how to do this efficiently.

Self-Reports and Psychometric Analyses

In most cases, we depend on patients (or survey respondents) to tell us about their experiences with stress, worry, mood states, and other symptoms of mental and physical disorder. In his review, Professor Goldberg noted important patterns in self-report data that suggest hierarchies of disorders. One pattern is that, across the spectrum of psychopathology, there seem to be commonalities among internalizing and externalizing disorders. Among internalizing conditions, there seem to be three patterns: general negative affect (neuroticism), positive affect (or a lack thereof), and fears or autonomic arousal.

Even if multiple latent dimensions are needed to account for patterns among self-reported symptoms, we still need to consider the magnitude of correlation among these dimensions. Studies that have employed nonorthogonal latent representations give different answers, and Professor Goldberg notes that some investigators have pruned the item set to make the dimensions seem less correlated. He also notes that, through semistructured interviews, clinicians are asked to find out whether depression or anxiety is "primary." This determination is presumably made by collecting more information from the patient about the timing of the complaints, perhaps after educating the respondent about the meaning of feeling "blue" versus feeling "anxious." Those who are seeking treatment for the first time, and survey respondents who have never sought treatment, might not have associated precise labels to facets of their distress. These conversations between interviewer and participant can help reduce the apparent correlation between low positive affect and fears/anxiety. The conversation might also reduce the overall variability of the nonspecific negative affect component of the complaints, as variability moves to the specific complaints.

Those who study the social cognition of survey responses, such as Norbert Schwarz (e.g., Schwarz 1998; Schwarz and Oyserman 2001) have argued that conscientious participants always view their survey responses in the context of conversational norms. Even if there is not a give and take, such as occurs in a semistructured interview, participants are likely to wonder what is expected of them. They realize that questions are being asked about undesirable characteristics, such as worry and emotional instability, and some might wonder if they will be viewed as defensive if they deny having worries, fears, or sadness. Alternatively, they might welcome the possibility of disclosing a difficult period, even if that period is outside the time frame of the question—a phenomenon called "telescoping" (Tourangeau et al. 2000). These kinds of effects might well account for the well-known "attenuation" pattern in psychiatric epidemiology, whereby the second wave of interviews yields consistently lower rates of complaints and disorders than the first wave. These effects can also account for initial improvement among help-seekers, who may be motivated to overreport in order to qualify for treatment.

Because these response effects are likely to be nonspecific across classes of complaints, such effects can lead to increased correlation among measures of anxiety and low positive affect and can also add to the variability of the overall neuroticism/negative affect dimension. The effects are likely to be made worse by complex questions that involve heavy demands on memory and social construction of personal history. I recommend that careful investigation of these response effects be added to the list of areas for further work provided by Professor Goldberg.

States and Traits

The issues of states and traits are critical both for understanding of the nature of disorders and for monitoring the response to treatment. Professor Goldberg warns us that measures of concepts defined as traits may well be affected by state variation. The social cognitive perspective just alluded to reminds us that clear state questions can be influenced by traits through the cognitive filter of question/norm interpretation.

For purposes of screening, it might not be important to distinguish between these trait and state components of responses; however, to answer the big questions of this meeting it seems that we would want better data on what is changing and what is not. I respectfully disagree with Professor Goldberg's suggestion that we focus on trait variation by putting the burden on respondents to tell us about their usual selves. I believe we need more data on how worries, fears, depressed affect, somatic problems, and low self-regard vary over time and over people. The fact that low positive affect is related to biological content, and has diurnal and seasonal variation, does not dissuade me from being interested in basic data on its daily variation. Indeed, the processes of disregulation of fears and positive affect might be as interesting as individual differences in levels of fears and positive affect over 2 weeks or 24 weeks. Neuroscientists such as Joe LeDeux and Bruce McEwen have been advocating more dynamic views of these processes.

Is it feasible to obtain more detailed information about basic processes over time? Recently, physicians who specialize in the diagnosis of hypertension have suggested that this is often feasible. Primary care physicians now have new tools for measuring ambulatory blood pressure over the course of a 24-hour day. Like psychiatrists' measures of distress, blood pressure is affected by context and time of day; these miniature recording devices provide an interesting picture of how a patient's blood pressure varies when he or she is out of the doctor's office. The average and extreme values of blood pressure help determine whether the patient should be treated for hypertension disorder. As new data are being collected about the relation of GAD and MDD, it would be nice to have data like that recorded in these devices.

As an example, daily diary methods might well be useful for persons who are at risk for either GAD or MDD or who seem to have one or both of these disorders. Diary methods might help distinguish short-term state fluctuations from trait variation. We still will continue to need longitudinal studies, like those reviewed by Professor Goldberg, to answer the questions about developmental course of the conditions. Diary studies imbedded in panel designs would allow mood-regulation patterns over time to be documented and interpreted.

Psychometric/Statistical Analysis

Professor Goldberg's paper highlights many of the statistical tools we have for modeling error processes and for assessing association among pathologic processes. These methods make different assumptions and, usually, it is impossible to verify the correctness of these assumptions. It is, however, possible to think critically about the assumptions and to carry out sensitivity analyses to determine whether a specific assumption can make or break an empirical inference. Most important, from my perspective, is to think carefully about how we interpret the latent variables. The traditional representation of factor-analytic and latent-trait models implies a causal path. We think about a liability for low positive affect, or high neuroticism/negative affect, or high autonomic arousal, as causing the emergence of symptoms such as sleep disturbance or low self-regard. In my view, these models make much more sense within the context of a genetically informative developmental study than in a factor analysis of cross-sectional data. In the latter case, it is difficult to determine which variables might be related to the emergence of a disorder as causal factors and which are genuine consequences of the disorder.

In the years ahead, we can consider implications of exploring other models, such as taxometric models (Waller and Meehl 1998), growth mixture models (Muthen and Shedden 1999; Nagin 1999), and nonparametric item response theory models (e.g., Meijer and Baneke 2004). There is also new work being done on full-information item response theory models related to the tripartite model (Gibbons et al. 2007). It will be of special interest to see if these models can represent the emergence of anxiety over time and whether a disposition for episodes of depression can be modeled in a way that allows for interactions of both genetic risk and environmental triggers.

Conclusion

Much can be learned from psychometric analyses of existing data, but it is useful to recognize that these data are likely to be affected by self-report processes that may complicate the separation of trait risk from state variation. Self-report biases can be minimized by asking questions about current condition and events over the past day. Although time-intensive data present real logistical problems, these problems are likely to be solvable in certain populations by using modern technology. Application of multivariate psychometric models to retrospective data can be informative but likely will not be definitive until the varying influences on symptom reports can be isolated. Analyses of dynamic processes over time offer the possibility of increasingly definitive answers to questions about relationships of GAD and MDD.

References

American Psychiatric Association: Diagnostic and Statistical Manual of Mental Disorders, 4th Edition. Washington, DC, American Psychiatric Association, 1994

Gibbons RD, Bock RD, Hedeker D, et al: Full-information item bifactor analysis of graded response data. Applied Psychological Measurement 31:4–19, 2007. Available at http://apm.sagepub.com/cgi/content/abstract/31/1/4. Accessed August 5, 2009.

Kraemer HC, Shrout PE, Rubio-Stipec M: Developing the diagnostic and statistical manual V: what will "statistical" mean in DSM-V? Soc Psychiatry Psychiatr Epidemiol 42:259–267, 2007

Meijer RR, Baneke JJ: Analyzing psychopathology items: a case for nonparametric item response theory modeling. Psychol Methods 9:354–368, 2004

Muthen B, Shedden K: Finite mixture modeling with mixture outcomes using the EM algorithm. Biometrics 55:463–469, 1999

Nagin DS: Analyzing developmental trajectories: a semiparametric, group-based approach. Psychol Methods 4:139–157, 1999

Schwarz N: Communication in standardized research situations: a Gricean perspective, in Social and Cognitive Approaches to Interpersonal Communication. Edited by Fussell SR, Kreuz, RJ. Mahwah, NJ, Lawrence Erlbaum Associates, 1998, pp 39–66

Schwarz N, Oyserman D: Asking questions about behavior: cognition, communication, and questionnaire construction. American Journal of Evaluation 22:127–160, 2001

Tourangeau R, Rips LJ, Rasinski K: The Psychology of Survey Response. New York, Cambridge University Press, 2000

Waller NG, Meehl PE: Multivariate Taxometric Procedures: Distinguishing Types From Continua. Thousand Oaks, CA, Sage Publications, 1998

6

THE BOUNDARY BETWEEN GENERALIZED ANXIETY DISORDER AND THE UNIPOLAR MOOD DISORDERS

Diagnostic and Psychometric Findings in Clinical Samples

Timothy A. Brown, Psy.D.

This chapter reviews and summarizes data from the Center for Anxiety and Related Disorders that bear on boundaries between DSM-IV (American Psychiatric Association 1994) generalized anxiety disorder (GAD) and the unipolar mood disorders (major depressive disorder [MDD] and dysthymic disorder). This work was conducted with clinical outpatient samples and has focused on the overlap and distinguishability of the disorders at the diagnostic and psychometric levels. Data reviewed here lead to the conclusion that although GAD and MDD/dysthymic disorder are closely related disorders, the overlap is not to an extent that these conditions should be combined (or eliminated) from DSM-V. Issues pertaining to the reorganization and dimensional classification of these disorders are also considered.

During the process of preparing DSM-IV, there was considerable debate as to whether GAD should be retained as a formal diagnostic category (Brown et al. 1994). In particular, some researchers argued that, given evidence of GAD's modest diagnostic reliability and high comorbidity with other anxiety and mood disorders, its features should be subsumed under the conditions with which it frequently co-occurs. Although GAD was retained as a distinct category in DSM-IV, the debate about GAD's diagnostic status has persisted. Unlike during the run-up to DSM-IV, when GAD's distinguishability with respect to a variety of disorders (e.g., obsessive-compulsive disorder [OCD]) was questioned (Brown et al. 1993), in recent times this debate has been more focused on the distinction between GAD and the unipolar mood disorders—fueled, in part, by compelling evidence that GAD and MDD share the same genetic liability (e.g., Kendler et al. 1992).

Diagnostic Findings

Data from our center could be viewed as bolstering concerns about the distinguishability of GAD from the mood disorders. In 2001, we published findings from our diagnostic reliability study of the DSM-IV anxiety and mood disorders, in which 362 patients underwent two independent administrations of the Anxiety Disorders Interview Schedule for DSM-IV–Lifetime version (ADIS-IV-L; Brown et al. 2001b). Although the diagnostic reliability of DSM-IV GAD had improved, relative to estimates based on its DSM-III-R (American Psychiatric Association 1987) definition ($\kappa = 0.65$ and 0.53 for DSM-IV and DSM-III-R, respectively; Di Nardo et al. 1993), the level of diagnostic agreement continued to be modest relative to other major anxiety disorder categories; for example, κ values for panic disorder with agoraphobia (PDA), social phobia, and OCD were 0.81, 0.77, and 0.75, respectively. Interestingly, MDD and dysthymic disorder joined GAD as the disorders associated with the lowest levels of diagnostic reliability ($\kappa = 0.59$ and 0.31, respectively). Brown et al. (2001b) also examined reasons for diagnostic disagreements that occurred between the ADIS-IV-L interviewers. In many cases, these disagreements did not involve other disorders. For instance, a common source of unreliability was a "threshold disagreement," in which both interviewers agreed that the features of a given disorder were present but disagreed as to whether the symptoms were severe enough to meet the threshold for a formal DSM-IV disorder. However, when diagnostic disagreements with GAD involved other disorders, most often the other condition was a mood disorder (i.e., 23 of these 35 disagreements involved MDD, dysthymic disorder, and in one case, bipolar disorder). It is also noteworthy that 10 of the 35 GAD disagreements involving other disorders were with anxiety disorder not otherwise specified (i.e., GAD-type presentations judged by one interviewer not to fully meet GAD diagnostic criteria). Along with the aforementioned "threshold disagreements," the high rate of disagreements with anxiety disorder not otherwise specified is a manifestation of the difficulties that arise from imposing a categorical diagnostic threshold on the number, severity, and duration of symptoms (see concluding paragraph of this chapter).

Results from our large-scale study on the diagnostic comorbidity of DSM-IV anxiety and mood disorders ($N=1,127$ patients) are consistent with findings from epidemiological studies that GAD and the mood disorders co-occur frequently (e.g., 74% of patients with GAD have lifetime mood disorders; Brown et al. 2001a). Yet several aspects of Brown et al. (2001a) indicated where comorbidity data based on DSM-IV diagnoses produced misleading findings in regard to overlap among disorders. For example, the presence of social phobia and specific phobia was associated with decreased likelihood of PDA, and vice versa, which would suggest that although these conditions possess overlapping features (e.g., situational avoidance, panic attacks), they co-occur relatively infrequently. However, it is likely that findings of significantly lower relative risks were artifacts of DSM-IV differential diagnosis and hierarchy rules (e.g., features of social phobia were judged to be better accounted for by PDA). A clear instance of this phenomenon is evident in findings on the comorbidity of GAD and mood disorders. For instance, when adhering strictly to DSM-IV diagnostic rules, the comorbidity between GAD and dysthymic disorder was 5%. However, when ignoring the hierarchy rule that GAD should not be assigned when it occurs exclusively during a course of a mood disorder, the comorbidity estimate increased to 90%. Such findings reflect how inquiry focused solely at the diagnostic level provides limited information about the discriminant validity of emotional disorders (e.g., diagnostic-level studies are bound to the diagnostic system being evaluated and are at increased risk for measurement error associated with categorical thresholds of the dimensional frequency and severity of symptoms). Accordingly, researchers should be mindful of this issue when interpreting the results of latent structural analyses of comorbidity, where DSM or ICD diagnoses serve as the binary units of analysis (e.g., Krueger 1999; Slade and Watson 2006); for detailed discussion of these limitations, see Brown and Barlow (2005). Indeed, such studies have often produced structures that are at odds with latent-structural analyses of dimensional ratings and clinical wisdom—for example, OCD as a "fear-based" disorder with close ties to PDA and social phobia (Slade and Watson 2006).

Psychometric Findings

Because of the observed limitations associated with using diagnoses as units of analyses, the majority of our work on classification of anxiety and mood disorders has employed dimensional indicators of the DSM-IV disorder constructs (e.g., Brown 2007; Brown et al. 1998; Campbell et al. 2003). Specifically, the features of the various disorders are rated dimensionally by both clinicians and patients, and these indicators are subjected to various types of latent-structural analyses. This approach is not completely divorced from the DSM-IV diagnostic system; that is, the constructs defined by DSM-IV are used as the starting point for developing the dimensional indicators used in the analyses. However, the advantages of this approach include the ability to better capture individual differences in disorder severity (compared with a binary indicator reflecting the presence/absence of disorder), as well as the true extent of diagnostic construct overlap because assessments are not based on categorical classification and DSM diagnostic decision rules (e.g., a better estimate of the overlap between GAD and MDD can be obtained because diagnostic hierarchy rules are not used in the dimensional ratings).

In one study in which this approach was used, Brown et al. (1998) conducted a confirmatory factor analysis of selected DSM-IV anxiety and mood disorder constructs (i.e., GAD, OCD, PDA, social phobia, and unipolar depression, or depression) in a sample of 350 patients assessed cross-sectionally with a variety of clinical and self-report dimensional ratings. Acceptable confirmatory factor analysis model fit was obtained for a solution that treated the five DSM-IV disorders as distinct constructs (notably, model fit was degraded when GAD and depression were collapsed into a single latent construct). Although no evidence of insufficient discriminant validity was obtained, factor correlations from the final confirmatory factor analysis model indicated that GAD's strongest relationship was with depression ($r=0.63$). Nonetheless, the covariance among all disorders was considerable, and the GAD factor was strongly related to other disorder constructs in addition to depression (e.g., factor correlations with OCD and PDA were 0.52 and 0.50, respectively).

In addition, Brown et al. (1998) tested models that involved the structural relations of the DSM-IV anxiety and mood disorder constructs and dimensions of the hierarchical model of anxiety and depression (i.e., negative affect, positive affect, autonomic arousal; Mineka et al. 1998). Of note, virtually all the considerable covariance of the DSM-IV disorder constructs was explained by the higher-order dimensions of negative affect and positive affect. Negative affect evidenced significant paths to all of the disorder constructs but had its strongest relationships with GAD and depression ($\gamma=0.74$ and 0.67, respectively), as well as PDA ($\gamma=0.65$). In accord with a reformulated hierarchical model of anxiety and depression (Mineka et al. 1998), positive affect had significant direct effects on depression and social phobia only ($\gamma=-0.29$ and -0.28, respectively), a result that was recently replicated in Brown (2007). Recent comorbidity and structural genetic findings have also revealed a differential relationship between mood disorders and social phobia, a relationship that could be seen as consistent with the existence of a temperamental vulnerability dimension specific to these two disorders (e.g., Brown et al. 2001a). Importantly, GAD has not shown these relations to positive affect; that is, low positive affect that is composed, in part, of low self-confidence/poor self-esteem (in addition to anhedonia) seems to be germane to depression and social phobia but not GAD.

Results of the structural models reported in Brown et al. (1998) indicate that the dimension of autonomic arousal was positively related to PDA only ($\gamma=0.67$).

The DSM-IV constructs of OCD and social phobia had no unique relation to autonomic arousal ($\gamma=0.02$ and -0.02, respectively), a finding that runs counter to proposals, based on factor analyses of binary classifications in epidemiological samples, to subclassify OCD and social phobia as "fear disorders" (e.g., Slade and Watson 2006; Watson 2005). Whereas depression evidenced no relationship with autonomic arousal, GAD was found to be inversely related to autonomic arousal; that is, when negative affect was held constant, an increase in GAD was associated with a decrease in autonomic arousal. In addition to representing another point of distinction between GAD and depression, this finding is in accord with laboratory studies that have shown that the process of worry leads to a suppression of autonomic arousal (e.g., Borkovec et al. 1993).

Recently, Brown (2007) extended these findings through a longitudinal study of 606 patients assessed with a broader range of dimensional indicators of DSM-IV disorder constructs and temperament (i.e., neuroticism/behavioral inhibition [N/BI]; behavioral activation/positive affect [BA/P]) than was observed in previous studies. In addition to replicating key findings from Brown et al. (1998)—for example, that N/BI and BA/P accounted for the cross-sectional covariance of the DSM-IV constructs and that BA/P was related to depression and social phobia but not GAD—this more-recent study examined the temporal covariation and directional relations among selected DSM-IV disorder constructs and temperament. Dimensional indicators were collected on three occasions during a 2-year interval. These data were subjected to parallel-process latent-growth models in which latent variables of the temperament and DSM-IV disorder constructs served as outcomes. Regressive paths and covariances among the growth factors (i.e., intercepts, slopes) in the parallel-process models provided estimates of the directional effects and temporal covariation of the various constructs. In one such model, it was found that the temporal covariation of depression and GAD over the 2-year period was not extreme ($r=0.30$); in fact, depression change was more strongly related to change in social phobia ($r=0.54$). Whereas the initial (i.e., Time 1) level of N/BI was strongly related to the initial levels of both depression ($r=0.77$) and GAD ($r=0.70$), initial N/BI predicted less temporal improvement in GAD (and social phobia) but was not predictive of change in depression. Finally, all the temporal covariance of the DSM-IV disorder constructs was accounted for by change in N/BI; that is, when N/BI was specified as a predictor, the temporal overlap among disorder constructs was reduced to zero.

Conclusion and Recommendations

Along with evidence from other lines of inquiry (e.g., epidemiological and biological studies), our clinical findings could be taken as indicating that the mood disorders are more closely related to GAD than are the anxiety disorders. Boundary issues remain at the DSM-IV diagnostic level—for example, high GAD/mood disorder comorbidity; the differential diagnosis of GAD and mood disorders is a common source of diagnostic unreliability. However, the results of these studies underscore several salient points of distinction at the psychometric level: GAD and depression possess differential relations with positive affect and autonomic arousability; the cross-sectional overlap of GAD and depression is not excessive; and the temporal covariation of these constructs is modest. Such findings lend support to retention of GAD and the mood disorders as separate diagnostic entities in DSM-V.

Nonetheless, some researchers have called for a reorganization of the emotional disorders in DSM-V to enhance recognition of the close relationships between GAD and the mood disorders. However, at this time, evidence does not support any current proposals for reorganization of the anxiety and mood disorders. As noted earlier, one such psychometrically based proposal (Watson 2005) subclassified GAD, unipolar mood disorders, and posttraumatic stress disorder as "distress disorders," and PDA, OCD, social phobia, and specific phobia as "fear disorders." Although this rearrangement would place GAD closer to the mood disorders, it obfuscates several important relationships—for example, it disassociates GAD from closely related anxiety disorders, such as OCD; fails to acknowledge the close relationship of PDA and posttraumatic stress disorder in regard to high autonomic arousability; and does not acknowledge the unique relationship of mood disorders and social phobia with low positive affect/behavioral activation (Brown 2007; Brown et al. 1997, 1998, 2001a, 2001b). Moreover, the so-called fear disorders would be misclassified in view of clinical evidence that, of these four conditions, only PDA is characterized by high autonomic arousal (Brown et al. 1997, 1998). An alternative proposal is to simply collapse all the anxiety and mood disorders into a single chapter in DSM-V without subclassification. Although perhaps more valid than the first proposal, this reorganization scheme also is not without its tensions (e.g., specific phobia and bipolar disorder would reside in the same chapter). In addition, although it recognizes the relationships that some anxiety disorders have with the mood disorders, this rearrangement would ignore the fact that some associations with somatoform disorders are just as salient (e.g., GAD and OCD with hypochondriasis; social phobia, OCD, and unipolar depression with body dysmorphic disorder).

Developers of DSM-V will grapple also with the prospect of incorporating dimensional elements into the classification system. Although the utility of dimensional classification has been recognized for more than three decades (e.g., Kendell 1975), no strong proposals have emerged with regard to how dimensional classification could be accomplished in DSM. Elsewhere (Brown and Barlow 2005), we have suggested that movement toward this goal could begin with basic research systems whereby dimensional ratings of severity are introduced to the extant DSM diagnostic categories and constituent symptom criteria—akin to the methods in the ADIS-IV-L (Brown 2007; Brown et al. 1998). This seems to be a relatively practical alternative because, if ultimately adopted into clinical practice, the categorical system would remain intact and the dimensional rating system could be optional in settings where its implementation is less feasible (e.g., primary care). Although not directly addressing the problem of high comorbidity, this strategy would address some of the chief complaints with DSM-IV, such as the poor reliability of categorical disorder specifiers—for example, mild, moderate, and severe MDD (Brown et al. 2001b)—and the failure to capture individual differences in disorder severity as well as other clinically significant features that are either subsumed by other disorders (e.g., GAD in mood disorders and posttraumatic stress disorder) or fall just below conventional thresholds due to a DSM technicality (e.g., subclinical or not otherwise specified diagnoses where the clinical presentation is a symptom or two short of a formal disorder). Because dimensional ratings would simply be added to the current diagnostic categories, this approach would have several other advantages, including 1) its basis on a preexisting and widely studied set of constructs (American Psychiatric Association 1994) and 2) the ability to retain functional analytic and temporal (duration) aspects of diagnosis that are difficult to capture in a purely psychometric approach. Moreover, it would provide a standardized assessment system that fosters across-site comparability in the study of dimensional models of psychopathology. Thus, this approach might be a prudent "first step" that would assist in determining the reliability and feasibility of more-ambitious dimensional systems (e.g., quantifying higher-order dimensions that convey disorder risk or prognosis).

References

American Psychiatric Association: Diagnostic and Statistical Manual of Mental Disorders, 3rd Edition Revised. Washington, DC, American Psychiatric Association, 1987

American Psychiatric Association: Diagnostic and Statistical Manual of Mental Disorders, 4th Edition. Washington, DC, American Psychiatric Association, 1994

Borkovec TD, Lyonfields JD, Wiser SL, et al: The role of worrisome thinking in the suppression of cardiovascular response to phobic imagery. Behav Res Ther 31:321–324, 1993

Brown TA: Temporal course and structural relationships among dimensions of temperament and DSM-IV anxiety and mood disorder constructs. J Abnorm Psychol 116:313–328, 2007

Brown TA, Barlow DH: Categorical versus dimensional classification of mental disorders in DSM-V and beyond. J Abnorm Psychol 114:551–556, 2005

Brown TA, Moras K, Zinbarg RE, et al: Diagnostic and symptom distinguishability of generalized anxiety disorder and obsessive-compulsive disorder. Behav Ther 24:227–240, 1993

Brown, TA, Barlow DH, Liebowitz MR: The empirical basis of generalized anxiety disorder. Am J Psychiatry 151:1272–1280, 1994

Brown TA, Chorpita BF, Korotitsch W, et al: Psychometric properties of the Depression Anxiety Stress Scales (DASS) in clinical samples. Behav Res Ther 35:79–89, 1997

Brown TA, Chorpita BF, Barlow DH: Structural relationships among dimensions of the DSM-IV anxiety and mood disorders and dimensions of negative affect, positive affect, and autonomic arousal. J Abnorm Psychol 107:179–192, 1998

Brown TA, Campbell LA, Lehman CL, et al: Current and lifetime comorbidity of the DSM-IV anxiety and mood disorders in a large clinical sample. J Abnorm Psychol 110:585–599, 2001a

Brown TA, Di Nardo PA, Lehman CL, et al: Reliability of DSM-IV anxiety and mood disorders: implications for the classification of emotional disorders. J Abnorm Psychol 110:49–58, 2001b

Campbell LA, Brown TA, Grisham JR: The relevance of age of onset to the psychopathology of generalized anxiety disorder. Behav Ther 34:31–48, 2003

Di Nardo PA, Moras K, Barlow DH, et al: Reliability of DSM-III-R anxiety disorder categories using the Anxiety Disorders Interview Schedule-Revised (ADIS-R). Arch Gen Psychiatry 50:251–256, 1993

Kendell RE: The Role of Diagnosis in Psychiatry. Oxford, Blackwell Scientific, 1975

Kendler KS, Neale MC, Kessler RC, et al: Major depression and generalized anxiety disorder: same genes, (partly) different environments? Arch Gen Psychiatry 49:716–722, 1992

Krueger RF: The structure of common mental disorders. Arch Gen Psychiatry 56:921–926, 1999

Mineka S, Watson D, Clark LA: Comorbidity of anxiety and unipolar mood disorders. Annu Rev Psychol 49:377–412, 1998

Slade T, Watson D: The structure of common DSM-IV and ICD-10 mental disorders in the Australian general population. Psychol Med 36:1593–1600, 2006

Watson D: Rethinking the mood and anxiety disorders: a quantitative hierarchical model for DSM-V. J Abnorm Psychol 114:522–536, 2005

7

MAJOR DEPRESSION AND GENERALIZED ANXIETY DISORDER IN THE NATIONAL COMORBIDITY SURVEY FOLLOW-UP SURVEY

Ronald C. Kessler, Ph.D.
Michael Gruber, M.S.
John M. Hettema, M.D., Ph.D.
Irving Hwang, M.A.
Nancy Sampson, B.A.
Kimberly A. Yonkers, M.D.

The American Psychiatric Association first introduced the diagnosis of generalized anxiety disorder (GAD) into DSM more than two decades ago, in DSM-III (American Psychiatric Association 1980). Prior to that time, GAD was conceptu-

---

Excerpts from "Co-Morbid Major Depression and Generalized Anxiety Disorders in the National Comorbidity Survey Follow-up" by R.C. Kessler, M. Gruber, J.M. Hettema, I. Hwang, N. Sampson, and K.A. Yonkers in *Psychological Medicine*, Volume 38, Issue 03, March 2008, pp 365–374.

Copyright © Cambridge University Press 2008. Reprinted with permission.

alized as one of the two core components of anxiety neurosis, with panic as the other component (American Psychiatric Association 1968). Recognition that GAD and panic, although they often occur together, are sufficiently distinct to be considered independent disorders led to their separation in DSM-III. In DSM-III, GAD was defined as uncontrollable and diffuse (i.e., not focused on a single major life problem) anxiety or worry that was excessive or unrealistic in relation to objective life circumstances and persisted for 1 month or longer. A number of related psychophysiological symptoms were also required to occur with the anxiety or worry.

Early clinical studies that evaluated DSM-III GAD, according to this definition, in clinical samples found that GAD seldom occurred in the absence of some other comorbid anxiety or mood disorder. Comorbidity between GAD and major depression was especially strong (Breslau 1985; Breslau and Davis 1985a), leading some commentators to suggest that GAD might better be conceptualized as a prodrome, residual, or severity marker of major depression than as an independent disorder (Brown et al. 1998; Cloninger et al. 1990; Offord et al. 1994). However, in these clinical studies, the comorbidity of GAD with other disorders was observed to decrease as the duration of GAD increased (Breslau and Davis 1985b). Based on this finding, the DSM-III-R committee on GAD recommended that the duration requirement for the disorder be increased to 6 months. This change was implemented in the final version of DSM-III-R (American Psychiatric Association 1987). Further changes in the definition of excessive worry and the required number of associated psychophysiological symptoms were made in DSM-IV (American Psychiatric Association 1994).

The issue of strong comorbidity of GAD with major depression was not resolved with these diagnostic changes. Indeed, a number of community epidemiological studies that used DSM-III-R and DSM-IV criteria found strong evidence of comorbidity between GAD and major depression (Grant et al. 2005; Kessler et al. 1996, 2005b). Attempts to explore the factor structure of comorbidity among Axis I led to the conclusion that GAD and major depression are both strongly related to a general "distress" factor (Krueger 1999; Krueger et al. 1998; Vollebergh et al. 2001) that also includes dysthymia, posttraumatic stress disorder (PTSD), social phobia, and, in at least one analysis (Slade and Watson 2006), neurasthenia. At the same time, longitudinal analyses show meaningful divergence between GAD and major depression both in risk factors (Moffitt et al. 2007) and in illness course (Fergusson et al. 2006).

The prospective evidence of somewhat different environmental risk factors for GAD and major depression is consistent with results of genetic epidemiological studies, which suggest that although the genes for GAD and major depression are very similar or possibly even identical, the environmental determinants of the two disorders are less strongly related (Kendler 1996; Kendler et al. 1992, 2007; Roy et al. 1995). Taken together with the prospective evidence for differential risk factors, these data suggest that, despite strong similarities that might lead them to be placed in the same diagnostic category in the upcoming revisions of the DSM and ICD systems (Watson 2005), GAD and major depression are distinct disorders. However, the body of prospective risk-factor evidence on which this conclusion is based is thin. This chapter adds to this body of evidence by presenting prospective data on patterns and risk factors for onset and persistence of GAD and major depression, based on a nationally representative two-wave panel survey of the household population of the United States.

Methods

SAMPLE

Data considered here are from the National Comorbidity Survey (NCS; Kessler et al. 1994) and the NCS follow-up survey (NCS-2; Kessler et al. 2003). The baseline NCS was a nationally representative survey of 8,098 respondents, ages 15–54 years, carried out between September 1990 and February 1992. Respondents were selected from a stratified, multistage area probability sample of households in the United States, as well as from a supplemental sample of students living in campus housing. The response rate was 82.4%. Interviews were conducted by professional survey interviewers and were administered in two parts. Part I, which included the core diagnostic interview, was administered to all NCS respondents. Part II, which included additional disorders and risk factors, was administered to a probability subsample of 5,877 respondents, including all respondents ages 15–24, all others with any lifetime DSM-III-R disorder assessed in Part I, and a random subsample of remaining Part I respondents. The Part II sample was weighted to adjust for differential probabilities of selection and for nonresponse bias. Further details about the NCS design are reported elsewhere (Kessler et al. 1994).

The NCS-2 sought to trace and re-interview the Part II NCS respondents a decade after their baseline interview. Of the original 5,877 respondents, 5,463 were successfully traced, of whom 166 were deceased. A total of 5,001 respondents were re-interviewed from the remaining 5,297, yielding a conditional response rate of 87.6%. The unconditional response rate, which takes into account the baseline NCS response rate of 82.4%, was 72.2% (0.876×0.824). NCS-2 respondents were assessed using an expanded version of the baseline NCS interview that asked about the onset, course, and severity of mental disorders during the years between the two surveys. Relative to other baseline NCS respondents, NCS-2 respondents were significantly more likely to be female, well educated, and residents of rural areas. A propensity score adjustment weight (Rosenbaum and Rubin 1983) was used to correct the NCS-2 sample for these discrepancies. Importantly, there was no difference between NCS-2 respondents and nonrespondents in their reports of baseline history of either major depressive episode (MDE) ($\chi^2_1 = 0.8$, $P = 0.39$) or GAD ($\chi^2_1 = 2.1$, $P = 0.16$).

DIAGNOSTIC ASSESSMENT

Lifetime DSM-III-R disorders were assessed in the baseline NCS with a modified version of the World Health Organization Composite International Diagnostic Interview (CIDI), Version 1.1 (Robins et al. 1988), a fully structured, lay-administered diagnostic interview. DSM-IV disorders that had first onsets in the decade between the two interviews were assessed in the NCS-2 by means of the CIDI Version 3.0 (Kessler and Ustun 2004). DSM organic exclusion rules were used in making diagnoses in both surveys. The NCS-2 assessment also considered first onsets of DSM-IV disorders, prior to the time of the baseline interview, that were not reported at baseline, as well as persistence of baseline disorders in the decade between the two interviews. Persistence was evaluated with a CIDI assessment of interval prevalence and charted with a life-history calendar for each year in the decade between the two interviews (Belli 1998). The life-history calendar method of retrospectively reconstructing event histories has been shown experimentally to produce significantly more accurate retrospective recall than more conventional survey methods (Belli et al. 2001).

Blind clinical re-interviews of a probability subsample of respondents were used in both surveys to assess the concordance of CIDI diagnoses with clinical diagnoses. The Structured Clinical Interview for DSM-III-R (Spitzer et al. 1992) was used to make the clinical diagnoses in the baseline NCS, whereas the Structured Clinical Interview for DSM-IV (First et al. 2002) was used in the NCS-2.

Good concordance between CIDI diagnoses and clinical diagnoses was found for MDE and for GAD in both surveys. In the NCS, the concordance of CIDI diagnoses with clinical diagnoses at the individual level, defined in terms of area under the receiver operating characteristic (ROC) curve, a measure that, unlike the more conventional kappa statistic, is not influenced by prevalence (Kessler et al. 2004), was 0.78 for MDE and 0.71 for GAD (Kessler et al. 1998). Aggregate comparisons found no significant difference in CIDI versus Standard Clinical Interview for DSM lifetime-prevalence estimates for either disorder in the NCS (McNemar $\chi^2_1 = 0.0$, $P = 0.94$ for MDE; $\chi^2_1 = 1.7$, $P = 0.20$ for GAD). In the NCS-2, the area under the ROC curve of the CIDI, in relation to clinical diagnoses, was 0.75 for MDE and 0.83 for GAD. Aggregate comparisons found that the CIDI prevalence estimate was significantly lower than the clinical estimate for MDE (McNemar $\chi^2_1 = 8.1$, $P = 0.004$) but did not differ significantly from the clinical estimate for GAD (McNemar $\chi^2_1 = 1.7$, $P = 0.19$) (Haro et al. 2006).

PROSPECTIVE RISK FACTORS

We considered three sets of risk factors: childhood adversities, parent history of common mental and substance disorders, and respondent personality. The childhood adversities included three dimensions of maltreatment (neglect, physical abuse, sexual abuse) and three dimensions of loss (parental death, parental divorce, any other long-term separation from a parent). The parent disorders included MDE, GAD, panic disorder, antisocial personality disorder, and alcohol-drug dependence. The personality dimensions included neuroticism, extroversion, and openness to experience.

Neglect was assessed both at baseline and again in the NCS-2. At baseline, respondents were asked a single yes/no question: "Were you seriously neglected as a child?" The NCS-2 used a more detailed assessment based on a five-question index that asked about the frequency (often, sometimes, rarely, or never) with which parents or caregivers made the respondent, as a child, do chores that were too difficult or dangerous for someone their age; left the respondent home alone or unsupervised when they were too young to be alone; failed to provide the respondent with things they needed (e.g., clothes, shoes, school supplies) because the caregivers wasted the family's money; failed to feed or prepare meals for the respondent; and ignored or failed to provide medical attention when the respondent was sick or injured. Cronbach's α, a measure of internal consistency reliability (Cronbach 1951), was 0.77 for the neglect scale made by summing each of these items with equal weight. Neglect was defined dichotomously, for purposes of the current review, either as a report at baseline of being seriously neglected as a child or a report in the second interview of at least two of the five experiences having happened either "often" or "sometimes."

Physical abuse was assessed by a question that asked respondents if they were ever physically abused as a child, as well as by a modified version of the Parent-Child Conflict Tactics Scales (Straus et al. 1998) that assessed frequency (often, sometimes, rarely, or never) of several types of major physical violence (kick, bite, or hit with a fist; hit or try to hit with an object; beat up; choke; purposefully burn or scald) perpetrated by parents and caregivers when the respondent was a child (Cronbach's $\alpha = 0.51$). Physical abuse was defined dichotomously, for purposes of the current report, as either reporting self-defined abuse or experiencing major physical violence "often."

Sexual abuse was defined dichotomously as repeatedly either being raped or sexually assaulted by a relative or step-relative, as a child. Rape was defined as "someone either having sexual intercourse with you or penetrating your body with a finger or object when you did not want them to, either by threatening you or using force, or when you were so young that you didn't know what was happening." Sexual assault was defined as "someone touching you inappropriately when you did not want them to." No distinction was made between rape and sexual assault in the analysis, based on preliminary evidence that the effects of the two different types of experience were very similar on the outcomes considered here.

Parental death and divorce were defined based on simple questions that asked respondents if either of their biological parents died or were divorced during the time the respondent was a child. Other long-term separation from a parent, the third measure of childhood loss, was defined based on the analysis of open-ended responses to a probe for clarification of a positive response to the question of whether the respondent lived with both his biological parents up through age 16. Some positive responses did not involve any actual loss, as when the respondent was adopted at birth and never knew his biological parents. Other positive responses did involve loss, as when a parent was imprisoned or had a long stay in a hospital or abandoned the family during the respondent's childhood, or when the respondent was taken out of the home by the juvenile justice or human services systems. Incidents involving separation were classified as instances of other long-term separation from a parent.

The baseline NCS evaluated parental history of MDE, GAD, antisocial personality disorder, and alcohol-drug dependence while the respondent was growing up, through use of the Family History Research Diagnostic Criteria (FHRDC; Endicott et al. 1978). The NCS-2 added a comparable assessment of parent panic disorder. Because no FHRDC criteria existed for GAD, we adopted the criteria developed for this purpose in the Virginia Twin Study (Kendler et al. 1992). The latter required a period of at least 1 month, not part of an obvious justified stress reaction, in which the parent was particularly tense, anxious, or worried and either received treatment or had at least three associated symptoms (from among those of being keyed up or on edge, irritable, restless, trouble falling asleep, and tiring easily).

The final set of risk factors involved respondent personality. Personality was assessed in the baseline NCS through a modified version of the Goldberg (1992) personality scales. Three dimensions of personality were assessed: neuroticism, extroversion, and openness to experience. Cronbach's α was 0.88 for neuroticism, 0.80 for extroversion, and 0.83 for openness to experience. All of these dimensions have consistently been documented, in personality research, to be core dimensions of personality (Goldberg 1990) that exhibit considerable stability over the adult years of life (Caspi et al. 2005). Neuroticism, in particular, also has been found to correlate with MDE and GAD (Hettema et al. 2006; Kendler et al. 1993). Extroversion has been found to correlate with depression, although less strongly than neuroticism (Enns and Cox 1997). Although there has been less research on the effects of openness to experience, at least one study found a Minnesota Multiphasic Personality Inventory personality style of high suppression—linked conceptually to low openness to experience—among combat veterans with comorbid anxiety and mood disorders (Engdahl et al. 1991).

STATISTICAL ANALYSES

Cross-tabulations were used to estimate lifetime prevalence and persistence of MDE and GAD. Discrete-time-survival analysis with person-year as the unit of analysis (Efron 1988) was used to study the prospective predictors of first onset and persistence of MDE and GAD. In addition to studying the risk factors described earlier in the models for onset and persistence of GAD, prior lifetime history of MDE was included as a time-varying predictor. MDE was "time-varying" in the sense that we took into consideration retrospectively reported information about age at onset of MDE in predicting later GAD. Parallel models were estimated to study the associations of risk factors, which included temporally primary GAD with the subsequent onset and persistence of MDE. Standard errors and confidence intervals were estimated in these equations using the Taylor series method (Wolter 1985) implemented in the SUDAAN software system (Research Triangle Institute 2002) to adjust for design effects. Multivariate significance was evaluated using Wald χ^2 tests based on design-corrected coefficient variance-covariance matrices. Statistical significance was evaluated consistently using two-tailed 0.05-level tests.

Results

PREVALENCE, AGE AT ONSET, AND PERSISTENCE

At the time of the baseline NCS, 21.2% of NCS-2 respondents met lifetime criteria for DSM-III-R MDE (Table 7–1). Some 9.6% of respondents, who had never experienced MDE as of baseline, had a first onset of DSM-IV MDE over the next decade, resulting in 28.8% of NCS-2 respondents possessing a lifetime history of MDE as of the second interview.

TABLE 7–1. Lifetime prevalence of major depressive episode (MDE) and generalized anxiety disorder (GAD) in the NCS-2 panel sample ($N=5,001$)

	MDE, % (SE)	GAD, % (SE)
Lifetime prevalence as of baseline	21.2 (0.8)	8.6 (0.5)
First onset by NCS-2[a]	9.6 (0.8)	3.6 (0.4)
Lifetime prevalence as of NCS-2	28.8 (0.9)	11.9 (0.6)

Note. NCS=National Comorbidity Survey.
[a]Among respondents without a baseline lifetime history of the disorder.

GAD is much less prevalent than MDE. As of the baseline NCS, 8.6% of NCS-2 respondents met lifetime criteria for DSM-III-R GAD (Table 7–1). Of baseline respondents who had never experienced GAD prior to this time, 3.6% had a first onset of DSM-IV GAD over the next decade, resulting in 11.9% of NCS-2 respondents with a lifetime history of GAD as of the second interview.

The age-of-onset distributions of MDE and GAD are very similar (Figure 7–1). Median age at onset in the NCS-2 sample was in the early 30s for both disorders (32 for MDE and 34 for GAD), with an interquartile range (25th–75th percentiles) of 21–44 for MDE and 22–42 for GAD. It should be noted that these medians are considerably later and the interquartile ranges considerably wider than for most anxiety disorders, impulse-control disorders, and substance-use disorders (Kessler et al. 2005a). These results, coupled with the fact that MDE and GAD are both highly comorbid, means that both these disorders are often temporally secondary to earlier-onset disorders (typically anxiety, impulse-control, or substance disorders) and that the age at onset of MDE and GAD often occurs a number of years after the onset of other temporally primary disorders.

COMORBIDITY OF MAJOR DEPRESSIVE EPISODE AND GENERALIZED ANXIETY DISORDER

A convenient way to examine MDE-GAD comorbidity, in a preliminary way, is to focus on the cross-classification of the three-category variables for whether the respondent 1) met lifetime criteria for MDE at baseline; 2) had a first onset of MDE between baseline and the NCS-2; or 3) never met lifetime criteria for MDE, as of the NCS-2, with the comparable three-category variable for GAD. As it turns out, the four degrees of freedom in this 3×3 table can be decomposed into four orthogonal 2×2 subtables, as follows: the baseline association between lifetime history of MDE and GAD (M1-G1); the prospective association between a baseline history of MDE and the subsequent first onset of GAD (M1-G2); the prospective association between a baseline history of GAD and the subsequent first onset of MDE (G1-M2); and the prospective association between subsequent onset of MDE and subsequent onset of GAD among respondents with no history of either disorder at baseline (M2-G2). The sum of the likelihood-ratio χ^2 values for these four 2×2 subtables is equal to the four-degree-of-freedom χ^2 test in the 3×3 table from which the four subtables can be derived.

Focusing first on M1-G1, 24.8% of respondents with a baseline history of MDE also had a baseline history of GAD, compared with 4.2% of respondents without a baseline history of MDE (Table 7–2). Thinking reciprocally, 61.3% of respondents with a baseline history of GAD also had a baseline history of MDE, compared with 17.5% of respondents without baseline MDE. These elevated percentages are equivalent to a statistically significant odds ratio of 7.5, between baseline history of MDE and baseline history of GAD. Turning to M1-G2, among

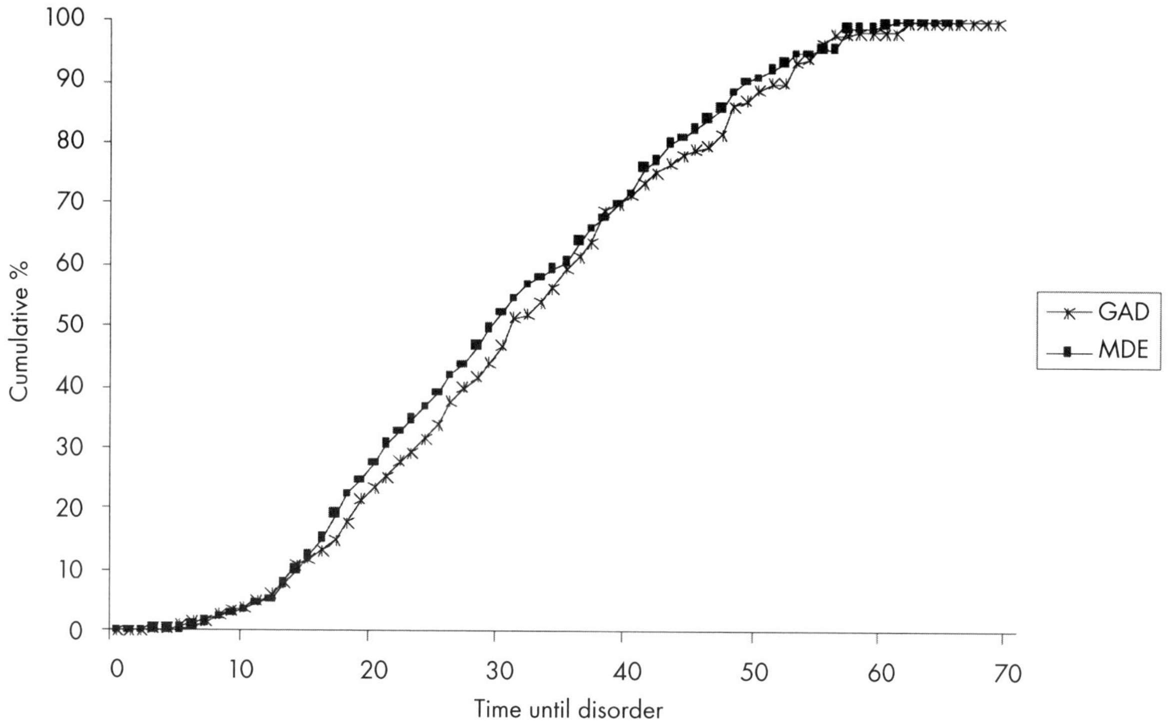

FIGURE 7-1. Age-at-onset distributions for major depressive episode (MDE) and generalized anxiety disorder (GAD) in the National Comorbidity Survey–2 panel sample (N=5,001). Median age at onset was 32 for MDE and 34 for GAD.

Time until disorder=age in years of respondent when disorder appeared.

respondents without a baseline history of GAD, the percentage who subsequently developed GAD was significantly higher among those with (6.7%), than those without (3.0%), a baseline history of MDE; this resulted in a statistically significant odds ratio of 2.3 between baseline MDE and the subsequent onset of GAD. In a similar way, among respondents without a baseline history of MDE, the percentage who subsequently developed MDE was significantly higher among those with (24.7%), than those without (8.9%), a baseline history of GAD, which resulted in a statistically significant odds ratio of 3.4 between baseline GAD and the subsequent onset of MDE. Finally, among respondents without a baseline history of either MDE or GAD, the proportion that subsequently developed GAD was significantly higher among those who also developed MDE (12.3%) than those who did not (2.1%). Thinking reciprocally, the proportion that subsequently developed MDE was significantly higher among those who also developed GAD (36.6%) than those who did not (8.0%). The resulting odds ratio between subsequent development of MDE and GAD was 6.6.

It is noteworthy that the MDE-GAD odds ratios, which involved associations without a temporal priority between the disorders (i.e., M1-G1 and M2-G2), are higher than those that involved a temporal priority (i.e., M1-G2 and G2-M1). This same pattern holds when we examine the associations separately within cohorts of respondents who were in adolescence (15–24 years of age), early adulthood (25–39), or middle age (40–54) at baseline (Table 7–3). All but two of the odds ratios in this disaggregated table are statistically significant. Odd ratios did not change significantly with increasing age, with the exception of one (M1-G2 middle 40+ cohort). In all cases, the cross-sectional M1-G1 and M2-G2 odds ratios are larger than the time-lagged M1-G2 and G1-M2 odds ratios. This last pattern is not surprising, because the cross-sectional odds ratios represent the accumulation of cross-lagged associations over the entire life course, up to the time of the survey, whereas the time-lagged associations represent only one-way associations over only a single decade.

TIME-LAGGED ASSOCIATIONS PREDICTING FIRST ONSET OF MAJOR DEPRESSIVE EPISODE AND GENERALIZED ANXIETY DISORDER

A more comprehensive way to examine time-lagged association is to use respondent reports about age at onset to carry out survival analyses, in which each of the two disorders is treated as a time-varying covariate that predicts the first onset of the other disorder. When that is done, the time-lagged odds ratio of temporally primary MDE predicting the subsequent onset of GAD is 2.7, whereas the time-lagged odds ratio of temporally primary GAD predicting the subsequent onset of MDE is 3.2 (see Table 7–4). Both of these associations are somewhat stronger among

TABLE 7–2. Decomposition of the association between major depressive episode (MDE) and generalized anxiety disorder (GAD) in the NCS-2 panel sample (N=5,001)

	Conditional prevalence								
	GAD among respondents				MDE among respondents				
	With MDE		Without MDE		With GAD		Without GAD		
Association	% (SE)	N	% (SE)	N	% (SE)	N	% (SE)	N	OR (95% CI)
M1-G1	24.8 (1.4)	1,442	4.2 (0.5)	3,559	61.3 (3.6)	531	17.5 (0.7)	4,470	7.5*(5.5–10.3)
M1-G2	6.7 (0.8)	1,103	3.0 (0.4)	3,367	—	—	—	—	2.3* (1.6–3.4)
G1-M2	—	—	—	—	24.7 (5.6)	192	8.9 (0.7)	3,367	3.4* (1.8–6.1)
M2-G2	12.3 (2.8)	311	2.1 (0.4)	3,056	36.6 (7.1)	116	8.0 (0.8)	3,251	6.6*(3.3–13.3)

Note. G1-M2=prospective association between baseline history of GAD and subsequent first onset of MDE; M1-G1=baseline association between lifetime history of MDE and GAD; M1-G2=prospective association between baseline history of MDE and subsequent first onset of GAD; M2-G2=subsequent onset of GAD among respondents with no history of either disorder at baseline; NCS=National Comorbidity Survey.
*Significant at the 0.05 level, two-sided test.

TABLE 7–3. Decomposition of major depressive episode (MDE)–generalized anxiety disorder (GAD) comorbidity in NCS-2 panel sample by cohort

	Cohort by age (y) at baseline		
	15–24 ($n=1,489$[a])	25–39 ($n=2,208$[a])	40–54 ($n=1,304$[a])
Association	OR (95% CI)	OR (95% CI)	OR (95% CI)
M1-G1	8.4* (4.5–15.7)	6.5* (4.4–9.9)	8.7* (5.2–14.4)
M1-G2	2.5* (1.4–4.6)	2.5* (1.5–4.2)	1.5 (0.5–4.2)
G1-M2	3.2 (0.9–11.9)	3.4* (1.6–7.5)	3.9* (1.2–13.0)
M2-G2	5.5* (2.3–12.9)	7.2* (2.7–19.0)	4.6* (1.3–17.0)

Note. G1-M2=prospective association between baseline history of GAD and subsequent first onset of MDE; M1-G1=baseline association between lifetime history of MDE and GAD; M1-G2=prospective association between baseline history of MDE and subsequent first onset of GAD; M2-G2=subsequent onset of GAD among respondents with no history of either disorder at baseline; NCS=National Comorbidity Survey.
[a]Unweighted sample size.
*Significant at 0.05 level, two-sided test.

respondents who were adolescents (15–24 years of age) than adults (25–54 years of age) at baseline (3.7 vs. 1.7–2.4 for MDE predicting GAD; 3.6 vs. 3.0–3.1 for GAD predicting MDE).

The time-lagged odds ratios varied dramatically as a function of time since onset of the temporally primary disorder. Focusing first on temporally primary MDE predicting subsequent GAD in the total sample, the odds ratio for MDE was 7.9 in the first 2 years after first onset of MDE, 4.7 in the next 3 years, 2.8 in the next 5 years, and 3.5 thereafter. In other words, risk of first onset of GAD was much more highly elevated in the first 2 years after the first onset of temporally primary MDE than in later years, with magnitude of this elevated risk decreasing over time. It is noteworthy that the elevated odds remained significant more than a decade after first onset of MDE. Furthermore, although all these odds ratios were somewhat more pronounced among respondents in the youngest cohorts, the generally positive and statistically significant pattern can be seen even in the oldest cohorts. Strikingly, the odds ratio associated with GAD occurring in the very same year as MDE was much higher than any of the time-lagged odds ratios (54.4 in the total sample; 40.7–51.9 in cohorts). We were unable, however, to distinguish temporal priority between MDE and GAD within a year in the NCS-2 data, so we have no way of knowing if these same-year onsets involved MDE that started before, after, or at the same time as GAD.

TABLE 7-4. Time-lagged associations between major depressive episode (MDE) and generalized anxiety disorder (GAD), involving one temporally primary disorder predicting the subsequent first onset of the other disorder, as a function of time since onset of the primary disorder and cohort in the NCS-2 panel sample (N=5,001)

Association	Total sample, OR (95% CI)	Cohort by age (y) at baseline, OR (95% CI)		
		15–24	25–39	40–54
Temporally primary MDE predicting subsequent GAD				
Total	2.7* (2.1–3.5)	3.7* (2.6–5.2)	2.4* (1.6–3.7)	1.7* (1.0–2.9)
0 years since MDE onset	54.4* (37.3–79.3)	51.9* (36.1–74.5)	50.0* (28.7–87.3)	40.7* (12.1–137.4)
1–2 years since MDE onset	7.9* (4.7–13.3)	9.3* (5.5–15.8)	5.7* (2.1–15.7)	4.7* (2.0–10.8)
3–5 years since MDE onset	4.7* (3.3–6.5)	6.6* (3.7–11.5)	2.5* (1.2–5.1)	2.4 (0.8–7.1)
6–10 years since MDE onset	2.8* (1.8–4.3)	4.0* (1.9–8.4)	2.3* (1.3–3.9)	0.2 (0.0–1.2)
11+ years since MDE onset	3.5* (2.4–5.0)	2.8* (1.0–8.0)	4.1* (2.5–6.5)	2.5* (1.3–4.8)
Temporally primary GAD predicting subsequent MDE				
Total	3.2* (2.3–4.3)	3.6* (2.2–6.0)	3.0* (2.0–4.6)	3.1* (1.7–5.6)
0 years since GAD onset	54.1* (37.0–79.1)	51.9* (35.9–74.9)	49.0* (27.9–86.1)	42.2* (12.0–148.1)
1–2 years since GAD onset	8.9* (5.5–14.4)	7.5* (3.5–16.2)	5.2* (2.2–12.5)	23.0* (7.7–68.7)
3–5 years since GAD onset	3.9* (2.4–6.4)	4.3* (2.2–8.2)	4.2* (1.9–9.6)	0.4 (0.1–2.2)
6–10 years since GAD onset	2.0* (1.2–3.3)	3.1* (1.2–8.3)	1.8* (1.0–3.4)	0.6 (0.1–3.3)
11+ years since GAD onset	2.8* (1.9–4.2)	1.6 (0.4–6.3)	3.4* (2.0–5.6)	3.0* (1.4–6.7)

Note. Based on a discrete-time-survival model, with person-year as unit of analysis, controlling for cohort (age at interview); gender; race-ethnicity; and person-year. NCS=National Comorbidity Survey. *Significant at 0.05 level, two-sided test.

Source. Reprinted from Kessler RC, Gruber M, Hettema JM, et al.: "Co-Morbid Major Depression and Generalized Anxiety Disorders in the National Comorbidity Survey Follow-up." *Psychological Medicine*, 38:365–374, 2008. Used with permission.

A similar pattern can be seen in the associations of temporally primary GAD with subsequent MDE. In the total sample, the GAD odds ratio was 8.9 in the first 2 years after onset of GAD, 3.9 in the next 3 years, 2.0 in the next 5 years, and 2.8 thereafter. As with MDE predicting later GAD, the odds ratio of temporally primary GAD remained significant even in the longest time lag in the oldest cohorts. The very high odds ratios associated with MDE occurring in the very same year as GAD that were seen in the models for MDE predicting subsequent GAD appeared again, finally, in the models for GAD predicting subsequent MDE.

OTHER PROSPECTIVE RISK FACTORS FOR FIRST ONSET OF MAJOR DEPRESSIVE EPISODE AND GENERALIZED ANXIETY DISORDER

Measures of childhood adversity, parental history of mental and substance disorders, and personality dimensions were introduced into the same survival equations to predict first onset of MDE and GAD. We were interested in both assessing the effects of these predictors on outcomes and examining the extent to which controlling for them explained the effects of MDE on subsequent GAD and the effects of GAD on subsequent MDE.

When considered one at a time, the majority of the childhood adversities were associated with significantly elevated risk of GAD in the total sample, with odds ratios in the range 1.4–1.8 (Table 7–5). These effects were largely confined, however, to onsets that occurred in childhood or adolescence (prior to age 25). Risk of subsequent first onset among respondents who never had GAD prior to age 25 was only significantly related to one of the childhood adversities (neglect among respondents in the age range 40–54).

Parental history of MDE, GAD, substance disorder, and panic disorder all predicted elevated risk of GAD in the total sample, with odds ratios of 1.5–1.6. More detailed analyses showed little evidence of consistent variation in these odds ratios based on number of parents with the disorder; sex of the parent with the disorder, in cases where only one had it; or the match between sex of disordered parent and sex of respondent (R.C. Kessler, M. Gruber, J.M. Hettema, et al., unpublished data, March 2008; results available on request). As with childhood adversities, the effects of parental disorders were confined to onsets that occurred in childhood or adolescence, although it should be remembered that the assessment of parental disorders focused on disorders present when the respondent was a child. We have no way of knowing about the effects of later-onset parent disorders.

Neuroticism was the only dimension of personality that was significantly associated with elevated odds of GAD in the total sample. Because personality was assessed only in the baseline NCS, the associations of personality with onset of GAD were examined only in the person-years subsequent to the baseline interview. No attempt was made to examine the associations between personality and retrospectively reported first onsets of GAD that occurred prior to the baseline interview. We were nonetheless able to examine the extent to which this prospective association varied by life-course stage. Unlike childhood adversity, we found a significantly elevated odds ratio of neuroticism with subsequent GAD in early adulthood (25–39 years of age; OR=1.4). In addition, extroversion was associated with significantly reduced odds of GAD onset in early adulthood (OR=0.7) but not in the total sample or at the other parts of the life course examined here.

The associations of childhood adversity, parental history of mental and substance disorders, and personality dimensions with subsequent first onset of MDE were somewhat more complex than the association with first onset of GAD. As with GAD, the majority of the childhood adversities were associated with significantly elevated risk of MDE in the total sample, with odds ratios in the range 1.4–2.2 (Table 7–6). The significant adversities in the total sample were the same in predicting both outcomes, but the odds ratios were generally somewhat higher in predicting MDE than GAD. Furthermore, unlike the situation with GAD, where the significant odds ratios were largely confined to onsets in childhood and adolescence, childhood adversities predicted first onset of MDE into early adulthood (ages 25–39), although not into middle age (ages 40–64). Furthermore, in the baseline adolescent cohorts, parental death significantly predicted subsequent onset of MDE (1.6) but not GAD (0.8), illustrating clearly the fact that environmental experiences sometimes have differential effects on MDE and GAD.

Parent history of mental and substance disorders significantly predicted respondent MDE. The total-sample odds ratios were somewhat more consistent and larger in predicting MDE than GAD. All five parent disorders were associated with significantly elevated risk of MDE in the total sample with odds ratios of 1.7–2.1, as compared with only four of the five that predicted onset of GAD with odds ratios of 1.5–1.6. As with GAD, there was little evidence of variation in these odds in their prediction of MDE based on number of parents with the disorder; sex of the parent with the disorder, in cases where only one had it; or the match between sex of disordered parent and sex of respondent (results not presented, but available on request). Furthermore, unlike the situation with GAD, in which the effects of parental disorders were confined to onsets in childhood or adolescence, the odds ratios of parent disorders with respondent onset of MDE were also significant both in early adulthood (all but substance disorder) and middle age (all five parent disorders).

Extroversion was associated with significantly reduced odds of MDE onset in middle age (OR=0.7) and was associated with elevated odds of MDE in adolescence (1.3). Although the association between extroversion and MDE was significant in two of the cohorts, it was inconsistently correlated (positive during childhood or adolescence, negative in middle age). The odds ratios of neuroticism predicting the subsequent onset of MDE are similar in magnitude to those predicting onset of GAD but are not significant. Openness to experience, finally, was

TABLE 7–5. Time-lagged associations of childhood adversities, parental history of mental disorders, and respondent personality with subsequent first onset of generalized anxiety disorder in NCS-2 panel sample (*N*=5,001)

Prospective risk factor	Total sample, OR (95% CI)	Cohort by age (y) at baseline, OR (95% CI)		
		15–24	25–39	40–54
Childhood adversity				
Neglect	1.7* (1.3–2.0)	2.1* (1.5–3.1)	1.1 (0.6–1.7)	2.0* (1.0–3.7)
Physical abuse	1.8* (1.4–2.4)	2.2* (1.5–3.2)	1.4 (0.9–2.2)	2.0 (0.8–4.6)
Sexual abuse	1.6* (1.1–2.2)	1.5* (1.0–2.4)	1.5 (0.9–2.5)	2.0 (0.5–8.4)
Death of parent	1.1 (0.7–1.8)	0.8 (0.4–1.5)	1.6 (0.8–3.5)	0.6 (0.2–2.1)
Divorce of parents	1.4* (1.1–1.8)	1.7* (1.2–2.5)	1.1 (0.7–1.9)	0.9 (0.4–2.1)
Other long-term separation	1.3 (0.7–2.1)	1.3 (0.7–2.6)	0.9 (0.3–2.6)	2.7 (0.7–10.9)
Parental history of mental disorders				
Major depressive episode	1.5* (1.2–2.0)	1.5* (1.1–2.2)	1.4 (0.9–2.3)	1.7 (0.9–3.4)
Generalized anxiety disorder	1.6* (1.2–2.1)	1.9* (1.4–2.7)	1.3 (0.8–2.1)	1.4 (0.7–2.7)
Panic disorder	1.5* (1.1–2.0)	1.7* (1.1–2.5)	1.0 (0.5–1.9)	2.1 (0.6–7.1)
Antisocial personality disorder	1.5 (0.6–3.6)	1.5 (0.6–3.6)	1.5 (0.6–3.6)	1.5 (0.6–3.6)
Substance disorder	1.5* (1.1–2.0)	1.4* (1.1–1.9)	1.5 (0.9–2.5)	1.5 (0.6–3.6)

TABLE 7-5. Time-lagged associations of childhood adversities, parental history of mental disorders, and respondent personality with subsequent first onset of generalized anxiety disorder in NCS-2 panel sample (*N*=5,001) *(continued)*

		Cohort by age (y) at baseline, OR (95% CI)		
Prospective risk factor	Total sample, OR (95% CI)	15–24	25–39	40–54
Respondent personality[a]				
Neuroticism	1.3* (1.1–1.5)	0.9 (0.6–1.4)	1.4* (1.1–1.7)	1.2 (0.9–1.6)
Extraversion	0.9 (0.7–1.1)	1.3 (0.7–2.5)	0.7* (0.6–0.9)	1.2 (0.8–1.7)
Openness to experience	1.0 (0.8–1.2)	1.0 (0.6–1.7)	0.9 (0.7–1.1)	1.3 (0.8–2.0)

Note. Based on a discrete-time-survival model with person-year as the unit of analysis, controlling for cohort (age at interview), gender, race-ethnicity, and person-year. NCS=National Comorbidity Survey.
[a]Estimated only in person-years subsequent to baseline interview among those without an onset of generalized anxiety disorder prior to baseline interview, due to fact that personality was assessed only as of time of baseline interview (*N*=4,470).
*Significant at 0.05 level, two-sided test.
Source. Adapted from Kessler et al. 2008.

TABLE 7–6. Time-lagged associations of childhood adversities, parental history of mental disorders, and respondent personality with subsequent first onset of major depressive episode in NCS-2 panel sample (*N*=5,001)

Prospective risk factor	Total sample, OR (95% CI)	Cohort by age (y) at baseline, OR (95% CI)		
		15–24	25–39	40–54
Childhood adversity				
Neglect	1.8* (1.5–2.1)	2.4* (1.9–3.0)	1.7* (1.1–2.4)	1.0 (0.5–1.9)
Physical abuse	2.2* (1.8–2.7)	2.6* (2.1–3.2)	2.1* (1.4–3.1)	1.4 (0.7–3.2)
Sexual abuse	1.8* (1.3–2.5)	2.0* (1.3–2.9)	1.8* (1.1–2.9)	1.6 (0.9–3.1)
Death of parent	1.1 (0.7–1.6)	1.6* (1.1–2.5)	0.5 (0.2–0.9)	1.2 (0.5–2.9)
Divorce of parents	1.4* (1.2–1.7)	1.2* (1.0–1.4)	1.7* (1.2–2.3)	1.7 (0.9–3.2)
Other long-term separation	1.1 (0.8–1.6)	1.1 (0.6–1.9)	0.7 (0.3–1.7)	1.9 (0.6–6.4)
Parental history of mental disorders				
Major depressive episode	1.8* (1.6–2.1)	2.3* (1.9–2.8)	1.4* (1.0–1.9)	1.8* (1.2–2.8)
Generalized anxiety disorder	1.8* (1.5–2.1)	2.3* (1.9–2.8)	1.4* (1.0–2.0)	1.5* (1.0–2.2)
Panic disorder	1.9* (1.5–2.4)	1.9* (1.5–2.5)	1.9* (1.3–2.8)	2.1* (1.3–3.5)
Antisocial personality disorder	2.1* (1.3–3.3)	2.1* (1.3–3.3)	2.1* (1.3–3.3)	2.1* (1.3–3.3)
Substance disorder	1.7* (1.4–2.0)	1.9* (1.6–2.4)	1.2 (0.9–1.6)	2.1* (1.3–3.3)

TABLE 7–6. Time-lagged associations of childhood adversities, parental history of mental disorders, and respondent personality with subsequent first onset of major depressive episode in NCS-2 panel sample (*N*=5,001) *(continued)*

Prospective risk factor	Total sample, OR (95% CI)	Cohort by age (y) at baseline, OR (95% CI)		
		15–24	25–39	40–54
Respondent personality[a]				
Neuroticism	1.2 (1.0–1.4)	1.3 (1.0–1.8)	1.2 (0.9–1.4)	1.2 (0.8–1.8)
Extroversion	0.9 (0.8–1.1)	1.3* (1.0–1.7)	1.0 (0.8–1.4)	0.7* (0.6–0.9)
Openness to experience	1.3* (1.1–1.5)	1.3 (1.0–1.7)	1.4* (1.1–1.8)	1.1 (0.9–1.4)

Note. Based on a discrete-time-survival model, with person-year as the unit of analysis, controlling for cohort (age at interview), gender, race-ethnicity, and person-year. NCS=National Comorbidity Survey.
[a]Estimated only in person-years subsequent to baseline interview among those without an onset of major depressive episode prior to baseline interview, due to fact that personality was assessed only as of time of baseline interview (*N*=3,559).
*Significant at 0.05 level, two-sided test.
Source. Adapted from Kessler et al. 2008.

more consistently correlated with MDE than GAD in the total sample (OR = 1.3) and in early adulthood (1.4), suggesting that people who are intellectually curious and otherwise open to new experiences have a specifically elevated risk for depression but not for generalized anxiety.

When controls were introduced for childhood adversities, parental history of mental and substance disorders, and personality, the significant time-lagged associations of temporally primary MDE with the subsequent first onset of GAD attenuated somewhat but remained statistically significant in the total sample (OR = 1.8); increased among respondents who were adolescents at baseline (5.0); and became insignificant in older cohorts (1.4–1.8). In the case of GAD predicting subsequent first onset of MDE, the introduction of controls led to more modest attenuation of associations, although these associations remained statistically significant in the total sample (OR = 2.8) as well as in the early adulthood and middle age subsamples (2.7–3.3) (results not presented, but available on request).

PERSISTENCE OF MAJOR DEPRESSIVE DISORDER AND GENERALIZED ANXIETY DISORDER IN THE DECADE BETWEEN THE TWO SURVEYS

Close to half (46.2%) of respondents with a history of MDE at baseline had one or more recurrences of an MDE in the intervening decade (Table 7–7). This persistence was inversely related to age, although the range in the proportion of baseline cases with persistent episodes in the youngest through oldest cohorts is relatively small (49.8%–40.6%). On average, baseline cases reported having an episode of recurrent MDE in 19.8% of the years between the two interviews, again with an inverse relationship to age and a relatively narrow range from the youngest to highest age groups in the sample (21.9%–16.4%).

Proportional persistence of GAD in the decade between the two surveys was only slightly higher than that of MDE, with 49.7% of baseline lifetime cases having persistent GAD in at least one intercurrent year. The mean proportion of years in episode of GAD between the two surveys, 27.4%, was also somewhat higher than the comparable proportion for MDE. However, the mean proportion was much higher for respondents who were in late adolescence at baseline (45.5%) than for older respondents (23.3%–25.7%), indicating that there was a much greater decrease in the persistence of GAD than MDE in middle age.

TIME-LAGGED ASSOCIATIONS PREDICTING PERSISTENCE OF MAJOR DEPRESSIVE EPISODE AND GENERALIZED ANXIETY DISORDER

We examined the time-lagged association between baseline history of MDE and the persistence of GAD over the decade between the NCS and NCS-2 in the sub-

TABLE 7–7. Persistence of baseline major depressive episode (MDE) and generalized anxiety disorder (GAD) (any episode and mean proportion of years in episode between baseline NCS and NCS-2) in total sample and by cohort

Cohort, age (y) at baseline	Any persistence[a] % (SE)	Mean proportion of years in episode[b] % (SE)	N
MDE			
15–24	49.8 (3.6)	21.9 (1.9)	313
25–39	48.1 (2.3)	21.1 (1.5)	698
40–54	40.6 (3.3)	16.4 (2.1)	431
Total	46.2 (1.8)	19.8 (1.0)	1,442
GAD			
15–24	75.9 (3.2)	45.5 (3.6)	74
25–39	44.2 (3.5)	23.3 (2.5)	258
40–54	46.5 (3.8)	25.7 (2.5)	199
Total	49.7 (2.4)	27.4 (1.7)	531

Note. NCS = National Comorbidity Survey.
[a]An episode of MDE lasting at least 2 weeks and an episode of GAD lasting at least 1 month, in any year subsequent to baseline.
[b]The mean proportion of years between the two surveys when the respondent had one or more episodes of MDE (2 weeks or longer) and one or more episodes of GAD (1 month or longer).

sample of respondents with a baseline history of GAD. We also examined the time-lagged association between baseline history of GAD and the persistence of MDE among respondents with a baseline history of MDE. An important asymmetry was found in these associations: that although history of GAD significantly predicted persistence of MDE both in the total sample (OR=1.8) and in cohort-specific subsamples (1.5–2.6), history of MDE did not significantly predict persistence of GAD in either the total sample (1.2) or in subsamples (1.1–1.3) (Table 7–8). It is noteworthy that these prediction equations controlled for age at onset of the outcome disorder, which was consistently associated with significantly decreased risk of recurrence. This means that early age at onset of both MDE and GAD are associated with high-recurrence risk of these disorders. Only in the case of MDE, however, did comorbidity also predict high-recurrence risk. Interestingly, we found that the association between comorbid GAD and persistence of MDE was unrelated to temporal priority in first onset of MDE and GAD (results not presented, but available on request).

TABLE 7–8. Time-lagged associations of baseline major depressive episode (MDE), predicting the persistence of generalized anxiety disorder (GAD), and of baseline GAD, predicting the persistence of MDE, by cohort in the NCS-2 panel sample

Association	Total sample, OR (95% CI)	Cohort by age (y) at baseline, OR (95% CI)		
		15–24	25–39	40–54
Baseline MDE predicting persistence of GAD				
MDE	1.2 (0.9–1.7)	1.2 (0.5–2.6)	1.1 (0.7–1.8)	1.3 (0.8–2.1)
Age at onset of GAD	0.9* (0.7–1.0)	0.9 (0.4–1.9)	0.8 (0.7–1.0)	0.8* (0.6–1.0)
n[a]	531	74	258	199
Baseline GAD predicting persistence of MDE				
GAD	1.8* (1.4–2.4)	2.6* (1.4–4.6)	1.5* (1.1–2.2)	1.9* (1.3–2.7)
Age at onset of MDE	0.8* (0.7–0.9)	0.4* (0.2–0.8)	0.7* (0.6–0.9)	0.9 (0.8–1.1)
n[a]	1,442	313	698	431

Note. Based on a discrete-time-survival model, with person-year as unit of analysis, controlling for cohort (age at interview), gender, race-ethnicity, and person-year. NCS = National Comorbidity Survey.
[a]Unweighted sample sizes.
*Significant at 0.05 level, two-sided test.

Source. Reprinted from Kessler RC, Gruber M, Hettema JM, et al.: "Co-Morbid Major Depression and Generalized Anxiety Disorders in the National Comorbidity Survey Follow-up." *Psychological Medicine*, 38:365–374, 2008. Used with permission.

OTHER PROSPECTIVE RISK FACTORS FOR THE PERSISTENCE OF MAJOR DEPRESSIVE EPISODE AND GENERALIZED ANXIETY DISORDER

Persistence of GAD in the total sample was significantly predicted by several childhood adversities (1.4–1.8) and by neuroticism (1.1) but not by any of the measures of parental history of mental or substance disorders (Table 7–9). We were unable to study the stability of these associations across cohorts due to sparse data. Persistence of MDE in the total sample was significantly predicted by a somewhat different set of childhood adversities (1.3–1.5); by parental panic disorder (1.3); and by two personality dimensions: neuroticism (1.1) and openness to experience (1.1). As with GAD, subsample associations in cohorts could not be examined because of sparse data.

When controls were introduced for childhood adversities, parental history of mental and substance disorders, and personality, the significant time-lagged associations of baseline history of MDE with the subsequent persistence of GAD remained insignificant (OR=1.1) (Table 7–10). In the case of GAD predicting persistence of MDE, the introduction of controls led to modest attenuation of the association, which remained statistically significant (1.7).

Discussion

The results discussed here are limited in three important ways.

1. The assessments of MDE and GAD were based on fully structured diagnostic interviews, likely to be less accurate than clinician-administered diagnostic interviews.
2. The data on age at onset and persistence were obtained retrospectively, which might have introduced additional measurement errors.
3. Although the risk factor data were gathered prospectively, the data were based on retrospective reports. Respondents may have forgotten events, made errors regarding the timing of events, or may have been biased in their recall by current mood states at the time of the baseline interview.

Each of these limitations restricts the inferences that can be drawn from this study and represents an area for improvement in future studies.

These limitations notwithstanding, this study provides useful new information about MDE-GAD comorbidity as well as about patterns and prospective predictors of MDE and GAD onset and persistence. With regard to basic patterns of lifetime comorbidity, the NCS-2 results—consistent with results of much previous research—document a strong cross-sectional association between MDE and

TABLE 7–9. Time-lagged associations of childhood adversities, parental history of mental disorders, and respondent personality with persistence of major depressive episode (MDE) and generalized anxiety disorder (GAD) between the two interviews in the NCS-2 panel sample

Association	MDE, OR (95% CI)	GAD, OR (95% CI)
Childhood adversity		
Neglect	1.5* (1.2–1.9)	1.8* (1.2–2.5)
Physical abuse	1.3* (1.0–1.7)	1.4* (1.0–1.8)
Sexual abuse	1.3* (1.1–1.6)	1.2 (0.8–1.8)
Death of parent	1.0 (0.7–1.5)	1.2 (0.7–2.1)
Divorce of parents	1.1 (0.9–1.3)	1.4 (1.0–2.0)
Other separation	1.4 (1.0–2.1)	1.1 (0.5–2.8)
Parental history of mental disorders		
MDE	1.2 (1.0–1.4)	1.1 (0.8–1.6)
GAD	1.2 (1.0–1.5)	1.2 (0.9–1.5)
Panic disorder	1.3* (1.0–1.7)	1.4 (0.9–2.1)
Antisocial personality disorder	1.0 (0.7–1.2)	1.0 (0.6–1.6)
Substance disorder	1.1 (0.9–1.3)	1.2 (0.9–1.6)
Respondent personality		
Neuroticism	1.1* (1.0–1.2)	1.1* (1.0–1.3)
Extroversion	0.9 (0.8–1.0)	0.9 (0.8–1.0)
Openness to experience	1.1* (1.0–1.2)	1.0 (0.8–1.2)
n[a]	1,442	531

Note. Based on a discrete-time-survival model, with person-year as unit of analysis, controlling for cohort (age at interview), gender, race-ethnicity, and person-year, predicting number of years in episode in the decade between the two interviews. NCS = National Comorbidity Survey.
[a]Unweighted sample sizes.

GAD. This previous research has been reviewed elsewhere (Belzer and Schneier 2004; Gorwood 2004; Kessler 2000; Noyes 2001). However, by virtue of having prospective data in a large representative sample, we were also able to decompose this cross-sectional association. We found significant reciprocal relationships between baseline history of one of these disorders and the subsequent first onset of the other disorder that are roughly comparable in size for MDE predicting subsequent GAD and for GAD predicting subsequent MDE.

A more detailed inspection of these cross-lagged associations showed that they varied with length of time since the onset of the temporally primary disorder. Specifically, odds of onset of the temporally secondary disorder were higher in each of

TABLE 7–10. Effects of controlling for childhood adversities, parental history of mental and substance disorders, and respondent personality on time-lagged associations of baseline major depressive episode (MDE), with persistence of generalized anxiety disorder (GAD), and of baseline GAD, predicting the persistence of MDE, by cohort in the NCS-2 panel sample

Association	Without controls, OR (95% CI)	With controls, OR (95% CI)
Baseline MDE predicting the persistence of GAD ($n=531$[a])		
MDE	1.2 (0.9–1.7)	1.1 (0.8–1.6)
Age at onset of GAD	0.9* (0.7–1.0)	0.9 (0.7–1.1)
Baseline GAD predicting the persistence of MDE ($n=1,442$[a])		
GAD	1.8* (1.4–2.4)	1.7* (1.3–2.2)
Age at onset of MDE	0.8* (0.7–0.9)	0.8* (0.7–1.0)

Note. Based on a discrete-time-survival model, with person-year as unit of analysis, controlling for cohort (age at interview), gender, race-ethnicity, and person-year. NCS=National Comorbidity Survey.
[a]Unweighted sample sizes.
*Significant at 0.05 level, two-sided test.

the first 2 years after the onset of the temporally primary disorder than in each of the next 3 years and higher in the 3rd–5th years after onset than in each of the ensuing years 6 through 10. Despite these decays, however, the elevated odds of onset of the secondary disorders remained statistically significant even after more than a decade beyond the onset of the temporally primary disorder.

Perhaps the most striking aspect of the temporality of the cross-lagged associations between history of one of the two disorders and the subsequent onset of the other was that the elevated odds ratio of same-year onset was enormous (54.1–54.4) in comparison with any of the time-lagged associations (2.0–8.9). The temporal priority in first onset of MDE and GAD in these instances is unknown because the NCS-2 only dated first onsets to their year of occurrence. We do know, however, that these same-year associations were so strong that more than one-third of all the excess lifetime co-occurrence of MDE and GAD, above that expected by chance, occurred among cases in which both disorders started in the same year. This last observation raises the question whether comorbid MDE-GAD with same-year onsets differs in some way from cases in which first onset of the two disorders occurred in different years. We investigated this issue and could find no evidence for such differentiation. In particular, persistence of MDE and GAD was found to be unrelated either to the temporal priority in first onset between the two disorders or to the number of years that separated age at onset of the temporally primary and secondary disorders.

We have no way of knowing exactly what the strong association between time since onset and risk of comorbidity might mean. It clearly implies, however, that the temporally primary disorder in such cases is more than a mere marker of stable constitutional risk, because the latter would not be expected to produce an association between time since first onset of the temporally primary disorder and risk of the secondary disorder.

The fact that there was an association between the primary disorder and subsequent risk of the secondary disorder also has implications for another argument in the literature: that GAD, even if it is often temporally primary, might be nothing more than a prodrome or severity marker of MDE rather than an independent disorder (Brown et al. 1998; Cloninger et al. 1990; Offord et al. 1994). If this argument were correct, the window of risk for secondary depression would be expected to be fairly short. That is, we would expect that GAD, if it were no more than a prodrome of MDE, would be associated with an elevated risk of MDE largely within the subsequent few months or year. The fact that this was not the case and that the majority of cases of temporally secondary disorders had onsets a number of years after the temporally primary disorders argues against this interpretation.

An alternative view of causal processes that link temporally primary GAD with secondary MDE argues that secondary depression is often an exhaustion response that occurs in response to unremitting chronic anxiety (Akiskal 1985). Primary anxiety, in this view, can be conceptualized as a stressor that promotes secondary depression when it becomes sufficiently impairing (Akiskal 1990; Durham et al. 1997). If this were the case, however, we would expect that the odds ratio for GAD predicting secondary MDE would become higher with the passage of time since onset of GAD. The fact that the opposite is the case argues against this interpretation.

A more likely scenario is that the cross-lagged associations between temporally primary and secondary disorders are due to the effects of unmeasured common causes; the effects of one disorder on the other; or to some combination of both kinds of effects. We know that stable effects of the former sort exist. Indeed, as noted in the introduction to this chapter, a number of population twin studies suggest that genetic influences are important common causes of MDE and GAD (Gorwood 2004; Kendler et al. 2007). However, we can think of no biologically plausible mechanism whereby a genetic common cause would lead to a time decay in the odds ratios linking onset of temporally primary disorders with subsequent onset of secondary disorders, of the sort seen in the NCS-2 data.

It is also worth noting, in this same regard, that common genetic causes cannot account for all the observed comorbidity between MDE and GAD, because the latter is higher than would be predicted, based solely on the heritability of MDE and GAD and the strength of the association between the genes for the MDE and GAD. This means that there also must be common environmental causes of MDE and GAD. The estimates in population twin studies suggest that the latter causes explain between one- and two-thirds of the significant comorbidity between MDE and GAD, assuming that the joint effects of genetic and environmental causes are additive.

We investigated a number of potentially important prospective risk factors for MDE and GAD that might be considered common causes. The majority of these were found to be significant prospective predictors of the first onset of both MDE and GAD in the total sample. Included here were four of six measures of childhood adversity, four of five measures of parental mental or substance disorder, and one of three baseline personality dimensions. Far fewer of these variables, only two childhood adversities and one personality dimension, were significant prospective predictors of the persistence of both MDE and GAD. However, statistical control for all these common predictors only explained a small proportion of the observed cross-lagged associations between MDE and GAD involving either onset or persistence. This could mean that we simply failed to measure common environmental causes important for explaining the cross-lagged associations between MDE and GAD.

Another possibility is that the occurrence of one of these two disorders, in itself, might increase risk of the subsequent onset of the second disorder, possibly through some type of sensitization or kindling phenomenon (Post and Weiss 1998). The fact that the odds ratio predicting first onset of the secondary disorder becomes smaller, rather than larger, over time argues against sensitization or kindling being a dominant process, but it is nonetheless plausible to think that this process might explain the association of history of the temporally primary disorder with long-term risk of subsequent onset of the secondary disorder. It is noteworthy and indirectly consistent with this possibility that the odds ratios associated with onset of temporally secondary disorders increase at 11+ years after onset of the temporally primary disorder for both MDE and GAD and that this pattern is especially pronounced for the older respondents.

An important implication of the possibility that temporally primary MDE or GAD might itself increase risk of the subsequent first onset of the other disorder is that successful treatment of the temporally primary disorder might be expected, in such a case, to reduce risk of onset of comorbidity. We are aware of no empirical research that has investigated this possibility. Given the high odds ratios associated with temporally primary MDE predicting the subsequent first onset of GAD in the 5 years after first onset of MDE, however, the sample size required to detect a preventive effect of this sort in an effectiveness trial framework with long-term (5-year) follow-up would not be prohibitive. It might be that this kind of experimental investigation is the only way to resolve the uncertainty regarding whether temporally primary MDE and GAD are causal risk factors for each other or only risk markers.

Although the prospective risk factors considered here did not explain the time-lagged associations between MDE and GAD, these factors are important in documenting several differences in the environmental determinants of the two disorders. Most notable in this regard are associations of parental death, extroversion (negative), and openness to experiences with MDE but not GAD and generally somewhat stronger and temporally more persistent associations of the majority of risk factors with MDE than with GAD. These differences provide concrete substantiation of the conclusions of previous researchers, based on analysis of population twin studies, that MDE and GAD have partially distinct environmental determinants (Kendler 1996; Kendler et al. 1992, 2007; Roy et al. 1995) and add to the evidence from one previous prospective study of differences in the risk factors for MDE and GAD (Moffitt et al. 2007).

The prospective risk factors considered here had less consistent associations with persistence than with onset of MDE and GAD. We also found that temporally primary MDE was not a significant prospective predictor of persistence of GAD. However, comorbid GAD was found to be a significant prospective predictor of persistence of MDE. This difference in the associations of comorbidity with the course of MDE and GAD in the prospective NCS-2 data is consistent with an earlier finding, based on the analysis of retrospective reports in the baseline NCS. This earlier finding was associated with an investigation of whether comorbidity is related more strongly to the persistence and severity of GAD than other anxiety or mood disorders (Kessler et al. 1994). The rationale of this analysis was that if GAD were a prodrome, residual, or severity marker of MDE, as early commentators suggested it might be (Brown et al. 1998; Cloninger et al. 1990; Offord et al. 1994), the persistence and severity of GAD would be much more strongly affected by comorbidity than would the persistence and severity of depression.

The results of the analysis showed that comorbidity is generally associated with increased severity and persistence for all anxiety and mood disorders, including MDE. Furthermore, the patterns involving GAD were generally similar to those for other such disorders, with the important exception that GAD is the only anxiety or mood disorder in which persistence—as indirectly indicated by recency, controlling for age at onset and time since onset—is unrelated to comorbidity. Yonkers et al. (1996) reported a similar result regarding the predictors of the clinical course of GAD in an analysis of the prospective Harvard/Brown Anxiety Disorders Research Project (HARP) study, in which comorbid MDE was found not to predict persistence of GAD. These findings, in conjunction with the clear evidence that comorbidity is significantly related to the course of MDE, means that, if anything, GAD behaves more like an independent disorder in this respect than does depression.

The HARP data also showed that the course of comorbid GAD was unrelated to whether the GAD is temporally primary or secondary (Salzman et al. 2001). We replicated this finding in the NCS-2 for both MDE and GAD. We also found that the significant prospective association between comorbid GAD and the persistence of MDE was unrelated to whether the GAD is temporally primary or secondary. These multiple findings of the irrelevance of temporal priority might be taken as evidence that both MDE and GAD operate as risk markers, rather than as causal risk factors, in predicting first onset of each other and, in the case of GAD, in predicting persistence of MDE. As noted earlier, however, it is likely that definitive resolution of this uncertainty will require an effectiveness trial that evaluates the impact of treatment of a temporally primary disorder on the subsequent onset of the other disorder.

References

Akiskal HS: Anxiety: definition, relationship to depression, and proposal for an integrative model, in Anxiety and the Anxiety Disorders. Edited by Tuma AH, Maser JD. Hillsdale, NJ, Lawrence Erlbaum Associates, 1985, pp 787–797

Akiskal HS: Toward a clinical understanding of the relationship of anxiety and depressive disorders, in Comorbidity of Mood and Anxiety Disorders. Edited by Maser JD, Cloninger CR. Washington, DC, American Psychiatric Press, 1990, pp 597–610

American Psychiatric Association: Diagnostic and Statistical Manual of Mental Disorders, 2nd Edition. Washington, DC, American Psychiatric Association, 1968

American Psychiatric Association: Diagnostic and Statistical Manual of Mental Disorders, 3rd Edition. Washington, DC, American Psychiatric Association, 1980

American Psychiatric Association: Diagnostic and Statistical Manual of Mental Disorders, 3rd Edition Revised. Washington, DC, American Psychiatric Press, 1987

American Psychiatric Association: Diagnostic and Statistical Manual of Mental Disorders, 4th Edition. Washington, DC, American Psychiatric Association, 1994

Belli RF: The structure of autobiographical memory and the event history calendar: potential improvements in the quality of retrospective reports in surveys. Memory 6:383–406, 1998

Belli RF, Shay WL, Stafford FP: Event history calendars and question list surveys: a direct comparison of interviewing methods. Public Opin Q 65:45–74, 2001

Belzer K, Schneier FR: Comorbidity of anxiety and depressive disorders: issues in conceptualization, assessment, and treatment. J Psychiatr Pract 10:296–306, 2004

Breslau N: Depressive symptoms, major depression, and generalized anxiety: a comparison of self-reports on CES-D and results from diagnostic interviews. Psychiatry Res 15:219–229, 1985

Breslau N, Davis GC: DSM-III generalized anxiety disorder: an empirical investigation of more stringent criteria. Psychiatry Res 15:231–238, 1985a

Breslau N, Davis GC: Further evidence on the doubtful validity of generalized anxiety disorder. Psychiatry Res 16:177–179, 1985b

Brown TA, Chorpita BF, Barlow DH: Structural relationships among dimensions of the DSM-IV anxiety and mood disorders and dimensions of negative affect, positive affect, and autonomic arousal. J Abnorm Psychol 107:179–192, 1998

Caspi A, Roberts BW, Shiner RL: Personality development: stability and change. Annu Rev Psychol 56:453–484, 2005

Cloninger CR, Martin RL, Guze SB, et al: The empirical structure of psychiatric comorbidity and its theoretical significance, in Comorbidity of Mood and Anxiety Disorders. Edited by Maser JD, Cloninger CR. Washington, DC, American Psychiatric Press, 1990, pp 439–462

Cronbach LJ: Coefficient alpha and the internal structure of tests. Psychometrika 16:297–334, 1951

Durham RC, Allan T, Hackett CA: On predicting improvement and relapse in generalized anxiety disorder following psychotherapy. Br J Clin Psychol 36:101–119, 1997

Efron B: Logistic regression, survival analysis, and the Kaplan-Meier curve. J Am Stat Assoc 83:414–425, 1988

Endicott J, Andreasen N, Spitzer RL: Family History Research Diagnostic Criteria. New York, Biometrics Research, New York State Psychiatric Institute, 1978

Engdahl BE, Speed N, Eberly RE, et al: Comorbidity of psychiatric disorders and personality profiles of American World War II prisoners of war. J Nerv Ment Dis 179:181–187, 1991

Enns MW, Cox BJ: Personality dimensions and depression: review and commentary. Can J Psychiatry 42:274–284, 1997

Fergusson DM, Horwood LJ, Boden JM: Structure of internalising symptoms in early adulthood. Br J Psychiatry 189:540–546, 2006

First MB, Spitzer RL, Gibbon M, et al: Structured Clinical Interview for DSM-IV Axis I Disorders, Research Version, Non-Patient Edition (SCID-I/NP). New York, Biometrics Research, New York State Psychiatric Institute, 2002

Goldberg LR: An alternative "description of personality": the big-five factor structure. J Pers Soc Psychol 59:1216–1229, 1990

Goldberg LR: The development of markers for the big-five factor structure. Psychol Assess 4:26–42, 1992

Gorwood P: Generalized anxiety disorder and major depressive disorder comorbidity: an example of genetic pleiotropy? Eur Psychiatry 19:27–33, 2004

Grant BF, Hasin DS, Stinson FS, et al: Prevalence, correlates, co-morbidity, and comparative disability of DSM-IV generalized anxiety disorder in the USA: results from the National Epidemiologic Survey on Alcohol and Related Conditions. Psychol Med 35:1747–1759, 2005

Haro JM, Arbabzadeh-Bouchez S, Brugha TS, et al: Concordance of the Composite International Diagnostic Interview Version 3.0 (CIDI 3.0) with standardized clinical assessments in the WHO World Mental Health Surveys. Int J Methods Psychiatr Res 15:167–180, 2006

Hettema JM, Neale MC, Myers JM, et al: A population-based twin study of the relationship between neuroticism and internalizing disorders. Am J Psychiatry 163:857–864, 2006

Kendler KS: Major depression and generalised anxiety disorder: same genes, (partly) different environments—revisited. Br J Psychiatry Suppl (30):68–75, 1996

Kendler KS, Neale MC, Kessler RC, et al: Generalized anxiety disorder in women: a population-based twin study. Arch Gen Psychiatry 49:267–272, 1992

Kendler KS, Neale MC, Kessler RC, et al: A longitudinal twin study of personality and major depression in women. Arch Gen Psychiatry 50:853–862, 1993

Kendler KS, Gardner CO, Gatz M, et al: The sources of co-morbidity between major depression and generalized anxiety disorder in a Swedish national twin sample. Psychol Med 37:453–462, 2007

Kessler RC: The epidemiology of pure and comorbid generalized anxiety disorder: a review and evaluation of recent research. Acta Psychiatr Scand Suppl (406):7–13, 2000

Kessler RC, Ustun TB: The World Mental Health (WMH) Survey Initiative Version of the World Health Organization (WHO) Composite International Diagnostic Interview (CIDI). Int J Methods Psychiatr Res 13:93–121, 2004

Kessler RC, McGonagle KA, Zhao S, et al: Lifetime and 12-month prevalence of DSM-III-R psychiatric disorders in the United States: results from the National Comorbidity Survey. Arch Gen Psychiatry 51:8–19, 1994

Kessler RC, Nelson CB, McGonagle KA, et al: Comorbidity of DSM-III-R major depressive disorder in the general population: results from the US National Comorbidity Survey. Br J Psychiatry Suppl (30):17–30, 1996

Kessler RC, Wittchen H-U, Abelson JM, et al: Methodological studies of the Composite International Diagnostic Interview (CIDI) in the US national comorbidity survey (NCS). Int J Methods Psychiatr Res 7:33–55, 1998

Kessler RC, Merikangas KR, Berglund P, et al: Mild disorders should not be eliminated from the DSM-V. Arch Gen Psychiatry 60:1117–1122, 2003

Kessler RC, Abelson J, Demler O, et al: Clinical calibration of DSM-IV diagnoses in the World Mental Health (WMH) version of the World Health Organization (WHO) Composite International Diagnostic Interview (WMHCIDI). Int J Methods Psychiatr Res 13:122–139, 2004

Kessler RC, Berglund P, Demler O, et al: Lifetime prevalence and age-of-onset distributions of DSM-IV disorders in the National Comorbidity Survey Replication. Arch Gen Psychiatry 62:593–602, 2005a

Kessler RC, Chiu WT, Demler O, et al: Prevalence, severity, and comorbidity of 12-month DSM-IV disorders in the National Comorbidity Survey Replication. Arch Gen Psychiatry 62:617–627, 2005b

Kessler RC, Gruber M, Hettema JM, et al: Co-morbid major depression and generalized anxiety disorders in the National Comorbidity Survey Follow-up. Psychol Med 38:365–374, 2008

Krueger RF: The structure of common mental disorders. Arch Gen Psychiatry 56:921–926, 1999

Krueger RF, Caspi A, Moffitt TE, et al: The structure and stability of common mental disorders (DSM-III-R): a longitudinal-epidemiological study. J Abnorm Psychol 107:216–227, 1998

Moffitt TE, Caspi A, Harrington H, et al: Generalized anxiety disorder and depression: childhood risk factors in a birth cohort followed to age 32. Psychol Med 37:441–452, 2007

Noyes R Jr: Comorbidity in generalized anxiety disorder. Psychiatr Clin North Am 24:41–55, 2001

Offord DR, Boyle M, Campbell D, et al: Mental Health in Ontario: selected findings from the Mental Health Supplement to the Ontario Health Survey. Toronto, Queen's Printer for Ontario, 1994

Post RM, Weiss SR: Sensitization and kindling phenomena in mood, anxiety, and obsessive-compulsive disorders: the role of serotonergic mechanisms in illness progression. Biol Psychiatry 44:193–206, 1998

Research Triangle Institute: SUDAAN: Professional Software for Survey Data Analysis. Research Triangle Park, NC, Research Triangle Institute, 2002

Robins LN, Wing J, Wittchen HU, et al: The Composite International Diagnostic Interview: an epidemiologic instrument suitable for use in conjunction with different diagnostic systems and in different cultures. Arch Gen Psychiatry 45:1069–1077, 1988

Rosenbaum PR, Rubin DB: The central role of the propensity score in observational studies for causal effects. Biometrika 70:41–55, 1983

Roy MA, Neale MC, Pedersen NL, et al: A twin study of generalized anxiety disorder and major depression. Psychol Med 25:1037–1049, 1995

Salzman C, Goldenberg I, Bruce SE, et al: Pharmacologic treatment of anxiety disorders in 1989 versus 1996: results from the Harvard/Brown anxiety disorders research program. J Clin Psychiatry 62:149–152, 2001

Slade T, Watson D: The structure of common DSM-IV and ICD-10 mental disorders in the Australian general population. Psychol Med 36:1593–1600, 2006

Spitzer RL, Williams JB, Gibbon M, et al: The Structured Clinical Interview for DSM-III-R (SCID), I: history, rationale, and description. Arch Gen Psychiatry 49:624–629, 1992

Straus MA, Hamby SL, Finkelhor D, et al: Identification of child maltreatment with the Parent-Child Conflict Tactics Scales: development and psychometric data for a national sample of American parents. Child Abuse Negl 22:249–270, 1998

Vollebergh WA, Iedema J, Bijl RV, et al: The structure and stability of common mental disorders: the NEMESIS study. Arch Gen Psychiatry 58:597–603, 2001

Watson D: Rethinking the mood and anxiety disorders: a quantitative hierarchical model for DSM-V. J Abnorm Psychol 114:522–536, 2005

Wolter KM: Introduction to Variance Estimation. New York, Springer-Verlag, 1985

Yonkers KA, Warshaw MG, Massion AO, et al: Phenomenology and course of generalised anxiety disorder. Br J Psychiatry 168:308–313, 1996

8

THE RELATIONSHIP OF GENERALIZED ANXIETY DISORDER AND MAJOR DEPRESSION OVER TIME

Valery N. Krasnov, M.D.

Close clinical relationships between anxiety and depression have been formulated in traditional psychiatry (Lewis 1934; Weitbrecht 1973). Similar, or the same, pathophysiological processes have been observed in several studies (Boyer 2000; Heimann 1978; Hole et al. 1972; Paul 1988). It is well known, from psychiatric practice dealing with recurrent depression, that in every next depressive episode the representation of anxiety components decreases while the representation of typically depressive ones (such as diurnal variations, diminished drive intensity and motivation for activity, and feeling of guilt) increases. The more restricted diagnostic category of generalized anxiety disorder (GAD) shows a large overlap of symptoms, conceptualized as comorbidity, in general population surveys (Kessler et al. 1994, 2005; Preisig et al. 2001; Regier et al. 1993, 1998; Wittchen et al. 2000, 2003) and among primary-care users (Olfson et al. 1997). Clinically, the distinctions between long-term anxiety disorders and major depression (specifi-

---

I thank general physicians and psychiatrists Drs. T. Dovjenko, N. Yaltseva, Y. Rivkina, and M. Chernetsov for their assistance in collecting clinical data within the Programme Recognition and Treatment of Depression in Primary Care.

cally regarding first depressive episode) are not clear cut. According to genetic evidence (Gorwood 2004; Kendler 1996; Kendler et al. 2007; Roy et al. 1995), these disorders appear to be outcomes of the same underlying diathesis.

We conducted a research program to study the prevalence of affective spectrum disorders in primary care settings. Results of this research also suggest transformation of anxiety disorders into depressive disorder, within one continuum.

Methods

Methods used in our research included a screening questionnaire, semistructured psychiatric interview, the Symptom Checklist-90–R (SCL-90-R), and the Hamilton Rating Scale for Depression (HAM-D; Hamilton 1960) and Hamilton Rating Scale for Anxiety (HAM-A; Hamilton 1959). The research design and tools used were developed in 1998–1999 with the assistance of Drs. D. Regier and D. Lozovsky of the U.S. National Institute of Mental Health. After a pilot study in several Russian cities, the screening instrument and some approaches in the primary care setting were modified somewhat to reflect specific cultural and technical conditions in Russia (Krasnov 1999; Krasnov et al. 2004).

Results

In 2000–2001, as a part of the program *Recognition and Treatment of Depression in Primary Care,* we screened for affective spectrum disorders in several territorial (general medical) polyclinics in three cities of Russia. Subjects of investigation were students or employed individuals ages 18–55 years.

During the first stage, we identified, with the help of a seven-item screening instrument, a group of outpatients with various affective spectrum disorders, which included subthreshold depression, anxiety, and somatoform (psychovegetative) disorders. This group consisted of 2,749 persons, 51.2% of the total 5,366 outpatients screened. Members of this group were offered a consultation with a psychiatrist concerning their symptoms, in a special "psychotherapeutic" room. Of this group, 1,919 (35.8% of all patients screened) agreed to this proposal and were interviewed by a psychiatrist. Based on the interviews, 1,616 (30.1% of all patients screened) were diagnosed as having depression according to ICD-10 criteria for a depressive episode; in 1,334 cases (24.8% of all patients screened), severity of depression was 15 or more on the HAM-D (see Table 8–1). The distribution of the ICD-10 depressive diagnoses is presented in Table 8–2. In accordance with the terms of the program, these persons could enter a 6-week course of medication with modern antidepressants, mainly sertraline.

For about 90% of the individuals who received treatment, depression was the dominant condition but was accompanied by subsyndromal or obvious moderate

TABLE 8–1. Recognition and treatment of depression in primary care settings in three cities of Russia during 2000–2001

Stage	Care provider	Results
1	Nurse/GP	5,366 out-patients screened, using special screening questionnaire
2	GP	2,749 (51.2%) of patients diagnosed with affective-spectrum disorders
3a	Psychiatrist	1,919 (35.8%) of patients interviewed by psychiatrist
3b	Psychiatrist	1,616 (30.1%) of patients diagnosed with depression
4	Psychiatrist/GP	1,334 (24.8%) of patients advised to have treatment with antidepressants (HAM-D score 15+)
5	Psychiatrist/GP/nurse	762 (14.2%) of patients completed 6-week course of treatment

Note. Subjects were students and employed persons aged 18–55 years. GP = general practitioner.

anxiety disorders. At the same time, there were different combinations of depression with anxiety and somatoform disorders, with similar SCL-90-R score levels of somatization, depression, and anxiety. Prevalent anxiety disorders, such as GAD or panic disorder, were diagnosed in only 238 (4.4%) individuals, who then were prescribed benzodiazepines, hydroxyzine, or beta-blockers.

In 2002–2003, a second screening with subsequent diagnostic procedures, following the same research design, took place in two polyclinics. This screening covered 4,020 persons, 2,046 of which (50.9%) had signs of affective spectrum disorders. A psychiatric interview helped to detect 1,178 (29.3% of all patients receiving the second screening) cases of depression, including 992 cases (24.7%) with scores 15 and higher on the HAM-D.

Of this latter subgroup, 138 people had been included in the sample of previous research in 2000–2001, and 34 of these patients had been diagnosed at that time with anxiety disorders, including 9 cases of GAD, 19 cases of "panic disorders," and 6 other cases of anxiety disorders. It should be borne in mind that the diagnostic category GAD was relatively new in Russian psychiatric practice and was usually replaced by other diagnostic formulas. During the period 2002–2003, the cases met the criteria of depressive episode. The formerly dominant anxiety was subordinated because of pronounced symptoms of depression.

TABLE 8–2. Distribution of ICD-10 diagnoses for patients diagnosed with depression by a psychiatrist, 2000–2001

Diagnosis	ICD-10 code	Proportion of diagnoses
Depressive episode	F 32	31.2%
Recurrent depressive disorder	F 33	24.1%
Chronic depressive disorder (mainly "double depression" with dysthymia)	F 34	26.3%
Mixed anxiety and depressive disorder	F 41.2	11.0%
Long-term depressive reaction	F 43.21	3.1%
Other diagnoses		4.3%

In 2004–2005, the diagnoses of another 28 patients from the observed sample were changed to "depression," including 13 patients formerly diagnosed with GAD. During the period of observation, some patients with mixed anxiety and depressive disorder qualified for secondary consultative aid and the conditions of these patients turned out to be closer to the strict criteria of depression.

Discussion

Almost all the cases observed were, in fact, combinations of anxiety and depression, with differing degrees of expression of these disorders. Attempts to diagnose anxiety disorders as hypothetically independent have failed, on the whole. There were only a few cases with stable prevalence of anxious symptoms that, in particular, met the criteria for GAD. However, even in these cases, depressive disorders were present also, at least at a subsyndromal level, although they were not perceived as disorders. It was the anxiety component that brought patients to the doctor.

It is noteworthy that so-called social phobia was hardly considered a basis for seeking help within the primary care system. Separate somatoform disorders without subdepressive and anxiety features were also identified in rare cases. In this connection, it seems to be important, especially for a choice of medication, to take into consideration the combination of depression and verified somatic disorders (Table 8–3). It should be mentioned that severe physical diseases, which need special control, and active somatic treatments have been excluded from the sample.

Thus, one can suggest a tendency for transformation of affective disorders, over time or in subsequent episodes, from prevalent anxiety symptoms to mixed anxiety-depressive syndrome and further on to depressive symptoms, per se. It seems like another argument in favor of a single pathogenetic entity for the major-

TABLE 8–3. Combinations of depression and somatic disorders in 1,616 outpatients with verified depression, 2000–2004

Disorder	Percentage
Cardiovascular disorders	20.2
Gastrointestinal disorders	18.2
Asthma and asthmatic bronchitis	4.3
Other disorders	6.9

ity of affective spectrum disorders. Then anxiety appears at the initial stage, or as the foreground primary effect, and tends to evolve in the direction of typical depression.

We suggest—and this suggestion is confirmed by our data from primary care—that depression has several stages of development:

- Prodrome with nonspecific symptoms of emotional and vegetative instability
- Anxious stage, including three substages: 1) situation anxiety with a concrete cause; 2) free-floating anxiety, with changing subjects of anxiety, mainly determined by chance; and 3) anxiety with no cause
- Depressive stage, including three substages: 1) depression with "anxious" elements within sadness condition; 2) depression with hidden anxiety, but with domination of sadness; and 3) depression with areactivity/hyporeactivity and psychomotor retardation.

Operational diagnosis registers only a concrete stage at the moment the patient is seeking help. Identifying dynamic aspects of diagnoses seems to be a task for future classifications.

Conclusion

In the polyclinical (primary care) population, frequent combinations of anxiety and depression, along with rare cases of "pure" anxiety (anxiety disorders) or depression, are in conflict with the concept of separate, comorbid disorders. Dynamic ratios and transitions between the two disorders are more a part of clinical reality. However, special diagnostic approaches, based on a dynamic analysis of clinical conditions, should be developed in order to detect these relations and tendencies. A dynamic hierarchy and multiple interrelationships between depression and anxiety should be taken into account in the development of future psychiatric diagnostic systems. It could be functional diagnostics that consider anxiety-depressive affective disorder as a cohesive entity.

Operational criteria for separate disorders offer no solution, although the use of such criteria is justified at initial stages of the diagnostic procedure. Most probably, the separate comorbid-disorder concept will maintain its ground, as far as combinations of affective disorders and somatic disorders are concerned. However, research also should aim at establishing the relationships between specific physical disorders and stage of affective disorder.

The symptoms of GAD share many features with depression and often represent the prodromal phase of major depressive disorder or residuum. Differences between these disorders reflect physiological (including emotional) reactivity much more than the psychopathology itself. The debates on distinction or unity of GAD and major depressive disorder should take into consideration long-term course, appropriate treatment, dynamic changes of symptomatology hierarchy, and reactivity to external factors.

References

Boyer P: Do anxiety and depression have a common pathophysiological mechanism? Acta Psychiatr Scand 102:24–29, 2000

Gorwood P: Generalized anxiety disorder and major depressive disorder comorbidity: an example of genetic pleiotropy? Eur Psychiatry 19:27–33, 2004

Hamilton M: The assessment of anxiety states by rating. Br J Med Psychol 32:50–55, 1959

Hamilton M: A rating scale for depression. J Neurol Neurosurg Psychiatry 23:56–62, 1960

Heimann H: Changes of psychophysiological reactivity in affective disorders. Arch Psychiat Nervenkr 3:223–231, 1978

Hole G, Gehring A, Blaser P: Vegetativum, Psychomotoric und Selbstbeurteilung in Langsschnittuntersuchungen depressiver Patienten. Fortschr Neurol Psychiatr 1:69–82, 1972

Kendler KS: Major depression and generalized anxiety disorder: same genes (partly) different environments—revisited. Br J Psychiatry 6:6, 1996

Kendler KS, Gardner CO, Gatz M, et al: The sources of comorbidity between major depression and generalized anxiety disorder in a Swedish national twin sample. Psychol Med 37:453–462, 2007

Kessler RC, McGonagle KA, Zhao S, et al: Lifetime and 12-month prevalence of DSM-III-R psychiatric disorders in the United States. Arch Gen Psychiatry 51:8–19, 1994

Kessler RC, Chiu WT, Demler O, et al: Prevalence, severity and comorbidity of 12-month DSM-IV disorders in the National Comorbidity Survey Replication. Arch Gen Psychiatry 62:617–627, 2005

Krasnov VN: The programme "Recognition and Treatment of Depression in Primary Care settings" (in Russian). Soc Clin Psychiatry 4:5–8, 1999

Krasnov VN, Dovjenko TV, Rivkina U, et al: Diagnostics and therapy of affective spectrum disorders in primary care, in Proceedings of the Russian Conference, Modern Tendencies in Organization of Psychiatry Services: Clinical and Social Aspects (in Russian), Moscow, Russia, Medpraktika-m, 2004, pp 66–68

Lewis AJ: Melancholia: a historical review. J Ment Sci 80:1–42, 1934

Olfson M, Fireman B, Weissman MM: Mental disorders and disability among patients in primary care group practice. Am J Psychiatry 154:1734–1740, 1997

Paul SM: Anxiety and depression: a common neurobiological substrate? J Clin Psychiatry 49(suppl):13–16, 1988

Preisig M, Merikangas KR, Angst J: Clinical significance and comorbidity of subthreshold depression and anxiety in the community. Acta Psychiatr Scand 104:96–103, 2001

Regier DA, Narrow WE, Rae DS, et al: The de facto US mental and addictive disorders service system: epidemiologic catchment area prospective 1-year prevalence rates of disorders and services. Arch Gen Psychiatry 50:85–94, 1993

Regier DA, Rae DS, Narrow WE, et al: Prevalence of anxiety disorders and their comorbidity with mood and addictive disorders. Br J Psychiatry Suppl (34):24–28, 1998

Roy MA, Neale MC, Pedersen NL, et al: A twin study of generalized anxiety disorder and major depression. Psychol Med 5:1037–1049, 1995

Weitbrecht HJ: Psychiatrie im Grundriss. Berlin, Springer Verlag, 1973

Wittchen HU, Kessler RC, Pfister H, et al: Why do people with anxiety disorders become depressed? A prospective-longitudinal community study. Acta Psychatr Scand 102:14–23, 2000

Wittchen HU, Beesdo K, Bittner A, et al: Depressive episodes: evidence for causal role of primary anxiety disorders? Eur Psychiatry 18:384–393, 2003

9

GENERALIZED ANXIETY DISORDER AND MAJOR DEPRESSION

Common and Reciprocal Causes

D. M. Fergusson, Ph.D.
L. J. Horwood, M.Sc.

In their chapter on the correlation/overlap between major depression and generalized anxiety disorder (GAD), Kessler et al. (see Chapter 7, this volume) produced evidence to suggest a possible reciprocal relationship between these two disorders. In this relationship, prior major depression was prognostic of later GAD and prior GAD was prognostic of later major depression.

Although their study produced evidence consistent with the view that major depression and GAD may be causally related disorders, their analysis does not fully distinguish between two processes that may lead to this relationship. First, major depression and GAD may be related as a result of common causal processes that lead these conditions to co-occur. Second, there may be causal processes in which a) the presence of major depression leads to increased risks of GAD or b) the presence of GAD leads to increased risks of major depression.

In this chapter, we use data gathered over the course of a longitudinal study of a birth cohort of New Zealand young adults to fit structural equation models that distinguish between the effects of common causes and cross-lagged or reciprocal relationships between major depression and GAD. Our findings contribute to the debate on whether these are separate disorders or the same disorder by examining the extent to which there may be causal relationships between these conditions over and above the effects of common causes.

Methods

Data analyzed here are from the Christchurch Health and Development Study (CHDS). The CHDS is a longitudinal study of a birth cohort of 1,265 children born in the Christchurch (New Zealand) urban region during mid-1977. This cohort has been studied, at regular periods, to the age of 25 years. The portion of the data described in this chapter involves a cohort of 953 individuals who were studied at ages 18, 21, and 25 years using measures of major depression and GAD.

ASSESSMENT METHODS

Assessment of Major Depression

At each interview, participants were questioned about major depressive symptoms occurring in the past month, the past 12 months, and the period back to the time of the previous assessment. Participants who at any time reported a depressive episode involving either of the two core-symptom criteria for major depression (feeling sad, miserable, or depressed or loss of interest in daily activities) were further questioned about the occurrence of other DSM-IV (American Psychiatric Association 1994) symptom criteria. For the purposes of the present analysis, a depressive-symptoms score was constructed for each assessment period, based on a count of the number of DSM-IV major depression symptom criteria reported at any time during the assessment period.

Assessment of Generalized Anxiety Disorder

At each interview, participants were questioned about the occurrence of episodes of feeling tense, anxious, or worried most of the time since the previous assessment. Young people who reported an episode lasting at least 1 month or longer were further questioned about the duration and source of the anxiety and associated DSM-IV symptoms. For the purposes of the present analysis, a GAD-symptom score was constructed for each assessment period based on a count of the number of anxiety symptoms reported from the following list of DSM-IV symptom criteria: feeling restless, keyed up, or on edge; getting tired very easily; having difficulty concentrating; feeling irritable; muscles feeling tense, sore, or aching; or having trouble getting asleep or staying asleep.

Greater detail on the study and measurement of both these disorders is given in Fergusson et al. (2006).

Results

Table 9–1 shows the matrix of polychoric correlations between measures of major depression and GAD at ages 18, 21, and 25 years. Inspection of correlations in this table leads to three general conclusions:

1. There is a general tendency for all measures at all times to be intercorrelated. This evidence of pervasive correlation across diagnostic categories and time hints at the presence of common causal origins of major depression and GAD.
2. Within time periods, there are substantial correlations between GAD and major depression, reflecting comorbidity of these conditions.
3. There is evidence that the presence of GAD and major depression at one time is predictive of GAD or major depression at another time, suggesting the presence of across-time stability.

These observations suggest that models of GAD and major depression need to take into account three causal structures: 1) effects of common causes on GAD and major depression; 2) potentially reciprocal effects of major depression and GAD; and 3) stability of these disorders across time.

TWO MODELS OF THE STRUCTURE OF MAJOR DEPRESSION AND GENERALIZED ANXIETY DISORDER ACROSS TIME

Figures 9–1 and 9–2 present two structural-equation models aimed at examining the roles of common causes, reciprocal effects, and stability in measures of GAD and major depression, measured at three times (18, 21, 25 years of age). The models assume that 1) the repeated measures of major depression (MDt; $t = 18, 21, 25$ years) reflect a common underlying causal factor, C1; and 2) the repeated measures of GAD ($GADt$; $t = 18, 21, 25$ years) reflect a common underlying causal factor, C2. Technically, the factors C1 and C2 are fixed effects that describe the fixed effects of common genes and environment on $GADt$ and MDt.

The models then describe the structure of the residual terms, MDt' and $GADt'$, using different causal structures.

1. Model 1 is a simultaneous reciprocal-cause model in which, after correction for the correlation between C1 and C2, major depression is causally related to GAD by the parameter B1 and GAD is causally related to major depression by the parameter B2. In addition, early major depression is related to later major depression and early GAD to later GAD.
2. Model 2 is a cross-lagged model that assumes that, after correction for the correlation between C1 and C2, major depression at time t is related to GAD at the next time of observation by the parameter B1 and GAD at time t is related

TABLE 9–1. Matrix of polychoric correlations between measures of major depression (MD) and generalized anxiety disorder (GAD) symptom scores, at ages 18, 21, and 25 years

Measure	18 years		21 years		25 years	
	MD	GAD	MD	GAD	MD	GAD
18 years—MD	1.00					
18 years—GAD	0.56	1.00				
21 years—MD	0.51	0.29	1.00			
21 years—GAD	0.41	0.41	0.51	1.00		
25 years—MD	0.38	0.19	0.48	0.29	1.00	
25 years—GAD	0.28	0.20	0.39	0.30	0.57	1.00

to major depression at the next time of observation by the parameter B2. This model provides an alternative to Model 1 by assuming a cross-lagged rather than simultaneous structure.

In terms of the issues raised by Kessler et al. (see Chapter 7, this volume), the critical issues focus on the values of B1, B2. Specifically, if there is a causal structure between major depression and GAD, after correction for common fixed causes, it is necessary for at least one of the parameters to be non-zero. Furthermore, the sizes of these parameters may provide some guidance about the direction of any reciprocal effects.

MODEL RESULTS

The models in Figures 9–1 and 9–2 were fitted to the data in Table 9–1 by means of weighted least squares. The results for each model are summarized in Table 9–2, which reports estimates of the model parameters and standard errors. In addition, the goodness of fit of each model is summarized by a series of indices.

Model Fit

For both models, the fit proved to be excellent, suggesting that the data in Table 9–1 are consistent with the proposed models. In terms of nonnested measures of fit, AIC (Akaike information criterion) and BIC (Bayesian information criterion), the fit of both models was very similar, with the result that the models cannot be discriminated between on the basis of goodness-of-fit.

Role of Common Causes

Both analyses show that the fixed-effect factors, C1 and C2, were perfectly correlated. This result implies that common fixed causes (genes, environment) were the same for both conditions.

Reciprocal Effects

The model of reciprocal causes (Figure 9–1) suggests that although major depression was related to GAD (B=0.88; $P<0.05$), GAD was not related to major depression (B=0.013; $P>0.50$). The cross-lagged model (Figure 9–2) leads to a similar finding, with lagged major depression predicting GAD (B=0.23; $P<0.01$) but lagged GAD not predicting major depression (B=0.05; $P>0.50$). Both models lead to the consistent conclusion that, if causal relationships exist between major depression and GAD (after correction for common factors), these relationships involve a unicausal association in which major depression leads to GAD but GAD does not lead to major depression.

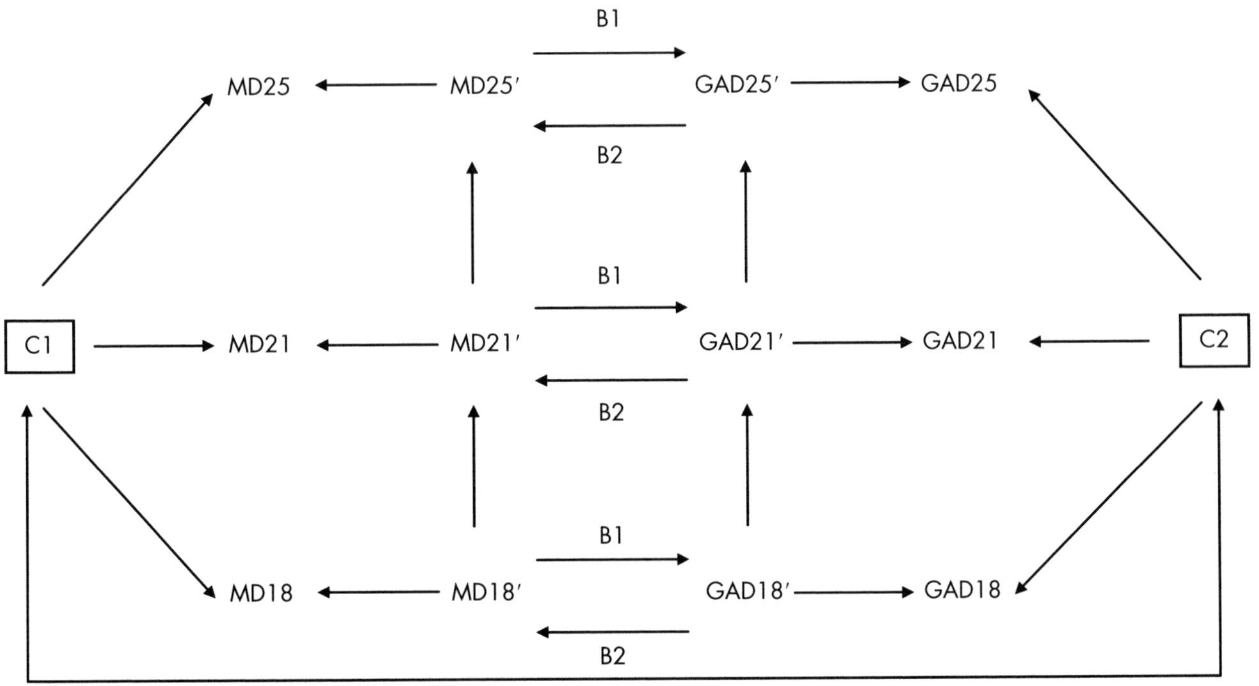

FIGURE 9–1. Reciprocal-cause model for major depression (MD) and generalized anxiety disorder (GAD) symptoms.

Note. MDt (t=18, 21, 25 years) are variables representing major depression symptoms at each time t; MDt' (t=18, 21, 25 years) are variables representing the components of MDt that are not explained by the common causal factor C1. $GADt$ (t=18, 21, 25 years) are variables representing GAD symptoms at each time t; $GADt'$ (t=18, 21, 25 years) are variables representing the components of $GADt$ that are not explained by the common causal factor C2. B1 and B2 are regression parameters representing the simultaneous reciprocal causal effects between MDt and $GADt$ at each time t.

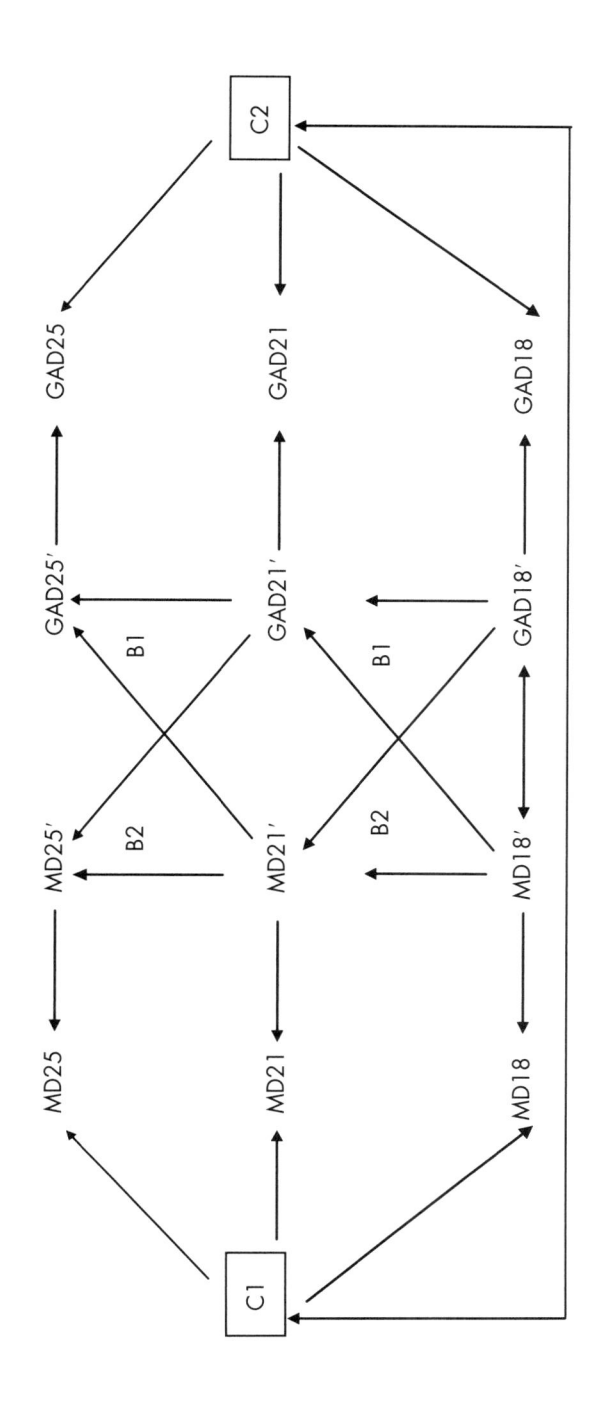

FIGURE 9–2. Cross-lagged model for major depression (MD) and generalized anxiety disorder (GAD) symptoms.

Note. MDt (t=18, 21, 25 years) are variables representing major depression symptoms at each time t; MDt' (t=18, 21, 25 years) are variables representing the components of MDt that are not explained by the common causal factor C1. GADt (t=18, 21, 25 years) are variables representing GAD symptoms at each time t; C2 is a fixed factor representing underlying common causes of GAD symptoms at each time t; GADt' (t=18, 21, 25 years) are variables representing the components of GADt that are not explained by the common causal factor C2. B1 is a regression parameter representing the lagged causal effects of MDt' on GAD symptoms at the next time of observation; B2 is a regression parameter representing the lagged causal effects of GADt' on major depression symptoms at the next time of observation.

TABLE 9–2. Summary of fitted model parameters and goodness-of-fit indices for reciprocal-cause and cross-lagged models

	Model 1 (reciprocal-cause)		Model 2 (cross-lagged)	
Measure	Parameter (SE)	P	Parameter (SE)	P
Factor loadings				
C1 → MD 18, 21, 25	0.57 (0.06)	< 0.0001	0.57 (0.07)	< 0.001
C2 → GAD 18, 21, 25	0.33 (0.10)	< 0.01	0.30 (0.11)	< 0.01
Factor correlation				
C1 ↔ C2	1.00	—	1.00	—
Structural parameters				
MD' → GAD' (B1)	0.88 (0.42)	< 0.05	0.23 (0.09)	< 0.01
GAD' → MD' (B2)	0.13 (0.33)	0.70	0.05 (0.07)	0.52
MD18' → MD21'	0.21 (0.15)	0.16	0.26 (0.10)	< 0.05
GAD18' → GAD21'	0.22 (0.09)	< 0.05	0.26 (0.07)	< 0.001
MD21' → MD25'	0.21 (0.14)	0.12	0.21 (0.10)	< 0.05
GAD21' → GAD25'	0.12 (0.07)	0.08	0.14 (0.07)	< 0.05
Disturbance covariances				
MD18' ↔ GAD18'	−0.29 (0.38)	0.46	0.40 (0.08)	< 0.001
MD21' ↔ GAD21'	−0.36 (0.36)	0.33	0.27 (0.08)	< 0.001
MD25' ↔ GAD25'	−0.30 (0.37)	0.22	0.34 (0.05)	< 0.34

TABLE 9–2. Summary of fitted model parameters and goodness-of-fit indices for reciprocal-cause and cross-lagged models *(continued)*

Measure	Model 1 (reciprocal-cause)		Model 2 (cross-lagged)	
	Indice	P	Indice	P
Goodness-of-fit indices				
Model chi square	$\chi^2_4 = 2.9$	0.58	$\chi^2_4 = 2.1$	0.71
RMSEA	0.00		0.00	
RMSR	0.014		0.015	
AIC	36.9		36.1	
BIC	136.5		135.8	

Note. The fitted models permitted the disturbances of the variables $MD t'$ and $GAD t'$ to be correlated within time 1 to allow for the fact that the structural models may not explain all of the observed associations between $MD t'$ and $GAD t'$ at each time. To simplify the model presentation, we did not depict these covariances in Figures 9–1 and 9–2, but the fitted covariances are reported above. AIC = Akaike information criterion; BIC = Bayesian information criterion; C1 = underlying causal factor for MD; C2 = underlying causal factor for GAD; GAD = generalized anxiety disorder; MD = major depression; RMSEA = root mean square error of approximation; RMSR = root mean square residual correlation.

Stability

Both models suggest some across-time stability in major depression and GAD, over and above the effects of common causes.

Discussion

Our analysis of these data leads to two major conclusions about the origins of the correlation and comorbidity between major depression and GAD.

1. In confirmation of a large amount of previous research, there is evidence to suggest GAD and major depression are influenced by common causal factors that account for much of the correlation and comorbidity between these conditions.
2. In confirmation of the suggestions put forward by Kessler et al. (see Chapter 7, this volume), there also is evidence of additional causal pathways, over and above the common causal factors.

Results of our analysis lead to the conclusion that, after common factors are taken into account, changes in depressive symptoms may lead to changes in GAD symptoms, but changes in GAD symptoms do not lead to changes in major depression symptoms. These results are only partially consistent with the conclusion drawn by Kessler et al. (see Chapter 7, this volume), who suggested a bidirectional relationship. Nonetheless, both studies are in agreement over the common point that there appear to be structural relationships between major depression and GAD over and above the effects of common causes.

It must be stressed that the work presented in this chapter is both exploratory and preliminary and is subject to a number of important caveats. First, it is important to recognize that the model focuses on symptoms of GAD and major depression rather than upon diagnostic measures, and findings for symptom-level data may not translate readily to diagnostic classifications. Second, the process of model fitting raises some complex technical issues. In particular, to solve the proposed model it has been necessary to use variables measured at one time as causes of the same measures at another time. Technically, such variables have been described as lagged endogenous variables, and the use of such variables in structural models may lead to potential conceptual and statistical problems. Conceptually, treating a variable as a cause of itself at a later time is a moot argument. Furthermore, these difficulties translate into problems of statistical estimation because the absence of information on causal factors, other than the variable itself, leads to estimation difficulties. To resolve these problems, the introduction of further measures (instruments) that identify sources of unique variation in major depression and GAD would be required.

For all of these reasons, it would be unwise to believe the analyses we have presented provide a definitive and unambiguous resolution to the issues that have been raised about the relationship between these two disorders. Nonetheless, our findings clearly suggest that a "common causes" model is not completely adequate to explain the correlation and comorbidity between major depression and GAD and that there are grounds for suspecting the existence of fine-grained relationships in which the onset of one condition may provoke the onset of the other. In turn, our findings favor the conclusions that major depression and GAD are two closely related conditions rather than being different expressions of the same underlying disorder.

References

American Psychiatric Association: Diagnostic and Statistical Manual of Mental Disorders, 4th Edition. Washington, DC, American Psychiatric Association, 1994

Fergusson DM, Horwood LJ, Boden JM: Structure of internalizing symptoms in early adulthood. Br J Psychiatry 189:540–546, 2006

10

CONFIRMATORY FACTOR ANALYSIS OF COMMON MENTAL DISORDERS ACROSS CULTURES

K. S. Jacob, M.D., Ph.D., MRCPsych
Martin Prince, M.D., MRCPsych
David Goldberg, D.M., FRCPsych

Common mental disorders are widely prevalent in primary care and are often disabling. Although the traditional depression-anxiety dichotomy has been generally accepted and employed in practice, the subcategorization of common mental disorders has been controversial. Clinical classifications have preferred categories, although dimensional models have been said to reflect clinical reality more accurately (Feinstein 1985). Attempts at sorting these issues have often employed the concept of "latent variables," unifying constructs that characterize responses to related groups of variables. The identification of such underlying factors greatly simplifies the description and understanding of complex phenomena like common mental disorders.

Studies of common mental disorders have often employed principal-component analysis to identify factors that parsimoniously describe correlations between observed depression and anxiety variables. Research from primary care has suggested that the two-factor model of anxiety and depression—although the two factors were found to be highly correlated—provided a slightly better fit than the one-factor solution (Goldberg et al. 1987). Many studies of patients of psychiatry clinics have also suggested similar two-factor solutions. From a review of studies that employed principal-component analyses of symptoms, personality, and illness characteristics of patients with affective disorders, it was found that most solutions were consistent with factors indicative of depression and anxiety (Mullaney 1984).

Exploratory factor analysis, however, has been criticized on many grounds (Dunn et al. 1993), including 1) subjectivity involved in the comparison of the observed factor structure with the hypothetical structure; 2) technique not being hypothesis driven; 3) small samples resulting in unstable latent variables; and 4) technique being sensitive to the psychometric properties of the scales employed.

Confirmatory factor analysis (CFA), on the other hand, allows for testing of various hypotheses about the structure of latent variables in the data (Bentler and Stein 1992; Cole 1987; Dunn et al. 1993). CFA can be employed to test whether different data sets have the same factor structure. Unlike exploratory factor analysis, which does not test a specified hypothesis on the factor structure of observed data, CFA allows for assessment of a particular hypothesized factor model. CFA, which examines the goodness of fit between the hypothesized model and the observed factor structure, eliminates the inherent "eyeballing" and consequent subjectivity of exploratory factor analysis.

Researchers have employed CFA to assess cross-cultural validity of the Euro-D, a late-life depression scale (The SHARE Project; Castro-Costa et al. 2008). CFA also has been employed to assess latent-variable models of common mental disorders (Jacob et al. 1998). This chapter compares data on common mental disorders from 11 different primary care populations. CFA was performed to assess whether data from these populations had the same factors structure.

Methods

DATA

Data sets from culturally diverse populations in 11 settings (community and primary care) in 7 countries were analyzed. Details of the data sets are given in Table 10–1.

ASSESSMENT OF COMMON MENTAL DISORDERS

All studies employed the Clinical Interview Schedule Revised (CISR; Lewis et al. 1992) to assess common mental disorders. This instrument is a standardized semi-structured interview designed to assess the mental states of people with nonpsychotic psychiatric morbidity. The CISR does not include interviews with clinical judgment and hence minimizes observer bias. Many aspects of interviewing style are prescribed by the interview, including the exact wording of most of the questions and specific rules for coding each symptom.

TABLE 10–1. Details of datasets

Country	Place	Setting	N	Age, y (SD)	Females, n (%)
Chile	Santiago	Primary care	1,701	35.08 (14.16)	1,129 (66.4%)
Chile	Santiago	Community	3,870	36.85 (13.76)	2,332 (60.3%)
Ethiopia	Addis Ababa		117		
India	Goa	Primary care	303	44.6 (14.3)	210 (69.3%)
India	Goa	Community	2,494	32.4 (8.1)	
India	Vellore	Primary care	350	34.7 (13.0)	244 (69.7%)
Pakistan		Community	86	25.7 (4.0)	86 (100%)
Tanzania			354	30.9 (10.9)	225 (63.6%)
Thailand			1,052	20.3 (2.9)	585 (55.6%)
United Kingdom	London	Primary care	404	35.7 (13.1)	257 (63.6%)
UK-NPMS Archive		Community	8,580	47.5 (15.2)	3,203 (37.3%)

Note. UK-NPMS=UK National Psychiatric Morbidity Survey.

The CISR has 14 subsections: somatic symptoms, fatigue, concentration, sleep problems, irritability, worry about physical health, depression, depressive ideas, worry, anxiety, phobia, panic, obsessions, and compulsions. Scores for subsections range from 0–4 (0–5 for depressive ideas). Ratings obtained can be presented for each symptom group and can be summed up to yield a total score. Algorithms also have been developed that allow an ICD-10 diagnosis. The CISR has been shown to have high interrater reliability and has been translated into many languages and employed in diverse cultures.

STATISTICAL ANALYSIS

Principal-Component Analysis

We calculated mean scores on all CISR subscales for data from all settings. Cronbach's alpha was also calculated. Principal-component analysis was performed, with varimax rotation. All factors with eigenvalues greater than 1 were considered significant.

Confirmatory Factor Analysis

A model that specifies relations between observed variables and latent factors was tested using CFA. We compared two models in which all item loadings were 1) constrained and 2) not constrained to be identical between countries. In each case, factor variances and covariances were sample specific. The χ^2 statistic was used to measure absolute fit of the model. The Akaike's Information Criterion (AIC), which adjusts the model χ^2 to penalize for model complexity, was also used with a lower value, suggesting better fit (Akaike 1987). Other indices of relative fit were also employed, because the χ^2 test is very sensitive to large sample size or to a violation of the multivariate normality assumption (Bentler and Bonett 1980). Indices of relative fit included:

1. *Goodness of Fit Index (GFI).* Values near 0 indicate poor fit, whereas values near 1.0 indicate good fit; values greater than 0.95 suggest a good fit whereas those above 0.90 suggest a satisfactory fit.
2. *Tucker-Lewis Index (TLI).* TLI (Tucker and Lewis 1973) indicates the proportion of covariation among indicators explained by the model, relative to a null model of independence, and is independent of sample size; values greater than 0.90 are considered satisfactory (Dunn et al. 1993; Marsh et al. 1996).
3. *Root Mean Square Error of Approximation (RMSEA).* RMSEA assesses badness-of-fit per degree of freedom in the model and is 0 if the model fits perfectly; RMSEA values of less than 0.05 indicate close fit and 0.05–0.08 reasonable fit of a model (Browne 1990).

Description of data and the principal-component analysis were conducted with SPSS 12 and CFA with AMOS 5 (Arbuckle 2003).

Results

Data from a total of 19,201 subjects from 7 countries and 11 settings were included in the analysis. Details related to age and gender are shown in Table 10–1. A majority of the data sets had a preponderance of women, with average ages between 30 and 50 years.

PRINCIPAL-COMPONENT ANALYSIS

Table 10–2 shows the results of our exploratory factor analysis. Most data sets had two factors with high eigenvalues and variance. However, many of these data sets also had one or two additional factors with lower eigenvalues and variance. Initial examination of the data also shows that these two factors could be labeled broadly "depression" and "anxiety." Nevertheless, a closer examination of factor loadings suggests marked variation between data sets on the items that load on each factor and also in the loading of each item.

CONFIRMATORY FACTOR ANALYSIS

Table 10–3 shows results of the CFA for the one-factor model. The unconstrained one-factor model fits moderately well according to all relative-fit indices. The fit of the fully constrained model (factor loadings set to be equal across samples) is significantly weaker statistically (χ^2 for difference between the two models = 5,497; df = 130; P < 0.0001). The relative-fit indices (e.g., GFI, TLI, RMSEA) also suggest much worse fit of the fully constrained model, particularly with respect to the AIC (nearly double that of the unconstrained model). The hypothesis of full-measurement invariance of the one-factor solution across samples is, therefore, rejected.

Inspection of the pattern of factor loadings in the unconstrained model suggests that most of the heterogeneity across samples arises from four symptoms: phobia, panic, obsessions, and compulsions. The first would seem to be a general anxiety/depression factor and the second a specific anxiety factor with the symptoms phobia, panic, obsession, and compulsion. Consequently, a two-factor solution was assessed, testing the hypotheses that 1) both the general anxiety/depression factor and specific anxiety factor were invariant across samples; and 2) only the general anxiety/depression factor is invariant across samples (partial measurement invariance).

All two-factor solutions for the unconstrained model, the partially constrained model, and the fully constrained model had poor indices of absolute fit, as indicated by the χ^2 values (Table 10–4). However, the measures of absolute fit for the fully and partially constrained models were worse than when factor loadings were

TABLE 10–2. Principal-component analysis with varimax rotation

	Two-factor solution		Factors eigenvalue > 1	Variables not captured in two-factor solution
Country, place, setting	One-factor	Two-factor		
Chile, community			2	Anxiety, obsession
% Variance	28.3	14.0		
Item loading	**Depression, fatigue** depressive ideas, sleep, concentration, irritability, somatic symptoms *worry, worry physical*	Phobia, panic, compulsion		
Chile, primary care			2	Worry physical, panic
% Variance	28.8	12.4		
Item loading	**Depression, fatigue, anxiety** depressive ideas, sleep somatic symptoms, concentration, *irritability, worry*	Phobia, obsession, *compulsion*		

TABLE 10–2. Principal-component analysis with varimax rotation *(continued)*

	Two-factor solution			
Country, place, setting	One-factor	Two-factor		Factors eigenvalue > 1	Variables not captured in two-factor solution

Country, place, setting	One-factor	Two-factor	Factors eigenvalue > 1	Variables not captured in two-factor solution
Ethiopia			4	Somatic symptoms, concentration, worry, worry physical, anxiety, compulsions, obsession
% Variance	39.2	10.4		
Item loading	**Depression, depressive ideas, irritability,** *fatigue*	**Phobia, panic** sleep		
India, Goa, community			4	Concentration, worry physical, anxiety, sleep, compulsions, obsession, phobia, panic, irritability
% Variance	17.0	15.5		
Item loading	**Depression, depressive ideas** worry	**Fatigue, somatic symptoms**		
India, Goa, primary care			4	Worry physical, worry, compulsions, phobia, panic
% Variance	32.1	8.9		

TABLE 10–2. Principal-component analysis with varimax rotation *(continued)*

	Two-factor solution			
	One-factor	Two-factor	Factors eigenvalue > 1	Variables not captured in two-factor solution
Country, place, setting				
India, Goa, primary care *(continued)*				
Item loading	**Depression, depressive ideas** fatigue, sleep, irritability, anxiety, *somatic symptoms, concentration*	Obsession		
India, Vellore, primary care				
% Variance	37.8	12.2		
Item loading	**Depression, depressive ideas, fatigue, concentration, worry physical** sleep, irritability, anxiety, worry *somatic symptoms*	Compulsions, obsessions *panic*	3	Phobia
Pakistan				
% Variance	46.5	11.1		
Item loading	**Depression, depressive ideas, fatigue, concentration, worry, irritability, anxiety, somatic symptoms** sleep, obsessions	Phobia, panic	3	Compulsions, worry physical

TABLE 10–2. Principal-component analysis with varimax rotation *(continued)*

Country, place, setting	Two-factor solution		Factors eigenvalue > 1	Variables not captured in two-factor solution
	One-factor	Two-factor		
Tanzania			3	Phobia, panic, compulsion, concentration, worry physical
% Variance	21.1	15.9		
Item loading	**Depression, depressive ideas** worry, irritability, obsessions	**Fatigue** sleep, somatic symptoms		
Thailand			3	Phobia, panic, compulsion, obsession, concentration, sleep, irritability
% Variance	16.3	17.6		
Item loading	**Depression, depressive ideas**	**Worry, anxiety, somatic symptoms, fatigue, worry physical**		
UK—Rotherhithe			3	Concentration, irritability, phobia
% Variance	25.3	17.1		
Item loading	**Panic** depression, depressive ideas, worry, worry physical, obsession, *compulsions*	**Somatic symptoms, fatigue** sleep		

TABLE 10–2. Principal-component analysis with varimax rotation *(continued)*

	Two-factor solution			
Country, place, setting	One-factor	Two-factor		Factors eigenvalue > 1	Variables not captured in two-factor solution

Country, place, setting	One-factor	Two-factor		Factors eigenvalue > 1	Variables not captured in two-factor solution
UK-NPMS Archive					
% Variance	37.0	7.9		2	Obsession
Item loading	**Depression, fatigue** depressive ideas, concentration, sleep, worry, anxiety, irritability *somatic symptoms, worry physical*	Phobia, panic, compulsion			
All data sets					
% Variance	32.2	13.54		2	Panic, obsessions
Item loading	**Depression, depressive ideas, fatigue** anxiety, concentration, irritability, sleep, somatic symptoms, worry *worry physical*	Compulsion, phobia			

Note. Item loading: **bold**=>0.70; regular=0.60–0.69; *italics*=0.50–0.59. Worry refers to general psychological health; worry physical refers to worry about physical health.

allowed to differ between samples. Similarly, the indices of relative fit (e.g., GFI, TLI, RMSEA) were reasonable for the unconstrained model but were poorer when partial or full constraints were applied.

The two-factor solution was marginally superior to the one-factor solution. Constraining both sets of factor loadings to be equal across samples resulted in a significant deterioration in goodness of fit, suggesting that the criteria for full-measurement invariance were not met. Constraining only the general anxiety/depression factor loadings to be equal across samples again resulted in deterioration in model fit, suggesting that these parameters also varied across samples and the criteria for partial-measurement invariance also were not met.

A detailed examination of the factor loading suggests that, for the specific anxiety factor of the two-factor model, there was wide variation in factor loading for symptoms of phobia, panic, obsessions, and compulsions, particularly in three south Asian samples—Vellore, Pakistan, and Goa Primary Care—and also a poor fit in the Ethiopia and Tanzania samples.

Discussion

This study employed CFA on many data sets from culturally diverse populations. Limitations of the study include that the data did not have a multivariate normal distribution and that sample sizes of some individual groups were small. However, the majority of populations included had large sample sizes, especially considering the fact that the models tested had only one- and two-factor solutions. Although the theory behind CFA requires large sample sizes and multivariate normal distributions, most applications of the technique have largely ignored this requirement, appealing, perhaps, to a general confidence in the robustness of most normally based statistical procedures (Jacob et al. 1998).

CFA was employed to test whether the different samples had a similar factor structure. The values suggest poor fit on χ^2, an absolute index of fit. However, this measure is often influenced by data sets with large sample sizes and by psychometric properties of instruments employed. Consequently, measures of relative indices of fit were employed to assess the goodness of fit. Nevertheless, the data sets had less than ideal fit, using the strict criteria of the relative-fit indices: the GFI (>0.95) and the TLI (>0.95).

The relative-fit indices of the one- and two-factor models, when fitted across data sets, with factor loadings allowed to vary between samples, suggested a reasonable fit. However, when these loadings were set to be equal across samples, a poorer fit was obtained, suggesting that the same one- and two-factor models do not fit well across all data sets. In addition, the one-factor and the two-factor (general anxiety/depression factor and specific anxiety factor) models had similar indices of fit, with the two-factor model marginally superior. Nevertheless, a detailed

TABLE 10–3. Confirmatory factor analysis comparing an unconstrained one-factor model with one in which factor loadings are constrained to be equal in all samples

Symptom	Vellore	Thailand	Pakistan	Tanzania (PC)	Goa	Chile	Chile (PC)	Goa (PC)	Ethiopia	Rotherhithe (PC)	UK NPMS	Constrained model
Fatigue	1.00	1.00	1.00	1.00	1.00	1.00	1.00	1.00	1.00	1.00	1.00	1.00
Concentration	0.62	0.75	0.84	0.66	0.65	0.77	0.86	0.98	0.75	1.24	0.70	0.75
Sleep	0.96	0.79	0.76	1.10	0.66	0.78	0.81	0.96	0.78	0.96	0.84	0.81
Irritability	0.76	1.28	1.18	0.97	1.53	0.93	0.95	0.89	1.01	1.00	0.79	0.89
Worry over physical health	0.94	0.65	0.15	1.23	1.10	0.45	0.68	0.88	0.68	0.80	0.46	0.52
Depression	1.16	0.80	1.17	1.81	2.05	0.93	1.25	1.31	1.02	1.37	0.81	0.94
Worry	0.88	1.46	1.07	1.16	0.16	0.91	0.95	0.93	0.90	1.45	0.95	0.79
Anxiety	0.75	0.41	1.09	0.91	1.64	0.51	1.24	1.22	0.31	1.07	0.65	0.69
Suicidality	1.31	1.05	1.16	1.60	2.25	0.94	1.18	1.43	1.27	1.44	0.80	0.95
Somatic	0.45	0.82	1.12	1.14	1.15	0.70	0.76	0.76	0.78	0.85	0.43	0.56
Phobia	0.03	0.46	0.05	0.44	0.39	0.43	0.26	0.07	0.37	0.49	0.32	0.32
Panic	0.59	0.13	0.27	0.36	0.15	0.35	0.48	0.67	0.77	0.81	0.23	0.27
Compulsion	0.04	0.59	0.08	0.39	0.24	0.29	0.22	0.05	0.15	0.64	0.22	0.21
Obsession	0.07	0.38	0.83	1.57	0.43	0.08	0.29	-0.01	0.19	1.11	0.36	0.19

TABLE 10–3. Confirmatory factor analysis comparing an unconstrained one-factor model with one in which factor loadings are constrained to be equal in all samples *(continued)*

Model fit indices	Unconstrained	Constrained
χ^2	6245	11742
df	847	977
χ^2 difference	—	5497
df	—	130
P value	—	<0.0001
GFI	0.95	0.91
TLI	0.87	0.78
RMSEA	0.018	0.024
AIC	6861	12098

Note. AIC=Akaike's information criterion; GFI=Goodness of Fit Index; PC=primary care; RMSEA=root mean square error of approximation; TLI=Tucker Lewis Index; UK-NPMS=UK National Psychiatric Morbidity Survey.

TABLE 10–4. Confirmatory factor analysis comparing an unconstrained two-factor model with models in which 1) all factor loadings are constrained to be equal in all samples (fully constrained), and 2) only anxiety/depression factor loadings are constrained (partially constrained)

Symptom	Vellore	Thailand	Pakistan	Tanzania (PC)	Goa	Chile	Chile (PC)	Goa (PC)	Ethiopia	Rother-hithe (PC)	UK-NPMS	Constrained model
				UNCONSTRAINED MODEL								
General anxiety/depression												
Fatigue	1.00	1.00	1.00	1.00	1.00	1.00	1.00	1.00	1.00	1.00	1.00	
Concentration	0.62	0.74	0.83	0.67	0.65	0.76	0.86	0.98	0.73	1.24	0.70	
Sleep	0.96	0.79	0.76	1.10	0.66	0.78	0.81	0.96	0.75	0.96	0.83	
Irritability	0.75	1.28	1.17	0.97	1.52	0.93	0.95	0.89	1.01	1.00	0.79	
Worry over physical health	0.94	0.66	0.15	1.24	1.08	0.45	0.67	0.88	0.68	0.79	0.46	
Depression	1.15	0.82	1.16	1.82	2.12	0.94	1.25	1.32	1.04	1.37	0.80	
Worry	0.88	1.47	1.07	1.16	0.16	0.91	0.95	0.93	0.90	1.46	0.95	
Anxiety	0.74	0.41	1.08	0.91	1.63	0.51	1.24	1.21	0.30	1.07	0.65	
Suicidality	1.30	1.07	1.15	1.60	2.31	0.94	1.17	1.43	1.27	1.45	0.79	
Somatic	0.44	0.82	1.11	1.14	1.13	0.70	0.75	0.76	0.78	0.86	0.43	

TABLE 10–4. Confirmatory factor analysis comparing an unconstrained two-factor model with models in which 1) all factor loadings are constrained to be equal in all samples (fully constrained), and 2) only anxiety/depression factor loadings are constrained (partially constrained) *(continued)*

Symptom	Vellore	Thailand	Pakistan	Tanzania (PC)	Goa	Chile	Chile (PC)	Goa (PC)	Ethiopia	Rother-hithe (PC)	UK-NPMS	Constrained model
				UNCONSTRAINED MODEL *(continued)*								
Specific anxiety												
Phobia	1.00	1.00	1.00	1.00	1.00	1.00	1.00	1.00	1.00	1.00	1.00	
Panic	315.4	0.27	25.4	0.81	0.39	0.77	1.64	12.9	2.55	1.56	0.70	
Compulsion	28.2	1.20	39.4	0.89	0.27	0.64	0.82	0.87	0.03	1.16	0.67	
Obsession	42.4	0.71	203.3	3.59	0.51	0.15	1.07	0.08	0.17	1.95	1.02	
Model-fit indices												
χ^2	5239											
df	836											
GFI	0.96											
TLI	0.90											
RMSEA	0.017 (0.016–0.017)											
AIC	5877											

TABLE 10–4. Confirmatory factor analysis comparing an unconstrained two-factor model with models in which 1) all factor loadings are constrained to be equal in all samples (fully constrained), and 2) only anxiety/depression factor loadings are constrained (partially constrained) *(continued)*

Symptom	Vellore	Thailand	Pakistan	Tanzania (PC)	Goa	Chile	Chile (PC)	Goa (PC)	Ethiopia	Rotherhithe (PC)	UK-NPMS	Constrained model
					PARTIALLY CONSTRAINED MODEL							
General anxiety/depression												
Fatigue	1.00											1.00
Concentration	0.76											0.76
Sleep	0.82											0.81
Irritability	0.88											0.88
Worry over physical health	0.53											0.53
Depression	0.95											0.95
Worry	0.80											0.80
Anxiety	0.69											0.68
Suicidality	0.96											0.95
Somatic	0.56											0.56

TABLE 10–4. Confirmatory factor analysis comparing an unconstrained two-factor model with models in which 1) all factor loadings are constrained to be equal in all samples (fully constrained), and 2) only anxiety/depression factor loadings are constrained (partially constrained) *(continued)*

Symptom	Vellore	Thailand	Pakistan	Tanzania (PC)	Goa	Chile	Chile (PC)	Goa (PC)	Ethiopia	Rotherhithe (PC)	UK-NPMS	Constrained model
PARTIALLY CONSTRAINED MODEL (continued)												
Specific anxiety												
Phobia	1.00	1.00	1.00	1.00	1.00	1.00	1.00	1.00	1.00	1.00	1.00	1.00
Panic	262.5	0.29	31.2	0.82	0.43	0.77	1.65	12.8	2.56	1.55	0.71	0.71
Compulsion	23.4	1.19	49.0	0.87	0.29	0.64	0.84	0.86	0.03	1.15	0.67	0.61
Obsession	35.5	0.69	255.4	3.39	0.54	0.15	1.09	0.06	0.17	1.91	1.01	0.58
Model-fit indices												
χ^2	9080											10438
df	926											956
χ^2 difference	—											—
df difference	—											—
P value	—											—
GFI	0.93											0.92
TLI	0.83											0.81
RMSEA	0.021											0.023
AIC	9,538											10,746

Note. AIC=Akaike's Information Criterion; GFI=Goodness of Fit Index; PC=primary care; RMSEA=root mean square error of approximation; TLI=Tucker Lewis Index; UK-NPMS=UK National Psychiatric Morbidity Survey.

examination of factor loadings for the two-factor model suggested wide variation in the symptoms phobia, panic, obsessions, and compulsions on the specific anxiety factor, especially for South Asian (India and Pakistan) and African countries (Ethiopia and Tanzania).

Measures of absolute fit and the use of conservative estimates of relative fit (e.g., GFI>0.95, TLI>0.95) suggest that both the one- and two-factor models do not fit well across data sets. Use of less-stringent criteria of relative fit (e.g., GFI>0.90, TLI>0.90) suggests a reasonable fit. However, the fact that when factor loadings were constrained across a data set, the goodness of fit deteriorated, suggests that the same models do not fit well across data sets.

Results of this study are similar to findings of previous CFAs on populations from Santiago, Rotherhithe, Ealing, and Harare (Jacob et al. 1998). The one-factor model, being a more parsimonious explanation, may be considered a better solution for common mental disorders in primary care and in the community.

Other evidence from primary care also suggests that the reality of primary care differs from that of psychiatric settings (Jacob 2006b). The issues involved are mentioned briefly.

1. There are differences between patients attending a psychiatric hospital and those who present to primary care. Patients who visit psychiatric facilities often have severe, complex, and chronic illness and are highly motivated to receive treatment from specialists. On the other hand, those who visit general practitioners have milder and less-distinct forms of illness, with concomitantly less psychosocial stress.
2. Differing conceptual models and perceptions are employed in different settings. Psychiatrists employ medical models, whereas general practitioners focus on the psychosocial context, stress, personality, and coping (Jacob 2006b).
3. In patients attending primary care, symptom scores on standardized interview schedules—for example, the CISR (Lewis et al. 1992)—are distributed continuously, with no point of rarity between cases and non-cases, making dichotomous clinical decision making difficult.
4. Mixed presentations of anxiety and depression are common in primary care.
5. Many patients who cross the case threshold do not have the full-syndrome attributes of depression or anxiety (Stein et al. 1995).
6. Labeling of patients with subsyndromal presentations based on distress and impairment essentially implies a lowering of the threshold for diagnosis (Zinbarg et al. 1994).
7. The most common presentation of psychiatric problems in primary care is with medically unexplained somatic symptoms (Tylee and Gandhi 2005). However, a significant number of such patients also mention the presence of simultaneous psychological stress or distress. The cultural background of the patient may determine the mode of presentation, that is, psychological or somatic symptoms.

Taken together, results of this study, along with other evidence, suggest the need for a different framework for primary care. These data argue for a different approach and perspective to diagnosing and managing such presentations (Jacob 2006b). It is possible that the symptoms of common mental disorders reflect general emotional distress. Replication of this study is needed in other populations using different measures of symptoms of common mental disorders.

References

Akaike H: Factor analysis and AIC. Psychometrika 52:317–332, 1987
Araya R: Common Mental Disorders and Detection by Primary Care Physicians. London, England, University of London, 2000
Araya R, Rojas G, Fritsch R, et al: Common mental disorders in Santiago, Chile: prevalence and socio-demographic correlates. Br J Psychiatry 178:228–233, 2001
Arbuckle JL: Amos 5.0 Update to the Amos User's Guide. Chicago, SPSS Inc, 2003
Bentler PM, Bonett DG: Significance tests and goodness of fit in the analysis of covariance structures. Psychol Bull 88:588–606, 1980
Bentler PM, Stein JA: Structural equation models in medical research. Stat Methods Med Res 1:159–181, 1992
Browne MW: MUTMUM PC: User's Guide. Columbus, OH, Ohio State University, 1990
Castro-Costa E, Dewey M, Stewart R, et al: Ascertaining late-life depression symptoms in Europe: an evaluation of the survey version of the EURO-D scale in 10 nations. The SHARE Project. Int J Methods Psychiatr Res 17:12–29, 2008
Cole DA: Utility of confirmatory factor analysis in test validation research. J Consult Clin Psychol 55:584–594, 1987
Dunn G, Everitt B, Pickles A: Modelling Covariances and Latent Variables using EQS, 1st Edition. London, England, Chapman and Hall, 1993
Feinstein AR: Clinical Epidemiology: The Architecture of Clinical Research. Philadelphia, PA, WB Saunders, 1985
Goldberg DP, Bridges K, Duncan-Jones P, et al: Dimensions of neurosis seen in primary-care settings. Psychol Med 17:461–470, 1987
Jacob KS: The diagnosis and management of depression and anxiety in primary care: the need for a different framework. Postgrad Med J 82:836–839, 2006b
Jacob KS, Everitt BS, Patel V, et al: The comparison of latent variable models of non-psychotic psychiatric morbidity in four culturally diverse populations. Psychol Med 28:145–152, 1998
Lewis GH, Pelosi A, Araya R, et al: Measuring psychiatric disorder in the community: a standardized assessment for use by lay interviewers. Psychol Med 22:465–486, 1992
Marsh HW, Balla JR, Hau KT: An evaluation of incremental fit indices: a clarification of mathematical and empirical properties, in Advanced Structural Equation Modeling: Issues and Techniques. Edited by Marcoulides GA, Schumacker RE. Mahwah, NJ, Lawrence Erlbaum Associates, 1996, pp 315–355
Mullaney JA: The relationship between anxiety and depression: a review of some principal component analytic studies. J Affect Disord 7:139–148, 1984

Stein MB, Kirk P, Prabhu V, et al: Mixed anxiety-depression in a primary-care clinic. J Affect Disord 34:79–84, 1995

Tucker L, Lewis C: A reliability coefficient for maximum likelihood factor analysis. Psychometrika 38:1–10, 1973

Tylee A, Gandhi P: The importance of somatic symptoms in depression in primary care. Prim Care Companion J Clin Psychiatry 7:167–176, 2005

Zinbarg RE, Barlow DH, Liebowitz M, et al: The DSM-IV field trial for mixed anxiety-depression. Am J Psychiatry 151:1153–1162, 1994

Commentary

COMMENTARY ON "CONFIRMATORY FACTOR ANALYSIS OF COMMON MENTAL DISORDERS ACROSS CULTURES"

Dan J. Stein, M.D., Ph.D.
Vikram Patel, M.Sc., MRCPsych, Ph.D.
Gerhard Heinze, M.D.

In Chapter 10, Jacob and colleagues note that previous work, based on principal-component analyses of psychiatric symptoms in primary care, has usually identified a two-factor solution of anxiety and depression. These authors carried out a confirmatory factor analysis—a more robust statistical method for testing hypotheses on the relationships between symptoms—on data derived from eight countries ($N>19,000$). For this work, they used the Revised Clinical Interview Schedule (CIS-R), a symptom-based structured interview that generates ICD-10 diagnoses of common mental disorders. They report that a two-factor model is again marginally superior to a single-factor solution. However, they note that even a two-factor solution had less than an ideal fit and that the patterns of symptoms loading on the two factors differed considerably across sites. Furthermore, these findings emphasize the high correlation between anxiety and depressive symptoms across sites, suggesting that a one-factor solution is more parsimonious. The authors also underscore the distinction between specialist and primary-care practices. Most cases of depression and generalized anxiety disorder (GAD) are encountered in primary care, where neurotic psychiatric syndromes may reflect general emotional distress and are less likely to be distinct from one another; where cultural background often influences the mode of presentation; and where classifications that reflect specialist psychiatric presentations are not necessarily useful.

In our response, we raise a number of issues about cross-cultural aspects of anxiety and depression and, in particular, about the practical implications of classification for mental health care in primary care within developing countries.

Different Approaches Within Cross-Cultural Psychiatry

Cross-cultural psychiatry offers a range of concepts and methods for approaching psychiatric disorders (Stein 1993; Stein and Williams 2002). Some clinicians who work in this area adopt a "classical," or "positivist," approach and emphasize that, throughout different parts of the world, psychiatric disorders have a universal form, albeit with somewhat varying local content. Data that show that particular depressive and anxiety symptoms are found across the globe, are closely correlated, and are associated with disability would seem to be consistent with such a view. Those who work in this perspective might expect the psychobiological correlates of depressive and anxiety symptoms to overlap but might caution that, because these correlates are not yet fully known, it is not possible to make claims about whether major depressive episode (MDE) and GAD are different forms of the same psychiatric disorder or different disorders altogether.

The development of structured diagnostic interviews and symptom-rating scales for use within a range of different settings is consistent with a classical approach to psychiatric classification insofar as it implies the existence of universal categories. A classical approach might argue that, provided semantic equivalence can be established across different translations of such instruments, the constructs measured in different settings are ultimately similar. Clearly, there is the risk that when words such as "depression" or "anxiety" are translated into other languages, there may be changes in meaning, with consequent differences in response patterns. A classical approach emphasizes, however, that, given that the characteristic features of depression and anxiety are so universal, semantic equivalence across translations is likely to be high.

A contrasting approach in cross-cultural psychiatry has taken a more "critical" or "hermeneutic" approach and argued that both the form and content of symptoms are determined by culture, with our nosologies themselves best understood as cultural artifacts. The arguments that psychiatric symptoms across cultures reflect general distress, that culture determines the mode of presentation, and that medical models of psychiatric symptoms are not necessarily useful would seem consistent with such a view. This perspective has different views about how best to intervene, but there is often an emphasis on eliciting and accepting the patient's own explanatory models of symptoms. The debate about how to classify MDE and GAD may be viewed as more reflective of the sociopolitics of psychiatry than informative about emotional distress, per se.

A number of authors have argued that the constructs of depression and anxiety have characteristics that reflect their origin in a Western nosology. For example, it has been suggested that the emphasis in diagnostic criteria for depression on psychological symptoms, in contrast to the emphasis on somatic features in conceptualizing mood disorder in other parts of the globe, reflects a peculiarly Western separation of mind and body (Kleinman 1988). To the extent that categories, which are socially constructed in particular contexts, are reified and inappropriately employed in other settings, a category fallacy is committed.

An Integrated Approach to Psychiatric Classification

We propose an integrated approach to cross-cultural psychiatric classification. Across cultures, in regular medical and psychiatric practice, clinicians might be able to integrate aspects of both the "classical" and "critical" views. We can conceptualize MDE and GAD as biomedical disorders caused by psychobiological mechanisms but also accept that they are necessarily expressed and experienced within particular sociocultural contexts. In psychiatric practice, there is at least some evidence that the psychobiologies of MDE and GAD differ, with corresponding differences required in interventions. These data are, however, preliminary. On the other hand, within the particular cultural context of primary care practice, one can understand why it might be useful to conceptualize depression, anxiety, and somatic symptoms as representing overlapping variations of expression of emotional distress in response to life stressors and difficulties. Nevertheless, ongoing advances in psychobiology and treatment indicate that this view is not always correct (Stein and Matsunaga 2001; Stein and Rapoport 1996).

Somatic symptoms are a common form of presenting symptoms, although the classical psychological symptoms of depression and anxiety also can be relatively easily elicited in both developing and developed countries. There is good evidence that symptoms of depression, GAD, and somatization are often comorbid—as well as more common in family members of probands than expected by chance—across a range of different settings, suggesting the existence of universal psychobiological mechanisms that underlie such confluences. At the same time, psychobiological mechanisms well may be altered by sociocultural features; expressions of distress seem to vary systematically from place to place and time to time. From a public health perspective, it would seem useful to emphasize the importance of recognizing the triad of symptoms of depression, anxiety, and somatization to primary care practitioners. Still, insofar as certain genes and environments predispose to particular symptoms within this triad, and to the extent that these symptoms respond to particular medications and psychotherapies, some degree of diagnostic "splitting" rather than "lumping" may be useful for etiological research.

In developing countries, the overwhelming majority of people with depressive, anxiety, and somatization symptoms will be seen in primary care. In these settings, many patients present with admixed symptoms—as is reflected in the chapter by Jacob and colleagues—where levels of comorbidity between depression, anxiety, and somatization symptoms are so high that distinctions between these disorders seem neither useful nor valid. Thus if we are to achieve the requirement of utility of a classification for public health and clinical practice from a global context, we must acknowledge that emotional and unexplained somatic symptoms cannot be easily separated in specific clusters. Discrete somatoform diagnoses are rare, and latent-trait and cluster analysis do not support main DSM-IV (American Psychiatric Association 1994) discrete categories. Emotional and somatoform diagnoses may load into one common factor ("internalizing" disorders). Furthermore, the relationships between somatic and depressive/anxiety symptoms are not unique to developing countries. Indeed, the recent World Mental Health Surveys have shown a strong linear relationship between the experience of somatic complaints (such as pain) and depressive and anxiety disorders in all settings of the surveys (Gureje et al. 2008).

On the other hand, some degree of diagnostic "splitting," rather than "lumping," is useful, even in resource-constrained environments. We propose, for public health and primary care at least, a broad or supraordinate category of dysphoric disorders, within which specific categories reflecting "prominent" depressive, somatic, or anxiety symptoms are proposed. This construct might be useful in guiding appropriate clinical interventions. Furthermore, a public health perspective would argue for sufficient resources to allow the recognition and treatment of a range of disorders other than the three sets of internalizing symptoms noted here (depression, GAD, somatization). For example, healthcare practitioners faced with patients presenting with panic disorder and obsessive-compulsive disorder may require knowledge that is not captured by very simple clinical guidelines for depression and anxiety (e.g., patients with panic disorder may need to be started on lower dosages of antidepressants than patients with most other mood and anxiety disorders, patients with obsessive-compulsive disorder may ultimately require higher dosages than would be used for a number of other disorders).

Conclusion

Cross-cultural data on the overlap of MDE/GAD and somatization are relatively sparse, and we commend the work of Jacobs and colleagues in addressing this overlap in a range of settings. In our brief commentary, we have taken a more conceptual approach, addressing some of the relevant cross-cultural theory and putting forward an integrated clinically based approach. More empirical work is needed to support the conclusions drawn here. Advances in our understandings of the psychobiology of internalizing disorders, their pharmacotherapy and psychotherapy, and how best to approach these conditions from a public health perspective will, hopefully, lead to a more valid and more useful psychiatric nosology in the future.

References

American Psychiatric Association: Diagnostic and Statistical Manual of Mental Disorders, 4th Edition. Washington, DC, American Psychiatric Association, 1994

Gureje O, Von Korff M, Kola L, et al: The relation between multiple pains and mental disorders: results from the World Mental Health Surveys. Pain 135:82–91, 2008

Kleinman A: Rethinking Psychiatry: From Cultural Category to Personal Experience. New York, Free Press, 1988

Stein DJ: Cross-cultural psychiatry and the DSM-IV. Compr Psychiatry 34:322–329, 1993

Stein DJ, Matsunaga H: Cross-cultural aspects of social anxiety disorder. Psychiatr Clin North Am 24:773–782, 2001

Stein DJ, Rapoport JL: Cross-cultural studies and obsessive-compulsive disorder. CNS Spectr 1:42–46, 1996

Stein DJ, Williams D: Cross-cultural aspects of anxiety disorders, in Textbook of Anxiety Disorders. Edited by Stein DJ, Hollander E. Washington, DC, American Psychiatric Publishing, 2002, pp 463–474

11

GENERALIZED ANXIETY DISORDER AND DEPRESSION

Childhood Risk Factors in a Birth Cohort Followed to Age 32 Years

Terrie E. Moffitt, Ph.D.
Avshalom Caspi, Ph.D.
HonaLee Harrington, B.A.
Barry Milne, Ph.D.
Maria Melchior, Sc.D.
David Goldberg, D.M., FRCPsych
Richie Poulton, Ph.D.

This chapter was prepared in response to a call for research that might inform how generalized anxiety disorder (GAD) should be characterized, in relation to depression, in forthcoming diagnostic systems (Kendler and Goldberg 2004). Proposals to collapse major depressive disorder (MDD) and GAD together in DSM-V would be supported if the two disorders share common antecedent risk factors. Here, we

---

Based on Moffitt TE, Caspi A, Harrington H, et al: "Generalized Anxiety Disorder and Depression: Childhood Risk Factors in a Birth Cohort Followed to Age 32." *Psychological Medicine* 37:441–452, 2007. Copyright © 2007, Cambridge University Press. Used with permission.

test whether prospectively assessed risk factors for MDD and GAD are similar or different. Prospective longitudinal research of this nature has been called for to help define the boundaries of mental disorders for DSM-V (Widiger and Clark 2000).

Six empirical observations point to a close association between MDD and GAD.

1. Epidemiological studies indicate that MDD and GAD co-occur beyond chance expectations (Angold et al. 1999; Mineka et al. 1998); among all disorders GAD is most comorbid with MDD (Kessler et al. 1996).
2. Twin studies have shown that MDD and GAD share joint genetic susceptibility (Kendler 1996), and among anxiety disorders, GAD is genetically closest to MDD (Kendler et al. 1995).
3. Personality studies have found that MDD and GAD share a continuously distributed vulnerability trait called "neuroticism" or "negative emotionality" (Barlow and Campbell 2000; Krueger et al. 1996; Watson et al. 2005).
4. Based on statistical models of the structure of psychopathology, MDD and GAD converge on the same latent internalizing factor (Krueger 1999; Krueger and Finger 2001; Krueger et al. 1998; Vollebergh et al. 2001).
5. Anxiety during childhood is a risk predictor for later MDD according to longitudinal studies (Breslau et al. 1995; Lewinsohn et al. 2000; Parker et al. 1999; Pine et al. 2001; Zahn-Waxler et al. 2000) and multigeneration family studies (Weissman et al. 2005).
6. MDD and GAD symptoms often respond to the same drugs (Kuzma and Black 2004).

These six observations have prompted speculation that MDD and GAD may be two clinical presentations of one disorder process, in which GAD-MDD co-occurrence is a sign of severity (Coryell et al. 1992; Merikangas et al. 2003; Mineka et al. 1998; Sartorius et al. 1996; Wittchen 1996; Zahn-Waxler et al. 2000). However, arguments also have been put forward that GAD and MDD should remain nosologically separate as independent diagnoses (Kessler 2005; Kessler et al. 2005), albeit grouped together with MDD in a new class to be entitled "distress disorders" (Watson et al. 2005). Thus, the relation between GAD and MDD and the nosological implications of that relation remain controversial (Kessler and Wittchen 2002; Wittchen et al. 2000).

A seventh type of evidence relevant to the classification of GAD and MDD would be information about antecedent risk predictors. Are risk factors for GAD and MDD the same or different? There is no shortage of studies that have reported risk factors for anxiety or for depression. However, such studies constitute two quite separate literatures, one for each disorder. Findings from these separate literatures could be compared, but such comparisons would confound any differences in risk factors with other differences between studies, such as differences in sample characteristics, research design, measurement age, or data collection methods (Phillips et al. 2005).

Systematic comparison, carried out within one cohort sample between GAD and MDD risk factors, is needed. Such a single-cohort comparison would offer the key additional advantage of being able to take comorbidity between GAD and MDD into account while making comparisons between them. Finally, such a comparison should ideally draw on risk factors measured prospectively before the onset of GAD and MDD, in order to document temporal precedence of risk factors. Prospective measurement also avoids relying on retrospective reports of risk factors, which may be biased by recall failure or by study participants' experiences of their disorders.

This chapter describes child and adolescent risk factors for adult MDD and GAD in the prospective-longitudinal Dunedin birth cohort. Our choice of risk factors for the present research was guided by Kendler's influential developmental model, which addresses the etiological complexity of internalizing disorders (Kendler et al. 2002). Although Kendler's review focused on pathways to depression, it incorporated all known antecedent risk factors for both depression and anxiety. The child/adolescent risk constructs specified were as follows: predisposing genetic influences (operationalized in our study as family history of anxiety or depression and maternal internalizing symptoms); exposure to an adverse family environment, including deprivation, abuse, or premature parental loss (operationalized as low childhood socioeconomic status, child maltreatment, and childhood parental absence due to death or marital dissolution); early onset anxiety and internalizing problems (operationalized as preschool inhibited temperament, childhood internalizing problems of anxiety and withdrawal, and childhood depression symptoms); conduct disorder (operationalized as childhood conduct problems); and a dysfunctional self-schema (operationalized as low adolescent self-esteem).

Predisposing personality traits were also specified (Kendler et al. 2002). We examined two adolescent personality trait measures that have featured prominently in the literature on depression and anxiety: negative emotionality and positive emotionality. Prior evidence suggests that high negative emotionality (e.g., high levels of neuroticism, alienation, irritability, stress reactivity) poses a common risk for depression and anxiety, whereas low positive emotionality (e.g., low levels of well-being, social potency, social closeness) poses specific risk, differentiating depression from anxiety (Watson 2005).

Elsewhere, we have described the longitudinal development of GAD and MDD in the Dunedin cohort from adolescence to adulthood and the comorbidity between the disorders (Moffitt et al. 2007). The odds ratio for cumulative MDD+GAD comorbidity in the cohort up to age 32 (OR=5.6; CI=3.9–7.2) resembled that from the National Comorbidity Survey (6.0 [NCS]; Kessler et al. 1996) and the NCS-Replication (6.4 [NCS-R]; Kessler et al. 2005).

The research question for this chapter is whether MDD and GAD have the same or different risk factors. However, because more than half of MDD and GAD cases are in the same individuals, this comorbid overlap necessarily must produce virtually identical risk factors for the two disorders. Therefore, tests for differential risk factors reported here isolate risk factors for GAD-only cases with no history of MDD and for MDD-only cases with no history of GAD, while including two further groups for comparison purposes: comorbid MDD+GAD and study members with no history of any mental disorder.

Method

SAMPLE

Participants were members of the Dunedin Multidisciplinary Health and Development Study (Moffitt et al. 2001). Of infants born in Dunedin, New Zealand between April 1972 and March 1973, 1,037 children (91% of eligible births; 52% male) participated in the first follow-up assessment at age 3 years, thereby constituting the base sample for the remainder of the study. Cohort families represented the full range of socioeconomic statuses in the general population of New Zealand's South Island and were, primarily, white. Participants attended the research unit for a full day of individual data collection. The Otago Ethics Committee granted ethical approval for each phase of this longitudinal study. Study members gave informed consent before participating. Assessments were carried out at ages 3, 5, 7, 9, 11, 13, 15, 18, 21, 26, and most recently 32 years, when we assessed 972 (96%) of the 1,015 Study members still alive in 2004–2005.

Cohort members who did not have diagnostic data from two or more of five periods (ages 18, 21, 26, 32 years and juvenile) were excluded when we defined diagnostic groups for comparison in this chapter; thus, 945 individuals were studied here, 8.6% with one missing diagnostic data point and 91.4% with no missing diagnostic data point.

MEASURES OF DISORDERS

Major Depressive Disorder at Ages 18, 21, 26, and 32 Years

MDD was diagnosed through structured interviews with study members, who used the Diagnostic Interview Schedule (Robins et al. 1989, 1995). Interviews were administered by healthcare professionals with tertiary degrees in clinical psychology, medicine, public health, or social work (not lay interviewers). At ages 18 and 21 years, diagnoses followed DSM-III-R (American Psychiatric Association 1987) and at ages 26 and 32 years, diagnoses followed DSM-IV (American Psychiatric Association 1994). Variable construction details, reliability and validity, and evidence of impairment for diagnoses in the cohort have been reported elsewhere (Feehan et al. 1994; Hankin et al. 1998; Newman et al. 1996). For example, attesting to validity, study members who were diagnosed with MDD at age 32 years self-reported their mean impairment resulting from MDD as 3.57 (SD=0.99) on a scale from 1 (some impairment) to 5 (severe impairment); 62% said they had received mental health services in the past year, and 31% said they took medication for their disorder. The past-year MDD prevalence of 14%, averaged across ages 15–32 years, for the Dunedin cohort is comparable with the past-year prevalence of 12% reported for 15- to 34-year-olds in the NCS (Kessler et al. 1993).

Generalized Anxiety Disorder at Ages 18, 21, 26, and 32 Years

GAD was diagnosed through instruments and procedures parallel to those described for MDD. To allow study of comorbidity, GAD was diagnosed if criteria were met, regardless of the presence of MDD. Attesting to validity, study members who were diagnosed with GAD at age 32 years self-reported their mean impairment resulting from GAD as 3.62 (SD=0.95) on a scale from 1 (some) to 5 (severe); 49% said they had received mental health services in the past year, and 25% said they took medication for their disorder. The past-year GAD prevalence of 7.0%, averaged across ages 18–32 years, for the Dunedin cohort is comparable with the past-year prevalence of 5.5% across all ages in the NCS (Kessler et al. 2005; published NCS data did not allow a comparison matched on age group).

For this chapter, GAD diagnoses followed the DSM-III (American Psychiatric Association 1980) 1-month criterion, instead of the DSM-IV 6-month duration criterion, because a 6-month criterion is stricter than MDD's 2-week criterion, a difference that would confound our comparisons between the two disorders on risk factors. Thus, all GAD cases in this chapter met full symptom criteria for GAD, but approximately one-half of the cases had a 6-month duration, whereas the other half met GAD criteria for some shorter period between 1 and 6 months. Twin research has shown that the etiology of GAD is the same, whether GAD lasts 6 months or 1–6 months (Kendler 1996). The NCS-R found that clinical significance and impairment were similar, whether GAD lasted 6 months or 1–6 months (Kessler et al. 2005). As occurred in the NCS-R, relaxing the duration criterion in the Dunedin Study increased the GAD prevalence rate—e.g., from 7.7% to 13.5% at age 32 years. However, as in the NCS-R (Kessler et al. 2005), associations between GAD and other study variables were virtually unaffected. Continuity from juvenile anxiety disorder to adult GAD was similar with the 6-month or 1-month duration criterion (OR=2.9 vs. 2.5), as was the female-to-male ratio for GAD (1.6:1 vs. 1.4:1). GAD-diagnosed study members' ratings of how much GAD symptoms had impaired their lives in the past year at age 32 years was similar with the 6-month or 1-month criterion (mean=3.81, SD=0.90 vs. mean=3.62, SD = 0.95), as was the percentage who received mental health services (55% vs. 49%). Most relevant here, longitudinal comorbidity was similar; with the 6-month or the 1-month criterion among MDD+GAD comorbid cases, anxiety onset occurred before, or concurrently with, MDD onset in 68% (6-month GAD criterion) versus 66% (1-month GAD criterion) of participants (Moffitt et al. 2007).

Juvenile Depression and Anxiety Disorder

Juvenile depression and anxiety were included in this study because ignoring participants' pre-adult disorder history would have created inaccurate classifications of pure, comorbid, and healthy groups. Diagnoses followed DSM-III criteria based on structured interviews that used the Diagnostic Interview Schedule for Children–Child Version (Costello et al. 1982). Diagnoses made at ages 11, 13, and 15 years have been described elsewhere (Anderson et al. 1987; Frost et al. 1989; McGee et al. 1990).

Indicators of Mental Health Service Use

Indicators of mental health service use were assessed through use of the Life History Calendar, a visual method (columns=time units, rows=events) that has been shown to enhance recall reliability (Belli et al. 2001; Caspi et al. 1996b). As part of the assessment of life events from ages 20 to 32 years, participants reported years in which they received mental health services (e.g., from a general practitioner, psychiatrist, psychologist, or emergency department) or took psychiatric medications for anxiety or depression. One-month test-retest reliability of the calendar was evaluated in a sample of 30 psychiatric outpatients; 10-year reports of service use and medication showed greater than 90% test-retest agreement.

MEASURES OF RISK FACTORS

Descriptions of variable construction and evidence of good construct validity and reliability (test-retest, interrater, and/or internal consistency, as appropriate) for each risk measure have been published previously; relevant citations are provided later.

Family History

Family history data were collected and cases identified by means of the interview protocol and case-definition algorithms of the Family History Screen (Thompson et al. 1980; Weissman et al. 2000). Histories were ascertained from separate interviews of three respondents per study family during 2003–2006. The 32-year-old study member, his or her mother, and his or her father (or an aunt, if a parent were unavailable) were all interviewed. Three informants reported for 78% of cohort families, two for 93%, and one for 97% of families. Reports characterized the study members' 4 biological grandparents, 2 biological parents, and 0–10 biological siblings (range = 1–16 members per family, mean = 9). We report here on the proportions of family members identified with symptoms of anxiety and depression.

Maternal Internalizing Symptoms

Maternal internalizing symptoms were measured with the Malaise Inventory (Rodgers et al. 1999), which assesses symptom complaints associated with anxiety and depression (e.g., insomnia, hopelessness, tension, somatic complaints). The inventory was completed by the mother when the study child was 5, 7, and 9 years old, and scores were standardized and averaged (McGee et al. 1985b).

Low Childhood Socioeconomic Status

Status was measured as the highest of father's or mother's occupation, using a six-point scale for New Zealand (Elley and Irving 1976); repeated measures over the first 15 years of the study child's life were averaged (Wright et al. 1999).

Maltreatment

Maltreatment at ages 3–11 years was ascertained through behavioral observations of rejecting mother–child interactions when the child was 3 years old; parental reports of harsh discipline at ages 7 and 9 years; two or more changes in primary caregiver before age 11; and retrospective reports by study members, when they were age 26, of exposure to injurious physical abuse or unwanted sexual contact before age 11 years. In the full sample, 9% of children experienced at least two indicators of maltreatment (Caspi et al. 2002).

Parental Loss

Loss of a parent was recorded from parents' reports—when their children were ages 3, 5, 7, 9, and 11 years—of whether a biological parent had become permanently absent from the family due to death, separation, or divorce (Jaffee et al. 2002).

Inhibited Temperament

Children's temperaments were assessed at ages 3–5 years through ratings made by staff members after they had observed a child in a 90-minute testing session, with an unfamiliar examiner, at the beginning and end of this age span (ages 3 and 5 years). Factor and cluster analyses reduced these ratings to three reliable temperament types (Caspi and Silva 1995; Caspi et al. 1996a), which has since been replicated in other samples (Asendorpf et al. 2001; Hart et al. 2003; Robins et al. 1996). We report here on the "inhibited" type.

Internalizing Problems

Internalizing problems present at ages 5–11 years were reported by parents and teachers based on the Rutter Child Scales, which assess characteristics such as worrying, unhappiness, misery, and fearfulness (Elander and Rutter 1996). Ratings made when the study child was 5, 7, 9, and 11 years of age were standardized and averaged (McGee et al. 1985a).

Conduct Problems

Conduct problems at ages 5–11 years were reported by parents and teachers using the Rutter Child Scales to assess characteristics such as fighting, bullying, stealing, tantrums, and lying (Elander and Rutter 1996). Ratings made when the study child was 5, 7, 9, and 11 years were standardized and averaged (Moffitt et al. 2001).

Psychiatrist's Count of Child's Depression Symptoms

Depression symptoms at age 9 years were measured through an interview of each child by a psychiatrist in 1981–1982. Fewer than 1% of children met full diagnostic criteria for MDD at age 9 years, but the count of symptoms was archived and is used here as a scale (Kashani et al. 1983).

Self-Esteem

At ages 11, 13, and 15 years, self-esteem of each child was assessed through adolescent self-report, using the Rosenberg Self-Esteem Scale (Rosenberg 1965), standardized and averaged across ages (Trzesniewski et al. 2006).

Personality Traits

Personality traits were assessed for each participant at age 18 years through self-report using the Multidimensional Personality Questionnaire (Patrick et al. 2002). Items of the Negative Emotionality scale measure interpersonal alienation, irritable-aggressive attitudes, and reactivity to stress. Items of the Positive Emotionality scale measure well-being, social potency, achievement, and social closeness. These two scales are relatively independent, internally consistent, and stable over time (Krueger et al. 1996).

STATISTICAL ANALYSES

Findings for categorical measures are reported as group percentages. Findings for continuous measures are reported as group means on z-scores standardized to a mean of 0 and standard deviation of 1 (the difference between two group means, for this representative cohort, may be interpreted as an effect size). Comparisons between diagnostic groups were tested using regression analysis; we report odds ratios for dichotomous risk measures and t-tests (associated with beta weights) for continuous risk measures. The sexes were combined to augment statistical power, but sex was controlled as a covariate. The purpose of this research was to compare risk factors across diagnostic groups, *not* to ascertain if any association between a risk factor and a diagnosis were unique or causal. Therefore, bivariate risk-diagnosis associations are presented; multivariate models were not performed.

Results

As an initial screening step, basic analyses tested which risk factors predicted MDD and which predicted GAD, by comparing the diagnostic groups against a healthy control group of study members who had never been diagnosed with any Axis I mental or substance-abuse disorder.

Study members with GAD differed significantly from healthy control subjects on all 13 risk factors (all $P<0.05$, tests not tabled). In a separate parallel analysis, study members with MDD differed from healthy control subjects on 11 of the 13 risk factors (all $P<0.05$, tests not tabled); the exceptions were childhood socioeconomic status and behavioral inhibition at age 3 years. However, as anticipated, the aforementioned two comparisons were not particularly informative because, given the high rate of comorbidity, a substantial proportion of GAD- and MDD-diagnosed study members were the same individuals, virtually guaranteeing these similar risk-factor associations. As such, the following analyses set the MDD+GAD group apart, to look specifically at MDD-only and GAD-only groups.

Four mutually exclusive groups were defined on the bases of their adult diagnostic status at ages 18, 21, 26, and 32 years and their juvenile diagnostic history from ages 11–15 years.

1. The MDD-only group was diagnosed with MDD in adulthood but never with GAD in adulthood or anxiety as a juvenile ($n=162$ pure cases of MDD).
2. The GAD-only group was diagnosed with GAD in adulthood but never with MDD in adulthood or as a juvenile ($n=52$ pure cases of GAD).
3. The MDD+GAD group comprised cohort members diagnosed with both disorders during the adult study period ($n=189$, 20% of the cohort).
4. No-diagnosis control subjects were cohort members never diagnosed with any disorder, as described earlier ($n=205$ healthy).

Table 11–1 compares the four groups, first on descriptors, then on risk factors. As a natural consequence of the greater prevalence of MDD among women, the MDD-only and MDD+GAD groups had more women, whereas the GAD-only group had more men. However, sex was controlled as a covariate in all group comparisons, so differential risk patterns for GAD versus MDD, as reported later, were not an artifact of any sex differences in risk factors.

TABLE 11–1. Prospective risk factors: comparisons of comorbid vs. non-comorbid cases of major depressive disorder (MDD) and generalized anxiety disorder (GAD)—defined cumulatively from ages 18 to 32 years—including influences of childhood disorder history

	Diagnostic groups (ages 18–32 y)				Planned group comparisons			
	Healthy control subjects, % (N=205)	MDD-only, % (N=162)	GAD-only, % (N=52)	MDD+GAD, % (N=189)	MDD-only vs. healthy control subjects	MDD-only vs. comorbid	GAD-only vs. healthy control subjects	GAD-only vs. comorbid
Group descriptors								
Birth cohort, N=945	22	17	6	20	OR=2.30 (1.5–3.6)	OR=1.03 (0.7–1.6)	OR=0.96 (0.5–1.8)	OR=2.5 (1.3–4.7)
Female[a]	42	62	40	63				
First MDD diagnosis by age 15 years		2		14		OR=8.67 (2.6–29.2)		
First anxiety diagnosis by age 15 years			12	37				OR=4.51 (1.8–11.3)
Recurrent MDD (two or more episodes)		27		61		OR=4.26 (2.7–6.7)		
Recurrent GAD (two or more episodes)			14	50				OR=6.70 (2.8–15.8)

TABLE 11–1. Prospective risk factors: comparisons of comorbid vs. non-comorbid cases of major depressive disorder (MDD) and generalized anxiety disorder (GAD)—defined cumulatively from ages 18 to 32 years—including influences of childhood disorder history *(continued)*

	Diagnostic groups (ages 18–32 y)				Planned group comparisons			
	Healthy control subjects, % (N=205)	MDD-only, % (N=162)	GAD-only, % (N=52)	MDD+GAD, % (N=189)	MDD-only vs. healthy control subjects	MDD-only vs. comorbid	GAD-only vs. healthy control subjects	GAD-only vs. comorbid
Group descriptors *(continued)*								
Received mental health services, ages 20–32 years	9	41	35	57	OR=6.78 (3.8–12.2)	OR=1.89 (1.2–2.9)	OR=6.16 (2.8–13.5)	OR=2.09 (1.1–4.1)
Took psychiatric medication, ages 20–32 years	5	22	19	39	OR=5.10 (2.4–10.8)	OR=2.30 (1.4–3.7)	OR=5.05 (1.9–13.3)	OR=2.25 (1.0–4.9)
Risk factors								
Family members with history of depression (mean pedigree members)	21	29	25	33	t=3.70, P<0.001	t=1.69, P=0.09	t=1.26, P=0.20	t=2.64, P=0.009

TABLE 11–1. Prospective risk factors: comparisons of comorbid vs. non-comorbid cases of major depressive disorder (MDD) and generalized anxiety disorder (GAD)—defined cumulatively from ages 18 to 32 years—including influences of childhood disorder history *(continued)*

	Diagnostic groups (ages 18–32 y)				Planned group comparisons			
	Healthy control subjects, % (N=205)	MDD-only, % (N=162)	GAD-only, % (N=52)	MDD+ GAD, % (N=189)	MDD-only vs. healthy control subjects	MDD-only vs. comorbid	GAD-only vs. healthy control subjects	GAD-only vs. comorbid
Risk factors *(continued)*								
Family members with history of anxiety disorder (mean pedigree members)	15	18	19	26	t=1.85, P=0.07	t=3.92, P<0.001	t=1.19, P=0.23	t=2.86, P=0.005
Maternal internalizing symptoms (mean z-score)	−0.24	−0.05	0.16	0.27	**t=2.12, P=0.035**	**t=2.76, P=0.006**	**t=2.70, P=0.007**	t=0.75, P=0.46
Childhood socioeconomic status (mean z-score)	0.13	0.20	−0.19	−0.09	t=0.61, P=0.54	**t=2.72, P=0.007**	**t=2.16, P=0.032**	t=0.43, P=0.67
Child maltreatment before age 11 years	3	9	14	14	**OR=2.60 (1.0–6.6)**	OR=1.56 (0.8–3.1)	**OR=4.49 (1.5–13.5)**	OR=1.00 (0.4–2.5)

TABLE 11–1. Prospective risk factors: comparisons of comorbid vs. non-comorbid cases of major depressive disorder (MDD) and generalized anxiety disorder (GAD)—defined cumulatively from ages 18 to 32 years—including influences of childhood disorder history *(continued)*

	Diagnostic groups (ages 18–32 y)				Planned group comparisons			
	Healthy control subjects, % (N=205)	MDD-only, % (N=162)	GAD-only, % (N=52)	MDD+ GAD, % (N=189)	MDD-only vs. healthy control subjects	MDD-only vs. comorbid	GAD-only vs. healthy control subjects	GAD-only vs. comorbid
Risk factors *(continued)*								
Lost parent before age 11 years	9	12	14	19	OR=1.50 (0.8–3.0)	OR=1.61 (0.9–2.9)	OR=1.62 (0.6–4.1)	OR=1.30 (0.5–3.3)
Inhibited temperament, ages 3–5 years	5	4	12	12	OR=0.75 (0.3–2.0)	OR=2.93 (1.2–7.1)	OR=2.31 (0.8–6.6)	OR=0.83 (0.3–2.2)
Internalizing problems, ages 5–11 years (mean z-score)	−0.23	−0.18	0.07	0.29	t=0.32, P=0.74	t=4.40, P<0.001	t=2.07, P=0.04	t=1.15, P=0.25
Conduct problems, ages 5–11 years (mean z-score)	−0.30	−0.17	0.06	0.09	t=2.50, P=0.013	t=2.93, P=0.004	t=2.70, P=0.007	t=0.67, P=0.50

TABLE 11–1. Prospective risk factors: comparisons of comorbid vs. non-comorbid cases of major depressive disorder (MDD) and generalized anxiety disorder (GAD)—defined cumulatively from ages 18 to 32 years—including influences of childhood disorder history *(continued)*

	Diagnostic groups (ages 18–32 y)				Planned group comparisons			
	Healthy control subjects, % (N=205)	MDD- only, % (N=162)	GAD- only, % (N=52)	MDD+ GAD, % (N=189)	MDD-only vs. healthy control subjects	MDD-only vs. comorbid	GAD-only vs. healthy control subjects	GAD-only vs. comorbid
Risk factors *(continued)*								
Depression symptom count, age 9 years (mean z-score)	−0.15	−0.20	0.10	0.19	t=0.33, P=0.74	**t=3.62, P<0.001**	t=1.44, P=0.15	t=1.30, P=0.19
Self-esteem, ages 11–15 years (mean z-score)	0.30	0.19	0.08	−0.34	t=0.67, P=0.50	**t=5.07, P<0.001**	t=1.65, P=0.10	**t=2.50, P=0.013**
Negative-emotionality, age 18 years (mean z-score)	−0.56	−0.04	0.09	0.48	**t=6.18, P<0.001**	**t=4.97, P<0.001**	**t=5.29, P<0.001**	**t=3.27, P=0.001**
Positive-emotionality, age 18 years (mean z-score)	0.26	−0.15	0.06	−0.10	**t=3.88, P<0.001**	t=0.44, P=0.66	t=1.35, P=0.18	t=.83, P=0.40

Note. Significant comparisons at an alpha criterion = 0.05 are bolded.
[a]Gender controlled in group comparisons.

MAJOR DEPRESSIVE DISORDER ONLY GROUP

Findings for the MDD-only group are shown in Table 11–1 and may be summarized thus:

1. The MDD-only group was distinguished from healthy control subjects by a worse family history of depression, as well as by more maternal internalizing symptoms.
2. The MDD-only group differed from healthy control subjects on family environment measures only on maltreatment.
3. The MDD-only group differed from control subjects on childhood behavior measures only by showing somewhat more conduct problems, although the MDD groups' conduct problems were not above the cohort mean.
4. On personality measures, the MDD-only group was distinguished from control subjects by significantly lower positive emotionality and higher negative emotionality scores.
5. Table 11–1 shows the MDD-only group was at markedly *lower* levels of risk than the MDD+GAD comorbid group, scoring significantly healthier on 9 of 13 risk measures.

GENERALIZED ANXIETY DISORDER ONLY GROUP

Findings for the GAD-only group are shown in Table 11–1. Inspection of these data shows that

1. On family history measures, the GAD-only group differed from healthy control subjects only in maternal internalizing symptoms.
2. In measures of family adversity, the GAD-only group differed from control subjects on low socioeconomic status and maltreatment.
3. As to childhood behavior, the GAD-only group differed from control subjects on both childhood internalizing problems and conduct problems and also had an elevated risk of inhibited temperament.
4. On personality measures, the GAD-only group was distinguished from healthy control subjects by worse scores on negative emotionality but not on positive emotionality. It should be noted, however, that the differences observed in childhood behavior reached only marginal significance; the comparison between the GAD-only group and control subjects had less statistical power than the comparison between the MDD-only group and control subjects.

Table 11–1 shows that, on the majority of childhood risk factors, the GAD-only group was *not* at significantly lower risk than the comorbid MDD+GAD group (the GAD-only group scored as poorly as the MDD+GAD group on 9 of

13 risk measures). This overall pattern of similar childhood risk for GAD-only and MDD+GAD was not merely an issue of low statistical power; the group-difference effect sizes were small.

MAJOR DEPRESSIVE DISORDER+GENERALIZED ANXIETY DISORDER GROUP

The comorbid MDD+GAD group also provided notable findings (Table 11–1). As a group, comorbid study members scored significantly worse than the GAD-only group on 3 of 13 risk factors; worse than the MDD-only group on 9 of 13 risk factors; and worse than healthy control subjects on all 13 risk factors (all $P<0.01$, tests not tabled). This MDD+GAD group was also characterized by younger onset, greater recurrence, and more use of mental health services and medications as compared with the pure MDD and GAD groups.

Discussion

This chapter reports new information, from a prospective longitudinal study, about risk factors for MDD and GAD. Our findings indicate that MDD and GAD share some, but not all, antecedent risk factors. Findings for each group are discussed here.

Adults who were diagnosed with both MDD and GAD had the most pronounced risk histories, as indicated by family psychiatric history, childhood adversity and behavior, and predisposing personality traits. This high-risk history is consistent with clinical outcomes in which individuals with comorbid MDD+GAD were set apart by having recurrent courses of both disorders and elevated health burdens as indicated by service and medication usages. Prior studies have shown that comorbidity is common and that individuals with comorbid MDD and GAD have more severe and persistent symptoms than do individuals with either single disorder only (Hagnell and Gräsbeck 1990; Lewinsohn et al. 1997; Merikangas et al. 2003; Moffitt et al. 2007; Murphy 1990; Pine et al. 1998; Wittchen et al. 2000). Our study adds that comorbid cases have more marked antecedent risk histories than do pure cases.

Another finding is that MDD, in the absence of comorbid GAD, was not strongly associated with risk factors during childhood. Indeed, pure MDD was predicted most strongly by family history of depression and adolescent personality traits (negative and positive emotionality). As anticipated from prior research findings, low positive emotionality predicted pure MDD but not pure GAD, suggesting that individuals with a high threshold for experiencing positive emotion are at specific risk for MDD (Watson 2005). This differential risk also seemed to apply to family history. A family history of depression predicted the MDD-only group more than it did the GAD-only group, a pattern reported previously (Klein et al. 2004; Wickramaratne and Weissman 1993).

A related finding about MDD was that non-comorbid MDD involved markedly lower levels of risk than comorbid MDD+GAD, as indicated by milder risk factors and less-extreme personality traits. This pattern suggests that adult MDD, occurring in the absence of any lifetime history of juvenile anxiety or GAD, might warrant special research focus to ascertain whether it has a unique etiology. Findings here suggest the hypothesis that pure adult MDD does not involve risk during childhood but instead could arise from genetic and personality predispositions that are only manifested as depression when predisposed individuals encounter stressful life events as adults. Previously, we reported fewer childhood risks for adult-onset than juvenile-onset MDD (Jaffee et al. 2002).

An additional finding is that GAD, whether comorbid or pure, was associated with several risk factors, across multiple domains of risk, during childhood: maternal internalizing symptoms, low socioeconomic status, maltreatment, inhibited temperament, internalizing and conduct problems, and high scores on negative emotionality. Moreover, GAD-only cases were similar to comorbid MDD+GAD on the level of many risks. This pattern for the GAD-only group (broad risks, levels similar to the comorbid group) contrasted against the pattern for the MDD-only group (somewhat narrower risks, lower levels than the comorbid group). These patterns find support in previous studies (Judd et al. 1998; Kessler et al. 1996, 1999, 2002; Ormel et al. 1994; Phillips et al. 2005; Wittchen et al. 2000). That GAD—with or without MDD—has its own set of risk factors that are not shared with pure MDD, is consistent with the view that the presence of GAD may signal a distinct developmental pathway to a more serious distress disorder (Kessler 2005).

Findings of this study should be considered in light of its potential limitations:

- Past Dunedin Study findings have generally mirrored those from other countries; however, additional research must check whether the findings we are reporting here transcend local conditions and ethnic variations.
- Although we focused on GAD because its relation to MDD is the subject of nosological debate, research should examine other anxiety disorders comorbid with MDD (Roy-Byrne et al. 2000; Stein et al. 2001).
- The gaps between Dunedin assessment windows may have led us to undercount cases. However, we suspect undercounting is trivial because only 4% of cohort members who reported on the Life History Calendar that they received mental health services in gaps between assessment years had escaped the study's diagnostic net (Moffitt et al. 2007). The gaps probably led us to undercount episodes and, consequently, to underidentify recurrence, but there is no reason to expect that missed episodes between assessments would be less, or more, comorbid. Any misassignment of cases with disorder that occurred in gaps between assessments in the healthy control group would have made group differences harder to detect.

- Our data are right-hand censored at age 32 years. There has been no prospective study conducted yet that can report whether comorbidity rates or risk predictors change across midlife; hence, continued follow-ups of this group are needed.
- Although we were able to examine prospective measures that operationalized the domains of risk specified by leading theorists (Kendler et al. 2002; Watson 2005), we were not able to include biological markers of the activity of the autonomic nervous system, stress hormones, or neurotransmitter systems. Such biomarkers may, in the future, prove essential for resolving nosological questions.

Some readers may find the cumulative prevalence rates of MDD and GAD in the Dunedin cohort unexpectedly high. Several factors may contribute to the Dunedin Study's high prevalence rates. We diagnosed GAD and MDD, regardless of the presence of other disorders, eschewing exclusionary criteria followed in most studies (and GAD was diagnosed with a 1-month minimum duration). Also, the cohort's 96% participation rate let us count disordered individuals overlooked by most studies. Moreover, after more than 30 years of participation with no confidentiality violation, longitudinal-study members are more forthcoming about psychiatric symptoms than participants in single-wave surveys. Dunedin diagnoses are based on concurrent symptom reports; lifetime cases are not undercounted due to failure to recall criterion symptoms from years past, as occurs in retrospective surveys. The prospective cumulative prevalence reported here comprises a sum of cases ascertained in a series of successive prospective past-year assessments, each of which diagnosed a percentage of the cohort very similar to the percentage diagnosed in the past-year assessments of surveys such as the NCS and NCS-R (Kessler et al. 1993, 1999, 2005).

Finally, expectations for lower cumulative prevalence come from retrospective surveys, which are known to underestimate lifetime disorder (Andrews et al. 2005; Kessler et al. 2002; Simon and VonKorff 1995). However, cumulative prevalence rates now emerging from prospective longitudinal studies in North Carolina, New York, and Oregon (Costello et al. 2003; Jaffee et al. 2005; Lewinsohn et al. 1993) are elevated similar to those in the Dunedin Study. We suspect that cumulative prevalence rates of GAD and MDD are, in reality, higher than previously estimated from one-wave retrospective surveys.

This chapter reports that, of the several risk factors studied, relatively few were clearly shared by MDD and GAD. GAD had specific risk factors not shared by MDD (childhood adversity and behavior), and MDD had specific risk factors not shared by GAD (predisposing family history and personality). These findings of differential risk factors point to partly different etiologies, which would not be consistent with collapsing the two into one disorder in future nosological systems. However, the clearest finding here was the similar broad, serious risk history among individuals who develop either pure GAD or comorbid MDD+GAD as adults. The comorbid group is common in the population and constitutes a substantial mental health burden (Moffitt et al. 2007). Antecedent risk factors confirmed here suggest prevention targets to reduce this burden.

References

American Psychiatric Association: Diagnostic and Statistical Manual of Mental Disorders, 3rd Edition. Washington, DC, American Psychiatric Association, 1980

American Psychiatric Association: Diagnostic and Statistical Manual of Mental Disorders, 3rd Edition, Revised. Washington, DC, American Psychiatric Association, 1987

American Psychiatric Association: Diagnostic and Statistical Manual of Mental Disorders, 4th Edition. Washington, DC, American Psychiatric Association, 1994

Anderson JC, Williams SM, McGee RO, et al: DSM-III disorders in preadolescent children: prevalence in a large sample from the general population. Arch Gen Psychiatry 44:69–76, 1987

Andrews G, Poulton R, Skoog I: Lifetime risk for depression: restricted to a minority or waiting for most? Br J Psychiatry 187:495–496, 2005

Angold A, Costello EJ, Erkanli A: Comorbidity. J Child Psychol Psychiatry 40:57–87, 1999

Asendendorpf J, Borkenau P, Ostendorf F, et al: Carving personality description at its joints: confirmation of three replicable personality prototypes for both children and adults. Eur J Pers 15:169–198, 2001

Barlow DH, Campbell LA: Mixed anxiety-depression and its implications for models of mood and anxiety disorders. Compr Psychiatry 41(suppl):55–60, 2000

Belli RF, Shay WL, Stafford FP: Event history calendars and question list surveys: a direct comparison of interview methods. Public Opin Q 65:45–74, 2001

Breslau N, Schultz L, Peterson E: Sex differences in depression: a role for pre-existing anxiety. Psychiatry Res 58:1–12, 1995

Caspi A, Silva PA: Temperamental qualities at age 3 predict personality traits in young adulthood: longitudinal evidence from a birth cohort. Child Dev 66:486–498, 1995

Caspi A, Moffitt TE, Newman DL, et al: Behavioral observations at age 3 predict adult psychiatric disorders: longitudinal evidence from a birth cohort. Arch Gen Psychiatry 53:1033–1039, 1996a

Caspi A, Moffitt TE, Thornton A, et al: The life history calendar: a research and clinical assessment method for collecting retrospective event-history data. Int J Methods Psychiatr Res 6:101–114, 1996b

Caspi A, McClay J, Moffitt TE, et al: Role of genotype in the cycle of violence in maltreated children. Science 297:851–854, 2002

Coryell W, Endicott J, Winokur G: Anxiety syndromes as epiphenomena of primary major depression: outcome and familial psychopathology. Am J Psychiatry 149:100–107, 1992

Costello A, Edelbrock C, Kalas R, et al: National Institute of Mental Health Diagnostic Interview Schedule for Children. Rockville, MD, National Institute of Mental Health, 1982

Costello EJ, Mustillo S, Erkanli A, et al: Prevalence and development of psychiatric disorders in childhood and adolescence. Arch Gen Psychiatry 60:837–844, 2003

Elander J, Rutter M: Use and development of the Rutter parents' and teachers' scale. Int J Methods Psychiatr Res 6:63–78, 1996

Elley WB, Irving JC: Revised socio-economic index for New Zealand. New Zealand Journal of Educational Studies 11:25–36, 1976

Feehan M, McGee R, Nada Raja S, et al: DSM-III-R disorders in New Zealand 18-year-olds. Aust N Z J Psychiatry 28:87–99, 1994

Frost LA, Moffitt TE, McGee R: Neuropsychological function and psychopathology in an unselected cohort of young adolescents. J Abnorm Child Psychol 98:307–313, 1989

Hagnell O, Gräsbeck A: Comorbidity of anxiety and depression in the Lundby 25-year prospective study on the pattern of subsequent episodes, in Comorbidity of Mood and Anxiety Disorders. Edited by Maser JD, Cloninger CR. Washington, DC, American Psychiatric Press, 1990, pp 139–152

Hankin BL, Abramson LY, Moffitt TE, et al: Development of depression from preadolescence to young adulthood: emerging gender differences in a 10-year longitudinal study. J Abnorm Psychol 107:128–140, 1998

Hart D, Atkins R, Fegley S: Personality and development in childhood: a person-centred approach. Monogr Soc Res Child Dev 68:1–109, 2003

Jaffee SR, Moffitt TE, Caspi A, et al: Early childhood risk factors differentiate child-onset versus adult-onset depression in a prospective, longitudinal study. Arch Gen Psychiatry 58:215–222, 2002

Jaffee SR, Harrington H, Cohen P, et al: Cumulative prevalence of psychiatric disorder in youths. J Am Acad Child Adolesc Psychiatry 44:406–407, 2005

Judd LL, Kessler RC, Paulus MP, et al: Comorbidity as a fundamental feature of generalized anxiety disorder: results from the National Comorbidity Study (NCS). Acta Psychiatr Scand Suppl 98:6–11, 1998

Kashani JH, McGee RO, Clarkson SE, et al: Depression in a sample of 9-year-old children. Arch Gen Psychiatry 40:1217–1223, 1983

Kendler KS: Major depression and generalised anxiety disorder: same genes, (partly) different environments—revisited. Br J Psychiatry 168:68–75, 1996

Kendler KS, Goldberg D: Depression and general anxiety disorders workgroup presentation, presented at the DSM-IV–ICD Conference Organized by the American Psychiatric Institute for Research and Education (APIRE), 2004

Kendler KS, Walters EE, Neale MC, et al: The structure of the genetic and the environmental risk factors for six major psychiatric disorders in women: phobia, generalised anxiety disorder, panic disorder, bulimia, major depression and alcoholism. Arch Gen Psychiatry 52:374–383, 1995

Kendler KS, Gardner CO, Prescott CA: Toward a comprehensive developmental model for major depression in women. Am J Psychiatry 159:1133–1145, 2002

Kessler RC: Evidence that generalized anxiety disorder is an independent disorder, in Generalized Anxiety Disorder: Symptomatology, Pathogenesis and Management. Edited by Nutt D, Rickels K, Stein D. London, England, Martin Dunitz Publishers, 2005, pp 1–8

Kessler RC, Wittchen H-U: Patterns and correlates of generalized anxiety disorder in community samples. J Clin Psychiatry 63:4–10, 2002

Kessler RC, McGonagle KA, Swartz M, et al: Sex and depression in National Comorbidity Survey 1: lifetime prevalence, chronicity and recurrence. J Affect Disord 29:85–96, 1993

Kessler RC, Nelson CB, McGonagle KA, et al: Comorbidity of DSM-III-R major depressive disorder in the general population: results from the US National Comorbidity Survey. Br J Psychiatry 168:17–30, 1996

Kessler RC, DuPont RL, Berglund P, et al: Impairment in pure and comorbid generalized anxiety disorder and major depression at 12 months in two national surveys. Am J Psychiatry 156:1915–1923, 1999

Kessler RC, Andrade LH, Bijl RV, et al: The effects of co-morbidity on the onset and persistence of generalized anxiety disorder in ICPE surveys. Psychol Med 32:1213–1225, 2002

Kessler RC, Brandenburg N, Lane M, et al: Rethinking the duration requirement for generalized anxiety disorder: evidence from the National Comorbidity Survey Replication. Psychol Med 35:1–10, 2005

Klein DN, Shankman SA, Lewinsohn PM, et al: Family study of chronic depression in a community sample of young adults. Am J Psychiatry 161:646–653, 2004

Krueger RF: The structure of common mental disorders. Arch Gen Psychiatry 56:921–926, 1999

Krueger RF, Finger MS: Using item response theory to understand comorbidity among anxiety and unipolar mood disorders. Psychol Assess 13:1–12, 2001

Krueger RF, Caspi A, Moffitt TE, et al: Personality traits are differentially linked to mental disorders: a multi-trait/multi-diagnosis study of an adolescent birth cohort. J Abnorm Psychol 105:299–312, 1996

Krueger RF, Caspi A, Moffitt TE, et al: The structure and stability of common mental disorders (DSM-III-R): a longitudinal-epidemiological study. J Abnorm Psychol 107:216–277, 1998

Kuzma JM, Black DW: Integrating pharmacotherapy and psychotherapy in the management of anxiety disorders. Curr Psychiatry Rep 6:268–273, 2004

Lewinsohn PM, Hops H, Roberts RE, et al: Adolescent psychopathology, I: prevalence and incidence of depression and other DSM-III-R disorders in high school students. J Abnorm Psychol 102:133–144, 1993

Lewinsohn PM, Zinbarg R, Seeley JR, et al: Lifetime comorbidity among anxiety disorders and between anxiety disorders and other mental disorders in adolescents. J Anxiety Disord 11:377–394, 1997

Lewinsohn PM, Rohde P, Seeley JR, et al: Natural course of adolescent major depressive disorder in a community sample: predictors of recurrence in young adults. Am J Psychiatry 157:1584–1591, 2000

McGee R, Williams SM, Bradshaw J, et al: The Rutter Scale for completion by teachers: factor structure and relationship with cognitive abilities and family adversity for a sample of New Zealand children. J Child Psychol Psychiatry 26:727–739, 1985a

McGee R, Williams SM, Silva PA: An evaluation of the Malaise Inventory. J Psychosom Res 30:147–152, 1985b

McGee R, Feehan M, William S, et al: DSM-III disorders in a large sample of adolescents. J Am Acad Child Adolesc Psychiatry 29:611–619, 1990

Merikangas KR, Zhang H, Avenevoli S, et al: Longitudinal trajectories of depression and anxiety in a prospective community study: the Zurich cohort study. Arch Gen Psychiatry 60:993–1000, 2003

Mineka S, Watson D, Clark LA: Comorbidity of anxiety and unipolar mood disorders. Annu Rev Psychol 49:377–412, 1998

Moffitt TE, Caspi A, Rutter M, et al: Sex Differences in Antisocial Behaviour: Conduct Disorder, Delinquency, and Violence in the Dunedin Longitudinal Study. Cambridge, United Kingdom, Cambridge University Press, 2001

Moffitt TE, Harrington H, Caspi A, et al: Depression and generalized anxiety disorder: cumulative and sequential comorbidity in a birth cohort followed prospectively to age 32 years. Arch Gen Psychiatry 64:651–660, 2007

Murphy JM: Diagnostic comorbidity and symptom co-occurence: the Stirling County Study, in Comorbidity of Mood and Anxiety Disorders. Edited by Maser JD, Cloninger CR. Washington, DC, American Psychiatric Press, 1990, pp 153–176

Newman DL, Moffitt TE, Caspi A, et al: Psychiatric disorder in a birth cohort of young adults: prevalence, comorbidity, clinical significance, and new cases incidence from age 11 to 21. J Consult Clin Psychol 64:552–562, 1996

Ormel J, VonKorff M, Ustun TB, et al: The common mental disorders and disability across cultures: results from the WHO Collaborative Study on Psychological Problems in General Health Care. JAMA 272:1741–1748, 1994

Parker G, Wilhelm K, Austin M-P, et al: The influence of anxiety as a risk to early onset major depression. J Affect Disord 52:11–17, 1999

Patrick CJ, Curtin JJ, Tellegen A: Development and validation of a brief form of the Multidimensional Personality Questionnaire. Psychol Assess 14:150–163, 2002

Phillips NK, Hammen CL, Brennan PA, et al: Early adversity and the prospective prediction of depressive and anxiety disorders in adolescents. J Abnorm Child Psychol 33:13–24, 2005

Pine D, Cohen P, Brook J, et al: The risk for early adulthood anxiety and depressive disorders in adolescents with anxiety and depressive disorders. Arch Gen Psychiatry 55:56–64, 1998

Pine DS, Cohen P, Brook J: Adolescent fears as predictors of depression. Biol Psychiatry 50:721–724, 2001

Robins LN, Helzer JE, Cottler L, et al: Diagnostic Interview Schedule, Version III-R. St Louis, MO, Washington University School of Medicine, 1989

Robins LN, Cottler L, Bucholz KK, et al: Diagnostic Interview Schedule for DSM-IV. St. Louis, MO, Washington University School of Medicine, 1995

Robins RW, John OP, Caspi A, et al: Resilient, overcontrolled, and undercontrolled boys: three replicable personality types. J Pers Soc Psychol 50:157–171, 1996

Rodgers B, Pickles A, Power C, et al: Validity of the Malaise Inventory in general population samples. Soc Psychiatry Psychiatr Epidemiol 34:333–341, 1999

Rosenberg M: Society and the Adolescent Self-Image. Princeton, NJ, Princeton University, 1965

Roy-Byrne P, Stang P, Wittchen H-U, et al: Lifetime panic-depression comorbidity in the National Comorbidity Survey: association with symptoms, impairment, course and help-seeking. Br J Psychiatry 176:229–235, 2000

Sartorius N, Ustun TB, Lecrubier Y, et al: Depression comorbid with anxiety: results from the WHO study on psychological disorders in primary health care. Br J Psychiatry 168:38–43, 1996

Simon GE, VonKorff M: Recall of psychiatric history in cross-sectional surveys: implications for epidemiologic research. Epidemiol Rev 17:211–227, 1995

Stein MB, Fuetsch M, Müller N, et al: Social anxiety and the risk of depression: a prospective community study of adolescents and young adults. Arch Gen Psychiatry 58:251–256, 2001

Thompson WD, Kidd JR, Weissman MM: A procedure for the efficient collection and processing of pedigree data suitable for genetic analysis. J Psychiatr Res 15:291–303, 1980

Trzesniewski KH, Donnellan MB, Brent M, et al: Low self-esteem during adolescence predicts poor health, criminal behavior, and limited economic prospects during adulthood. Dev Psychol 42:381–390, 2006

Vollebergh WAM, Iedema J, Bijl RV, et al: The structure and stability of common mental disorders: the NEMESIS Study. Arch Gen Psychiatry 58:597–603, 2001

Watson D: Rethinking the mood and anxiety disorders: a quantitative hierarchical model for DSM-V. J Abnorm Psychol 114:522–536, 2005

Watson D, Gamez W, Simms LJ: Basic dimensions of temperament and their relation to anxiety and depression: a symptom-based perspective. J Res Pers 39:46–66, 2005

Weissman MM, Wickramaratne P, Adams P, et al: Brief screening for family psychiatric history: the family history screen. Arch Gen Psychiatry 57:675–682, 2000

Weissman MM, Wickramaratne P, Nomura Y, et al: Families at high and low risk for depression: a 3-generation study. Arch Gen Psychiatry 62:29–36, 2005

Wickramaratne PJ, Weissman MM: Using family studies to understand comorbidity. Eur Arch Psychiatry Clin Neurosci 243:150–157, 1993

Widiger T, Clark AL: Toward DSM-V and the classification of psychopathology. Psychol Bull 126:946–963, 2000

Wittchen H-U: Critical issues in the evaluation of comorbidity of psychiatric disorders. Br J Psychiatry 168:9–16, 1996

Wittchen HU, Kessler RC, Pfister H, et al: Why do people with anxiety disorders become depressed? A prospective-longitudinal community study. Acta Psychiatr Scand Suppl 406:14–23, 2000

Wright BRE, Caspi A, Moffitt TE, et al: Reconsidering the relationship between SES and delinquency: causation but not correlation. Criminology 37:175–194, 1999

Zahn-Waxler C, Klimes-Dougan B, Slattery MJ: Internalizing problems of childhood and adolescence: prospects, pitfalls, and progress in understanding the development of anxiety and depression. Dev Psychopathol 14:442–466, 2000

12

ARE THERE EARLY ADVERSE EXPOSURES THAT DIFFERENTIATE DEPRESSION AND ANXIETY RISK?

Marcus Richards, Ph.D.
David Goldberg, D.M., FRCPsych

Evidence strongly suggests that depression and anxiety are closely associated. These two psychiatric disorders co-occur in population-based studies (Angold et al. 1999); appear to share genetic risk in twin studies (Kendler 1996; Kendler et al. 1992); do not readily separate in mathematical modeling (e.g., see Krueger et al. 1998); are correlated with the personality trait of neuroticism (e.g., see Longley et al. 2006); and respond to the same psychological and pharmacological interventions (Kuzma and Black 2004; National Institute for Clinical Excellence 2004) and one of them, anxiety, in childhood is a risk factor for the other, depression, in adulthood (e.g., see Parker et al. 1999). However, little is known about the effects of early adverse environmental exposures on the relationships between the disorders and whether any such exposures operate as differential risk factors for anxiety or depression.

The Medical Research Council National Survey of Health and Development (NSHD)—also known as the British 1946 birth cohort—provides an opportunity to investigate this question, because this survey obtained prospective information from mothers of cohort members on a range of adverse exposures during childhood. The Present State Examination (PSE) was then administered to cohort members themselves in mid adulthood.

Using this information, Rodgers (1990a) conducted an extensive analysis of associations between perinatal factors, socioeconomic and home conditions of origin, family composition and structure, childhood illness, parental behavior and health, childhood cognitive ability and schooling, and PSE scores at 36 years. Results are summarized separately for men and women in Table 12–1.

Table 12–1 also includes results obtained when our team conducted a more conservative analysis (5% level of significance) of the data. For men, factors remaining in the model at the 5% level were: father's age at birth (older than 42 years); death of the father (between 5–11 years); temporary separations (over 4 weeks and in-care/fostered); and high maternal neuroticism. For women, factors remaining in the model at the 5% level were: parental divorce or separation; serious chronic illness between birth and 15 years; poor maternal management; high maternal neuroticism; paternal mental and physical illness; no religious upbringing; and special schooling. The special schooling factor is almost certainly explained by learning disability, because this was subsequently shown to be associated with a fivefold increase in risk of PSE caseness (Index of Definition [ID] of 5 or more) in this cohort, independently of father's social class, mother's education, family size, overcrowding, parental divorce or death, and severe illness up to age 5 years (Richards et al. 2001).

Two recent studies also have refocused attention on associations between intermediate mental health phenotypes and adult psychiatric disorders. Again, using data from the British 1946 birth cohort, Coleman et al. (2007) showed that approximately 70% of adolescents, who were rated as having internalizing disorder, had a mental disorder at age 36, 43, or 53 years compared with approximately 25% of mentally healthy adolescents. However, these authors did not attempt to differentiate adult anxiety from depression either in adolescence or in adulthood. Similarly, Moffitt et al. (2006), using the Dunedin Multidisciplinary Health and Development Study, found that having internalizing disorders in childhood differentiated patients with major depressive disorder (MDD) in early to mid-adulthood as well as patients with generalized anxiety disorder (GAD) from normal control subjects. Again, however, this study did not directly contrast anxiety and depression.

All these findings, therefore, guided the study described in this chapter, which tested whether key early adverse exposures (associated with the PSE) and intermediate mental health phenotypes differentially predicted anxiety or depression when these were separated from the overall PSE score.

The Medical Research Council National Survey of Health and Development

The NSHD initially consisted of 5,362 children of non-manual and agricultural workers and a random sample of one in four of manual workers selected from all

TABLE 12–1. Early environment and the Present State Examination at 36 years

Environment	Factor	Effect
Perinatal factors	Birth weight	No association for men or women
	Older father (44+ years)	Higher score in men
	Breastfeeding duration	No association for men or women
Socioeconomic status, home conditions	Registrar General social class of father	No association for men; higher scores in women born to unskilled manual fathers
	Housing tenure	Higher scores in men and women from council (public) housing
	Overcrowding at age 4 years	Higher scores in women (borderline significance in men)
	Other material home conditions (age, repair, cleanliness of house; cleanliness, clothing of survey member)	No association for men or women
	Parental education	No association for men or women
Family composition, structure	Family size	Higher scores in people from larger families, particularly women (not independent of housing tenure, overcrowding)
	Divorce or separation	Higher scores in women (particularly if before age 5 years)
	Permanent separation from mother	No association for men or women; high study drop out in this group
	Death of sibling	No association for men or women

TABLE 12–1. Early environment and the Present State Examination at 36 years *(continued)*

Environment	Factor	Effect
Family composition, structure *(continued)*	Death of parent	Higher scores in men, particularly if father lost at ages 5–11 years; effect disappeared if mother remarried
	Employment-related absence of father	No association
	Daytime absence of mother before school age	No association
	Separation from parents	Higher scores if separation longer than 1 month; effect lost in women if early chronic illness/disability excluded
	Temporary residential care/foster parenting	Higher scores in men if stay longer than 1 month
Childhood illness	Hospital early admission	Higher scores in men if longer than 4 weeks; probably accounted for by separation from mother
	Early serious illness	Higher scores in women with chronic illness/disability ($n=22$)
	School absenteeism	Higher scores in women for later school years, possibly confounded by personality/behavioral characteristics
Parental behavior and health	Maternal management	Higher scores for children of mothers rated poorest managers
	Parental interest in education	Higher scores in women whose parents showed least interest
	Religious upbringing	Higher scores in women with no religious upbringing (meaning of "religious" unclear)

TABLE 12–1. Early environment and the Present State Examination at 36 years *(continued)*

Environment	Factor	Effect
Parental behavior and health *(continued)*	**Parental health**	Higher scores in daughters of fathers with physical and mental ill health, offspring of mothers with mental illness (neuroticism better predictor), and daughters of mothers with physical illness
Cognitive ability	**General ability, age 15 years**	No association in men; higher scores in women with low ability (threshold effect, corroborated by Richards et al. [2001] for learning disability)
Schooling	Type of school	No association for men or women, except if attended special schools (probably reflects learning disability)
	Changing schools	Higher scores in women who attended multiple primary schools (explained by parental divorce/separation)

Note. Univariate associations reported by Rodgers 1990a; 5% level of significance from Richards et al. 2001.
Text in **bold** represents associations significant at the 5% level.

single births within marriage that occurred in England, Scotland, and Wales during 1 week in March 1946. The cohort has been studied on 21 occasions since birth, most recently in 1999 at age 53 years, when sample size was 3,035 (Wadsworth et al. 2005). In 1982, when cohort members were 36 years old (the age at which mental health outcomes for the present study were obtained), 3,754 cohort members were traced (86.3% of those who were still alive and resident in the United Kingdom), and 3,322 of these were interviewed. In 1999, the cohort was shown to be a representative sample, in most respects, of the U.K. population legitimately and singly born in the immediate postwar era. Exceptions were an overrepresentation among nonresponders of individuals never married, those of lowest literacy, those always in manual occupational social class, and those with psychiatric disorder (Wadsworth et al. 2005).

Study Methods

In the study described in this chapter, the influences of early adverse exposures upon risk for later depression and anxiety were analyzed as described in the following sections.

ADULT ANXIETY AND DEPRESSION SYNDROMES

Of the 3,322 survey members interviewed in 1982 at age 36 years, 3,293 underwent a shortened version of the PSE (Wing and Sturt 1978; Wing et al. 1974, 1977). This version of the PSE consisted of the first 48 items (symptoms) of the Ninth Edition, with the exceptions of items 2, 3, and 13, which do not contribute to the scoring procedure; the inclusion of items 97, 98, 99, and 103; the addition of three general questions on affect over the previous year; and the inclusion of the standard PSE question on treatment for "nerves," extended to cover the past year. Details of nurse interviewer recruitment and training, along with the reliability and validity of this instrument in the NSHD, were reported by Rodgers and Mann (1986). To avoid any ambiguities that might arise from the manner in which the CATEGO algorithm subsumes anxiety symptoms into depression classes, orthogonal Anxiety and Depression PSE outcomes were derived as follows

- The normal comparison group ($n=2,884$) comprised PSE CATEGO classes XN or NO (not serious) or an ID less than 4.
- The anxiety only group ($n=201$) included PSE CATEGO classes Anxiety Neurosis or Phobic Neurosis and an ID of 4 or more.
- The depression only group ($n=171$) was composed of PSE CATEGO classes Retarded Depression or Neurotic and Simple Depression combined, with General Anxiety or Situational Anxiety syndromes of severity less than ++ and an ID of 4 or more.
- The mixed anxiety and depression group ($n=37$) comprised PSE CATEGO classes Retarded Depression or Neurotic and Simple Depression combined, with General Anxiety or Situational Anxiety syndromes of ++ severity and an ID of 4 or more.

Twenty-two survey members who completed the PSE interview were classified as schizophrenic, between ages 16 and 43 years, and were excluded from this study (15 from the normal group, 4 from the depression only group, and 3 from the mixed anxiety and depression group). This classification was based on the application of DSM-III-R (American Psychiatric Association 1987) criteria to clinical material extracted from hospital case notes (from sources that included the Mental Health Enquiry), correspondence with general practitioners, and NSHD survey data (Jones et al. 1994). No clinical case ascertainment was undertaken using these or any other sources for any other type of psychiatric disorder in NSHD.

Final numbers for the PSE groups were as follows: normal comparison group = 2,869; anxiety only group = 201; depression only group = 167; and mixed anxiety and depression group = 34.

EARLY ADVERSE EXPOSURES

Early adverse exposures examined included:

- Father's age at birth, entered as a continuous variable.
- Death of a parent between birth and age 15 years.
- Separation from parents from birth to age 6 years, dichotomized as "up to or longer than 4 months."
- Parental divorce or separation between birth and age 15 years.
- Maternal neuroticism, measured by the self-report Maudsley Personality Inventory (Eysenck 1958), when the cohort member was aged 15 years. Scores ranged from 0–6 and were dichotomized into 4 or less and 5 or 6, which yielded categories with a similar frequency to that of adolescent internalizing disorder.
- Chronic illness between birth and age 5 years was defined as a physical, usually nonfatal condition that lasted longer than 3 months in a given year or necessitated a period of continuous hospitalization of more than 1 month. Any such condition was coded according to the ICD-8 system (World Health Organization 1967). For the purpose of the present analysis, this variable was dichotomized into "none or any" condition, although to avoid overlap with Learning Disability, "mental retardation" (ICD-9 codes 310–313; $N=51$) was treated as missing data. The most common conditions were "congenital" (codes 740–759; $n=90$), followed by conditions of "early infancy" (codes 760–779; $n=52$), then "acute specific bacterial and virus infections of childhood" (codes 032–034, 052, 055–057, 072; $n=49$), and "pneumonia and bronchitis, asthma" (codes 480–493; $n=49$).
- Maternal management when the cohort member was aged 4 years was rated during the relevant home-based interview by a health visitor and scored as among the best, average, or among the worst. Because only 49 mothers fell into the worst category, these were merged with the average category. Thus the indicator variable was dichotomized to good or average/poor.
- Parental health when the cohort member was aged 15 years was self-reported by the mother, who was also asked about the health of her husband. In both cases, health was rated as excellent, good, average, not very good, or poor and dichotomized for the present analysis as excellent to average or poorer than average.
- Mild learning disability was assigned to cohort members if they scored between 2–3.33 SD units below the mean on the general ability score of the Group Ability Test AH4 (Heim 1955), equivalent to an IQ score range 50–69. This was

in line with ICD-10 criteria for mild learning disability (F70; World Health Organization 1992). The AH4 is a 130-item timed test, with separate verbal and nonverbal sections that are summed to yield the general ability score and was administered at age 15 years (Pigeon 1968). The verbal items consist of analogies, comprehension, and numerical reasoning, whereas the nonverbal items consist of matching, spatial analysis, and nonverbal reasoning. An adequate measure was not available to assess whether participants met the ICD-10 criterion of impaired adaptive behavior.

INTERMEDIATE PHENOTYPES

- Neuroticism at age 13 years was assessed by self-report, using the Pintner Aspects of Personality Inventory (Pintner and Folando 1938; Pintner et al. 1937). As with maternal neuroticism, the score was dichotomized to yield categories with a similar frequency to that of adolescent internalizing disorder.
- Adolescent internalizing disorder was based on teacher ratings when survey members were aged 13 and 15 years, covering a range of personality, behaviors, and attitudes. Factor analysis revealed a factor representing anxiety/depression and internalizing emotions and behaviors (Rodgers 1990b). Items that loaded on this factor consisted of "timid child," "rather frightened of rough games," "extremely fearful," "always tired and washed out," "usually gloomy and sad," "avoids attention," "very anxious," "unable to make friends," "diffident about competition," "frequently daydreaming in class," and "becomes unduly miserable or worried in response to criticism." Cronbach's alpha values for these items were 0.68 and 0.71, at 13 and 15 years, respectively. Adolescents were classified as having internalizing disorder if they scored above the 95th percentile on this factor (Coleman et al. 2007), since a prevalence of 5% corresponds to reported prevalences of adolescent anxiety and depression.

STATISTICAL METHODS

Linear or logistic regression (as appropriate) was used to test associations between early adverse exposures and PSE subgroup membership. For each exposure, comparisons were made between normal and anxiety groups; normal and depression groups; and anxiety and depression groups. For each comparison, gender and the exposure-by-gender interaction terms were initially entered. If the latter term was significant at the 10% level or less, the analysis was stratified by gender but otherwise was run for men and women combined. Because of their low frequency ($n=34$), the mixed anxiety and depression group was not included in these comparisons.

Results

Descriptive statistics for the early adverse exposures and intermediate phenotypes, tabulated against each PSE outcome, are shown in Table 12–2. Although inspection of the continuous variable means suggests there were little differences between the PSE groups in father's age at birth of the cohort member, there was a visible trend toward higher maternal neuroticism in the anxiety and mixed groups. For nearly all of the dichotomous variables, cell sizes were small for the clinical groups, particularly so for the mixed group. Nevertheless, there were visible trends toward higher proportions of people in the clinical groups who had been exposed to adverse conditions than were found in the normal group, particularly for exposures involving separation from parents, poor parental health, and for cohort members with learning disabilities. The risk appears to be highest in the mixed group, although this latter trend should, of course, be regarded with caution in view of the low numbers. Finally, it can be seen that risk of intermediate phenotypes (adolescent neuroticism and internalizing disorder) was more likely in the clinical groups, although no clear pattern was observed in regard to risk for anxiety and depression; people with high adolescent neuroticism were most likely to be in the depression group, whereas people with high internalizing disorder were more likely to belong to the anxiety and mixed groups.

Logistic regression was then used to test these comparisons, with the results shown in Table 12–3. In regard to comparisons with the normal group, men who had undergone separation from their parents for more than 1 month by age 6 years had more than twice the risk of being in the anxiety group. When the separation from parents and parental divorce variables were combined to represent separation from the parents for any reason, women showed significantly higher risk of being in the depression group than the normal group (RR=2.71 [1.60, 4.60], $P<0.001$) and showed significantly higher risk of being in the depression group compared to the anxiety group (RR=2.42 [1.12, 5.06], $P=0.02$), the effect of which was not attenuated by controlling for total PSE score.

Men and women who, when they were 15 years old, had a parent in poor health or who could have been classified as having mild learning disability at that age had a significantly higher risk of being in the anxiety or depression groups, compared with people in the normal group. This effect was particularly evident for learning disability, which was associated, in men and women, with a threefold risk of membership in the anxiety group and more than sixfold risk for women of being in the depression group.

In terms of intermediate phenotypes, people with high self-rated neuroticism scores at 13 years of age were twice as likely to be in the depression group compared with the normal group, whereas adolescent internalizing disorder, according to teacher ratings, strongly differentiated people with anxiety from the normal group. However, there was no difference in risk when the anxiety and depression

TABLE 12–2. Descriptions of study groups

Exposure	Normal group	Anxiety group	Depression group	Mixed group
N	2,869	201	167	34
Father's age at birth of cohort member, y[a]	32.02 (6.43)	31.82 (6.78)	31.69 (6.87)	31.71 (6.69)
Maternal neuroticism	163 (6.6%)	17 (9.6%)	9 (6.9%)	3 (10.3%)
Death of parent by age 15 years	191 (6.7%)	10 (5.0%)	9 (5.4%)	5 (14.7%)
Separation from parents by age 6 years	203 (7.8%)	18 (9.8%)	16 (11.3%)	5 (15.6%)
Parental divorce or separation by age 15 years	160 (6.8%)	16 (9.6%)	13 (9.8%)	5 (20.8%)
Chronic illness by age 5 years	142 (5.0%)	5 (2.5%)	12 (7.3%)	6 (17.6%)
Sub-optimum maternal management	1,319 (50.1%)	94 (51.4%)	69 (46.9%)	18 (56.3%)
Poor parental health at age 15 years	223 (9.5%)	25 (14.8%)	19 (15.2%)	4 (15.4%)
Learning disability at age 15 years	58 (2.4%)	12 (7.0%)	12 (9.2%)	1 (3.2%)
Neuroticism at age 13 years	160 (6.7%)	17 (10.3%)	19 (14.7%)	2 (7.4%)
Internalizing disorder at age 13–15 years	154 (7.5%)	25 (18.1%)	14 (12.5%)	5 (20.8%)

[a]Means and standard deviations.

TABLE 12–3. Risk ratios for Present State Examination outcome (normal vs. anxiety, normal vs. depression, anxiety vs. depression) by early adverse exposures (shown separately for men and women where the exposure × sex interaction was significant at <0.10)

	Group comparison		
Exposure	Normal vs. anxiety	Normal vs. depression	Anxiety vs. depression
Father's age at birth of cohort member[a]	M: −0.09 (−0.41, 0.24) P=0.60 F: 0.22 (−0.08, 0.52) P=0.14	M: 0.05 (−0.28, 0.38) P=0.60 F: 0.08 (−0.23, 0.38) P=0.63	M: 0.01 (−1.84, 1.86) P=0.99 F: 0.04 (−1.25, 1.33) P=0.95
Maternal neuroticism	1.50 (0.89, 2.53) P=0.13	1.05 (0.52, 2.10) P=0.90	0.70 (0.30, 1.62) P=0.40
Death of parent by age 15 years	0.73 (0.38, 1.41) P=0.35	0.80 (0.40, 1.60) P=0.52	1.09 (0.43, 2.74) P=0.86
Separation from parents by age 6 years	M: 2.28 (1.09, 4.78) P=0.03 F: 0.88 (0.43, 1.78) P=0.71	1.50 (0.88, 2.58) P=0.14	M: 0.46 (0.13, 1.62) P=0.23 F: 1.98 (0.80, 4.92) P=0.14
Parental divorce or separation by age 15 years	1.45 (0.84, 2.49) P=0.18	M: 0.30 (0.04, 2.24) P=0.24 F: 2.22 (1.15, 4.26) P=0.02	1.02 (0.47, 2.21) P=0.96
Chronic illness by age 5 years	0.49 (0.20–1.22) P=0.12	1.51 (0.82, 2.78) P=0.19	3.06 (1.06, 8.88) P=0.04[b]
Sub-optimum maternal management at age 4 years	1.05 (0.78, 1.42) P=0.74	0.88 (0.63, 1.23) P=0.46	0.84 (0.54, 1.29) P=0.42
Poor parental health at age 15 years	1.66 (1.06, 2.59) P=0.03	1.71 (1.03, 2.84) P=0.04	M: 0.31 (0.08, 1.18) P=0.09 F: 1.71 (0.78, 3.72) P=0.18
Learning disability at age 15 years	3.10 (1.63, 5.90) P=0.001	M: 1.62 (0.38, 6.95) P=0.52 F: 6.68 (3.14, 15.01) P<0.001	1.34 (0.58, 3.10) P=0.42
Neuroticism at age 13 years	1.59 (0.94, 2.70) P=0.08	2.39 (1.43, 4.00) P<0.001	1.50 (0.75, 3.03) P=0.25
Externalizing disorder at ages 13–15 years	2.74 (1.72, 4.35) P<0.001	1.77 (0.99, 3.17) P=0.06	0.65 (0.32, 1.31) P=0.23

[a]Linear regression for continuous variable.
[b]Higher risk of depression than anxiety, slightly strengthened by adjusting for overall Present State Examination score.

groups were compared with each other. In fact, the only exposure variable to differentiate the anxiety group from the depression group, in this way, was chronic illness by age 5 years, which was associated with greater risk of depression than anxiety, an effect that persisted after controlling for overall PSE score. However, this was probably the net result of the trend toward a protective effect of early chronic illness in the anxiety group compared with the normal group, and the trend toward the risk effect of this variable in the depression group compared with the normal group.

To check whether potential differences between the anxiety and depression groups were being suppressed by differences in clinical severity, all other comparisons between these two groups were re-run, controlling for total PSE score. However, the results were not substantially altered.

It was not possible to investigate whether the teacher ratings of "very anxious" and "usually gloomy and sad" at 13 or 15 years of age differentially predicted PSE anxiety-only or depression-only, because these teacher ratings co-occurred too frequently.

Discussion

In this prospective longitudinal birth cohort study—broadly representative of the U.K. population born immediately after World War II—a range of early adverse exposures and two intermediate phenotypes were examined as possible differential risk factors for anxiety and depression in midlife. Selection of these factors was guided by the earlier work, in this same cohort, of Rodgers (1990a) on associations between environmental factors during childhood and adolescence and the total PSE score at age 36 years; and by the work of Moffitt et al. (2006). Consistent with the overall conclusions of Rodgers (1990a), we found little evidence that early adverse exposures reliably predicted PSE classes in midlife and little evidence that these exposures differentiated cohort members with anxiety only from those with depression only. There also was no evidence that the intermediate phenotypes of adolescent neuroticism and internalizing disorder differentiated cohort members in this way.

Several limitations of the present study should be noted, the most important of which is lack of statistical power. In fact, for most exposures in the anxiety and depression groups, the frequencies of risk categories were so low that the demonstration of effects at the 5% level is all the more remarkable. However, poor parental health, which differentiated both anxiety and depression from normality by an equal degree, did not differentiate anxiety from depression. This was also the case for learning disability, which was very strongly associated with risk of anxiety or depression. Investigation of these findings in a far larger sample is required before these conclusions can be accepted or rejected with any degree of certainty. In this context, it is worth noting Rodgers's (1990a) comment that, when individual factors appeared to have strong associations with adult symptoms, this was for small groups with particularly adverse circumstances, in marked contrast to the more graded associations of early environment with cognitive development (Douglas 1964; Richards and Sacker 2003; Richards and Wadsworth 2004) and with physical growth (Kuh and Wadsworth 1989), in this cohort.

Another important limitation, also originally raised by Rodgers (1990a), is that the study remit of the NSHD in its early years was broadly health-based, and data collected during these years were not specifically chosen for their potential to predict psychiatric symptoms. Missing, in particular, is detailed prospective information on parental interaction and information of any kind on maltreatment, including physical or sexual abuse, the long-term serious mental health effects of which are well known (e.g., see Brown and Anderson 1991).

Finally, it is worth noting that the anxiety and depression outcomes were based on a single measure, the PSE, at 36 years.

With these limitations in mind, the results of this study are consistent with other lines of evidence that suggest anxiety and depression are too closely interlinked to be easily dissociated, whether by descriptive prevalence studies, risk factor studies, mathematical modeling, or intervention studies. This was the case, even when these two sets of PSE symptoms were deliberately disaggregated into orthogonal groups. To the extent that these orthogonal groups represent MDD and GAD, data from the 1946 birth cohort do not support the possibility that these two disorders are unrelated or only distally related. However, these data are not able to distinguish whether they are either different forms of the same disorder or closely related disorders. Further evidence is required from large, long-term prospective studies in which early adverse exposures, including those of abuse and maltreatment, are well characterized and repeated measures enable MDD and GAD to be identified as stable phenotypes.

References

American Psychiatric Association: Diagnostic and Statistical Manual of Mental Disorders, 3rd Edition Revised. Washington, DC, American Psychiatric Association, 1987

Angold A, Costello EJ, Erkanli A: Comorbidity. J Child Psychol Psychiatry 40:57–87, 1999

Brown GR, Anderson B: Psychiatric morbidity in adult inpatients with childhood histories of sexual and physical abuse. Am J Psychiatry 148:55–61, 1991

Coleman I, Wadsworth MEJ, Croudace TJ, et al: Forty-year psychiatric outcomes following assessment for internalizing disorder in adolescence. Am J Psychiatry 164:126–133, 2007

Douglas JWB: The Home and the School. London, England, MacGibbon and Kee, 1964

Eysenck HJ: A short questionnaire for the measurement of two dimensions of personality. J Appl Psychol 43:14–17, 1958

Heim AW: Manual for the Group Test of General Intelligence AH4. London, England, National Foundation for Educational Research, 1955

Jones PJ, Rodgers B, Murray R, et al: Child developmental risk factors for adult schizophrenia in the British 1946 birth cohort. Lancet 344:1398–1402, 1994

Kendler KS: Major depression and generalised anxiety disorder: same genes, (partly) different environments—revisited. Br J Psychiatry 52:374–383, 1996

Kendler KS, Neale MC, Kessler RC, et al: Major depression and generalized anxiety disorder: same genes, (partly) different environments? Arch Gen Psychiatry 49:716–722, 1992

Krueger RF, Caspi A, Moffitt TE et al: The structure and stability of common mental disorders (DSM-II-R): a longitudinal-epidemiological study. J Abnorm Psychol 107:216–277, 1998

Kuh D, Wadsworth M: Parental height, childhood environment and subsequent adult height in a national birth cohort. Int J Epidemiol 18:663–668, 1989

Kuzma JM, Black DW: Integrating pharmacotherapy and psychotherapy in the management of anxiety disorders. Psychol Assess 13:1–12, 2004

Longley SL, Watson D, Noyes R Jr, et al: Panic and phobic anxiety: associations among neuroticism, physiological hyperarousal, anxiety sensitivity, and three phobias. J Anxiety Disord 20:718–739, 2006

Moffitt TE, Caspi A, Harrington H, et al: Generalized anxiety disorder and depression: childhood risk factors in a birth cohort followed to age 32. Psychol Med 37:1–12, 2006

National Institute for Clinical Excellence: Depression: Management of Depression in Primary and Secondary Care—NICE Guidance. London, England, National Institute for Clinical Excellence, 2004. Available at http://www.nice.org.uk/Guidance/CG23. Accessed March 2009

Parker G, Wilhelm P, Austin MP, et al: The influence of anxiety as a risk to early onset major depression. J Affect Disord 52:11–17, 1999

Pigeon DA: Details of the fifteen years tests, in All Our Future, Appendix 1. Edited by Douglas JWB, Ross JM, Simpson HR. London, England, Davies, 1968, pp 194–197

Pintner R, Folando G: Four retests of a personality inventory. J Ed Psychol 29:93–100, 1938

Pintner R, Loftus JJ, Forlando G, et al: Aspects of Personality Inventory: Test and Manual. Yonkers, NY, World Book, 1937

Richards M, Sacker A: Lifetime antecedents of cognitive reserve. J Clin Exp Neuropsychol 25:614–624, 2003

Richards M, Wadsworth MEJ: Long-term effects of early adversity on cognitive function. Arch Dis Child 89:922–927, 2004

Richards M, Maughan B, Hardy R, et al: Long-term affective disorder in people with mild learning disability. Br J Psychiatry 179:523–527, 2001

Rodgers B: Adult affective disorder and early environment. Br J Psychiatry 157:539–550, 1990a

Rodgers B: Behaviour and personality in childhood as predictors of adult psychiatric disorder. J Child Psychol Psychiatry 31:393–414, 1990b

Rodgers B, Mann SA: The reliability and validity of PSE assessments by lay interviewers: a national population survey. Psychol Med 16:639–700, 1986

Wadsworth MEJ, Butterworth SL, Hardy R, et al: The life course design: an example of benefits and problems associated with study longevity. Soc Sci Med 57: 2193–205, 2005

Wing JK, Sturt E: The PSE-ID-CATEGO System: Supplementary Manual. Mimeo. London, England, Institute of Psychiatry, 1978

Wing JK, Cooper JE, Sartorius N: Present State Examination. Cambridge, United Kingdom, Cambridge University Press, 1974

Wing JK, Nixon JM, Mann SA, et al: Reliability of the PSE (ninth edition) used in a population study. Psychol Med 7:505–516, 1977

World Health Organization: International Classification of Diseases, 8th Revision. Geneva, Switzerland, World Health Organization, 1967

World Health Organization: International Statistical Classification of Diseases and Related Health Problems, 10th Revision. Geneva, Switzerland, World Health Organization, 1992

13

EPISODES AND DISORDERS OF GENERAL ANXIETY AND DEPRESSION

Ian M. Goodyer, M.D.

Theoretical Issues in Current Classifications

Currently, generalized anxiety disorder (GAD) and major depressive disorder (MDD) are classified in two distinct sections of DSM-IV (American Psychiatric Association 1994). MDD is classified as a mood disorder (296.2X) and GAD (300.02) as an anxiety disorder. A read of the introduction of these two sections in the DSM-IV manual indicates clearcut weaknesses in the current classifications of these clusters of mental phenomena.

The first weakness is that both operational definitions for the two conditions contain emotion criteria. MDD alone can be diagnosed if patients qualify, via the presence of sad emotion, empty feelings, or, specifically in childhood, irritability.

Inspection of the GAD criteria indicates that this diagnosis also requires a distinct emotion qualifier, defined as excessive anxiety or worry. The initial problem here is to allow the term "anxiety," to be used as a general category and a qualifying criterion for diagnosis. A further weakness in GAD is the inclusion of a second emotion state, "irritability," to be counted as a symptom, rather than a qualifier as in major depression. The presence of irritability as a clinical symptom in both MDD and GAD is also the first of a number of opportunities for double counting a single phenomenon toward two "distinct" diagnoses.

Interestingly, the rules for GAD (sections D, E and F, 300.2) indicate that anxiety mood symptoms are "trumped" by the presence of a "mood disorder." This implicit hierarchical assumption that the mood states of depression are more important than those of anxiety is not supported with any argument, merely stated. Presumably, the technical issue is that short-term episodes of depression count when they occur within longer-term GAD. If they did not, then the prevalence of depression would, no doubt, drop. This makes the temporal criteria of considerable clinical significance in determining diagnosis. Thus, the ability of the researcher and clinician to distinguish between these two clusters is guided by the timing qualifier, the hierarchical statement, and some social context used in the definition of GAD.

MDD criteria state five symptoms (emotion plus four others) should be present in a 2-week period, whereas GAD criteria (emotion plus three symptoms) state change should be present for 6 months. Timing parameters also dictate the use of the terms *episode* and *disorder*. Furthermore, a recurrence of MDD can be diagnosed in a very short time frame, compared with GAD, for which recurrence can be determined only over a relatively long time scale. There is no clearcut rationale for either of these time points in the classification system. Finally, for MDD, one episode is also a qualifier for a disorder, whereas for GAD, there is no episode, only disorder.

ADDITIONAL SYMPTOMS

From the additional-symptom perspective, MDD has 6 symptom sections, with approximately 12 symptom features to consider, once a mood qualifier is met. If four other symptoms are present, then an episode of MDD can be diagnosed. In contrast, GAD has six symptoms available to consider, within one section. If three more of these symptoms are present, then disorder (not episode) is diagnosed. GAD requires that the worry not be confined to the symptoms themselves (i.e., "I am worried about having a panic attack") or be about embarrassment, being alone, or being ill. This makes the emotion of anxiety/worry more pervasive in nature. Inspection of these symptom domains—the presence of which determines "MDD episode" and "GAD disorder," shows remarkable overlap (see Figure 13–1).

The emotion state "irritability" has a further conditional ambiguity, because it is used as a qualifier mood for depression in childhood and adolescence but not in adulthood. Adults can be irritable, but if irritability is present as a symptom, it can only count as a secondary symptom for GAD. From the theoretical perspective, the emotion qualifiers for both MDD and GAD are in the main primary emotion states. In contrast, irritability is a secondary relational state—that is, an observed inference from the behavior of one person, by another. The appropriate primary emotion state for irritability is anger. However, anger does not appear at all in the DSM-IV index.

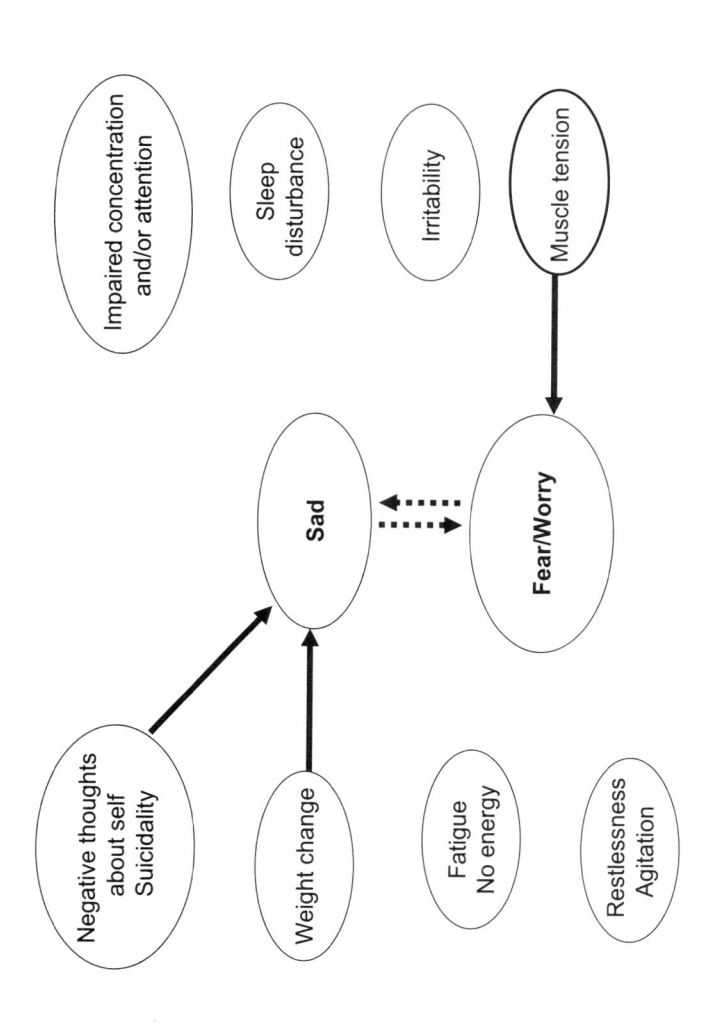

FIGURE 13–1. Major depressive and generalized anxiety disorder symptom domains.

Emotions, Feelings, and Moods

The three terms *emotions, feelings,* and *moods* have been used interchangeably throughout history to denote an alteration from a general state of well-being. Well-being, itself, is almost never defined, except via circular, or exclusion, terminology—for example, as a state of competence and the absence of negative states of mind. Affective neuroscience has focused on delineating the primary emotions, considered to be hard wired in the brain and essential to psychological integrity and adaptive behavioral function in the presence of different social stimuli. The six "basic" emotions identified to date are fear, anger, disgust, sadness, happiness, and surprise. Current neuroscientific research has made progress toward validating that some of these emotions are, indeed, "hard wired" or, more specifically, have neural substrates that subserve their activity at a conscious psychological level (Calder 2003; Calder et al. 2001; Damasio et al. 2000; Hariri and Holmes 2006; May 2002). A summary of the flow of basic emotion states is summarized in Figure 13–2.

IMPLICATIONS FOR DIAGNOSES

GAD refers to "excessive" worry, a secondary emotion term—that is, "looking worried," implying a deviation from the norm (it would be better to denote this as fear). This is a dimensional perspective, which is distinct from using the term "abnormal," to imply a categorical distinction.

If you meet symptom and time criteria, the assessment that finally makes you "clinical," is that you no longer function at the personal or social level in the way that you previously did. This requirement raises issues concerning the detection of those who are impaired with low symptoms or who fail time criteria for GAD. Already, these issues have been shown to be a matter of some concern in the first two decades of life (Angold et al. 1999).

The emotion state "happy" can be logically inferred to extrapolate to hypomania or mania, but whether there is a true relationship between individual differences in happiness and the liability for excessive happiness—to be associated with hypomania/mania—is far from clear.

Conclusions Based on Theory and Concept of Major Depressive Disorder and Generalized Anxiety Disorder Diagnoses

ARE MDD AND GAD SEPARATE CATEGORIES?

MDD and GAD are not, theoretically, separate categories.

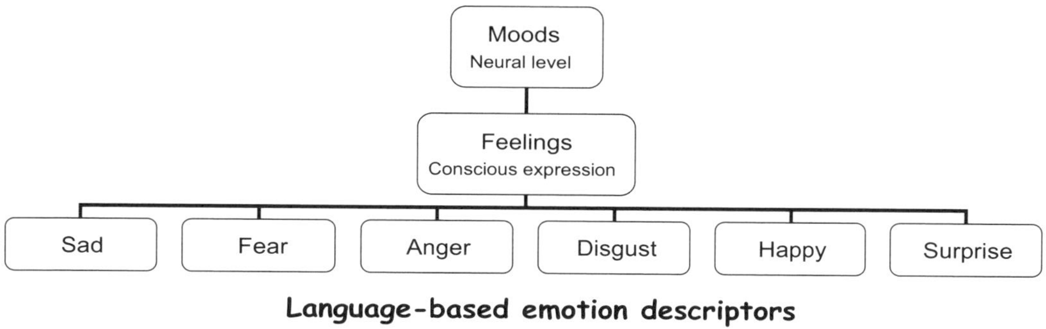

Episodes and Disorders of General Anxiety and Depression

```
Moods
Neural level
   │
Feelings
Conscious expression
   ├── Sad
   ├── Fear
   ├── Anger
   ├── Disgust
   ├── Happy
   └── Surprise
```

Language-based emotion descriptors

FIGURE 13–2. Flowchart of moods, feelings, and emotion states.

SHOULD MDD AND GAD BE CLASSIFIED IN THE SAME CATEGORY?

Yes, these disorders should be classified in the same category. The precise nomenclature at the categorical and syndrome levels is not straightforward and depends on assumptions made. There are some clear theoretical guidelines:

Category of Disorder

Mood disorders remain a logical choice of category for these two disorders and would map onto current neuroscientific advances in the field of affective neuroscience. This category would afford the possibility of a stronger scientific partnership between neuroscience and psychopathology than has been achieved hitherto. Future classifications may be informed by a greater understanding of the neural systems that subserve emotion language labels.

Emotion Qualifiers

Only primary emotions should be used as emotion qualifiers for a mood episode or disorder. Anger should be considered as a replacement for the term *irritability* as an emotion label qualifier. There appears to be no theoretical justification for the current differential use of the term *irritability* in MDD and GAD criteria.

Time Qualifiers

Time qualifiers need to be reviewed for both MDD and GAD. Standardizing time qualifiers for episode and disorder may reduce the risk of double counting and, therefore, of inflation of diagnoses.

ARE MDD AND GAD SUBTYPES OR SUBFORMS OF ONE DISORDER?

MDD and GAD are probably subtypes. First, there may be distinct forms of MDD-only and GAD-only. Second, there is likely to be a third, mixed disorder. A mixed state will likely present with differential signs and symptoms in differing episodes, fluctuating over time, perhaps as is seen, for example, in bipolar disorder.

The Clinical Evidence

The outstanding epidemiology research of Moffitt and colleagues (Chapter 11)—which was provided for use in this chapter—assumed that there were two disorders, as defined in the DSM system, and that longitudinal study of both would help unravel their relationships to each other over time. The authors' extensive follow-up was key to examining the comorbid relationships, because four repeat estimates of diagnosis—at 18, 21, 26, and 32 years of age—gave the best opportunity for a robust examination of diagnostic interplay, over this 14-year period. The basic difficulties within the DSM system noted earlier were, however, not entirely negated by longitudinal design alone. Moffitt and colleagues stated "GAD was diagnosed, regardless of other disorders" and MDD was also allowed to be diagnosed in the presence of any other disorder, at the same time. The results confirmed last-year prevalences of 14% for MDD and 4% for GAD. Recurrences were 50%–60% for MDD and 50% for GAD. This work demonstrated a three-group type model, with MDD-only, GAD-only, and a mixed group. The mixed group appeared more impaired and had elevated healthcare use compared with the "pure" groups. A key finding was the observation that recurrence was virtually synonymous with comorbidity over time (MDD+GAD) and that 12% of the cohort had this mixed disorder. Recurrence rate was not given but presumably was more frequent for MDD—that is, it was MDD "episodes" recurring within GAD "disorder" that was being reported.

By suggesting a much more detailed look at latent correlational structures at the symptom level in future studies, the authors showed they were fully aware of the diagnostic difficulties. Such an examination would advance a previous preliminary look at symptom profiles, at one time point, within MDD in female adolescents, where it was noted that the symptom pattern of depression and the sensitivity and specificity of self-reported symptoms with disorder varied with age (Cooper and Goodyer 1993; Goodyer and Cooper 1993). Moffitt and colleagues noted that the prevailing notion that GAD "develops" into MDD was no more common in their data than MDD "developing into GAD."

Conclusions From the Dunedin Study
ARE MDD AND GAD SEPARATE CATEGORIES?

The findings of Moffitt and colleagues from the Dunedin study provided partial support for a three-form model: depression, anxiety, and a mixed diagnosis. The latter diagnosis was more severe over time and presented with a variability of mood and cognitive features that remained underspecified.

SHOULD MDD AND GAD BE CLASSIFIED IN THE SAME CATEGORY?

Yes, MDD and GAD should be classified in the same category. The precise nomenclature at the categorical and syndrome level is not straightforward and depends on assumptions made. It is important that future studies examine the patterning of symptoms ascertained within a diagnosis at each assessment and over time.

ARE MDD AND GAD SUBTYPES OR SUBFORMS OF ONE DISORDER?

The interplay between MDD and GAD, over time, in the severely impaired mixed group in the Dunedin Study (Chapter 11) suggested that the mix of both disorders should be considered as a distinct subtype from the more stable single form, over time. The three-form classification—that is, MDD-only, GAD-only, and mixed type—was somewhat supported by the data from this study. However, this classification does require double counting of some symptoms. There could be better use of the terms *episode* and *disorder* in future classifications. Currently, these definitions are seriously hampered by the time qualifiers between MDD and GAD being so different. Perhaps a 1-month qualifier should apply to an episode for MDD and GAD; this would have the benefits of both removing likely sporadic adjustment reactions from the MDD group (also, perhaps, stop some unnecessary treatment actions on relatively well people) and being able to assign GAD to an episode within the same time frame. The term "disorder" could be reserved for patients with two or more episodes only (for further reading, see American College of Neuropsychopharmacology guidelines on remission and recurrence for depression; Rush et al. 2006).

Risk Factors and the Nature of Major Depressive Disorder and Generalized Anxiety Disorder

Chapters 11 and 12 in this monograph describe aspects of risk for MDD and GAD. A key suggestion raises the possibility for somewhat different risk processes differentiating MDD, GAD, and the mixed disorder. The strength of the prospective data from the Dunedin study favors the three-form solution (Chapter 11). Risks used in both studies spanned genetic and environmental influences. It is not clear whether activation mechanisms for an episode of any form may be distinct, because this was not formally investigated in either study. Overall, however, the data from the Dunedin cohort indicate that earlier-onset GAD may be a marker for a pathway toward a relatively more severe mixed disorder emerging in late adolescence and early adult life. Risk factor profiles are sufficiently different between MDD- and GAD-only forms to suggest partially distinct etiologies. Marcus Richards reports findings from the Medical Research Council National Survey of Health and Development (Chapter 12). This major survey was not focused on mental health outcomes, and the data are, therefore, somewhat more limited for addressing the current questions regarding MDD and GAD. Perhaps the key finding is one commensurate with that of observations from the Dunedin study—that a range of early childhood and adolescent risk factors for psychopathology do not predict onsets of MDD in early life. There is fairly clear evidence for greater aggregation of anxiety and depression than disaggregation when different data and/or methods were used, in an attempt to separate the disorders.

Conclusions

ARE MDD AND GAD SEPARATE CATEGORIES?

The risk findings provide no support for continuing with classifications of MDD and GAD as separate disorders in different categories.

SHOULD MDD AND GAD BE CLASSIFIED IN THE SAME CATEGORY?

Again, the risk findings support the notion that MDD and GAD should be classified in the same category. The risks used are devoid of putative biomarker data but are comprehensive in their coverage of those markers that have been measured in epidemiological studies, to date.

The suggestion has been made that MDD and GAD should be considered as "distress" disorders in DSM-V. This change is not supported by the evidence. First, putatively distressing risk factors are not associated with all forms, or all episodes, over time. Second, none of the studies presented actually defined or measured distress. This type of data would be helpful before consigning mental disorders to such a category. Third, without full lifetime data, we risk the development of yet another incomplete category. Fourth, the rationale of a phenomenological system is, in part, to remain as free as possible from inference and interpretation.

ARE MDD AND GAD SUBTYPES OR SUBFORMS OF ONE DISORDER?

The current risk evidence suggests MDD and GAD are not one disorder, and a three-form diagnostic system of MDD-only, GAD-only, and a mixed disorder should be retained.

Summary

The current classification of MDD and GAD is no longer tenable. Major theoretical and conceptual errors are undermining the ascertainment of valid evidence about these phenomena. Prospective data using the diagnostic system to detect and follow these syndromes are therefore, limited by these difficulties. The Dunedin study demonstrated that, even given these major problems, we appear to have sufficient evidence to state that:

- MDD and GAD are not, truly, separate categories and should be classified together in a revised DSM system.
- Within that system, there is sufficient evidence to consider three forms: MDD-only, GAD-only, and a mixed condition.
- These three forms cannot be considered as one disorder.

A new "distress" category would require defining and validating and is a complex topic in itself. In addition, the likelihood that kindling occurs, altering the putative mechanisms for episode onset of MDD for some individuals (Kendler et al. 2001) by at least two differing pathways—one probably genetic, the other probably via illness effects on the brain—does not support "distress" as providing added value for a new generic category.

My own view is that the category of mood disorders should be redefined to incorporate conditions characterized by an excess of one or more observable basic emotions that result in personal impairment. A classification of mood disorders might be considered within which one set of forms involved an excess of negative, diminished-positive, or excess-of-positive emotion states. Such states would arise from latent dysregulation of the neural systems that subserve mood activation and control and give rise to emotion states. Figure 13–3 illustrates a starting point of such a classification.

These emotion states would initially be considered clinical episodes if they met specific additional criteria and led to personal impairment. Duration criteria would be standardized to 1-month history, with impairment for a clinical episode. Disorder might be reserved for recurrent episode illnesses, which tend to occur in around 60% of clinically referred cases (Dunn and Goodyer 2006). Mixed states could not be ruled out from single-state presentations.

Issues and Prospects

Moffitt and colleagues pointed out the shortcomings of not looking at latent-trait characteristics of symptoms and dimensions of "depression" and "anxiety." Growth models on longitudinal data would be of considerable additional value here. The Dunedin finding that there was a fluctuating mixed state of MDD+GAD over many years seems reminiscent of bipolar characteristics. Perhaps we could learn more from a closer inspection of the episodes and symptom profiles in this study.

Finally, there is a need for a much better understanding of the intermediate biology of these conditions. First, there is a strongly emerging literature on the role

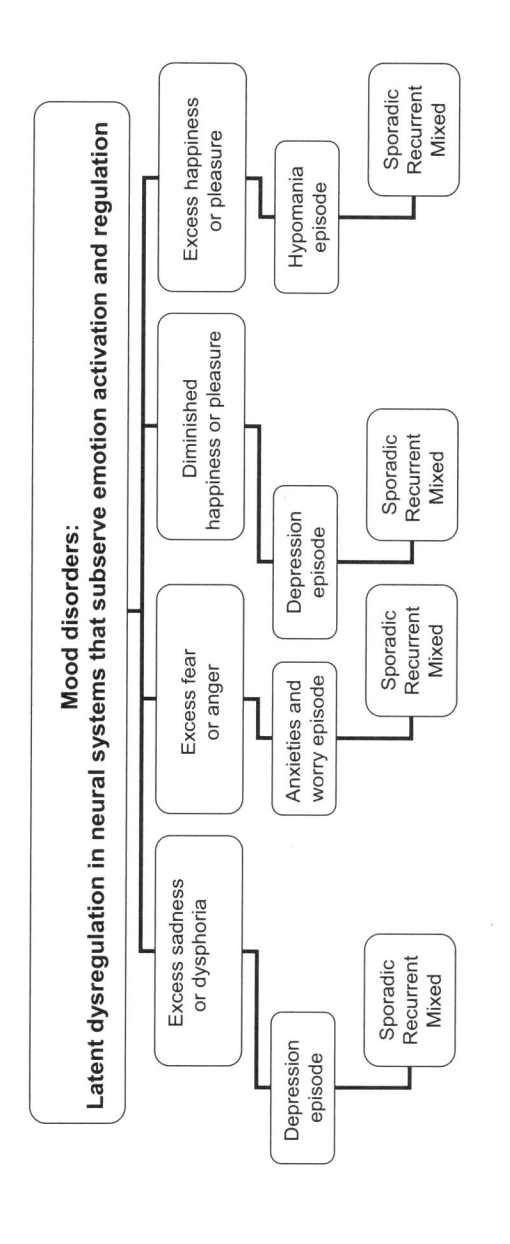

Episodes and Disorders of General Anxiety and Depression 267

FIGURE 13–3. Mood disorders: latent dysregulation in neural systems that subserve emotion activation and regulation.

of specific serotonin vulnerabilities (Caspi et al. 2003; Cervilla et al. 2007) for depression, which have significant implications for the integrity of mood-sensitive neural circuitry (Ernst et al. 2006; Neumeister et al. 2006; Roberson-Nay et al. 2006). Second, there is a robust relationship between the physiology of the stress system, as indexed by cortisol differences, and the emergence, course, and outcomes of depressive episodes (Goodyer et al. 2000, 2009; Harris et al. 2000). Third, serotonergic-sensitive functions, such as are seen in reward, punishment, and motivational systems (Ernst et al. 2006), are corticoid sensitive as well and deserve further scrutiny in an effort to discriminate the neural bases of different forms of MDD, GAD, and mixed MDD+GAD disorders.

References

American Psychiatric Association: Diagnostic and Statistical Manual of Mental Disorders, 4th Edition. Washington, DC, American Psychiatric Association, 1994

Angold A, Costello EJ, Farmer EM, et al: Impaired but undiagnosed. J Am Acad Child Adolesc Psychiatry 38:129–137, 1999

Calder AJ: Disgust discussed. Ann Neurol 53:427–428, 2003

Calder AJ, Lawrence AD, Young AW: Neuropsychology of fear and loathing. Nat Rev Neurosci 2:352–363, 2001

Caspi A, Sugden K, Moffitt TE, et al: Influence of life stress on depression: moderation by a polymorphism in the 5-HTT gene. Science 301:386–389, 2003

Cervilla JA, Molina E, Rivera M, et al: The risk for depression conferred by stressful life events is modified by variation at the serotonin transporter 5HTTLPR genotype: evidence from the Spanish PREDICT-Gene cohort. Mol Psychiatry 12:748–755, 2007

Cooper PJ, Goodyer IM: A community study of depression in adolescent girls, I: estimates of symptom and syndrome prevalence. Br J Psychiatry 163:369–374, 1993

Damasio AR, Grabowski TJ, Bechara A, et al: Subcortical and cortical brain activity during the feeling of self-generated emotions. Nat Neurosci 3:1049–1056, 2000

Dunn V, Goodyer IM: Longitudinal investigation into childhood- and adolescence-onset depression: psychiatric outcome in early adulthood. Br J Psychiatry 188:216–222, 2006

Ernst M, Pine DS, Hardin M: Triadic model of the neurobiology of motivated behavior in adolescence. Psychol Med 36:299–312, 2006

Goodyer IM, Cooper PJ: A community study of depression in adolescent girls, II: the clinical- features of identified disorder. Br J Psychiatry 163:374–380, 1993

Goodyer IM, Herbert J, Tamplin A, et al: Recent life events, cortisol, dehydroepiandrosterone and the onset of major depression in high-risk adolescents. Br J Psychiatry 177:499–504, 2000

Goodyer IM, Bacon A, Ban M, et al: Serotonin transporter genotype, morning cortisol and subsequent depression in adolescents. Br J Psychiatry 195:39–45, 2009

Hariri AR, Holmes A: Genetics of emotional regulation: the role of the serotonin transporter in neural function. Trends Cogn Sci 10:182–191, 2006

Harris TO, Boranyi S, Messari S, et al: Morning cortisol as a risk factor for subsequent major depressive disorder in adult women. Br J Psychiatry 177:505–510, 2000

Kendler KS, Thornton LM, Gardner CO: Genetic risk, number of previous depressive episodes, and stressful life events in predicting onset of major depression. Am J Psychiatry 158:582–586, 2001

May TS: Emotions and the brain: linking affective disorders to brain regions. Lancet Neurol 1:80, 2002

Neumeister A, Hu XZ, Luckenbaugh DA, et al: Differential effects of 5-HTTLPR genotypes on the behavioral and neural responses to tryptophan depletion in patients with major depression and controls. Arch Gen Psychiatry 63:978–986, 2006

Roberson-Nay R, McClure EB, Monk CS, et al: Increased amygdala activity during successful memory encoding in adolescent major depressive disorder: an FMRI study. Biol Psychiatry 60:966–973, 2006

Rush JA, Kraemer HC, Sackeim HA, et al: Report by the ACNP Task Force on Response and Remission in Major Depressive Disorder. Neuropsychopharmacology 31:1841–1853, 2006

14

ARE MAJOR DEPRESSION AND GENERALIZED ANXIETY DISORDER THE SAME OR DIFFERENT DISORDERS?

Discussion of the Dunedin and Medical Research Council Birth Cohort Studies and the Three-Generation High Risk Study

Myrna M. Weissman, Ph.D.
Virginia Warner, M.P.H.
Priya Wickramaratne, Ph.D.

This chapter was prepared in response to a request from the Research Planning Committee on Depression and Generalized Anxiety Disorder, jointly sponsored by the American Psychiatric Association, National Institutes of Health, and the World Health Organization. This committee seeks to design research that will inform and help refine future revisions of the diagnostic classifications of DSM-IV (American Psychiatric Association 1994). The question posed here was "How should generalized anxiety disorder [GAD] be characterized, in relationship to major depressive disorder [MDD], in the revision, DSM-V?"

Proposals to collapse MDD and GAD into one diagnostic group in DSM-V would be supported if 1) the two disorders share common antecedent risk factors; 2) prospectively assessed risk factors for MDD and GAD are similar; 3) one disorder transmits the other disorder between generations; or 4) one disorder predicts the other disorder, across the life span.

In this chapter, we discuss the evidence presented in the chapters by Moffitt and colleagues (Chapter 11) and Richards and Goldberg (Chapter 12) and then ask similar questions about GAD and MDD from our own high-risk longitudinal study of three generations. Moffitt and colleagues and Richards and Goldberg looked at antecedent risks; the former also examined cumulative and sequential comorbidity. Our high-risk study looks at transmissions between generations and longitudinal diagnostic predictions.

Antecedent Risk Factors (Dunedin and Medical Research Council Birth Cohort Studies)

The data presented in Chapter 11 came from the 1972–1973 Dunedin birth cohort of 1,037 subjects followed to age 32 years (Moffitt et al. 2007a, 2007b). Childhood disorders were diagnosed by means of the Diagnostic Interview Schedule for Children. Adult GAD and MDD were diagnosed at ages 18, 21, 26, and 32 years through use of the Diagnostic Interview Schedule. Childhood risk factors were obtained between ages 3–11 years from parents and teachers. Because DSM-III (American Psychiatric Association 1980) did not include juvenile GAD, overanxious disorder was substituted for juveniles. The duration criterion was 1 month for GAD, and no hierarchies were included. The strengths of this study are the use of one birth cohort, so that age was constant; a high retention rate; and multiple assessments between ages 18 and 32 years. The diagnostic group was divided at ages 18–32 years into four groups and compared on a host of descriptive and childhood risk factors. The four groups were:

1. MDD-only, defined as having MDD in adulthood, with no GAD as an adult or juvenile ($n=162$)
2. GAD-only, defined as having GAD in adulthood but not having MDD as an adult or juvenile ($n=52$)
3. MDD+GAD, defined as having both disorders during adulthood ($n=189$)
4. Healthy control subjects, defined as not having any disorder ever ($n=205$)

The major findings summarized from Moffitt et al. (2007a) were that MDD-only and GAD share some, but not all, antecedent risk factors. Few risk factors were clearly shared by the MDD- or GAD-only groups. Comorbid MDD+GAD was antedated by highly elevated risk factors, broadly across all domains. MDD+GAD was further characterized by the earliest onset of disorder, most frequent recurrence, and greatest use of mental health services and medication. The GAD-only group had levels of risk factors similar to the elevated levels for comorbid MDD+GAD; generally, the MDD-only group did not. The GAD-only group had risks during childhood not shared by the MDD-only group in the domains of adverse family environment (low socioeconomic status, more maltreatment) and childhood behavior (internalizing problems, conduct problems, somewhat more-inhibited temperament). MDD-only subjects had risks not shared by GAD-only subjects in the domains of family history of depression and personality (low positive emotionality).

Specific antecedent risk factors for adult MDD-only, versus GAD-only, suggested partly different etiological pathways. Many risk markers were shared by GAD and the comorbid form, MDD+GAD, which suggests that the presence of GAD may signal a pathway toward a more severe disorder. These findings point to partly different etiologies and suggest that GAD and MDD should not be collapsed into one disorder in future diagnostic systems.

The Richards data in Chapter 12 come from the Medical Research Council National Survey of Health and Development (British 1946 birth cohort), which obtained prospective information from mothers of the birth cohort members and also looked at adverse exposures in childhood. The cohort has been studied 21 times since birth. A shortened version of the Present State Examination was administered when the subjects were age 36 years. Eighty-six percent of the original sample of 3,754 participants was traced and assessed, and the CATEGO (ICD) algorithm was used. The strengths of this study included the use of a birth cohort, multiple assessments, and good subject retention. The three groups examined were:

1. Depression only, defined as retarded, neurotic, or simple depression without general or situational anxiety ($n=131$)
2. Anxiety only, defined as anxiety, or phobic neurosis ($n=201$)
3. Normal control subjects, defined as no serious disorder ($n=2,882$)

The survey was not originally designed to predict psychiatric symptoms; thus, potentially relevant risk factors on family interaction and maltreatment were not included, as the authors noted. Risk factors included demographics; death or divorce of a parent; maternal neuroticism; chronic medical illness and health of parent or child; learning disability; and one assessment of maternal management of the home when the cohort was age 4. Intermediate phenotypes of cohort neuroticism or internalizing disorder were obtained in adolescence. Data were presented on maternal neuroticism; death of parent by age 15 years; separation from parent by age 6 years; parental divorce or separation by age 15 years; chronic illness by age 5 years; and suboptimal maternal management at age 4 years.

These data showed few risk factor differences between anxiety and depression, and the authors concluded that there is little evidence that early adverse exposure predicted disorder in midlife or predicted differential anxiety-only or depression-only. The authors noted the lack of power and lack of more-relevant risk factors.

There is lack of clarity as to the denominator in the British cohort study; in the "Methods" section, the authors stated that the data derived from interviews with the birth cohort at age 36 years, in 1982. The sample at that time was 3,754 individuals traced, with 86.3% ($n=3,239$) alive and residing in the United Kingdom. In the Richards and Goldberg chapter, Table 12–2 was based on 3,214 subjects, with 2,882 (89.6%) comprising the normal comparison group with no serious mental illness; 201 (6.2%) with anxiety only; and 131 (4.0%) with depression only. No data were presented on comorbid anxiety and MDD.

Cumulative and Sequential Comorbidity in the Dunedin Birth Cohort

The second paper by Moffitt et al. (2007b), on cumulative and sequential comorbidity, used data obtained from the sample when participants were between ages 11 and 32 years and looked at the sequence of onset of GAD and MDD. Although the GAD/MDD relationship was strong, the developmental relationship was more symmetric than previously presumed. One-third of the sample had GAD onset first, a third had depression first, and a third had concurrent onset of depression and anxiety. MDD was not necessarily primary over GAD. The authors made an important point about cumulative comorbidity, in which both disorders occur during a lifetime but not necessarily at the same time. Therefore, cross sections of brief periods can underestimate the true extent to which individuals experience the two disorders. Alternatively, clinical studies may overestimate because of the well-documented tendency of persons with two disorders to come for treatment.

Transmission and Longitudinal Predictions (Three-Generation High Risk Study)

We present data from our 20-year longitudinal study of families at high and low risk of depression by virtue of the depression status of the first generation. Data are available on three generations. The first and second generations have been interviewed directly for a maximum of four times over 20 years, and the third generation for a maximum of two times. A fifth wave, approximately 25 years since the study began, includes functional and structural magnetic resonance imaging and genotyping in a partial sample and eventually may provide more refined answers to the questions. The sample presented in this chapter includes the first generation that had second- or third-generation offspring.

The first generation, the grandparents (G_1), are average age 63 years ($n=91$); the second generation, the parents (G_2), are average age 36 years ($n=224$); and the third generation, the grandchildren (G_3), are average age 12 years ($n=161$). The full details of methods, sampling, and results were given in Weissman et al. (2005, 2006). Eighty-five percent of the G_2 and 93% of G_1 groups were interviewed using the Kiddie-Schedule for Affective Disorders and Schizophrenia for juveniles, the Schedule for Affective Disorders and Schizophrenia for adults, and DSM criteria, which evolved over the years to DSM-IV. All interviews were conducted by clinically experienced mental health professionals who were blinded to the diagnoses of the other generations and were conducted independently of other family members. Lifetime rates and ages-at-onset of disorder were obtained. The strengths of our study are direct assessment of the sample at different ages and the availability of three generations. The limitations are the sample size and the fact that the study was not designed to answer the questions posed here, regarding GAD- or MDD-only. All conclusions are tentative.

No diagnostic hierarchies were ever used for GAD. Duration for GAD was 6 months, except for the first waves of G_1, which used 2 weeks. Because GAD was not a childhood disorder in DSM-III, we used the same procedures described by Moffitt et al. (2007a). Childhood overanxious disorder was used in the first two waves of G_2, when they were juveniles. Mood disorders, including MDD not otherwise specified, were used with prepubertal subjects. Because we had longitudinal assessments of G_2 and G_3 across different developmental phases and did not have a birth cohort, we looked at longitudinal outcome by age at onset, categorized as prepubertal, adolescent, or adulthood onset.

We have used the same diagnostic classification for GAD and MDD as Moffitt et al. (2007a, 2007b). The exception is that, instead of healthy control subjects—as used by Moffitt and colleagues (Chapter 11) and Richards and Goldberg (Chapter 12)—we used study participants in whom neither of the two disorders was present as control subjects. The classification GAD- or MDD-only refers to either disorder without the other disorder, as in the Moffitt et al. and Richards and Goldberg studies.

The questions we are addressing in this analysis are:

1. Do G_1 diagnoses of MDD and GAD transmit to G_2 and G_3?
2. Does childhood GAD predict childhood-, adolescent-, or adult-onset MDD?

DOES G_1 DIAGNOSIS OF MDD/GAD PREDICT TRANSMISSION TO G_2?

Adjusted for age and correlation within families, MDD-only in G_1 was associated with *increased* rates of MDD and comorbid MDD in G_2 and *not* with increased rates of GAD-only (Table 14–1). Moreover, GAD-only in G_1 was *not* associated with increased rates of MDD-only, GAD-only, or comorbid MDD+GAD. The rates of MDD in G_2 were higher in G_1 with MDD-only as compared with comorbid MDD. Interestingly, the lack of transmission of GAD-only was not found when other anxiety disorders were studied (see bottom of Table 14–1). MDD-only in G_1 was associated with increased rates of phobias or any anxiety disorder in G_2. The discrepant results on risk factors between the Dunedin and Medical Research Council birth cohort studies might be due to the use of GAD-only in the Dunedin study and mixed-anxiety groups in the U.K. study.

DOES G_1 DIAGNOSIS OF MDD/GAD PREDICT TRANSMISSION TO G_3?

The analyses in G_3 adjusted for GAD and MDD in G_2. MDD-only in G_1 was associated with *increased* rates of MDD-only in G_3 and *not* with increased rates of GAD-only in G_3 (Table 14–2). GAD-only in G_1 did *not* transmit MDD in G_3. As with G_2, the lack of transmission of GAD in G_3 was *not* found when other anxiety disorders were examined (see bottom of Table 14–2). MDD in G_1 transmitted phobias and any anxiety disorder to G_3. Results were similar when the analyses were rerun without adjusting for GAD and MDD in G_2.

In summary, two studies that used very different methods—a top-down design with direct interviews of family members, blind to proband status (our study), and a bottom-up family history that used a brief family history screen (Dunedin study)—resulted in comparable findings on the transmission of MDD between generations and on the nontransmission of MDD to GAD between generations.

Prevalence of Major Depressive Disorder and Generalized Anxiety Disorder Only and Sequence of Onset

Lifetime GAD-only and, to a lesser extent, MDD-only, were not highly prevalent in our index sample, G_1, or in the Dunedin and United Kingdom birth cohorts (Table 14–3). None of these studies were community based probability samples; hence, selection factors were operative. However, it is likely that GAD-only and, to a lesser extent, MDD-only, are not widely prevalent lifetime diagnoses when no hierarchies are used.

Longitudinal studies, including our own, generally show that anxiety disorders (but not necessarily GAD) are the first presentation in juveniles, particularly prepubertal subjects, and that MDD follows in adolescence and young adulthood. As noted by Moffitt et al. (2007b), lifetime diagnosis, which cumulates disorders across a lifetime up to the time of ascertainment, is likely to show comorbidity, although the disorders do not occur at the same time.

TABLE 14–1. Does G_1 diagnosis of major depressive disorder (MDD)/generalized anxiety disorder (GAD) predict transmission to G_2?

	G_1 diagnosis				Group comparisons			
	Neither	MDD-only	GAD-only	Comorbid	MDD-only vs. neither	GAD-only vs. neither	MDD-only vs. comorbid	GAD-only vs. comorbid
N (G_1)	75	43	10	96				
G_2 diagnoses	n (%)	n (%)	n (%)	n (%)	OR (95% CI)[a]	OR (95% CI)[a]	OR (95% CI)[a]	OR (95% CI)[a]
Neither	50 (66.7)	7 (16.2)	6 (60.0)	42 (43.8)	1.0	1.0	1.0	1.0
MDD-only	19 (25.3)	27 (62.8)	4 (40.0)	41 (42.7)	9.2 (3.4, 24.9)***	1.7 (0.4, 6.7)	3.5 (1.4, 9.1)**	0.6 (0.2, 2.5)
GAD-only	1 (1.3)	1 (2.3)	0 (0.0)	2 (2.1)	7.6 (0.4, 138.1)	NE	3.3 (0.3, 44.0)	NE
Comorbid	5 (6.7)	8 (18.6)	0 (0.0)	11 (11.5)	8.7 (2.1, 35.5)**	NE	3.4 (1.0, 11.8)	NE
					HR (95% CI)[b]	HR (95% CI)[b]	HR (95% CI)[b]	HR (95% CI)[b]
Phobia	11 (14.7)	17 (39.5)	1 (10.0)	32 (33.3)	3.1 (1.3, 7.1)*	0.6 (0.1, 3.0)	1.3 (0.6, 2.6)	0.3 (0.1, 1.2)
Any anxiety	21 (28.0)	28 (65.1)	2 (20.0)	50 (52.1)	3.0 (1.5, 6.1)**	0.6 (0.2, 2.1)	1.4 (0.8, 2.7)	0.3 (0.1, 1.0)*

Note. G_1=Generation 1; G_2=Generation 2; HR=hazard ratio; NE=not estimable due to presence of small cells.
[a]Analyses were conducted by fitting logistic regression models, adjusting for age, with "neither" as reference group. [b]Analyses were conducted by fitting proportional hazards models adjusting for age and correlation within family.
*P<0.05; **P<0.01; ***P<0.001.

TABLE 14–2. Does G_1 diagnosis of major depressive disorder (MDD)/generalized anxiety disorder (GAD) predict transmission to G_3?

	G_1 diagnosis				Group comparisons				
	Neither	MDD-only	GAD-only	Comorbid	MDD-only vs. neither	GAD-only vs. neither	MDD-only vs. comorbid	GAD-only vs. comorbid	
$N(G_3)$	60	29	11	61					
G_3 diagnoses	n (%)	n (%)	n (%)	n (%)	OR (95% CI)[a]	OR (95% CI)[a]	OR (95% CI)[a]	OR (95% CI)[a]	
Neither	56 (93.3)	16 (55.2)	8 (72.7)	50 (81.9)	1.0	1.0	1.0	1.0	
MDD-only	3 (50.0)	12 (41.4)	3 (27.3)	9 (14.7)	7.2 (1.6, 32.5)*	3.6 (0.6, 23.2)	2.4 (0.7, 7.9)	1.2 (0.2, 6.1)	
GAD-only	0 (0.0)	0 (0.0)	0 (0.0)	1 (1.6)	NE	NE	NE	NE	
Comorbid	1 (1.7)	1 (3.4)	0 (0.0)	1 (1.6)	4.5 (0.2, 83.9)	NE	3.7 (0.2, 65.0)	NE	
					HR (95% CI)[b]	HR (95% CI)[b]	HR (95% CI)[b]	HR (95% CI)[b]	
Phobia	6 (10.0)	15 (51.7)	1 (9.1)	9 (14.7)	3.2 (1.2, 9.1)*	0.7 (0.1, 4.5)	2.4 (1.1, 5.8)*	0.5 (0.1, 3.0)	
Any anxiety	9 (15.0)	19 (65.5)	3 (27.2)	12 (19.7)	4.2 (1.8, 9.8)***	1.5 (0.4, 4.9)	3.7 (2.0, 6.7)***	1.3 (0.5, 3.5)	

Note. G_1 = Generation 1; G_2 = Generation 2; G_3 = Generation 3; HR = hazard ratio; NE = not estimable due to presence of small cells.
[a]Analyses were conducted by fitting logistic regression models, adjusting for age and G_2 GAD and MDD, with "neither" as reference group.
[b]Analyses were conducted by fitting proportional hazards models, adjusting for age, G_2 GAD and MDD, and correlation within family.
*$P<0.05$; **$P<0.01$; ***$P<0.001$.

TABLE 14–3. Lifetime rates of generalized anxiety disorder (GAD), major depressive disorder (MDD), and comorbid MDD+GAD in the three-generation, Dunedin, and Medical Research Council studies

Study	GAD without MDD, %	MDD without GAD, %	MDD+GAD, %
Three-generation[a]	2	16	48
Dunedin	6	17	37
Medical Research Council	6	4	NA

Note. NA=Not available.
[a]Generation 1.

What Is the Sequence of Onset of Major Depressive Disorder and Generalized Anxiety Disorder?

Looking at G_2, where we had 20-year data across the developmental range, among those participants who had comorbid GAD and MDD we found that 37.5% of G_2 had an onset of GAD *before* MDD; 25% had an onset of MDD *before* GAD; and 37.5% had an onset of GAD and MDD at the same time. We also concluded that MDD is not, necessarily, primary over GAD. These findings are comparable with those of Moffitt et al. (2007b).

Does Childhood Generalized Anxiety Disorder Predict Major Depressive Disorder at Different Developmental Periods in G_2 or G_3?

Childhood GAD in G_2 did *not* predict an onset of MDD in childhood, adolescence, or adulthood (Table 14–4). For the G_3 generation, childhood GAD in G_3 *did not* predict an onset of childhood mood disorders in G_3. However, although not shown here, for the G_2 generation, there was a statistically significant cross-sectional association between childhood GAD and childhood MDD, along with a trend for a cross-sectional association between GAD and adolescent or adult MDD. These associations were independent of parental MDD. In G_3, there was a trend for a cross-sectional association between any mood disorder and GAD. This later association was also independent of parental MDD (Warner et al. 2008).

TABLE 14–4. Does childhood general anxiety disorder (GAD) predict major depressive disorder (MDD) in G_2 or G_3 across developmental phases?

Generation with childhood GAD	Subsequent disorder	Hazard ratio (95% CI)
G_2	Childhood-onset MDD[a]	1.5 (0.3, 8.0)
	Adolescent-onset MDD[a]	1.4 (0.2, 12.3)
	Adult MDD[a]	NE
G_3	Childhood-onset mood disorder[b, c]	4.6 (0.4, 60.5)

Note. G_2 = Generation 2; G_3 = Generation 3; NE = not estimable due to presence of small cells.
Analyses were conducted by fitting a proportional hazards model; for childhood MDD, "childhood overanxious disorder or GAD" was treated as a time-dependent covariate; for adolescent- and adult-onset MDD, "childhood overanxious disorder or GAD" was entered as a dummy variable; onset ages were categorized as childhood, before age 13; adolescent, age 13–18; adult, age 19+.
[a]Adjusted for G_2 age, parental MDD, and correlation within family.
[b]Defined as MDD, dysthymia, or depressive disorder not otherwise specified that met probable or definite DSM-IV criteria.
[c]Adjusted for G_3 age, parent and grandparent MDD, parent GAD, and correlation within family.
Source. Data from Warner et al. 2008.

We conducted analyses (not shown here) to determine whether the well-established effect of parental MDD on offspring MDD was mediated by offspring anxiety. We used both proportional-hazards models and probit models in the context of path analysis of dichotomous variables. The main distinction between these models, in the context of our analysis, was that the outcome (MDD in offspring), as well as the hypothesized mediating variable (anxiety in offspring), represented presence or absence of the relevant disorder in the proportional-hazards model. In contrast, for the path analysis, the outcome as well as the hypothesized mediator represented the liability (or vulnerability) to the respective disorders. Parental MDD was treated as a dichotomous outcome that measured the presence/absence of MDD in a parent in both analyses.

Our results show that some subtypes of anxiety, other than GAD, mediate the effect of parental MDD on offspring MDD diagnosis (results from proportional-hazards model) as well as offspring vulnerability to MDD (results from path analysis, using a probit model). In addition, we found that offspring vulnerability to anxiety disorder explained a greater proportion of the effect of parental MDD on offspring vulnerability to MDD (results from path analysis) when compared with the proportion of the effect of parental MDD on the diagnosis of MDD than was explained by offspring anxiety diagnoses. Our findings suggest that the *vulnerability* to anxiety and depression might be more strongly related than the *lifetime diagnoses* of anxiety and depression in offspring, for these particular anxiety disorders, and might explain a greater proportion of the effect of parental MDD (Warner et al. 2008).

Conclusions From the Three-Generation Study

In summary, data from our three-generation study have led to some conclusions pertinent to our initial question of how GAD should be characterized relative to MDD in DSM-V:

1. GAD-only or MDD-only, as a lifetime diagnosis, is less common than comorbid GAD and MDD in clinical samples and also, it seems, in community samples—such as the two birth-cohort studies considered here. This could be due to the sequence of presentation of anxiety and depression over a lifetime in different developmental phases. Current prevalence at a point in time may find subjects with GAD-only or MDD-only; however, when these disorders are cumulated over a lifetime—as is done in calculation of lifetime rates—many subjects are found to have had both disorders, although not necessarily at the same time. Therefore, this pattern of comorbidity is reflected in lifetime rates.
2. MDD transmits MDD and comorbid MDD, but not GAD, to the next generation, and vice versa.
3. MDD does transmit other anxiety disorders; these findings were consistent across generations.
4. Prepubertal-onset GAD does not predict MDD in adolescent- or adult-onset MDD, but cross-sectionally, prepubertal-onset GAD may be associated with prepubertal-onset MDD.
5. Other anxiety disorders might predict later MDD.
6. MDD is not necessarily primary over GAD in onset.

Conclusion

Although our group and Moffitt and colleagues used quite different experimental designs, based on our findings regarding familial transmission and course of MDD and GAD, we would agree with Moffitt et al. (2007a, 2007b) that there is a distinction between GAD and MDD that, in part, points to different etiologies. Our findings are not consistent with collapsing GAD and MDD into one disorder in future nosologic systems.

Our conclusions are at variance with the British birth cohort study (see Richards and Goldberg, Chapter 12, this volume). Differences between this study and ours are likely due to use of different diagnostic criteria. The ICD system lumps anxiety disorders and does not separate out GAD. However, Moffitt et al. (2007a, 2007b) and our group used DSM criteria and separated out GAD and MDD, without any hierarchies.

We agree with Moffitt et al. (2007a, 2007b) that biological markers are essential for resolving nosological questions. In this regard, we have undertaken functional and structural magnetic resonance imaging studies and genotyping in our sample. About 200 individual samples of both measures have been collected to date, and preliminary results have been recently published (Peterson et al. 2009). Startle reaction and electroencephalographic data are available on approximately 170 subjects and also might be useful if a sufficient number of the sample fall into these diagnostic groups. This work is in progress.

References

American Psychiatric Association: Diagnostic and Statistical Manual of Mental Disorders, 3rd Edition. Washington, DC, American Psychiatric Association, 1980

American Psychiatric Association: Diagnostic and Statistical Manual of Mental Disorders, 4th Edition. Washington, DC, American Psychiatric Association, 1994

Moffitt TE, Caspi A, Harrington H, et al: Generalized anxiety disorder and depression: childhood risk factors in a birth cohort followed to age 32. Psychol Med 37:441–452, 2007a

Moffitt TE, Harrington H, Caspi A, et al: Depression and generalized anxiety disorder: cumulative and sequential comorbidity in a birth cohort followed prospectively to age 32 years. Arch Gen Psychiatry 64:651–660, 2007b

Peterson BS, Warner V, Baneal R, et al: Cortical thinning in persons at increased familial risk for major depression. Proc Natl Acad Sci 106:6273–6278, 2009

Roberson-Nay R, McClure EB, Monk CS, et al: Increased amygdala activity during successful memory encoding in adolescent major depressive disorder: an FMRI study. Biol Psychiatry 60:966–973, 2006

Warner V, Wickramaratne PJ, Weissman MM: The role of fear and anxiety in the familial risk for major depression: a three-generation study. Psychol Med 38:1543–1556, 2008

Weissman MM, Wickramaratne PJ, Nomura Y, et al: Families at high and low risk for depression: a 3-generation study. Arch Gen Psychiatry 62:29–36, 2005

Weissman MM, Wickramaratne P, Nomura Y, et al: Offspring of depressed parents: 20 years later. Am J Psychiatry 163:1001–1008, 2006

Appendix: Answers to Questions Posed by the Research Planning Committee on Major Depressive Disorder and Generalized Anxiety Disorder

1. Given the available information, do the data best support the hypothesis that MDD and GAD are different forms of the same disorder, closely related disorders, or distally related disorders?

   The risk factor, longitudinal, and family transmission data, based on the studies using DSM and no hierarchies, suggest that GAD and MDD are distally related disorders.

2. What are the implications of the conclusion for point 1 for DSM-V? Specifically:
   - Should MDD and GAD be considered as they are in DSM-IV, in separate categories?
   - Should MDD and GAD be classified in the same category, as subforms or subtypes of the same disorder? If in the same category, should GAD be moved into "Mood Disorders?"
   - Should MDD be moved into "Anxiety Disorders?"
   - Should a new category be created?

   Keep GAD and MDD in separate categories and do not use hierarchies. If MDD and GAD were collapsed, you would miss subjects, especially juveniles, who develop GAD and never have MDD. Because we know little about the pathophysiology of these disorders, it would be premature and possibly misleading for researchers to collapse them.

3. What new data could be gathered that would help to address, more definitively, the relationship between MDD and GAD?

   Several genetic and magnetic resonance imaging studies of MDD and of anxiety in the United States and United Kingdom are available and ongoing (e.g., Peterson et al. 2009; Roberson-Nay et al. 2006). An effort should be made to determine whether, with these tools, important differences can be found between GAD and MDD. Clinical and epidemiological studies have reached their limits in trying to answer these questions. A deeper understanding requires the addition of new methods, and this work is going on now. The DSM classifications do not preclude disaggregating the disorders for research into more-refined hypothesized stress systems. In fact, such disaggregations are likely essential for research.

15

TOWARD A PRIMARY-CARE FRIENDLY DSM-V CLASSIFICATION OF EMOTIONAL DISORDERS

An Integrative Approach

J. Ormel, Ph.D.
M. J. Manley, Ph.D.

Depressive and anxiety disorders are highly prevalent across the life span and around the world (Alonso et al. 2004; Kessler and Üstün 2008). In addition to causing distress and functional impairment, these disorders generate an enormous global burden of socioeconomic disadvantage (Ormel et al. 2008). A thorough understanding of the etiology of the disorders is needed in order to develop effective preventive interventions and successful treatments. A reliable and valid diagnostic classification system that carves nature at its joints would benefit clinical practice by informing prognosis, treatment, etiology and pathogenesis, research and teaching, communication, and reimbursement. Although the DSM-IV (American Psychiatric Association 1994) and ICD-10 (World Health Organization 1992) classifications of depressive and anxiety disorders have substantial clinical utility and have facilitated scientific progress, a number of general and more-specific problems have been encountered.

Various problems have been noted in the use of DSM classification in primary care settings, and many of these problems have been attributed to the complexity and specialty orientation of DSM, because it has been developed by psychiatrists working in specialty settings. A general practitioner is often the first point of contact for psychiatric diagnosis and treatment and, in many countries, is the gatekeeper to specialist care. A general criticism of DSM-IV is that it insufficiently accounts for the distinctive features of primary care, which include a high prevalence of self-limiting and subthreshold cases; mixed-symptom patterns, in which anxiety, stress, and depressive symptoms blend into all sorts of combinations; and comorbidity with physical disorders and medically unexplained somatic symptoms. In addition, many primary care physicians are under the pressure of great time constraints, often having more than 2,500 patients.

These problems have led to the development of primary-care versions of DSM and ICD (American Psychiatric Association 1995; World Health Organization 1994). Despite improvements, these versions are generally considered insufficient, and most general practitioners, at least in the Netherlands, prefer the International Classification for Primary Care (Lamberts and Wood 1987). A DSM classification system that has high utility across a wide variety of general and mental healthcare settings is needed.

This chapter addresses frequently noted problems and takes into account the particulars of depression and anxiety in primary care as well as the needs of general practitioners (Eisenberg 1992a, 1992b; Goldberg and Huxley 1992; Ormel et al. 1990, 1993; Tiemens et al. 1999; Üstün and Sartorius 1995; van Os et al. 2004). We propose a revision that ameliorates some problems with the current classification system, improves the utility of DSM for primary care, and preserves the strong characteristics of DSM.

Basic Positions on Mental Disorders and Psychiatric Nosology

Before we delve into problems with the current classification system and offer a new system, there are three important issues worth addressing that frame our thinking about mental disorders and the classification of psychopathology. Our positions on these issues in psychiatric nosology are often implicit but probably have an important influence on the way we think about the classification of mental disorders. Therefore, we want to make our positions as explicit as possible.

The first fundamental issue deals with the opposing concepts of "essentialism" and "nominalism." Zachar and Kendler (2007) define *essentialism* as a belief that mental disorders exist independent of our classifications. Essentialists argue that mental disorders are part of the reality of the human condition and that classifications should reflect that reality. In contrast, steadfast *nominalists* argue that classifications should have utility but do not reflect any deeper truths about the world. Moderate nominalists are in between these two positions, and we are of moderate-nominalist minds.

In addition, depression, anxiety, and adjustment disorders can be viewed as syndromes—that is, relatively homogeneous (i.e., statistically correlated) sets of symptoms—rather than distinct nosological entities such as infectious diseases and cancers. Our current knowledge about the functioning of the brain is still too limited to fully elucidate the brain pathologies possibly underlying emotional disorders. Until such knowledge is available, nosological entities are both hard to prove and difficult to refute.

A second basic issue is whether mental disorders are best understood as illnesses, with discrete boundaries (categorical model), or as the pathological ends of functional dimensions (continuous model). Proponents of the categorical model posit that mental disorders are "discrete categories that are defined by nonarbitrary boundaries between what is inside and what is outside" (see Chapter 1). Supporters of the continuum viewpoint, however, argue that mental disorders represent essentially arbitrary cutoffs on objective continua, such as depressed mood and fear, in a way analogous to operational definitions of high blood pressure and osteoporosis in medicine. From this perspective, differences between individual mental disorders themselves, and between illness and normality, are quantitative rather than qualitative and thus are differences of degree rather than kind. The totality of available evidence consistently points toward continua. Data from primary care clearly show positive linear relationships between severity and disability, recognition of disorder by the general practitioner, treatment, and outcome (Das-Munshi et al. 2008; Ormel et al. 1991, 1993; Wohlfarth et al. 1993).

A third basic issue regards validators, which have been proposed to examine similarity between mental disorders (e.g., see Robins and Guze 1970; Kendler 1984). For each validator, the degree to which disorders resemble one another can be mapped if sufficient knowledge is available. Kendler distinguished three classes of validators: antecedent (etiology, including familial aggregation, genetics, personality, life events, social support); concurrent (neural and cognitive bases, as assessed by neuroimaging, neurophysiology, and cognitive tests); and predictors (course, diagnostic stability, disability, treatment response). If the evidence for all, or most, validators point in the same direction, conclusions are easily drawn. If not, weights are needed to integrate the validators into a hierarchy of importance. Two hierarchies are generally considered: the primacy of clinical similarity (symptom patterns, age at onset, course, treatment response) versus the primacy of etiology, pathogenesis, and neural bases. The latter validators are occasionally mentioned as primary classification principles but are not really applicable yet, due to lack of knowledge of pathogenesis and neural bases. Neuroimaging, neurophysiology, and cognitive databases, which pertain to generalized and other anxiety disorders, are too immature to allow for reliable comparisons (see Chapter 2). Until these databases advance, we are advocates of clinical similarity as the primary validator, followed by etiology.

General Problems in DSM-IV Classifications of Anxiety, Depression, and Adjustment

DSM has been an asset to the discipline of psychiatry, thanks to its characteristics of systematic design; explicit definitions; operational criteria; and evidence-based (where possible at time of construction), consensus-based, and international orientation. This has led to considerable reliability in the use of psychiatric diagnoses. However, the validity of the DSM is still debated, in part, because of the proliferation of psychiatric diagnostic categories from slightly more than 100 in DSM-I (American Psychiatric Association 1952) to more than 350 in DSM-IV.

One problem resulting from the current classification system is the considerable heterogeneity within most disorder categories in terms of symptom pattern, natural history, treatment response, etiology, and neurobiological abnormalities. For instance, taking major depressive disorder (MDD) as an example, both population-based and clinical laboratory-based studies have found that a large number of rather different sets of five or more MDD symptoms results in a diagnosis of MDD; that MDD episodes last from 2 weeks to many years; and that large individual differences exist in both treatment response and neurobiological abnormalities. The within-category heterogeneity has prompted the question of whether diagnostic lumping has gone too far.

Another problem is that high levels of lifetime and cross-sectional comorbidity have been reported for specific anxiety and depressive symptoms and disorders, not only in specialty patients but also in population-based samples and primary-care patients. Overall lifetime comorbidities between MDD and anxiety disorders—in particular, generalized anxiety disorder (GAD) and panic disorder—are very high, usually greater than 75%. This has led some researchers to wonder whether diagnostic splitting has overshot its purpose and others to wonder whether a new diagnostic category of mixed anxiety and depressive disorder is needed.

Specific Problems in DSM-IV Classifications of Anxiety, Depression, and Adjustment Disorders

DISTINCTIVENESS OF MAJOR DEPRESSION VERSUS GENERALIZED ANXIETY DISORDER AND OTHER ANXIETY DISORDERS

In successive editions of the DSM, GAD has undergone a series of diagnostic revisions that have moved it away from its original affiliation with panic disorder and closer to MDD (see Chapter 2). This evolution of GAD has brought into question its place in future psychiatric classification. However, as elaborated in more detail later, similarities between MDD and GAD are not so different from those seen between MDD and the other major anxiety disorders. This perspective, in turn, extends the nosological questions from only MDD and GAD to the other anxiety disorders. The following six points are largely based on Hettema's review in Chapter 2:

1. At the phenotypic level, factor-analytic studies of population-based data have found two broadband, high-order factors, one loading highly on internalizing disorders and accounting for the association among anxiety and depressive disorders, and the other factor loading highly on externalizing disorders and accounting for the association between substance use and antisocial personality disorders (Krueger 1999; Slade and Watson 2006; Vollebergh et al. 2001).
2. Although GAD and MDD share most of their genetic risks and personality vulnerability factors, such as neuroticism (e.g., see Fanous et al. 2002; Hettema et al. 2006; Jardine et al. 1984; Kendler et al. 2006), a great deal of evidence suggests that this relationship may not be unique to GAD and MDD. For example, other anxiety disorders, particularly panic disorder—as well as social phobia and agoraphobia—share this risk and vulnerability with both GAD and MDD, although not to the same degree (Chantarujikapong et al. 2001; Hettema et al. 2006; Kendler et al. 2003b). Specific phobias, in particular, blood-injury and situational phobias, seem to be relatively genetically independent from the anxiety disorders and MDD (Emmelkamp and Wittchen 2009; Hettema et al. 2005).
3. Although evidence is sparse, there appears to be only partial overlap between environmental etiological factors, in particular, stressful life events, which predispose to MDD, GAD, and the other anxiety disorders; this is consistent with findings of modest environmental correlations between these disorders from twin studies. There is limited evidence that the experience of humiliation and entrapment, together with loss, is a more potent predictor of MDD than of GAD, whereas the experience of dangerous events is more predictive of GAD (Brown et al. 1995; Kendler et al. 2003a). Few data are available for the other anxiety disorders, thus it is unclear how generalizable, or specific, the GAD findings are.
4. A fairly consistent asymmetry in the course of MDD and GAD has been found: GAD predates the onset of, and transitions into, MDD more frequently than the other way around. Overall, the specific phobias, and to a lesser extent GAD and the other anxiety disorders, tend to be more chronic and unremitting than MDD. Prospective studies from childhood into young adulthood, looking forward (Hofstra et al. 2002) or backward (Gregory et al. 2007), suggest similar but not identical developmental pathways for the anxiety disorders, with phobic disorders having the earliest age at onset, the highest level of homotypic continuity, and the smallest risk of lifetime and cross-sectional MDD comorbidity (see Emmelkamp and Wittchen 2009).

5. Analyses that compare role functioning in MDD and anxiety disorders generally find roughly equal levels of impairment, suggesting that disability may be a nonspecific marker of illness severity (Ormel et al. 1994, 2008). Consistent with this idea is the finding that diagnostic group (including mixed anxiety and depression) had no association with disability after adjustment for total symptom score, whereas a large independent effect of total symptom score on all impact measures was found after adjustment for diagnosis (Das-Munshi et al. 2008).
6. Most tricyclic antidepressants as well as serotonin-specific and serotonin-norepinephrine reuptake inhibitors seem equally moderately effective for MDD and anxiety disorders, albeit limited evidence exists for GAD. This is not true for the benzodiazepines, which show clear efficacy for anxiety symptoms, most anxiety disorders, GAD, and social phobia but not for MDD (Schatzberg and Cole 1978). Thus, the pharmacological evidence suggests only a partial overlap in treatment response between MDD and the anxiety disorders.

IS SPECIFIC PHOBIA DIFFERENT FROM THE REST (OTHER PHOBIAS OR OTHER ANXIETY DISORDERS)?

The category "specific phobias" ("simple phobia" in DSM-III [American Psychiatric Association 1980]) includes phobias of public places, speaking, heights, closed spaces, blood-needle injury, snakes and animals, and so on. There is accumulating evidence for a specific genetic vulnerability of specific phobia (Emmelkamp and Wittchen 2009; Hettema et al. 2003, 2005; Marks 1987), although some earlier studies (Kendler et al. 1992; Skre et al. 1993) found only support for a broad anxiety-spectrum genetic vulnerability factor. The *phenotypic* architecture of the emotional disorders seems to consist of two correlated common factors: the first factor of "anxiety-misery" loads primarily on MDD, dysthymia disorder, and GAD, whereas the second factor of "fear" loads strongly on specific phobias (Krueger 1999; Vollebergh et al. 2001). Panic disorder and social phobia have intermediate positions, with loadings on both factors.

The *genetic* architecture of the internalizing disorders largely reflects the phenotypic structure, with two common additive genetic factors (Emmelkamp and Wittchen 2009; Kendler et al. 2003b). The first factor loads primarily on MDD, GAD, and panic disorder, whereas the second factor of "fear" loads strongly on situational and animal phobias. Agoraphobia and social phobia were intermediate but closer to MDD and GAD than to the specific phobias. Other work, which addressed only anxiety disorders, also suggested two common genetic factors, with the first loaded primarily on GAD, panic disorder, social phobia, and agoraphobia, and the second loaded strongly on situational and animal phobias (Hettema et al. 2003, 2005). Blood-injury phobia seems to hold an intermediate position, with genetic correlation with both agoraphobia and other specific phobias (Emmelkamp and Wittchen 2009).

A relatively distinct position for specific phobias in the internalizing domain is consistent with latent-trait analyses of Present State Examination data from general-population samples, primary-care attendees, and psychiatric outpatients (T. Croudace, I. Colman, P. Jones: "The Latent Structure of PSE Symptoms in a Birth Cohort," manuscript submitted for publication, 2007; Ormel et al. 1995). These analyses strongly suggested the existence of three dimensions: 1) situational and phobic anxiety and avoidance; 2) nonspecific anxiety, characterized by free-floating anxiety and various symptoms relating to tension, irritability, and restlessness; and 3) depression. Although depression and nonspecific anxiety were strongly correlated, the fear dimension had relatively low correlations with the other two dimensions. This three-dimensional structure was replicated by Croudace et al. (T. Croudace, I. Colman, P. Jones: "The Latent Structure of PSE Symptoms in a Birth Cohort," manuscript submitted for publication, 2007) in a large, population-based, 36-year-old cohort, making it likely that the two-dimensional solutions found earlier (Grayson et al. 1990) that failed to demonstrate phobic anxiety were due to the exclusion of phobic avoidance (Goldberg 2008).

Such a relatively distinct position for specific phobias is also consistent with recent neurobiological insights into the shared and unique components of specific fears and generalized anxiety (Depue and Lenzenweger 2006; Patrick and Bernat 2006). Although fear and anxiety share enhanced amygdala reactivity, these separate emotions seem to differ in how much of the broader fear-anxiety system is sensitized. In individuals with nonspecific anxiety, the affiliated anxiety system of the extended amygdala (including the bed nucleus of the stria terminalis) seems to be sensitized, as well as the core fear system (i.e., nucleus amygdala). There is also evidence of an imbalance in the amygdala-prefrontal circuitry in anxiety (Bishop 2007).

ADJUSTMENT DISORDERS: NEGLECTED BUT RELEVANT

Adjustment disorder is a disorder in DSM-IV that has been neglected by psychiatric research but is highly prevalent in primary care. This disorder is defined as

- Emotional or behavioral symptoms that develop in response to an identifiable psychosocial stressor(s), within 3 months of onset of the stressor(s); where symptoms lead to significant impairment of social or occupational role or to marked distress, in excess of what would be expected from exposure to the stressor(s);
- Stress-related disturbance does not meet criteria for another specific Axis-I disorder and is not merely an exacerbation of a preexisting Axis-I or Axis-II disorder;
- Symptoms do not represent bereavement; and
- Symptoms do not persist for more than an additional 6 months, once the stressor (or its consequences) has terminated.

Six subtypes of adjustment disorder are distinguished as: with anxiety, depressed mood, mixed anxiety and depressed mood, with disturbance of conduct, with mixed disturbance of emotions and conduct, and unspecified.

A remarkable feature of this definition is its link to an etiological agent. This link does create some problems. First, it is at odds with the fact that etiology was specifically rejected as a classification principle in DSM. Second, it creates problems in the demarcation from normality, because it does not specify when a reaction is in excess of a normal and expectable reaction and what constitutes significant role impairment and marked distress. Third, the demarcation from other, more-severe, pathology is awkward because it is simply defined as "not meeting the criteria for another specific Axis-I disorder," regardless of whether the criteria for adjustment disorder are still met. Without this exclusion criterion, adjustment disorder would badly overlap with MDD and anxiety disorders. Finally, it is very hard, especially for primary care physicians, to judge whether the disturbance "is not merely an exacerbation of a preexisting Axis-I or Axis-II disorder." In all, adjustment disorder is a rather hybrid concept, with a stress reaction at its core; the disorder is poorly demarcated by time limits, symptom thresholds of specific mental disorders, and difficult-to-assess thresholds.

A Proposal for the Classification of Emotional Disorders

Table 15–1 presents our proposed classification, at a rather general level. Its hierarchical structure has three levels: a single broadband first-order domain of emotional (or internalizing) disorders, with four second-order spectrum categories, each consisting of one or more disorders, with or without further subtypes.

Following Watson (2005) and Tackett et al. (2008), we have assigned bipolar disorder a spectrum category of its own, and posttraumatic stress disorder has been placed in the category of distress disorders, because there is accumulating evidence from different research domains that this disorder falls within the anxious-misery spectrum (Grillon and Davis 1997; Watson 2005). Obsessive-compulsive disorder, not included in our classification, might also need a category of its own, given the limited evidence that points to this disorder as falling halfway on the distress, nonspecific anxiety, and fear spectra, with characteristics from each of these spectra (e.g., Tackett et al. 2008). In contrast to Watson (2005), we distinguish between two anxiety spectra, nonspecific anxiety disorders and fear disorders, because these spectra are somewhat different in terms of symptoms, age at onset, continuity, and etiology.

TABLE 15–1. Proposed classification of emotional disorders

Broad-band level		Emotional (or internalizing) disorder		
Spectrum categories	Bipolar	Distress	Nonspecific anxiety[a]	Fear
Specific disorders (some have minor and major variants)	Type 1 Type 2 Cyclothymia	Major depression Dysthymia Posttraumatic stress disorder	Generalized anxiety disorder[a] Panic disorder[a]	Agoraphobia Social phobia Situational phobia
Subtypes		e.g., subtypes of depression	e.g., subtypes of panic disorders	e.g., subtypes of social phobia[b]

Note. Definition of disorders is the same as in DSM-IV.
[a]If GAD were not considered a mental disorder, but seen as high-trait anxiety, and panic disorder were moved to the fear spectrum, the spectrum category "General Anxiety Disorders" could be dropped.
[b]See, for instance, Bögels and Stein 2009; Cox et al. 2003.

ADDITIONAL CHARACTERISTICS OF THE PROPOSED CLASSIFICATION

Hierarchical Structure

An important characteristic of the proposed classification is its hierarchical structure. The three-level hierarchical structure:

- Accounts for, and is consistent with, the existence of both co-occurring disorders and "pure" disorders;
- Accounts for, and is consistent with, the existence of both shared and disorder-specific (genetic) risk factors; and
- Helps to counter the enormous within-category heterogeneity in symptom pattern, natural history, etiology, and treatment response.

In addition to the hierarchical structure, we propose to make a distinction between minor (subthreshold) and major (definite) disorder, for some disorders. Although not all disorders will benefit from a subthreshold, or minor, version, such a version might be useful for MDD, GAD, and some fear disorders, in particular, agoraphobia and social phobia. A distinction between minor and major disorder has four advantages:

1. The minor-major distinction does justice to the clinical significance (associated distress and impairment, reason for visit) of subthreshold syndromes in primary care, without dropping the clinically relevant categorical approach.
2. The problematic category of adjustment disorder is rendered unnecessary and is therefore unneeded in DSM-V. Although the symptom pattern of adjustment disorder is still recognized as a mental health problem, the problematic features of time limits, linkage to a stressor (etiology-based), and the difficult-to-define criterion of excess disturbance is avoided.
3. In combination with the possibility of grading severity within the major disorder category, the minor-major distinction reflects the critical importance of severity for understanding the degree of impairment, treatment decisions, and outcome in primary care and specialty settings (Goldberg and Huxley 1992; Ormel et al. 1991; Prince et al. 2008).
4. This distinction accounts for the high prevalence of mixed anxiety-depression cases in primary care settings and general population samples that do not meet the criteria for any specific mental disorder currently but have considerable public health and clinical significance (Das-Munshi et al. 2008). This mixed category could be diagnosed as minor depression and minor anxiety—thus, as co-occurring minor disorders.

Classification of History

An important feature of the DSM-IV classification of MDD is that it records history; it may be fruitful to extend this to some of the anxiety disorders. Although the episodic nature of major depression is well established (although full recovery is relatively rare), the episodic course of anxiety and fear disorders has not been studied as well. The available evidence suggests that the concept of episodes might be relevant for anxiety disorders, except for the specific phobias, which show substantially higher degrees of homotypic continuity than has been found for other anxiety or depressive disorders (Wittchen 2005). First, for MDD, if the index episode is a recurrence, the disorder is classified as recurrent; if not, it is classified as single-episode. It might be worthwhile to record the number of previous MDD episodes, because preventive cognitive-behavioral therapies seem to be most effective when the patient has had four or more previous episodes (e.g., Bockting et al. 2005; Conradi et al. 2008). Second, it is indicated whether the current episode of MDD is chronic, that is, has lasted for more than 2 years. Third, DSM-IV rates the extent of recovery between episodes as with, versus without, full interepisode recovery. Finally, DSM-IV distinguishes dysthymic disorder: a chronic disturbance of mood, less severe than MDD, lasting at least 2 years.

These differentiations trigger interesting questions. For instance, are similar systems of history of interest for the anxiety and fear disorders? Is the waxing and waning of severity and avoidance, in the course of anxiety and fear disorders, of such a degree that the notion of episodes makes sense?

Prognostic Classification

Prognosis generally serves three major functions in patient care: it guides treatment decisions, provides a norm by which to monitor course, and, for patients, reduces uncertainty of what to expect. Prognosis is even more important in primary care than in specialty care because the general practitioner—working under considerable time constraints—is the first physician to see the patient and often serves as a gatekeeper who decides whether specialty care is needed. Especially when stepped-care programs are in place, prognosis is essential for deciding at which step treatment has to start. Prognosis informs decisions as to whether treatment should be limited to watchful waiting or take the form of a minimal intervention, such as psychoeducation or self-help material; a moderately intensive intervention, such as phone-administered cognitive-behavioral therapy or mono-medication; or whether a more intensive intervention, including consultation, switching/augmentation, and brief psychotherapy by a primary care psychologist, is warranted.

A prognostic classification makes sense only if two conditions are met: 1) the course of the disorder is somewhat predictable, based on information available to the physician or easily obtained at the time the prognosis is made (attainable accuracy); and 2) this potential can be realized, with good reliability, by the average general practitioner. It is likely that both conditions can be met by physicians in most primary care settings. van den Brink et al. (2001; Brink et al. 2002) investigated both issues using an independent patient sample. They found that the 1-year course predicted by the best-fitting model, based on information available to the physician (such as history, familial history), substantially correlated with the observed course. They subsequently found that about half the potential predictability was realized by the primary care physicians, with a correlation of 0.42 between physician-given prognosis and observed course. This suggests that implementing prognostic classification is possible and worthwhile and, also, that there is room for improvement in prognostic skills among primary care physicians.

Because most diagnostic categories are fairly uninformative regarding prognosis, it probably would be worthwhile to record prognosis by means of a separate specifier. To be clinically useful, prognosis should roughly discriminate among self-limiting within a few months; self-limiting within 4–12 months although treatment will speed up recovery; persistent, chronic, or recurrent, without treatment; and longstanding incurable problems. Based on Goldberg and Huxley's (1992) classification of emotional distress, a treatment-relevant prognostic classification could look like this:

1. Minor disorder that requires recognition and discussion that gives advice and hope.
2. Emotional disorders that require specific psychiatric interventions.
3. Longstanding emotional disorders—associated with intractable social disadvantage and/or personal vulnerability—that require social support and social interventions.

A prognostic classification should be simple, explicitly link diagnosis and treatment, reflect the real-life diagnostic process, and explicitly consider patients with difficult-to-treat chronic and recurrent disorders.

Two Alternative Classifications

Two reasonable alternative classifications should be considered, each of which consists of three spectra, excluding obsessive-compulsive disorder. In the first alternative, proposed by Watson (2005), GAD is part of the distress spectrum and panic disorder part of the fear spectrum. In the second alternative, GAD is not considered a mental disorder but instead is interpreted as reflecting high neuroticism or trait anxiety. Neuroticism represents a substantially heritable high-order personality trait of feelings, thoughts, and behaviors and is characterized by dysphoria, anxiety, tension, and emotional reactivity. Neuroticism is strongly correlated with emotional distress and disorders, particularly with MDD, GAD, and panic disorder (Duncan Jones et al. 1990; Hettema et al. 2004; Kendler et al. 1993; Ormel et al. 2004). Correlations with specific phobias are smaller but still significant, especially with social phobia and agoraphobia. These correlations appear to be due largely to shared genetic influences (Fanous et al. 2002). Twin analyses have shown a very strong genetic correlation between neuroticism and GAD (0.80) and a somewhat weaker correlation (0.55) between neuroticism and MDD (Hettema et al. 2004). These findings suggest considerable overlap between neuroticism and (subthreshold) GAD. Thus, GAD may reflect, primarily, high trait-negative affect (see Brown et al. 1998; Mineka et al. 1998; Watson et al. 1984). Panic disorder, GAD's most important companion in the general-anxiety spectrum, could be moved to the specific-fears spectrum, which then might be more appropriately labeled "anxiety disorders."

Conclusion

This chapter was developed on the nosological relationship between MDD and GAD in the context of the DSM-V working group. This group has addressed the core question of whether MDD and GAD are different forms of the same disorder, closely related disorders, or distinct disorders. Rather than make isolated changes to a domain as complex and interrelated as the emotional disorders, we have sought to develop a classification that uses a comprehensive and integrative approach and takes the other anxiety and adjustment disorders into account.

Our proposed classification's three-level hierarchical structure—consisting of spectrum categories, specific disorders, and subtypes—addresses a number of problems in the DSM-IV classification. The spectra reduce diagnostic splitting and, by grouping disorders together, account more parsimoniously for comorbidity by explicitly acknowledging the underlying common features (e.g., fear). Further consideration will need to be given to the nosology of GAD; the continued classification of GAD as a disorder, or a shift to it being labeled high-trait anxiety, has implications for our proposed classification and warrants further research.

The DSM-IV and ICD-10 classification systems suffer from a number of problems that limit their utility for general practitioners. One of the central aims of our proposed revision is a classification system that is applicable in both specialty and primary care settings, thus removing the need for different versions for different treatment settings. The classification of emotional disorders that we have detailed here takes into account some of the issues and cases that primary care physicians encounter, including subthreshold cases and patients with mixed-symptom patterns. Identifying and treating patients with both minor and major disorder, recording the history of the disorder, and classifying prognosis all have potential value as additional sources of data that will serve to advance our understanding of the epidemiology and development of effective treatments for this group of disorders. It is our hope that this improved classification system will inspire research, advance the dialogue about nosology, and lead to improved identification and treatment of emotional disorders, particularly in primary care settings.

References

Alonso J, Angermeyer MC, Bernert S, et al: Prevalence of mental disorders in Europe: results from the European Study of the Epidemiology of Mental Disorders (ESEMeD) project. Acta Psychiatr Scand Suppl (420):21–27, 2004

American Psychiatric Association: Diagnostic and Statistical Manual: Mental Disorders. Washington, DC, American Psychiatric Association, 1952

American Psychiatric Association: Diagnostic and Statistical Manual of Mental Disorders, 3rd Edition. Washington, DC, American Psychiatric Association, 1980

American Psychiatric Association: Diagnostic and Statistical Manual of Mental Disorders, 4th Edition. Washington, DC, American Psychiatric Association, 1994

American Psychiatric Association: Diagnostic and Statistical Manual of Mental Disorders, 4th Edition, Primary Care Version. Washington, DC, American Psychiatric Association, 1995

Bishop SJ: Neurocognitive mechanisms of anxiety: an integrative account. Trends Cogn Sci 11:307–316, 2007

Bockting CL, Schene A, Spinhoven P, et al: Preventing relapse/recurrence in recurrent depression with cognitive therapy: a randomized controlled trial. J Consult Clin Psychol 73:647–657, 2005

Bögels S, Stein M: Social phobia, in Stress-Induced and Fear Circuitry Disorders. Edited by Andrews A, Charney D, Sirovatka P, et al. Washington, DC, American Psychiatric Association, 2009, pp 59–75

Brink RH van den, Ormel J, Tiemens BG, et al: Predictability of the one-year course of depression and generalized anxiety in primary care. Gen Hosp Psychiatry 24:156–163, 2002

Brown GW, Harris TO, Hepworth C: Loss, humiliation and entrapment among women developing depression: a patient and non-patient comparison. Psychol Med 25:7–21, 1995

Brown TA, Chorpita BF, Barlow DH: Structural relationships among dimensions of the DSM-IV anxiety and mood disorders and dimensions of negative affect, positive affect, and autonomic arousal. J Abnorm Psychol 107:179–192, 1998

Chantarujikapong S, Scherrer JF, Xian H, et al: A twin study of generalized anxiety disorder symptoms, panic disorder symptoms and post-traumatic stress disorder in men. Psychiatry Res 103:133–145, 2001

Conradi HJ, de Jonge P, Ormel J: Cognitive-behavioural therapy v. usual care in recurrent depression. Br J Psychiatry 193:505–506, 2008

Cox BJ, McWilliams LA, Clara IP, et al: The structure of feared situations in a nationally representative sample. J Anxiety Disord 17:39–101, 2003

Das-Munshi J, Goldberh D, Bebbington PE, et al: Public health significance of mixed anxiety and depression: beyond current classification. Br J Psychiatry 192:171–177, 2008

Depue RA, Lenzenweger MF: A multidimensional neurobehavioral model of personality disturbance, in Personality and Psychopathology. Edited by Krueger RF, Tackett JL. New York, Guilford, 2006, pp 210–261

Duncan-Jones P, Fergusson DM, Ormel J, et al: A model of stability and change in minor psychiatric symptoms: results from three longitudinal studies. Psychol Med 38:1–28, 1990

Eisenberg L: Treating depression and anxiety in primary care: closing the gap between knowledge and practice. N Engl J Med 326:1080–1084, 1992a

Eisenberg L: Treating depression and anxiety in the primary care setting. Health Aff (Millwood) 11:149–156, 1992b

Emmelkamp PM, Wittchen H-U: Specific phobias, in Stress-Induced and Fear Circuitry Disorders: Refining the Research Agenda for DSM-V. Edited by Andrews G, Charney D, Sirovatka P, et al. Washington, DC, American Psychiatric Association, 2009, pp 77–101

Fanous A, Gardner CO, Prescott CA, et al: Neuroticism, major depression and gender: a population-based twin study. Psychol Med 32:719–728, 2002

Goldberg D: Towards DSM-V: the relationship between generalized anxiety disorder and major depressive episode. Psychol Med 38:1671–1675, 2008

Goldberg D, Huxley P: Common Mental Disorders: A Biosocial Model. London, England, Routledge, 1992

Grayson D, Bridges K, Cook D, et al: The validity of diagnostic systems for common mental disorders: a comparison between the ID-CATEGO and the DSM-III systems. Psychol Med 20:209–218, 1990

Gregory AM, Caspi A, Moffitt TE, et al: Juvenile mental health histories of adults with anxiety disorders. Am J Psychiatry 164:301–308, 2007

Grillon C, Davis M: Fear-potentiated startle conditioning in humans: explicit and contextual cue conditioning following paired versus unpaired training. Psychophysiology 34:451–458, 1997

Hettema JM, Annas P, Neale MC, et al: A twin study of the genetics of fear conditioning. Arch Gen Psychiatry 60:702–708, 2003

Hettema JM, Prescott CA, Kendler KS: Genetic and environmental sources of covariation between generalized anxiety disorder and neuroticism. Am J Psychiatry 161:1581–1587, 2004

Hettema JM, Prescott CA, Myers JM, et al: The structure of genetic and environmental risk factors for anxiety disorders in men and women. Arch Gen Psychiatry 62:182–189, 2005

Hettema JM, Neale MC, Myers JM, et al: A population-based twin study of the relationship between neuroticism and internalizing disorders. Am J Psychiatry 163:857–864, 2006

Hofstra MB, van der Ende J, Verhulst FC: Child and adolescent problems predict DSM-IV disorders in adulthood: a 14-year follow-up of a Dutch epidemiological sample. J Am Acad Child Adolesc Psychiatry 41:182–189, 2002

Jardine R, Martin NG, Henderson AS: Genetic covariation between neuroticism and the symptoms of anxiety and depression. Genet Epidemiol 1:89–107, 1984

Kendler KS: Paranoia (delusional disorder): a valid psychiatric entity. Trends Neurosci 7:14–17, 1984

Kendler KS, Neale MC, Kessler RC, et al: The genetic epidemiology of phobias in women: the interrelationship of agoraphobia, social phobia, situational phobia and simple phobia. Arch Gen Psychiatry 49:273–281, 1992

Kendler KS, Neale MC, Kessler RC, et al: A longitudinal twin study of personality and major depression in women. Arch Gen Psychiatry 50:853–862, 1993

Kendler KS, Hettema JM, Butera F, et al: Life event dimensions of loss, humiliation, entrapment, and danger in the prediction of onsets of major depression and generalized anxiety. Arch Gen Psychiatry 60:789–796, 2003a

Kendler KS, Prescott CA, Myers J, et al: The structure of genetic and environmental risk factors for common psychiatric and substance use disorders in men and women. Arch Gen Psychiatry 60:929–937, 2003b

Kendler KS, Gatz M, Gardner CO, et al: Personality and major depression: a Swedish longitudinal, population-based twin study. Arch Gen Psychiatry 63:1113–1120, 2006

Kessler RC, Üstün TB: The WHO Mental Health Surveys: Global Perspectives on the Epidemiology of Mental Disorders. Cambridge, United Kingdom, Cambridge University Press, 2008

Krueger RF: The structure of common mental disorders (see comments). Arch Gen Psychiatry 56:921–926, 1999

Lamberts H, Wood M: ICPC: International Classification of Primary Care (Oxford Medical Publications). Oxford, United Kingdom, Oxford University Press, 1987

Marks IM: Fears, Phobias and Rituals: Panic, Anxiety, and Their Disorders. Oxford, United Kingdom, Oxford University Press, 1987

Mineka S, Watson D, Clark LA: Comorbidity of anxiety and unipolar mood disorders. Annu Rev Psychol 49:377–412, 1998

Ormel J, van den Brink W, Koeter MW, et al: Recognition, management and outcome of psychological disorders in primary care: a naturalistic follow-up study. Psychol Med 20:909–923, 1990

Ormel J, Koeter MW, van den Brink W, et al: Recognition, management, and course of anxiety and depression in general practice. Arch Gen Psychiatry 48:700–706, 1991

Ormel J, Oldehinkel AJ, Brilman EI, et al: Outcome of depression and anxiety in primary care: a three-wave 3½-year study of psychopathology and disability. Arch Gen Psychiatry 50:759–766, 1993

Ormel J, VonKorff M, Üstün TB, et al: Common mental disorders and disability across cultures: results from the WHO Collaborative Study on Psychological Problems in General Health Care. JAMA 272:1741–1748, 1994

Ormel J, Oldehinkel AJ, Goldberg DP, et al: The structure of common psychiatric symptoms: how many dimensions of neurosis? Psychol Med 25:521–530, 1995

Ormel J, Oldehinkel AJ, Vollebergh W: Vulnerability before, during, and after a major depressive episode: a 3-wave population-based study. Arch Gen Psychiatry 61:990–996, 2004

Ormel J, Petukhova M, Chatterji S, et al: Disability and treatment of specific mental and physical disorders across the world. Br J Psychiatry 192:368–375, 2008

Patrick CJ, Bernat CM: The construct of emotion as a bridge between personality and psychopathology, in Personality and Psychopathology. Edited by Krueger RF, Tackett JL. New York, Guilford, 2006, pp 174–209

Prince MJ, de Rodriguez JL, Noriega L, et al: The 10/66 Dementia Research Group's fully operationalised DSM-IV dementia computerized diagnostic algorithm, compared with the 10/66 dementia algorithm and a clinician diagnosis: a population validation study. BMC Public Health 8:219, 2008

Robins E, Guze SB: Establishment of diagnostic validity in psychiatric illness: its application to schizophrenia. Am J Psychiatry 126:983–987, 1970

Schatzberg AF, Cole JO: Benzodiazepines in depressive-disorders. Arch Gen Psychiatry 35:1359–1365, 1978

Skre I, Onstad S, Torgersen S, et al: A twin study of DSM-III-R anxiety disorders. Acta Psychiatr Scand 88:85–92, 1993

Slade T, Watson D: The structure of common DSM-IV and ICD-10 mental disorders in the Australian general population. Psychol Med 36:1593–1600, 2006

Tackett JL, Quilty LC, Sellbom M, et al: Additional evidence for a quantitative hierarchical model of mood and anxiety disorders for DSM-V: the context of personality structure. J Abnorm Psychol 117:812–825, 2008

Tiemens BG, VonKorff M, Lin EH: Diagnosis of depression by primary care physicians versus a structured diagnostic interview: understanding discordance. Gen Hosp Psychiatry 21:87–96, 1999

Üstün TB, Sartorius N (eds): Mental Illness in General Health Care: An International Study. Hoboken, NJ, Wiley, 1995

van den Brink RH, Ormel J, Tiemens BG, et al: Accuracy of general practitioner's prognosis of the 1-year course of depression and generalised anxiety. Br J Psychiatry 178:18–22, 2001

van Os TW, van den Brink RH, Tiemens BG, et al: Are effects of depression management training for general practitioners on patient outcomes mediated by improvements in the process of care? J Affect Disord 80:173–179, 2004

Vollebergh WA, Iedema J, Bijl RV, et al: The structure and stability of common mental disorders: the NEMESIS study. Arch Gen Psychiatry 58:597–603, 2001

Watson D: Rethinking the mood and anxiety disorders: a quantitative hierarchical model for DSM-V. J Abnorm Psychol 114: 522–536, 2005

Watson D, Clark LA, Tellegen A: Cross-cultural convergence in the structure of mood: a Japanese replication and a comparison with U.S. findings. J Pers Soc Psychol 47:127–144, 1984

Wohlfarth TD, van den Brink W, Ormel J, et al: The relationship between social dysfunctioning and psychopathology among primary care attenders. Br J Psychiatry 163:37–44, 1993

World Health Organization: International Statistical Classification of Diseases and Related Health Problems, 10th Revision. Geneva, Switzerland, World Health Organization, 1992

World Health Organization: The ICD-10 Classification of Mental and Behavioural Disorders. Primary Health Care Version. Geneva, Switzerland, World Health Organization, 1994

Zachar P, Kendler KS: Psychiatric disorders: a conceptual taxonomy. Am J Psychiatry 164:557–565, 2007

16

PSYCHOSOCIAL ORIGINS OF DEPRESSIVE AND ANXIETY DISORDERS

George W. Brown, Ph.D.

Most research on the etiological role of psychosocial factors in depressive and anxiety disorders has dealt with *proximal* factors. However, in this chapter, I place particular emphasis on studies that used the Life Events and Difficulties Schedule (LEDS; Brown and Harris 1978). Investigators, blind to any history of psychiatric disorder, make judgments about *likely* threats, taking the broader context into account to assess the impact of an event on key plans and purposes. Thus, a woman's husband unexpectedly announcing that he is leaving would not be rated severe if it emerged she had been having an affair for some time and had even gone so far as to visit a lawyer to discuss leaving her husband. Only an event likely to convey severe threat 2 weeks after occurrence is taken into account; an event that resolves earlier does not raise risk.

Similarly, life events also are significant factors in anxiety disorders. However, the meaning of events tends to differ for the two conditions, with "loss" more often associated with depression and "danger" with anxiety. Most research has focused on women, although there is some indication that the findings hold broadly for men as well (e.g., Nazroo et al. 1997).

This relatively straightforward etiological picture is complicated by the fact that, although the majority of *depressive* episodes are preceded by a severely threatening event, the events are rarely sufficient to provoke an onset. Onset usually requires the presence of at least one, and more usually two, ongoing psychosocial "vulnerability" factors. The importance of these has been established in prospective studies. An "interpersonal" factor reflects shortcomings in core relationships, whereas a "psychological" factor reflects internal characteristics, such as low self-esteem (e.g., see Brown 1998, Figure 1). A surprising finding on the role of the *current* environment has been that, although *anxiety* disorders are equally likely to be provoked by a severe event, they are much less responsive to other aspects of the environment. Indeed, background factors important for depression, such as degree of social support, appear to play no role.

However, etiological research also needs to concern itself with the life course as a whole and particularly with neglect and abuse in childhood and adolescence. There is a large literature related to childrearing experiences and common mental disorders. A recent review described this literature as vast and, despite frequent methodological shortcomings, concluded there is a surprising consistency in suggestions that parental rejection is important for both depressive and anxiety disorders (Rapee 1997). One of the obvious limitations of the research has been a failure of many studies—including the majority of the most recent—to deal with the full range of behavior that can be involved in such maltreatment; frequently, these studies have dealt only with abuse and, often, only sexual abuse (Brown 2002a). In light of this, I place particular emphasis here on research that has used the Childhood Experiences of Care and Abuse (CECA) instrument, an investigator-based measure that gathers material retrospectively and covers all aspects of maltreatment (Bifulco et al. 1994; Brown 2006; Brown et al. 2007a, 2007b).

In placing emphasis on studies that have used London-based measures, I have persuaded myself that this degree of self-absorption is justified, because the investigator-based approach of these studies to collection and rating of social and clinical material—with an almost obsessive concern with dating—represents the most effective way, at present, of tackling etiological questions.

I am primarily concerned with three observations that bear on the usefulness of DSM diagnostic criteria:

1. There are both similarities and differences in psychosocial factors involved in the etiologies of anxiety and depressive disorders. What are the implications of these factors? As already noted, the disorders are similar in that severely threatening life events and early abuse and neglect substantially increase risks for both; however, the "meaning" of provoking life events tends to differ, and other current background factors, which apparently are important for depression, have little relevance for anxiety. In addition, there are within diagnostic differences; for example, the prevalence of simple phobias, unlike other anxiety disorders, does not relate to early abuse and neglect.
2. It is clear that depressive and anxiety disorders often occur together (e.g., Kaufman and Charney 2000; Kessler 2000; Levine et al. 2001; Robins and Regier

1990), and the similarity of etiological risk factors raises the question of the contributions of these factors to their substantial comorbidity.
3. Anxiety disorders commonly precede depressive disorders. What are the implications of this?

Some Background Features of the London Studies

The London study, to which I will most often refer, was prospective and based on women living in Islington, an inner-city area. The women were first seen in the early 1980s, when they had at least one child living at home. Sampling concentrated on working-class women because earlier research had indicated that these women were more at risk of a depressive disorder once they had children (Brown and Harris 1978; Brown et al. 1987). Single mothers were included, irrespective of social class, and formed a fifth of the sample.

Women were questioned about their psychiatric states and personal circumstances in the year before our first contact, and this interview was repeated a year later. Many women were seen again, and on average, a period of just over 4 years was covered by the interviews. A shortened version of the Present State Examination was used at each contact (Wing et al. 1974), with a threshold for "caseness" of depression somewhat higher than the Research Diagnostic Criteria (Spitzer et al. 1978). For anxiety disorders, the DSM-III-R (American Psychiatric Association 1987) system was employed; the disorders were dealt with in terms of a hierarchy, with the ranking of panic, agoraphobia, generalized anxiety disorder (GAD), social phobia, simple phobia, and mild agoraphobia[1] (Brown and Harris 1993).

As would be expected from our inclusion criteria, prevalence rates were somewhat higher than has been found in large-scale national surveys (Brown and Harris 1993, Table 3). Community cases of depression are very rarely bipolar or melancholic; we dealt, essentially, with "neurotic" depression, although many women exhibited a fair number of vegetative symptoms characterized as "endogenous" (Kay et al. 1969; Kendall 1976; Kiloh and Garside 1963). Episodes tended to remit within a matter of months, but approximately one in four episodes lasted at least 1 year (Brown and Moran 1994).

---

[1]See Brown and Harris (1993) for full details of the ratings. Mild agoraphobia was defined in terms of having a relatively normal life style—for example, the woman travels unaccompanied, when necessary, such as to work or to shop but otherwise avoids traveling alone (American Psychiatric Association 1987, p. 239).

ASSOCIATION OF EARLY ADVERSITY WITH ADULT DEPRESSION AND ANXIETY

There is now convincing evidence that early abuse or neglect is associated with a raised risk of adult depression (Brown et al. 1994; Durbin et al. 2000; Kendler et al. 1997; Kessler et al. 1997a; Lara and Klein 1999; Lara et al. 2000).

In Islington, the CECA index was based on the presence of at least one of three adverse experiences before the age of 17 years: 1) parental indifference, covering physical and emotional neglect; 2) physical abuse from anyone at home, consistent with Strauss' definition (Strauss et al. 1980), and 3) sexual abuse from anyone, which involved, at a minimum, touching of genitals and breasts, excluding willing contact in teenage years (see Brown and Harris 1993 for details).

Such early adversity was associated with a doubling of risk of an adult depressive episode onset and quadrupling of one lasting at least 1 year (Brown and Moran 1994). Early adversity was also substantially associated with anxiety disorders. With the diagnostic hierarchy outlined earlier, there were associations with four of the six component-anxiety diagnoses. I refer here to these associated diagnoses as *core* conditions. Panic had the largest association, with agoraphobia, GAD, and social phobia having much the same level of risk (Table 16–1). Early adversity was unrelated to simple phobia or mild agoraphobia (Table 16–1). An earlier published account cited a number of findings consistent with these results, particularly the high risk associated with panic disorder (Brown and Harris 1993, Table 3). Since then, a number of similar findings have been published, although most of these studies dealt only with abuse.

TABLE 16–1. Anxiety disorders (with and without depression), by childhood adversity, for 404 women in the Islington study

DSM-III-R anxiety (hierarchical)	Childhood adversity, % (*n*)	Odds ratio	*P*
Panic disorder	64 (14/22)	8.7	< 0.001[a]
Agoraphobia, GAD, social phobia	43 (30/70)	3.7	< 0.001[a]
Simple phobia or mild agoraphobia	19 (6/32)	1.1	NS
Other women	17 (47/280)		

Note. GAD=generalized anxiety disorder; NS=not significant.
[a]Core anxiety.

A prospective study of young people from a New Zealand birth cohort considered the experience of panic, when these subjects were seen at 21 years of age. There was a marked association with physical and sexual abuse, even after adjustment for potential confounding factors, such as parental history of anxiety (Goodwin et al. 2004). Of particular interest, the conclusion of these investigators was that, despite this link, interparental violence was unrelated to later panic. A Canadian study of an adult population that also dealt only with physical and sexual abuse found higher rates of anxiety and depressive disorders, with the associations apparently stronger for women than men (MacMillan et al. 2001; see also de Graaf et al. 2003).

A number of studies have considered the possibility of specific effects, although again most of these have dealt only with abuse. Sexual abuse is highly correlated with other forms of abuse and neglect; therefore, large sample sizes probably would be required to establish whether sexual abuse has a specific effect (Brown 2006). There was no evidence from the Islington study that various aspects of early maltreatment were linked differently with anxiety, compared with depression or with diagnostic subgroups within anxiety. This observation also has held for an outpatient clinic population that, in general, replicated the findings of the Islington inquiry (Young et al. 1997). A Canadian survey, which again dealt only with abuse, has reported nonspecific effects (MacMillan et al. 2001). However, a study of 68 women who met DSM-III-R criteria for major depression found evidence that severe sexual abuse was associated most strongly with comorbid anxiety (Harkness and Wildes 2002). The question of specificity is therefore probably best seen as unsettled (see also Stein et al. 1996). Early maltreatment covers such a wide range of experiences that a number of neurophysiological and psychological systems probably are influenced and, despite the weight of negative evidence, the presence of some specific effects would not be surprising.

COMORBID ANXIETY AND DEPRESSION

Table 16–2 provides basic data about the prevalence of the various anxiety disorders in the Islington subjects during the 12-month period before the first interview as well as data about the extent to which these disorders were associated with depression. Only *core* anxiety conditions were associated with early adversity, and only these conditions had substantial overlap with depression and, therefore, with comorbidity.

The comorbid episodes overlapped, except for a few that occurred within a matter of a few weeks, thus Table 16–2 deals with *concurrent* rather than *successive* comorbidity (Angold et al. 1999). This has the advantage that the recall period is, at most, only a matter of a few years. Although somewhat different findings might emerge from dealing with episodes separated by longer periods of time, I am not aware of any evidence (Kessler et al. 1998). In reviewing other research, I also deal with population samples, because the selective nature of a patient series makes it difficult to study etiological questions with any confidence (Angold et al. 1999).

TABLE 16–2. DSM-III-R depression by hierarchical diagnoses of anxiety, for 404 women in the Islington study during 12 months before first interview

DSM-III-R anxiety (hierarchical)	Overall distribution in population, % (n)		Depression during previous 12 months, %	
Core anxiety disorders				
Panic	3.7 (15)	⎤	67	⎤
Agoraphobia	2.0 (8)	⎥ 167	50	⎥ 56
Generalized anxiety disorder	9.4 (38)	⎥	55	⎥
Social phobia	1.2 (5)	⎦	40	⎦
Remaining anxiety disorders				
Mild agoraphobia/simple phobia	7.4 (30)		13	
Total for anxiety disorders	*23.8 (96)*		*43*	
Depression with no anxiety	7.7 (31)			

In studying comorbidity, we were influenced by a puzzling related set of findings. Although social support from a core social tie reduces the chance of depression, once an event has occurred (Brown and Harris 1986; Brown et al. 1986; Veil and Baumann 1992), this does not hold for anxiety disorders. This is despite the fact they are provoked by the onset of severely threatening life events and that support might be expected to reduce the insecurity involved (Finlay-Jones 1989). A study of general-practice patients that focused on support from family and a confidant also concluded that different environmental variables predict liability to depression and anxiety (Goldberg et al. 1990). One possibility is that for anxiety risk is particularly associated with neurological changes resulting from early adversity and much less influenced by adult experience. We therefore included an index of *adult adversity* that covered adulthood, other than the 12 months before our contact, based on the presence of *any* of the following: 1) death of a child at any age; 2) death of a partner; 3) separation from a partner or divorce; 4) two or more induced abortions; 5) sexual abuse in adulthood; and 6) physical violence in a partnership. As expected, this index was associated with childhood adversity, with an odds ratio of 2.92. It also was related to current vulnerability factors relevant for depression, such as poor support and low self-esteem. This suggests that, although crude, the index was probably strong enough to test whether adult adverse experience is more important for depression than for core anxiety disorders.

Our analysis treated anxiety and depression as separate dependent variables and used the resulting 16-fold table, which included childhood and adult adversity indices, to fit log-linear models. This showed that although depression was associ-

TABLE 16–3. Presence of comorbid disorder in year before first interview and number of risk factors (i.e., early adversity, past marital violence, and single motherhood) for mothers in the Islington study

Risk factors, N	Comorbid disorder prevalence, %	Relative risk
3	54	16.1
2	17	5.4
1	10	3.3
0	3	1.0

Note. $\chi^2 = 46.13$; $df = 3$; $P < 0.001$; $N = 404$ mothers.
Source. For more detail, see Table 3 in Brown and Moran 1997.

ated with both conditions, anxiety related only to early maltreatment; however, with larger numbers, a modest effect from the adult index might be found for anxiety (Brown et al. 1993). This result again suggests that anxiety is less sensitive to adult experience, other than to events close to the point of onset.

The key question of in what way the two distal factors contributed to comorbidity remains to be discussed. In any population, a certain amount of comorbidity will arise by chance; for example, if the prevalences of core anxiety and depression were each 20%, one would expect 4% (0.2×0.2) of the population to have both conditions. Over and above this *chance comorbidity*, there may be additional *nonchance* comorbidity.

Chance comorbidity reflects the prevalence of specific conditions in a population and will be greater to the extent that the rates of these conditions are increased. Part of chance comorbidity can be attributed to the effects of etiological factors—in the present instance, to early and adult adversity—to the extent that these factors elevate the prevalence of one or both disorders.

The overall rates of depression and core anxiety disorders among Islington women were 30.9% and 22.7%, respectively. It follows that comorbid anxiety and depression would be expected, by chance, to form 7.1% of the total sample (0.309×0.227×404). This represents 45% of the 64 comorbid conditions that were actually found.

However, this chance comorbidity itself can be divided into two components. Baseline comorbidity could be calculated by multiplying the relevant rates among those *without* the two risk factors under consideration—in the present instance, among those without either childhood or adult adversity. This was 14.8% of all those with a comorbid condition, which means that the remaining 29.7% was due to the background risk factors (see left side of Figure 16–1).

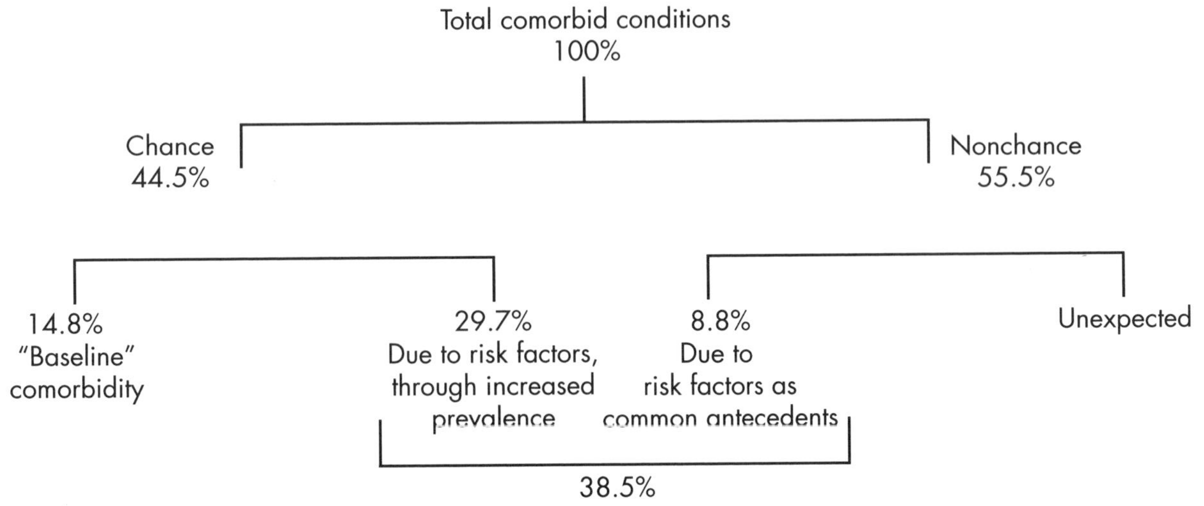

FIGURE 16–1. Contributions of baseline prevalence and distal risk factors to 64 comorbid conditions among women in the Islington study.

Note. The 12-month period covered in Table 16–2 has been extended to the whole study period to increase number.

How many of the comorbid conditions were due to the presence of the two prior risk factors, rather than to chance, remains to be established. For this estimation, we employed log-linear modeling, which gave a figure of 8.8% of the total, as explained by the common effect of childhood adversity on the two disorders (see Brown et al. 1993 for details). These results are summarized in Figure 16–1, which shows that 46.7% of the comorbid conditions remain unexplained.

To sum up, the main contribution of the two distal risk indices in explaining comorbidity was the result of their increasing the prevalences of core anxiety and depressive disorders in the Islington population, thereby increasing the likelihood that the types of disorder would occur together by *chance*. In addition, there was a modest contribution from childhood adversity acting as a common antecedent factor for both disorders. Together, the two contributions accounted for just under 40% of the comorbidity. If comorbidity due to baseline prevalence is added, just under half the comorbidity remains to be explained. I return later to this point and to the fact that simple phobias and mild agoraphobia were excluded from consideration.

ROLE OF LIFE EVENTS IN THE ONSET AND COURSE OF ANXIETY AND DEPRESSIVE DISORDERS

Consideration of the role of life events and ongoing difficulties in the onset of common psychiatric disorders has a lengthy history (Brown and Harris 1986; Kendler et al. 2002). Since the original research—which used the LEDS with both a patient sample of depressed men and women, ages 18–65 years, and a general-population sample of women of the same age (Brown and Harris 1978)—research has shown that the majority of onsets of both depressive and anxiety disorders have a severe event occurring not long before onset. In addition, a tendency for different aspects of the meaning of events has been shown to be associated with depression and anxiety (Brown and Harris 1986). *Loss* defined as loss involving either a person, role, or cherished idea has been associated with depression, and *danger* defined as the possibility of some future loss has been associated with anxiety (Finlay-Jones and Brown 1981).

Although there have been further refinements related to the role of humiliating and entrapping events for depression, this early work is still relevant, particularly for the understanding of comorbidity. It is important to keep in mind that the same event might involve both loss and danger. A woman who learns that her son has been arrested for selling drugs would be considered to have lost a cherished idea about her son—if she previously had no knowledge of such behavior—but she also might experience danger in the sense of her likely concern about the long-term implications of the event. It is also possible for a woman to experience both emotions, via distinct events; for example, to experience "loss" from the loss of a job held for many years and "danger" from fears related to her husband's heart attack. In all such instances, as with the rating of severity, the investigator-based ratings ignore any account, on the woman's part, of how she felt about the event. (This is achieved by withholding from raters such information, as well as any information about whether a psychiatric disorder was involved.)

The original study used a rating of anxiety disorder with a particularly high threshold; one that would have excluded the majority of those with GAD (see Brown and Harris 1993, Table 1). It is therefore significant that the findings of this study were replicated in the later Islington sample, where investigators used DSM-III-R criteria, with a lower threshold that included more instances of anxiety and, particularly, of GAD (Table 16–4).

Because the great majority of onsets involved a severe event, to simplify the presentation, Table 16–4 deals only with onsets associated with an event. The italicized results represent the type of event predicted to occur for each of the three types of disorders. It is clear that danger events predominated for the pure anxiety disorders and loss events for pure depression. For comorbid conditions, experiences of both loss *and* danger predominated (see Brown 1993).[2] As noted earlier, since this 1993 study it has been established that depression tends to be provoked by severe events that involve either humiliation or entrapment (Brown et al. 1995). However, such events almost always also involve a loss, and the implications of the results concerning loss and danger are unchanged.

Other workers, using similar ratings, have reported consistent findings (e.g., Cooke and Hole 1983; Kendler et al. 2003). Eley and Stevenson (2000) studied 13-year-old twins and found some evidence for an association between loss and depression and strong evidence for an association between danger and anxiety disorder. In the light of the findings noted earlier concerning anxiety disorders and support, it is interesting that children with depression, but not anxiety, were more likely to report lack of an intimate confidant than those in the normal comparison series. In terms of their design, these investigators concluded that the associations observed were not the result of genetic influence.

A study by Surtees (1995) is particularly interesting because it employed an alternative approach by studying groups of women experiencing similar events: "danger" from a partner recently surviving a myocardial infarction while remaining at risk of another, and "loss" from a partner's death. Depression and anxiety were defined by DSM-III-R diagnostic rules. The women were seen soon after the event and at a follow-up interview. The pre-event and post-event findings were much as expected. After the event, women in the coronary group showed a threefold increase in anxiety but no comparable increase in depression, whereas women

---

[2]The numbers in Table 16–4 were increased, compared with the published account, by including onsets that occurred outside the first follow-up year. Differences were similar in both data sets.

TABLE 16–4. Types of severe event that preceded onset of depression or anxiety disorders for women in the Islington study

Event type	Pure depression, % (n)	Mixed depression and anxiety, % (n)	Pure anxiety, % (n)
Loss	*52 (12)*	11 (2)	11 (2)
Danger	21 (5)	28 (5)	*63 (11)*
Loss + danger	26 (6)	*61 (11)*	26 (5)

Note. Italics represent results predicted by specificity hypothesis.
$\chi^2 = 18.71$; $df = 4$; $P < 0.02$.

in the bereaved group exhibited an eightfold increase in depression and a twofold increase in anxiety, as assessed with the LEDS.

There was no attempt to assess how far a loss due to death might have also conveyed "danger," for example, due to concern about the woman's ability to continue to pay for a large mortgage taken out not long before. The Islington findings, in any case, suggest that contextual ratings dealing with *likely* meaning have gone only part of the way in dealing with such joint meanings. The importance of this is underlined by the fact that a study of the elderly has shown that an anxiety disorder often follows the death of a partner (De Beurs et al. 2000). Such a response makes a good deal of sense, given that upon a partner's death, long-established routines often are broken; therefore, a sense of "danger" would not necessarily be inappropriate. However, contextual ratings, in their present form, only take account of tangible features of context to define danger, such as with the mortgage example. Given that the importance of specific meaning has been established, there is a case for supplementing contextual ratings with self-reports about feelings (see Lemyre and Lee 2006 for an example), although this does not rule out the possibility of further development of contextual ratings.

As an example of the kind of thing that might be possible, I considered onsets of pure anxiety and pure depression among the Islington women, where *only* a danger event had been considered to be present. If the event involved a core role, particularly as a mother or wife/partner, I rated whether or not the woman might have felt herself to be in some way responsible or whether the event had reflected negatively on her competence. Learning of her adolescent son's second arrest for selling hard drugs would be rated positively, but not a son's being attacked in a local street on his way home from school. All other events were classed as "external" in the sense that the circumstances surrounding the event made it too distant from her core responsibilities for her, in strictly logical terms, to have felt blame or incompetence—for example, a violent partner from whom she had separated finding out her address, despite her taking many precautions, or learning of the spread of her father's cancer after what had appeared to be a successful surgery. Table 16–5 shows there was a marked difference in the type of danger event, with, as predicted, those events preceding depression more often having negative implications for the performance of a core role. However, this exercise is intended as no more than illustrative of what might be possible. In particular, unlike in the published data, ratings were not made blind to diagnosis.

Further evidence for specificity is suggested by the fact that, in the same Islington population, more than half the women who had recovered or improved from an episode of depression that lasted at least 20 weeks did so after a positive event, although in a quarter of the women the event was also considered severely threatening—for example, a violent husband going to live with someone else while leaving her with many debts. For this recovery group, such positive events occurred six times more often than did a similar event during a comparable 20-week period of depression not characterized by recovery/improvement. The majority of these positive events were "fresh-start" type, defined by their likelihood of reversing or ameliorating loss or deprivation and likelihood of conveying hope as opposed to loss and entrapment (Brown et al. 1992). (Events that involved psychiatric treatment were excluded, but clearly might, at times, have had such a connotation.)

By contrast, recovery and improvement from anxiety disorders tended to be associated with events likely to increase security. "Anchoring" events were the most important, reflecting increased regularity and predictability in an activity or relationship. These events mostly concerned situations such as finalizing a divorce or separation, "settling down" with a man, a change in housing (e.g., a transition from rental housing to home ownership), or change in employment status (e.g., from unemployment to regular employment). Approximately 60% of remissions of mixed conditions were preceded by at least one positive event, with a clear tendency for "fresh starts" and "anchoring" to be involved (Brown et al. 1992; Table 2).

The study by Surtees (1995) reviewed earlier included a third group of women who had sought the protection of a Woman's Aid Refuge because of violence of a partner. These women were found to have a twofold reduction in depression but *no* change in the prevalence of anxiety disorder, a result consistent with the London research, because the move to the Refuge involved a "fresh start" rather than an "anchoring" event.

Positive events, using the London scheme, were shown by another research center to be important for remission of both depressive and anxiety conditions (Neeleman et al. 2003). This finding raised the important point that most of the person-linked risk factors for delayed remission, such as poor support and network size, also reduced the probability of occurrence of a positive event. However, this study did not confirm the role of anchoring events for anxiety disorders (Leenstra et al. 1995). The authors noted that this might be related to the very low incidence of such events in their population.

TABLE 16–5. Details of "danger" events, which occurred prior to onset of pure anxiety and pure depressive disorders for women in Islington study

Disorder	External	Role-related responsibility	
		Low	Some
Anxiety	7	3	2
Depression	0	1	4

Note. $\chi^2 = 18.71$; $df = 2$; $P < 0.001$.

A sense of lack of control has been implicated in the origins of both anxiety and depression, but these findings suggest that, insofar as a sense of lack of control contributes, different processes may be involved. The onset and course of depression is intimately related to a person's current social milieu (Brown 2002b; Gilbert 1992; Gilbert and Allan 1998). With this in mind, the likely relevance of lack of control for the onset of depression has been illustrated by a special analysis of severe events that involved separation from a core tie or infidelity. In order to pursue the question of control, events involving humiliation were distinguished by whether the woman took *some* initiative in ending the relationship following the event, for example, by acting at once to finish a relationship upon discovering an infidelity.

When a third category—women who took the initiative in promoting a separation—was included, a clear gradient in depressive onset emerged (see Brown 1998, Table 18.6). There was a threefold difference in risk of an onset between a woman being left by her boyfriend after being told she was no longer attractive ("no control"), and one where a single mother, badly wanting a secure sexual relationship, finishes a relationship in which she had set great store because of a man's unacceptable behavior and her realization that he would be impossible to live with ("control"). Those women rated as having "partial control" were at intermediate risk of depression. In a sense, they behaved as though they felt forced to act immediately once the humiliation had occurred. This exercise suggests that, insofar as control is relevant, it would involve ability to influence an aversive situation and a perception of being in control, with the two by no means necessarily coinciding (Miceli and Castelfranchi 2005; Weems and Silverman 2005). In more general terms, it is likely that awareness of the implications of an event is usually critical; for example, in events that convey entrapment in a highly punishing situation, such as a woman who is crippled by arthritis and in a markedly unpleasant marriage being told by her doctor that medicine could not help her further.

By contrast, although events that trigger anxiety also suggest the importance of a sense of lack of control, this, as already noted, appears to be unrelated to aspects of the current environment, such as the level of core support. There is thus the possibility that the provoking event evokes the "memory" of past trauma and that the etiological process is largely unconscious. Lang et al. (2000) discussed evidence for automaticity of fear reactions, often hyperreactivity to minimal threat cues, and evidence that the physiological responses in fear may be independent of slower, language-based appraisal processes. The two broad systems of obvious relevance are the protective system, involving the amygdala—closely linked to fear conditioning—from which anxiety disorders may be derived, and the preservative system, which is rewarding and responds to appetitive stimulation, for depression (Davis 1992; Ninan and Berger 2001). However, such a difference may well be no more than a difference of degree; events that provoke a depressive onset almost certainly also involve non-language-based systems, such as attachment. It also has been noted that memories of childhood trauma can be evoked by an event that provokes depression (Gilbert et al. 2003).

COMORBIDITY AND THE CONTRIBUTION OF LIFE EVENTS

On the assumption that contrasting life events—such as "loss" versus "danger" and "fresh start" versus "anchoring"—influence different brain systems evolved to be adaptive, the findings I have reviewed here suggest that the diagnostic rules of DSM-III-R, to a surprising extent, reflect disorders based on different neurophysiological systems. These findings raise the further question of how far such events contribute to comorbidity over and above the effects of distal risk factors, particularly that of early maltreatment. An answer is made difficult by the fact that such maltreatment partly influences the prevalences of both by increasing the incidence of severe events. Parental maltreatment, for example, is highly related to conduct problems among girls, which in turn relate to increased discordant core sexual relationships and events in adulthood associated with them (e.g., Brown et al. 2007a; see also Champion et al. 1995).

A larger sample than that of the Islington study would be necessary for an adequate answer to how far these events in adulthood make an independent contribution to comorbidity. However, given the importance of the question, it is perhaps worthwhile to present data that might anticipate the conclusions of a larger study. Table 16–6 gives diagnostic details of the status of core anxiety and depressive *onsets* that occurred during the 4-year study period[3] among Islington women. Because episodes starting outside the period have been excluded, there are 49 rather than the 64 comorbid conditions shown in Figure 16–1.

---

[3]In order to be consistent with the earlier analysis of comorbidity, only the first onset of each condition in the study period was taken. An analysis based on all onsets gave, essentially, the same result.

TABLE 16–6. Details of comorbidities for onsets of core anxiety and depressive disorders that occurred during 4-year study period for women in Islington study

Type of disorder onset	% (n)
Joint onset	21 (23)*
Anxiety preceded depression	5 (6)*
Depression preceded anxiety	2 (2)*
Chronic anxiety at start of study preceded depression	16 (18)*
Anxiety alone	14 (16)
Depression alone	42 (47)
Total	100 (112)

Note. Based on first onset during study period. If all onsets were analyzed, essentially the same pattern emerged. Fifteen comorbid conditions, included in Figure 16–1, were excluded because anxiety and depression were both present at start of study period and the type of onset was unclear.
*Comorbid conditions.

It is notable that *joint onsets* form almost half (23/49) the comorbid episodes. The association of loss and danger events with such onsets is, of course, the way in which life events contribute to comorbidity. Just more than half (11/20) of those who had experienced both loss *and* danger were without either early or adult adversity. Because these women would not have been taken into account in the earlier analysis, which dealt only with the contribution of distal risk factors, life events might make a modest, or possibly substantial, additional contribution to comorbidity over and above that of early adversity.

As a whole, the findings concerning comorbidity can be taken nearer the lives of women in Islington by considering the experience of single mothers, whose numbers have increased considerably in recent years, particularly in inner-city areas such as Islington (Utting 1995). In the United Kingdom, single mothers accounted for 8% of females with dependent children in 1971 and 21% in 1992 (Haskey 1994; Office of Population Censuses and Surveys 1994). It has been well established that these mothers are at greater risk for depression (e.g., Davies et al. 1997; Forgatch et al. 1988); in Islington, their risk was double that of other mothers. The elevated risk also held for anxiety disorders. However, this was almost entirely limited to *mixed* anxiety and depressive conditions, with a relative risk of 3.2, compared with other mothers. On their own, the incidences of anxiety and depression were unrelated to single motherhood (Brown and Moran 1997).

In terms of psychosocial risk factors, prior marital violence was three times more frequent among single mothers (45% vs. 13%). It seems reasonable to assume that the kind of life events involved in such violence often involved both danger and humiliation and, in this way, contributed to comorbidity. An additive index—based on the occurrence of violence, together with single motherhood and childhood adversity—in the year before our first contact was highly related to mixed conditions (Table 16–4).

ANXIETY AS A VULNERABILITY FACTOR FOR MAJOR DEPRESSION

I have already noted that anxiety disorders tend to take a chronic course. Among Islington women, at the time of our first contact 81% of the core anxiety disorders had lasted 1 year and 65% had lasted at least 2 years. This tendency to persist is also reflected by the fact that, in the 4-year study period, three-quarters of all such disorders were present at the point we first saw the participants. A German sample that used DSM-III-R criteria and covered a 7-year period confirmed that chronic symptoms were the most frequent pattern of illness (Wittchen et al. 2000).

The same German study showed that anxiety disorders typically antedated depression. Anxiety also was associated with a raised risk of major depression or dysthymia, the course of which was predominantly episodic, with full remissions. These findings held up in a large Dutch community sample first seen in childhood and adolescence and followed up 14 years later (Roza et al 2003; see also Essau 2003; de Graaf et al. 2003; Goodwin 2002; Parker et al. 1997, 1999). Such a time order is equally clear over shorter periods of time (e.g., Heron et al. 2004; Hettema et al. 2003). In Islington, using the total study period of 4 years, there was a 4.9-fold greater chance of an anxiety disorder leading to depression than the reverse, and there was no difference in risk of anxiety during a depressive episode when compared with depression-free periods (Brown and Harris 1993, p. 149). (In this estimate, no account was taken of anxiety that occurred more than a year before first interview. When this was included, risk remained high, at 3.45, i.e., 29 onsets of depression/ 118.6 years of prior anxiety.)

It remains unclear what mechanisms are involved in these relationships (Wittchen et al. 2000). The increased risk of depression is not necessarily related to the anxiety itself. Although the Islington research found an increased risk of depression in the presence of either subclinical depression or anxiety that had lasted at least 1 year, once psychosocial risk factors, such as ongoing severe difficulties and severe events, were taken into account, there was no association with onset of depression (Brown et al. 1986). However, simple phobia and mild agoraphobia were included in this analysis. Because these disorders have no association with depression (see Brown and Harris 1993, Table 1), their inclusion was unnecessary. A reanalysis of the data, in which only core anxiety conditions were used, did show a link, although this involved only a quarter of the depressive onsets and, as might be expected, all these onsets were also associated with either the interpersonal risk factor or low self-esteem.[4] Clearly, future research should take account of the contribution of such psychosocial factors.

Two further points are relevant. First, *subclinical* depression is an established risk factor for major depression (Moerk and Klein 2000; see also Judd et al. 1997; Kessler et al. 1997b), and this often accompanies chronic anxiety. For example, 43% (10/23) of cases in which the onset of depression occurred with chronic anxiety were also associated with chronic subclinical depression. Second, given the role of chance in comorbid conditions, some of the onsets of depression associated with ongoing anxiety will simply be due to the fact that anxiety more often takes a chronic course.

LONG-TERM OUTCOME OF JOINT ONSETS AND A PUZZLING ANOMALY

Among the Islington women, almost half the comorbid conditions that occurred during the 4-year period were joint onsets (Table 16–6). Published data about the long-term course of these conditions are limited. In Islington, there was a tendency for depression to remit first.[5] If the 23 joint onsets shown in Table 16–6 are considered, there was a remission during the study period of at least one of the two conditions for 13 subjects. For nearly half of those women (6/13), this involved remission of both anxiety and depression; however, for 86% (6/7) of the rest, depression remitted first. This finding is reminiscent of results from a population survey in the Outer Hebrides in which the rates of pure chronic anxiety were greater among the most socially integrated women (churchgoers and those working on small farms), and rates of depression greater among the least integrated (Brown and Prudo 1981; Prudo et al. 1981). Among the most integrated women, it was very common for either an anxiety disorder or a joint condition of anxiety and depression to occur after the death of a close relative and especially after the death of a parent or sibling. In such circumstances, the anxiety disorder tended to persist for many years, regardless of whether it occurred alone or with depression. Any accompanying depression usually remitted fairly quickly (Prudo et al. 1984).

---

[4]Based on unpublished data that used the first follow-up year of 330 Islington women. Partial odds ratios with 95% confidence intervals were 8.8 (2.9–26.8) for "interpersonal risk," 2.8 (1.2–6.4) for "low self-esteem," and 6.0 (1.9–18.8) for "core anxiety lasting at least one year." Only 8 of the 32 onsets were associated with such core anxiety.
[5]It is possible that the comorbid cases excluded in Table 16–6 (because onset of both conditions occurred before the study period) had a somewhat different clinical course, with more of the depression occurring in the context of ongoing chronic anxiety. Nonetheless, given that joint onsets are common, it is important to consider this question.

The close association of anxiety disorder with such "loss" among the integrated women runs counter to the findings reviewed earlier on the nature of provoking events and is more consistent with findings, also cited earlier, related to anxiety among the elderly. In these integrated Hebridean women, the severity and chronic course of the anxiety years was notable, and this was typically within the context of highly supportive kinship ties. We were struck by the intensity of the emotional ties with close kin—an observation similar to findings in an anthropological study of another Gaelic-speaking community off the coast of Ireland, where kin ties were so close that the pattern had been for many married couples not to live together because of a sense of disloyalty to their parents (Fox 1978). In short, the findings are an extreme instance of the apparent failure, discussed earlier, of supportive ties to ameliorate the experience of anxiety.

Findings of an exploratory analysis of monozygotic female twins may be relevant (Kendler and Gardiner 2001). A cluster analysis indicated three groups of depressed women. One group stood out as curiously free from psychosocial risk factors. As children, they demonstrated vulnerability and anxiety and higher rates of phobia. Perhaps because parents had had a sense of this vulnerability, these children had experienced higher rates of parental protectiveness than their co-twins. In adulthood, they reported lower rates of life events and relationship problems. Barlow (1988) has drawn attention to the argument of Andrews (1966) that excessive dependency, as a result of a markedly overprotected childhood, may be a predisposing factor for anxiety disorders. Work with monkeys also has suggested that an overprotected childhood may deprive one of an opportunity to develop a sense of mastery and control, and the development of a specific focus of anxious apprehension may be a function of the experience of a negative event. This speculation simply underlines how much more there is to learn.

CHILDHOOD EXPERIENCE AND COMORBIDITY

My account in this chapter has emphasized the importance of a lifespan perspective. It is therefore appropriate to point out important gaps in our knowledge. Anxiety disorders often start in adolescence and early adulthood and frequently take a highly chronic course. It follows that adult samples are often unhelpful about circumstances that surrounded the original onset of the disorder. For example, in the Islington study, simple phobias and mild agoraphobias were particularly likely to have started well before our contact with the women, and it proved impossible to carry out an analysis of the role of life events in the onset of these disorders.

One study, which used data from the U.S. National Comorbidity Survey (Kessler 1994), analyzed retrospective data about early life experiences of people 15–54 years of age; the data covered 12 negative life events and 10 chronic childhood adversities (Magee 1999). There was some hint of specific effects for different kinds of phobia—for example, experiences of violence at the hands of one or more adults and verbal aggression between parents had unique effects on specific phobias. However, although this was a significant and interesting study, its main message must be how little we know.

Although life events have been shown to play a role in childhood disorders, there is some indication that the findings are not so clear-cut as with adults (e.g., Goodyer 1990; Goodyer et al. 1985, 1987). Sandberg et al. (2001) found that life events played a role but concluded that there were differences between adult and childhood experiences and emphasized the importance in childhood of ongoing stressful difficulties (see also Goldberg and Goodyer 2005). However, these investigators probably drew too sharp a distinction between childhood and adult experiences. Figure 16–2 illustrates, for the adult Islington sample, just how important ongoing background vulnerability factors—defined by the presence of adverse interpersonal relationships and usually relating to a core sexual tie or ongoing low self-esteem—were in adulthood. Severe events that occurred during a 12-month period formed the basis of this analysis. Although risk of a depressive onset was 47% in the presence of both factors and 26% for one factor, the risk was only 5% for those women with neither factor[6] (see Brown et al. 1987 for measurement details).

Something similar in terms of background factors probably holds for children who experience parental abuse or neglect. What is likely to differ between childhood and adolescence is the development of highly committed social roles, which leaves adult women open to increased risk in the context of a matching life event—for example, a woman who is markedly committed to the role of mother finds out that her child has been systematically stealing from her and taking drugs (see Brown et al. 1987 for an account of the importance of role commitment). However, Goodyer et al. (2000) found that, in an adolescent sample, the most important class of "loss" events associated with the onset of depression involved the failure of previously held expectations in an interpersonal relationship (within family or between friends), and this might reflect the beginning of adult-type role commitments.

Nonetheless, we are clearly some way short of a comprehensive model of relevant psychosocial factors in childhood and adolescence, which, at a minimum, must take account of the role of events and ongoing difficulties in the context of

---

[6]This is unpublished data on the impact of severe events on risk for onset of depressive disorders and includes additional material from a prospective study of a high-risk sample of mothers (see Bifulco et al. 1998 for details). For the purposes of this chapter, "psychological" vulnerability was based only on the presence of low self-esteem and excluded ongoing anxiety and depression that did not reach criteria for major depression, which had been included in the "psychological index" used in earlier published accounts.

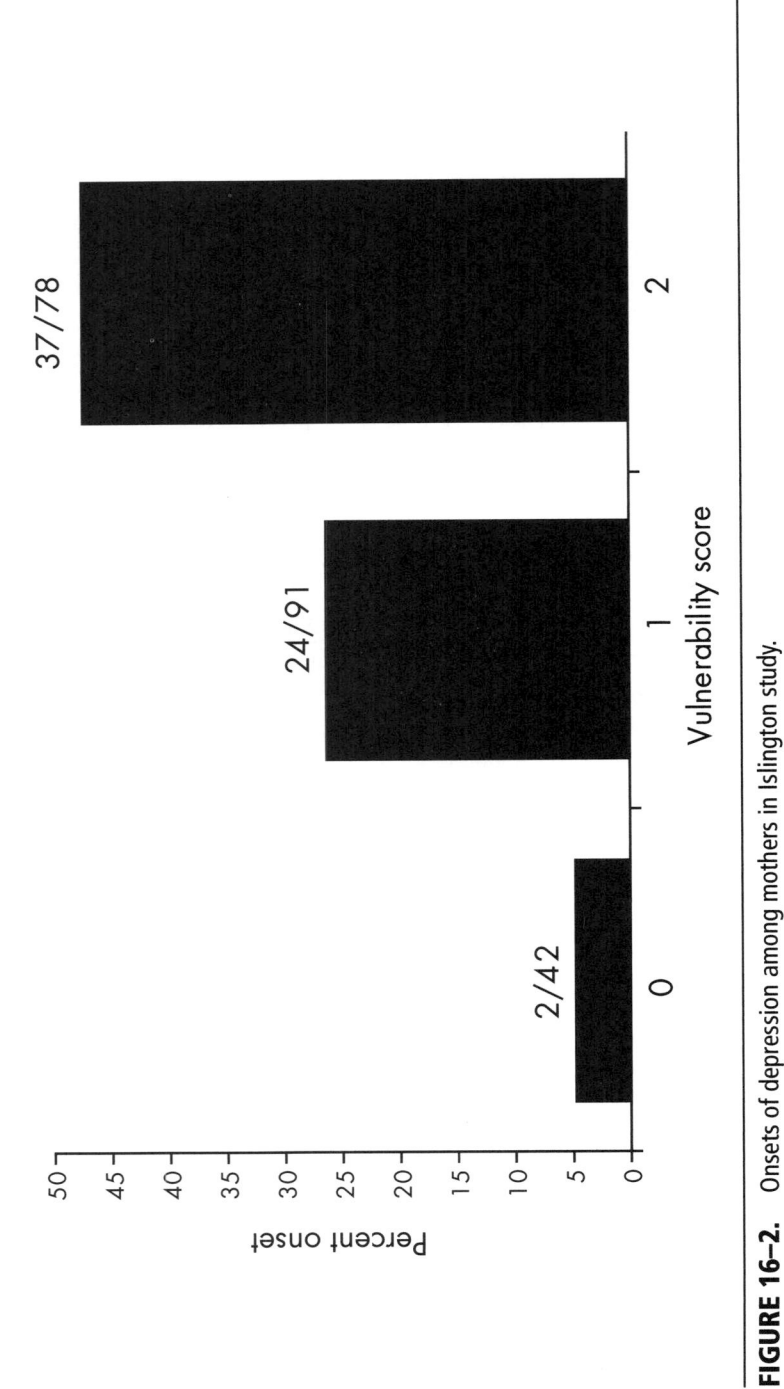

FIGURE 16–2. Onsets of depression among mothers in Islington study.

Note. Each woman had a severe event during a 12-month follow-up period. Events were only counted as provoking if they occurred within 6 months of onset of disorder; 211 events occurred. Vulnerability score was based on presence at first interview of either interpersonal risk or low self-esteem.

parental abuse and neglect. There is a particular need for studies that cover childhood, adolescence, and early adulthood (Goldberg and Goodyer 2005). There are formidable practical and ethical problems related to the collection of material about parental abuse and neglect while subjects are still children, but these problems are not insuperable (Brown 2006; Brown et al. 2007b).

Significant work in this area is beginning to emerge. Studies based on the prospective Christchurch Development Cohort have begun to deal with these problems by collecting data in young adulthood, although so far these studies have focused only on sexual and physical abuse. One report has shown that sexual abuse between ages 16 and 21 years, even after controlling for that in childhood, still has an odds ratio for anxiety and depression of 1.8 and 1.9 using DSM-IV criteria (American Psychiatric Association 1994; Fergusson et al. 2002). In a further report, these researchers have shown that a measure of anxious and withdrawn behavior at age 8 years strongly predicted anxiety disorders in early adulthood, after controlling for sexual and physical abuse and other family factors, such as witnessing interparental violence. However, after these controls were applied, this finding held, only to a modest extent, for depression (Goodwin et al. 2004). Research like this, clearly, begins to provide a foundation for genuine insights into the long-term link of early adverse experience with comorbidity in adulthood.

Generalized Anxiety Disorder and Depression and Final Comments

I believe that the implications of the association of GAD with depression are best explored in the context of the study of anxiety disorders as a whole. Among the Islington women, as already discussed, this analysis indicated that simple phobia and mild agoraphobia differed from other anxiety disorders. There was, for example, no indication that these phobias were associated with a risk of a depressive onset.[7] These phobias also stood out as unrelated to early adversity. Fundamental differences may well be involved. A family study has shown a much higher risk of simple phobia among first-degree relatives of simple phobic probands, although there was no evidence that this relationship held for other anxiety or phobic DSM-III-R conditions (Fyer et al. 1990).

A genetic study of monozygotic female twins found that situational or animal phobias stood out as distinct (Kendler and Gardiner 2001; see also Kendler et al. 1992). On the other hand, the U.S. National Comorbidity Survey found that sim-

---

[7]This result is not reported in Brown and Harris (1993): 1.3 onsets of depression (3/209 years) occurred during periods of simple phobia or mild agoraphobia, compared with 5.0 onsets (57/1070.5 years) for those without any DSM-III-R disorder.

ple phobias, like other anxiety disorders, did predict later depression, albeit with a lower odds ratio than GAD or panic (Kessler et al. 1996), and another large inquiry found that these phobias predicted elevated rates of GAD (Kessler et al. 2002). However, our Islington analysis was based on a hierarchical scheme in which simple phobia and mild agoraphobia were lowest. Such women, presumably, also were able to develop a comorbid core anxiety condition. It is possible the lack of an association of phobias with depression among the Islington women might be related to the fact that we were dealing with conditions that were, in some way, milder given their lack of any overlap with other anxiety conditions. Perhaps the failure of fear to generalize beyond the immediate phobic response is critical in the relationship of phobias with depression—that is, fear fails to generalize beyond an immediate "alerting" stimulus, which holds for core anxiety conditions.

A number of recent commentators have seen GAD as overlapping uncomfortably with depression. A review that largely dealt with the statistical manipulation of symptoms urged the current folk taxonomy be abandoned, but in practice, the main recommendation was no more than to ally GAD with depression (Clark and Watson 2006). However, the most significant conclusion, from our consideration of a range of anxiety disorders, was that the findings that concerned core anxiety disorders and depression held equally for GAD when considered alone. The data provided no evidence that GAD related any differently to distal risk factors, nor did GAD emerge as related any differently with later depressive episodes. Somewhat more than half (13/23) of the instances of ongoing anxiety that led to a depressive onset involved GAD, with the average duration of the anxiety episode before the depressive onset probably exceeding 5 years. This estimate is likely to be too low, because we did not always attempt to date the actual beginning of episodes that clearly had lasted many years.

GAD occurred more frequently than all other core anxiety disorders (Table 16–2), a result that probably holds more generally (e.g., Hunt et al. 2002). There was also some suggestion of the distinctiveness of GAD in terms of depression. Although almost two-thirds (41/64) of the mixed anxiety and depressive conditions involved GAD, 41% of GAD episodes were free of major depression, a result similar to the 42% found in the U.S. National Comorbidity Survey (Kessler et al. 1999). Results from two national comorbidity surveys in the United States have indicated that GAD and major depression have roughly equivalent degrees of impairment. Such findings are consistent with the two types of disorder being independent of each other (Kessler et al. 1999).

Perhaps the most significant data concerns the reasons for the substantial comorbidity of depression and core anxiety, because this association could easily lead to the assumption that the disorders have much in common. Indeed, I suspect this is one of the main, if often unstated, reasons for the current unease with existing diagnostic schemes. It is therefore significant that, among the Islington women, at least half, and perhaps substantially more, of the comorbidities of core anxiety disorders and depression was due to their chance associations. These associations, as discussed earlier, resulted from the influence of early maltreatment on rates of both conditions in the general population and the influence of a severely threatening life event, or events, in adulthood in bringing about both disorders by conveying danger *and* loss. Also relevant is the fact that emotional and practical support appear to have a much greater influence on depression and that the type of positive event, related to remission, may well differ for depression and core-anxiety conditions. Again, nothing has emerged to suggest that GAD differed from other core anxiety disorders on any of these counts.

The spirit of my review in this chapter has been one of exploration. I can therefore perhaps be excused for not spending much time listing necessary caveats. The emphasis I have given to research in London has obvious limitations: relatively small samples were employed, the work concentrated on women under 65, and findings might well be significantly different for men (e.g., MacMillan et al. 2001) and the elderly (Lenze et al. 2001). The findings concerning GAD and depression, which I have just reviewed, clearly require replication.

However, despite these limitations, it is possible to add that there has been a considerable amount of corroboration, from other research centers, of a number of the findings I have reported, and as far as I have managed a reasonably comprehensive review, very little by way of noncorroboration has been reported. Also, the findings related to GAD are perhaps sufficient to suggest the wisdom of some caution in recommending changes to the current classification.

In terms of the more-general picture, there are important issues I have not had space to cover. I have failed to discuss the possibility that adverse family experience, related to the attachment system, might play a role in comorbidity independently of the role of early abuse and neglect, although I am not aware of convincing data on this point (Shear 1996; Wood et al. 2003). I have not considered genetic and family studies, although some research points to conclusions not inconsistent with the emphasis I have placed on distal and proximal risk factors (see discussion in Klein et al. 2003). My neglect of the genetic literature partly relates to the puzzling almost-total lack of attention in such studies dealing with comorbidity to the role of early abuse and neglect (e.g., Middeldorp et al. 2005), although such experience could easily be incorporated (e.g., Kendler et al. 2002). However, I expect this lack of attention to be corrected in the future. It is also possible that the development of molecular genetics will reduce some of the need for very large samples, which need probably partly explains the superficial measurement of psychosocial risk factors in much genetic research.

References

American Psychiatric Association: Diagnostic and Statistical Manual of Mental Disorders, 3rd Edition Revised. Washington, DC, American Psychiatric Association, 1987

American Psychiatric Association: Diagnostic and Statistical Manual of Mental Disorders, 4th Edition. Washington, DC, American Psychiatric Association, 1994

Andrews JDW: Psychotherapy of phobias. Psychol Bull 66:455–480, 1966

Angold A, Costello EJ, Erkanli A: Comorbidity. J Child Psychol Psychiatry 40:57–87, 1999

Barlow DH: Anxiety and Its Disorders: The Nature and Treatment of Anxiety and Panic. New York, Guilford, 1988

Bifulco A, Brown GW, Harris TO: Childhood experiences of care and abuse (CECA): a retrospective interview measure. J Child Psychol Psychiatry 35:1419–1435, 1994

Bifulco A, Brown GW, Moran P, et al: Predicting depression in women: the role of past and present vulnerability. Psychol Med 28:39–50, 1998

Brown GW: Life events and affective disorders: replications and limitations. Psychosom Med 55:248–259, 1993

Brown GW: Loss and depressive disorders, in Adversity, Stress and Psychopathology. Edited by Dohrenwend BP. New York, Oxford University Press, 1998, pp 358–370

Brown GW: Measurement and the epidemiology of childhood trauma. Semin Clin Neuropsychiatry 7:66–79, 2002a

Brown GW: Social roles, context and evolution in the origins of depression. J Health Soc Behav 43:255–276, 2002b

Brown GW: Childhood maltreatment and adult psychopathology, in Relational Processes in DSM-V. Edited by Beach SRH, Wamboldt MZ, Kaslow NJ, Heyman RE, et al. Washington, DC, American Psychiatric Publishing, 2006, pp 107–122

Brown GW, Harris TO: Social Origins of Depression: A Study of Psychiatric Disorder in Women. London, England, Tavistock Press, 1978

Brown GW, Harris T: Stressor, vulnerability and depression: a question of replication. Psychol Med 16:739–744, 1986

Brown GW, Harris TO: Aetiology of anxiety and depressive disorders in an inner-city population, 1: early adversity. Psychol Med 23:143–154, 1993

Brown GW, Moran P: Clinical and psychosocial origins of chronic depressive episodes, 1: a community survey. Br J Psychiatry 165:447–456, 1994

Brown GW, Moran P: Single mothers, poverty and depression. Psychol Med 27:21–33, 1997

Brown GW, Prudo R: Psychiatric disorder in a rural and an urban population, 1: aetiology of depression. Psychol Med 11:581–599, 1981

Brown GW, Bifulco A, Harris T, et al: Life stress, chronic sub clinical symptoms and vulnerability to clinical depression. J Affect Dis 11:1–19, 1986

Brown GW, Bifulco A, Harris T: Life events, vulnerability and onset of depression: some refinements. Br J Psychiatry 150:30–47, 1987

Brown GW, Lemyre L, Bifulco A: Social factors and recovery from anxiety and depressive disorders: a test of specificity. Br J Psychiatry 161:44–54, 1992

Brown GW, Harris TO, Eales MJ: Aetiology of anxiety and depressive disorders in an innercity population, 2: comorbidity and adversity. Psychol Med 23:155–165, 1993

Brown GW, Harris TO, Hepworth C, et al: Clinical and psychosocial origins of chronic depressive episodes, II: a patient enquiry. Br J Psychiatry 165:457–465, 1994

Brown GW, Harris TO, Hepworth C: Loss, humiliation and entrapment among women developing depression: a patient and non-patient comparison. Psychol Med 25:7–21, 1995

Brown GW, Craig TK, Harris TO, et al: Child specific and family wide risk factors using the retrospective Childhood Experience of Care and Abuse (CECA) instrument: a life-course study of adult chronic depression, 3. J Affect Disord 103:225–236, 2007a

Brown GW, Craig TK, Harris TO, et al: Validity of retrospective measures of early maltreatment and depressive episodes using the Childhood Experience of Care and Abuse (CECA) instrument: a life-course study of adult chronic depression, 2. J Affect Disord 103:217–224, 2007b

Champion LA, Goodall G, Rutter M: Behaviour problems in childhood and stressors in early adult life, 1: a 20 year follow up of London school children. Psychol Med 25:231–246, 1995

Clark LA, Watson D: Distress and fear disorders: an alternative empirically based taxonomy of "mood" and "anxiety" disorders. Br J Psychiatry 189:481–483, 2006

Cooke D, Hole D: The aetiological importance of stressful life events. Br J Psychiatry 135:397–400, 1983

Davies L, Avison WR, McAlpine DD: Significant life experiences and depression among single and married mothers. J Marriage Family 59:294–308, 1997

Davis M: The role of the amygdala in conditioned fear, in The Amygdala: Neurobiological Aspects of Emotion, Memory and Mental Dysfunction. Edited by Aggleton JP. New York, Wiley, 1992

De Beurs E, Beekman ATF, Deeg DJH, et al: Predictors of change in anxiety symptoms of older persons: results from the Longitudinal Aging Study Amsterdam. Psychol Med 30:515–527, 2000

de Graaf R, Bijl RV, Spijker J, et al: Temporal sequencing of lifetime mood disorders in relation to comorbid anxiety and substance abuse disorders. Soc Psychiatry Psychiatr Epidemiol 38:1–11, 2003

Durbin CE, Klein DN, Schwartz JE: Predicting the 2½-year outcome of dysthymic disorder: the roles of childhood adversity and family history of psychopathology. J Consult Clin Psychol 68:57–63, 2000

Eley TC, Stevenson J: Specific life events and chronic experiences differentially associated with depression and anxiety in young twins. J Abnorm Child Psychol 28:383–394, 2000

Essau CA: Comorbidity of anxiety disorders in adolescents. Depress Anxiety 18:1–6, 2003

Fergusson DM, Swain-Campbell NR, Horwood LJ: Does sexual violence contribute to elevated rates of anxiety and depression in females? Psychol Med 32:991–996, 2002

Finlay-Jones R: Anxiety, in Life Events and Illness. Edited by Brown GW, Harris T. New York, Guilford, 1989

Finlay-Jones R, Brown GW: Types of stressful life event and the onset of anxiety and depressive disorders. Psychol Med 11:803–815, 1981

Forgatch MS, Patterson GR, Skinner ML: A mediational model of the effect of divorce on antisocial behaviour in boys, in Impact of Divorce, Single Parenting, and Stepparenting on Children. Edited by Hetherington EM, Arasteh JD. Mahwah, NJ, Lawrence Erlbaum Associates, 1988

Fox R: The Tory Islanders: A People of the Celtic Fringe. Cambridge, United Kingdom, Cambridge University Press, 1978

Fyer AJ, Mannuzza S, Gallops MS, et al: Familial transmission of simple phobias and fears. Arch Gen Psychiatry 47:252–256, 1990

Gilbert P: Depression: The Evolution of Powerlessness. Hove, United Kingdom, Lawrence Erlbaum Associates, 1992

Gilbert P, Allan S: The role of defeat and entrapment (arrested flight) in depression: an exploration of an evolutionary view. Psychol Med 28:584–597, 1998

Gilbert P, Cheung MS-P, Grandfield T, et al: Recall of threat and submissiveness in childhood: development of a new scale and its relationship with depression, social comparison and shame. Clin Psychol Psychother 10 108–115, 2003

Goldberg D, Goodyer I: The Origins and Course of Common Mental Disorders. New York, Routledge, 2005

Goldberg DP, Bridges K, Cook D, et al: The influence of social factors on common mental disorders: destabilization and restitution. Br J Psychiatry 156:704–713, 1990

Goodwin RD: Anxiety disorders and the onset of depression among adults in the community. Psychol Med 32:1121–1124, 2002

Goodwin RD, Fergusson DM, Horwood LJ: Early anxious/withdrawn behaviours predict later internalizing disorders. J Child Psychol Psychiatry 45:874–883, 2004

Goodyer IM: Life Experiences, Development, and Childhood Psychopathology. Chichester, UK, Wiley, 1990

Goodyer IM, Kolvin I, Gatzanis S: Recent undesirable life events and psychiatric disorder in childhood and adolescence. Br J Psychiatry 147:517–523, 1985

Goodyer IM, Kolvin I, Gatzanis S: The impact of recent undesirable life events in psychiatric disorders in childhood and adolescence. Br J Psychiatry 151:179–184, 1987

Goodyer IM, Herbert J, Tamplin A, et al: Recent life events, cortisol, dehydroepiandrosterone and the onset of major depression in high-risk adolescents. Br J Psychiatry 177:499–504, 2000

Harkness KL, Wildes JE: Childhood adversity and anxiety versus dysthymia comorbidity in major depression. Psychol Med 32:1239–1249, 2002

Haskey J: Estimated numbers of one-parent families and their prevalence in Great Britain in 1991. Popul Trends Winter (78):5–19, 1994

Heron J, O'Connor TG, Evans J, et al: The course of anxiety and depression through pregnancy and the postpartum in a community sample. J Affect Disord 80:65–73, 2004

Hettema JM, Prescott CA, Kendler KS: The effects of anxiety, substance use and conduct disorders on risk of major depressive disorder. Psychol Med 33:1423–1432, 2003

Hunt C, Issakidis C, Andrews G: DSM-IV generalized anxiety disorder in the Australian National Survey of mental health and well-being. Psychol Med 32:649–659, 2002

Judd LL, Akiskal HS, Paulus MP: The role and clinical significance of subsyndromal depressive symptoms (SSD) in unipolar major depressive disorder. J Affect Disord 45:5–18, 1997

Kaufman J, Charney D: Comorbidity of mood and anxiety disorders. Depress Anxiety 12(suppl):69–76, 2000

Kay DW, Garside RF, Roy JR, et al: "Endogenous" and "neurotic" syndromes of depression: a 5- to 7-year follow-up of 104 cases. Br J Psychiatry 115:389–399, 1969

Kendell RE: The classification of depression: a review of contemporary confusion. Br J Psychiatry 129:15–27, 1976

Kendler KS, Gardiner CO: Monozygotic twins discordant for major depression: a preliminary exploration of the role of environmental experiences in the aetiology and course of illness. Psychol Med 31:411–423, 2001

Kendler KS, Neale MC, Kessler RC, et al: The genetic epidemiology of phobias in women: the interrelationship of agoraphobia, social phobia, situational phobia, and simple phobia. Arch Gen Psychiatry 49:273–281, 1992

Kendler KS, Walters EE, Kessler RC: The prediction of length of major depressive episodes: results from an epidemiological sample of female twins. Psychol Med 27:107–117, 1997

Kendler KS, Gardner CO, Prescott CA: Toward a comprehensive developmental model for major depression in women. Am J Psychiatry 159:1133–1145, 2002

Kendler KS, Hettema JM, Butera F, et al: Life event dimensions of loss, humiliation, entrapment, and danger in the prediction of onsets of major depression and generalized anxiety. Arch Gen Psychiatry 60:789–796, 2003

Kessler RC: The National Comorbidity Survey of the United States. Int Rev Psychiatry 6:365–376, 1994

Kessler RC: The epidemiology of pure and comorbid generalized anxiety disorder: a review and evaluation of recent research. Acta Psychiatr Scand Suppl (406):7–13, 2000

Kessler RC, Nelson CB, McGonagle KA, et al: Comorbidity of DSM-III-R major depressive disorder in the general population: results from the US National Comorbidity Survey. Br J Psychiatry Suppl (30):17–30, 1996

Kessler RC, Davis CG, Kendler KS: Childhood adversity and adult psychiatric disorder in the US National Comorbidity Survey. Psychol Med 27:1101–1119, 1997a

Kessler RC, Zhao S, Blazer DG, et al: Prevalence, correlates, and course of minor depression and major depression in the National Comorbidity Survey. J Affect Disord 45:19–30, 1997b

Kessler RC, Stang PE, Wittchen H-U, et al: Lifetime panic-depression comorbidity in the National Comorbidity Survey. Arch Gen Psychiatry 55:801–808, 1998

Kessler RC, DuPont RL, Berglund P, et al: Impairment in pure and comorbid generalized anxiety disorder and major depression at 12 months in two national surveys. Am J Psychiatry 156:1915–1923, 1999

Kessler RC, Andrade LH, Bijl RV, et al: The effects of comorbidity on the onset and persistence of generalized anxiety disorder in the ICPE surveys. Psychol Med 32:1213–1225, 2002

Kiloh LG, Garside RF: The independence of neurotic depression and endogenous depression. Br J Psychiatry 109:451–463, 1963

Klein DN, Lewinsohn PM, Rhode P, et al: Family study of comorbidity between major depressive disorder and anxiety disorders. Psychol Med 33:703–714, 2003

Lang PJ, Davis M, Ohman A: Fear and anxiety: animal models and human cognitive psychophysiology. J Affect Disord 61:137–159, 2000

Lara ME, Klein DN: Psychosocial processes underlying the maintenance and persistence of depression: implications for understanding chronic depression. Clin Psychol Rev 19:553–570, 1999

Lara ME, Klein DN, Kasch KL: Psychosocial predictors of the short-term course and outcome of major depression: a longitudinal study of a nonclinical sample with recent-onset episodes. J Abnorm Psychol 109:644–650, 2000

Lemyre L, Lee JE: Triangulation of self-report and investigator-rated coping indices as predictors of psychological stress: a longitudinal investigation among public utility workers. Work 27: 89–100, 2006

Leenstra AS, Ormel J, Giel R: Positive life change and recovery from anxiety and depression. Br J Psychiatry 166:333–343, 1995

Lenze EJ, Mulsant BH, Shear MK, et al: Comorbidity of depression and anxiety disorders in later life. Depress Anxiety 14:86–93, 2001

Levine J, Cole DP, Chengappa KN, et al: Anxiety disorders and major depression, together or apart. Depress Anxiety 14:94–104, 2001

Levitan RD, Rector NA, Sheldon T, et al: Childhood adversities associated with major depression and/or anxiety disorders in a community sample of Ontario: issues of comorbidity and specificity. Depress Anxiety 17:34–42, 2003

MacMillan HI, Fleming JE, Streiner DL, et al: Childhood abuse and lifetime psychopathology in a community sample. Am J Psychiatry 158:1878–1883, 2001

Magee WJ: Effects of negative life experiences on phobia onset. Soc Psychiatry Psychiatr Epidemiol 34:343–351, 1999

Miceli M, Castelfranchi C: Anxiety as an "epistemic" emotion: an uncertainty theory of anxiety. Anxiety Stress Coping 18:291–319, 2005

Middeldorp CM, Cath DC, Van Dyk R, et al: The comorbidity of anxiety and depression in the perspective of genetic epidemiology: a review of twin and family studies. Psychol Med 35:611–624, 2005

Moerk KC, Klein DN: The development of major depressive episodes during the course of dysthymic and episodic major depressive disorders: a retrospective examination of life events. J Affect Disord 58:117–123, 2000

Nazroo JY, Edwards AC, Brown GW: Gender differences in the onset of depression following a shared life event: a study of couples. Psychol Med 27:9–19, 1997

Neeleman J, Oldehinkel AJ, Ormel J: Positive life change and remission of non-psychotic mental illness: a competing outcomes approach. J Affect Dis 76:69–78, 2003

Ninan PT, Berger J: Symptomatic and syndromal anxiety and depression. Depress Anxiety 14:79–85, 2001

Office of Population Censuses and Surveys: Census: Households and Family Composition (Topic reported monitor). London, England, Office of Population Censuses and Surveys, 1994

Parker G, Wilhelm K, Asghari A: Early onset depression: the relevance of anxiety. Soc Psychiatry Psychiatr Epidemiol 32:30–37, 1997

Parker G, Wilhelm K, Mitchell P, et al: The influence of anxiety as a risk to early onset major depression J Affect Disord 52:11–17, 1999

Prudo R, Brown GW, Harris T, et al: Psychiatric disorder in a rural and an urban population, 2: sensitivity to loss. Psychol Med 11:601–616, 1981

Prudo R, Harris T, Brown GW: Psychiatric disorder in a rural and an urban population, 3: social integration and the morphology of affective disorder. Psychol Med 14:327–345, 1984

Rapee RM: Potential role of childrearing practices in the development of anxiety and depression. Clin Psychol Rev 17:47–67, 1997

Robins LN, Regier DA (eds): Psychiatric Disorders in America: The Epidemiological Catchment Area Study. New York, Free Press, 1990

Roza SJ, Hofstra MB, Van der Ende MS, et al: Stable prediction of mood and anxiety disorders based on behavioral and emotional problems in childhood: a 14-year follow-up during childhood, adolescence and young adulthood. Am J Psychiatry 160:2116–2121, 2003

Sandberg S, Rutter M, Pickles A, et al: Do high-threat life events really provoke the onset of psychiatric disorders in children? J Child Psychol Psychiatry 42:523–532, 2001

Shear MK: Factors in the etiology and pathogenesis of panic disorder: revisiting the attachment-separation paradigm. Am J Psychiatry 153:125–136, 1996

Spitzer RL, Endicott J, Robins E: Research diagnostic criteria: rationale and reliability. Arch Gen Psychiatry 35:773–782, 1978

Stein MB, Walker JR, Anderson G, et al: Childhood physical and sexual abuse in patients with anxiety disorders and in a community sample. Am J Psychiatry 153:275–277, 1996

Strauss JS, Downey TW, Ware S: Treating children and adolescents in the same psychiatric inpatient setting. Am J Orthopsychiatry 50:165–168, 1980

Surtees PG: In the shadow of adversity: the evolution and resolution of anxiety and depressive disorder. Br J Psychiatry 166:583–594, 1995

Utting D: Family and Parenthood: Supporting Families, Preventing Breakdown. York, United Kingdom, Joseph Rowntree Foundation, 1995

Veil HOF, Bauman U (eds): Life Events and Social Support: Possibilities for Primary Prevention. Washington, DC, Hemisphere Publishing, 1992

Weems CF, Silverman WK: An integrative model of control: implications for understanding emotion regulation and dysregulation in childhood anxiety. J Affect Disord 91:113–124, 2005

Wing JK, Cooper JE, Sartorius N: The Measurement and Classification of Psychiatric Symptoms: An Instruction Manual for the Present State Examination and CATEGO Programme. London, Cambridge University Press, 1974

Wittchen HU, Kessler RC, Pfister H, et al: Why do people with anxiety disorders become depressed? A prospective-longitudinal community study. Acta Psychiatrica Scand Suppl (406):14–23, 2000

Wood JJ, McLeod BD, Sigman M, et al: Parenting and childhood anxiety: theory, empirical findings and future directions. J Child Psychol Psychiatry 44:134–151, 2003

Young EA, Abelson JL, Curtis GC, et al: Childhood adversity and vulnerability to mood and anxiety disorders. Depress Anxiety 5:66–72, 1997

Commentary

COMMENTARY ON "PSYCHOSOCIAL ORIGINS OF DEPRESSIVE AND ANXIETY DISORDERS," PART 1

Sidney Zisook, M.D.

In this discussion of Dr. Brown's chapter (Chapter 16), I begin with a brief summary of his key points and create a "scorecard" of the degree to which each point supports the alternative hypotheses that, based on psychosocial risk factors, major depressive disorder (MDD) and generalized anxiety disorder (GAD) are 1) the same disorder, 2) closely related disorders, or 3) distally related disorders.

Following this summary, I point to emerging evidence from several lines of investigation that may bear on the questions at hand. The evidence includes recently published results that shed additional light on the specificity of life events and onsets of MDD and GAD; data from studies on a specific stressor, bereavement; findings from a large, multisite treatment study of MDD, the Sequenced Treatment Alternatives to Relieve Depression (STAR*D); and a summary of how the prevailing data on psychosocial stressors help clarify the diagnostic relationship of MDD and GAD. Finally, I suggest what further steps might be taken.

Key Points of Dr. Brown's Chapter

In Chapter 16, "Psychosocial Origins of Depressive and Anxiety Disorders," Dr. Brown reviewed data from several longitudinal studies, particularly his own London-based studies that targeted working-class mothers living in Islington. In these studies, subjects were seen for an initial assessment and 1 year later, and many were seen again over an average period of about 4 years. Using a state-of-the-art instrument to measure psychosocial risk factors, the Life Events and Difficulties Schedule, data were gathered on childhood and adolescent adversity, adult life events, recent events, social support, and other known vulnerability factors (Brown and Harris 1978).

After reviewing his own methodologically rigorous series of studies, supplemented by discussions of related longitudinal investigations from other research centers, Dr. Brown concluded that any reclassification of MDD and GAD as the same disorder, or very closely related disorders, would be premature. Table 1 provides Dr. Brown's key points related to the relationship between MDD and GAD and includes my own subjective ratings of which of the three alternative hypotheses his data best support.

The Dunedin Study on Childhood Risk Factors in a Birth Cohort to Age 32

To specifically address the question of how antecedent risk predictors might help clarify the diagnostic relationship between GAD and MDD, Moffitt et al. (2007) prospectively measured risk factors across multiple domains, including adverse family environments and personality traits, and used structured diagnostic interviews for MDD and GAD during childhood and at various intervals during young adulthood. DSM-IV (American Psychiatric Association 1994) criteria were utilized, with two exceptions: GAD diagnoses used a 1-month rather than 6-month duration criteria, and to allow for comorbidity, GAD was diagnosed if criteria were met, regardless of the presence of MDD. Measures were chosen to incorporate known antecedent risk factors for both depression and anxiety and included family history, maternal internalizing symptoms, socioeconomic status, maltreatment, parental loss, inhibited temperament, internalizing problems, conduct problems, depression symptoms in childhood, self-esteem, and personality.

The sample was divided into four groups based on juvenile diagnostic histories and cumulative adult diagnostic status at ages 18, 21, 26, and 32 years: Healthy control subjects ($n=205$), MDD-only ($n=162$), GAD-only ($n=52$), and MDD+GAD ($n=189$). Table 2 provides a summary of risk factors that differentiate MDD from healthy control subjects and the comorbid group as well as factors that differentiate GAD from healthy control subjects and the comorbid group.

Overall, the findings of Moffitt et al. (2007) indicated that MDD and GAD share some, but not all, risk factors. The first finding to stand out is that there were more comorbid cases than cases of either MDD alone or GAD alone. For comorbid cases, onset of GAD occurred before, or concurrently with, onset of MDD in 66%

TABLE 1. Psychosocial risk scorecard

Psychosocial risk domain	Rating
Minimal evidence various aspects of early adversity (physical/sexual abuse, neglect) link differently with MDD or GAD	1
GAD more chronic than MDD Quality of social support buffers effects of severely threatening life events on onset of MDD but not on GAD GAD occurs earlier in life with a more chronic course MDD is associated with both childhood and adult adversity (previous to the immediate 12-month period); GAD associated only with early maltreatment If remission occurs in mixed cases, MDD almost always remits first	3
Specific types of current life events relate differently to risks for MDD and GAD "Loss" events (especially humiliating and/or entrapping) associated with onset of MDD "Danger" events associated with onset of GAD (and other core anxiety disorders) If danger event involves self blame or sense of incompetence to perform a core role, may be more likely to provoke MDD If danger event "external" (no self blame or incompetence) more likely to provoke anxiety disorder For comorbid conditions, experiences of both loss and danger predominate	2–3
Specific types of positive life events relate differently to recovery/ improvement from MDD and GAD "Fresh-start" (provide hope) events associated with improvement/ recovery from MDD "Anchoring" (increase security) events associated with recovery/ improvement in anxiety disorder Tendency for both "fresh-start" and "anchoring" events to be associated with improvement in "mixed" conditions	2–3

TABLE 1. Psychosocial risk scorecard *(continued)*

Psychosocial risk domain	Rating
Much MDD-GAD comorbidity cannot be explained by chance occurrence of two separate conditions or by common effects of childhood adversity	2
Single motherhood strong risk for mixed episodes but not for MDD or GAD alone	
Almost half comorbid cases involve joint onsets	
Anxiety associated with increased risk of onset of MDD or dysthymia	
Most of mixed MDD/anxiety disorder cases involve GAD	
41% of GAD cases free of MDD	
GAD related in same way to distal risk factors as other core anxiety disorders	
GAD clear risk for later MDD	
More than half the instances of ongoing anxiety disorders leading to MDD involved GAD	

Note. 1 = supports Hypothesis 1: MDD and GAD same disorder; 2 = supports Hypothesis 2: MDD and GAD closely related; 3 = supports Hypothesis 3: MDD and GAD distally related.
GAD = generalized anxiety disorder; MDD = major depressive disorder.

of occurrences. The comorbid MDD+GAD group differed from the healthy control group on all 13 risk factors. Overall, the GAD-only group shared more risk factors with the MDD+GAD group than did the MDD-only group. Both the MDD-only and the GAD-only groups differed from healthy control subjects on the following risk factors: maternal internalizing symptoms, childhood maltreatment before age 11 years, conduct problems before ages 5–11 years, and negative emotionality at age 18. The MDD-only group differed from healthy control subjects on two additional risk factors: family history of MDD and lack of positive emotionality at age 18. The GAD-only group differed from healthy control subjects on low childhood socioeconomic status and internalizing problems at ages 5–11 years.

The authors concluded that because MDD had specific risk factors not shared by GAD (predisposing family history and personality), and GAD had specific risk factors not shared by MDD (childhood adversity and behavior), the findings "point to different etiologies which would not be consistent with collapsing the two into one disorder in future nosological systems" (Moffitt et al. 2007, p. 9). However, the frequency of comorbidity and the many shared risk factors between pure MDD and pure GAD also point to a reasonably close relationship between

MDD and GAD. Furthermore, if the study had included a broader spectrum of depression and anxiety conditions, such as dysthymic disorder and subsyndromal depression (Akiskal 1998; Barbee et al. 2003; Barlow and Campbell 2000; Judd et al. 1998), the relationship might well have appeared even closer.

Bereavement Studies

Few experiences are associated with as much fear and anxiety as the death of a close friend or relative. Often considered the most distressing and disruptive event of ordinary life, the loss of a loved person may generate profound psychosocial consequences for the bereaved. When close, long-term attachment bonds are severed, the survivor must deal with often-overwhelming effects of loss and "aloneness," now in the absence of an important support person who heretofore had helped the survivor cope with adversity. Thus it is no surprise that the death of a loved one is associated with the onset or exacerbation of a number of psychiatric disorders, including both depression and anxiety (De Beurs et al. 2001; Onrust and Cuijpers 2006; Zisook et al. 1990b). Although depressive symptoms and syndromes are the disorders most often linked to the stress of bereavement (Zisook and Kendler 2007), lingering symptoms of anxiety may be much more prevalent than often is appreciated.

A biphasic protest-despair primate response to separation provides a model for infant and human responses to threatened or real loss. When infant monkeys are separated from their mothers in the first year of life, most initiate an anxious-agitated search for the mother, called the *protest* phase. Only after the initial search fails to retrieve the mother does the infant monkey give up the search and retreat into a retarded-despair state, the *despair* phase (Mineka and Suomi 1978). Similar biphasic patterns have been described in young children's responses to prolonged physical separation from their mothers (Spitz 1946) and in human adults' responses to deaths of loved ones (Bowlby 1980).

Bowlby (1980) described the initial protest response as a prototype for anxiety in adults and despair as the prototype for depression (Alloy et al. 1990). Along those same lines, Parkes (1986) declared grief to be an *anxiety reaction,* whereas Clayton et al. (1974) considered it to be a model for *reactive depression.* In fact, all of these interpretations may be correct. Thus, it is no surprise that the prevalence of both mood and anxiety disorders is considerably elevated in bereavement (Onrust et al. 2006).

Most studies of widowhood have emphasized symptoms rather than syndromes or disorders. A notable exception is a study presented by Jacobs et al. (1990a, 1990b) that utilized a modified Structured Clinical Interview for DSM-III (American Psychiatric Association 1980), given to bereaved spouses 6 and 12 months following their losses. Over 40% of bereaved spouses had at least one type of anxiety disorder during the first year of bereavement. Higher than expected prevalence rates

TABLE 2. Prospective risk factors: comparisons of comorbid versus non-comorbid cases of major depressive disorder (MDD) and generalized anxiety disorder (GAD)—defined cumulatively, from ages 18 to 32 years

	Planned group comparisons			
	A MDD-only vs. healthy control subjects	B MDD-only vs. comorbid	C GAD-only vs. healthy control subjects	D GAD-only vs. comorbid
Group descriptors				
Female[a]	62% vs. 42%	—	—	40% vs. 63%
First MDD diagnosis by age 15		2% vs. 14%		12% vs. 37%
First GAD diagnosis by age 15				
Recurrent MDD		27% vs. 61%		14% vs. 50%
Recurrent GAD				
Received mental health services, ages 20–32 years	41% vs. 9%	41% vs. 57%	35% vs. 9%	35% vs. 57%
Psychiatric medication, ages 20–32 years	22% vs. 5%	22% vs. 39%	19% vs. 5%	19% vs. 39%
Risk factors				
Proportion of family members with MDD	29% vs. 21%	25% vs. 33%		
Proportion of family members with GAD		18% vs. 26%		19% vs. 26%
Maternal internalizing symptoms (mean Z score)	$P=0.035$	$P=0.006$	$P=0.007$	
Childhood socioeconomic status (mean Z score)		$P=0.007$	$P=0.032$	

TABLE 2. Prospective risk factors: comparisons of comorbid versus non-comorbid cases of major depressive disorder (MDD) and generalized anxiety disorder (GAD)—defined cumulatively, from ages 18 to 32 years *(continued)*

	Planned group comparisons			
	A MDD-only vs. healthy control subjects	B MDD-only vs. comorbid	C GAD-only vs. healthy control subjects	D GAD-only vs. comorbid
Risk factors *(continued)*				
Child maltreatment before age 11 years	9% vs. 3%		14% vs. 3%	
Lost a parent before age 11 years				
Inhibited temperament, ages 3–5 years		4% vs. 12%		
Internalizing problems, ages 5–11 years (mean Z score)		$P<0.001$	$P=0.04$	
Conduct problems, ages 5–11 years (mean Z score)	$P=0.013$	$P=0.004$		
Depression symptom count, age 9 years (mean Z score)		$P<0.001$	$P=0.007$	
Self-esteem, ages 11–15 years (mean Z score)		$P<0.001$		$P=0.013$
Negative emotionality, age 18 years (mean Z score)	$P<0.001$	$P<0.001$	$P<0.001$	$P=0.001$
Positive emotionality, age 18 years (mean Z score)	$P<0.001$			

Note. Significant comparisons at $P \leq 0.05$ presented as percentages, or P values. GAD duration ≥ 1 month.
[a]Gender was controlled in group comparisons.
Source. Data from Moffitt et al. 2007.

were found for both panic and generalized disorders throughout the first year, for agoraphobia in the first 6 months, and for social phobia in the latter 6 months.

Several longitudinal studies on consequences of bereavement provide data that demonstrate the frequency and persistence of both depressive and anxiety symptoms (Clayton et al. 1968, 1974; Lindemann 1944; Maddison and Viola 1968; Parkes 1964; Zisook and Shuchter 1985, 1986; Zisook et al. 1990b). Table 3 shows the frequencies of selected anxiety symptoms 2 months after spousal bereavement according to data taken from the San Diego Widowhood study (Mulvihill and Shuchter 1990). Mean Hopkins Symptom Scale scores were stable from 2 to 7 months and remained substantially higher for bereaved spouses than for the married companion group (Zisook et al. 1990a). Risk factors for the elevations in the general anxiety factor on the Hopkins Symptom Scale showed some overlap with risk factors for depression—that is, both increased in younger persons, those who considered themselves still grieving, and those with past histories of MDD—whereas female gender, low income, and tense/incompatible relationships with the deceased spouse were associated with anxiety but not with depression.

Although the bereavement data do not, in and of themselves, answer the question of whether MDD and GAD are closely or distally related, the data do provide some theoretical rationale for the link between MDD and GAD as well as for the commonly found sequence of anxiety symptoms preceding depression. Given the oft-observed pattern of anxiety followed by depression in primates, human infants, and adults separated from a significant other; results of several longitudinal studies that demonstrated a high prevalence of both depression and anxiety following the death of a loved one; and the unique role of the stress of death of a loved one in the onset of late-life MDD and anxiety, the most logical conclusion from bereavement studies is that MDD and "clinically meaningful anxiety" are closely related phenomena. Whether the "clinically meaningful anxiety" translates to GAD is yet to be determined.

Sequenced Treatment Alternatives to Relieve Depression (STAR*D)

STAR*D was a large, multisite study designed to define, prospectively, which of several treatments are most effective for outpatients with nonpsychotic MDD who have had unsatisfactory clinical outcomes to an initial and, if necessary, subsequent treatments(s). Although few psychosocial risk factors were obtained, results of the study did reveal some findings relevant to the relationship between MDD and GAD. First, almost half (44%–46%) the patients had anxious depression (Fava et al. 2004, 2006). Patients with anxious MDD had a much more severe form of MDD than did those with nonanxious MDD; were more likely to have comorbid GAD (65%); and were less likely to remit with standard treatments.

TABLE 3. Selected anxiety symptoms at month 2, San Diego Widowhood Study

Symptom	%
Tense, keyed up	27
Nervousness	24
Trouble concentrating	20
Difficulty making decisions	17
Fearful	14
Feelings easily hurt	14
Restlessness	13
Suddenly scared	11
Feeling uneasy in crowds	10
Pains in chest	10
Nervous when left alone	9
Numbness, tingling	7
Weakness	7

Source. Data from Zisook et al. 1990.

Perhaps even more to the point of this discussion are the results of an ancillary STAR*D study that assessed children, ages 7–17 years, of depressed mothers who were enrolled in the treatment trial. Nearly half the children had current psychiatric disorders, including disruptive behavior (22%), anxiety (16%), and depressive (10%) disorders. Maternal comorbid GAD was selectively associated with an increased lifetime prevalence of anxiety disorders in children, but this finding fell short of conventional levels of statistical significance ($P=0.06$) (Pilowsky et al. 2006). Thus, anxiety disorders were even more prevalent than depressive disorders in the offspring of currently depressed mothers, and maternal comorbid GAD was associated with a possible increased risk for anxiety in the children. These findings suggest a close relationship between MDD and GAD but do not identify the extent to which the association is familial, genetic, or environmental.

A subsequent analysis, which assessed the extent to which improvements in maternal depressive symptoms predicted changes in children's diagnoses and symptoms, provided some insight into this question (Weissman et al. 2006). In that analysis, remission of maternal depression after 3 months of medication treatment was significantly associated with reductions in the children's diagnoses and symptoms. Although the small sample size precluded statistical analyses on each disorder individually, the changes in rates of diagnoses between children of mothers whose MDD did or did not remit were significantly different for the class of internalizing (including depressive and anxiety disorders; $P=0.03$) but not externalizing disorders. Similarly, internalizing symptoms also decreased significantly

(P<0.001) in children of mothers who remitted compared with children of mothers whose MDD did not remit. These findings suggest an environmental influence (the impact of maternal MDD and remission) on depression and anxiety in offspring living at home. Again, these findings support a relationship between MDD and anxiety disorders, although not specifically with GAD.

Conclusion

How close is the relationship between MDD and GAD? Even after reviewing Dr. Brown's comprehensive chapter, in which he described his own elegant series of studies and other relevant studies from diverse samples around the world that have dealt with psychosocial risk factors for MDD and anxiety disorders, no firm answer to the key question about the relationship between MDD and GAD has emerged.

Supplementing Dr. Brown's chapter, as I have done here, with 1) a review of a very recently published and methodologically rigorous longitudinal study that followed a birth cohort from ages 1–32 years; 2) data gathered from several separation and bereavement studies; and 3) findings from a large MDD treatment study, which also studied children of depressed mothers, may have added more questions but has not provided a definitive answer to the question of whether, and to what degree, MDD and GAD are related. At best, all these data suggest that MDD and GAD *are* related, but the nature and proximity of their relationship remain to be determined.

I am skeptical that further studies on life events and adversity—although interesting, important, and revealing—will shed further light on this key question. In part, my skepticism relates to the complexity of reliably and validly linking reports of life events to onset, persistence, and offset of mood and anxiety disorders, although the development and refinement of the Life Events and Difficulties Schedule, as described by Brown, has gone a long way to resolving many of the roadblocks. A second reason for my skepticism relates to drawing conclusions regarding the relationships of disorders to each other based on shared etiology. Thus, just because A may cause B, C, and D, it does not follow that B, C, and D are the same, or even closely related, disorders. Smoking has been linked to cancer, heart disease, and osteoporosis, but these are three very different disorders. Similarly, bereavement has been associated not only with the onsets of MDD and GAD but also of breast cancer (Lillberg et al. 2003). Clearly, this causal link does not suggest that MDD and breast cancer are identical or even closely related disorders.

One caveat is worth mentioning. The wisdom of drawing conclusions based on shared etiology may be dependent on what shared etiological factors are examined. In other words, if MDD and GAD share an underlying biological or genetic basis, yet differ somewhat in presentation depending on environmental factors, this would imply a closer relationship than if MDD and GAD were completely biologically different, yet only arose under very similar environmental conditions.

With the foregoing as background, I return to the three questions we were asked to address:

1. *Given the available information, do the data best support the hypothesis that MDD and GAD are: a) different forms of the same disorder, b) closely related disorders, or c) distally related disorders?* The psychosocial risk data, in and of themselves, suggest that MDD and GAD are related but leave open the proximity of the relationship. Although psychosocial risk factors are not identical, they appear to be more similar than different. In the context of other domains that have examined the relationship of MDD and GAD (e.g., phenomenology, genetics, comorbidity, and treatment), the predominance of data suggests a close relationship.
2. *What are the implications of the conclusions for question 1 for DSM-V?* These conclusions support a reclassification that puts MDD and GAD under a "family" of disorders, along the lines suggested by Watson (Clark and Watson 2006; Watson 2005). Figure 1 displays Watson's structural model. As Watson pointed out, additional research is needed on posttraumatic stress disorder and obsessive-compulsive disorder.
3. *What new data could be gathered that would help to address, more definitively, the relationship between MDD and GAD?* As discussed, I do not believe it will be the psychosocial risk domain that ultimately will clarify fully the relationship between MDD and GAD. That said, further studies ideally should be prospective, use representative samples, include genetic and other biological assessments, and measure a full range of the pleiomorphic manifestations of these disorders—that is, minor depression, dysthymic disorder, major depression, double depression, mixed anxiety and depression, subthreshold GAD, GAD, comorbid MDD and GAD, and possibly depressive and anxious temperaments (Akiskal 1998; Barbee et al. 2003; Barlow et al. 2000; Judd et al. 1998). It would be advantageous to simultaneously obtain dimensional symptom scales rather than merely (predetermined) DSM diagnostic categories in future work. If we had symptom data across many dimensions from large epidemiological samples and performed the equivalent of an exploratory factor analysis, it would be interesting to see what conclusions might emerge. Also, it might be useful to follow a cohort exposed to the same life event, such as bereavement, to further assess factors related to onset, persistence, and offset of mood and anxiety disorders. The rationale for selecting bereavement as the prototype stressor is that it is common, serious, dateable, irreversible, and known to be an important risk for both MDD and GAD. Finally, continued follow-up of the birth-cohort study reviewed here (Moffitt et al. 2007), and possibly even following the sample into the next generation, could yield interesting and useful results.

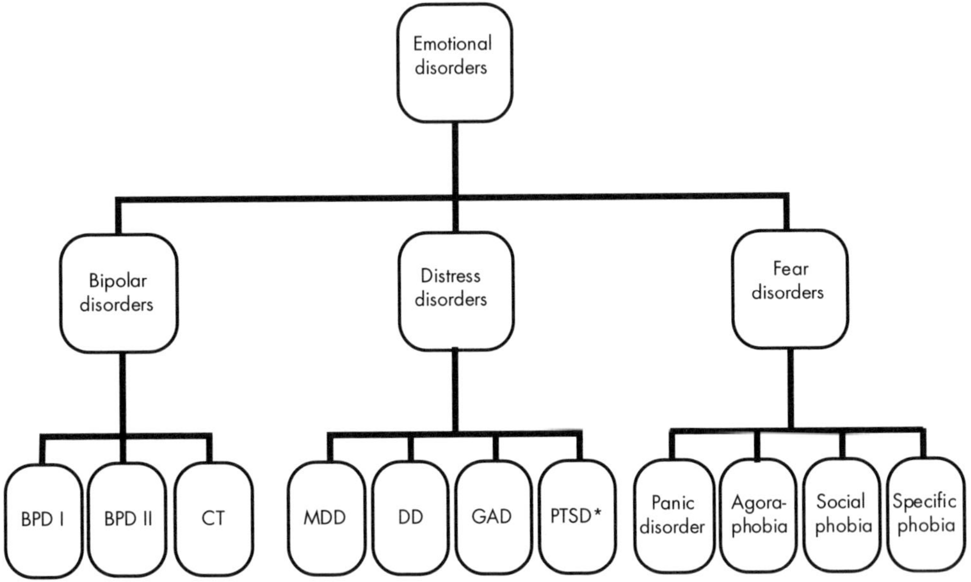

FIGURE 1. Watson's Structural Model for Reclassification of Mood and Anxiety Disorders.

*More work needed on PTSD and OCD.

BPD=bipolar disorder; CT=cyclothymic disorder; DD=dysthymic disorder; GAD=generalized anxiety disorder; MDD=major depressive disorder; OCD=obsessive-compulsive disorder; PTSD=posttraumatic stress disorder.

Source. Data from Watson 2005.

References

Akiskal HS: Toward a definition of generalized anxiety disorder as an anxious temperament type. Acta Psychiatr Scand Suppl 393:66–73, 1998

Alloy LB, Kelly KA, Mineka S, et al: Comorbidity of anxiety and depressive disorders: a helplessness-hopelessness perspective, in Comorbidity of Mood and Anxiety Disorders. Edited by Maser JD, Cloninger CR. Washington, DC, American Psychiatric Association, 1990

American Psychiatric Association: Diagnostic and Statistical Manual of Mental Disorders, 3rd Edition. Washington, DC, American Psychiatric Association, 1980

American Psychiatric Association: Diagnostic and Statistical Manual of Mental Disorders, 4th Edition. Washington, DC, American Psychiatric Association, 1994

Barbee JG, Billings CK, Bologna NB, et al: A follow-up study of DSM-III-R generalized anxiety disorder with syndromal and subsyndromal major depression. J Affect Disord 73:229–236, 2003

Barlow DH, Campbell LA: Mixed anxiety-depression and its implications for models of mood and anxiety disorders. Compr Psychiatry 41:55–60, 2000

Bowlby J: Attachment and Loss: Loss, Sadness and Depression, Vol 3. New York, Basic Books, 1980

Brown GW, Harris TO: Social Origins of Depression: A Study of Psychiatric Disorder in Women. London, England, Tavistock Press, 1978

Clark LA, Watson D: Distress and fear disorders: an alternative empirically based taxonomy of the "mood" and "anxiety" disorders. Br J Psychiatry 189:481–483, 2006

Clayton PJ, Desmarais L, Winokur G: A study of normal bereavement. Am J Psychiatry 125:168–178, 1968

Clayton PJ, Herjanic M, Murphy GE, et al: Mourning and depression: their similarities and differences. Can J Psychiatry 19:309–312, 1974

De Beurs E, Beekman A, Geerlings S, et al: On becoming depressed or anxious in late life: similar vulnerability factors but different effects of stressful life events. Br J Psychiatry 179:426–431, 2001

Fava M, Alpert JE, Carmin CN, et al: Clinical correlates and symptom patterns of anxious depression among patients with major depressive disorder in STAR*D. Psychol Med 34:1299–1308, 2004

Fava M, Rush AJ, Alpert JE, et al: What clinical and symptom features and comorbid disorders characterize outpatients with anxious major depressive disorder: a replication and extension. Can J Psychiatry 51:823–835, 2006

Jacobs S, Hanson MS, Kasl S, et al: Anxiety disorders during acute bereavement, in Grief and Bereavement in Contemporary Society, Vol 1. Edited by Chigier E. Tel Aviv, Israel, Freund Publishing House Ltd, 1990a

Jacobs S, Hansen F, Kasl S, et al: Anxiety disorders during acute bereavement: risk and risk factors. J Clin Psychiatry 51:269–274, 1990b

Judd LL, Akiskal HS, Maser JD, et al: A prospective 12-year study of subsyndromal and syndromal depressive symptoms in unipolar major depressive disorders. Arch Gen Psychiatry 55:694–700, 1998

Lillberg K, Verkasalo PK, Kaprio J, et al: Stressful life events and risk of breast cancer in 10,808 women: a cohort study. Am J Epidemiol 157:415–423, 2003

Lindemann E: Symptomatology and management of acute grief. Am J Psychiatry 101:141–148, 1944

Maddison D, Viola A: The health of widows in the year following bereavement. J Psychosom Res 12:297, 1968

Mineka S, Suomi SJ: Social separation in monkeys. Psychol Bull 85:1376–1400, 1978

Moffitt TE, Caspi A, Harrington H, et al: Generalized anxiety disorder and depression: childhood risk factors in a birth cohort followed to age 32. Psychol Med 37:441–452, 2007

Mulvihill M, Shuchter SR: Widowhood and anxiety. Psychiatr Med 8:99–116, 1990

Onrust SA, Cuijpers P: Mood and anxiety disorders in widowhood: a systematic review. Aging Ment Health 10:327–334, 2006

Parkes C: Recent bereavement as a cause of mental illness. Br J Psychiatry 110:298, 1964

Parkes C: Bereavement: Studies in Grief in Adult Life, 2nd Edition. London, England, Tavistock, 1986

Pilowsky DJ, Wickramaratne PJ, Rush AJ, et al: Children of currently depressed mothers: a STAR*D ancillary study. J Clin Psychiatry 67:126–136, 2006

Spitz RA: Anaclitic depression. Psychoanal Study Child 2:313–347, 1946

Watson D: Rethinking the mood and anxiety disorders: a quantitative hierarchical model for DSM-V. J Abnorm Psychol 114:522–536, 2005

Weissman MM, Pilowsky DJ, Wickramaratne PJ, et al: Remissions in maternal depression and child psychopathology: a STAR*D-Child report. JAMA 295:1389–1398, 2006

Zisook S, Kendler KS: Is bereavement-related depression different than non-bereavement-related depression? Psychol Med 37:779–794, 2007

Zisook S, Shuchter SR: Time course of spousal bereavement. Gen Hosp Psychiatry 7:95–100, 1985

Zisook S, Shuchter S: The first four years of widowhood. Psychiatr Ann 16:288, 1986

Zisook S, Mulvihill M, Shuchter SR: Widowhood and anxiety. Psychiatr Med 8:99–116, 1990a

Zisook S, Schneider D, Shuchter SR: Anxiety and bereavement. Psychiatr Med 8:83–96, 1990b

Commentary

COMMENTARY ON "PSYCHOSOCIAL ORIGINS OF DEPRESSIVE AND ANXIETY DISORDERS," PART 2

Donna E. Stewart, M.D., FRCPC

Professor Brown's beautifully written and compellingly argued chapter (Chapter 16) is based on an elegant series of community studies that examined depression and anxiety from a life course perspective, which he conducted in London, England.

Professor Brown discussed three issues to frame his argument for the usefulness of DSM diagnostic criteria: 1) the similarities and differences in psychosocial risk factors for anxiety and depressive disorders, 2) the contributions of the similar risk factors to the comorbidities of anxiety and depression, and 3) the implications of the fact that anxiety disorders often precede depressive disorders.

He began by reminding us that most depressive episodes are preceded by a severely threatening event, such as loss, but this event is usually insufficient, in itself, to provoke a depressive episode. Depression also usually requires that certain distal vulnerability factors, such as low self-esteem or childhood or adolescent abuse, are present. Moreover, certain protective factors, such as social support, may mitigate against the depressive episode, even if the threat is severe. On the other hand, anxiety disorders are equally likely to be provoked by a severely threatening event and past adversity but are much less responsive to current environmental and social support.

Similarities and Differences in Psychosocial Risk Factors for Anxiety and Depression

I will not repeat the details of Professor Brown's studies, other than to remind the reader that they were carried out in mothers in inner-city London. These women were interviewed to determine their psychiatric states and personal circumstances; the interviews were repeated 1 year and 4 years later. "Caseness" was determined for anxiety and depressive disorders using the Present State Examination and DSM-III-R (American Psychiatric Association 1987) criteria. The Childhood Experiences of Care and Abuse index was based on at least one of 1) parental physical and emotional abuse, 2) physical abuse by anyone at home, and 3) sexual abuse. Early adversity was associated with a double risk of adult-depression onset and a quadruple risk of the depression lasting at least 1 year. Early adversity also was associated with panic, agoraphobia, generalized anxiety disorder (GAD), and social anxiety but unrelated to simple phobia or mild agoraphobia.

Complementary and similar findings also have been described by other investigators. My colleague in Canada, Dr. Harriet MacMillan, has found stronger associations between childhood abuse and anxiety and depression in women compared with men (MacMillan et al. 2001). There is no evidence from these studies that shows specific effects of abuse on depressive or anxiety disorders, although other studies have made such claims (Harkness and Wildes 2002). Clearly, further work is needed to clarify this matter.

One of the problems with many studies on childhood-related neglect and abuse is how adversity is defined. In one highly cited study with high prevalence rates of abuse, a child qualified as having experienced childhood sexual abuse if adult genitalia of the opposite sex had been seen repeatedly before age 18 (Badgley 1989). Not only are the definitions problematic, or even nonexistent in some studies, but the negative affect that accompanies depression is likely to darken perception of childhood experiences (Watson et al. 1988). Clinicians are familiar with patients who relate stories of childhood physical neglect and abuse and who sometimes, after recovery, discount them as being minor, culturally common, or "part of growing up." This comment is by no means an attempt to discount the seriousness of childhood abuse or neglect, but is simply a reflection of the impact of depression on perception. It may, however, shed some light on why patients with depression, and especially chronic depression, are more likely to report childhood neglect and abuse in cross-sectional studies. Notably, this is a less-than-satisfactory explanation for anxiety following childhood adversity.

Moreover, it is difficult to quantify the degree of adversity, or its meaning to the individual, as Professor Brown has carefully pointed out. It bears mentioning that not only does childhood adversity correlate with depression and anxiety disorders, there also are strong associations between childhood adversity and substance abuse and dependence, antisocial personality disorder, borderline personality disorder, somatization, and posttraumatic stress disorder (Duncan et al. 1996). Accordingly, adversity appears to be a nonspecific stressor for several psychiatric disorders. Considered together, these findings do not, in my mind, justify combining, or keeping separate, depression and GAD in a new classification of mental disorders.

Comorbid Anxiety and Depression

Professor Brown found that "core" anxiety conditions (panic, agoraphobia, GAD, and social phobia) had an association with early adversity and a substantial overlap with depression, either occurring concurrently or successively. He reminded us that depression, more than anxiety, is ameliorated by social support. The work of Sir David Goldberg, in a family practice setting, also concluded that different environmental variables predicted liability to depression and anxiety (Goldberg et al. 1990). Professor Brown then described an adult adversity index, the findings from which correlated well with his childhood adversity index and with poor support and low self-esteem (known risk factors for depression). His subsequent analysis showed that depression was associated with both childhood and adult adversity, whereas anxiety was associated only with childhood adversity. He postulated that perhaps childhood adversity causes brain changes that lead to later anxiety disorders. He also noted that anxiety is less affected by later experiences, other than those close to the point of onset. He then calculated chance and nonchance comorbidity of anxiety and depression and found that the main contribution of the distal risk indices in explaining comorbidity was the result of their increasing the prevalence of core anxiety and depressive disorders in the Islington population, thereby increasing the chances the disorders would occur together by chance. The contribution for childhood adversity acting as a common antecedent, plus the baseline prevalence in the community, together explains about 50% of the comorbidity. Although this is an impressive contribution, it also means that there are other equally important factors to be considered!

Most of these studies were conducted in women, and it is well known that women experience twice the prevalence of depression and anxiety disorders, during their childbearing years, as do men (Kessler 2003). What are some of the factors— beyond abuse and neglect—that explain the high prevalence and comorbidity of depression and anxiety in women? Clearly, there are genetic factors to consider, especially in view of the work by Caspi et al. (2003), Kendler (2003a, 2003b), and others. Recent work by Caspi and Moffitt (2006) discussed gene–environment interactions and made the case for combining epidemiology with experimental neurosciences. Hormonal factors cannot escape attention, because the rising and falling incidence rates of depression and anxiety so closely mirror menarche and menopause (Soares et al. 2005). General social adversity, such as poverty and discrimination, disproportionately affects women. Women generally work for less pay than men in equivalent jobs and often lack the legal or union protection of permanent positions. Women are socialized to be compliant and nurturing, which does not serve them well in the work force, especially in a globalized competitive economy. Also, women have been shown to ruminate more about problems, a characteristic that impairs effective problem solving and action and predisposes them to both depression and anxiety.

The burden of motherhood cannot be disregarded. Although society likes to portray happy stay-at-home moms with content, well-behaved children, the reality is usually quite different. The tedium of changing diapers, preparing food, cleaning the house, and amusing children is not the lark that some envision. This situation is burdensome, in different ways, both to women with few skills and interests and to women who have had successful careers before motherhood (Diaz-Granados 2006). To mothers in poverty, often isolated from other adult company—especially in the case of single mothers—this must be extremely challenging! It is not surprising that many mothers succumb to depressive and/or anxiety disorders. I was intrigued by Professor Brown's finding that mixed anxiety and depressive conditions had a relative risk of 3.2 for single mothers compared with other mothers, but the incidence of either anxiety or depression alone was not related to single motherhood. Professor Brown rationalizes this high comorbidity by pointing out the threefold prevalence of marital violence (that may involve both danger and humiliation) in single mothers and the high prevalence of childhood adversity in this group. Our recent review of the literature supports these findings (Wang and Gucciardi 2006).

If adversity disproportionately affects women, compared with men, in the developed Western world, what is it like in less-fortunate countries? We currently are engaged in a study, funded by the Canadian Institutes of Health Research, in three lower-, middle-, and upper-income countries. In this study, we are looking at selected social policies that have particular relevance to women's health and, also, at a basket of selected mental- and physical-health indicators. The study is not yet completed, but I can tell you that good social policies make a large difference to women's mental health and especially to rates of depressive and anxiety disorders. There is also more comorbidity of depression and anxiety disorders in women than in men in low-, middle-, and high-income countries. This is especially true when one looks at the comorbidity of depressive episodes and GAD. How much this is due to adversity in childhood or adulthood is unknown. Interestingly, psychiatrists in those countries struggle, just as we do, in trying to disentangle the symptoms of GAD and depression to determine the primary diagnosis. At a recent international psychiatric conference, one experienced psychiatrist stated he had "never seen pure GAD without depression and seldom seen depression without anxiety."

This brings us to another topic: the perception of the clinician or researcher of the meaning or severity of symptoms may be very different from that of the patient, often a woman. Several studies have now confirmed the importance of "loss, especially humiliation or entrapment," for depression, and "danger," for anxiety. As Professor Brown astutely points out, the same provoking event may involve both loss and danger. However, it is uncommon for researchers to ask the personal meaning of the event for the individual. Moreover, we also know, from clinical practice, that patients may attribute or experience these symptoms differently from clinicians. We have all seen patients who look profoundly depressed who, on questioning, deny depression but complain of severe tension or anxiety. The opposite is also true. These observations all strengthen the case for the inclusion in practice and research of self-reports about feelings and their meanings.

I was delighted to note that Professor Brown also looked at recovery from depression and anxiety. The importance of positive life events, especially those with the potential for a "fresh start," was prominent for improvement in depression. In fact, positive events occurred six times more frequently than in a comparable 20-week period of depression not characterized by improvement. These positive events seemed to offer hope of ameliorating the loss in depressive disorders, or the entrapment in anxiety disorders. In the case of improvement in anxiety disorders, the events seemed to increase security or "anchoring." Not surprisingly, 60% of remissions of mixed conditions were preceded by an event with the potential for a fresh start and anchoring. Again, it would be useful to know more about how patients view events in their lives and how much control they perceive they may really have.

After many years of psychiatric practice, I continue to be surprised that some of my assumptions about the likely meaning of a patient's life events turn out to be so wrong. A successful middle-aged businessman with a 6-month history of GAD, panic, and depression that had failed to respond to antidepressants, was recently referred by his family doctor. His childhood in an overly protective, closely knit Italian family was, if anything, overindulgent. He remembers it as "warm and safe, because my mother and father were very loving and my father made all the decisions." His father's opinions were very important to him, and he was "devastated" when his father died 10 years ago. He confided that, despite the fact that life had been good to him, he was now unhappily married, had two children, and had started a secret affair with a female colleague a year earlier. He stated that his symptoms coincided with his realization that he no longer loved his wife and wanted to divorce her. Were his symptoms due to worry about his children, wife, elderly mother, economic stability, change, or other common concerns? No. On discussion, his greatest fear was how an older company shareholder, a "fatherly" man whose opinion he now valued above all others, would view him. Once he had clarified this concern and discussed his situation with the older man, who was nonjudgmental, he felt freed. His anxiety and depression lifted over the course of a few days, and he initiated divorce proceedings. Whoever would have guessed the source of his distress? His own comment is illustrative: "I feel back in control of my life." I was reminded of this man while reading about Professor Brown's joint-onset cases, patients who had experienced both loss and danger but were without early or adult adversity.

In summing up this section, I note the high comorbidity of general anxiety and depressive disorders, the clinical difficulty of teasing these disorders apart, and the meanings of symptoms to patients. I remain skeptical about the utility of keeping these problems separate in a new classification. It seems likely that major depression and general anxiety disorders are manifestations of a similar underlying disease process that differs in phenotype between individuals and even in the same individual, over time, depending on genetics, vulnerability, and environment.

I am joined in my skepticism by Professor David Watson of the University of Iowa, who in an excellent 2005 paper criticized the DSM-IV (American Psychiatric Association 1994) divisions into diagnostic classes, on the basis of the subjective criterion of "shared phenomenologic factors" (Watson 2005). He suggested, after a lengthy review of the literature, that this system should be replaced by an empiric-based structure that reflects the actual similarities of anxiety and mood disorders. He pointed out that a review of genetic studies (Mineka et al. 1998) concluded that depression is genetically indistinguishable from GAD and that both are distress-based disorders (Clark and Watson 2006). Moreover, cross-cultural studies in 14 countries over 5 continents (Krueger et al. 2003) "showed that a two-factor model of internalizing and externalizing syndromes provided a good fit to data from each country." Watson also pointed out the difficulties caused by hierarchical exclusion rules, which drastically reduce the base rates of GAD in a sample and attenuate its association with syndromes, such as major depression. By reconceptualizing DSM-IV classification of mood and anxiety disorders as a qualitative hierarchical model, he arrived at a classification in which major depressive disorder, GAD, dysthymic disorder, and posttraumatic stress disorder are placed side-by-side under the "distress disorders," or negative-affect disorders, and are distinguished from the "fear disorders," which include other anxiety disorders. Interestingly, antidepressant drugs are equally effective for each of these "distress disorders" but somewhat less so for the "fear disorders," which respond better to behavioral interventions. In summing up this discussion, I find the evidence for grouping major depressive disorder and GAD into a "distress disorders" group (also termed by some as "anxious-misery") to be more compelling than for keeping them separate, as in DSM-IV.

Anxiety Disorders Often Predate Depressive Disorders

Professor Brown pointed out that anxiety disorders typically pursue a chronic course and frequently antedate depression. Depressive disorders typically run an episodic course, with remissions, as demonstrated in many epidemiological studies. However, this increased risk of depression is not necessarily related to anxiety, because psychosocial factors, personality variables, cognitive style, and chance occurrence may play vital roles. The fact that depressive disorders remitted before anxiety in the Islington study may simply reflect the natural course of depression as a remitting and recurring disorder.

In the Islington study and others, GAD occurred more frequently than all other core anxiety disorders, and two-thirds of all mixed conditions involved GAD and depression. Both conditions had equivalent degrees of impairment. Although GAD may precede depression, these findings do not convince me that these are separate disorders.

Conclusion

Professor Brown provides an elegant exposition of his illuminating studies over many years. Despite his findings, and for the reasons I have discussed here, I am not persuaded of the utility of keeping GAD and depression separate in a new classification. Perhaps, more controversially, I do not think that psychosocial studies, as important as these are for other reasons (new knowledge, clinical understanding, and policy), are likely to lead us to a better classification system. I think the key insights are more likely to evolve from genetic, neuroimaging, epidemiological, and pharmacological-interactive (Kennedy et al. 2007) studies and that the insights gained will lead not only to better understanding but to more effective treatments as well!

References

American Psychiatric Association: Diagnostic and Statistical Manual of Mental Disorders, 3rd Edition Revised. Washington, DC, American Psychiatric Association, 1987

American Psychiatric Association: Diagnostic and Statistical Manual of Mental Disorders, 4th Edition. Washington, DC, American Psychiatric Association, 1994

Badgley RF: Prevalence of child sexual abuse. Can J Public Health 80:296–298, 1989

Caspi A, Moffitt TE: Gene-environment interactions in psychiatry: joining forces with neuroscience. Nat Rev Neurosci 7:583–590, 2006

Caspi A, Sugden K, Moffitt TE, et al: Influence of life stress on depression: moderation by a polymorphism in the 5-HTT gene. Science 301:386–389, 2003

Clark LA, Watson D: Distress and fear disorders: an alternative empirically based taxonomy of "mood" and "anxiety" disorders. Br J Psychiatry 189:481–483, 2006

Diaz-Granados N: The epidemiology of depression, in A Literature Review on Depression Among Women. Edited by Diaz-Granados N, Stewart DE. Toronto, Canada, Ontario Women's Health Council, 2006, pp 17–28

Duncan RD, Saunders BE, Kilpatrick DE, et al: Childhood physical assault as a risk factor for PTSD, depression, and substance abuse: findings from a national survey. Am J Orthopsychiatry 66:437–448, 1996

Goldberg DP, Bridges K, Cook D, et al: The influence of social factors on common mental disorders: destabilization and restitution. Br J Psychiatry 156:704–713, 1990

Harkness KL, Wildes JE: Childhood adversity and anxiety versus dysthymia comorbidity in major depression. Psychol Med 32:1239–1249, 2002

Kendler KS, Hettema JM, Butera F, et al: Life event dimensions of loss, humiliation, entrapment, and danger in the prediction of onsets of major depression and generalized anxiety. Arch Gen Psychiatry 60:789–796, 2003a

Kendler KS, Prescott CA, Myers J, et al: The structure of genetic and environmental risk factors for common psychiatric and substance use disorders in men and women. Arch Gen Psychiatry 60:929–937, 2003b

Kennedy SH, Konarski JZ, Segal ZV, et al: Differences in brain glucose metabolism between responders to CBT and venlafaxine in a 16-week randomized controlled trial. Am J Psychiatry 164:778–788, 2007

Kessler RC: Epidemiology of women and depression. J Affect Disord 74:5–13, 2003

Krueger RF, Chentsova-Dutton YE, Markon KE, et al: A cross-cultural study of the structure of comorbidity among common psychopathological syndromes in the general health care setting. J Abnorm Psychol 112:437–447, 2003

MacMillan HL, Fleming JE, Streiner DL, et al: Childhood abuse and lifetime psychopathology in a community sample. Am J Psychiatry 158:1878–1883, 2001

Mineka S, Watson D, Clark LA: Comorbidity of anxiety and unipolar mood disorders. Annu Rev Psychol 49:377–412, 1998

Soares CN, Steiner M, Provst J: Effects of reproductive hormones and SERMS on the central nervous system, in Menopause: A Mental Health Practitioner's Guide. Edited by Stewart DE. Washington, DC, American Psychiatric Press, 2005, pp 33–56

Wang S, Gucciardi E: Lone mothers, in A Literature Review on Depression Among Women. Edited by Diaz-Granados N, Stewart DE. Toronto, Canada, Ontario Women's Health Council, 2006, pp 103–113

Watson D: Rethinking the mood and anxiety disorders: a quantitative hierarchical model for DSM-V. J Abnorm Psychol 114:522–536, 2005

Watson D, Clark LA, Carey G: Positive and negative affectivity and their relation to anxiety and depressive disorders. J Abnorm Psychol 97:346–353, 1988

17

THE RELATIONSHIP BETWEEN GENERALIZED ANXIETY DISORDER AND MAJOR DEPRESSIVE EPISODE

David Goldberg, D.M., FRCPsych

In this conference, our task was to produce new findings from research in order to influence any changes that might be made to DSM-V in the relationship between the two common disorders, generalized anxiety disorder (GAD) and major depressive episode (MDE). Kendler (Chapter 1) opened the conference by reminding us of the changing definitions of GAD since DSM-III (American Psychiatric Association 1980) and asked whether one should give more emphasis to causal relationships, which explore the etiology of each disorder, or to descriptive relationships, based upon clinical characteristics. In the event, both approaches were used. Kendler also asked whether we should continue with clinical categories or whether continuous measures, such as dimensions, were preferable.

There was general agreement that, as defined at present, GAD and MDE are not the same disorder and could not be merged usefully into a single illness. There

---

Based on Goldberg D: "The Relationship Between Generalized Anxiety Disorder and Major Depressive Episode." *Psychological Medicine* 38:1–5, 2008. Copyright © Cambridge University Press 2008. Used with permission.

also was general agreement that the two disorders share a number of features but that there are some differences in the etiological factors associated with each one.

Factors Shared by Both Disorders

SHARED CAUSAL FEATURES

In his comprehensive review of the field, Hettema (Chapter 2) argued that family, twin, and high-risk transmission studies all indicate that GAD and major depressive disorder (MDD) share some, if not most, of their genetic risk factors (Kendler et al. 1992; Roy et al. 1995). Hettema also showed that the genetic risk for each disorder was mainly shared: a genetic correlation of approximately +0.96 was shared about equally between variance related to neuroticism and variance unrelated to it (Hettema et al. 2006). Neuroticism was common to both disorders, and families of each showed an elevated incidence of anxiety disorders. Moffitt et al. (2007a) reported that negative emotionality, which is closely related to neuroticism, also is shared. In this study, parents of children with either disorder were more likely to show low care and high overprotection; both disorders were associated with parental neglect as well as both sexual and physical abuse during childhood. Periods of parental separation also were shared, and both disorders were more likely to show personality disorders—although there were inconsistent differences between them in the kinds of personality disorder. Similar findings were reported from the repeat U.S. National Comorbidity Survey: childhood risk factors for both disorders were almost identical, with all three forms of abuse and parental divorce being more common in the early lives of each (Kessler et al. 2005).

Moffitt et al. (2007a) showed that, in the Dunedin cohort, some of these findings were confirmed, and persons with both disorders were more likely to have a higher rate of anxiety disorders in other family members; have mothers with high rates of internalizing disorders; and have been maltreated relative to normal control subjects. Persons with both disorders had lower self-esteem and higher neuroticism in adolescence than did those with either disorder alone. Richards and Goldberg (Chapter 12) presented data from the Medical Research Council National Survey of Health and Development (Wadsworth et al. 2003), which showed that, in comorbid cases, individuals were more likely to have experienced chronic illness before age 5 years and parental divorce or separation by age 15 years. With such similarities in etiological factors—shown by Hettema and Moffitt and colleagues in this volume—much of the observed comorbidity in adult life is inevitable.

SHARED DESCRIPTIVE FEATURES

Hettema et al. (2006) argued that there is a female preponderance in each disorder, with higher rates of each, in middle age, among persons who are separated and divorced, have low income, and are unemployed. Odds ratios for comorbidity between the two disorders were 6.9, 8.2, and 6.4, respectively, in the Dunedin study, the National Comorbidity Survey, and the National Comorbidity Survey Replication. Kessler (in press) presented data from the National Comorbidity Survey Follow-up and showed that the cumulative age-at-onset curves for the two disorders were identical. Parental divorce was more common for persons with both disorders than for control participants.

Furukawa and colleagues (Chapter 4) presented meta-analyses showing that benzodiazepines, antidepressants, and azapirones were effective in reducing counts of both depressive and anxious symptoms in cases of both GAD and MDE. One possible explanation was that persons with either disorder have some symptoms of both, whereas another explanation was that any psychotropic drug can be shown to be superior to placebo. However, the observations also could be explained if the two diagnostic entities were, in fact, the same.

INTERMEDIATE PHENOTYPES

In Moffitt et al.'s (2007a) Dunedin study, both persons with GAD and those with major depressive disorder were more likely to have experienced conduct problems between the ages of 5–11 years and to have elevated counts of internalizing symptoms by age 18 years. This study also showed that the longer symptoms of either disorder lasted, the more likely comorbidity became; after 3 years all cases that started as anxiety, and almost all cases of depression, had become comorbid.

Factors Specific to Generalized Anxiety and Major Depression

SPECIFIC CAUSAL FACTORS

Depression has an additional familial aggregation component (see Chapters 2, 7, and 11, this volume). In the Dunedin prospective cohort study, it was shown that persons with comorbid disorders had the highest rates of childhood maltreatment, mothers' internalizing symptoms, and neuroticism reported by an informant during childhood relative to persons without either disorder. Study participants with GAD had the next highest rates as well as higher inhibited temperament and informant-rated neuroticism. Participants with GAD also experienced more maltreatment during childhood than did those with MDE. Moffitt and colleagues (see Chapter 11) speculated that GAD is a more severe disorder than depression.

Among working class women in North London, pure depression was more likely to be preceded by loss events; pure anxiety, by danger events; and comorbid anxiety and depression, by a combination of both sorts of events (Finlay-Jones and

Brown 1981). This comorbidity was directly proportional to the number of risk factors. Hettema (Chapter 2) and Brown (Chapter 6) showed that these findings have been partially replicated by others.

INTERMEDIATE PHENOTYPES

Social support has been found to reduce the risk of MDD, overall, in most studies (Paykel 1994; see also Chapter 6), but one population study in Oslo suggested that social support has little association with GAD (Cramer et al. 2005). In contrast to earlier claims, MDE preceded GAD almost as often as GAD preceded MDE (Moffitt et al. 2007b).

SPECIFIC DESCRIPTIVE FEATURES

The most striking differences between anxiety and depression are, undoubtedly, in their underlying biology (see Chapter 3), a conclusion underpinned by much research in depression, but rather less in anxiety disorders. Martin and Nemeroff summarized these differences for us, as discussed in the following sections.

Neuroimaging Studies

Depression activates the dorsal insular cortex and the anterior cingulate cortex, whereas anxiety activates the ventral insular cortex and deactivates the posterior cingulate cortex. The amygdala is overactive at rest in depression but is not overactive at rest in anxiety; however, the amygdala becomes overactive during anxiety provocation. The ventrolateral subregional cortex is associated with both GAD and MDD, and successful treatment with antidepressant drugs influences frontal cortical activity in both disorders.

Neuroendocrine Studies

Major depression is characterized by hypothalamic-pituitary-adrenal axis overactivity (HPA), and hypothalamic-pituitary-thyroid (HPT) axis alterations are common, but the hypothalamic-pituitary-gonadal (HPG) axis is underactive. There have been fewer neuroendocrine studies in GAD, but although there is some evidence of HPG underactivity, activity of both HPA and HPT axes are usually normal. Neuropeptide Y is decreased in depression and may be a neural correlate of resiliency to mood and anxiety disorders, whereas cholecystokinin provokes panic and anxiety but not depression.

Neurotransmitters

The well-documented effectiveness of selective serotonin reuptake inhibitors in treatment of both depression and anxiety disorders likely results from the diverse role of 5-HT in the central nervous system and the manifold effects of these drugs rather than a common underlying pathophysiology of serotonergic circuits. MDE is associated with normal autonomic activation, whereas GAD is associated with autonomic arousal. It was also pointed out that each disorder has characteristic, and distinct, somatic symptoms.

Psychometric Aspects of Anxious and Depressive Symptoms

Negative affect (or neuroticism) is a common characteristic of all internalizing disorders, including the closely related fear disorders. However, MDE is characterized by low positive affect and GAD by normal positive affect (Krueger 1999). Depressive states are associated with memory biases for negative information about the self, whereas anxiety is associated with automatic attentional biases for threatening material (see Chapter 5).

Although the purpose of this conference is to discuss GAD and MDE, several speakers pointed out that "like was not being compared with like." To do this, we would need to compare GAD with depressions that have lasted 6 months, or MDE with anxiety states that have lasted as little as 2 weeks. Kessler came close to the latter situation by considering different decision rules for the duration of GAD and shortening the requirement from 6 months to 1 month (Kessler et al. 2005). This had the effect of approximately doubling the lifetime prevalence (from 6.1 at 6 months to 12.7 at 1 month). For GAD, 1-month episodes were comparable with 6-month episodes in terms of onset, persistence, impairment during episodes, comorbidity, parental GAD, and sociodemographic correlates.

When the relationship between depressive and anxious symptoms is considered, we realize that the two sets of symptoms are linked inextricably. Two of the research interviews (Revised Clinical Interview Schedule and Present State Examination) used in studies presented by speakers from the United Kingdom employed the same time frame for diagnoses—the past month. When this was done, the two sets of symptoms were even more highly correlated than the two diagnoses of GAD and MDE. Jacob and colleagues (Chapter 10) quoted work in six developing countries using the Clinical Interview Schedule and showed that a single-factor solution provided almost as good a fit as a two-factor (anxiety and depression) solution. These high correlations between the symptom dimensions—as opposed to the diagnoses of GAD and MDE—occur because many patients with "anxiety only" also have subsyndromal levels of depression, and vice versa.

It is clear that that long-term vulnerability factors—both genetic and environmental—are common to both disorders, but because GAD is defined to last much longer than MDE, it may well need more long-term vulnerability factors. This is consistent with findings from the longitudinal studies quoted. If we consider

MDE, one can argue that sometimes severe-loss events will be followed by brief episodes of depression. Kessler's (see Chapter 7, this volume) finding of a greater tendency for participants with MDE to be "open to experience" would fit with the observation that only a minority of those who have experienced a severe-loss event go on to develop MDE. The attentional biases associated with each disorder fit well with the partial association with life events associated with threat and loss.

Categories or Dimensions?

Dimensions allow consideration of the severity of a disorder, which often has treatment implications. The provision of three degrees of severity of depression by both ICD-10 (World Health Organization 1992) and DSM-IV (American Psychiatric Association 1994) has been useful in that optimal treatments for each are not the same (National Institute for Clinical Excellence 2004). These are pseudodimensional categories and argue for severity measures—thus dimensional measures—to be available when differences in clinical management are indicated.

Conclusion

Those conference participants who considered the two disorders to be "distally related" were influenced by the biological differences described here, by the extra aggregation of depression in families of patients with MDE, and by the (rather small) differences in causal factors involved in the two disorders. For these people, it followed that the two disorders should remain in separate categories.

Persuasive as the biological data undoubtedly are, they are hardly conclusive. They have been arrived at by considering extreme ends of a continuous distribution, and they fail to take into account the most common type of distressed patient seen in general medical practice. Although these conferees were agreed that depression and anxiety are not the same disorder, others thought that the two disorders were "closely related." Hettema (see Chapter 2, this volume) reminded us that panic disorder shares comorbidity with MDE, and Angst and colleagues (see commentary on Chapter 2) reminded us that, in the Zurich study, GAD was more closely related to bipolar disorder than to MDE. In Krueger's (1999) analysis of data from the National Comorbidity study, although the tetrachoric correlations were highest between MDE and GAD, correlations between the other internalizing disorders were almost as high. However close or distant the disorders are, the causes of each are almost the same, and the symptom dimensions themselves are closely related.

References

American Psychiatric Association: Diagnostic and Statistical Manual of Mental Disorders, 3rd Edition. Washington, DC, American Psychiatric Association, 1980

American Psychiatric Association: Diagnostic and Statistical Manual of Mental Disorders, 4th Edition. Washington, DC, American Psychiatric Association, 1994

Cramer V, Torgersen S, Kringlen E: Quality of life and anxiety disorders: a population study. J Nerv Ment Dis 193:196–202, 2005

Finlay-Jones R, Brown GW: Types of stressful life event and the onset of anxiety and depressive disorders. Psychol Med 11:803–815, 1981

Hettema JM, Neale MC, Myers JM, et al: A population-based twin study of the relationship between neuroticism and internalizing disorders. Am J Psychiatry 163:857–864, 2006

Kendler KS, Neale MC, Kessler RC, et al: Major depression and generalized anxiety disorder: same genes, (partly) different environments? Arch Gen Psychiatry 49:716–722, 1992

Kessler RC, Brandenburg N, Lane M, et al: Rethinking the duration requirement for generalized anxiety disorder: evidence from the National Comorbidity Survey Replication. Psychol Med 35:1073–1082, 2005

Krueger RF: The structure of common mental disorders. Arch Gen Psychiatry 56:921–926, 1999

Moffitt TE, Caspi A, Harrington H, et al: Generalized anxiety disorder and depression: childhood risk factors in a birth cohort followed to age 32. Psychol Med 37:441–452, 2007a

Moffitt TE, Harrington H, Caspi A, et al: Depression and generalized anxiety disorder: cumulative and sequential comorbidity in a birth cohort followed prospectively to age 32 years. Arch Gen Psychiatry 64:651–660, 2007b

National Institute for Clinical Excellence: Depression: Management of Depression in Primary and Secondary Care. London, England, British Psychological Society, Royal College of Psychiatrists, and Gaskell, 2004. Available at http://www.nice.org.uk/nicemedia/pdf/CG23fullguideline.pdf. Accessed July 31, 2009.

Paykel ES: Life events, social support and depression. Acta Psychiatr Scand Suppl 377:50–58, 1994

Roy MA, Neale MC, Pedersen NL, et al: A twin study of generalized anxiety disorder and major depression. Psychol Med 25:1037–1049, 1995

Wadsworth ME, Butterworth SL, Hardy RJ, et al: The life course prospective design: an example of benefits and problems associated with study longevity. Soc Sci Med 57:2193–2205, 2003

World Health Organization: International Statistical Classification of Diseases and Related Health Problems, 10th Revision. Geneva, World Health Organization, 1992

INDEX

Page numbers printed in **boldface** *type refer to tables or figures.*

Adinazolam, 60
ADIS-IV-L, 132, 136
Adjustment disorders, 288–292, 294
Adolescence. *See also* Childhood experiences
　internalizing disorder and, 248
　personality trait measures and, 219
　stressful life events as predictor of adult GAD/MDD in, 24
Adrenocorticotropic hormone (ACTH), 54
Adult adversity, 308–309
Adversity. *See* Adult adversity; Childhood experiences
Affective spectrum disorders, 172–176
Age. *See* Adolescence; Age at onset; Childhood experiences; Elderly
Age at onset
　National Comorbidity Survey follow-up study and, 146, **147**, 148–152
　of phobic disorders, 289
AIC (Akaike information criterion), 183, 194
Alprazolam, 73, **81**, **83**, **84**
Amygdala, and neuroanatomy of GAD/MDD, **49**, 50–51, 291, 316, 358
Anger, and irritability, 258
Animal phobias, 5, 290, 323–324
Antecedent validators, and nosologic relationship between GAD and MDD, 16–28, 32, **33**, 287. *See also* Validators

Antidepressants. *See also* Selective serotonin reuptake inhibitors; Tricyclic antidepressants
　CRF activation and stress-induced behavioral responses to, 55
　neuroanatomy of GAD/MDD and, 46–47, 50
　neuropeptide Y and, 57
　study of differences in effectiveness of for GAD/MDD, 72–99
Antisocial personality disorder, 27
Anxiety. *See also* Anxiety disorders; Anxiety reaction
　amygdala and neuroanatomy of, 50
　cultural constructs of depression and, 213
　early adverse exposures and differentiation of risk for depression and, 241–253
　GAD and subsyndromal forms of, 93, 107
　problems in DSM-IV classification of, 288–292
　psychometrics and relationship between depression and, 113–117, 359–360
　psychosocial factors in etiology of, 303–325, 333–345, 347–353
　self-report scales for symptoms of, 110

Anxiety disorders. *See also* Anxiety; Anxious-misery disorders; Generalized anxiety disorder; Posttraumatic stress disorder
  comorbidity with MDD and other, 30, 31
  depressive disorders predated by, 352–353
  developmental pathways for, 289
  family studies of GAD and, 17, 18–19, 20
  genetic relationships between MDD, GAD, and other, 20–21
  muscle tension and, 63
  structural model for reclassification of, 344
Anxiety reaction, grief as, 337
Anxiolytics, and cholecystokinin receptor–selective antagonists, 58. *See also* Buspirone
Anxious-misery disorders, 113, 114, 115
Apomorphine, 62
Assessment, of GAD/MDD. *See also* Diagnosis
  confirmatory factor analysis and, 192, 194
  study of common and reciprocal causes, 180
Asymmetry, in diagnostic systems, 10
Attenuation pattern, in psychiatric epidemiology, 128
Australian Twin Register, 2, 26
Autonomic arousal, and relationship between GAD and mood disorders, 134–135
Azapirones, study of effectiveness of for GAD/MDD, 72–99

Behavioral activation/positive affect (BA/P), 112–113, 135
Behavioral activation system (BAS) and behavioral inhibition system (BIS), 112
Benzodiazepines
  cholecystokinin and, 58
  differences in effectiveness for GAD/MDD, 72–99, 107, 290
  treatment of anxiety disorders and, 60
Bereavement studies, 337, 340
BIC (Bayesian information criterion), 183
Biology, and history of classification systems, 8. *See also* Genetics; Neurobiology
Bipolar II disorder, 42
Bipolar disorder
  classification of emotional disorders and, 292, **293**
  DSM criteria and association of GAD with, 42, **43**
Blood-injury phobia, 5, 290
Borderline personality disorder, 27
Box score, and validators, 3
British 1946 birth cohort study, 241–253, 272–274, **279**, 282, 356
"Buffering theory of social support," 25
Bupropion, **82, 83**
Buspirone, 78, **81, 84, 85**. *See also* Anxiolytics

Canada
  childhood adversity and rates of adult anxiety or depression in, 307
  gender and associations between childhood abuse and adult anxiety or depression in, 348
  Life Events Scale and study of GAD/MDD in, 24
Canadian Institutes of Health Research, 350
CATEGO algorithm, 246, 273. *See also* ICD-Catego system
Categorical viewpoint, and relationship between GAD and MDD, 11, 113–114, 287, 360
Causal factors
  conceptual issues in classification and, 9–10
  relationship between GAD and MDD and, 179–189, 356, 357–358
CCDANCTR-Studies database, 77, 88

Center for Anxiety and Related Disorders, 131
Cerebrospinal fluid (CSF), 54
Chance comorbidity, 309, **310**
Child abuse. *See also* Childhood experiences
  effects of on risk for adult GAD/MDD, 23, **33**
  problem with definition of, 348
  as risk factor for adult depression/anxiety in London study, 306
  as risk factor for GAD/MDD in Dunedin birth cohort study, 223, **228**
  as risk factor for GAD/MDD in National Comorbidity Survey follow-up study, 143–144, 152, **154, 156, 162**
Childhood experiences. *See also* Child abuse; Risk factors
  adverse exposures and differentiation of risk for depression and anxiety, 241–253
  association of adverse with adult depression and anxiety, 306–307
  comorbidity in London study and, 320–323
  GAD as predictor of MDD and, 279–281
  nosologic relationship between GAD and MDD, 21–23
  risk factors for GAD/MDD in Dunedin birth cohort study and, 217–235, 334–337
  risk factors for GAD/MDD in National Comorbidity Survey follow-up study and, 153, **154–157**, 158, 161, **162, 163**, 165
Childhood Experiences of Care and Abuse (CECA), 304, 306, 348
Chile, and cross-cultural study of confirmatory factor analysis, **193, 196, 202, 204–207**, 208
Cholecystokinin, 53, 58

Christchurch Health and Development Study (CHDS), 180, 323
Chronic illness, as childhood factor in later development of depression and anxiety, **244**, 247, **250, 251**, 252
Cingulate cortex, 47, **49**, 50, 51
Citalopram, **82, 83**
Cladistics, and biological classification, 8
Classification. *See also* Categorical viewpoint; Dimensional approach; Generalized anxiety disorders; Integrated approach; Major depressive disorder
  categorical vs. dimensional approaches to, 360
  conceptual issues in, 4–10
  DSM rules for assigning disorders in, 7–8
  emotional disorders in primary care settings and, 285–298
  empirical issues in, 3–4
  of GAD and MDD as subtypes, 262, 264, 265
  nosologic history of GAD/MDD and, 1–2
  philosophical issues in, 4, 286–287
  review of issues in nosologic relationship between GAD and MDD, 15–34, 41–44
  risk factors and, 264–265
  structural model for, **344**
  theoretical issues in current, 257–258, 260, 262
Clinical Interview Schedule—Revised (CISR), 192, 194, 208, 211
Clinical research interviews, and relationships between anxiety and depression, 113, 359
Clinical sampling, vs. epidemiological sampling as conceptual issue in classification, 8–9
Clonidine, 62
Cochrane Collaboration Depression, Anxiety, and Neurosis Group (CCDAN), 74

Cognitive ability, and risk factors for GAD/MDD, **245**
Cognitive-behavioral therapy, and brain activity in patients with MDD, 46
Common causes model, 179, 189
Comorbidity. *See also* National Comorbidity Survey/Replication
  cumulative and sequential in Dunedin birth cohort study, 274
  dimensional approach to diagnostic categories and, 118
  of DSM-IV anxiety and mood disorders, 133
  London study and, 307–311, 316–318, 320–323
  nosologic relationship between GAD and MDD, 41–42
  of personality disorders with GAD/MDD, 28
  predictive validators and lifetime rates of for GAD/MDD, 30, **31**, **33**
  prevalence of for GAD/MDD, 146, 148, 288, 307–311, 316–318, 320–323
  psychosocial factors and, 307–311, 316–318, 320–323, 349–352
  recurrence of GAD/MDD as synonymous with, 263
  risk factors for GAD/MDD in Dunedin birth cohort study and, 232
  risk factors for GAD/MDD in London study and, **336**, **338–339**
  three-generation study and pattern of, 281
Composite Diagnostic Interview, 114
Composite International Diagnostic Interview (CIDI), 142
Conceptual issues, and relationship between GAD and MDD, 4–10
Concurrent comorbidity, 307
Concurrent validators, and nosologic relationship between GAD and MDD, 28, **29**, 32, **33**, 287. *See also* Validators

Conduct problems, and childhood risk factors for GAD and MDD, 224, **229**, 231
Confirmatory factor analysis (CFA)
  cross-cultural study of, 191–209, 211–215
  psychometric findings and, 134
Continuum viewpoint, on relationship between GAD and MDD, 11, 287
Control, lack of as psychosocial factor in anxiety and depression, 315
Convergent validity, of treatment responses for GAD/MDD, 98
Co-occurring anxiety and major depression, 118
Cortical-limbic neural networks, and neuroanatomy of GAD/MDD, 51
Corticotropin-releasing factor (CRF), **52**, 54, 55, 57
Cortisol, and neuroendocrinology of GAD/MDD, 54
Critical approach, to cross-cultural psychiatry, 212–213
Cross-cultural studies. *See also* Culture
  of confirmatory factor analysis, 191–209, 211–215
  two-factor model of internalizing and externalizing syndromes and, 352
Cross-lagged model, for GAD/MDD symptoms, 181, 183, **185**, **186–187**, 188
Culture. *See also* Cross-cultural studies
  constructs of depression and anxiety in, 213
  disproportionate impact of adversity on women and, 350
  somatic symptoms in primary care settings and, 208–209, 214
Cyclothymia, **293**

Danger, and psychosocial factors in anxiety and depression, 311–313, **315**
Data analysis, for study of effectiveness of psychotropics for GAD and MDD, 76

Death, of parent as risk factor for GAD/MDD, 144, 153, **154, 156, 162,** 166, 247, **250, 251**
Demographics, and concurrent validators for relationship between GAD and MDD, 28, **29, 33**
Depression. *See also* Major depressive disorder; Postpartum depression
 anxiety disorders predating, 352–353
 cultural constructs of anxiety and, 213
 diagnosis and treatment of in primary care settings in Russia, **173, 174, 175**
 early adverse exposures and differentiation of risk for anxiety and, 241–253
 hypothyroidism as cause of refractory, 57
 MDD and subsyndromal forms of, 93, 107
 problems in DSM-IV classification of, 288–292
 psychometrics and relationship between anxiety and, 111–117
 psychosocial factors in etiology of, 303–325, 333–345, 347–353
 self-report scales for symptoms of, 110
 symptoms of in children, 224
Descriptive features, and relationship between GAD and MDD, 356–357, 358–359
Despair phase, and bereavement studies, 337
Diagnosis. *See also* Assessment; Diagnostic validity
 distinguishability of GAD from mood disorders and, 132–133
 emotions, feelings, and moods in, 260
 psychometrics and, 113–114, 115–117, 118–119, 126–127
 relationship between treatment and, 71–72
Diagnostic Interview Schedule, 113, 220
Diagnostic Interview Schedule for Children—Child Version, 222

Diagnostic validity, for GAD/MDD, 98
Diary methods, for persons at risk of GAD and MDD, 129
Diazepam, **79, 84**
Dimensional approach, to diagnostic categories
 categorical approach vs., 360
 DSM-IV and, 136–137
 psychometrics and, 118–119, 126–127
Disability. *See also* Learning disability
 concurrent validators for relationship between GAD and MDD, 28, **33**
 as marker of illness severity for MDD and anxiety disorders, 290
Discrete-time-survival analysis, 145
Disorder, timing parameters in use of term, 258, 264
Distress disorders, and subclassification of GAD and mood disorders, 136, 265, 266
Divorce, and risk factors for GAD/MDD, 144, **154, 156, 162,** 247, **250, 251**
Dorsal prefrontal cortex (dPFC), 47, **48,** 51
DSM-III
 association of GAD with bipolar disorder and, 42, **43**
 latent-trait analysis and, 116, **117**
 nosologic history of GAD and, 1
 rules for assigning disorders to categories of, 7
 separation of GAD and panic in, 140
 time criterion for GAD diagnosis in, 221
DSM-III-R
 association of GAD with bipolar disorder and, 42, **43**
 British 1946 birth cohort study and, 246
 diagnostic reliability of GAD and, 132
 duration requirement for GAD in, 140
 nosologic history of GAD/MDD and, 2

DSM-IV
   associated psychophysiological symptoms of GAD in, 140
   association of GAD with bipolar disorder and, 42, **43**
   debate on retention of GAD as diagnostic category in, 131–132
   diagnostic relationship between GAD and mood disorders, 136
   diagnostic reliability of GAD and, 132
   general problems in classification of anxiety, depression, and adjustment in, 288–292
   Hamilton Rating Scale for Depression and, 97
   multiple cutpoints and implied continuum for GAD/MDD in, 126–127
   nosologic history of GAD and, 2
   primary care settings and, 286, 297
   study of effectiveness of psychotropics for GAD/MDD and, 72
   time criterion for GAD diagnosis and, 221
DSM-IV-TR, heterogeneity of groupings for closely related disorders in, 5
DSM-V. *See* Classification; Generalized anxiety disorder; Major depressive disorder
Duloxetine, **82**
Dunedin Multidisciplinary Health and Development Study, 114, 219, 220–35, 242, 263–264, 265–266, 272–274, **279**, 334–337, 356, 357
Dutch Nemesis Study, 114
Dysthymia
   classification of, **293**, 295
   comorbidity of with GAD, 30, **31**

Early Developmental Stages of Psychopathology Study, 21–22
Education, and risk factors for GAD/MDD, **245**
Elderly, stressful life events and risk of depression/anxiety in, 24

Emotions. *See also* Negative affect; Positive affect
   classification of mood disorders and, 265, **267**
   operational definitions for and classification of GAD/MDD, 257, 262
   symptoms of GAD/MDD and, 260, **261**
Empirical issues, and review of interrelationship between GAD and MDD, 3–4
Epidemiological sampling, vs. clinical sampling as conceptual issue in classification, 8–9
Epidemiology. *See* Etiology; Prevalence
Episode, timing parameters in use of term, 258, 264
Escitalopram, 78, **79**, **82**
Essentialism, as philosophical issue in classification, 11, 286–287
Estrogen, and neuroendocrinology of mood and anxiety, 56
Ethiopia, and cross-cultural study of confirmatory factor analysis, **193**, 197, 201, **202**, **204–207**, 208
Etiology
   as approach to nosologic classification, 7–8
   environmental factors in GAD/MDD and, 289
   psychosocial factors in depressive and anxiety disorders, 303–325
Exhaustion response, to chronic anxiety in secondary depression, 164
Exploratory factor analysis, 192, 195
Externalizing factors. *See also* Internalizing factors and disorders
   genetic relationships among MDD, GAD, and other anxiety disorders, 20, 21
   risk factors for GAD/MDD and, **251**
Extroversion, and risk factors for GAD/MDD, 144, 153, **155**, **157**, **162**, 166

Factor analysis, and relationships between categorical diagnoses of anxiety and depression, 113–114, 120, 289
Familial aggregation, and genetics of relationship between GAD and MDD, 16–21, **33**
Family history. *See also* Parents and parenting
  risk factors for GAD/MDD in British 1946 birth cohort study and, **243–244**
  risk factors for GAD/MDD in Dunedin birth cohort study and, 222–223, **227**, **228**, 231, 232–233, 234
  risk factors for GAD/MDD in National Comorbidity Survey follow-up study and, 144, 152, 153, **154–157**, 158, 161, **162**, **163**, 165
Family History Research Diagnostic Criteria (FHRDC), 144
Family History Screen, 222
Family studies, of compared risk of GAD/MDD in relatives of probands, 17, **18–19**, 20
Fear disorders
  psychometrics and relationships between anxiety and depression, 113–114, 115
  subclassification of OCD and social phobia as, 135, 136
Feighner criteria, 2
Fixed-effect analyses, 76
Fluoxetine, **82**, **83**
Frontal cortex, differential disruption of in GAD/MDD, 46–47
Funnel-plot analyses, 76, 93
"Future of Psychiatric Diagnosis: Refining the Research Agenda for Depression and Generalized Anxiety Disorders, The" (conference), 1

GABA (γ-aminobutyric acid), **59**, 60
Galanin, **53**, 58

Gender. *See* Women
Generalized anxiety disorder (GAD). *See also* Anxiety disorders; Classification; Comorbidity; Diagnosis; Neurobiology; Prevalence; Psychometrics; Psychopharmacology; Risk factors; Symptoms
  causes of and reciprocal relationship between MDD and, 179–189
  conceptual issues in review of relationship between MDD and, 4–10
  debate on retention of as diagnostic category in DSM-IV, 131–132
  empirical issues in review of relationship between MDD and, 3–4
  nosologic history of, 1–2
  philosophical issues in review of relationship between MDD and, 11
  psychosocial factors and relationship between MDD and, 342–345
  review of issues in nosologic relationship between MDD and, 15–34, 41–44
  risk predictors and diagnostic relationship between MDD and, 334–337
  study of relationship with MDD over time, 171–176
  subsyndromal anxiety and, 93, 107
  summary of conclusions on relationship between MDD and, 355–360
  theoretical issues in current classification of, 257–258, 260, 262
Genetics. *See also* Family studies; Twin studies
  familial aggregation and relationship between GAD and MDD, 16–21, 27–28, **33**
  neuroticism and correlation between GAD and MDD, 26
  specific phobia and, 290, 297

Gepirone, 84, 85
Germany, and study of relationship between anxiety and depression, 318
Global Assessment of Functioning scale, 112, 119
Glucocorticoid, 54
Goodness of Fit Index (GFI), 194
Group Ability Test, 247–248

Hamilton Rating Scale for Anxiety (HAM-A), 72, 73, 74, 75, 76, 77, **86–87**, 88, **91–92**, 93, **96**, 97, 98, 107, 110, 172
Hamilton Rating Scale for Depression (HAM-D), 72, 73, 75, 76, 77, 88, **89**, 93, **94–95, 96** 97, 98, 107, 110, 172
Harvard/Brown Anxiety Research Project (HARP), 27, 166
Hopkins Symptom Scale, 340
Hospital Anxiety and Depression Scale, 77
Hydroxyzine, **81**
Hypomania, 42
Hypothalamic-pituitary-adrenal (HPA) axis, 51, **52–53**, 54–55, 358
Hypothalamic-pituitary-gonadal (HPG) axis, 51, **52–53**, 55–56, 358
Hypothalamic-pituitary-thyroid (HPT) axis, 51, **52–53**, 56–57, 358
Hypothyroidism, 56–57

ICD-8, 247
ICD-9, 4
ICD-10, 174, 194, 211, 248, 297
ICD-Catego system, 116, **117**. *See also* CATEGO system
India, and cross-cultural study of confirmatory factor analysis, **193, 197, 198**, 201, **202, 204–207**, 208
Inflammatory state, MDD as, 63
Inhibition, and risk factors for GAD/MDD, 223, **229**, 231
Insular cortex, 47, **48**
Integrated approach, to classification, 213–214, 285–298

Integrative hierarchical model, of relationship between GAD and MDD, 115
Intermediate phenotypes, of GAD and MDD, 357
Internalizing factors and disorders. *See also* Externalizing factors
 genetic relationships between MDD, GAD, and other anxiety disorders, 20–21, 290
 risk factors for GAD/MDD and, 224, **228, 229**, 231, 248, **250**
International Classification for Primary Care, 286
"Interpersonal" psychosocial factors, 304
Iowa Depression and Anxiety Scales, 110
Ipsapirone, 61
Ireland, and anthropological study of Gaelic-speaking community, 320
Irritability, as symptom of GAD/MDD, 257, 258, 262
I-squared statistics, 76

Joint onset, of anxiety/depression, 317, 319–320

Kiddie-Schedule for Affective Disorders and Schizophrenia, 275

Labile states, and psychometrics, 111–113, 128–129
Last observation carried forward (LOCF), 76
Latent class analysis, and psychometrics, 118
Latent-trait analyses, and psychometrics, 115–117, 120, 125–126
Learning disability, as risk factor for anxiety/depression, 247–248, 249, **250**, 251, 252
Life events. *See also* Childhood experiences; Stress
 comorbidity in London study and, 321
 etiology of GAD/MDD and, 289, 303, 335

role of in onset and course of anxiety/
depression, 311–318
role of in risk of GAD/MDD, 24–25,
33
Life Events and Difficulties Schedule
(LEDS), 303, 311, 334
Life Events Scale, 24
Life History Calendar, 233
Limbic region, and neuroanatomy of
GAD/MDD, 47, 50–51
London studies, 305–323, 357–358
Longitudinal predictions, and three-
generation high risk study, 274–282
Lorazepam, **80, 83**
Loss, definition of, 311–313. *See also*
Bereavement studies; Death; Parents
and parenting

Major depressive disorder (MDD). *See also*
Classification; Comorbidity;
Diagnosis; Neurobiology; Prevalence;
Psychometrics; Psychopharmacology;
Risk factors; Symptoms
  causes of and reciprocal relationship
  between GAD and, 179–189
  conceptual issues in review of relation-
  ship between GAD and, 4–10
  empirical issues in review of
  relationship between GAD and,
  3–4
  nosologic history of, 2
  philosophical issues in review of
  relationship between GAD and,
  11
  psychosocial factors and relationship
  between GAD and, 342–345
  review of issues in nosologic
  relationship between GAD and,
  15–34, 41–44
  risk predictors and diagnostic
  relationship between GAD and,
  334–3347
  study of relationship with GAD over
  time, 171–176

subsyndromal depression and, 93,
107
summary of conclusions on
relationship between GAD and,
355–360
theoretical issues in current
classification of, 257–258, 260,
262
Malaise Inventory, 223
Maternal internalizing symptoms, 223,
228
Maudsley Personality Inventory, 247
Medial prefrontal cortex (mPFC), 46, **48**,
51
Medical Research Council Birth Cohort
Study. *See* British 1946 birth cohort
study
Medicine, approaches to classification in
other branches of, 9. *See also* Chronic
illness; Primary care settings
Memories, of childhood trauma, 316
Mental health service use, and risk factors
for GAD/MDD, 222, **227**
Minnesota Multiphasic Personality
Inventory, 144
Mixed anxiety-depression, 118
Montgomery-Åsberg Depression Rating
Scale (MADRS), 73, 75, 77
Mood, and basic emotions, 260, **261**
Mood disorders
  amygdala and neuroanatomy of,
  50
  diagnostic findings on relationship
  between GAD and, 132–135
  emotions and classification of, 266,
  267
  family studies of GAD and, 17,
  18–19, 20
  structural model for reclassification of,
  344
Multidimensional Personality
Questionnaire, 224
Multivariate analyses, of self-report
personality scales, 110–111

National Comorbidity Survey/Replication (NCS/NCS-R), 20, 27, **29**, 30, 42, 113, 114, 139–167, 219, 221, 320, 324, 356, 357

National Epidemiologic Survey on Alcohol and Related Conditions (NESARC), 27, 28, **29**

National Hospital Discharge Survey, 118

National Survey of Health and Development (NSHD), 241, 242–245, 253, 264

Negative affect. *See also* Emotions
diagnostic findings on relationship between GAD and mood disorders, 134
psychometrics and relationship between anxiety and depression, 110–111, 114, 115, 119–120
risk factors for GAD/MDD in Dunedin birth cohort study and, **230**

NEO Personality Inventory—Revised, 26

Netherlands. *See also* Dutch Nemesis Study
study of childhood and adolescent precursors of adult anxiety and depression, 318
use of classifications systems in primary care settings, 286

Neurobiology
descriptive features of anxiety and depression, 358–359
differences in responses to psychotropics in GAD/MDD, 105–108
functional neuroanatomy of GAD/MDD, 46–51
neuroendocrinology of GAD/MDD and, 51–59
neurotransmitters and influences on GAD/MDD, 58–62
somatic symptoms of GAD/MDD and, 63
of specific phobias, 291
summary of conclusions and implications for research, 63–64

Neuroendocrinology, of GAD/MDD, 51–57, 358

Neuroimaging studies, 46–51, 358

Neuropeptides, influence of on mood and anxiety, **52**, 57–58

Neuropeptide Y, **52**, 57, 358

Neuroticism
antecedent validators for GAD/MDD and, 25–26
classification of GAD and, 296–297
psychometrics of depression and, 111–113
risk factors for GAD/MDD and, 144, 152–153, **155**, **157**, 161, **162**, 247, 248, 249, **250**, **251**

Neuroticism/behavioral inhibition (N/BI), 112, 113, 120, 135

Neurotransmitters, influence of on GAD and MDD, 58–62, 358–359

New York, and prevalence rates, 234

New Zealand, and longitudinal studies of relationship between GAD and MDD, 179–189, 220–235, 307. *See also* Dunedin Multidisciplinary Health and Development Study

N-methyl-D-aspartate (NMDA), 60

Nominalism, as philosophical issue in classification, 11, 286–287

Norepinephrine, **59**, 61, 62

North Carolina, and prevalence rates for GAD/MDD, 234

Nosology. *See* Classification

Obsessive-compulsive disorder (OCD)
amygdala and neuroanatomy of, 50
association between bipolar and major depressive disorders, 43
classification of, 292
fear disorders and, 135

Openness to experience, and personality factors in GAD/MDD, 153, **155**, **157** 158, 161, **162**, 166, 360

Orbital frontal cortex (OFC), 46, **48**, 51

Oregon, and prevalence rates for GAD/MDD, 234

Index 373

Outcomes
  in joint onset of anxiety and depression, 319–320
  measures of for study of effectiveness of psychotropics for GAD/MDD, 73

Panic disorder
  association between MDD and bipolar disorder, **43**
  childhood adversity in London study and, **306, 308**
  comorbidity of with GAD and MDD, 30, **31**, 133, 288
  family studies of GAD/MDD and, 17, **18**
  genetic relationship among GAD, MDD, and, 21, 289, 290
  neuroanatomy and, 46
  proposal for classification of emotional disorders and, **293**, 297
Paralimbic region, and neuroanatomy of GAD/MDD, 47, 50–51
Parent Bonding Instrument, 22
Parent-Child Conflict Tactics Scales, 143
Parents and parenting. *See also* Death; Divorce; Family history
  anxiety/depression in London study and, 317–318
  childhood environment and validator findings for GAD/MDD, 21–23, **33**
  loss of as risk factor for adult GAD/MDD, 223, **229**
  prevalence of anxiety and depression in women and, 350
  risk factors for GAD/MDD in British 1946 birth cohort study and, **244–245**, 247, 249, **250, 251**
Pakistan, and cross-cultural study of confirmatory factor analysis, **193, 198**, 201, **202**, 204–**207**, 208
Paroxetine, 46, **80**, 82
Path analysis, 280
Patient history, and DSM-IV classification of MDD, 295

Persistence, of GAD/MDD in National Comorbidity Survey follow-up study, 158–159, **160**, 161, **162, 163**, 166
Personality
  antecedent validators for GAD/MDD and, 25–28, **33**
  multivariate analyses of self-report scales of, 110–111
  risk factors for GAD/MDD in Dunedin birth cohort study and, 219, 224, 231, 234
  risk factors for GAD/MDD in National Comorbidity Survey follow-up study and, 144, 152–153, **154–157**, 158, **162, 163**, 165
Personality disorders, relationship between MDD and, 27, **33**
Phenotypic architecture, of emotional disorders, 290
Philosophical issues, in review of relationship between GAD and MDD, 11
Phobias. *See also* Simple phobias; Situational phobias; Social phobia; Specific phobias
  association between bipolar disorder and MDD, **43**
  depression in London study and, 323–324
  developmental pathways for, 289
Pintner Aspects of Personality Inventory, 248
Positive affect. *See also* Emotions
  diagnostic findings on relationship between GAD and mood disorders, 134
  psychometrics of anxiety/depression and, 111, 115, 119, 120
  risk factors for GAD/MDD in Dunedin birth cohort study and, **230**
Positive and Negative Affect Schedule (PANAS), 112, 113
Postpartum depression, 56

Posttraumatic stress disorder (PTSD)
childhood sexual abuse and, 23
classification of, 292, **293**
frontal cortex and, 46
genetic correlation between GAD, panic disorder, and, 21
neuroendocrinology of, 55, 57
Predictive validators, and nosologic relationship between GAD and MDD, 30, **31**, 32, **33**, 287. *See also* Validators
Present State Examination (PSE), 113, 116, 117, 241, 242, **243–245**, 246, 247, 249, **251**, 252, 253, 272, 291, 305, 348, 359
Prevalence, of GAD and MDD
of affective spectrum disorders in primary care settings, 172–176
Dunedin birth cohort study and, 234
London study and, 305
in longitudinal studies, 276, **279**
National Comorbidity Survey follow-up study and, 145–146
Primary care settings
classification of emotional disorders and, 285–298
differences between patients of psychiatric hospitals and, 208
prevalence of affective spectrum disorders in, 172–176
Principal-component analysis, and cross-cultural study of GAD/MDD, 195, **196–200**
Probit models, 280
Prognostic classification, of emotional disorders, 295–296
Proportional-hazards models, 280
Protest phase, and bereavement studies, 337
Proximal factors, in depressive and anxiety disorders, 303
Psychological dimensions, and psychometrics of anxiety/depression, 114–115

Psychometrics
of anxious and depressive symptoms, 113–117, 359–360
clinical diagnoses with latent-trait analyses and, 115–117, 125–126
clinical research interviews and relationship between anxiety and depression, 113
diagnostic findings on relationship of GAD to mood disorders, 133–135
dimensional approach to diagnostic categories and, 118–119, 126–127
latent class analysis and, 118
linkages between psychological dimensions and clinical categories, 114–115
multivariate analyses of self-report personality scales and, 110–111
relationships between categorical diagnoses found by factor analysis, 113–114
self-report scales for symptoms of anxiety/depression and, 110, 127–128
stable traits and labile states in depression and, 111–113, 128–129
statistical analysis and, 129
Psychopharmacology. *See also* Antidepressants; Anxiolytics; Benzodiazepines; Selective serotonin reuptake inhibitors; Treatment
risk factors for GAD/MDD and, **227**
study of effectiveness of psychotropics for GAD/MDD, 72–99, 105–108
Psychosocial factors, in etiology of depressive and anxiety disorders, 303–325, 333–345, 347–353. *See also* Social support
Public health, and integrated approach to psychiatric classification, 214

Sleep disorders, 5
Sleep polysomnography, 63
Social phobia. *See also* Phobias
  childhood adversity in London study
    and, 306, 308
  classification of emotional disorders
    and, 293, 297
  comorbidity of with GAD/MDD, 31,
    133
  differential relationship between mood
    disorders and, 134, 290
  negative and positive affect in, 115
  primary care system in Russia and,
    174
Social support. *See also* Psychosocial
  factors
  reduction in depression or anxiety and,
    308, 349, 358
  risk factors for GAD/MDD and, 25,
    32, 33
Socioeconomic status, during childhood
  as risk factor for GAD/MDD, 223,
    228, 231, 243
Somatic symptoms
  cultural factors for psychiatric
    problems in primary care settings
    and, 208–209, 214
  diagnosis of depression in primary care
    settings in Russia and, 174, 175
  integrated approach to psychiatric
    classification and, 213–214
  neurobiology of GAD/MDD and, 63
Specificity, of stressful life events as
  predictor of GAD/MDD, 24–25, 32
Specific phobias, 31, 133, 289, 290–291,
  297. *See also* Phobias
Stable traits, and psychometrics, 111–113,
  128–129
Standardized mean difference (SMD), 76
STAR*D study, 56, 340–342
Statistical analysis
British 1946 birth cohort study and,
  248
Dunedin birth cohort study and,
  224–225

Structured Clinical Interview for
  DSM-III, 337, 340
Structured Clinical Interview for
  DSM-III-R, 142
Structured Clinical Interview for
  DSM-IV, 142
Subclinical depression, as risk factor for
  major depression, 319
Substance use disorders
  association between bipolar and major
    depressive disorders, 43
  childhood sexual abuse and, 23
  comorbidity of with GAD/MDD, 30,
    31
  family studies of GAD/MDD and, 17,
    18
Subtypes and subtyping
  of adjustment disorders, 292
  classification of GAD/MDD and, 262,
    264, 265
  system of for schizophrenia, 4, 5
Successive comorbidity, 307
SUDAAN software system, 145
Sweden, and association between social
  support and GAD, 358
Swedish Twin Registry, 2, 20, 26
Symptom Checklist—90—Revised, 44,
  172
Symptoms. *See also* Somatic symptoms
  associated psychophysiological of
    GAD in DSM-IV, 140
  conceptual issues in study of
    relationship between GAD and
    MDD, 6
  current classification of GAD/MDD
    and, 258, 259

Structural model, for reclassification of
  mood and anxiety disorders,
  344
MDD, 55. *See also* Life events
Stress, and neuroendocrinology of GAD/
  psychometrics and, 129
principal-component analysis and, 194
up study and, 145
National Comorbidity Survey follow-

Index 375

Randomized, controlled trials (RCTs), 72
Raskin Depression Scale, 77, 97
Reactive depression, 337
Receiver operating characteristics (ROC) curve, 142
Reciprocal causes, and relationship between GAD and MDD, 179–189
Recognition and Treatment of Depression in Primary Care (2000–2001), 172
Recurrences, of GAD/MDD comorbidity over time and, 263
in National Comorbidity Survey follow-up study, 158, 159
Regional cerebral blood flow (rCBF), and neuroanatomy of GAD/MDD, 46, 50
Research Diagnostic Criteria, 1, 2, 305
Research Planning Committee on Depression and Generalized Anxiety Disorder, 271, 283
Revised Clinical Interview Schedule, 359
RevMan 4.2.8 software, 76
Risk factors. *See also* Childhood experiences
classification of GAD/MDD and, 264–265
conceptual issues in classification and, 9–10
different environmental factors for GAD/MDD and, 140–141
Dunedin Multidisciplinary Health and Development Study and, 220–35, 242, 263–264, 265–266, 272–274, 334–337
British 1946 birth cohort study and, 241–253, 272–274
National Comorbidity Survey follow-up study and, 143–144, 152–158, 161, 165–166, 272–274
Root Mean Square Error of Approximation (RMSEA), 194
Rosenberg Self-Esteem Scale, 224
Russia, and study of affective spectrum disorders in primary care settings, 172–176

San Diego Widowhood Study, 340, 341
Schedule for Affect Disorders and Schizophrenia, 275
Schizophrenia, subtyping system for, 4, 5
Scotland, and study of psychosocial factors in anxiety/depression, 319–320
Screening, for affective spectrum disorders in Russia, 172–173
Selective serotonin reuptake inhibitors (SSRIs), 55, 60, 358–359
Self-esteem, and childhood risk factors for GAD and MDD, 224, 230
Self-reports
clinical diagnosis of GAD/MDD and, 6
scales for symptoms of anxiety/depression and, 110, 127–128
Sensitivity analyses, and study of effectiveness of psychotropics for GAD and MDD, 77, 88, 93
Sequenced Treatment Alternatives to Relieve Depression (STAR*D) study, 56, 340–342
Serotonin, and neurotransmitter abnormalities in GAD/MDD, 59, 60–61
Serotonin-norepinephrine reuptake inhibitors, 290
Serotonin transporter (SERT), 59, 61
Sertraline, 78, 82, 83
Sexual abuse. *See also* Child abuse
definition of, 348
effects of on risk for adult MDD and anxiety disorders, 23, 307, 323
prospective risk factors for GAD/MDD in National Comorbidity Survey follow-up study and, 143–144, 154, 156, 162
Simple phobias, 5, 290, 306. *See also* Phobias
Simultaneous reciprocal-cause model, 181, 184, 186–187, 188
Situational phobias, 5, 290, 291, 293, 323–324. *See also* Phobias

psychometrics of anxiety/depression and, 113–117, 359–360
self-report scales for anxiety/depression and, 110

Tanzania, and cross-cultural study of confirmatory factor analysis, **193, 199,** 201, **202, 204–207,** 208
Telescoping, in psychiatric epidemiology, 128
Testosterone, and neuroendocrinology of GAD, 55
Thailand, and cross-cultural study of confirmatory factor analysis, **193, 199, 202, 204–207**
Three-factor model, of relationship between anxiety and depression, 112, 114, 115
Three-form classification, 263, 264
Three-generation high-risk study, 274–282
Three-level hierarchical structure, of proposed classification, 294, 297
Threshold disagreement, and DSM-IV criteria for GAD, 132
Thyroid-stimulating hormone (TSH), 56–57
Thyrotropin-releasing hormone (TRH), 56–57
Thyroxine, 56
Time
study of relationship of GAD/MDD over, 171–176
parameters for use of terms *disorder* and *episode,* 258, 264
Time-lagged associations, and National Comorbidity Survey follow-up study, 148–152, **154–157,** 158–159, **160, 162, 163,** 164
Trait/state problem, in psychometrics, 112
Transmission, of GAD/MDD in three-generation high-risk study, 274–282
Treatment. *See also* Cognitive-behavioral therapy; Psychopharmacology
daily diary methods and, 129

diagnosis of depression in primary care settings in Russia and, **173**
relationship between diagnosis and, 71–72
Triazolobenzodiazepine, 88
Tricyclic antidepressants. *See also* Antidepressants
effectiveness of for GAD/MDD, 290
neurotransmitters and, 60
Triiodothyronine, 56
Tucker-Lewis Index (TLI), 194
Twin studies
genetic relationship between GAD and MDD, 20, 297
genetics of situational or animal phobias and, 323–324
reviews of findings from, 2
vulnerability to depression and, 320
Two-dimensional solution, to relationship between anxiety and depression, 116

United Kingdom. *See also* British 1946 birth cohort study; London studies
cross-cultural study of confirmatory factor analysis in, **193, 199, 200, 202, 204–207**
research interviews used by studies in, 359
study of early adverse exposures and differentiation of depression and anxiety risk in, 241–253

Validators. *See also* Antecedent validators; Concurrent validators; Predictive validators
conceptual issues in review of relationship between GAD and MDD, 5–6, 6–7, 287
neurobiological profiles of GAD/MDD and, 106
empirical issues in review of relationship between GAD and MDD, 3–4
Venlafaxine, 78, **79,** 80, **82,** 83
Ventrolateral prefrontal cortex, 47, **48**

Ventromedial prefrontal cortex (vmPFC), 47, **48**
Vietnam Era Twin Registry, 21
Violence, and psychosocial factors in anxiety and depression, 317–318
Virginia Twin Registry (VTR), 2, 20, 21, 22, 23, 24, 26, 114, 144
Vulnerability, and psychosocial factors in anxiety/depression, 304, 318–319, 359–360

Woman's Aid Refuge, 314
Women. *See also* London studies
  association between child abuse and adult depression or anxiety in, 348
  prevalence and comorbidity of anxiety/depression in, 349–351
World Mental Health Surveys, 214

Zurich Study, and association of GAD with bipolar II disorder, 42